Modules in Applied Mathematics: Volume 2

Edited by William F. Lucas

Modules in Applied Mathematics

Volume 1
Differential Equation Models
Martin Braun, Courtney S. Coleman, and Donald A. Drew, *Editors*

Volume 2
Political and Related Models
Steven J. Brams, William F. Lucas, and Philip D. Straffin, Jr., *Editors*

Volume 3
Discrete and System Models
William F. Lucas, Fred S. Roberts, and Robert M. Thrall, *Editors*

Volume 4
Life Science Models
Helen Marcus-Roberts and Maynard Thompson, *Editors*

Political and Related Models

Edited by
Steven J. Brams, William F. Lucas,
and Philip D. Straffin, Jr.

With 28 Illustrations

Springer-Verlag
New York Heidelberg Berlin

Steven J. Brams
Department of Politics
New York University
New York, NY 10003
USA

William F. Lucas
School of
Operations Research
Cornell University
Ithaca, NY 14853
USA

Philip D. Straffin, Jr.
Department of Mathematics
Beloit College
Beloit, WI 53511
USA

AMS Subject Classifications: 00A69; 90D12, 45; 90A05-08, 14, 30

Library of Congress Cataloging in Publication Data
Modules in applied mathematics.
Includes bibliographies.
Contents: —v. 2. Political and related models / edited by Steven J. Brams, William F. Lucas, and Philip D. Straffin, Jr.
1. Mathematics—1961– . 2. Mathematical models. I. Lucas, William F., 1933–
QA37.2.M6 1982 510 82-10439

This book was prepared with the support of NSF grants Nos. SED77-07482, SED75-00713, and SED72-07370. However, any opinions, findings, conclusions, and/or recommendations herein are those of the authors and do not necessarily reflect the views of NSF.

Softcover reprint of the hardcover 1st edition 1978

Typeset by Asco Trade Typesetting Ltd., Hong Kong

9 8 7 6 5 4 3 2 1

ISBN-13: 978-1-4612-5432-4 e-ISBN-13: 978-1-4612-5430-0
DOI: 10.1007/978-1-4612-5430-0

Preface

The purpose of this four volume series is to make available for college teachers and students samples of important and realistic applications of mathematics which can be covered in undergraduate programs. The goal is to provide illustrations of how modern mathematics is actually employed to solve relevant contemporary problems. Although these independent chapters were prepared primarily for teachers in the general mathematical sciences, they should prove valuable to students, teachers, and research scientists in many of the fields of application as well. Prerequisites for each chapter and suggestions for the teacher are provided. Several of these chapters have been tested in a variety of classroom settings, and all have undergone extensive peer review and revision. Illustrations and exercises are included in most chapters. Some units can be covered in one class, whereas others provide sufficient material for a few weeks of class time.

Volume 1 contains 23 chapters and deals with differential equations and, in the last four chapters, problems leading to partial differential equations. Applications are taken from medicine, biology, traffic systems and several other fields. The 14 chapters in Volume 2 are devoted mostly to problems arising in political science, but they also address questions appearing in sociology and ecology. Topics covered include voting systems, weighted voting, proportional representation, coalitional values, and committees. The 14 chapters in Volume 3 emphasize discrete mathematical methods such as those which arise in graph theory, combinatorics, and networks. These techniques are used to study problems in economics, traffic theory, operations research, decision theory, and other fields. Volume 4 has 12 chapters concerned with mathematical models in the life sciences. These include aspects of population growth and behavior, biomedicine (epidemics, genetics and bio-engineering), and ecology.

These four volumes are the result of two educational projects sponsored by The Mathematical Association of America (MAA) and supported in part by the National Science Foundation (NSF). The objective was to produce needed material for the undergraduate curriculum. The first project was undertaken by the MAA's Committee on the Undergraduate Program in Mathematics (CUPM). It was entitled Case Studies and Resource Materials for the Teaching of Applied Mathematics at the Advanced Undergraduate Level, and it received financial support from NSF grant SED72-07370 between September 1, 1972 and May 31, 1977. This project was completed under the direction of Donald Bushaw. Bushaw and William Lucas served as chairmen of CUPM during this effort, and George Pedrick was involved as the executive director of CUPM. The resulting report, which appeared in late 1976, was entitled *Case Studies in Applied Mathematics*, and it was edited by Maynard Thompson. It contained nine chapters by eleven authors, plus an introductory chapter and a report on classroom trials of the material.

The second project was initiated by the MAA's Committee on Institutes and Workshops (CIW). It was a summer workshop of four weeks duration entitled Modules in Applied Mathematics which was held at Cornell University in 1976. It was funded in part by NSF grant SED75-00713 and a small supplemental grant SED77-07482 between May 1, 1975 and September 30, 1978. William F. Lucas served as chairman of CIW at the time of the workshop and as director of this project. This activity lead to the production of 60 educational modules by 37 authors.

These four volumes contain revised versions of 9 of the 11 chapters from the report *Case Studies in Applied Mathematics*, 52 of the 60 modules from the workshop Modules in Applied Mathematics, plus two contributions which were added later (Volume 2, Chapters 7 and 14), for a total of 63 chapters. A preliminary version of the chapter by Steven Brams (Volume 2, Chapter 3), entitled "One Man, *N* Votes," was written in connection with the 1976 MAA Workshop. The expanded version presented here was prepared in conjunction with the American Political Science Association's project Innovation in Instructional Materials which was supported by NSF grant SED77-18486 under the direction of Sheilah K. Mann. The unit was published originally as a monograph entitled *Comparison Voting*, and was distributed to teachers and students for classroom field tests. This chapter was copyrighted by the APSA in 1978 and has been reproduced here with its permission.

An ad hoc committee of the MAA consisting of Edwin Beckenbach, Leonard Gillman, William Lucas, David Roselle, and Alfred Willcox was responsible for supervising the arrangements for publication and some of the extensive efforts that were necessary to obtain NSF approval of publication in this format. The significant contribution of Dr. Willcox throughout should be noted. George Springer also intervened in a crucial way at one point. It should be stressed, however, that any opinions or recommendations are those of the particular authors, and do not necessarily reflect the views of NSF, MAA, the editors, or any others involved in these project activities.

There are many other individuals who contributed in some way to the realization of these four volumes, and it is impossible to acknowledge all of them here. However, there are two individuals in addition to the authors, editors and people named above who should receive substantial credit for the ultimate appearance of this publication. Katherine B. Magann, who had provided many years of dedicated service to CUPM prior to the closing of the CUPM office, accomplished the production of the report *Case Studies in Applied Mathematics.* Carolyn D. Lucas assisted in the running of the 1976 MAA Workshop, supervised the production of the resulting sixty modules, and served as managing editor for the publication of these four volumes. Without her efforts and perseverance the final product of this major project might not have been realized.

July 1982 W. F. LUCAS

Preface for Volume 2

One of the major developments in mathematics in recent decades has been the spread of the mathematical approach into many other disciplines and into new problem areas. The social sciences have been a major benefactor of this trend. Some areas of subjects such as economics have become highly mathematical. Although the use of mathematical models has been relatively less rapid in the field of political science, there are already many interesting and useful results; this subject is ripe for further substantial mathematical development. Subjects such as social choice, voting systems, committee decisions, coalitional behavior, fair division and strategic interactions have a major mathematical component, and they are instrinsically very interesting subjects from an analytical perspective. This volume contains chapters on voting schemes, committee decision making, coalitional values and equitable distribution, weighted voting systems, and apportionment. In addition to these topics in political science, there are a few chapters concerned with problems in environmental, ecological and social science.

The first chapter by Thompson provides a general discussion of the process of applied mathematics and the nature of mathematical modeling. Chapter 6 by Thrall and Perry and Chapter 8 by Maceli provide somewhat atypical introductions to basic working tools for the social scientists. The former chapter is an elementary introduction to vectors and matrices in a format appropriate for those in the social, decisional and operational sciences. This is in contrast to the more common presentations which are given in terms of purely mathematical or physical terminology and concepts. The chapter by Maceli on random response techniques addresses the important problem of how to collect reliable data from individuals when seeking answers to sensitive questions to which they may not reply honestly.

Chapters 2 and 3 analyze some specific voting systems. Bolger is concerned primarily with schemes which provide proportional representation, whereas Brams provides a comparison of different nonranked voting schemes. A procedure called approval voting is emphasized, and it appears highly suitable for multicandidate voting situations such as primary elections. Chapter 12 by Rice models some important aspects of decision making in a committee.

Chapter 4 by Lucas and Billera and Chapter 5 by Heaney are concerned with coalitions (of individuals or other entities), their associated values, and the equitable allocations of such group costs or benefits to the participants. These chapters (as well as Chapters 2 and 3) are particularly appropriate for open-ended modeling at quite elementary levels. Chapter 4 also provides a simple introduction into the nature of multiperson cooperative games requiring only high school level mathematical prerequisites. Chapter 5 addresses an environmental problem and intermunicipality cooperation.

Chapters 9, 10 and 11 provide a fairly detailed presentation of measuring power in weighted voting systems. Power is a fundamental concept in politics, and the power indices for weighted voting provide one of the few applications for which a somewhat reasonable measure of power has been determined. The chapters by Lucas and Straffin cover mostly the well-known Shapley–Shubik index and Banzhaf–Coleman index (Chow parameters), whereas the chapter by Deegan and Packel proposes an additional measure of power. The power indices have been implemented in many real world applications in voting. There have been several court rulings in which the power indices have been accepted. For example, about half of the county governments in New York state have made use of weighted voting in the past fifteen years. The theory of simple games arising out of weighted voting situations is based upon a rather fundamental mathematical structure which also appears in other mathematical contexts, both pure and applied.

The apportionment problem presented in the final chapter of this volume is concerned with allocating discrete quantities in an equitable manner. It arises in assigning the number of representatives to each district in a legislative assembly, e.g., the U.S. House of Representatives. However, it also arises in many other allocation problems concerning discrete entities that arise in a variety of fields such as statistics, numerical analysis, optimal assignment problems, and fair division theory. The recent axiomatic approach to this problem by M. L. Balinski and H. P. Young has provided a superb illustration of the basic role of axioms in modeling, especially in the social and decisional sciences.

Chapter 13 by Cobb introduces some basic ideas about stochastic difference equations with some interesting interpretations in sociology. Chapter 7 by Hayslett is a collection of bibliographical materials on ecology and the environment which are suitable for classroom use as well as for private study. These two chapters, as well as most others in this volume, contain many illustrations, exercises and projects which are highly appropriate for contemporary courses on mathematical modeling.

July 1982

Steven J. Brams
William F. Lucas
Philip D. Straffin, Jr.

Contents

Contents of the Companion Volumes

VOLUME 1. DIFFERENTIAL EQUATION MODELS

VOLUME 3. DISCRETE AND SYSTEM MODELS

VOLUME 4. LIFE SCIENCE MODELS

Part I. Population Models

CHAPTER 1

The Process of Applied Mathematics

Maynard Thompson*

1. Introduction

In discussing the applications of mathematics in the undergraduate curriculum, one is inclined to begin with a precise definition of what is meant by applied mathematics. There are many informative discussions of the nature of what is commonly referred to as applied mathematics, for example, [4], [10], [12], and [13], and it is not our purpose here to expand on these. Instead, we shall initially adopt a relatively informal approach, avoiding definitions and relying on comments and examples to convey ideas. It is our hope that the reader will acquire from this chapter an appreciation of the process that is exemplified in the modules that comprise this book and its three companion volumes.

If one views mathematics in a very broad sense as rigorous, logical thinking, then the scholar or student whose approach to his discipline involves a precise identification of the concepts, definitions, and assumptions and the deduction of consequences from these assumptions through logical argument is doing applied mathematics. Our point of view here is much narrower. We have in mind only those studies in which a situation arising outside of mathematics is clarified by making appropriate use of mathematical ideas and techniques that are accessible to an undergraduate.

When we speak of the applications of mathematics, it is clear that we mean applying mathematics to something. That something can, of course, be another branch of mathematics. However, we shall exclude from our discussion the use of the mathematics originating in one branch (e.g.,

* Department of Mathematics, Indiana University, Bloomington, Indiana 47401.

probability) to the study of problems arising in another (e.g., analysis). This choice reflects the purpose of these materials and does not imply that such uses are unimportant or uninteresting. Rather, they are simply outside the scope of this collection. We concentrate on the use of mathematics to study situations that arise in the everyday world of business, government, industry, etc., or in another discipline. There is an expanding range of situations for which mathematics yields useful conclusions, and even more which have been studied using mathematics. The goal of the process of applying mathematics is to learn something about the situation that either was unknown or not firmly supported prior to the mathematical investigation.

To be more precise, we ought to speak of the use of the ideas and techniques of the mathematical sciences rather than simply those of mathematics, which for many means pure mathematics. Indeed, it may be that statistics and computer simulation are the most appropriate tools to use on a problem arising in urban planning. Many of the more interesting problems are sufficiently complex that one needs to utilize concepts from several branches of the mathematical sciences to make progress. This amalgamation of methods from several mathematical areas is one of the common characteristics of applied mathematics. In the future, when the phrase "use of mathematics" occurs, it is to be interpreted in the broad sense just described.

The application of mathematical methods to a precisely formulated problem is one part of the process of applying mathematics. Another important component of that process has come to be referred to as modeling. Although the term has been used in many different ways in the literature, it is a useful descriptor and we shall use it freely. Our use of the term will become precise in the next section.

2. Applied Mathematics as a Process

Applied mathematics is a science that is concerned with the interaction between pure mathematics and another subject—another academic discipline or some aspect of the everyday world. One of the more useful analyses of the way in which this interaction takes place is due to Dr. H. O. Pollak. (Another, ascribed to J. L. Synge, may be found in [4], p. 12.) This organization provides a profitable starting point for our discussion, and it is appropriate to summarize it here. Briefly, the process can be viewed as consisting of five phases:

(i) Identification of the problem in the scientific setting.
(ii) Formulation of a mathematical model.
(iii) Solution of the mathematical problems that arise in the study of the model selected.
(iv) Development of algorithms and associated computer programs for relevant computations.

(v) Explanation and interpretation of the results in the context of the original problem and the communication of this information to the interested audience. Evaluation of the results.

It is uncommon for a mathematician to play a significant role in phase (i). Usually the situation is being studied by a scientist (or manager or doctor), and it is this individual who recognizes the importance of the issues and the possible relevance of mathematical techniques. It may happen that the subject is studied intensively, perhaps for an extended period, data are collected, and the results summarized in empirical laws before a systematic effort is made to provide supporting theory. In business and industrial settings, it is not uncommon for problems to be solved solely on the basis of experience or ad hoc techniques prior to the recognition that mathematical methods may be helpful. Recently, however, the utility of mathematics is more widely appreciated and it is increasingly common to turn quickly to the search for mathematical solutions to problems. Since this is written for mathematicians, it is worthwhile to add the cautionary note that the minor role usually played by mathematicians in this phase is very appropriate. Indeed, at present few mathematicians have the scientific knowledge to judge the importance of the issues or to interpret the results of experiments. This may well change as more mathematicians move from the fringes to the center of active research in other disciplines.

Phase (ii), is frequently the most crucial and most difficult part of the entire process. Usually it is a very creative activity carried out by a mathematically knowledgeable scientist or by a scientist and mathematician working jointly. Model building, or theory construction as it is sometimes called by social scientists, consists of examining the situation carefully, identifying what is important and what is not, and selecting (or creating) a suitable mathematical structure. A model has two components: a mathematical structure (primitive terms, definitions, and axioms) and an identification between the concepts of the real situation and those in the mathematical system. In general the particular structure selected is chosen because it has some theorems (predictions) that are known to be consistent with the data of the original situation. Of couse, the goal is to use the mathematical system to deduce new information about the situation or to provide firm support for known results. Generally, in the process of identifying those aspects of the original situation that are to be retained, one also simplifies it as much as possible. In this phase such simplifications are made on a scientific and not a mathematical basis. The meaning of each simplification or idealization should be carefully considered with respect to its meaning in the original setting. Obviously it is essential that the simplifications not be so radical that the theorems of the related mathematical system cease to provide valid predictions about the actual situation. On the other hand, it may be necessary that some simplification take place in order that the resulting mathematical system be manageable. The problems of deciding what is important and what is not and which simplifications are legitimate and which are not are major ones and require experience and ingenuity. Clearly the activity must be carried out by an investigator who is thoroughly familiar with the actual situation and the basic scientific principles of the field.

Depending on the situation being investigated, there may be several different mathematical structures that provide useful mathematical models. For example, a situation in economics may involve consumer demand as one of the quantities of interest. The model may be significantly different depending upon whether this demand is viewed as a deterministic or probabilistic quantity, and the conclusions based on the model may differ as well. In many cases there will be several alternative models, and there may well be no "best" model. That is, one model may lead to predictions of one sort that agree well with observations, while another model leads to predictions of a different sort that agree well with experiments. An example of this from elementary physics is the dual wave and particle models for light. The wave model for light provides explanations for the main phenomena of physical optics: reflection and refraction, dispersion, polarization, and diffraction. However, the photoelectric effect, which is difficult to understand in the wave model, is perfectly comprehensible in the particle model.

The creation of a mathematical model includes the selection of a mathematical structure and a correspondence between that structure and the original situation. Thus specific questions regarding the original situation carry over into specific mathematical questions. Phase (iii) is concerned with the study of these mathematical questions. It is this activity that is usually thought of as applied mathematics and which provides the content for most applications-oriented undergraduate courses. Actually much of what goes on in this phase is indistinguishable on the surface from pure mathematics, only the motivation is different. It is important, however, to keep in mind that the mathematical problem has a connection with the physical (or social or everyday) world. If the problem must be modified for mathematical reasons, then the relationship of the modified problem with the original one, and consequently with the physical world, must be carefully analyzed.

It is easy to formulate apparently straightforward models for relatively simple situations that lead to extremely difficult mathematical problems. Sometimes these problems fit neatly into a well-understood mathematical topic, more often they do not. At the research level, this will often lead to the creation of new mathematics. At the undergraduate level, it leads to the reformulation of the situation in different, hopefully more tractable, mathematical terms, or to computation. Since the goal is the understanding of the original situation, resorting to computational methods or computer simulation is an acceptable alternative to developing a new mathematical theory for many applications, and for most of them at the undergraduate level. However, one ought not to turn to computation or simulation too readily. Often a deeper understanding of the original situation or the mathematical representation that has been selected leads to a fruitful approach to the mathematical problems.

The use of computation and simulation, identified as phase (iv), has been discussed briefly above. Although occasionally the result of the mathematical analysis of phase (iii) is a useable analytic expression, more frequently this result requires computation to have meaning for the original problem. For example, the result might be a theorem concerning information transmission in a complex organization. To be useful the theorem may require large amounts of data to be organized and represented cleverly in incidence matrices so as to display certain patterns. In all but trivial cases, this representation cannot be carried out by hand, and one must develop computer programs to handle the data in order that the mathematics be useful. It may happen that the development of a mathematical theory is quite straightforward while the invention of appropriate algorithms is very difficult and requires considerable ingenuity. The solution of these problems frequently hinges on deep understanding of the mathematics as well as skill in taking full advantage of the capabilities of the computer. The efficient use of a computer may also be an important issue. While a factor of 10 in computer time may seem unimportant from a theoretical point of view, it may make the difference between the feasibility and infeasibility of a certain approach to an industrial problem.

There is finally the task of interpreting and evaluating the results in terms of the original problem, phase (v). The scientist who is applying mathematics must have sufficient familiarity with the original situation to be capable of interpreting and translating his results into the language and setting of the initial problem.

It is not uncommon to proceed through phases (i)–(iv) and find when reaching phase (v) that the results are not useful when viewed as statements about the original situation. In such a case one normally assumes that the mathematical analyses and computations of phases (iii) and (iv) are correct and therefore looks more closely at phases (i) and (ii), especially, (ii). We noted above that model building is crucial: an inadequate or inappropriate model may well lead through the mathematics to useless or even nonsensical conclusions. This holds independent of the quality of the mathematics used. A model based on concepts or assumptions that are deficient in some fundamental way will not produce useful results no matter how elegant the mathematical arguments used in its development.

Even if the predictions are wrong in detail, there may still have been some gain from the activity. At a minimum the situation has been examined critically with a view to identifying the underlying principles. The model building may have uncovered implicit assumptions that may or may not hold up under examination. Also, if a theory is presented in verbal form and fails, it is easy for the proponents to claim that it is essentially correct and only minor adjustments are necessary. On the other hand, if the theory is developed as a mathematical model one can more easily determine the validity of such claims. A formulation of the assumptions as individual axioms may make it easy to isolate the difficulty and modify the offending axioms instead of discarding the entire model.

3. The Construction and Use of Mathematical Models

Since the model building portion of the process described in the preceding section plays such a central role, we shall consider it in somewhat greater detail. It involves the identification of certain concepts and relations as the essential ones in the situation being studied. Typically this includes an idealization and approximation of the real situation resulting in its replacement by another that is simpler in some sense but that retains the essential features of the original. Initially, the concepts singled out as fundamental may be closely identified with real things, e.g., with individuals in a population, molecules in a gas, or automobiles on a freeway, even though they may no longer be thought of as behaving strictly as real things. That is, a rat is thought of as moving instantaneously from one compartment in a maze to another, a molecule is thought of as a perfectly elastic sphere, or a population of herbivores is thought of as uniformly distributed over its range. As the model building continues, the entities are viewed less as real things and more as elements in a mathematical system. The crux of modeling is the selection of an appropriate mathematical structure and useful identifications between the concepts and relations of the original situation and those of the mathematical system. Usually there is no single best system. There may be several systems that are natural to consider and, consequently, several models for the same situation. It may happen that one of the models is distinctly preferable to the others in the sense that it accounts for the known facts and data more adequately. In such a case, one normally retains that model and discards the others. There have been a number of crucial experiments specifically designed to evaluate a model or to distinguish between models. The celebrated experiment of Michelson and Morley to detect the motion of the earth through the ether and the experiements in 1960 by W. K. Estes comparing the linear model and the all-or-none model for paired-associate learning are examples. It is more common, however, that one model accounts for some observations and another model accounts for others, but that no one model accounts for all. The model(s) to be retained then depends upon which aspects of the situation are of most interest to the investigator. Among the first questions that the model builder should ask are: Which aspects of the situation am I most concerned that my model include, and which have the most bearing on the detailed questions of interest to me?

Frequently a situation is studied by beginning with a simple model and cycling through the process outlined in Section 2 several times rather than by starting with a comprehensive model. The advantages of such an approach are that simple models tend to be more tractable mathematically, and that by adding assumptions one or a few at a time it may be quite clear just which assumptions lead to which conclusions. The disadvantage, and it is a very real one, is that an oversimplified model may lead to such poor predictions when compared with observations that one loses faith in the whole approach. However, a recognition of the evolutionary nature of the modeling process, and a realization that models are in general not all-encompassing are usually sufficient to overcome this difficulty.

There is today no treatise that provides a definitive discussion of the theory and practice of model building. It is not even clear that such an undertaking is a reasonable one. However, there are some classifications of models, not all of them widely accepted, that provide a useful framework for comparisons. The following system, admittedly incomplete and without many desirable fine distinctions, includes several of the categories common in the literature.

i. Models for Insight and Models for Decisions. Model building concerned primarily with providing insight into a situation or system arising outside of mathematics has as its goal the identification of the basic processes that operate in that situation and the selection of a mathematical system and correspondences between the components of the original system and the mathematical one, which illuminate the behavior of the original system. Models for decisions are designed with more specific goals in mind. Typically one is interested in making a decision or selecting a course of action so as to accomplish certain ends. The selection is to be made on the basis of the information resulting from a study of a model for the original system. Models for decision making often culminate in the development of a technique, frequently including an algorithm or simulation to be implemented on a computer, which provides solutions to specific problems or all problems of a certain class. Markov chain models for concept acquisition in mathematical psychology are usually viewed as models for insight, whereas dynamic programming models for industrial production tend to be models for decisions. In many cases an investigation has both aspects and the model is designed to provide a solid logical foundation for decision making.

ii. Deterministic and Stochastic Models. Deterministic models, i.e., models based on the assumption that if there were sufficient information at one instant in time or at one stage in a process then the entire future of the system could be precisely predicted, have been widely used in the physical sciences and engineering. Stochastic models, those which describe the behavior of the system in probabilistic terms, have had their most extensive applications to situations arising in the social and life sciences. Of course, stochastic models have been used successfully in physics, e.g., statistical mechanics, and deterministic models have been used in the social and life sciences. The model of Lewis Richardson for arms races and the Lotka–Volterra models for interacting populations are examples of models arising in political science and population biology, respectively, which when expressed in mathematical terms lead to systems of ordinary differential equations. Many systems have been modeled in both terms. It may be that a deterministic model is selected as a first approximation to a stochastic one, and sometimes a blend of the two is appropriate. It should not be assumed that the results (or predictions) based on one type of model are necessarily better (or worse) than results based on the other. The decision as to which type of model should be constructed depends on the situation being studied and the goals of the study. It is ultimately a choice of the model builder.

iii. Continuous and Discrete Models. Some situations lend themselves naturally to description in terms of continuous quantities, e.g., space or time, and others are just as naturally phrased in discrete terms, e.g., the number of automobiles produced in an hour. Even situations that initially appear to be described in terms of a continuous parameter may upon closer examination admit a natural discretization. For example, a biological population may be thought of as evolving through time. However, if observations are made periodically or if seasonal variations play a major role, then a description of the system in discrete terms may be very appropriate. There is frequently a choice and the mathematical analysis is usually quite different in the two cases. For example, difference equations may replace differential equations in a discrete model of a biological system. If computation on a digital computer is involved, then it will be necessary to return to discrete terms eventually.

iv. Analytic and Simulation Models. Mathematicians tend to be better satisfied with the results of a study if their conclusions can be expressed in analytic form. This may be an analytic solution to a specific problem, or an investigation carried out largely in analytic terms and culminating in an algorithm. In either case the results can be summarized in statements recognizable as mathematical theorems. However, the complexity of actual situations may force one to admit, at least for the time being, the inadequacy of analytic techniques and to turn to simulation. One can form a mathematical model and simulate the resulting mathematical system or one can simulate the original system more or less directly. Of course, there are various blends of analytic and simulation methods, and the simulation itself may take any of a number of forms. Psychological experiments frequently involve the simulation of an actual experience by a contrived one, interactive simulation between a human and a machine is a common training technique, and a complex engineering system, such as a nuclear reactor, may be simulated before it is constructed. In most instances simulation involves an analog or digital computer. There are instances in which simulation may be useful even though analytic solutions can be obtained. For example, it may be that the effect of changes in the parameters of a system on the results obtained from the model is made clearer by several simulation runs than by an examination of analytic expressions. In interpreting the results of simulation, it is worthwhile to keep in mind that if a system is sufficiently complex to require simulation methods, then the model building is likely to be difficult. For instance, simulation is frequently necessitated by the inclusion of various types of random behavior in the model, e.g., random demands subject to empirically deduced probability distributions in an economic model. In such cases the results of a simulation or of several simulation runs only give estimates subject to statistical error, and the conclusions must be accompanied by some assessment of the associated random fluctuations. Although simulation is sometimes referred to as a "last resort," it is a powerful method which, if used wisely, is capable of providing information that can be obtained in no other manner.

There have been some very useful models constructed for phenomena arising in the social and life sciences. For example, probability models in genetics, (Mendel's laws), logistic growth models for fruit fly populations, and input–output models in economics (for which Leontief received the 1973 Nobel Prize in Economics). Mathematical programming models have a well-deserved reputation for effectiveness in business decision making. However, most of the credibility of mathematical models rests on their unusual effectiveness in the physical sciences and engineering. One could list numerous scientific phenomena whose understanding has been facilitated by the thoughtful use of mathematics. We illustrate such applications by considering what is probably the best known model of all.

4. Planetary Motion: The Evolution of a Model

The creation of a systematic explanation of the apparent motions of the planets as viewed from the earth is a major accomplishment of human intellect. The problem is one that has its origins in ancient history and also one that has attracted attention in this century. The scientific effort devoted to its study has been enormous. We shall survey the subject briefly, emphasizing the modeling aspect of the various theories. There is ample literature available containing the details (e.g., [5], [11], [13], [17], [18]).

Some of the earliest attempts to explain astronomical observations adopted a view of a fixed flat earth covered by a spherical celestial dome. In the fourth century B.C., the Greeks began with such a view and devised a model that largely accounted for the data then available. This model was formulated in terms of real though somewhat idealized objects and relations. It assumed a fixed earth with a sphere containing the fixed stars rotating about it. The "seven wanderers"—the sun, moon, and five planets—moved between the earth and the celestial dome. The Greeks intended to construct combinations of uniform circular motions centered in the earth by which the movements of the seven wanderers among the fixed stars could be represented. The assumption of uniform circular motion was based on nonscientific, or at best psuedoscientific justifications. Each body was supposed to be moved by a set of interconnecting, rotating spherical shells. Aristotle utilized the system and introduced 55 shells to account for the data available to him. In its mathematical form this model was a geometrical one. Its predictions were consistent with observations, at least to within the accuracy of the time. It was however, inadequate in two respects. First, as observations became better the model required continual refinement, and second, since each planet was assumed to remain at a fixed distance from the earth, the variations in brightness of the planets as they moved could not be explained.

Ptolemy modified this system in the second century A.D. to obtain better agreement with the data. In a simple version of his theory, each planet was assumed to move in a small circular orbit (epicycle) in the period of its actual motion through the sky, while the center of this orbit moved around the earth on a large orbital circle (deferent). The deferent and epicycle alone were insufficient to account for the observed irregularities in planetary motion, and Ptolemy also introduced the equant, an axis of uniform motion off center within the deferent. Only from this position would the planet appear to move with uniform angular velocity. The earth was assumed to be off center in the opposite direction from the equant with respect to the center of the deferent. This system provided adequate flexibility for the planets other than Mercury; with a slight modification it would serve for Mercury also.

Early in the sixteenth century Copernicus became dissatisfied with the Ptolemaic equant, which seemed to him to violate the principle of uniform circular motion, and he proposed modifications involving more epicycles, off-center deferents, and finally a heliocentric (sun-centered) system. It is interesting that his early defense of the heliocentric system is based entirely on esthetics, particularly on a plea for simplicity. He proposed that the earth and the other planets revolved around the sun in uniform circular orbits. Since his model retained the assumption that the basic motions of the planets were circular, it was also necessary to retain the epicycle concept to account for variations in the brightness and apparent velocity of the planets as viewed from the earth. This model was based on geometry, as was Ptolemy's, and not on physics. Indeed, the editor of one of Copernicus' major works writes "But these hypotheses need not be true or even probable," and "If they provide a calculus consistent with the observations, that alone is sufficient."

Toward the end of the sixteenth century a Swedish astronomer, Tycho Brahe, collected masses of detailed observations on the motions of the planets. Tycho seems to have viewed Copernicus as a builder of hypothetical geometric models, and, in an attempt to formulate models incorporating the apparent physical reality of a sluggish, massive earth, he proposed another geocentric model. It is not his model for which he is accorded his status in astronomy, however, it is for his systematic observations that provided the foundations for future work. Johannes Kepler inherited Tycho's records and he undertook to modify Copernican theory to fit these observations. He was particularly bothered by the orbit of Mars whose large eccentricity made it difficult to fit into a deferent-epicycle system. He was eventually led to make a very creative step, a complete break with the Platonic–Pythagorean uniform circular motion hypotheses that had so dominated astronomy. He posed as a model for the motions of the planets the following three assumptions, usually referred to as Kepler's laws:

(1) The planets revolve around the sun in elliptical orbits with the sun at one focus (1609).
(2) The radius vector from the sun to a planet sweeps out equal areas in equal times (1609).
(3) The squares of the periods of revolution of any two planets are in the same ratio as the cubes of their mean distances from the sun (1619).

These empirical laws are simply statements of observed facts. They are, however, perceptive and especially useful formulations of the regularities noted in the observations. Along with the identification of these laws, Kepler hypothesized a physical mechanism, a force emanating from the sun, which accounted for the motion of the planets. This model accounted very well for the accumulated observations and set the stage for the next refinement.

The models developed up to the middle of the seventeenth century had an empirical or geometrical basis with a minimum of support from physics. Isaac Newton's theory of gravitation provided simultaneously a physical interpretation and a concise and elegant mathematical description of cosmological phenomena. The combination of the laws of motion and the universal law of gravitation furnished a mathematical system from which the motions of the planets could be deduced. In this setting the motion of a planet could be determined by first considering the two-body system consisting of the planet and the sun. The motion of this system was easy to determine, and the results were the three laws of Kepler. These predictions are good first approximations since the sun is the dominant mass in the solar system and the planets are widely separated. However, according to the law of gravitation, each planet is also subject to forces due to each of the other planets, and these forces result in perturbations of the elliptical orbits predicted on the basis of the two-body model. A careful examination of the orbit of a specific planet resulted in the identification of perturbations due to each of the remaining known planets. If these perturbations did not account for the total of the observed deviations from the behavior predicted on the basis of a two-body model, then one might try to account for the remainder by assuming the existence of a yet unknown planet. Estimates on the size and location of the hypothesized planet could be obtained and a search initiated. In fact, this is the sequence of events that resulted in the discovery of Uranus, Neptune, and Pluto. It is an impressive triumph for the mathematical system proposed by Newton that minute discrepencies between theory and observations could lead to the discovery of unknown and in fact unanticipated planets.

Even the remarkable model of Newton does not account for all the data and there has been further refinement in this century. Small perturbations in the orbit of Mercury, unexplainable in Newtonian mechanics, provided some motivation and support for the development of the theory of relativity. The modified version of the Newtonian theory incorporating relativistic corrections appears to be adequate for existing data. New data or revised interpretations of existing data may of course necessitate further revision.

Any of the models mentioned here can be formalized. That is, one can identify the basic concepts that are important, e.g., force, mass, and position, select some as undefined terms, and provide precise definitions of the others. The resulting mathematical system can be studied as an abstract structure without reference to its origin or to any possible real-world meaning of the terms.

The attempts to account for the motion of the planets described here illustrate several aspects of model building. First, and perhaps most vividly, the typical cycling through the model building process is demonstrated. Some of the successive refinements are clearly defined major departures from previous efforts, while others are simply minor modifications. These revisions were initiated for varying reasons. Copernicus was primarily concerned with simplifying the Ptolemaic model while Newton was interested in finding physical and mathematical principles from which Kepler's laws (among others) could be deduced. The search for a simple model based on a few easily understood principles is characteristic of modeling. Also, in addition to modifications based on a desire for simplicity or elegance, the refinement of a model necessitated by new data is illustrated. What has not been discussed, other than the brief mention of the geocentric model of Tycho Brahe, are the many dead ends and useless models that were considered in the process of discovering useful models. Some such efforts have been recorded in the literature, many more have been lost.

5. An Example from Psychology

The model for physical phenomena known as classical or Newtonian mechanics, which provided one of the models sketched in the preceding section, has several desirable characteristics. First, the mathematical laws are simple and their relation to well-understood physical concepts is clear. Next, the model is quite comprehensive and it can be used to study an enormous variety of situations in physics and engineering. It is unnecessary to construct a number of variations of the model to account for the results of different kinds of experiments. Thus, to cite a simple example, the motion of a cylinder rolling down an inclined plane can be described using the same basic principles as are used to describe the motion of a water droplet leaving a garden hose. Finally, there is (nearly universal) confidence in the results or theorems that follow from an analysis of the model. It is accepted that the model does indeed illuminate the underlying physics of the situation.

On the other hand, the models constructed for use in the social and life sciences and in business do not in general have this simplicity and comprehensiveness, and they have sometimes inspired less confidence in their users. Typically the basic concepts and mathematical relations may be relevant only to a rather restricted set of situations, and the degree to which they illuminate the underlying scientific or business problem may be less than totally clear. In addition, problems of parameter estimation may severely restrict the utility of otherwise promising models. It is, of course, by no means the case that models in the physical sciences are always simpler and more useful than models in the social and life sciences. For example, relatively simple mathematical models have proved effective in genetics ([7], [8]) and in learning theory. Applications of mathematics to learning theory are especially interesting because of the variety of models that have been developed to account for the experimental evidence. It is useful to comment briefly on this field since it illustrates the development of models very different from those of mechanics.

Paired-associate learning is one of the topics included under the general designation of verbal learning. In a typical paired-associate learning experiment, a subject is presented with a list of stimulus-response pairs, one pair at a time. For example, one pair in the list might be XW-4. Here XW is the stimulus member and 4 is the response member. Depending upon the particular experimental design being used, the subject might be presented with a stimulus and given a short time to respond before the associated response member appears. This routine is repeated for each item on the list. A trial is one presentation of the entire list. Usually the order of the items is determined randomly for each trial. The experiment will proceed either for a fixed number of trials or until a criterion level is reached. For example the criterion level might be two successive errorless trials.

A major objective of a learning theory is to confirm or predict a learning curve, a measure of performance as a function of time. For paired-associate learning, one usually takes the measure of performance to be the proportion of correct responses and the time as the trial number. This objective is usually not sufficiently refined and several reasonable models with two or three free parameters can be made to agree adequately with empirical learning curves by a careful selection of parameter values. Consequently, one normally has to use other methods of selecting between alternative models. For example, one might base a distinction between models on a detailed analysis of response sequences.

We mention the basic ideas of two models to indicate the possibilities.

A detailed discussion of these two models is included in [1], [3], and [15]. Alternative models are proposed in the references just cited and in [16] and [20]. Bush and Mosteller compare eight of the common learning models in [2].

Of the many versions of the linear model, the following is probably the most elementary. Consider a specific item in the list and let P_n be the probability that the subject makes a correct response to that item on trial n. It is reasonable to suppose that P_{n+1} depends in some way on P_n. Various rationales (see [3], p. 51 and [15], p. 3) can be given to support the assumption that

$$P_{n+1} = \alpha A + (1 - \alpha)P_n,$$

where A is the asymptotic value of P_n for large n, and α is a parameter that must be estimated from the data.

One of the alternatives to the linear model is the all-or-none (or one-element) model. The view of the learning process that underlies the all-or-none theory is very different from that of the linear model. In a simple version of the all-or-none view of learning, the subject is supposed to be in one of two states, the learned state (L) or the unlearned state (U). During each trial the subject either remains in L or U or makes a transition from U to L. It is assumed that once the subject reaches state L, it remains there. If the subject is in state L, it is supposed to make only correct responses, while if it is in state U, it may or may not make correct responses by chance. Finally, it is assumed that the subject begins in the unlearned state U. In one direction these assumptions can be given an intuitive rationale and in the other direction they can be made quite precise (see Section 3.1 of [1]).

It is natural to take a Markov chain as a mathematical system whose structure is appropriate for the all-or-none model: A Markov chain model of the simple version described above has a transition matrix of the form

$$\begin{array}{c} \\ L \\ U \end{array}\!\!\begin{array}{c} \begin{array}{cc} L & \quad U \end{array} \\ \begin{bmatrix} 1 & 0 \\ c & 1-c \end{bmatrix} \end{array},$$

where c is a learning parameter. It is not learning but responses that are observed in experiments, and the connection between state occupancy and response is given by

$$Pr[\text{correct response} \mid \text{state } L] = 1,$$

$$Pr[\text{correct response} \mid \text{state } U] = \beta,$$

where β is a response parameter. It is customary to estimate β in advance from the number of response alternatives available to the subject. Thus the predictions based on this model will be functions of the single parameter c, which must then be estimated from the data.

The predictions of these two rather different models are analyzed and compared in [1], Chapter 3 and [15], Chapter 2. In the linear model, learning is viewed as a change in response probability from one trial to the next. Thus each presentation of an item is assumed to increase the probability of a correct response. On the other hand, as its name implies, the all-or-none model is based on the assumption that the effect of a single presentation is either to produce complete learning of the association or no learning at all. For a specific set of data, it is reasonable to expect that one should be able to choose between the models based on these rather different hypotheses. This is the case in the comparisons cited above.

6. Concluding Remarks

There are two points to which we return for emphasis. The first relates to the criterion of simplicity frequently mentioned earlier in this paper. The idea is an imprecise one, and the degree of simplicity or complexity ascribed to a model is frequently dependent upon the observer. However, it usually happens that when a situation is modeled in full generality, the resulting mathematics is sufficiently peculiar to the situation that one encounters difficulties in taking advantage of known results. The alternative then to developing a new mathematical theory is to make simplifications that bring the mathematical systems arising from the model within the scope of known theories. These theories may have been developed in the analysis of a model created in the study of another situation. This brings us to the second point. One of the major advantages of using mathematics to describe scientific phenomena is that its use enhances markedly the possibility of recognizing similarities between situations that may appear superficially quite different. These similarities may allow the use of results that were derived in the analysis of a model constructed for the purpose of studying a very different situation. For example, results on linear inequalities derived by J. Farkas in his study of an engineering problem have proved to be very useful in studying linear programming problems that arise in economics and business. The recognition of a common mathematical structure may even lead to the identification of new scientific principles. This is exemplified in the biological least-action principles identified by noting the similarities in models for biological systems and those for physical systems ([6], [9], [17]).

We conclude with a comment that is somewhat out of place in this article but entirely appropriate for these four volumes. The repeated successes of certain individuals in creating and developing mathematical models for scientific phenomena indicates quite clearly that model building can be learned. It is not as clear that it can be taught in the same way as most academic subjects. The novice needs to be an observer initially and then, as quickly as possible, a doer. A beginner benefits considerably by observing the process of applied mathematics in action. To this end, it may be that examples that are not original but that are new and meaningful to the student serve as well as new examples created for the purpose. However, modeling is not learned by watching others build models, even if this includes some of the false starts and failures that are so common, but rather by becoming actively and personally involved in the modeling process. To be sure, there will be frustrations and futile efforts, but only through participation can one gain understanding and facility in applying mathematics.

References

The references provided in this list are cited in the paper. Those selected for examples in Sections 4 and 5 were chosen because they give attention to the model building aspect of the work.

1. Atkinson, R. C., G. H. Bower, and E. J. Crothers. *An Introduction to Mathematical Psychology*. John Wiley and Sons, New York, 1966.
2. Bush, R. R., and F. Mosteller. "A Comparison of Eight Models," in *Studies in Mathematical Learning Theory*, R. R. Bush and W. K. Estes, eds. Stanford University Press, Stanford, California, 1961.
3. Bush, R. R., and F. Mosteller. *Stochastic Models for Learning*. John Wiley and Sons, New York, 1955.
4. Coulson, C. A. *The Spirit of Applied Mathematics*. Clarendon Press, Oxford, 1953.
5. Gingerich, O. "Copernicus and Tycho," *Sci. Am.*, *229* (1973).
6. Goel, N. S., S. C. Maitra, and E. W. Montroll. *Nonlinear Models of Interacting Populations*. Academic Press, New York, 1971.
7. Karlin, S., and M. Feldman. "Mathematical Genetics: A Hybrid Seed for Educators to Sow," *Int. J. Math. Educ. Sci. Technol.*, *3* (1972), 169–189.
8. Karlin, S. "Some Mathematical Models of Population Genetics," *Am. Math. Monthly*, *79* (1972), 699–739.
9. Kerner, E. H. *Gibbs Ensemble: Biological Ensemble*. Gordon and Breach, New York, 1972.
10. Klamkin, M. S. "On the Ideal Role of an Industrial Mathematician and Its Educational Implications," *Am. Math. Monthly*, *78* (1971), 53–76. See also the many references provided with this article.
11. Koestler, A. *The Sleepwalkers*. Macmillan Company, New York, 1959.
12. Lin, C. C. "Objectives of Applied Mathematics Education," *SIAM Rev.*, *9* (1967), 293–311.
13. Pollak, H. O. "Applications of Mathematics," in *Mathematics Education*. University of Chicago Press, Chicago, Illinois, 1970.
14. Ravetz, J. "The Origins of the Copernican Revolution," *Sci. Am.*, *215* (1966).
15. Restle, F., and J. G. Greeno. *Introduction to Mathematical Psychology*. Addison-Wesley Publishing Company, Reading, Massachusetts, 1970.
16. Restle, F. *Mathematical Models in Psychology*. Penguin Books, Middlesex, England, 1971.
17. Samuelson, P. A. "A Biological Least-Action Principle for the Ecological Model of Volterra-Lotka," *Proc. Nat. Acad. Sci. USA*, *71* (1974), 3041–3044.
18. *The Scientific World of Copernicus*. ed. B. Biénkowska, Forword by Z. Kopal. D. Reidel Publishing Company, Dordrecht, Holland, 1973.
19. Small, R. *An Account of the Astronomical Discoveries of Kepler* with a Forword by W. D. Stahlman. University of Wisconsin Press, Madison, Wisconsin, 1963.

20. Sternberg, S. "Stochastic Learning Theory," in *Handbook of Mathematical Psychology*, Vol. II, R. D. Luce, R. R. Bush, and E. Galanter, eds. John Wiley and Sons, New York, 1963.
21. Wigner, Eugene P. "The Unreasonable Effectiveness of Mathematics in the Natural Sciences," *Comm. Pure Appl. Math.*, XIII (1960), 1–14.

The references listed below, while not cited in the paper, provide additional sources of information and examples. Some of the items are concerned with applications to particular situations or classes of situations, and others illustrate and study the model building process.

Apostel, Leo. "Towards the formal study of models in the non-formal sciences," in *The Concept and the Role of the Model in Mathematics and Natural and Social Sciences*, H. Freudenthal, ed. Gordon and Breach, New York, 1961.

Bailey, Norman T. J. *The Mathematical Approach to Biology and Medicine*. John Wiley and Sons, New York, 1967. See especially Chapter 3, "The Process of Scientific Research."

Ball, R. J. "Econometric Model Building," in *Mathematical Model Building in Economics and Industry*, M. G. Kendall, ed. Hafner Publishing Company, New York, 1968.

Bergstrom, A. R. *Selected Economic Models and their Analysis*. New York, American Elsevier Publishing Company, 1967. See especially Chapter 1, "Introduction."

Cohen, Hirsh. "Mathematics and the Biomedical Sciences" in *The Mathematical Sciences*. The MIT Press, Cambridge, Massachusetts, 1969.

Dantzig, George B. *Linear Programming and Extensions*. Princeton University Press, Princeton, New Jersey, 1963.

Dyson, Freeman J. "Mathematics in the Physical Sciences" in *The Mathematical Sciences*. The MIT Press, Cambridge, Massachusetts, 1969.

Kemeny, J. G., and J. L. Snell. *Mathematical Models in the Social Sciences*. Ginn/Blaisdell, Waltham, Massachusetts, 1962. See especially Chapter 1.

Kendall, M. G. "Model Building and Its Problems," in *Mathematical Model Building in Economics and Industry*, M. G. Kendall, ed. Hafner Publishing Company, New York, 1968.

Kowal, Norman E. "A Rationale for Modeling Dynamic Ecological Systems," in *Systems Analysis and Simulation in Ecology*, Bernard C. Patten, ed. Academic Press, New York, 1971.

Luce, R. D., and H. Raiffa. *Games and Decisions*. John Wiley and Sons, New York, 1957.

Maki, Daniel P., and M. Thompson. *Mathematical Models and Applications*. Prentice-Hall, Englewood Cliffs, New Jersey, 1973. See especially Chapter 1, "Basic Principles."

Rapoport, Anatol. "Lewis F. Richardson's Mathematical Theory of War," *J. Conflict Resolution, 1* (1957), 244–299.

Saaty, Thomas L. *Mathematical Methods of Operations Research*. McGraw-Hill Book Company, New York, 1959. See especially Chapters 1 and 3.

Saaty, Thomas L. *Topics in Behavioral Mathematics*. Mathematical Association of America, Washington, D. C., 1973.

Simon, Herbert A. "Some Strategic Considerations in the Construction of Social Science Models," in *Mathematical Thinking in the Social Sciences*, Paul Lazarsfeld, ed. The Free Press, Glencoe, Illinois, 1959.

Suppes, Patrick. "A Comparison of the Meaning and Uses of Models in Mathematics and Empirical Sciences," in *The Concept and The Role of the Model in Mathematics and Natural and Social Sciences*, H. Freudenthal, ed. Gordon and Breach, New York, 1961.

Several of the NSF Chautauqua-Type Short Courses (sponsored cooperatively by AAAS and NSF) have Study Guides that contain examples of mathematical modeling.

Those courses offered during 1974–75 for which study guides were prepared are listed together with the lecturer(s) below.

Behavior-Genetic Analysis, Jerry Hirsch.
Patterns of Problem Solving, Moshe F. Rubinstein.
Public Policy Analysis: Theory and Some Applications, Elinor Ostrom.
Water Polution, David Kidd.
Conflict Regulation, Paul E. Wehr.
Mathematical Modeling and Computing in the Physical, Biological, and Social Sciences, William Dorn and Jack Cohen.
Atmospheric Sciences, Vincent J. Schaefer and Volker A. Mohnen.

CHAPTER 2

Proportional Representation

Edward Bolger*

1. Introduction

Suppose the voters of a certain school district are to elect five of their members to represent them on the local school board. Suppose also that approximately one-fifth of the voters are women and one-fifth are black males. What type of voting system should be used if we wish to give the women and the blacks the *opportunity* to elect at least one woman and one black (assuming there are women and blacks among the nominees)? A widely used voting method in the United States is the method of *plurality voting* in which each voter may cast up to a total of five votes (if five are to be elected). The voter casts one vote or no votes for a given candidate. The five candidates with the largest vote totals are declared elected.

With say 8000 voters and five to be elected, it is clear that, under plurality voting, a coalition C of 4001 members can elect five candidates of its choice by giving each of its five candidates 4001 votes. The most any other candidate could receive is 3999 votes.

Exercises

1. Show that under plurality voting a coalition consisting of a majority of the voters can always sweep the election.
2. Give an example to show that a minority might sweep an election.
3. For the above illustration (8000 voters, five to be elected), determine the coalition sizes needed to guarantee the election of 1, 2, $\cdots$, 5 candidates. Assume plurality voting is to be used.

* Department of Mathematics and Statistics, Miami University, Oxford, Ohio 45056.

A voting method used in several states (see Glasser [5] and Young [12]) to elect members to a corporate board is the method of cumulative voting. In these notes, *cumulative voting* is the method in which each voter may cast a total of e votes (assuming e is the number to be elected), distributing these e votes (not necessarily in integral units) among as many candidates as desired. For example, a voter may cast one vote for each of e candidates. Or, the voter may cast $e/2$ votes for each of two candidates. The e candidates with the most votes are declared elected.

If, under cumulative voting, a coalition C of 4001 members (out of 8000 voters) ran a full slate of five candidates, then its "lowest ranking" candidate, say C_5, could not receive (from coalition C) more than 4001 votes. If the remaining 3999 voters each cast 1.1 votes for some other candidate D, then D would have more votes than C_5, and C_5 would not be elected.

In the next section we shall demonstrate that cumulative voting usually provides the opportunity for proportional representation. (It should be noted that this method does not *force* a member of a group, say a woman, to cast all her votes for a woman candidate. She may cast her votes as she pleases.)

One of the major arguments against the use of cumulative voting for corporate directors is that, because it does usually provide proportional representation, it may promote factional strife and thus seriously affect the efficiency of the company. For more on this point and for other arguments against cumulative voting, see Axley [1] and Young [12]. For a comprehensive attack on the concept of proportional representation, see Hermens [6].

EXERCISES

4. With cumulative voting, does it make any difference how many votes a voter may cast? For instance, if with $e = 8$ each voter could cast up to 16 votes, would the strategy of a coalition be different than if each voter could cast a total of eight votes?

5. Show that under each of the voting methods discussed so far (and indeed under any "reasonable" voting method), a candidate who receives more than $N/(e + 1)$ votes must be declared elected. Here, N is the total number of votes cast.

2. Cumulative Voting

In what follows, we shall let v be the total number of voters, N the total number of votes cast, and e the number to be elected. We assume $v > e$.

Theorem 1 and Lemma 1 indicate why cumulative voting can provide the opportunity for proportional representation.

Theorem 1. *Under cumulative voting, a coalition C of n voters can guarantee the election of* $[ne/v]$ *candidates, where* $[y]$ *stands for the largest integer less than or equal to y.*

PROOF. Let $x = [ne/v]$. Then coalition C may cast ne/x votes for each of x candidates. We shall show that it is impossible for each of $e - x + 1$ other candidates to receive at least ne/x votes. Indeed, it is easy to see that since $x \leq ne/v$, we have

$$\frac{e - x + 1}{x} \geq \frac{e - (ne/v) + 1}{(ne/v)}.$$

It follows that

$$(e - x + 1) \cdot \frac{ne}{x} \geq \left(e - \frac{ne}{v} + 1\right) \cdot \frac{ne}{(ne/v)}$$
$$= ve - ne + v > (v - n)e.$$

The result follows since $(v - n)e$ is the total number of votes that can be cast by the other $v - n$ voters. □

EXAMPLE. Suppose $n = 46$, $v = 81$, $e = 8$. According to the previous theorem, a coalition of 46 voters can elect $[(46/81) \cdot 8] = 4$ candidates by giving each of its four candidates $(46)(8)/4 = 92$ votes. Actually, the coalition can elect five candidates by giving each of them 368/5 votes. The reader should verify this latter claim.

The above example leads us to wonder if the result in the above theorem can be sharpened. In order to accomplish this, we use the following lemma.

Lemma 1. *Under cumulative voting, a coalition C of n voters can quarantee the election of k candidates if and only if*

$$\frac{n}{k} > \frac{v - n}{e - k + 1}$$

or, equivalently, if $n(e + 1) > kv$.

PROOF. A coalition of n voters can give each of k candidates ne/k votes. The least popular of $e - k + 1$ other candidates could receive no more than $(v - n)e/(e - k + 1)$ votes. Thus the coalition of n voters can guarantee the election of k candidates if $(ne/k) > (v - n)e/(e - k + 1)$. On the other hand, if $n/k \leq (v - n)/(e - k + 1)$, then the other $v - n$ voters can block the election of the kth candidate of coalition C. (In case of equality, a tie might result.) □

Corollary. *A coalition of n voters can guarantee the election of* $[(ne/v) + 1]$ *candidates if* $[(ne/v) + 1] \cdot v < n(e + 1)$.

EXAMPLE. Let $v = 81$ and $e = 8$. A coalition of size 55 can guarantee the election of six candidates since $(6)(81) < (55)(9)$.

EXERCISES

6. Suppose $n = 41$, $v = 81$, $e = 8$. Under cumulative voting, how many candidates should a coalition of 41 voters support and how many votes should the coalition give to each of its candidates? Assume that the candidates supported by coalition C will receive no support from the other voters.
7. (Continuation). Answer the same questions for a coalition of 60 members.
8. Either prove directly or deduce from the above lemma that if $kv < n(e + 1)$, then $(e - k + 1)v \geq (v - n)(e + 1)$.
9. Prove that a coalition can elect k candidates if its size is at least $\{[kv/(e + 1)] + 1\}$.

There remains the question as to whether a coalition can guarantee that it will elect more than its "fair share."

10. Prove that $n(e + 1) < [(ne/v) + 2] \cdot v$. (Assume $n \leq v$.)
11. Conclude that under cumulative voting a coalition of n voters cannot guarantee that it will elect more than

$$\begin{cases} \dfrac{ne}{v} \text{ candidates if } \dfrac{ne}{v} \text{ is an integer,} \\ \left[\dfrac{ne}{v} + 1\right] \text{ candidates if } \dfrac{ne}{v} \text{ is not an integer.} \end{cases}$$

It appears that if one is interested in "proportional representation," then cumulative voting would be a reasonable voting method. However, in English-speaking countries, "proportional representation" is often identified with the method of the single transferable vote, which will be described briefly (and incompletely) in the next section. For a complete description of the method of single transferable voting, see Lakeman and Lambert [9], especially Appendices IV and V. For a description of several other proportional representation schemes, also see Rae [10].

STV (single transferable voting) was used to elect city council members in several U.S. cities including New York, Cincinnati, Ashtabula, and Hamilton, Ohio but is no longer used in any of these cities. For a list of places where STV has been used, see Lakeman and Lambert [9]. Critics of STV claim that it strengthens factions and promotes extremist groups, that it leads to inefficient government, and that it weakens the two-party system (see Hermens [6]). Proponents of STV claim that STV has often been dropped when an "undesirable" minority appears to have an opportunity to elect one of its members. For a defense of STV, see Hoag and Hallett [7], and Humphreys [8].

3. Single Transferable Vote

Each voter ranks in descending order of preference as many (or as few) candidates as he or she pleases (ties are not allowed). At the first count, a voter's vote goes entirely to the candidate ranked first on the voter's ballot. However, if a candidate receives at least q votes where

$$q = \left[\frac{v}{e+1} + 1\right],$$

then that candidate is declared elected. If at the first count fewer than e candidates are elected, then we define for each elected candidate C (if any) the *surplus* to be the number $V(C)$ of votes received by candidate C minus q. These surplus votes are then transferred to the next remaining active (i.e., not yet elected or eliminated) candidate on the voters' lists. There are several methods of transfer. The method recently used by the American Mathematical Society involves transferring to the next remaining active candidate

$$\frac{V(C) - q}{V(C)}$$

votes. This method is also used to elect members of the Irish Senate (Bergh [2]). Thus if $q = 25$ and a candidate received 100 votes, then 75/100 votes would be transferred to the next remaining active candidate on each of the voters' ballots that had originally been assigned to the elected candidate. If, after all surpluses have been dealt with, fewer than e candidates have been elected, then some candidates shall be eliminated and the votes currently assigned to them transferred to the next remaining active candidate on the voter's ballot. There are several methods for deciding whom to eliminate, but basically one eliminates the candidates with the lowest vote total. The process continues (including transfer of surpluses created by the elimination of candidates) until either e candidates have been declared elected (by receiving q votes) or until further elimination will no longer affect those to be ultimately elected. (If only k candidates receive q votes, then the remaining $e - k$ candidates declared elected are those with the largest vote totals.) The fact that proportional representation is usually obtained is related to the following theorem.

Theorem 2. *If* $eq \leq v$, *then* $n \geq [ne/v] \cdot q$.

PROOF. $v \geq eq \Rightarrow 1 \geq eq/v \Rightarrow n \geq (ne/v) \cdot q \geq [ne/v] \cdot q$. □

It follows that a coalition of n voters can, under STV, elect $[ne/v]$ candidates provided $eq \le v$. We now investigate conditions under which $eq \le v$.

Lemma 2. *If* $q = [v/(e+1)] + 1$, *then* $(e+1)(q-1) \le v \le q(e+1) - 1$. *The proof is left as an exercise for the reader.*

Theorem 3. *If* $e < q$, *then* $eq \le v$.

Proof. $e < q \Rightarrow e + 1 \le q \Rightarrow eq \le eq + q - e - 1 \Rightarrow eq \le (e+1)(q-1) \le v$. □

Theorem 4. *If* $v > e(e+1)$, *then* $eq \le v$.

Proof. $v > e(e+1) \Rightarrow q > e$. □

Theorem 5. *If* $e^2 \le v \le e(e+1)$, *then* $eq \le v$.

Proof. The result is trivial if $v = e(e+1)$, so consider the case where $e^2 \le v < e(e+1)$. Then

$$\frac{e^2}{e+1} \le \frac{v}{e+1} < e \Rightarrow \left[\frac{e^2}{e+1} + 1\right] \le \left[\frac{v}{e+1} + 1\right] < e + 1 \Rightarrow$$

$$e \le q < e + 1 \Rightarrow q = e,$$

and hence $eq = e^2 \le v$. □

Combining the previous two theorems, we get

Theorem 6. *If* $v \ge e^2$, *then* $eq \le v$.

Exercises

12. For $v = 25, 30, 35$, and 40, find the first value of e for which $eq > v$.

13. Construct an example of an election in which no candidate receives q votes.

Example. Let $v = 170$ and $e = 16$, so that $q = 11$. Consider a coalition of 85 voters. Under cumulative voting, this coalition could effect the election of $[(ne/v)] = 8$ candidates. Is this also true under STV? Suppose the coalition's candidates are $C_1, C_2, \cdots, C_8$, and each member of the coalition ranks C_8 last. Further suppose that these eight candidates have no other support. Then the first seven will all be elected before any candidates are excluded (since transfer of surplus occurs before any elimination). C_8 will then have eight votes. If there were nine other candidates each with nine votes, then C_8 would not be elected and the coalition would not elect its proportional share.

NOTE. The problem in the preceding example is that $eq > v$. One way out of this difficulty is to redefine $q = (v + 1)/(e + 1)$ (and no longer require q to be an integer). It is left as an exercise for the reader to show that if $v \geq e$ and if $q = (v + 1)/(e + 1)$, then $eq \leq v$. Another solution (suggested by Robert M. Thrall of Rice University) would be to lower the quota to 10 after one candidate is elected with 11 votes, i.e., to reevaluate the quota after election of each candidate.

Another major advantage of STV is that it usually results in a small proportion of "wasted" votes. A vote is wasted if it is cast for a candidate who cannot use it (either because this candidate already has enough votes to be elected or will eventually be defeated). Empirical studies support the claim that a small proportion of votes are wasted with STV. One can, of course, construct examples where most of the votes are wasted even when using STV. This usually only happens when the voters list too few choices.

With cumulative voting, a very popular candidate might receive far more votes than needed. Similarly, votes may be wasted on unpopular candidates. In the sequel, we shall consider modifications of cumulative voting that alleviate these difficulties.

4. Cumulative Voting with Transfer of Surplus

Let $q = (ve + 1)/(e + 1)$. Let $V(A)$ be the total number of votes assigned to candidate A. Declare A elected if $V(A) \geq q$. (Wc are assuming here that the basic voting method used is cumulative voting.)

EXERCISE

14. Why is it impossible for more than e candidates to receive q votes each?

Definition. If $V(A) \geq q$, then $V(A) - q$ is called A's surplus.

Declare all candidates with nonnegative surpluses elected. Now let A be the candidate with the largest surplus. Call a candidate B a remaining active candidate if $V(B) < q$. Now transfer to the only remaining active candidates $V(A) - q$ votes, leaving candidate A with the q votes needed for election. We consider now the problem of which $V(A) - q$ votes should be transferred.

NOTE. At this point it might be appropriate to consider several procedures for choosing the votes to be transferred. For example, transfer the first $V(A) - q$ votes encountered or select at random.

The method to be followed here is essentially the same as that used in the preceding section under STV. That is, if voter i originally cast $V_i(A)$ votes for candidate A, transfer $V_i(A)[(V(A) - q)/V(A)]$ of voter i's votes from candidate A to voter i's remaining active candidates. If voter i has no remaining active candidates, make no transfer for voter i.

EXAMPLE. Let $v = 89$ and $e = 10$ so that $q = 81$. Suppose $V(A) = 243$. Then 162 votes may be transferred from A. Suppose further that voter i had cast three votes for A. We transfer $3 \cdot (162/243) = 2$ votes to voter i's remaining active candidates.

This still leaves the question of how many of the votes to be transferred should be assigned to each of the remaining active candidates on a given voter's list.

NOTE. At this point one might wish to discuss several possibilities, such as
(1) transfer all to the candidate receiving the highest number of votes from voter i.
(2) share the transferable votes equally.

We shall transfer "proportionately." To this end, let V_i' be the total number of votes cast by voter i for his remaining active candidates. Then transfer to candidate B

$$\frac{V_i(B)}{V_i'} \cdot \frac{V(A) - q}{V(A)} \cdot V_i(A) \text{ votes.}$$

EXAMPLE. Let $v = 89$, $e = 10$, and $V(A) = 243$. Then, as above, $q = 81$. Suppose voter i had cast his votes:

A	3
B	3
C	2
D	2

Then we transfer

$$\tfrac{3}{7} \cdot \tfrac{2}{3} \cdot 3 \text{ votes to B,}$$

$$\tfrac{2}{7} \cdot \tfrac{2}{3} \cdot 3 \text{ votes to C,}$$

$$\tfrac{2}{7} \cdot \tfrac{2}{3} \cdot 3 \text{ votes to D,}$$

provided B, C, and D are remaining active candidates. Thus, after the transfer, voter i's votes are distributed as follows:

A	1
B	$\frac{27}{7}$
C	$\frac{18}{7}$
D	$\frac{18}{7}$

EXERCISES

15. Note that the total number of votes cast by voter i is still 10, and the proportion assigned to B (of those assigned to B, C, and D) is still 3/7. Show that these properties hold in general.

16. Let $v = 100$ and $e = 8$. Suppose candidate A initially receives 356 votes.
    a) Determine the value of q.
    b) What is A's surplus?
    c) Suppose voter i had cast four votes for candidate A. How many of voter i's votes would be transferred from candidate A?
    d) Suppose voter i had cast his votes:

A	4
B	2
C	1
D	1

Assuming B, C, and D are remaining active candidates, how many of voter i's votes will be transferred to B, C, and D, respectively?

NOTE. One might wish to allow the voter to list on the ballot some candidates to whom he or she wishes to assign initially 0 votes. The transfer process would be the same as above until the voter has no remaining active candidates with positive numbers of votes (on the voter's ballot). The transferred votes would then be shared equally by the candidates with 0 votes. This might aid a coalition that grossly underestimates its size.

EXAMPLE. Let $v = 100$ and $e = 8$, so that $q = 89$. Consider a coalition C, which knows its size is between 25 and 55 members. In order to play it safe, the coalition could run a slate of four candidates, instructing its members to cast their votes for these four candidates in the proportions 89 : 89 : 21 : 1. Then if its size is 25, its four candidates will receive 89, 89, 21, and 1 votes, respectively. On the other hand, if its size is 55, then its four candidates will receive 979/5, 979/5, 231/5, and 11/5 votes, respectively. In the latter case, 534/5 votes are wasted on each of its two leading candidates. Under transferable voting, the coalition would (by casting its votes in the proportions 89 : 89 : 21 : 1) elect two candidates if its size is between 25 and 33, three candidates if its size is between 34 and 44, and four candidates if its size is between 45 and 55. Moreover, if the coalition size were 55 and if the coalition had given some token support to a fifth candidate (or if one could transfer votes to a candidate listed with 0 votes), then the coalition's fifth candidate would eventually receive 84 votes from the coalition and might be elected if the opposition is not united.

EXERCISES

17. In the above example, what might happen to coalition C under standard (nontransferable) cumulative voting if the size of coalition C were 25 and it ran a slate of four candidates, dividing its votes equally among the four candidates?

18. Let $v = 89$ and $e = 10$, so that $q = 81$. Consider a coalition C which knows its size is between 9 and 24 members.
    a) If its size is 9, how many candidates should coalition C be able to elect? What if its size is 24?
    b) Assuming transferable cumulative voting, how many candidates should coalition C support and how many votes should be assigned to each of its candidates by each of its members?

It would obviously be desirable to have a voting system in which a coalition could do just as well by instructing its members to cast equal numbers of votes for the coalition's candidates. In the next section we consider such a system.

5. Cumulative Voting with Transfer of Surplus and Elimination of Low-Ranking Candidates

In this section we shall consider cumulative voting with transfer of surplus but we shall add one new feature. If after all transfers of surplus votes, fewer than e candidates have been declared elected, then the candidate with the lowest vote total shall be eliminated, and the votes currently assigned to the eliminated candidate by voter i shall be transferred to voter i's remaining active candidates in accordance with the proportional transfer process described in the preceding section. (In case of a tie, the candidate to be eliminated shall be chosen at random.) The process continues (including transfer of surpluses created by elimination of candidates) until either e candidates have been declared elected (by receiving q votes) or until further elimination will no longer affect those to be ultimately elected. If only k candidates receive q votes, then the remaining $e - k$ candidates declared elected are those with the largest vote totals. This voting method will be called cumulative transferable voting (CTV).

EXAMPLE 1. Suppose voter i had cast his votes:

A	6
B	2
C	1

and candidate A is to be eliminated. The six votes assigned to A shall be transferred, four going to B and two to C.

EXAMPLE 2. Let $v = 100$ and $e = 8$, so that $q = 89$. Consider again a coalition C, which knows its size is between 25 and 55 members. The coalition can support *eight* candidates, instructing its members to cast one vote each for its eight candidates. Consider the worst case where the size of the coalition is 25. The opposition, after the transfer of all surpluses (and assuming the opposition is united), will have elected exactly six candidates since $6 \cdot 89 < 600$ whereas $7 \cdot 89 > 600$. Since fewer than eight candidates have been declared elected, the candidate with the lowest vote total is eliminated. Assuming that none of the opposition has cast a single vote for any of the coalition's candidates, the elimination process will continue until six of the coalition's candidates have been eliminated, leaving the remaining two candidates with more than 89 votes each.

Recall that under standard (i.e., nontransferable) cumulative voting, a coalition of n voters can guarantee the election of k candidates if and only if $kv < n(e + 1)$. If k is the largest such positive integer, then the coalition can elect k candidates by giving each of its k candidates ne/k votes. (Actually, there are instances where a coalition should adopt the strategy of supporting $k + 1$ candidates, one more than its "share." For more on strategies connected with cumulative voting, see Brams [4] and Sawyer and MacRae [11].) However, in order to elect its share of the candidates *under standard cumulative voting, a coalition must have a fairly accurate estimate of its size*. Otherwise it may end up electing fewer candidates than it should.

One of the more famous examples of the use of standard cumulative voting is the 1883 election of the board of directors of the Sharpsville Railroad Company. (See Brams [4] and Glasser [5].) There were two coalitions, one controlling 53% of the votes, the other controlling 47% of the votes. The majority coalition ran a full slate of six candidates, whereas the minority ran a slate of four candidates. Each coalition divided its votes equally among its candidates. As a result, the minority elected four candidates and the majority elected only two candidates. *Had they used CTV, each coalition would have elected three candidates.*

Exercise

19. Let $v = 81$ and $e = 8$. Assuming standard cumulative voting, how many candidates can a coalition of size 54 "safely" support, assuming each of the members of the coalition votes only for members of the coalition and assuming the coalition's candidates receive equal numbers of votes from the coalition.

If we allow transfer of surplus and elimination of low ranking candidates, then a *coalition can quarantee it will elect its share of the candidates even though it has no idea of its size. This can be accomplished by directing each of its members to cast one vote for each of e candidates* selected in advance by the coalition. To see this, let C be a coalition of (unknown) size n. Let k be the largest integer such that $kv < n(e + 1)$. It follows (see Exercise 6) that $(e - k + 1)v \geq (v - n)(e + 1)$. Now if the opposition runs $e - k + 1$ other candidates, its lowest ranking candidate cannot receive more than $(v - n)e/(e - k + 1)$ votes. But

$$\frac{v-n}{e-k+1} \leq \frac{v}{e+1} \Rightarrow \frac{(v-n)e}{e-k+1} \leq \frac{ve}{e+1} < \frac{ve+1}{e+1},$$

so that the opposition does not have $e - k + 1$ quotas. After elimination of $e - k$ of coalition C's candidates, each of coalition C's remaining candidates will have ne/k votes and, since $ne/k > (v - n)e/(e - k + 1)$, coalition C will elect at least k candidates.

Thus a coalition need not concern itself with the number of candidates it should run. The coalition can support a full slate of candidates.

EXERCISE

20. Prove that if $kv < n(e + 1)$, then $ne \geq kq$.

We conclude from the above exercise that if a coalition C can guarantee the election of k candidates under standard cumulative voting, *then this coalition can elect, under CTV, k candidates.*

6. An Illustration of the Use of Cumulative Voting

Cumulative voting is used in Illinois to elect representatives to the Illinois General Assembly. Each party may run a slate of one, two, or three candidates (with three to be elected in each district). Each voter has three votes that he may distribute 3 : 0, 2 : 1, 3/2 : 3/2, or 1 : 1 : 1 among three candidates. (For a description of how the number and the names of the candidates are chosen, see Blair [3].) The majority party often ran a slate of only two candidates, even when the majority controlled more than 75% of the votes. This may have been done out of fear that their percentage might fall below 75%, although it has been suggested that, in some districts, there is an unwritten agreement that the majority will run only two candidates. (For a further discussion of the strategies of the parties, see Brams [4] and Sawyer and MacRae [11].) If they were to adopt CTV, each party could run a slate of three candidates and be guaranteed that it will elect its proper share of the representatives.

7. STV versus CTV

Assuming proportional representation is the goal, which (if either) of STV and CTV should be used?

NOTE. The instructor might wish to pose the above question for classroom discussion and/or a class project. Some obvious differences are

(1) STV requires that each voter rank his choices with ties not allowed.
(2) CTV, although allowing ties, requires that each voter decide how many votes to give to each of his candidates.
(3) It is easier to design a voting machine for STV.

Whether CTV is a practical voting system or just another mathematician's folly is unknown at this writing. A biased sample of political scientists indicated that the system has some merit. The author would appreciate receiving reactions to CTV.

References

1. Axley, Ralph, E. "The Case Against Cumulative Voting," *Wisconsin Law Review* (1950), 278–287.
2. Bergh, George van den. *Unity in Diversity*. Batsford, London, 1956.
3. Blair, George S. "Cumulative Voting: An Effective Electoral Device in Illinois Politics," *Studies in Social Sciences*, University of Illinois Press, *45* (1960).
4. Brams, Steven J. *Game Theory and Politics*. The Free Press, New York, 1975.
5. Glasser, Gerald J. "Game Theory and Cumulative Voting for Corporate Directors," *Management Sci.*, *5* (1959), 151–156.
6. Hermens, F. A. *Democracy or Anarchy*? The Abbey Press, St. Meinrad, Indiana, 1941.
7. Hoag, Clarence, and Hallett, Jr., George. *Proportional Representation*, The Macmillan Company, New York, 1926.
8. Humphreys, John H. *Proportional Representation*, Methuen and Co. Ltd., London, 1911.
9. Lakeman, Enid, and Lambert, James. *Voting in Democracies*, Faber and Faber, London, 1955.
10. Rae, Douglas. *Political Consequences of Electoral Laws*, Yale University Press, New Haven, Connecticut, 1967.
11. Sawyer, Jack, and MacRae, Duncan. "Game Theory and Cumulative Voting in Illinois: 1902–1954," *Am. Political Science Review*, *56* (1962), 937 f.
12. Young, George H. "The Case for Cumulative Voting," *Wisconsin Law Review*, January 1950, 49–56.

Notes for the Instructor

Objectives. This module discusses some of the mathematical aspects of two voting schemes designed to provide proportional representation. It is suitable for use in freshman mathematics and political science courses.

Prerequisites. A course in precalculus mathematics that included properties of simple inequalities.

Time. This module can be completed in about two hours of class time.

CHAPTER 3
Comparison Voting[1]

Steven J. Brams*

1. Preview: Do the Rules of the Game Make a Difference?

As a preview of the subsequent analysis, imagine the following hypothetical situation. Assume that the five most recent Democratic presidents all lived at the same time (the present). All decide to seek their party's presidential nomination in the first presidential primary in New Hampshire. You are a registered Democratic voter in New Hampshire and can vote for any candidate. If the candidate with the most votes wins in a plurality election, which candidate would you vote for? (Your judgment should be based not on the specific policies advocated by these presidents at the time they served, but instead on their competence to solve problems and their effectiveness as political leaders.)

[Conduct in class a secret-ballot election among Jimmy Carter, Lyndon Johnson, John Kennedy, Harry Truman, and Franklin Roosevelt. Do not announce the results of the election.]

Now assume that the election rules change to permit a runoff between the top two vote-getters if no candidate receives a majority of votes in the plurality election.

[Conduct in class a secret-ballot election and announce the results only if no candidate receives a majority of votes. Then, given that no candidate

[1] This module is based in part on material contained in Brams [2], Brams [4], Brams and Fishburn [7], and Brams [5]. The latter two works contain detailed citations to the literature not given here. A booklength treatment and extension of results in this module, which was published as an Innovative Instructional Unit (Test Edition) by the American Political Science Association in 1978, can be found in Brams and Fishburn [6].

* Department of Politics, New York University, New York, N.Y. 10003.

receives a majority of votes, conduct a secret-ballot runoff election. Do not announce the results of the runoff.]

Next assume that in the plurality election, each voter can cast either a vote for a candidate (indicated by a + 1 after his name on the ballot), or a vote against a candidate (indicated by a − 1 after his name on the ballot), but not both. In other words, a voter can cast either a "positive" vote for his most-preferred candidate, or a "negative" vote against his least-preferred candidate, but he cannot vote for/against more than one candidate. Each candidate's negative votes are subtracted from his positive votes to give him a "net vote" total (which may be negative). The candidate with the most net votes—the highest positive number or, that failing, the lowest negative number—wins. There is no runoff election even if no candidate's net vote is positive.

[Conduct in class a secret-ballot election with negative voting allowed. Do not announce the results of the election.]

Finally, assume that negative voting is not allowed, but a voter can cast a single positive vote for as many candidates as he wishes. In other words, he can vote for between one and five candidates; he does so by writing on his ballot the names of all candidates he chooses to support. (This form of voting is called "approval voting" since a voter can approve of as many candidates as he wishes.) There is no runoff election.

Ballots

I. *Plurality election:* Vote for one.
 1. Jimmy Carter
 2. Lyndon Johnson
 3. John Kennedy
 4. Harry Truman
 5. Franklin Roosevelt

II. *Runoff election* (between top two vote-getters in plurality election if no candidate receives a majority): Vote for one.
 1. Jimmy Carter
 2. Lyndon Johnson
 3. John Kennedy
 4. Harry Truman
 5. Franklin Roosevelt

III. *Negative voting election:* Vote for one (+1) or against one (−1), but not both.
 1. Jimmy Carter
 2. Lyndon Johnson
 3. John Kennedy
 4. Harry Truman
 5. Franklin Roosevelt

IV. *Approval voting election:* Vote for one or more.
 1. Jimmy Carter
 2. Lyndon Johnson
 3. John Kennedy
 4. Harry Truman
 5. Franklin Roosevelt

[Conduct in class a secret-ballot election under approval voting. Now announce the winner(s) under (1) plurality voting, (2) plurality voting with a runoff, (3) negative voting, and (4) approval voting.]

Exercises

1. Try to explain similarities or differences in the election results under the four different election rules.
2. Which of the four rules seems "fairest"? Specify criteria.
3. Is there an election rule that you would prefer to any of the four that does not require voters either to rank the candidates or to allocate different numbers of votes among them? Why? [Conduct in class a secret-ballot election under this rule and compare the result with those under the four previously postulated rules.]
4. [Conduct in class reruns of all the elections under the different rules, but now by a show of hands instead of by secret ballot.] Try to explain why a knowledge of the secret-ballot election results does or does not change the outcome in each case. (You may think of the earlier secret-ballot results as a poll, with later balloting taking account of information provided by the poll.)
5. Assume that you are a member of the committee in the House of Representatives or Senate in the General Court of New Hampshire (its state legislature) charged with responsibility for drafting a bill to change the law governing preferential voting, and the selection of delegates to national party conventions, in the New Hampshire presidential primary. What language would you suggest to implement the election rule you consider most desirable?

Note. With respect to voting in the New Hampshire presidential primary, the current law (58:5-a, effective September 13, 1977) reads as follows:

> Every qualified voter, eligible to vote in the election of his party, shall have opportunity at such presidential preference primary to vote his preference, on the ballot of his party, for his choice for one person to be the candidate of his political party for president of the United States and one person to be the candidate of his political party for vice president of the United States, either by writing the names of such persons in blank spaces to be left in said ballot for that purpose, or by marking a cross or check mark opposite the printed names of the persons of his choice, as in the case of other primaries.

With respect to the apportionment of delegates to the national party conventions, the law (57:8) says:

> Based on the total of the votes cast statewide for each presidential candidate, the secretary of state shall determine the percentage of the total votes received by each presidential candidate of a political party, and apportion the number of delegates each of the successful candidates are entitled to receive. The apportionment shall be determined by the proportion of votes cast for each presidential candidate whose name was on the ballot that bears to the total votes cast for all presidential candidates of the same political party at such election, rounded to the nearest whole number. A presidential candidate shall receive at least 10% of the total vote cast in his political party to be eligible for a percentage of the apportioned delegates.

2. Introduction

It has been proposed by George A. W. Boehm [1] that voters in an election be allowed either to cast a vote for or a vote against one candidate, but not both. Under this scheme, as indicated in Section 1, a candidate's "negative" votes would be subtracted from his "positive" votes to determine his *net vote*, and the candidate with the highest net vote would win.

Boehm argues that the introduction of negative votes in United States presidential elections would force the candidates to appeal to the voters with positive programs, not just try to be the least unpopular candidate in the race. To prevent a candidate from winning who had little popular appeal, but who otherwise might be preferred because he attracted few negative votes, Boehm suggests that a threshold (say, at least 10% of the total votes cast) be set that a winning candidate's net vote would have to exceed for him to be elected.

In this module, I shall show that there is never any incentive for a voter to cast a negative vote in a two-candidate race, except to register his dissatisfaction with one of the candidates or possibly prevent the leading candidate from obtaining the number of net votes required to be elected (if there is a minimum threshold that must be met). Because a voter can always bring about the same outcome with a positive vote as with a negative vote in a two-candidate race without a minimum threshold, negative votes are superfluous in such a contest.

To be sure, the psychological impact of negative votes may be considerable, especially in the case where the net vote of the "winner" is negative. However, if one's reason for casting negative votes is to ensure or prevent the election of a candidate, then a negative vote against a candidate always has the same effect on the outcome as a positive vote for the other candidate if there is no minimum threshold.

In three-candidate races, by contrast, negative votes may be uniquely advantageous: A voter can definitely do better, in some circumstances, by casting a negative vote against a candidate rather than a positive vote for either of the other two candidates. This fact will be demonstrated both in the case in which the candidate with a plurality wins and the case in which there is a runoff election between the top two vote-getters in the plurality contest if no candidate wins a majority of votes.

In races with more than three candidates, I shall show that some of the advantages of negative voting break down, and it is useful to ask whether the *idea* of negative voting can be incorporated in a voting scheme that allows for the fuller expression of voter preferences. Indeed, it will be shown that a simple generalization of the idea of negative voting that allows a voter to cast "approval" votes for one *or more* candidates is equivalent to a negative voting strategy in specific cases.

More generally, however, approval voting opens up possible voting strategies for a voter that a single positive or a single negative vote does not permit. Not only may it lead to more desirable strategy choices for individual voters, but it may also produce more desirable outcomes for a plurality or majority of voters than could be achieved by restricting voters to a single positive or single negative vote. According to criteria to be set forth later, several general results for approval voting will be established that allow comparisons with other systems that permit voters to vote for no more than one, no more than two, $\cdots$, candidates, without ranking them according to their preferences.

The possible effects of poll announcements on the voting behavior of individuals, and on election outcomes, will then be discussed and illustrated for an actual election. Finally, an application of the theoretical analysis to voting in the 1968 multicandidate presidential election in the United States will be presented.

As new concepts are introduced in this module, they are italicized and defined. Many examples are given throughout the module, both in the text and the exercises, to illustrate the analysis, which builds up gradually to include general results we call theorems. In most but not all cases, once a theorem is stated, a proof is offered to establish its validity.

Although this style of analysis is still uncommon in political science, it is being more and more used in rigorous scientific treatments of a variety of subjects. Its main advantage is that it allows one to make statements that are valid, or logically true—that is, that can be derived step by step from a set of assumptions and are always true if the conditions of the theorem are met. To the extent that these statements describe a real-life situation or class of events, they offer generalizations, not just specific illustrations, of what will follow under the given conditions.

These generalizations are particularly important when we compare voting systems and try to establish which are superior according to specified criteria. When we look at an actual election, on the other hand, our interest is not in general results but in specific changes that might have occurred had a different voting system been used. This is precisely the question asked in Section 9, where I report on an attempt made to reconstruct from survey data what the outcome would have been in the 1968 presidential election had approval voting been used.

3. Negative Voting in Two-Candidate Contests

To fix ideas, let us first examine the effect of negative voting in a two-candidate contest. Assume that X and Y are two candidates running for office, and every voter has a preference scale defined over these candidates. He may prefer X to Y, which we indicate by the scale (X, Y), Y to X, which we indicate by the scale (Y, X), or be indifferent between the two candidates, which we indicate by the scale $(X - Y)$.

Given negative voting, every voter has four *strategies*: (1) vote for X (X); (2) vote against X ($\bar{X}$); (3) vote for Y (Y); (4) vote against Y ($\bar{Y}$). (We ignore the strategy of abstaining, because it cannot change the outcome of voting by all other voters, which is the focus of our subsequent analysis.) A voter is *rational* if he chooses a strategy that is *undominated*: There is no other strategy that is as good in all contingencies, and, in at least one contingency, better.

"Contingencies" are the *states of nature* that can arise from the voting of all the *other* voters. If there are n voters, there are 4^{n-1} states of nature since the $n - 1$ other voters can each choose one of their four possible strategies.

However, many of these states of nature lead to the same *result*, which we define to be the ordered pair (x, y), where x is the net vote cast for X and y is the net vote cast for Y by the $n - 1$ other voters. In fact, to determine the undominated strategies of a voter, we have to concern ourselves with only a relatively few results—those in which the vote of a single voter can make a difference in the outcome.

A voter's vote can *make a difference* if and only if it makes or breaks a tie. In a two-candidate race, a voter can break a tie (of the $n - 1$ other voters) if the result is $x = y$, he can make a tie if $x = y - 1$ or $y = x - 1$. For all other results (i.e., where $|x - y| > 1$), a voter's vote would not change the *outcome*, which we define to be the candidate—or candidates, in the case of a tie—who receives the larger net vote and is thereby elected.

If there is a tie, presumably one candidate will eventually be selected, perhaps by some random device. In evaluating this outcome, we assume that a voter allows for the possibility that either candidate will eventually be selected. Thus, if his preference scale is (X, Y), it follows that he will rank the tied outcome X/Y "in the middle"—$(X, X/Y, Y)$; if his preference scale is $(X - Y)$, then $(X - X/Y - Y)$ since indifference between X and Y implies indifference among X, X/Y, and Y.

I have already indicated that in two-candidate contests there are only three results of voting by the $n - 1$ other voters in which a voter's vote is

Table 1. Outcomes in Two-Candidate Contest with Negative Voting

Strategies of voter	Relevant results for $n - 1$ other voters: $n - 1$ (even)	$n - 1$ (odd)	
	$x = y$	$x = y - 1$	$y = x - 1$
X	X	X/Y	X
$\bar{X}$	Y	Y	X/Y
Y	Y	Y	X/Y
$\bar{Y}$	X	X/Y	X

decisive: $x = y$; $x = y - 1$; $y = x - 1$. Since the strategy a voter chooses cannot change the outcome associated with any other result, these are the only results relevant to the determination of undominated strategies. The outcomes generated by a voter's four strategies for these results in a two-candidate contest are shown in Table 1.

Notice that the outcomes associated with strategy $\bar{X}$ are exactly the same as those associated with strategy Y, and the outcomes associated with strategy $\bar{Y}$ are exactly the same as those associated with strategy X, for all relevant results. Since a voter who casts a negative vote against one candidate can always do as well by casting a positive vote for the other candidate, both these strategies are undominated and a negative vote is not uniquely advantageous in a two-candidate contest.

In Section 4, I shall show that in a three-candidate contest among X, Y, and Z, there is one situation in a plurality election in which casting a negative vote is definitely preferable to casting a positive vote. Even when the plurality election is followed by a runoff election between the top two vote-getters, negative voting may still be advantageous. But first we deal with the case without a runoff.

4. Negative Voting in Three-Candidate Contests without a Runoff

Consider three-candidate contests in which the candidate with the most votes wins (plurality elections). If there is no single plurality winner, a voter evaluates tied outcomes in the manner described earlier.

In Table 2, outcomes associated with the 16 relevant results and six strategies of each voter are shown for a plurality election. Numerical examples are also given in Table 2 for the subsets of relevant results that are the same except for the order in which x, y, and z are listed in the triple (x, y, z).

Thus, for example, there are three relevant results in which two candidates are tied with the same number of votes and the third candidate has one more vote than the other two. These results are indicated in the first three columns of Table 2: Z has the extra vote in column 1, Y in column 2, and X in column 3. The numerical example given above these three columns in Table 2, $(x, y, z) = (0, 0, 1)$, illustrates the case in which Z has the extra vote.

In Table 3, the undominated strategies of a voter are given for four different preference scales. The four preference scales given in Table 3 include all preference scales indistinguishable except for order. Thus, while the three outcomes X, Y, and Z can be permuted in six different ways ($3! = 3 \times 2 \times 1 = 6$), the five permutations different from (X, Y, Z) are indistinguishable except for order. Similarly, there are two preference scales indistinguishable from $(X, Y - Z)$ except for order (either Y or Z is ranked

Table 2. Outcomes in Three-Candidate Contest with Negative Voting

	Relevant results (and examples) for $n-1$ other voters															
	$(x, y, z) = (0, 0, 1)$			$(x, y, z) = (1, 1, 0)$			$(x, y, z) = (0, 0, -2)$			$(x, y, z) = (2, 1, 0)$						$(x, y, z) = (0, 0, 0)$
	1	2	3	4	5	6	7	8	9	10	11	12	13	14	15	16
Strategies of voter	$x = y = z-1$	$x = z = y-1$	$y = z = x-1$	$x-1 = y-1 = z$	$x-1 = z-1 = y$	$y-1 = z-1 = x$	$x-1 = y-1 > z$	$x-1 = z-1 > y$	$y-1 = z-1 > x$	$x-1 = y > z$	$x-1 = z > y$	$y-1 = x > z$	$y-1 = z > x$	$z-1 = x > y$	$z-1 = y > x$	$x = y = z$
X	X/Z	X/Y	X	X	X	$X/Y/Z$	X	X	Y/Z	X	X	X/Y	Y	X/Z	Z	X
$\bar{X}$	Z	Y	$X/Y/Z$	Y	Z	Y/Z	Y	Z	Y/Z	X/Y	X/Z	Y	Y	Z	Z	Y/Z
Y	Y/Z	Y	X/Y	Y	$X/Y/Z$	Y	Y	X/Z	Y	X/Y	X	Y	Y	Z	Y/Z	Y
$\bar{Y}$	Z	$X/Y/Z$	X	X	X/Z	Z	X	X/Z	Z	X	X	X/Y	Y/Z	Z	Z	X/Z
Z	Z	Y/Z	X/Z	$X/Y/Z$	Z	Z	X/Y	Z	Z	X	X/Z	Y	Y/Z	Z	Z	Z
$\bar{Z}$	$X/Y/Z$	Y	X	X/Y	X	Y	X/Y	X	Y	X	X	Y	Y	X/Z	Y/Z	X/Y

Table 3. Undominated (Dominant) Strategies for Four Preference Scales with Negative Voting

Preference scales	Undominated (dominant) strategies
(X, Y, Z)	$X, \bar{Z}$
$(X, Y - Z)$	(X)
$(X - Y, Z)$	$(\bar{Z})$
$(X - Y - Z)$	$X, \bar{X}, Y, \bar{Y}, Z, \bar{Z}$

first), and two indistinguishable from $(X - Y, Z)$ except for order (either X or Y is ranked last). If the order in which indifference is indicated is irrelevant, indifference among the three outcomes is obviously given by one scale: $(X - Y - Z)$.

In the subsequent analysis, I assume that the preference relation (P) and indifference relation (I) that underlie the scales of individual voters are *transitive*: if A, B, and C are any three candidates, APB and BPC imply APC; and AIB and BIC imply AIC. This assumption ensures that for a voter with preference scale (X, Y, Z) or $(X - Y - Z)$, for example, it is always true that (X, Z) in the case of the former, $(X - Z)$ in the case of the latter.

For two of the four preference scales in Table 3, $(X, Y - Z)$ and $(X - Y, Z)$, there is only one undominated strategy of a voter. A unique undominated strategy is necessarily *dominant*—as good as, and in at least one contingency better than, any other strategy—which means it is an unequivocally best choice, whatever result shown in Table 2 occurs.

Let us verify this for a voter with preference scale $(X, Y - Z)$. To do so, we must compare the outcomes associated with his dominant strategy X with the outcomes associated with his five other strategies for the 16 relevant results. To begin with, note that the outcomes associated with strategy X are at least as good as the outcomes associated with his five other strategies. Thus, for example, if strategy X does not yield his first choice X as an outcome, neither do his other strategies.

Is strategy X better than every other strategy in at least one contingency? For result 5, it yields X, which is a better outcome for our voter than strategies $\bar{X}$, Y, $\bar{Y}$, and Z—which all can lead to nonpreferred outcomes Y or Z—offer. But strategy X is also better than strategy $\bar{Z}$, because even though it leads to the same outcome as X for relevant result 5, X leads to a better outcome than $\bar{Z}$ for relevant result 6 ($X/Y/Z$ versus Y). In this contingency, strategy X allows for the possibility that outcome X will be chosen, but strategy Z always ensures that nonpreferred outcome Y will be chosen. Thus, we have shown that X is a dominant strategy for a voter with preference scale $(X, Y - Z)$: It leads to outcomes at least as good as, and sometimes better than, any other strategy.

The fact that $\bar{Z}$ is dominant when the preference scale of a voter is $(X - Y, Z)$ demonstrates that a negative vote is uniquely advantageous in this situation. While it leads to no better an outcome than strategy X or strategy Y for 13 of the 16 relevant results, it leads to a definitely superior outcome for three results (better than X for results 6, 9, and 15; better than Y for results 5, 8, and 14). We say that $\bar{Z}$ *dominates* X and Y (as well as all other strategies) for a voter with preference scale $(X - Y, Z)$.

In words, the preference scale $(X - Y, Z)$ of a voter says that he is indifferent between two candidates (X and Y) but definitely prefers them to the third candidate (Z). In such a situation, it is always rational for a voter to cast a negative vote against Z rather than a positive vote for either of the two candidates, X and Y, that he prefers.

EXERCISES

6. Verify that X and $\bar{Z}$ are undominated strategies for a voter with preference scale (X, Y, Z).

7. What strategy dominates Y for a voter with preference scale (X, Y, Z)?

5. Negative Voting in Three-Candidate Contests with a Runoff

What if the election is not decided in the three-candidate plurality contest but in a runoff between the top two vote-getters? For the purpose of comparing negative voting in a single plurality contest with voting in a plurality contest followed by a runoff, assume for now that—consistent with most present-day procedures—a voter cannot cast a negative vote in the plurality contest. Then the undominated (dominant) strategies for the four preference scales, given earlier in Table 3, are shown in Table 4. Comparing undomi-

Table 4. Undominated (Dominated) Strategies for Four Preference Scales without Negative Voting

Preference scales	Undominated (dominant) strategies
(X, Y, Z)	X, Y
$(X, Y - Z)$	(X)
$(X - Y, Z)$	X, Y
$(X - Y - Z)$	X, Y, Z

nated and dominant strategies in the two tables, we see that when a voter's strategy of voting against his last choice ($\bar{Z}$) is unavailable, it may be advantageous for him to vote for his second choice [Y if his preference scale is (X, Y, Z)], or either one of his first choices [X or Y if his preference scale is $(X - Y, Z)$].

Can a voter's choice of these apparently inferior strategies, when he is restricted to casting only a positive vote, be rectified in a runoff? If we assume, as is common in many jurisdictions that allow for a runoff between the top two vote-getters, that the runoff occurs if and only if no candidate in the plurality election receives a majority of votes, the answer is "not necessarily." In other words, the restriction of voters to a single positive vote may again force them to choose inferior strategies, compared with strategies available under negative voting, even when a runoff is permitted.

An example will help to clarify this point. Assume that there are five voters, whose preference scales are as follows: (1) $(X, Y - Z)$; (2) $(X, Y - Z)$; (3) $(Y, X - Z)$; (4) $(Y, X - Z)$; (5) (X, Y, Z). From Table 4, we know that voters 1–2 and voters 3–4 have dominant strategies: vote for X and vote for Y, respectively. Now, if voters are restricted to a single positive vote in the plurality election, voter 5 has two undominated strategies (given that he has no information about the preference scales of the other voters and therefore cannot predict how they will vote): vote for X or vote for Y (see Table 4). Clearly, strategy X would be preferable if X and Y were tied and Z were out of the running; on the other hand, strategy Y would be preferable if Y and Z were tied and X were out of the running.

Regardless of which undominated strategy voter 5 chooses, either X or Y will receive a majority of votes and there will be no runoff. If voter 5 chooses strategy Y, however, and Y thereby obtains a majority of votes, three of the five voters (1, 2, and 5) will be dissatisfied. For X is the so-called *Condorcet winner*, that is, the candidate preferred by a majority of voters in pairwise contests between each of the other candidates, Y and Z. In a pairwise contest between X and Y, X would be preferred by voters 1, 2, and 5; similarly, these voters would also prefer X to Z in a pairwise contest between those two candidates. Yet, if all voters but voter 5 choose their dominant strategies, and voter 5 chooses his undominated strategy Y, Y will defeat the Condorcet winner X.

Would negative voting have prevented the choice of Y in a plurality election with a runoff if there were no majority winner (of net votes)? The answer is "yes," because, whichever of his undominated strategies voter 5 chose in the plurality election—X or $\bar{Z}$ (see Table 3)—he would have prevented the election of Y. If he had voted for X, X would have defeated Y 3 votes to 2, and there would have been no runoff. If he had voted against Z, the plurality contest would then have resulted in a 2-to-2 tie between X and Y (with Z's net vote being -1), and X would have won in the runoff since voter 5 would prefer him to Y.

Clearly, allowing for a runoff in a plurality contest restricted to positive voting does not necessarily recapture the advantages of negative voting; specifically in our example, lead to the election of the Condorcet winner. Permitting negative voting, on the other hand, does lead to the election of the Condorcet winner, at least in our example, if there is a runoff between the top two vote-getters when neither finalist receives a majority of votes. In addition, our example suggests that if there is a Condorcet winner, negative voting is better able to find him, though I postpone a further discussion of this question until a generalization of negative voting is offered in Section 6.

In summary, we have seen that although negative voting offers no unique advantage to a voter in two-candidate contests, negative votes in a plurality contest among three candidates—with or without a runoff between the top two—may be uniquely advantageous for a voter, depending on his preference scale. In addition, negative voting can ensure the selection of a Condorcet winner when a runoff does not.

As we shall see in Section 6, however, the apparent advantages of negative voting do not carry through to plurality contests with more than three candidates. Yet, a simple generalization of negative voting in more populous contests can prevent the most undesirable outcomes from occurring, given voters can make a dichotomous division of the candidates. In particular, if all voters can divide the candidates into two categories, "acceptable" and "unacceptable," the candidate who is acceptable to the most voters will be elected when the voters choose their dominant strategies. Such strategies, as will be proven in Section 7, always exist.

EXERCISE

8. With negative voting, verify that strategy $\bar{Z}$ does not dominate strategy X for a voter with preference scale (X, Y, Z), but does dominate X for a voter with preference scale $(X - Y, Z)$. What does this difference suggest about when the advantages of negative voting will be greatest in an electorate?

6. Advantages of Approval Voting

Consider a four-candidate contest among the set of candidates $(\{W, X, Y, Z\})$. If a voter has preference scale $(W - X, Y - Z)$, and he can cast either one positive or one negative vote, whom should he vote for or vote against?

It is not necessary to construct a table of relevant results for four-candidate plurality contests to show that this voter has four undominated strategies: Cast a positive vote for W or X (strategies W and X) or cast a negative vote against Y or Z (strategies $\bar{Y}$ and $\bar{Z}$). Clearly, if the result of voting by the $n - 1$ other voters is (0, 0, 0, 0), casting a positive vote for either W or for X are the only strategies that ensure the election of a preferred candidate (W or X). If the results are either (1, 0, 1, 0) or (0, 1, 1, 0), casting a negative vote against Y is the only strategy that ensures the election of a preferred candidate in both contingencies; similarly, if the results are (1, 0, 0, 1) or (0, 1, 0, 1), casting a negative vote against Z is the only strategy that ensures the election of a preferred candidate in both contingencies. In both the latter cases, negative votes eliminate a nonpreferred candidate and thereby make a preferred candidate the winner.

But in these examples there is a strategy, if a voter can cast more than one positive vote, that is as good as, and for at least one relevant result better than, any of the four "best" (undominated) strategies described above. For a voter with preference scale ($W - X$, $Y - Z$), this strategy is to cast two positive votes, one for W and one for X.

For the two results (1, 0, 1, 1) and (0, 1, 1, 1), this strategy ensures the election of one of one's more-preferred candidates, whereas none of the four undominated strategies under negative voting can offer this assurance for both results. In the case of all other results, including those described previously for which the four undominated negative voting strategies are best, casting two positive votes for W and X is a strategy that cannot be improved upon.

Thus, the strategy of casting two positive or "approval" votes for W and X is as good as, and in at least one contingency better than, any of the four undominated strategies described earlier of casting a single positive or a single negative vote. Hence, it dominates these four strategies. If there are m candidates, voting that allows a voter to cast m or fewer positive or approval votes, but no more than one vote for each candidate, we call *approval voting*.

The reason that negative voting does not yield as good a set of outcomes for all relevant results as approval voting in our example is because of the restriction of a voter to only one positive or one negative vote. If there are m candidates, this means that a voter can cast a positive vote in m ways, and a negative vote in m ways, giving him a total of $2m$ strategies. (If we also include the abstention strategy of casting no positive votes for all candidates, or the equivalent strategy of casting no negative votes for all candidates, a voter has $2m + 1$ strategies.) By contrast, under approval voting, a voter can cast either an approval vote or no vote for each of the m candidates, giving him 2^m voting strategies. (Since, however, the abstention strategy of casting no approval votes is equivalent to the strategy of casting m approval votes for all the candidates, a voter has $2^m - 1$ nonequivalent strategies.) Because $2^m - 1 > 2m + 1$ if $m > 3$, approval voting in general allows a voter more voting strategies in multicandidate races.

When $m = 3$, $2^m - 1 = 2m + 1 = 7$, and negative voting yields the same outcomes as approval voting. The reason is that, eliminating the abstention strategy, six strategies remain under both types of voting. Clearly, the three positive voting strategies in which one positive vote is cast for one of the three candidates are also approval strategies, and the three negative voting strategies in which one vote is cast against one of the three candidates

Table 5. Numbers of Admissible Voting Strategies for Three Voting Systems with Four Candidates

Preference scale	No. of admissible strategies for: Approval voting	Negative voting	Plurality voting
Dichotomous			
$(W, X - Y - Z)$	1	1	1
$(W - X - Y, Z)$	1	1	3
$(W - X, Y - Z)$	1	4	2
Trichotomous			
$(W - X, Y, Z)$	2	4	3
$(W, X, Y - Z)$	2	4	2
$(W, X - Y, Z)$	4	2	3
Multichotomous			
(W, X, Y, Z)	4	4	3

are equivalent to approval strategies in which two positive votes are cast for the other two candidates. Thus, when there are three candidates, the strategies and outcomes under negative voting and approval voting are equivalent.

One might note that "disapproval" voting (negative voting for more than one candidate) is in general equivalent to approval voting, given that the candidate with the fewest negative votes wins. The reason is evident: A voter who casts positive votes under approval voting for one subset of candidates would cast negative votes for the complementary subset under disapproval voting. Since both forms of voting change the difference in the vote between the approved and disapproved candidates by one vote, they both yield the same outcomes.

It may be feared that since the number of approval voting strategies increases exponentially with the number of candidates, approval voting may well overwhelm voters with a wealth of options. For example, if there are as few as four candidates, there are $2^4 - 1 = 15$ approval voting strategies. If we assume, however, that the salient consideration for a voter with a given preference scale is the number of these voting strategies that are undominated or dominant, then this number is not necessarily greater under approval voting than under the other forms of voting we have considered.

To illustrate this fact, define a strategy for a voter with a given preference scale to be *admissible* if and only if it is either undominated or dominant. Then the number of admissible voting strategies for plurality voting (no runoff), negative voting, and approval voting among a set of four candidates (W, X, Y, Z) are shown in Table 5 for all distinct preference scales (except that indicating indifference among all candidates). Note that three scales are *dichotomous* (divide candidates into two subsets, among whose members a voter is indifferent), three are *trichotomous* (divide candidates into three subsets), and one is *multichotomous* (divides candidates into more than three subsets).

It is apparent from Table 5 that approval voting generally offers fewer admissible strategies to a voter than the other voting systems when a voter's preference scale is dichotomous. When a voter's preference scale is trichotomous, approval voting offers more admissible strategies than the other two systems for one preference scale, $(W, X - Y, Z)$. In the case of the single multichotomous scale, approval voting and negative voting offer a voter the same number of admissible strategies. Thus, although approval voting may offer more admissible strategies than the other systems, as when a voter's preference scale is $(W, X - Y, Z)$, it may also offer fewer admissible strategies than the others, as when a voter's preference scale is dichotomous. Hence, it is not generally true that approval voting will overwhelm voters with a wealth of *viable* options (Brams and Fishburn [7], Fishburn [8]).

EXERCISES

9. What are the four admissible approval voting strategies of a voter with preference scale $(W, X - Y, Z)$? Prove that each strategy is admissible by indicating the result or results for which it yields a uniquely best outcome for the voter.

10. For three candidates, show by enumeration that the number of admissible strategies of a voter under approval and negative voting is *always* equal to or less than the number of his admissible strategies under plurality voting, except when a voter is indifferent to all the candidates.

7. General Results for Approval Voting

The first general results we shall establish for approval voting relate to optimal strategies.

Theorem 1. *If a voter has dichotomous preferences, he has a dominant strategy under approval voting: Vote for all members of his preferred subset. We call this strategy his* approval strategy.

PROOF. Consider a strategy (N) in which a voter does *not* vote for all members of his preferred subset. Then this strategy is dominated by a voter's approval strategy (A), because for at least one result of voting by the $n - 1$ other voters, A would give a preferred candidate who did not receive a vote under N more votes than any other candidate and hence make him the winner. For results in which A would not make this preferred candidate the winner, it would either create a tie between him and another winning candidate or have no effect on the outcome. Thus, a voter's approval strategy cannot prevent the choice of another candidate (if a tie is created or the outcome is unaffected), but it will ensure the choice of a preferred candidate for at least one result. Hence, this strategy dominates a strategy of not voting for all members of one's preferred subset.

Consider a strategy (M) in which a voter votes for all members of his preferred subset *plus* one or more candidates who are members of his nonpreferred subset. Then this strategy is dominated by his approval strategy, because for at least one result of voting by the $n - 1$ other voters, M would give a nonpreferred candidate more votes than any other candidate and hence make him the winner. For results in which M would not make this nonpreferred candidate the winner, it would either create a tie between him and another winning candidate or have no effect on the outcome. Thus, a voter's approval strategy cannot prevent the choice of another candidate (if a tie is created or the outcome is unaffected), but it will prevent the choice of a nonpreferred candidate for at least one result. Hence, this strategy dominates a strategy of voting for all members of one's preferred subset plus one or more candidates who are members of one's nonpreferred subset.

By a similar argument, one can show that a voter's approval strategy dominates his strategy of voting for some (but not all) members of his preferred subset and some (but not all) members of his nonpreferred subset. Since this strategy dominates all other voting strategies under approval voting, it is a dominant strategy. □

Theorem 2 reverses the implication of Theorem 1.

Theorem 2. *If a voter has a dominant strategy under approval voting, his preferences are dichotomous.*

PROOF. The proof is by contradiction. Assume that a voter's preferences are *not* dichotomous. Then there are two possibilities:

(1) He is indifferent among all the candidates, in which case he does not have a dominant strategy since all his strategies are undominated.
(2) He can divide the set of candidates into more than two disjoint subsets, with at least one member, such that the following preference ordering holds: Each member of a first subset, among whom the voter is indifferent, is preferred to each member of a second subset; each member of the second subset, among whom the voter is indifferent, is preferred to each member of a third subset; and so on.

In fact, for possibility (2) the division into subsets can be read off directly from a voter's preference scale. The first subset contains the candidate(s) that the voter most prefers but among whom he is indifferent; the second subset contains the candidate(s) the voter next most prefers but among whom he is indifferent; and so on.

By assumption, there are at least three nonempty disjoint subsets into which the candidates can be divided for possibility (2). Without loss of generality, assume that the voter's preferences are trichotomous, and let candidates X, Y, and Z be the only members of the first, second, and third subsets, respectively. For a voter with preference scale (X, Y, Z), consider the following results (x, y, z) of voting by the $n - 1$ other voters: (i) (2, 2, 0); (ii) (0, 2, 2). For result (i), a voter has no better strategy than to vote for X, thereby making his most-preferred candidate the winner; for result (ii), a voter has no better strategy than to vote for Y, or for X and Y, thereby making his next most-preferred candidate the winner. Now, for a strategy of a voter with preference scale (X, Y, Z) to be dominant, he *must* vote for Y in the case of result (ii), but he *cannot* vote for Y in the case of result (i), so there is a contradiction.

Thus, no strategy exists that is best for a voter for all results of voting by the other voters. Hence, a voter does not have a dominant strategy if his preferences are not dichotomous. Consequently, only if a voter has dichotomous preferences will he have a dominant strategy under approval voting. □

Taken together, Theorems 1 and 2 establish the logical equivalence between dichotomous preferences and the existence of a dominant strategy under approval voting. Theorem 1 also says what this strategy is for a voter with dichotomous preferences—vote for all members of his preferred subset.

To be sure, not all voters may have dichotomous preferences. Let us assume, however, that instead of asking voters to rank candidates, we ask them simply to distinguish acceptable from unacceptable candidates—and not discriminate among candidates within these two classes. If this division of candidates into two classes meets the conditions of Theorem 1—that is, if all voters are truly indifferent among members of each class, however they make the division—they will have dominant strategies under approval voting: their approval strategies of voting only for the candidates they deem acceptable.

We shall next characterize the nature of outcomes under approval voting, given that all voters can divide the set of candidates into acceptable and unacceptable classes, among whose members each voter is indifferent. (If all voters make only a two-way division, of course, they have dichotomous preferences.)

Theorem 3. *If all voters have dichotomous preferences, and they choose their approval strategies, a candidate wins under approval voting if and only if he is a Condorcet winner.*

Proof. By definition, a winning candidate under approval voting is judged acceptable by more voters than any other candidate. Since we assume that the voters who consider each candidate acceptable in a plurality election do not change their judgment in a pairwise contest, a winning candidate in the plurality election will remain a winner in each pairwise contest, and vice versa. □

Thus, unlike many other voting procedures, under which a winning candidate may not be a Condorcet winner, approval voting always produces a Condorcet winner, given that voters only distinguish between acceptable and unacceptable candidates (i.e., they have dichotomous preferences). Of course, a winning candidate under approval voting—even when voters are able to divide the candidates into acceptable and unacceptable classes, and choose their dominant strategies—may not be acceptable to a majority of voters. The most that can be said of the winning candidate in such a situation is that (i) he will be acceptable to more voters than any other candidate; and (ii) in a pairwise contest with every other candidate, he will be acceptable to a majority of voters who consider either one or both candidates of the pair acceptable.

Approval voting has other desirable properties if all voters have dichotomous preferences. To describe these, first we need some definitions. A voting *strategy* is *sincere* if and only if, whenever it includes voting for some candidate, it also includes voting for all candidates preferred to him. A voting *system* is *sincere* for a set of voters if and only if no voter in the set has an admissible strategy that is insincere.

Theorem 4. *If all voters have* dichotomous *preferences, every system is sincere; if some voters have* trichotomous *preferences but no multichotomous preferences, approval voting is uniquely sincere; if some voters have* multichotomous *preferences, no voting system is sincere.*

The proof of this theorem, which applies to all voting systems in which a voter cannot rank candidates but can only vote for one candidate, one or two candidates, $\cdots$, m or fewer candidates, is beyond the scope of this module and is given elsewhere (Brams and Fishburn [7]). We can, however, illustrate it by referring to the results for the three nonranked voting systems given in Table 5.

We leave for an exercise verification that (i) for the three dichotomous preference scales given in Table 5, admissible strategies under approval voting, negative voting, and single plurality are all sincere; (ii) for the three trichotomous scales, only the admissible strategies under approval voting are all sincere. To illustrate the third part of Theorem 4, consider the four admissible approval voting strategies for the multichotomous scale: vote for (1) $\{W\}$; (2) $\{W, X\}$; (3) $\{W, Y\}$; (4) $\{W, X, Y\}$. Clearly, (3) is not sincere since it does not include voting for X, who is preferred to Y.

To show when it would be advantageous for a voter to choose his insincere admissible strategy $\{W, Y\}$, assume that he thinks that the result of voting by the other voters might be either (i) (1, 1, 0, 0) or (ii) (0, 0, 1, 1). Then his only admissible strategy that simultaneously ensures the election of W in the case of (i), and the election Y (and the defeat of Z) in the case of (ii), is $\{W, Y\}$.

The problem with such an insincere strategy is that if the result of voting by the other voters is, say, (0, 1, 1, 1), the voter's next-worst choice Y is elected. On the other hand, if the voter had chosen his sincere admissible strategy $\{W, X, Y\}$, the voter's next-best choice X would have been elected. Thus, the voter has reason to regret his insincerity.

This cannot happen, however, if the voting system is sincere and voters choose admissible strategies. Although a voter may not obtain his best choice under such a system, after the election he cannot regret having failed to vote for a candidate (X in the above example) preferred to the lowest-ranked candidate he voted for (Y in the above example).

There is still a stronger criterion than sincerity that may be used to characterize voting systems. A voting system is *strategy-proof* for a set of voters if and only if every voter in the set has exactly one strategy that is admissible (in which case this strategy must be sincere).

Theorem 5. *If all voters have* dichotomous *preferences, approval voting is uniquely strategy-proof; if some voters have* trichotomous *or* multichotomous *preferences, no voting system is strategy-proof.*

Like Theorem 4, the proof of Theorem 5 is beyond the scope of this module and is given elsewhere (Brams and Fishburn [7]). From Table 5, however, it can readily be ascertained that for the four-candidate case, and the three voting systems under consideration, (i) approval voting is the only system in which a voter has just one admissible strategy for all dichotomous preferences, namely, his approval strategy; (ii) no system, including approval voting, limits a voter to just one admissible (sincere) strategy when preferences are trichotomous or multichotomous.

Like sincerity, strategy-proofness seems a desirable property for a voting system to possess. If a voter has only one admissible strategy, he will never have an incentive to deviate from it for strategic reasons even if he knows the result of voting by all the other voters.

Sincerity, on the other hand, does not imply such stability but rather says that whatever admissible strategy a voter chooses, he will vote for *all* candidates above the lowest-ranked candidate that his admissible strategy includes. Thus, if a candidate that a sincere voter votes for wins, the sincere voter can rest assured that he could not have brought about the election of a more-preferred candidate by choosing a different admissible strategy.

A voting system that encourages sincere voting, it seems, would probably produce higher voter turnout. By allowing voters to tune their preferences more finely, and forcing them to make insincere choices for strategic reasons less often, approval voting may well stimulate more voters to express themselves at the polls and enhance their positive attitudes toward the system.

Taken together, Theorems 4 and 5 establish that approval voting is the most sincere and strategy-proof of all systems in which a voter can vote for, but not rank, candidates. Yet, we should not forget the limitations of these and the other results; strategy-proofness, as well as the existence of dominant strategies (Theorems 1 and 2)—which is closely related—depends entirely on the preferences of all voters' being dichotomous. So does the assured selection of a Condorcet winner under approval voting (Theorem 3). Only the weaker criterion of sincerity extends to trichotomous preferences under approval voting; for multichotomous preferences, there seem to be no significant desiderata that distinguish approval voting strategies and outcomes from those that other nonranked voting systems offer the voter.

Despite the restriction of our positive results to dichotomous and trichotomous preferences, multicandidate races in which voters make only two- or three-way preference divisions of the candidates seem quite common. We shall say more about the relationship of our theoretical results to empirical data in Section 9, but first we assay some possible effects of poll announcements on voting strategies and outcomes.

Exercises

11. For plurality voting and approval voting, list the admissible strategies for dichotomous preference scale $(W - X, Y - Z)$ and for trichotomous preference scale $(W - X, Y, Z)$.
12. Verify that these strategies are sincere under the two voting systems for dichotomous preference scale $(W - X, Y - Z)$, but only under approval voting are these strategies sincere for trichotomous preference scale $(W, X - Y, Z)$.

8. The Possible Confounding Effects of a Poll[2]

We know from Theorem 3 that if not all voters have dichotomous preferences, a non-Condorcet winner may be elected under approval voting. As an example, consider an election among a set of four candidates $\{W, X, Y, Z\}$ where the electorate consists of four voters whose preference scales are as follows: (1) (Y, W, X, Z); (2) (Y, W, X, Z); (3) (Y, X, W, Z); (4) (Z, X, W, Y). Assume that each voter judges the three candidates he ranks highest to be "acceptable," his last choice "unacceptable." Then, under approval voting, W and X will each receive 4 votes, Y 3 votes, and Z 1 vote. Yet, Y is the Condorcet winner if we take account of the complete preference scales of the voters, though he loses to both W and X under approval voting.

Curiously, if a pollster announced the above results before the election, and voters changed their votes to distinguish between the two likely winners W and X, each voter would have an incentive to divide acceptable and unacceptable candidates as follows (indicated by a slash): (1) $(Y, W/X, Z)$; (2)

[2] Much of the material in this section was suggested to me by Philip D. Straffin, Jr.

$(Y, W/X, Z)$; (3) $(Y, X/W, Z)$; (4) $(Z, X/W, Y)$. By voting only for his favorite candidate of the two, either W or X, each voter would make his vote "count" for one of the likely winners (but not the other).

Now the results of the election would be that W and X would each receive 2 votes, Y 3 votes, and Z 1 vote, so Y, the Condorcet winner, would be elected. However, if the preferences of voters 3 and 4 were (Y, W, X, Z) and (Z, W, X, Y), respectively, W would defeat the Condorcet winner Y by 4 votes to 3 after the results of the poll were announced.

So far I have shown by examples that if the preferences of voters are not dichotomous, a Condorcet winner may not be elected under approval voting. Neither is a Condorcet winner guaranteed election by a poll that induces voters to adjust their voting strategies to distinguish between the top two candidates in the poll. However, we can prove one general result that relates Condorcet winners and polls.

Theorem 6. *If one of the top two candidates indicated by a poll is a Condorcet winner, this candidate will always defeat the other top candidate if voters adjust their voting strategies after the poll.*

PROOF. By assumption, voters adjust their strategies to distinguish between the top two candidates. But this is the same distinction they would make in a pairwise contest between these two candidates, so the Condorcet winner (who by definition defeats every other candidate in a pairwise contest) will defeat the other top candidate after the poll announcement. □

Note that the sufficient condition for this theorem, that the Condorcet winner be one of the top two candidates indicated by the poll, was not met by our earlier examples. That this condition is not necessary is shown by the previous example in which the Condorcet winner is elected after the poll announcement, though he is not one of the top two candidates in the poll.

The restriction of voters today to only one vote in plurality elections probably leads to the election of non-Condorcet winners more frequently than would approval voting. To see how approval voting might have counteracted this problem in a real-life case, consider the 1970 New York race for the United States Senate among James R. Buckley, Charles E. Goodell, and Richard L. Ottinger. Although the conservative candidate, Buckley, won this election, probably a majority of voters would have preferred either of the more liberal candidates—Goodell or Ottinger—who collectively got 61% of the vote to Buckley's 39%.[3]

Suppose one-half of the 24% who supported Goodell and the 37% who supported Ottinger had felt truly indifferent between these two candidates. Had they been able to cast approval votes for both Goodell and Ottinger (their dominant strategy under approval voting), then Goodell would have

[3] For reasons why voters support third-party candidates under plurality voting, see Riker [15].

received about 42% of the vote, Ottinger 49%, and Buckley would have finished last. Likewise, a runoff election between Buckley and the leading liberal candidate, Ottinger, probably also would have resulted in the defeat of Buckley. We see, therefore, that in a real-life instance either approval voting or a run-off election would probably have prevented the will of the majority from being thwarted. (As was shown in Section 5, however, negative [and approval] voting may not produce the same outcome as a run-off election.)

In the 1970 Senate race in New York, it seems plausible to assume that the preference scales of supporters of Buckley (B), Goodell (G), and Ottinger (O) were (B, G, O), (G, O, B), and (O, G, B), respectively. If we also assume that Buckley supporters considered only B acceptable, but Goodell and Ottinger supporters considered both G and O acceptable, then G and O would have tied with the most votes, and Buckley again would have finished last under approval voting.

If, however, we assume that in addition to the mutual support that Goodell and Ottinger supporters confer on each other, Buckley supporters considered Goodell acceptable, then Goodell would have emerged as the clear-cut winner. In fact, Stratmann [18] estimates, based on work reported in Stratmann [17], that under approval voting Goodell would have won with about 59% of the vote to about 55% each for Buckley and Ottinger: Whereas Buckley and Ottinger would have received significant support from Goodell voters, Goodell would have benefited from the support of *both* Buckley and Ottinger voters.

Now suppose there was a poll that indicated Goodell and Ottinger to be the top two candidates. Then, under approval voting, supporters of each of the three candidates would be motivated to make the following divisions between acceptable and unacceptable candidates in their preference scales: B—(B, G/O); G—(G/O, B); O—(O/G, B). Paradoxically, Goodell, the candidate with the fewest supporters, would get the most votes—from both his and Buckley's supporters.

This result is not as paradoxical as it first seems when one realizes that Goodell is the Condorcet winner: He would defeat both Buckley and Ottinger in pairwise contests by getting the votes of the third candidate. In fact, as the Condorcet winner, and one of the top two candidates in the poll, we know from Theorem 6 that Goodell *must* defeat the other top candidate in the poll (Ottinger) after the poll announcement.

Surprisingly, it is possible for a candidate who is not one of the top two in the poll to defeat, after the poll announcement, one of the top two in the poll. Even if one of the top two is a Condorcet winner, who by Theorem 6 will always defeat the other top candidate, he may still lose after the poll to a third and lower-standing candidate. As an example of this bizarre circumstance, assume there are a set of three candidates $\{X, Y, Z\}$ and six classes of voters with the following numbers of members and preference scales for the candidates:

(1) 10: (X, Y, Z)
(2) 10: (X, Z, Y)
(3) 9: (Y, X, Z)
(4) 10: (Y, Z, X)
(5) 15: (Z, X, Y)
(6) 11: (Z, Y, X)

If all voters consider the top two candidates acceptable under approval voting, the outcome is Z—46, X—44, and Y—40. (Note: Z also wins in plurality voting: all voters vote only for their top single candidate—getting 26 votes to X's 20 and Y's 19. Moreover, Z is the Condorcet winner, defeating both X and Y 36 to 29; Y again comes in last, losing to X in a pairwise contest 35 to 30.)

After the poll announcement identifying Z and X as the top two candidates, the six classes of voters will make the following divisions between acceptable and unacceptable candidates:

(1) 10: $(X, Y/Z)$
(2) 10: $(X/Z, Y)$
(3) 9: $(Y, X/Z)$
(4) 10: $(Y, Z/X)$
(5) 15: $(Z/X, Y)$
(6) 11: $(Z, Y/X)$

(Note: If the previous division of voting for the top two candidates already distinguished between Z and X, the voter makes no adjustment in his previous strategy.) Now Y, the former last-place candidate, wins with 40 votes, Z, the Condorcet winner, gets 36 votes, and X gets 29 votes.

Clearly, poll announcements that voters react to in the manner we have postulated may drastically alter election outcomes. As in the previous example, they may elevate last-place candicates to first place, and, in the process, may even topple Condorcet winners (Z in the example). Indeed, in the 1970 New York race for Senate, there is good reason to believe that Goodell was the Condorcet winner (as I suggested earlier), but in the election he came in a poor third. At least in part his poor showing seems attributable to some of his supporters who, viewing the real contest in the end to be one between Buckley and Ottinger (as the polls indicated), drifted toward one or the other of the two front-runners.

To recapitulate, we have seen in this section that four combinations of outcomes are possible—winning and losing, with or without a poll—under approval voting. In fact, all voting systems of the kind discussed are vulnerable to possible manipulation by the publication (or nonpublication) of poll results. Although it is hard to assess the degree to which poll announcements actually affect voting behavior, and even change election outcomes,[4] our model of poll effects at least shows up some potential problems of polling in a democratic society.

[4] For a review of empirical evidence, see Brams [2, pp. 67–70].

EXERCISES

13. Assume that the number (N) of supporters of Buckley, Goodell, and Ottinger are such that $N(B) > N(O) > N(G)$, but no group of supporters commands a majority of votes. If the preferences of each group of supporters are as given in the text, show that the Condorcet winner is the approval voting winner if each voter considers his top two choices acceptable, but his last choice unacceptable. Does this relation hold if each voter considers only his top choice acceptable?

14. If "vote for I" is a strategy under plurality voting, define the *corresponding strategy* under approval voting to be the (sincere) strategy, "vote for I and all candidates preferred to I." Find an example where "vote for I" under plurality voting produces a different winner than its corresponding strategy under approval voting. Can this occur if the winner under plurality voting is a Condorcet winner?

9. Approval Voting and Presidential Elections

Several desirable properties of approval voting in multicandidate elections have been described in previous sections. As a practicable reform, Kellett and Mott [11] have made a strong case that approval voting be adopted in presidential primaries, which, at least in the early stages, often involve several candidates running for their party's nomination. When Kellett and Mott asked a sample of 225 Pennsylvania voters to "vote for any candidates whose nomination you can support" in the 1976 presidential primary (eight Democratic candidates and eight Republican candidates were listed on two sample ballots), 72% of those voting chose to support two, three, or four candidates.

A case for approval voting in national party conventions can also be made. As in primaries, the main effect would probably be to give comparatively more support to moderates that most delegates find acceptable, comparatively less to extremists who are only acceptable to ideological factions in their party.

If there had been approval voting in the 1972 Democratic convention, it seems at least doubtful that George McGovern would have been his party's nominee. Not only did he not have strong support from his party rank and file (Keech and Matthews [10, p. 212]), but he also was not accorded any reasonable chance of winning in the general election.

Although most general elections are, for all intents and purposes, two-candidate contests, since 1900 there have been several serious bids by third-party candidates in presidential elections (Mazmanian [13]). The most notable challenges in the first quarter of the century were in 1912, when Theodore Roosevelt won 27.4% of the popular vote, and in 1924, when Robert La Follette won 16.6% of the popular vote.

More recently, Harry Truman faced defections from both wings of the Democratic Party in 1948. The Progressive Party candidate, Henry Wallace, and the States' Rights Party candidate, Strom Thurmond, each captured

2.4% of the popular vote. Nevertheless, Truman was able to win 49.6% of the popular vote to Republican Thomas Dewey's 45.1%.

The most serious challenge by a minor-party candidate since World War II was that of George Wallace in the 1968 presidential election. This is the election I shall analyze in some detail to try to assess the possible effects of approval voting in a presidential election.

More recently, Eugene McCarthy ran as a third-party candidate in the 1976 presidential election. Playing the spoiler role, McCarthy sought to protest what he saw to be the outmoded procedures and policies of the Democratic Party, for whose nomination he had run in 1968 and 1972. Although McCarthy garnered only 0.9% of the popular vote, his candidacy may have cost Jimmy Carter four states, which Gerald Ford won by less than what McCarthy polled. In the end, of course, Carter did not need the electoral votes of these states, but had he lost in a few states that he won by slim margins, these McCarthy votes could have made the difference in the election outcome. Similarly, John Anderson's much more substantial 6.6% vote total in the 1980 presidential election could have contributed significantly to Jimmy Carter's 41.0% total, but even with all Anderson's votes, Carter would have fallen well short of Ronald Reagan's 50.7%.

I turn now to an analysis of the third-party challenge by George Wallace's American Independence Party in 1968. As with Strom Thurmond's support twenty years earlier, Wallace's support was concentrated in the South. Although Wallace had no reasonable chance of winning the presidency, it seemed at the time that he had a very good chance of preventing both Richard Nixon and Hubert Humphrey from winning a majority of electoral votes, thereby throwing the election into the House of Representatives. There Wallace could have bargained with these candidates for major policy concessions—in particular, weaker enforcement of civil rights statutes and a halt to busing.

Wallace captured 13.5% of the popular vote and was the victor in five states, winning 46 electoral votes. He came close to denying Nixon, who got 43.4% of the popular vote to Humphrey's 42.7%, an electoral-vote majority.

Would this outcome have been different, or would its magnitude have significantly changed, if there had been approval voting in 1968? Presumably, all voters who voted for one of the three candidates would not have changed their votes. But how many would have cast second approval votes, and for whom would they have voted?

The best information available to answer this question was collected in the University of Michigan Survey Research Center's 1968 National Election Study. Data derived from a "feeling thermometer" assessment of candidates, whereby respondents are asked to indicate warm or cold feelings toward the candidates on a 100-degree scale, may be used to define an "acceptability" scale for candidates, from which plausible approval voting strategies of voters can be surmised.

Taking account of both the reported votes of the respondents (the survey was taken just after the election) and their feeling-thermometer assessments of the candidates, D. R. Kiewiet [12] developed a set of rules for assigning approval votes to respondents.[5] After adjusting reported voting by the sample to reflect the actual voting results, he estimated that Nixon would have increased his vote total to 69.8% (a 58% increase over the 44.1% in the survey who reported voting for Nixon), Humphrey would have increased his vote total to 60.8% (a 44% increase over the 42.3% in the survey who reported voting for Humphrey), and Wallace would have increased his vote total to 21.3% (a 58% increase over the 13.5% in the survey who reported voting for Wallace).

Kiewiet drew several conclusions from his analysis. First, plurality voting nearly deprived Nixon of his victory: Although many voters were certainly not wildly enthusiastic about Nixon, more than a two-thirds majority probably considered him at least acceptable. Second, although most of the additional approval votes Nixon and Humphrey would have received would have come from each other's supporters, Wallace supporters, according to the rules used for assigning approval votes, would have cast more than twice as many approval votes for Nixon as for Humphrey.

It is this factor which largely explains Nixon's 9% approval-voting edge over Humphrey. Wallace also would have benefited from approval voting. In fact, his estimated 21% approval voting share exactly matches the percentage who reported they would vote for him two months before the election (Scammon and Wattenberg [16, pp. 171–172]). If there had been approval voting, Wallace almost surely would not have lost most of his original supporters, and probably would have picked up some support from the major-party voters as well, to capture approval votes from more than one-fifth of the electorate.

Perhaps the most interesting conclusion we can derive from these estimates is that Nixon was undoubtedly the Condorcet winner. Kiewiet estimates that Nixon would have defeated Wallace in a pairwise contest 81.5 to 18.5% and would have defeated Humphrey 53.4 to 46.6%, given the propensity of Wallace voters to favor Nixon.

Several objections can be raised against Kiewiet's estimates and indeed against virtually any estimates based on assumptions about how the attitudes or "feelings" of voters would translate into voting behavior. Rather than dwelling on these, however, let us consider a rather different set of estimates made by Kiewiet based on more "strategic" assumptions.

These assumptions reflect the view of most voters in 1968 that only Humphrey and Nixon stood a serious chance of winning the election. After all, even at his high point in the polls, Wallace commanded the support of barely more than one-fifth of the electorate. Consistent with our poll model

[5] For a related effort, applied to primaries, to translate 1972 feeling-thermometer data into electoral outcomes under a variety of decision rules, see Joslyn [9].

in Section 8, then, it is plausible to assume that voters would cast approval votes to distinguish between Humphrey and Nixon.

More specifically, Kiewiet assumed that (i) Humphrey and Nixon supporters would vote for Wallace, if they also approved of him, but would not vote for the other major-party candidate; (ii) all Wallace voters would vote for either Humphrey or Nixon, but not both, in addition to Wallace. As he put it,

> In effect, a poll indicating Wallace had no chance of winning would, under approval voting, turn the election into two elections: the first, a pairwise contest between Nixon and Humphrey, wherein all voters would choose one or the other; the second, a sort of referendum for Wallace, who would receive approval votes from voters who wished to support him even if he could not win the election.

In operational terms, Kiewiet postulated that Humphrey and Nixon supporters would vote for their first choice and, in addition, for Wallace if the latter's thermometer rating exceeded 50. Wallace supporters, on the other hand, were assumed always to cast a second approval vote for the major-party candidate they gave the highest thermometer rating to, no matter what this rating was. Thereby Wallace voters were "forced" to be rational in accordance with the assumptions of the poll model.

What estimates does this set of assumptions yield? Nixon would have received 53.4% of the popular vote and Humphrey 46.6%, the same percentages given earlier had they been in a pairwise contest, and Wallace 21.3%. Thus, the approval voting percentages of Humphrey and Nixon would have been substantially reduced over those estimated earlier (69.8 and 60.8% respectively), but Wallace would have come out exactly the same (21.3% estimated earlier) since the "strategic" assumptions do not alter the voting behavior of Wallace supporters for Wallace.

The two sets of estimates for Humphrey and Nixon probably bracket the percentages the candidates would actually have received had there been approval voting in 1968. Whichever set gives the better estimates, Nixon in either case would have been the clear-cut winner in the popular-vote contest because of the much broader support he, rather than Humphrey, would have received from Wallace supporters.

The Electoral College also magnified Nixon's narrow popular-vote victory because he won by slim margins in several large states. However, speaking normatively, I believe this fact should have no bearing on the outcome. Much more significant is the fact that Nixon was the first or second choice of most voters and hence more acceptable than any other candidate. This, I believe, is the proper criterion for the selection of a president—and other democratically elected officials as well.

It is also interesting to note that approval voting would probably obviate the need for a runoff election in most multicandidate presidential elections if the Electoral College were abolished. No winning candidate in a presidential election has ever received less than 40% of the popular vote, with the exception of Abraham Lincoln in 1860, who got 39.8%. It seems highly unlikely that a candidate who is the first choice of 40% of the electorate would not be approved of by as many as one-sixth of the remaining voters and thereby receive at least 50% support from the electorate.

The legitimacy of election outcomes in the eyes of voters would certainly be enhanced if the winning candidate received the support of a majority of the electorate. This would be true even if he was the first choice of fewer voters than some other candidate, because this fact would not show up in the approval-voting returns.

By comparison, the proposed popular-vote amendment to abolish the Electoral College provides for a runoff between the top two vote-getters if neither receives at least 40% of the vote. This seems an unnecessary provision if more than 50% approve of the winning candidate. Of course, if no candidate wins even a majority of approval votes, then a runoff can still be conducted to ensure a majority winner.

But this would probably not be necessary in most presidential elections unless approval voting itself produces major changes in candidate strategies and election outcomes. Beyond these changes, however, approval voting could effect a fundamental alteration in the two-party system itself by encouraging additional parties or candidates to enter the fray. Fringe candidates, it seems, would probably drain little support from centrist candidates because, for strategic reasons, fringe candidate supporters would probably also tend to vote for a centrist. Additional centrist candidates, on the other hand, might draw support away from major-party nominees if they (the new centrists) were perceived as serious contenders.

The question that is hard to answer, in the absence of experience, is whether such contenders could position themselves in such a way as to displace the major-party candidates. If so, presumably they would be motivated to run, giving voters more viable alternatives from which to choose, and, in the process, weakening the two-party system. Their election, however, would probably not produce drastic policy changes in public polices since they would not be viable if they were unacceptable to numerous middle-of-the-road voters.

Barring unforeseen changes, it seems likely that at the same time approval voting would give some additional support to strong minority candidates like George Wallace, it would also help centrist candidates, including perhaps nominees of new parties, both in winning their party's nomination in the primaries and conventions and prevailing against more extreme candidates in the general election. Coupled with the greater opportunity it affords voters to express their preferences, and the greater likelihood it provides the winning candidate of obtaining majority support, approval voting would seem to be an overlooked reform that now deserves to be taken seriously.

EXERCISES

15. Assume in a three-candidate presidential election with approval voting that candidate *A* gets 40% of the vote, candidate *B* 50% of the vote, and candidate *C* 60% of the vote. If no voters cast three approval votes, how many voters cast two approval votes?
16. Assume candidate *A* is the first choice of 40% of the voters and candidate *B* the first choice of 50% of the voters. How many "second-choice" approval votes did candidate *C* receive? Does he "deserve" to be the winner?
17. Assume all candidate *B*'s supporters consider *C* their second choice. What would be the outcome of a contest between *A* and *C*?
18. Now assume that all candidate *A*'s supporters also consider *C* their second choice. What would be the outcome of a contest between *B* and *C*? Is *C* the Condorcet winner?

10. Summary and Conclusions

We began our comparison of different voting systems by looking at negative voting in two- and three-candidate plurality contests, with and without a runoff. Negative voting seemed unjustified in two-candidate contests since a voter can in general bring about the same outcome by casting a positive vote.

True, if there were a cutoff point for net votes, below which no candidate could be elected, a voter could succeed in preventing the election of the leading candidate by casting a negative vote against him, whereas a positive vote for his opponent might not prevent the leading candidate's election. But given a minimum threshold, the circumstance in which the loss of one net vote pushes the leading candidate below the threshold seems too remote a possibility to justify a switch to negative voting in two-candidate contests.

On the other hand, casting a negative vote in three-candidate plurality contests seems justified by the fact that this strategy may lead to outcomes as good as, and sometimes better than, one could achieve by casting a positive vote. Moreover, restricting a voter to only one positive vote may lead to a situation in which a Condorcet winner is not elected.

The limitations of negative voting only become evident in plurality contests with more than three candidates. In such contests, even if a voter can divide the candidates into two classes, acceptable and unacceptable, a single positive or single negative vote may not enable him fully to express his (dichotomous) preferences either for his preferred candidates or against his nonpreferred candidates.

I showed that approval voting, which allows a voter to cast a single "approval" vote for one or more candidates, meets this problem, but it is no panacea for the voter who wants to discriminate among more than two classes of candidates. If and only if a voter has dichotomous preferences will he have a dominant strategy: vote for all his acceptable, or preferred, candidates.

If all voters have dichotomous preferences and choose their dominant, or approval, strategies, then the winning candidate will always be the Condorcet winner. Approval voting, by forcing all voters to act *as if* distinctions among their "approved" and "nonapproved" candidates do not matter, always results in the selection of a candidate who is acceptable to more voters than any other candidate. If these distinctions do matter, however, a Condorcet winner may not be elected, as was illustrated.

Although every voting system is sincere for voters with dichotomous preferences, only approval voting is sincere for voters with trichotomous preferences as well. Dichotomous preferences, on the other hand, are required to ensure that approval voting is strategy-proof, which no other nonranked voting system is.

Polls that induce voters to adjust their voting strategies to distinguish between the top two vote-getters identified in the poll may produce a variety of results, including the demotion of a Condorcet winner to nonwinning status and the promotion of a non-Condorcet winner to winning status. Several of these possible effects were illustrated for the Buckley–Goodell–Ottinger 1970 Senate race in New York.

Approval voting seems to offer important advantages in multicandidate presidential elections, both at the nomination stage in primaries and party conventions and at the general election stage. Among other things, it would probably (i) increase voter turnout, (ii) increase the likelihood of a majority winner in plurality contests and thereby reinforce the legitimacy of election outcomes, and (iii) help centrist candidates without, at the same time, denying voters the opportunity to express their support for more extremist candidates.

Approval voting might encourage additional candidates to run, however, and thereby weaken the two-party system. While it would probably make more centrist candidates viable, it seems unlikely that it would produce drastic policy shifts.

Evidence for the centrist bias of approval voting was provided by two sets of estimates made of the likely outcome in the 1968 three-candidate presidential election had there been approval voting. Both sets of estimates indicated that Nixon would have won decisively, but Wallace would have made a much stronger showing than he did.

In a way, approval voting is a compromise between plurality voting and more complicated schemes like the Borda count which require voters to rank candidates. In my opinion, the latter schemes are too complicated and unnecessary in elections in which there is only a single winner. (Elections in which there are multiple winners, such as to a committee or council, would also seem well suited for approval voting, but that is a subject for another work.) On the other hand, approval voting is not only quite easy to understand, even if some of its theoretical implications are not so obvious, but it also seems an eminently practicable scheme that could readily be implemented on existing voting machines.[6]

EXERCISE

19. Determine how candidates in your city or state are chosen in primaries and general elections. From election, survey, or other data, try to assess whether the will of the majority was expressed in recent multicandidate elections. Do you think negative or approval voting would have changed any outcomes, and why? Recommend any election reforms that you believe are supported by your research.

Solutions to Selected Exercises

Section 4:

6. For all relevant results, X and $\bar{Z}$ lead to at least as good outcomes as all other strategies; for results 2, 4, 7, 12, and 16, X is better than $\bar{Z}$, but for results 9 and 15, $\bar{Z}$ is better than X. Since X does not dominate $\bar{Z}$, and $\bar{Z}$ does not dominate X, they are undominated strategies.

7. $\bar{Z}$.

Section 5:

8. See 6. For results 2, 4, 7, 12, and 16, $\bar{Z}$ leads to outcomes as good as X for a voter with preference scale $(X - Y, Z)$; for results 9 and 15, $\bar{Z}$ leads to better outcomes, so it is a dominant strategy. The advantages of negative voting are probably greatest when there is indifference between candidates, at least if there are only three.

9. W, $\{W, X\}$, $\{W, Y\}$, $\{W, X, Y\}$.
   W is uniquely best for result (0, 0, 0, 0); $\{W, X\}$ is better than $\{W\}$ and $\{W, Y\}$ for result (0, 2, 0, 2) and better than $\{W, X, Y\}$ for result (1, 0, 1, 1); $\{W, Y\}$ is better than $\{W\}$ and $\{W, X\}$ for result (0, 0, 2, 2) and better than $\{W, X, Y\}$ for result (1, 1, 0, 1); $\{W, X, Y\}$ is better than $\{W\}$ and $\{W, X\}$ for result (0, 0, 2, 2) and better than $\{W, Y\}$ for result (0, 1, 0, 1).

10. Admissible strategies of a voter under negative voting are given in Table 3. (There is an equivalent approval voting strategy for every negative voting strategy, given three candidates.) For each of the four preference scales of voters, the number of admissible negative/approval strategies is less than or equal to the number of plurality strategies, given in Table 4.

[6] For a very different theoretical argument in support of approval voting, as well as some empirical observations on its practicability, see Weber [19], [20] and Merrill [14].

Section 7:

11. Dichotomous—$(W - X, Y - Z)$. Approval: $\{W, X\}$; Single plurality: W, X.
    Trichotomous—$(W - X, Y, Z)$. Approval: $\{W, X\}, \{W, X, Y\}$; Single plurality: W, X, Y.

12. For trichotomous preference scale $(W - X, Y, Z)$, strategy Y under plurality is not sincere: It involves voting for a less-preferred candidate (Y) without also voting for a more-preferred candidate (W or X). All other strategies are sincere.

Section 8:

13. *Top two choices acceptable:* B—1, G—3, O—1, so G wins. Since G defeats O, 2–1, G is the Condorcet winner.
    Top choice acceptable: B—1, G—1, O—1. Since $N(B) > N(O) > N(G)$, B wins. The outcome of a contest between each pair of candidates is a "1–1 tie," with the third vote indeterminate, so there is no Condorcet winner. However, if one assumes that the third vote is split evenly between each candidate in the pair, B defeats the other two candidates and so is the Condorcet winner.

14. *Example:* Set of three candidates $\{X, Y, Z\}$, and three classes of voters with the following numbers of members and preference scales for the candidates: (1) 1—(X, Y, Z); (2) 6—(Y, X, Z); (3) 6—(Z, X, Y).
    Under plurality voting, assume that two class (2) voters, and two class (3) voters, vote for X; all other voters vote for their most-preferred candidates. The outcome is: X—5, Y—4, Z—4. Moreover, X is the Condorcet winner. If voters chose their corresponding strategies under approval voting, however, the outcome would be: X—5, Y—6, Z—6.

Section 9:

15. 50%.

16. 60–10% (first choice) = 50% (second choice).

17. A—40%; C—60%.

18. B—50%; C—50%. C is not the Condorcet winner since B and C tie in a pairwise contest.

References

1. Boehm, George A. W. "One Fervent Vote against Wintergreen," mimeographed, 1976.
2. Brams, Steven J. "One Man, *n* Votes," mimeographed. Module in Applied Mathematics, Mathematical Association of America, 1976.
3. Brams, Steven J. *Paradoxes in Politics: An Introduction to the Nonobvious in Political Science.* Free Press, New York, 1976.

4. Brams, Steven J. "When Is It Advantageous to Cast a Negative Vote?," *Lecture Notes in Economics and Mathematical Systems* (*Mathematical Economics and Game Theory: Essays in Honor of Oskar Morgenstern*, R. Henn and O. Moeschlin eds.), *141*. Springer-Verlag, Berlin (1977), 564–572.
5. Brams, Steven J. *The Presidential Election Game*. Yale University Press, New Haven, 1978.
6. Brams, Steven J., and Fishburn, Peter C. *Approval Voting*. Birkhäuser, Boston, (in press).
7. Brams, Steven J. and Fishburn, Peter C. "Approval Voting," *American Political Science Review*, *72* (1978), 831–847.
8. Fishburn, Peter C. "A Strategic Analysis of Nonranked Voting Systems," *SIAM Journal on Applied Mathematics*, *35* (1978), 488–495.
9. Joslyn, Richard A. "The Impact of Decision Rules in Multicandidate Campaigns: The Case of the 1972 Democratic Presidential Nomination," *Public Choice*, *25* (1976), 1–17.
10. Keech, William R. and Matthews, Donald R. *The Party's Choice*. Brookings Institution, Washington, D.C., 1976.
11. Kellett, John, and Mott, Kenneth. "Presidential Primaries: Measuring Popular Choice," *Polity*, *9* (1977), 528–537.
12. Kiewiet, D. Roderick, "Approval Voting: The Case of the 1968 Presidential Election," *Polity*, *12* (1979), 170–181.
13. Mazmanian, Daniel A. *Third Parties in Presidential Elections*. Brookings Institution, Washington, D.C., 1974.
14. Merrill, Samuel III. "Approval Voting: A 'Best Buy' Method for Multicandidate Elections?" *Mathematics Magazine*, *52* (1978), 98–101.
15. Riker, William H. "The Number of Political Parties: A Reexamination of Duverger's Law," *Comparative Politics*, *9* (1976), 93–106.
16. Scammon, Richard M., and Wattenberg, Ben J. *The Real Majority: An Extraordinary Examination of the American Electorate*. Coward, McCann, & Geoghegan, New York, 1970.
17. Stratmann, William C. "The Calculus of Rational Choice," *Public Choice*, *18* (1974), 93–105.
18. Stratmann, William C. Personal communication (September 21, 1977).
19. Weber, Robert James. "Comparison of Voting Systems," mimeographed, 1977.
20. Weber, Robert James. "Multiply-Weighted Voting Systems," mimeographed, 1977.

Notes for the Instructor

This module has several interrelated learning objectives:

(i) To introduce students to decision-theoretic and game-theoretic concepts (e.g., strategy, state of nature, outcome matrix, dominance);
(ii) To impart a precise meaning to rational choices, both of individuals and collectivities;
(iii) To illustrate formal analysis and develop an ability to reason deductively;
(iv) To embed the formal analysis in a concrete context, the study of voting systems, both extant and proposed, to justify its utility as a tool for policy analysis;
(v) To show how this analysis can be applied retrodictively to empirical data on elections;

(vi) To encourage normative judgments, based on both formal and empirical analysis.

The mathematical requirement for reading this module is a reasonably good background in high school mathematics. For students with this background, however, some parts of this module may still be difficult to understand and may require several readings to comprehend fully.

For instructors who also feel uneasy with some of this material, my suggestion is that they encourage their students to try to figure out, "dope out," what is being said in free and open discussion. This interactive mode should resolve most difficult points, because I believe all the reasoning is quite straightforward. It is simply more condensed and more rigorous than what is found in most political science textbooks. (For a justification of this kind of more formal, deductive analysis, and a statement of how it differs from nondeductive analysis, see the last part of Section 2.)

Both students and instructors unfamiliar with formal analysis cannot develop much understanding and appreciation of the contents of this module without doing the exercises at the end of most sections. Generally speaking, these provide illustrations of the main concepts and ideas in each section and thereby help to supplement the examples, and fill in details of the analysis, given in the text. Answers to all exercises that involve calculations or verifications are given above.

How does one motivate the hypothetico-deductive thinking that this module requires? I have tried to do this in Section 1. By conducting in class a hypothetical election under different rules, the same ones analyzed later in the module, I believe students will quickly develop an appreciation of the fact that election procedures, and the information available to voters about how others vote, can make a difference in what strategies are optimal and in the outcome chosen. Students are also encouraged in this section to judge the fairness of the various rules, think up new rules, and ponder how the current law in New Hampshire governing the conduct of the presidential primary would have to be changed to implement any proposed election reforms.

CHAPTER 4
Modeling Coalitional Values

William F. Lucas*
Louis J. Billera*

1. Introduction

The idea of a set of elements along with elementary notions about subsets are fundamental concepts in modern mathematics and are well-known to contemporary mathematics students. These elementary concepts, together with some method for assigning numbers to various subsets of a given set, are often sufficient to begin applying the techniques of mathematical modeling to a good number of interesting and nontrivial applications. Many important situations are characterized to a large extent by describing the set of participants involved and the values achievable by certain subsets of these participants. Such applications occur in economics and politics, business and operations research, the social and environmental sciences, and elsewhere.

Our problems will begin with a set of participants who will be referred to as *players*. The set of players may consist of a group of individual citizens, an assembly of political parties, a collection of economic agents, a set of business corporations or labor unions, an alliance of nations, a meeting of individual decision makers, as well as the ordinary players in a parlor game. Next, one can frequently assign, in some natural or straightforward manner, some sort of *value* to the different subsets of the set of players. A subset of players will be referred to as a *coalition*. In many instances, it is convenient to represent such coalitional values by a real number. Such values may in some way measure economic worth, political influence, taxes or subsidies, voter's power, social position, or merely points or monetary payments in a

* School of Operations Research and Industrial Engineering, Cornell University, Ithaca, New York 14853.

common game. Such values may only be of a binary nature, such as distinguishing between winning or losing in some contest such as an election. These coalitional values may depend only upon the particular subset considered, or they may also relate to how the remaining players partition themselves into coalitions. So the value of a certain coalition may be given by a single number, or this value may vary depending upon how the complementary coalition subdivides itself into subsets.

Given a set of players and the coalitional values for its subsets, one can consider an array of interesting questions about how these values (power, wealth, etc.) should or will be distributed among the participants. The resulting allocations may be arrived at by some bargaining procedure, by some ethical principle or equity concept, by a fair division scheme, by a ruling of a civil or family authority, or by some other social mechanism. The set of all realizable distributions of the available values to the players can often be represented by rather elementary concepts from algebra and geometry.

The object of this chapter is to present several illustrations of mathematical modeling that are suitable for use in the undergraduate classroom and that make use of only elementary mathematical notions. These can be employed in the traditional lecture–homework format, or preferably in a more open-ended or discovery approach in which the students attempt to develop their own techniques and solutions. The main goal is for students to obtain hands-on experience in the art of creating and analyzing nonroutine mathematical models. These examples do relate to the theory of multiperson cooperative games, although knowledge of this subject is *not* required. So a secondary purpose of this paper is to provide illustrations of how this theory is applied and thus to motivate students to undertake additional studies in this direction. This approach should also demonstrate that the theory of n-person cooperative games can be studied and applied without any prior knowledge of noncooperative game theory, in particular without knowledge of matrix games. Our examples are taken from straightforward bargaining situations, exchanges in economic markets, taxing diseconomies caused by pollution or development, equitable sharing of costs among different types of users of a service, distribution of voting power, and similar situations. These illustrations are drastic simplifications of the sorts of problems found in real applications. Nevertheless, the basic techniques employed here can and have been extended to realistic case studies as will be indicated in some of the references mentioned throughout this chapter.

2. Basic Concepts

2.1. Players and Coalitions

We shall begin our problems by focusing on a set of distinct elements. The elements in our models will be the participants in some sort of social interaction, and these participants will be called *players*. We shall label the players by the natural numbers $1, 2, \cdots, n$ and denote the *set of all players* by

$$N = \{1, 2, \cdots, n\}.$$

The natural number n will thus represent the nth player as well as the total number $n = |N|$ of participants involved in our models.

We shall be concerned with the various subsets of N, i.e., sets S whose elements are also elements of N. This is denoted by $S \subset N$, and such subsets are referred to as *coalitions*. The set of all subsets of N is denoted by 2^N. For example, if $N = \{1, 2, 3\}$, then

$$2^N = \{\varnothing, \{1\}, \{2\}, \{3\}, \{1, 2\}, \{1, 3\}, \{2, 3\}, N\},$$

where $\varnothing$ denotes the empty set. The relation of "being a subset of" is pictured in Fig. 4.1 (a lattice diagram or cube).

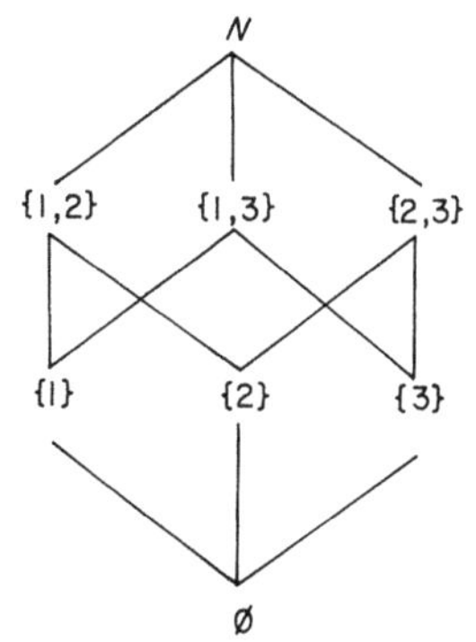

Figure 4.1

Exercises

1. Prove that the number $|2^N - \{\varnothing\}|$ of nonempty coalitions (subsets) of the player set N is $2^n - 1$.
2. Prove that for any n there is always just one more nonempty coalition with an odd number of players than there is such coalitions with an even number of players.
3. Show that the number of coalitions S in N with precisely $s = |S|$ players is given by the $(s + 1)$st term in the binomial expansion of $(1 + 1)^n$.

4. Show how the lattice of coalitions for $N = \{1, 2, 3\}$ corresponds to the vertices of a cube in which each vertex is denoted by three coordinates with entries of either 0 or 1.

5. Draw the lattice of all coalitions (including the empty set $\varnothing$) for $N = \{1, 2, 3, 4\}$.

6. Show that the lattice of subsets for the set $N = \{1, 2, 3, 4\}$ corresponds to a four-dimensional cube.

7. Students familiar with the definitions of relation, function, and cartesian product can determine the number of (binary) relations on N, the number of functions from N into N, the number of one-to-one correspondences from N onto N, and the number of elements (i.e., ordered pairs) in $N \times N$.

2.2. Values and Games

In many applications it is possible to assign some measure or *value* $v(S)$ to some or all of the coalitions S in N. Often the values $v(S)$ can be expressed as real numbers. In practice it may represent in some fashion the worth or power achievable by this coalition if the players in S act in unison in order to obtain some payoff or goal. Thus $v(S)$ may be taken as the maximum coalitional payoffs or outcomes that the group S can guarantee itself when this subset undertakes joint action, and this value can be realized or exceeded independently of how the players in the complementary coalition N–S act. In other words $v(S)$ describes the largest amount of some good or "utility" that the coalition S can be certain to obtain if they act in a cooperative manner. In other instances it seems reasonable to choose $v(S)$ as the amount to which the coalition S can be restricted to by its "opponents" in N–S. In any event, such values frequently arise in a very natural or obvious way in many applications. Such values may be merely approximations or estimates of some monetary or other measure available to S in some interaction involving the players in N. Nevertheless, focusing on such values may prove to be most insightful in modeling their activities, and they may very well be an essential ingredient in any quantifiable investigation of related social actions and outcomes. A rule (or function) v that assigns a real number $v(S)$ to each coalition S in N is called a *characteristic function*. We can express this as $v\colon 2^N \to R$, where R denotes the real numbers. It is common to assume that $v(\varnothing) = 0$ for the empty set $\varnothing$.

The idea of a characteristic function v for a set of players N is the starting point of the theory of multiperson cooperative games as introduced in the classical work by von Neumann and Morgenstern [25]. The pair (N, v) is referred to as a *game*, or more precisely as an *n-person cooperative game in characteristic function* (or *coalitional*) *form*. However, no familiarity with aspects of this theory is necessary in order to pursue the models in this paper.

2.3. Examples

Consider three players, 1, 2 and 3, who are allowed to split \$10 among themselves in any way they wish as long as a simple majority (i.e., two or three of the three players) agrees to the split. This can be represented by the characteristic function v where

$$v(\{1\}) = v(\{2\}) = v(\{3\}) = 0,$$

and

$$v(\{1, 2\}) = v(\{1, 3\}) = v(\{2, 3\}) = v(\{1, 2, 3\}) = 10.$$

Assume an old house is worth \$10,000 to its current owner, \$20,000 to a woman who will turn it into business offices, and \$30,000 to a man who will level it and construct a parking lot. A reasonable representation by a characteristic function v is

$$v(\{1\}) = 10{,}000 \quad v(\{2\}) = v(\{3\}) = v(\{2, 3\}) = 0$$

$$v(\{1, 2\}) = 20{,}000 \quad v(\{1, 3\}) = 30{,}000 \quad v(\{1, 2, 3\}) = 30{,}000,$$

where $1 =$ owner, $2 =$ woman, and $3 =$ man. For example, if 1 and 3 form a coalition, then 1 can sell the house to 3, and the value of 30,000 will be realized.

Many of the following exercises as well as other examples in this paper are taken from publications and notes by L. S. Shapley and M. Shubik. Many of these will also appear in Shubik's book in 1982.

Exercises

Determine a characteristic function v for each of the following game-type situations.

8. *Seller and Two Buyers.* A parcel of land is worth \$100,000 to the farmer who now owns it, \$200,000 to a potential industrial user as a plant site, and \$250,000 to a possible subdivider for a housing tract.

9. *Pure Bargaining or Unanimity Game.* A private foundation located in the state will give the n counties in the state a *total* (or sum) of \$100,000,000 to be used for research on water pollution control, provided that all the counties can agree to the final distribution of money among themselves. These must be no complaint by anyone to the state government. If there is no unanimous agreement, then the foundation will withhold all of the funds.

10. *Deterrence.* Each country i possesses its own wealth w_i, and assume that any one of the n countries is capable of destroying the total wealth of any number of other countries.

11. *Disposal.* It costs each one of six neighboring lumber mills \$10,000 per month to burn its own scrap wood in a huge oven. However, each company can burn the

scrap of any number of mills at the same cost as burning just its own scrap. First, assume there are no transportation costs. Second, reconsider this problem and assume a \$1000 expense per month to ship from any one mill to another. Third, redo this problem when each company can burn the scrap for up to a total of four companies at the same cost as just its own, but it reaches its capacity at four.

12. *Post Office*. Each one of n citizens *must* mail \$10 to one of the *other* citizens.

13. Each one of Oskar and Otto has two similar right shoes, and each one of Edmund and Elwood has three such left shoes. A matching pair of shoes is worth \$30, but any number of unmatched shoes by themselves is worth nothing.

14. *The Treasure of Sierra Madre*. A group of n persons discovers in the mountains a lost treasure of many gold ingots worth \$1,000,000 each. It takes two people to carry out one ingot, and no one can return for more than one trip since the word will get out before then.

2.4. Voting Games

In many voting situations the outcome is either a win or a loss, either the bill passes or fails to pass. In such voting games it is common to represent the characteristic function as $v(S) = 1$ when S is a winning coalition and $v(S) = 0$ when S loses. Games with values of just 0 or 1 are referred to as *simple games*.

In many, but not all, such voting schemes, the value $v(S)$ may depend only upon the number $s = |S|$ of players in the coalition S. Situations in which the outcome depends only upon the size of S are called *symmetric games*. Existence of symmetry or certain other properties may simplify the listing of a characteristic function for a game.

Exercise

15. Which games in Section 2.3 are symmetric games?

Many voting systems can be represented as *weighted majority games* in which there is a quota q and a weight w_i for each player i. A coalition S wins whenever $\sum_{i \in S} w_i \geq q$. These are represented as $[q; w_1, w_2, \cdots, w_n]$. One usually assumes that $q > (w_1 + w_2 + \cdots + w_n)/2$.

Exercises

Describe the characteristic function for the following simple games. Also represent these games as weighted majority games (except for the Canada and Projective Plane games that have no such representation). Prove that the Projective Plane game has no representation as a weighted majority game.

16. *Veto Power*. Any two (or three) of the three players 1, 2, and 3 can pass a bill except that player 1 has veto power over all legislation.

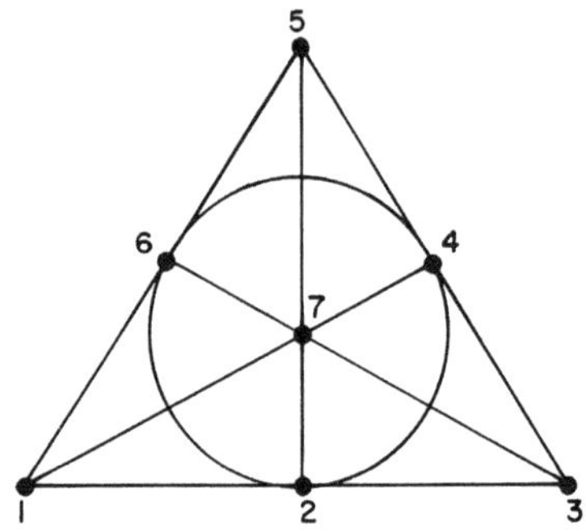

Figure 4.2

17. *Majority Rule.* An n-person simple game in which a coalition wins whenever it has more than half of the players.
18. *Australia.* The seven-person game in which each of the six states has one vote, the federal government has two votes (plus one more in the case of a tie), and majority rules.
19. *U. N. Security Council.* [39; 7, 7, 7, 7, 7, 1, 1, 1, 1, 1, 1, 1, 1, 1, 1].
20. *Tompkins County Board.* [8; 5, 3, 2, 1, 1, 1, 1, 1].
21. *Canada.* The following scheme has been proposed for amending the Canadian Constitution: veto power is held by Ontario, by Quebec, by any three of the four Atlantic provinces, by the three prairie provinces together, and by British Columbia along with any one of the prairie provinces. (The federal government also has a veto, but do not consider this part.)
22. The seven points and seven lines in the simplest finite projective plane geometry are indicated in Fig. 4.2. Consider the points as the seven players, and assume that a coalition wins if and only if it contains the three points of some line (including the circle as a "line").

For more discussion on voting games and power indices, including many exercises and suggested projects, see the paper by Lucas [14] and the module by Straffin [22].

In Appendix III of Farquharson's book [5], he discusses a symmetric five-person game described by the French writer and political philosopher J. J. Rousseau (1712–1778) in *Du Contract Social* (1762), which goes as follows.

(i) There are five (ordinary) players, and a Bank. The latter is a "non-strategic player," but acts to maximize its gains and minimize losses.
(ii) At each round the players are divided into two teams: a Big Team of three players and a Small Team of two players. Membership in the teams "rotates," so that in the game of ten rounds each player is in Big Team six times and in Small Team four times.

(iii) At each round every player may *nominate* one or other of the two teams.

(iv) The Bank then chooses at each of the ten rounds *any* one of the *nominated* teams (i.e., a team that obtains at least one nomination), and pays each of its members \$10 and collects \$10 from each member of the other team.

Rousseau considered three cases.

(a) *The State of Nature.* Each player always nominates his own team, and the Bank always chooses Small Team, so that in ten rounds every player will win four times and lose six times for a net loss of \$20 each.

(b) *The Social Contract.* All five players agree to form an Assembly, and to each nominate *only* the team selected by majority vote on each round. Each player *must* obey this "law of the Assembly." If each player votes for his own team, then only the Big Team is nominated and the Bank will be obliged to choose it each time. In ten rounds a player wins six times and loses four times for a net gain of \$20.

(c) *The Party System.* Assume that some m of the players form a party in the Assembly, and agree to always vote in the Assembly for the team in each round that gives the greatest advantage to the party members as a group. For example, if $m = 3$ and Small Team has two of the three party members, then it is chosen by the Assembly. In ten rounds, when $m = 3$, each Party member wins seven times and loses three times for a net gain of \$40, whereas the nonparty members lose \$40 each.

EXERCISES

23. Give the characteristic function for this game when the coalitions act as a Party and the law of the Assembly holds. Recall that the game consists of ten rounds.

24. Can you give a brief rationale to explain Rousseau's hostility to the existence of political parties.

3. Some Experiments

3.0. Introduction

In real applications, one must perform the frequently difficult task of determining the set N of n players and the characteristic function v as well as seeking some sort of "solutions" for the problem. On the other hand, one can get a general feeling for problems and potential outcomes in this area by first performing some laboratory or classroom-type experiments in which N and v are given. In this section we shall avoid the chore of selecting a suitable v, and proceed directly to some examples in which these values are known.

These examples can be treated as experiments to be run in a classroom setting. A group of students can act as the players, and they can bargain among themselves to determine how to split up some object of value such as money, some books, and so forth. On the other hand, the typical class is hardly the ideal place for running such experiments, since there are normally various disturbances such as time limits, social pressures, and imperfect communication. Nevertheless, some insights into bargaining behavior, equity considerations, prejudices, and the dynamics of coalition formation can often be gained from such crude and poorly run experiments.

3.1. A Simple Majority Game

Let us return to an earlier example in which there were three players labeled 1, 2, and 3, and the amount of \$10 to be given to any coalition of two or three players if this particular coalition will agree among its members on how to split the \$10 between the *three* players. The characteristic function v was given as

$$v(\{1\}) = v(\{2\}) = v(\{3\}) = 0,$$
$$v(\{1, 2\}) = v(\{1, 3\}) = v(\{2, 3\}) = v(\{1, 2, 3\}) = 10.$$

This game is referred to in the literature as a three-person simple majority game or as a three-person constant-sum game. In general, a game is *constant-sum* if $v(S) + v(N - S) = v(N)$ for all coalitions S. [Recall that we let $v(\varnothing) = 0$ for the empty coalition $\varnothing$.] This is also an example of a symmetric game.

The players are allowed to communicate freely and to bargain or arrive at agreements in whatever way they wish. If no agreement is forthcoming, then each player ends up with nothing. This is sufficient information to engage in a stimulating classroom encounter.

One can model this game as follows. The final distribution of wealth among the three players can be represented by a three-dimensional vector $x = (x_1, x_2, x_3)$, where x_i is the payoff to the ith player, $i = 1, 2$, and 3. If we assume that money is infinitely divisible, then we can represent all possible payoffs by the relation

$$x_1 + x_2 + x_3 = 10 \text{ or } 0.$$

We can assume that no player will accept less than zero, i.e., that

$$x_i \geq 0 \quad \text{for} \quad i = 1, 2 \text{ and } 3.$$

In the formal theory, the set

$$A = \{x: x_1 + x_2 + x_3 = 10, \quad x_1 \geq 0, x_2 \geq 0, x_3 \geq 0\}$$

is called the set of *imputations*. So the problem for the players is to decide on a vector x in A or else to settle for the noncooperative solution in which each player gets zero.

In most experiments, the resulting outcomes usually approximate either the midpoint (10/3, 10/3, 10/3), which seems like a natural equity or fair division solution as suggested by the symmetry of this game, or one of the three points (5, 5, 0), (5, 0, 5), or (0, 5, 5) for which one of the two-person ("minimal winning") coalitions splits evenly among themselves and excludes the remaining player.

3.2. A Veto Power Game

Consider the game

$$v(\{1\}) = v(\{2\}) = v(\{3\}) = v(\{2, 3\}) = 0,$$
$$v(\{1, 2\}) = v(\{1, 3\}) = v(\{1, 2, 3\}) = 10$$

in which the agreement of two players is necessary to split \$10, but player 1 has veto power over any decision. This can also be viewed as a market in which player 1 has a commodity, and \$10 can be created if he sells it to player 2 or 3.

The set of realizable outcomes $x = (x_1, x_2, x_3)$ is the same as in our previous example. In practice, player 1 tries to play off players 2 and 3 against each other and attempts to settle on some outcome such as $(10 - \varepsilon, \varepsilon, 0)$ or $(10 - \varepsilon, 0, \varepsilon)$, which is close to the point (10, 0, 0), where ε denotes a small positive number. However, if players 2 and 3 join together in a coalition, then they also possess veto power in this alliance. So symmetry between 2 and 3 suggest a possible outcome of $(10 - 2a, a, a)$ where the number a is in the range $0 < a < 5$.

An interesting tale related to this example, in which Walt Disney imagines playing off a (nonexistant) second banker against his creditor (the Bank of America), is given in Chapter 9 of the book by John McDonald [17].

3.3. Game with a Core

Consider the three-person game in which

$$v(\{1\}) = v(\{2\}) = v(\{3\}) = 0,$$
$$v(\{1, 2\}) = 8, \quad v(\{1, 3\}) = 6, \quad v(\{2, 3\}) = 5,$$
$$v(\{1, 2, 3\}) = 10.$$

This can be interpreted as follows. The coalition $\{1, 2, 3\}$ has \$10 to split among themselves if they only agree on how to divide it. The coalition

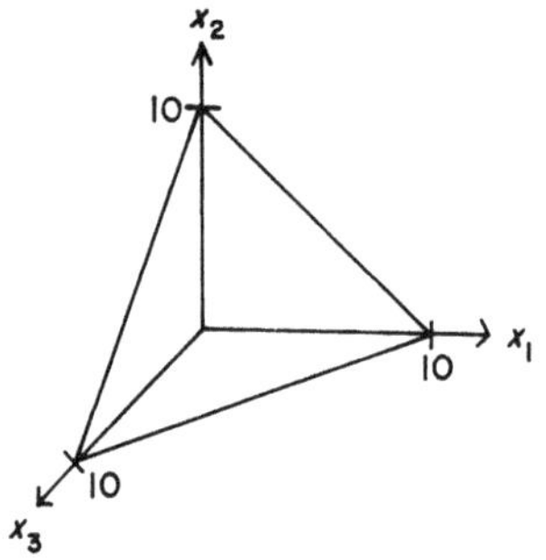

Figure 4.3

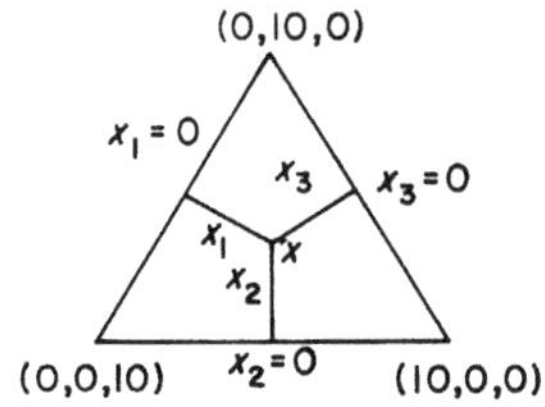

Figure 4.4

$\{1, 2\}$ can divide up \$8 among the *three* players (usually leaving player 3 with nothing). And similarly, coalitions $\{1, 3\}$ can divide \$6, and $\{2, 3\}$ can split \$5. The set of all realizable distributions (x_1, x_2, x_3) are

$$x_1 + x_2 + x_3 = 10, \quad x_1 + x_2 + x_3 = 8,$$

$$x_1 + x_2 + x_3 = 6, \quad x_1 + x_2 + x_3 = 5, \quad (0, 0, 0).$$

Usually the final outcome is in the set of imputations

$$A = \{x : x_1 + x_2 + x_3 = 10; \quad x_i \geq 0, i = 1, 2 \text{ and } 3\},$$

since such x "dominate" any of the other realizable distributions. The "simplex" A can be represented geometrically as indicated in either Figure 4.3 or Figure 4.4.

For any game (N, v), the set of all x in A which satisfies the conditions

$$\sum_{i \in S} x_i \geq v(S) \quad \text{for all} \quad S \subset N$$

is called the *core* of the game, and is denoted by C. The core for our example consists of all $x \in A$, such that $x_1 + x_2 \geq 8$, $x_1 + x_3 \geq 6$, and $x_2 + x_3 \geq 5$. It consists of those points in the inverted small triangle in Fig. 4.5. The core has vertices (4, 4, 2), (5, 3, 2), and (5, 4, 1).

In experiments with this example, the subjects usually do settle on some point in the core. However, other outcomes can result; e.g., the coalition $\{1, 3\}$ may argue for some point on the dotted line segment joining (5, 3, 2) to (13/2, 0, 7/2).

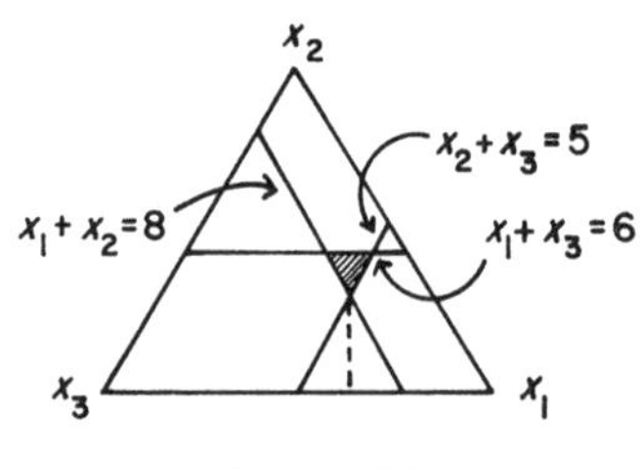

Figure 4.5

EXERCISES

25. Determine the core C for the two previous examples in this section.
26. Discuss whether the one-point core in the veto power game is likely to be achieved in experiments.
27. Describe the core for the three-person game with $v(\{1, 2, 3\}) = 10$, $v(\{1, 2\}) = 9$, $v(\{1, 3\}) = 7$, $v(\{2, 3\}) = 4$, and $v(\{1\}) = v(\{2\}) = v(\{3\}) = 0$.
28. Describe the core for some of the games described in Section 2, including some exercises.

3.4. Some Four-person Examples

Consider the four-person game with

$$v(\{1, 2, 3, 4\}) = 100, \quad v(\{1, 2\}) = v(\{3, 4\}) = 50,$$
$$v(S) = 0 \quad \text{for all other} \quad S \subset N = \{1, 2, 3, 4\}.$$

In practice, players 1 and 2 bargain over how to split the 50, and, similarly, coalition $\{3, 4\}$ decides how to divide their 50. The set of imputations is

$$A = \{x : x_1 + x_2 + x_3 + x_4 = 100, \quad x_i \geq 0 \quad \text{for} \quad i = 1, 2, 3, \text{and } 4\},$$

and the core is

$$C = \{x \in A : x_1 + x_2 = 50 = x_3 + x_4\}.$$

This can be interpreted as player 1 has an item that he can sell to player 2 for 50 units. Also, 3 can similarly sell an item to 4. The tetrahedron A and square C are pictured in Fig. 4.6.

Consider the extension of the above game to the case where players 1

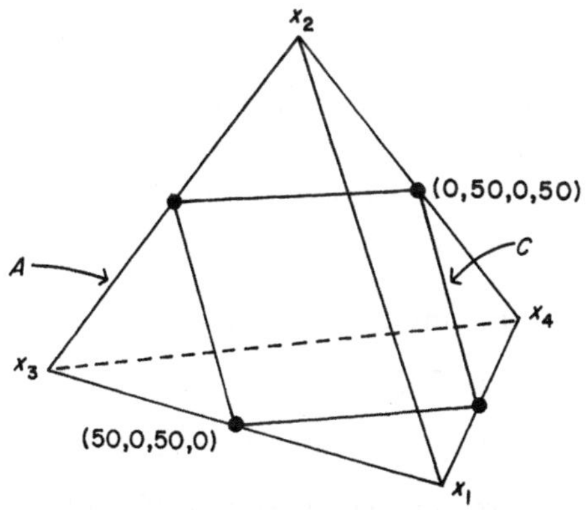

Figure 4.6

and 3 can sell to either players 2 or 4. For example, 1 and 3 may each own a desert full of oil, and 2 and 4 import oil for their industrialized economies. The characteristic function now becomes

$$v(\{1, 2\}) = v(\{1, 4\}) = v(\{2, 3\}) = v(\{3, 4\}) = 50,$$

$$v(T) = 50 \quad \text{for all three-person coalitions } T,$$

$$v(\{1, 2, 3, 4\}) = 100, \quad v(S) = 0 \quad \text{for all other } S \subset N.$$

The core now consists of the line segment joining points (50, 0, 50, 0) and (0, 50, 0, 50). Coalition $\{1, 3\}$ can form a cartel and split most of the potential gain, whereas $\{2, 4\}$ can boycott the market until they share evenly in most of the profit. Note that the outcomes in the core require each producer to sell at the same "price."

Two other four-person constant-sum experiments are described in detail in Section 12.3 of Luce and Raiffa [15].

EXERCISES

29. Show that the four-person game with

$$v(\{1, 2, 3\}) = v(\{1, 2, 4\}) = v(\{1, 3, 4\}) = v(\{2, 3, 4\}) = 75,$$

$$v(\{1, 2, 3, 4\}) = 100, \quad v(\{3, 4\}) = 60,$$

$$v(S) = 0 \quad \text{for all other } S \subset N = \{1, 2, 3, 4\}$$

has an empty core.

30. Show that if $v(\{3, 4\}) = 50$ (rather than 60) in exercise (29), then the core is a single point.

3.5. A Rich Aunt

Davis and Maschler [4, pp. 236–242] discuss a five-person game with a story similar to the following. A rich aunt (player 1) can enter into a partnership with any one of four nephews (players 2, 3, 4, and 5) and make 100 units if this pair agrees upon the split. The only other alternative is for all four nephews to have her declared incompetent and then obtain the 100 units for themselves. The characteristic function is

$$v(\{1, 2\}) = v(\{1, 3\}) = v(\{1, 4\}) = v(\{1, 5\}) = 100,$$

$$v(T) = 100 \quad \text{for any } T \supset \{1, i\} \text{ for } i = 2, 3, 4 \text{ or } 5,$$

$$v(\{2, 3, 4, 5\}) = 100,$$

$$v(S) = 0 \quad \text{for all other } S \subset N = \{1, 2, 3, 4, 5\}.$$

The question is what is a reasonable division of 100 between the aunt and one nephew. The opinions of several well-known game theorists were collected by Davis and Maschler [4]. This game makes for a simple but interesting experiment.

3.6. References

There is a great volume of literature on game theory experiments, and it is easy to make up many additional examples. The interested reader can consult journals such as *Behavioral Science* and *The Journal of Conflict Resolution*; e.g., the special issues on game theory that appeared in Volume 7, No. 1, January 1962 and Volume 6, No. 1, March 1962, respectively. Other sources of simple experiments are Part V of Shubik [21], Thrall, Coombs, and Davis [24], and Maschler's report [16].

4. Some Pollution Models

4.0. Introduction

A problem of major concern to our modern technologically oriented society is pollution. Many of our industrial activities produce bad effects such as pollution and depletion of resources as well as desired economic and social benefits. A production process consists of inputs, intended outputs, and byproducts. The latter are also referred to as joint-products or externalities. They often have a negative value such as the case with pollution, but in some cases they may be of positive value. One of the ongoing changes in modern society is to hold the producer responsible for such undesirable effects, i.e., to include such externalities in their statistics or general bookkeeping and to be accountable for them. The problem is to determine the best compromise solution for such endeavors and how to distribute the resulting costs in an equitable manner. Some very simple illustrations of how one might begin to model and to gain insight into such multiperson activities are given in this section. We focus on those aspects of these problems that are concerned with the formation and evaluation of coalitions.

4.1. The Symmetric Lake Game

An elementary model of lake pollution has been described by Shapley and Shubik [20]. There are n industrial plants located along the edge of a particular lake. To simplify this example, assume that the problem is symmetrical, i.e., each plant has the same relevant inputs and outputs, and each is affected equally by any pollution. Assume that each plant must take in the same amount of clean water from the lake each day, and that it then releases this water in a polluted state back into the lake. The options and costs involved are as follows.

(i) Each plant must pay c dollars per day to clean its intake water for *each one* of the plants (including itself) that are releasing dirty water directly into lake. That is, *each one* of the n plants pays uc dollars per day if u of the n plants are polluting.
(ii) Each plant has the option of installing a filter that will clean its output water before it enters the lake. The expense of this cleaning operation is b dollars per day for each company that chooses to do so.
(iii) To make our problem interesting we assume that

$$0 < c < b < nc.$$

We also assume that each plant is individually owned and that each owner's goal is to minimize his costs for each day. None of the owners are fishermen nor have other interests in the environment or in conservation.

Some insights may be obtained if we focus on the costs of various sized coalitions of players. Perhaps the participants can benefit economically if some of them enter into an agreement to install filters for their outflows. We can assume, for example, that no filters are used currently, and that the owners realize that potential gains may be realized if they were to be installed.

(i) An individual player i when acting alone sees his *value* as

$$v(\{i\}) = -nc,$$

i.e., he pays c dollars for each of the n plants that are polluting. If he alone were to install a filter, his *costs* would increase to $(n - 1)c + b$, i.e., his *value* would decrease to $-(n - 1)c - b$.
(ii) On the other hand, if the grand coalition N of all n players were to form and each agreed to clean his outflow, then the daily value to the total group would be

$$v(N) = -nb,$$

since each owner would be paying b each day. So the net social gain due to cooperation of the full group is

$$(-nb) - (-n(nc)) = -n(b - nc) = n(nc - b) > 0.$$

(iii) If it is unlikely that full cooperation can be reached, then it is important to focus on the value of intermediate sized coalitions S in which the number of players s is between 1 and n. A cooperating coalition S can decide to have none, some, or all of its players clean there outflow; but they must assume that the players in N–S whom they do not control will continue to pollute. It is sufficient to consider only the two cases

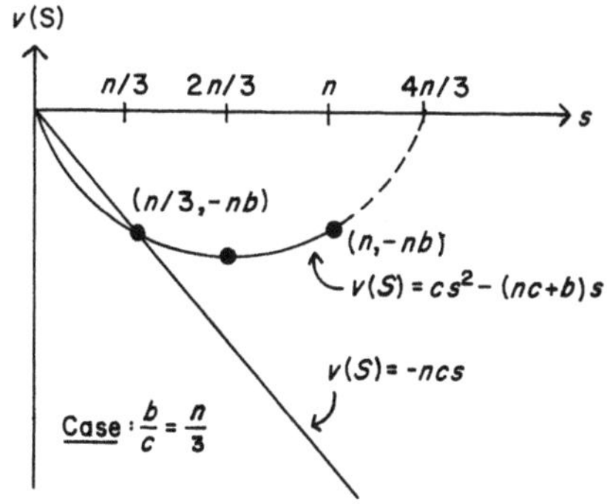

Figure 4.7

in which none or all of the players in S use filters. The resulting value for the coalition S is

$$v(S) = \max\{-snc, -sb - s(n - s)c\}$$
$$= \begin{cases} -snc & \text{if } sc \leq b \\ -snc + s(sc - b) & \text{if } sc \geq b. \end{cases}$$

If a coalition S is large enough ($s > b/c$), then they can as a group gain the amount $s(sc - b) > 0$ by cooperating. There are no economic benefits for a coalition of smaller size.

A graph of the curve $v(S)$ versus s for the special case when $b/c = n/3$ appears in Fig. 4.7.

Exercises

31. Verify the intercepts, intersection points, end points, and vertex for the curves in Fig. 4.7.
32. Repeat exercise (31) for other cases such as $b/c = n/4$ or $b/c = 4n/5$.

When $b < nc$, then the natural and most equitable "solution" to this game is for each owner to install a filter at a cost of b dollars per day to each. The imputation $(-b, -b, \cdots, -b)$ is in the core of this game, i.e., no coalition S can achieve more than $-sb$ by acting on its own. The core of this game is a rather large set as is the case for the class of "convex" games that includes this example. Note that as s increases, the amount that each additional player contributes to a coalition also increases when $s > b/c$. This incremental quantity is negative at first but becomes positive for value of s to the right of the vertex of the parabola in Fig. 4.7. This is the well-known bandwagon or snowballing effect. If a player obtains precisely that gain which he brings to a coalition when he joins it, then he should hold out as long as possible.

Note that any agreement to install filters is one that must be verifiable by some sort of inspection procedure. Otherwise, a particular player may decide to not filter and thus pay only c rather than b. This will also cost every other player the amount c. Hence, our cooperative agreement is "unstable" in this sense. This type of situation is an example of the famous "Prisoner's Dilemma" game mentioned in Section 4.3.

EXERCISES

33. Consider the Lake Pollution game when the cost to clean the intake water is only $(u - 1)c$ for each player, where u is the number of polluters. That is, the lake has the ability to clean up the pollution caused by one of the polluting factories. Determine the core for this game. What would be the most economical and fair "solution" to this game.

34. Construct an example of a nonsymmetrical lake pollution game in which different plant capacities cause different costs c_i and b_i to clean inflows and outflows. Analyze this game and recommend an equitable solution.

35. The lake game is an example of diffuse pollution. Often pollution can be voluntarily directed toward another active participant or a bystander. Consider the *Symmetric Garbage Game* in which each of the n players has one bag of garbage which he must dispose of by dropping it in another player's yard. The payoff to any player is $-u$ if u other players dispose of their garbage in his yard. Determine the characteristic function value $v(S)$ for each coalition S of s players. Is the core of this game empty or not? Is this game constant-sum? What do you expect to happen?

4.2. The River Game

If our polluting factories are located along a flowing river, then we have an example of involuntary directed pollution. Each plant intakes water that has been polluted by the plants upstream, whereas each owner releases his dirty water on only those plants that are downstream from his. A simple example of this sort appears in the book by McDonald [17, pp. 355–358].

McDonald then goes on in his Chapter 14 to discuss the *Oil Game in Maine* in a nontechnical manner but in the terminology of cooperative multiperson games. There are great economic benefits available to certain groups in the State of Maine and elsewhere if oil refineries and ports for supertankers are developed there, where they have the only natural deep water facilities on the eastern or southern coasts of the United States. On the other hand, enormous environmental, social, or economic costs may also result. This case is somewhat like the river game since the currents (and thus an oil slick) flow southward along the coast from the Canadian provinces above (which can independently expand their ports) down to Cape Cod.

EXERCISES

36. Analyze some river pollution games for various values of n in which the costs to clean inflow for the similar plants depend upon the number of upstream polluters, and the cost for one plant to clean its outflow is b. In each case, recommend "reasonable" solutions. Plants downstream may wish to subsidize those upstream if the latter filter their discharge.

37. Analyze some example like Exercise 36 in which the plants have different capacities, and thus different costs to clean inflow or outflow.

In Chapter 5, this volume, Heaney [9] discusses how three cities along a river can reduce their total sewerage costs by cooperation, and how such savings could be distributed. His models do not assume additive pollution as those above. Heaney has applied such models to real situations in the State of Florida. Some game theory solution concepts have also been proposed to allocate costs for a water resource development project in Japan [23]. Some other mathematical models for water pollution appear in several recent books, e.g., [3] and [10].

In the area of Ithaca, New York, there have been recent intercommunity cooperative efforts in constructing a sewer system as well as a new water supply system. In the latter case the town of Ithaca went independently of the city of Ithaca. As a result, both communities are now paying very much higher water bills in this example of noncooperative behavior. It would be an interesting project to study other possible solutions for this game (which has unfortunately already been played out) to see what savings would have been possible and how they could have been distributed in an equitable manner. The reader may be able to find such problems suitable for projects in communities located near his residence.

4.3. Other Pollution Models

In their paper, Shapley and Shubik [20], also describe a problem in which the inputs are ore and coke and the outputs are iron plus a dirty cloud of smoke. In this *Smelting Game* the group payoff is proportional to the number of units of iron produced by them diminished slightly by the amount of smoke in the air. Some players begin with ore and others with coke. This example is another case involving diffuse pollution. Whether this game has an empty core or not depends in a nontrivial way upon the number and types of players involved, as well as on the cost of the diseconomy smoke. Analyzing these cases and recommending reasonable or likely solutions make for interesting class modeling problems. Several extensions and variations of this game to nonsymmetric cases, directed (downwind) pollution, and so forth can easily be created. K. O. Kortanek and others at Carnegie–Mellon University propose in some reports how game theory solution concepts called nucleoli can be employed to tax air polluters.

Many pollution problems, as well as a great number of other social interactions, can be modeled as *n-person Prisoner's Dilemma* games. The famous two-person prisoner's dilemma is due to A. W. Tucker in 1950 and is discussed in a multitude of publications. There are many ways in which the two-person case can be generalized to the multiperson games, and a fine analysis of this appears in the article by Hamburger [8]. By introducing different interpretations for his cases, one can generate a great number of modeling exercises and projects. The n-person prisoner's dilemma and repeated play of such games model what are probably among the most frequently occurring activities in every day social interactions.

5. Equitable User's Fees

5.0. Introduction

There are many instances in which some service is provided to different types of users, and one wishes to charge a user's fee to recover some or all of the expense of operating the service facility. If there are different sorts of customers who use the facility to different extents, then it is reasonable to vary the charges or taxes to them according to how little or how much of the service they may use. The problem is how to assess such fees in an equitable way. One wishes to distribute the cost fairly relative to usage in such a way as to recover a certain known level of expenditures. Such problems frequently arise in the public domain, in services such as transportation and communications, where the provider of the service would like merely to recoup the expenses required for maintaining the facilities without making a profit.

Sometimes the service and rates already exist, but some change in technology or the number of users creates a surplus profit or new deficit. The question then becomes one of how the customers should share in such gains or losses. Many classical economic arguments about the marginal cost caused by each user do not seem fair and such schemes may not generate the level of income desired. Some examples, along with some coalitional considerations, are given in this section.

5.1. Airport Landing Fees

Assume that a small city maintains an airport with one runway that is 5000 ft long. It costs them \$150,000 per year to run this service and they wish to recover this amount in landing fees. Last year they had 3000 landings. These were by five general classes of planes, and each type required a different length of runway to make a safe landing. The number of landings of planes in the five classes were 300, 1000, 500, 800, and 400; the respective minimum safe landing distances in feet are 1000, 2500, 3500, 4000, and 5000. This information is illustrated in the following tabulation.

Plane type		1	2	3	4	5
No. of landings		300	1000	500	800	400
Feet of runway	0	1000	2500	3500	4000	5000
No of users of runway section		3000	2700	1700	1200	400
Cost per section		$30,000	45,000	30,000	15,000	30,000
Total cost						$150,000
Fee per landing		c_1	c_2	c_3	c_4	c_5

One approach to assigning landing fees is to charge each plane for the number of feet of runway that it requires. All 3000 landings make use of the "first" section of runway that is 1000 ft long (i.e., one-fifth of the total length). Hence, each user should pay his share for at least this part of the runway, and planes of type 1 should pay for only this part of the runway. The expense for this fifth of the runway can be taken as $150,000/5 = $30,000. Therefore each landing by a plane of type 1 should be assessed

$$c_1 = \$30{,}000/3000 = \$10 = c_1'.$$

Let us continue with this rather "one-dimensional" and "additive" type of argument. There are 2700 planes that make use of the second section of the runway in addition to the first section. They should also pay the cost of $150,000(3/10) = $45,000 for this length of runway. Hence, a plane of type 2 should be charged the amount

$$\begin{aligned} c_2 &= c_1 + \$45{,}000/2700 = \$10 + \$16.67 = \$26.67 \\ &= c_1 + c_2'. \end{aligned}$$

Likewise, planes of types 3, 4, and 5 should also pay for the expense of the third section of runway, which is again $30,000. Hence, each landing by a plane of type 3 should be charged at the rate of

$$\begin{aligned} c_3 &= c_1 + c_2' + \$30{,}000/1700 = c_2 + \$17.65 \\ &= \$44.32 = c_2 + c_3'. \end{aligned}$$

Similarly, the landing fee for a plane of type 4 is

$$\begin{aligned} c_4 &= c_1 + c_2' + c_3' + \$15{,}000/1200 \\ &= c_3 + \$12.50 = \$56.82 = c_3 + c_4', \end{aligned}$$

and for a plane of type 5 is

$$\begin{aligned} c_5 &= c_1 + c_2' + c_3' + c_4' = c_4 + \$30{,}000/400 \\ &= c_4 + \$75.00 = \$131.82 = c_4 + c_5'. \end{aligned}$$

One can verify that this schedule of fees will provide an income equal (up to round-off error) to the expenses (for last year). And we have divided the costs of each section of the runway equally among all the users of that segment. Any plane that uses several sections must pay an incremental fee for each such section.

A paper by Littlechild and Owen [12] discuss the above approach for the general case, and they present real data for the airport in Birmingham, England in 1968–1969.

There are many extensions of the idealized example presented above that can be pursued, and some suggestions appear in the following exercises.

Exercises

38. Assume in our example that 40% of the runway costs are "fixed" costs and do not depend upon the length of the runway in any manner, and thus should be spread equally among all the users. Only the remaining 60% depends upon the type of plane. Recompute "equitable" landing fees in this case.

39. The argument above was rather one-dimensional in the sense that it did not depend upon the width or depth of the runway. Assume that some "smaller" planes also require less-wide runways (making up your own numbers), and compute fair landing fees based upon an "area" rather than a "length" of runway used.

40. Extend (39) to a "volume" argument in which some "heavier" types of planes require a thicker runway to land on. A couple of years ago there was a debate in Portland, Maine, about new fees. They were reinforcing the runway since Delta Airlines wished to introduce a few flights each day with heavier planes.

41. Another approach to assessing fees might be to base them to some extent upon the number of passengers; or the capacity of the various planes as determined by the number of seats, the weight capacity, the weight of plane, or the number of people actually flying. Consider an example of this type and compute such fees. Discuss whether any of these are reasonable schemes.

42. It would be an interesting project to determine the various expenses involved in maintaining a small city or rural county airport. In addition to runway expense, there are costs for the terminal, fuel, and repair facilities, roads, and parking, interest on bonds, general overhead, and personnel, etc. Such costs are often covered by various government subsidies and taxes to residents of the area as well as by users. Analyze such a problem for some small local airport with a view toward recommending a more equitable way to distribute these expenses.

43. An airport usually has income from sources other than just landing fees. These include rental of space to airlines, car rental agencies, food or drink concessions or game rooms, as well as charges for parking or to taxis. (The current landing fees in Ithaca were agreed upon only after many months of negotiations with Allegheny Airlines, which had essentially a monopoly position. The latter suggested increasing other sources of revenue. It appears now as though free parking at the airport will soon come to an end.) Analyze a local airport, considering both income and expenses, and recommend how these should be altered to reflect real use of the facilities.

44. Is it fair to have the big trailer trucks on our highways paying so much more in taxes than the ordinary car owners?

45. Discuss the policy of a restaurant that charges any table sitting only for the one most expensive meal ordered by someone at the table.

In our considerations above, we have not stressed the idea of coalitions as such. One way to do this for a problem on providing services is as follows. Consider each individual service incident as a player and a set of such acts as a coalition. For example, the players in our landing fees game are the individual landings and not the particular planes, owners of a fleet, or particular pilots. In this case, the cost to service a coalition then depends upon the "largest" player in the coalition. The runway must be long enough for the plane with the longest landing distance. A doorway may be designed for the tallest person who is likely to use it. Many services attempt to be able to handle the peak load. In such cases, it is natural to take the value of a coalition to be the negative of the cost to service this most expensive user.

If the example above is represented as a game in the manner just described, then one can apply the different solution concepts from the multiperson cooperative game theory to our example to see what outcomes result. It turns out [12] that the procedure described above corresponds to the Shapley value of the game, which is considered as an equity solution concept in game theory. It is the unique solution that satisfies three axioms, which correspond to principles one would desire to have in any scheme considered as fair.

Another game theoretical solution concept that gives a unique outcome for each game is the nucleolus, and it has also been applied to the Airport Landing Fees game. This was first suggested by Richard Spinetto and is discussed in a paper by Littlechild [11].

5.2. WATS Telephone Lines

A heavy user of long distance telephone "lines" may be able to reduce his costs by renting a certain number of lines, called WATS lines, from the phone company. He does not actually control particular lines, but he can use up to a certain number of lines at no additional cost. Lines to a few different areas (or bands) cost different amounts. One question concerns how to best select a distribution of different WATS lines so as to minimize one's total expected costs. A second question then arises as to how one should distribute the resulting savings among the users in an equitable way. Such rates should depend upon the region called, the time and type of day when placed, and the length of the call.

If one considers each particular calling instant as a player, then one can model this latter problem as a game with a continuum of players, and the game theory solution concepts such as the Shapley value for nonatomic games [2] can be employed to set equitable charges. Some numerical computations are required to approximate the integrals that arise in the continuous model. This problem has been analyzed for the phone system at Cornell University by a group in Operations Research. The resulting set of fair phone rates has been adopted by the University.

6. Economic Markets

6.1. Markets

A simple exchange economy is determined by the bundles of goods that the individual traders bring to the market place along with the different preferences or desires that the individual traders have for the bundles they can take home from the market. Assume that there is a group $N = \{1, 2, \cdots, n\}$ of n traders labeled $1, 2, \cdots, n$; that there are m commodities that will similarly be indexed by $1, 2, \cdots, m$. Each trader i enters the market with his original commodity bundle described by $w^i = (w_1^i, w_2^i, \cdots, w_m^i)$, where w_j^i is the number of units of good j that trader i has in this initial endowment. We shall also assume that each trader i has a real valued utility function u_i, which expresses his preferences. Values $u_i(x)$ are defined for all realizable distributions $x = (x_1, x_2, \cdots, x_m)$ of goods, and i prefers vector x to vector y if and only if $u_i(x) > u_i(y)$. One normally assumes that the functions u_i have certain properties such as continuity and concavity, i.e., $u_i(\lambda x + (1 - \lambda)y) \geq \lambda u_i(x) + (1 - \lambda)u_i(y)$, whenever $0 \leq \lambda \leq 1$.

Consider a coalition $S \subset N$ of traders. The players in S can make any reallocation of goods among themselves that satisfies the conservation law

$$\sum_{i \in S} x^i = \sum_{i \in S} w^i,$$

where $x^i = (x_1^i, x_2^i, \cdots, x_m^i)$ describes the bundle distributed to i. Assuming that the group utility is the sum of its member's utility, the goal of coalition S is to choose the x^i so as to maximize the total utility to their group, i.e., to determine the x^i so as to realize

$$v(S) = \max \sum_{i \in S} u_i(x^i).$$

Any final settlement must take into account all of the coalitional values $v(S)$ determined in this way.

6.2. The Coffee Break

Assume that there are three workers 1, 2, and 3 who bring the four commodities (coffee, tea, sugar, and cream) to their morning coffee break. Player 1 brings two units of coffee, but likes to drink tea with cream. Player 2 has one unit of tea and prefers to drink coffee with sugar, whereas player 3 has two units of sugar and three units of cream, and desires to drink coffee with sugar and cream. We can represent these initial endowments as

$$w^1 = (2, 0, 0, 0),$$
$$w^2 = (0, 1, 0, 0),$$
$$w^3 = (0, 0, 2, 3),$$

and assume that the player's utility functions are

$$u_1(x) = \min\{x_2, x_4\},$$
$$u_2(x) = \min\{x_1, x_3\},$$
$$u_3(x) = \min\{x_1, x_3, x_4\}.$$

Here $u_i(x)$ gives the number of drinkable cups of beverage that worker i can make for himself from the ingredients represented by x.

One can then compute the coalitional values $v(S)$ for the various subsets S of $N = \{1, 2, 3\}$. For example, if player 1 were ill and did not come to work, then the coalition $\{2, 3\}$ would have to do the best they can without 1. The resulting characteristic function is

$$v(\{1\}) = v(\{2\}) = v(\{3\}) = v(\{1, 2\}) = v(\{2, 3\}) = 0,$$
$$v(\{1, 3\}) = 2, \quad v(\{1, 2, 3\}) = 3.$$

The set of imputations is

$$A = \{(u_1, u_2, u_3) : u_1 + u_2 + u_3 = 3; \quad u_1, u_2, u_3 \geq 0\},$$

and the core is

$$C = \{(u_1, u_2, u_3) \in A : u_1 + u_3 \geq 2\}.$$

No coalition has the power to block a distribution x which gives rise to utility outcome $u = (u_1, u_2, u_3)$ in the core. These sets are illustrated in Fig. 4.8.

Exercises

46. Analyze the Coffee Break game when the initial endowments are $w^1 = (2, 1, 0, 1)$, $w^2 = (0, 2, 0, 3)$, and $w^3 = (1, 1, 4, 1)$; when the players have the same utility functions.

47. Analyze the Coffee Break game when player 2 goes on a diet and no longer takes any sugar with his coffee.

48. Determine the vertices of the core in the game in Exercise 47.

49. Assume that there are three countries and four commodities: corn, wheat, steel, and aluminum. Country 1 has two units of corn, 2 has one unit of wheat, and 3 has two units of each of steel and aluminum. Country 1 needs wheat and aluminum, 2 needs corn and steel, and 3 needs corn, steel, and aluminum. The value of any

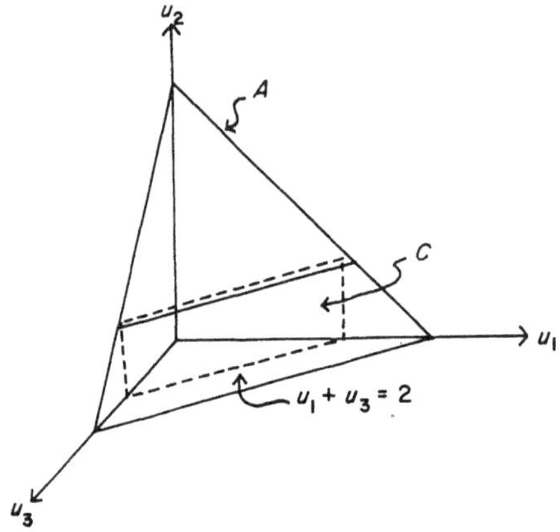

Figure 4.8

coalition is the total number of units they possess that any member of their coalition has a need for. Show that the characteristic function for this game of *International Trade* is as follows. Note that we count those units that a country already possesses and has a need for.

$$v(\{1\}) = v(\{2\}) = 0, \quad v(\{3\}) = 4,$$

$$v(\{1, 2\}) = 3, \quad v(\{1, 3\}) = 6, \quad v(\{2, 3\}) = 4,$$

$$v(\{1, 2, 3\}) = 7.$$

Determine A and C for this game.

50. Assume that there are r players with a house to sell and l players who wish to purchase a house. A gain of one unit is achieved whenever two players of different types get together for an exchange. Let $n = r + l$ and express the characteristic function values for all coalitions in this n-person *House Market* game.

A basic paper on game theoretical models for economic markets with "side payments" is by Shapley and Shubik [19]. Many extensions of their work to games without side payments and for alternate assumptions about the utility functions have also been published. An important theorem in most such models is that the core is always a nonempty set. In many such cases the core also contains the "equilibrium" outcome for the game. The latter is a solution concept for noncooperative multiperson games, and it often has an interpretation related to the "prices" of the goods. Another important research problem is the determination of which types of games are realizations of some economic market.

6.3. The Farmer's Market

Many other approaches to modeling economic exchanges also exist. Some models begin with "demand curves or surfaces," which may, for example, give the quantity to be sold as a function of the price of the good. Many models also take a noncooperative approach to the problem. The main solution concept in such models is that of an equilibrium point. The players are at an equilibrium point if none of these economic agents can change their "strategy" unilaterally and expect to do better. If all the players but one continue to use a particular equilibrium strategy, then the deviant player cannot achieve a higher payoff than at this equilibrium outcome.

Consider a symmetric market situation in which each one of ten local farmers has 150 bushels of tomatoes that he must sell at the market this Saturday, or else they will rot. These farmers have a cooperative, and they all agree that the estimated market price per bushel (in dollars) will be

$$P = 10 - \frac{Q}{100},$$

where Q is the total number of bushels taken to the market. (Actually, the price will bottom out and hold constant at 10 cents per bushel if 990 or more bushels are trucked in.)

Exercises

51. Consider this as a cooperative situation in which the farmers as a group can agree on a fixed number of bushels that each one should ship to the market so as to maximize their profits. If each farmer can be trusted to hold to this agreement, then what amount should each one bring to the market?

52. Consider this as a noncooperative situation. The farmer's cooperative can recommend the number of bushels that each one should bring to the market. However, it must now be a symmetric equilibrium point, so that no one independent-minded farmer in the group can gain by unilaterally deviating from this suggested quantity. Assume that no farmer can communicate with another after they leave the meeting at which they agree on the best equilibrium point, since they still have the old party line. Determine the best symmetric equilibrium point for them. Are there other symmetric equilibria? Is the answer to Exercise 51 an equilibrium point? Can you find a nonsymmetric equilibrium point?

Some other very simple economic situations are modeled as cooperative games in a paper by Shapley [18], including examples concerned with landowners.

7. Business Games

7.0. Introduction

The recent popular book by McDonald [17] describes some dozen major business interactions from a game theoretical point of view. This theory has provided him with a framework for writing about American business in *Fortune* magazine over the past few decades. In this final section we present two models from the business-industrial realm.

7.1. The Communication Satellite Game

In Chapter 11 of his book, McDonald details a game concerning which American corporation would put up a domestic communication satellite. A few historical highlights leading up to this game will be mentioned first. In 1960 the American nonmilitary balloon satellite, Echo 1, was put up by NASA, and the potential for a technological revolution in this industry appeared as a possibility. Comsat and AT&T's Telstar satellite appeared in 1962. Hughes Aircraft orbited the syncronous Early Bird in 1965. This required only a few "fixed" satellites to "cover" the earth, as well as simpler transmitting and receiving stations on the ground. The economic feasibility of a new system then seemed likely. In 1970 the Nixon administration declared an "open sky" policy and encouraged the interested companies to undertake cooperative efforts in this development. A license to produce a system had to be approved by the Federal Communication Commission (FCC). These events paved the way for a ten-person game.

Before long there were ten corporate groups, or players, in addition to one nonstrategic "player" (the FCC), involved in this game. There was not enough business for all of them to put up their own "bird." Some had the necessary technology, whereas others had sufficient communications "traffic" to ensure a profit. Thus room for cooperation did exist. The ten groups were AT&T, Comsat, Hughes, the Networks (ABC, CBS, NBC), Western Union, General Telephone (GT&E), RCA, MCI Lockheed, Western Tel, and Fairchild.

This game of ten-players was too complicated to study analytically in full detail, since there are 1,023 coalitions, but an extensive description is given by McDonald. Many coalitions were very unnatural for various reasons and did not have to be considered seriously. However, McDonald did analyze one important "subgame" involving the three players GT&E (G), Hughes (H), and Western Union (W). These three did consider various possible coalitions among themselves and undertook negotiations. McDonald, who has interviewed many of the experts and decision makers in this game, estimated the characteristic function values for this subgame to be

$$v(\{G\}) = 1, \quad v(\{H\}) = 2, \quad v(\{W\}) = 3,$$

$$v(\{H, W\}) = 8, \quad v(\{G, W\}) = 6.5,$$

$$v(\{G, H\}) = 8.2, \quad v(\{G, H, W\}) = 7.$$

These values are not as simple as something like expected profits, but reflect many nonquantifiable values such as corporate image or even long-run

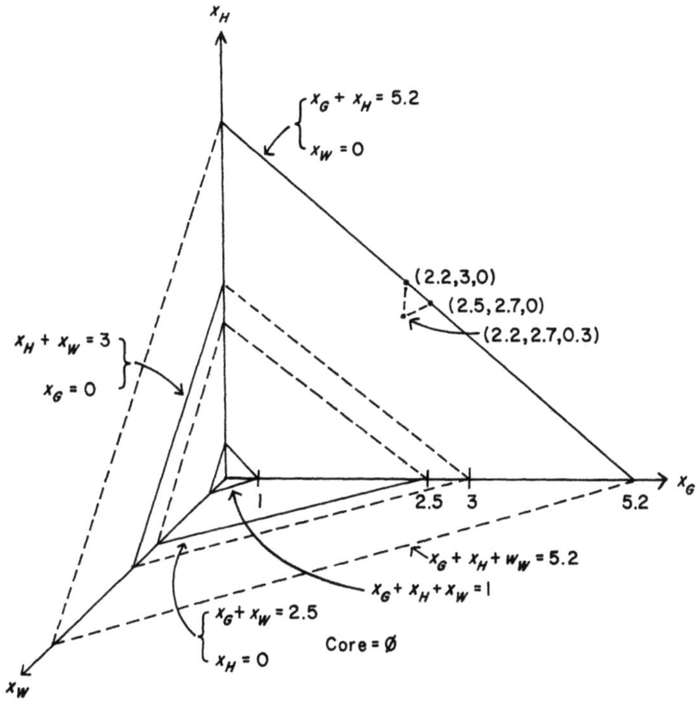

Figure 4.9

survival. Clearly, such values are very gross and imprecise measures, and any resulting modeling with them should be suspicious. Nevertheless, they are about the best the decision makers can supply, and using them might provide some insights. The determination of these values are discussed in much more detail in McDonald's chapter.

Let us assume that we can normalize these coalitional values by subtracting off those values for the one-person coalitions, i.e., the value a corporation places in going it alone. The resulting values are

$$v(\{G\}) = v(\{H\}) = v(\{W\}) = 0,$$
$$v(\{H, W\}) = 3, \quad v(\{G, W\}) = 2.5,$$
$$v(\{G, H\}) = 5.2, \quad v(\{G, H, W\}) = 1.$$

Assuming side payments, the resulting realizable distributions $x = (x_G, x_H, x_W)$ of these values are indicated in Fig. 4.9.

From Fig. 4.9, it appears as though G and H should form a coalition and split 5.2, whereas W gets its fall-back value of 0 (really 3 before normalization). It also appears as though H should obtain the value $2.7 + \varepsilon$ and that G should get $2.5 - \varepsilon$ for $0 \leq \varepsilon \leq .3$. If G were to demand more than 2.5 from H, then he is asking for more than G and W could obtain in coalition against

H. Similarly for $x_H > 3$. Note that the core of this game is empty, but just "barely so", since certain changes in the coalitional values of 0.3 would generate a nonempty core. Player W does have a little bargaining power (i.e., 0.3) with which to upset the coalition $\{G, H\}$. One way for $\{G, H\}$ to neutralize this threat by W would be to allocate a small side payment to him. Hence, an outcome such as

$$(x_G, x_H, x_W) = (2.3, 2.8, 0.1)$$

is not unreasonable.

It is interesting to note that in the real-world application both W and $\{G, H\}$ did request that they be given a license for a satellite system (which, in a sense, only left them in the resulting game that would follow this first stage). However, the FCC first turned them down and suggested that all three players go together with one satellite system. There was some question of W's plans and its technological situation and the chance that its customers may have to pay in case of failure. The three players reviewed their position and again requested the FCC to let W go it alone while H and G would cooperate. However, this time they offered to make a small side payment from H to W in terms of the transfer of some confidential technological information that would reduce the perceived risk in W's plan.

McDonald's story had to end with events of a few years ago. Since that time W has put up a satellite. Several other players, e.g., IBM, have since entered the picture and a more involved corporation game is still in progress.

EXERCISE

53. Change the value of $v(\{G, H\})$ from 5.2 to 6, and find the core for the resulting game.

7.2. The Chemical Companies

A four-person game involving two chemical companies and two fabricating concerns has been described by S. L. Anderson and E. A. Traynor in [1]. Each of two chemical companies C_1 and C_2 can supply either of two fabricating companies F_1 and F_2 with a new product that can be made into clothing and sold at a profit. On the other hand, each chemical company can develop its own fabricating facilities and outlets. Similarly, each fabricator can construct the required chemical plant by itself. However, antitrust laws prohibit cooperation between any two corporations in the same industry.

The seven possible coalition structures (or partitions of the players into subsets) are

(i) $\{\{C_1\}, \{C_2\}, \{F_1\}, \{F_2\}\}$
(ii) $\{\{C_1, F_1\}, \{C_2\}, \{F_2\}\}$

(iii) $\{\{C_1, F_2\}, \{C_2\}, \{F_1\}\}$
(iv) $\{\{C_1\}, \{C_2, F_1\}, \{F_2\}\}$
(v) $\{\{C_1\}, \{C_2, F_2\}, \{F_1\}\}$
(vi) $\{\{C_1, F_1\}, \{C_2, F_2\}\}$
(vii) $\{\{C_1, F_2\}, \{C_2, F_1\}\}$

and the respective payoffs (expected profits) to these coalitions in these particular coalition structures are given in [1] as

(i) 25, 15, 75, 100
(ii) 300, 25, 110
(iii) 500, 30, 85
(iv) 28, 200, 105
(v) 30, 425, 90
(vi) 400, 600
(vii) 700, 300.

This description in terms of a "partition function" gives rise in a natural way to the characteristic function v with values

$$v(\{C_1\}) = 25, \quad v(\{C_2\}) = 15, \quad v(\{F_1\}) = 75,$$
$$v(\{F_2\}) = 100, \quad v(\{C_1, F_1\}) = 300, \quad v(\{C_1, F_2\}) = 500,$$
$$v(\{C_2, F_1\}) = 200, \quad v(\{C_2, F_2\}) = 425.$$

It seems most likely that coalition structure (vi) or (vii) would form. One could argue (e.g., by way of the theory of bargaining sets as is done in [1]) that the respective final distributions to the four players (C_1, C_2, F_1, F_2) should be somewhere in the ranges

(vi) $(x_1, x_2, 300 - x_1, 425 - x_2)$,
(vii) $(y_1, y_2, 200 - y_2, 500 - y_1)$,

where the two-dimensional vectors $x = (x_1, x_2)$ and $y = (y_1, y_2)$ are in the the ranges indicated by Fig. 4.10.

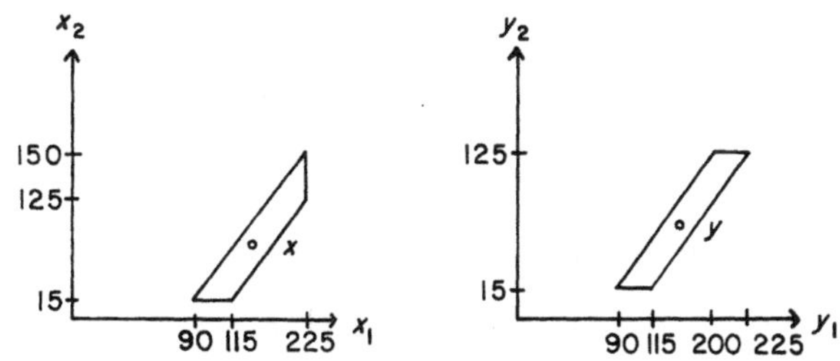

Figure 4.10

EXERCISES

54. Give an argument to justify the assertion made above about the range of the final distribution of the profits.

55. If coalition structure (ii) were actually to form, what range would you expect the final outcome to fall in? What if (v) formed?

56. Determine the core C for this game.

7.3. Other Cooperative Games

A cooperative game related to the sharing of gains from regional cooperation in providing electrical power is described by Gately [6].

Many interactions that exhibit cartel-type behavior are also suitable for analysis by means of the multiperson games. See, for example, the model by Gately, Kyle, and Fischer [7] and the discussion in Lucas [13] concerning the world oil market. Noncooperative games have been used by G. Owen and R. M. Thrall to study U.S. energy policy. Inspection games investigated by A. J. Goldman and others are important in nuclear energy if weapons proliferation is to be avoided.

References

1. Anderson, S. L., and Traynor, E. A. "An Application of the Aumann-Maschler n-person Cooperative Game" in *Recent Advances in Game Theory*, Princeton University Conference, Oct. 4–6, (1961) 265–270. (Out of print.)
2. Aumann, R. J., and Shapley, L. S. *Values of Nonatomic Games*, Princeton University Press, Princeton, 1974.
3. Brebbia, C. A., editor, *Mathematical Models for Environmental Problems*, John Wiley and Sons, New York, 1976.
4. Davis, M., and Maschler, M. "The Kernel of a Cooperative Game," *Naval Research Logistics Quarterly*, *12* (1965), 223–259.
5. Farquharson, R., *Theory of Voting*, Yale University Press, New Haven, Connecticut, 1969.
6. Gately, D., "Sharing the Gains from Regional Cooperation: A Game Theoretic Application to Planning Investment in Electric Power" *International Economic Review*, *15* (1974), 195–208.
7. Gately, D., and Kyle, J. F. with D. Fischer. "'Optimal' Strategies for OPEC's Pricing Decisions," Discussion Paper, Center for Economic Research, New York University, New York, Nov. 1976, 43 pp.
8. Hamburger, H. "n-person Prisoner's Dilemma," *Journal of Mathematical Sociology*, *3* No. 1 (1973), 27–48.
9. Heaney, J. P., "Urban Wastewater Management Planning," Chapter 5 in this Volume.
10. Keinath, T. M., and Waneilista, M. P. editors. *Mathematical Modeling for Water Pollution Control Processes*, Ann Arbor Science Publishers, Ann Arbor, Michigan, 1975.

11. Littlechild, S. C., "A Simple Expression for the Nucleolus in a Special Case," *International Journal of Game Theory*, *3* Issue 1 (1973), 21–29.
12. Littlechild, S. C., and Owen, G. "A Simple Expression for the Shapley Value in a Special Case" *Management Science*, *20* (1973), 370–372.
13. Lucas, W. F., "On Mathematics in Energy Research," in *Energy, Mathematics and Models*, SIAM Conference on Energy at Alta, July 7–11, 1975, edited by F. S. Roberts (1976) 253–263.
14. Lucas, W. F., "Measuring Power in Weighted Voting Systems." Chapter 9 in this volume.
15. Luce, R. D., and Raiffa, H. *Games and Decisions: An Introduction and Critical Survey*, Wiley and Sons, New York, 1957.
16. Maschler, M. "Playing an *n*-Person Game, An Experiment," Econometric Research Program, Research Memo. No. 73, Princeton University (Feb. 1965). (Out of Print).
17. McDonald, John. *The Game of Business*, Doubleday, Garden City, New York, 1975; paperback, Anchor, 1977.
18. Shapley, L. S. "The Value of a Game as a Tool in Theoretical Economics," P-3658, RAND Corp., Santa Monica (Aug. 1967), 16 pp.
19. Shapley, L. S., and Shubik, M. "On Market Games", *Journal of Economic Theory*, *1* (June 1969), 9–25.
20. Shapley, L. S., and Shubik, M. "On the Core of an Economic System with Externalities", *American Economic Review*, *LIX*, *4* (Sept. 1969) 678–684.
21. Shubik, M. editor. *Game Theory and Related Approaches to Social Behavior: Selections*, John Wiley and Sons, New York, 1964.
22. Straffin, P. D. Jr., "Power Indices in Politics", Chapter 11 in this Volume.
23. Suzuki, M., and Nakayama, M. "The Cost Assignment of the Cooperative Water Resource Development: A Game Theoretical Approach," *Management Science*, *22* (June 1976) 1081–1086.
24. Thrall, R. M., Coombs, C. H., and Davis, R. L. editors. *Decision Processes*, John Wiley and Sons, New York, 1960.
25. Von Neumann, J., and Morgenstern, O. *Theory of Games and Economic Behavior*, Princeton University Press, Princeton, 1944, 2nd ed., 1947; 3rd ed., 1953.

Notes for the Instructor

Objectives. To present some nontypical illustrations of mathematical modeling that assume only elementary mathematical concepts. Intended for use by the instructor in more open-ended modeling courses, as well as in traditional courses. The models are concerned with coalition formation, values of coalitions, and distribution of gains.

Prerequisites. Elementary algebra and geometry, and elementary set theory. This module can be used in different ways at various undergraduate course levels. It is self-contained. No knowledge of game theory is required.

Time. Various lengths of time, from one lecture to about one month of class time, can be spent on this module. Term projects related to this material are also possible.

CHAPTER 5
Urban Wastewater Management Planning

James P. Heaney*

1. Introduction

By way of a hypothetical example, we shall describe how decisions are made to expend public monies to control water pollution in a river system. Federal guidelines require that the technical, economic, financial, environmental, and socio-political aspects of the problem be evaluated. Thus, multiple and often conflicting objectives exist. Also, planning is undertaken on an area-wide or river basin level, wherein we must deal with numerous political jurisdictions. The analyst, especially if he is trained only in one discipline, has a strong tendency to define the "problem" as being one that requires primary input from his area of specialization. The hard question is to try to allocate successfully the available resources in such a way that the highest assurance of making the correct decision is obtained. The quality of the analysts' efforts are gauged by the quality of the information for making the decisions and not on their independent value as worthwhile scientific investigations.

The example will describe a hypothetical case. After reading through the case, you can explore numerous avenues of inquiry within this general framework. The main character in the scenario is a practicing professional who is trained in mathematics and has had some exposure to the social sciences and/or engineering.

* Department of Environmental Engineering Sciences, University of Florida, Gainesville, Florida 32611.

2. Description of the Study Area and the Scenario

The urbanized area is comprised of three cities, Thrallsville, Bramsberg, and Straffin, which are presently discharging raw sewage into the nearby Lucas River. The general location map is shown in Fig. 5.1. Each city is required to reduce the pollution by constructing a sewage treatment plant alone or in conjunction with the other cities.

You are the head of the Perry County Planning Department. In addition to a small technical staff, you are able to consult with faculty from nearby Buxious University regarding special problems. After some preliminary discussions with your staff you decide to examine the technical aspects of the problem first.

3. Environmental Engineering Design

Professor Foster advises you that the pollution control regulations require that a secondary treatment plant be installed at each of the cities. Such a plant removes 90% of the pollution. You had hoped to remove all of the pollution but he says that it is technically infeasible.

The cost of a secondary sewage treatment plant can be estimated using

$$C_T = 730{,}000Q^{0.712}, \tag{1}$$

where C_T = present value of capital plus operation and maintenance cost based on 8% interest over 20 yr; Q = wastewater flow in cubic feet per second (cfs).

Note that there are economies of scale in building sewage treatment plants, i.e., $\Delta C/\Delta Q$ decreases as Q gets larger. Thus, it may be cheaper to pipe the wastewater from Thrallsville and Bramsberg to Straffin and construct a single larger plant. Piping costs can be estimated using

$$C_P = 6600Q^{0.51}L, \tag{2}$$

where C_P = present value of capital plus operation and maintenance costs based on 8% interest over 20 yr; Q = wastewater flow in cubic feet per second (cfs); L = pipe length in 1000 ft.

4. Economic Analysis

Professor Gibbs, a resource economist, describes pollution as an external diseconomy, i.e., the production decisions of one unit in the system impose adverse effects on other units. He explains a model of a rational economic

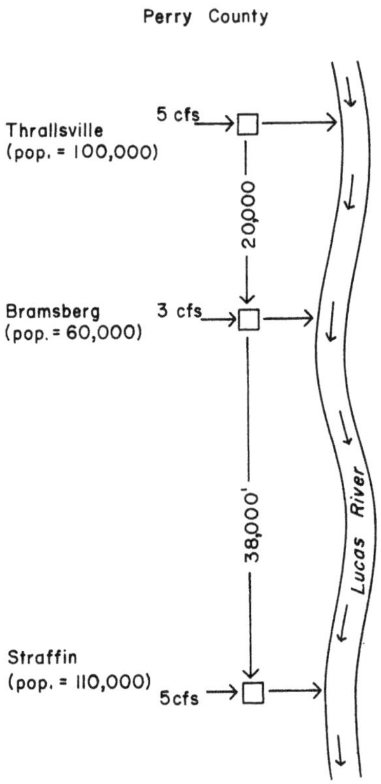

Figure 5.1 Location of the three cities.

man seeking to maximize profits or minimize costs given certain technologic alternatives, associated price, and cost guides.

Within the context of your problem, he asks you to find the least costly way of meeting the specified pollution control standards. With only three cities he suggests that you enumerate all possibilities. The results are shown below.

OPTION 1. Each city builds its own plant

$$\begin{aligned} C(1) &= 730{,}000(5)^{0.712} = \$2{,}300{,}000 \\ C(2) &= 730{,}000(3)^{0.712} = 1{,}600{,}000 \\ C(3) &= 730{,}000(5)^{0.712} = \$2{,}300{,}000 \\ \text{Total cost} &= \$6{,}200{,}000 \end{aligned}$$

OPTION 2. Cities 1 and 2 consider a plant at 2. City 3 builds its own plant.

$$C(12) = \min. \begin{cases} 730{,}000(5+3)^{0.712} + 6600(5)^{0.51}(20) = \$3{,}500{,}000 \\ \qquad C(1) \qquad + \qquad C(2) \qquad = \$3{,}900{,}000 \end{cases}$$

$$\begin{aligned} C(12) &= \$3{,}500{,}000 \\ C(3) &= \underline{\ \ 2{,}300{,}000} \\ \text{Total cost} &= \$5{,}800{,}000 \end{aligned}$$

OPTION 3. City 1 builds its own plant. Cities 2 and 3 consider a plant at 3.

$$C(23) = \min. \begin{cases} 730{,}000(3 + 5)^{0.712} + 6600(3)^{0.51}(38) = \$3{,}650{,}000 \\ \quad C(2) \quad + \quad C(3) \quad = \ \ 3{,}900{,}000 \end{cases}$$

$$\begin{aligned} C(1) &= \$2{,}300{,}000 \\ C(23) &= \underline{\ \ 3{,}650{,}000} \\ \text{Total cost} &= \$5{,}950{,}000 \end{aligned}$$

OPTION 4. City 2 builds its own plant. Cities 1 and 3 consider a plant at 3.

$$C(13) = \min. \begin{cases} 730{,}000(5 + 5)^{0.712} + 6600(5)^{0.51}(58) = \$4{,}630{,}000 \\ \quad C(1) \quad + \quad C(3) \quad = \ \ 4{,}600{,}000 \end{cases}$$

$$\begin{aligned} C(13) &= \$4{,}600{,}000 \\ C(2) &= \underline{\ \ 1{,}600{,}000} \\ \text{Total cost} &= \$6{,}200{,}000 \end{aligned}$$

No better than option 1. Delete from further consideration.

OPTION 5. Cities 1, 2, and 3 consider a plant at 3.

$$C(123) = \min. \begin{cases} 730{,}000(5 + 3 + 5)^{0.712} + 6600(5)^{0.51}(20) + 6600(8)^{0.51}(38) = \$5{,}560{,}000 \\ \quad C(12) \quad + \quad C(3) \quad = \ \ 5{,}800{,}000 \\ \quad C(23) \quad + \quad C(1) \quad = \ \ 5{,}950{,}000 \\ \quad C(13) \quad + \quad C(2) \quad = \ \ 6{,}200{,}000 \end{cases}$$

$$C(123) = \$5{,}560{,}000$$

Thus, from the viewpoint of economic efficiency, the best overall solution is to pipe the wastes from Thrallsville and Bramsberg to Straffin and build one large plant at that point.

5. Financial Analysis

Given that the least costly solution is a single plant, some mechanism is needed to apportion this cost among the three cities. Professor Packel, an expert on public finance, says that there are numerous ways to assign these costs. The method most commonly used in the waste treatment field is the use of facilities method. The procedure is to assign each city a share of the cost based on his proportional share of the use measured in flow rate. We decide to follow this seemingly reasonable procedure. The results are presented below.

(1) Thrallsville		
(a) Pipeline from Thrallsville to Bramsberg	=	$ 300,000
(b) 5/8 of pipeline from Bramsberg to Straffin	=	450,000
(c) 5/13 of treatment plant at Straffin	=	1,745,000
Total cost	=	$2,495,000
(2) Bramsberg		
(a) 3/8 of pipeline from Bramsberg to Straffin	=	$ 274,000
(b) 3/13 of treatment plant at Straffin	=	1,046,000
Total cost	=	$1,320,000
(3) Straffin		
(a) 5/13 of treatment plant at Straffin	=	$1,745,000
(4) Total cost	=	$5,560,000

This cost-sharing procedure does apportion the entire cost of the project among the three cities. We should like to check how each city would react to this arrangement. The results are disappointing, for while the overall plan is financially better for Bramsberg and Straffin, it is more expensive for Thrallsville ($2,495,000 versus $2,300,000). Professor Packel points out that this situation sometimes occurs. He suggests that you might find some concepts from cooperative n-person game theory to be helpful.

The use of game theory is very helpful. Its axioms of fairness would not allow Thrallsville to be assessed a cost that is higher than its cost of independent action. Indeed you see that it is straightforward to construct a three-person cooperative game in characteristic function, wherein the characteristic function is defined as the savings to a coalition from cooperation. Thus, the savings ($\$ \times 10^3$) are

$$v(1) = v(2) = v(3) \qquad = 0$$
$$v(12) = C(1) + C(2) - C(12) \qquad = 400$$

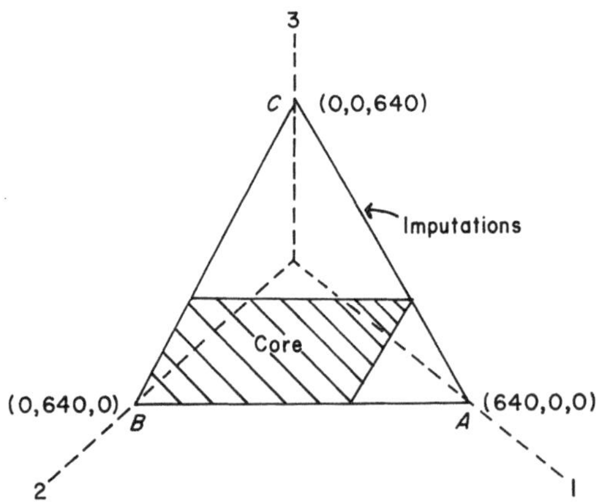

Figure 5.2. Imputations and core of the three-city game.

$$\begin{aligned} v(23) &= C(2) + C(3) - C(23) &&= 250 \\ v(13) &= C(1) + C(3) - C(13) &&= \ \ 0 \\ v(123) &= C(1) + C(2) + C(3) - C(123) &&= 640 \end{aligned}$$

Note, that coalition (13) is inessential, i.e., $v(13) = v(1) + v(3)$.

The set of imputations and the core of the game are shown graphically in Fig. 5.2. Equilateral triangle ABC delimits the set of imputations, i.e.,

$$x(i) \geq 0 \quad i = 1, 2, 3$$

$$\sum x(i) = v(123),$$

where $x(i)$ = savings alloted to player i.

The additional constraints to delimit the boundaries of the core are

(a) $x(1) + x(2) \geq 400$, which is bounded by alloting (640 − 400) units to $x(3)$ and the balance to either $x(1)$ or $x(2)$. Thus, the two additional data points are (400, 0, 240) and (0, 400, 240).
(b) $x(2) + x(3) \geq 250$ generates two additional data points (390, 250, 0) and (390, 0, 250).
(c) $x(1) + x(3) \geq 0$ generates two additional data points (0, 640, 0) and (0, 640, 0), which are simply the original point B since the coalition is inessential.

The core is shown as the shaded portion of the equilateral triangle. We would like our cost-sharing point to fall within the core. In general, at most six data delimit the core boundaries. In this example, they are (counting point B twice)

(1) (400, 0, 240)
(2) (0, 400, 240)
(3) (390, 250, 0)
(4) (390, 0, 250)
(5) (0, 640, 0)
(6) (0, 640, 0)

Professor Packel suggests that the Shapley value might give a reasonable solution. Shapley assumes that each member should get the incremental value he brings to the coalition averaged over the $n!$ coalition formation sequences. In this case, the sequences are

(123) (213) (312)

(132) (231) (321)

Thus

$$\begin{aligned} x(1) &= \tfrac{1}{3}[v(1) - v(\phi)] + \tfrac{1}{6}[v(12) - v(2)] \\ &\quad + \tfrac{1}{6}[v(13) - v(3)] + \tfrac{1}{3}[v(123) - v(23)] \\ &= \tfrac{1}{3}(0) + \tfrac{1}{6}(400) + \tfrac{1}{6}(0) + \tfrac{1}{3}(640 - 250) \\ x(1) &= 196, \end{aligned}$$

where $v(\phi) \equiv 0$.
Similarly,

$$x(2) = 322, \quad x(3) = 122.$$

Note that

$$\sum x(i) = 640.$$

This solution is in the core. Indeed, it is the same solution you would get if you simply averaged the above six corner points. Thus, you are satisfied that the financial arrangements are reasonable.

6. Environmental Impact Statement—Ecology

The results of the economic analysis indicate that option $5 > 2 > 3 > 1$.[1] State environmental regulations require that an environmental impact statement be prepared. Professor Zahavi, the Ecology Professor, suggests an intensive field survey of the Lucas River. Following this investigation, the study team recommends that three plants be built because of their better reliability. Thus, option 1 is their first choice, followed by 2 or 3, with 5 being their lowest choice.

This really complicates matters since the ecologists' and economists' solutions are in direct conflict. Furthermore, attempts to relate "reliability" to dollars prove futile. Thus, we are at an impasse.

Also, in accordance with environmental regulations, a public hearing to elicit citizen's input is required. This is the next item on the work plan.

7. Public Participation

Your next stop is at the Department of Speech and Communications to get some insight into how to organize a public hearing. After lengthy discussion you decide to hold a televised meeting at Bramsberg High School auditorium. As director of the planning staff, you chair the meeting with members of your staff available to answer questions. A brochure describing the alternatives and their economic, environmental, and financial implications is sent to every taxpayer in Perry County.

The meeting is a lively one with many people making presentations. Highlights, as reported in the Bramsberg Bugle, are listed below.

(1) Members of Ecoalert feel that plan 1 must be selected irrespective of cost. We cannot afford to risk "killing" the river.

[1] The symbol $>$ indicates "is preferred to,"

(2) The Lucas River Canoe Association favors plan 5 to keep the river unpolluted upstream of that point.
(3) Mayer Deegan of Thrallsville strongly favors building his own plant to stimulate the economy in his area.
(4) Numerous upper-income residents from Straffin oppose plan 5 because they do not want to have sewage from other cities transported to their city.
(5) The Perry County Board of Education, while sympathetic to environmental control, feels that it is more vital to initiate the middle school construction program that has been delayed for three years due to lack of funds. They present a petition with 1000 signatures.
(6) Mr. Knight, a retired lawyer, questions the legitimacy of the public hearing. He wants to know how the final choice is to be made.
(7) The citizens against higher taxes urge support for plan 5 because it is the least costly.
(8) Mayor Loucks from Straffin protests that his city should pay less than recommended by plan 5 because they have to put up with the numerous inconveniences associated with the construction.
(9) Mayor Haith from Bramsberg argues that Straffin should pay a larger share of the cost because they will gain jobs for their constituents.

Overall the hearing lasts 6 hr during which 500 pages of testimony are submitted by 83 people. You now realize that this is quite a sensitive issue. Next, you contact Professor Mayer to see if she can suggest techniques from political science that might prove helpful in resolving this issue.

8. Political Science

Your readings in political science make frequent mention of one man, one vote as the appropriate principle to select the best plan. Thus, your first thought is to set up a county-wide referendum to choose among the various alternatives. You describe this proposed procedure to your advisers and receive the following reactions.

(1) Professor Foster, your engineering adviser, opposes a referendum. He feels that this is a technical question that should be decided by the experts. Politics should be kept out! He recommends that the technical staff should make the decision.
(2) Professor Gibbs, the economics consultant, is opposed to considering any plan other than 5, the economically optimal one. He feels it would be irrational to select any other plan.
(3) Professor Mayer feels that four alternatives are too many to consider in a referendum because the voters will be confused. No plan is apt to receive a majority of votes so that a runoff would be necessary.

(4) Each mayor feels strongly that the chosen plan should be favored by a majority of his constituents. This would require additional referenda.

After consulting with Professor Mayer you decide to reject suggestions to let the experts make the selection. You are convinced that this is a social choice problem wherein we shall, by some mechanism, aggregate the preferences of all individuals into a single social choice mechanism. Professor Mayer advises that no single, best way to determine the appropriate social choice exists. She does suggest evaluating the relative power of the various cities using the Shapley–Shubik index that is identical to the Shapley value except that the characteristic function is defined as follows

$$v(S) = \begin{cases} 1 \Leftrightarrow S & \text{is a winning coalition} \\ 0 \Leftrightarrow S & \text{is a losing coalition.} \end{cases}$$

Thus, $v(S) - v((S) - \{i\})$ will be zero if player i joins a coalition that is already a winner, or joins a losing coalition that remains a loser with player i. Only when player i converts a losing coalition to a winning one is he pivotal. His relative power depends on the number of times he is pivotal.

Alloting one vote per thousand persons, and requiring a simple majority to win, then a three-city quota game can be constructed. Let

$$[q; w_1, w_2, w_3]$$

denote the quota game where

$$q = \text{the quota needed to win,}$$

$$w_i = \text{number of votes owned by player } i, \quad i = 1, 2, 3.$$

For this case, the game is

$$[136; 100, 60, 110].$$

The coalition formation sequences are listed below. The pivot is circled.

1②3 2①3 3①2

1③2 2③1 3②1

For this case, the Shapley–Shubik index, expressed as a vector ϕ, is $\phi = [1/3, 1/3, 1/3]$. All cities have equal power. This seems unfair to the two larger cities. Next, a two-thirds quota is used, or

$$[181; 100, 60, 110].$$

The resulting vector is $\phi = [1/2, 0, 1/2]$. In this case, Bramsberg is powerless, or in game theory parlance, it is a "dummy." Thus, this approach is rejected. In general, city 2 has relative power of 0, 1/6, or 1/3, depending on the quota. His nominal relative power is 60/270 = 0.22. Thus, he is either under- or over-represented. Similar results occur for Thrallsville and Straffin. Thus, this procedure is abandoned.

Representatives from the three cities meet with the technical staff to try to reduce the number of alternatives under consideration. After lengthy discussion, it is decided that alternative 3 can be eliminated because it is dominated by alternative 2, since its cost is higher and it offers the same environmental quality.

For the remaining three alternatives, each city is asked to rank the three alternatives denoting by *A* their first choice, *B* their second choice, and *C* their third choice. The results are shown below:

⟨Plan⟩	⟨City⟩ 1	2	3
1, three plants	A	C	B
2, two plants	B	B	A
3, one plant	C	A	C

Clearly no plan is unanimously preferred. Plan *B* does offer two cities their second choice and one city its first choice so it would be expected to be preferred. But city 1 opposes this solution because it does not feel that city 2 should receive equal representation due to its smaller size. At this point, what would you do?

9. Epilogue

The intent of presenting this exercise is to allow you to see the wide variety of considerations that enter into a real world decision-making problem. While this is a hypothetical situation, actual planning studies costing $150 million are underway throughout the United States that are going through the same general thought processes. These studies, funded by the U.S. Environmental Protection Agency, are underway in most urbanized areas of the United States. You may wish to contact your local regional planning council or council of governments and inquire about the status of these so called "208" studies.

Notes for the Instructor

Objectives. This module is designed to provide a scenario for a mathematics-modeling course that seeks to examine applications of mathematical principles to an important public decision making problem. Following presentation of the technical, economic, environmental, social, and political aspects of the problem, the students can pursue several avenues of inquiry ranging from repeating the same type of analysis with a modified set of assumed conditions to in-depth evaluation of one phase of the study. The text is oriented toward illustrating the role of models in a particular decision-making process rather than emphasizing modeling as the end product.

Prerequisites.
(A) General: The student should be juniors or seniors with mathematical background through algebra and some background in economics, sociology, political science, and/or physical sciences, and engineering.
(B) Specific: Introductory material on economic and voting games using n-person game theory would need to be presented. General background from a text such as F. S. Roberts, *Discrete Mathematical Models*, Prentice-Hall, Inc., 1976 would serve very well, especially the following: Chapter 6, n-Person Games; Chapter 7, Group Decision-making and Chapter 8, Measurement and Utility.

Time. One to six weeks.

I use this scenario in a senior course for environmental engineering science students. The objective is to impress upon them the importance of evaluating the total decision problem and the necessity of providing the client with the best possible information upon which to base his decision. They are taught to allocate their time among the many tasks to be accomplished and to finish the work for the subtasks and move on to the rest of the study. Naturally, because of the overall complexity of the problem, there is a strong tendency to procrastinate in the hope of finding more data or to get a more refined model running properly.

If you are in or near a large city, they are probably undertaking a "208" study of urban water pollution. You may wish to have a representative talk to your class to describe his problems. The students could work on the problems as a joint venture or you could use the scenario as a basis for generating problems for them.

CHAPTER 6

An Everyday Approach to Matrix Operations

Robert M. Thrall*
E. L. Perry†

Introduction

From a historical point of view, it is clear that interaction between mathematics and other disciplines has been twofold. First, mathematics has been applied to other disciplines, and second, problems from other fields have helped stimulate the development of certain types of mathematics. This two-way interaction has long been evident in the case of physics, where application of mathematics to certain physical problems, such as the relationship between velocity, distance, and acceleration, in turn spurred new developments in mathematics, particularly in calculus and differential equations.

In this module, we wish to emphasize the second interaction. We shall take everyday examples from newspapers, sports, business, and use them to motivate the development of the standard operations on vectors and matrices. Although these operations are usually introduced at the beginning of any linear algebra or finite mathematics course, they are seldom motivated by real-world examples. The instructor gives the definitions of these operations and then expects the student to wait until later in his or her mathematical career to learn their practical significance. Unfortunately, many of the students may drop out of mathematics before they actually reach the point of seeing the applications. It is our contention that when the definitions are motivated by real-world examples, not only will the student be more inclined to want to pursue mathematics further but also the actual definition itself will be easier to learn and to remember.

The examples that we use are taken from areas where, in most cases, the

* Department of Mathematical Sciences, Rice University, Houston, Texas 77251.
† TRW, Inc., Webster, Texas 77598.

number of possibilities is discrete (either finite or countably infinite), and hence the entries in our matrices and vectors will be integers or rational numbers. This does not reflect a defect in our method but merely points out the fact that many simple real-world problems deal with discrete mathematics. It is precisely in this setting that matrices become most useful.

Although written for a different audience, this paper is in the spirit of Appendix B of Spivey and Thrall [1]. We have taken the ideas presented there and enlarged upon them, bringing in many other outside examples.

1. Introduction to Vectors and Matrices

In everyday life, we often must deal with "stacks" or "collections" of numbers. For example, in a baseball game, at the end of each half inning the announcer gives a list such as

2 runs
3 hits
1 error
2 left on base. (1)

The shopping list that many men or women carry with them to the store would be another example. One such list is

1 loaf of bread
2 pounds of coffee
6 potatoes
2 pounds of cheese. (2)

Each day in the newspaper, there is a column of numbers on the stock-market page that is of considerable interest to many people. A portion of the column might be

American Income	$39\frac{1}{2}$
Hammond Corp.	26
White Eagle	25
Turncoat Industries	$19\frac{1}{4}$
Zefco Products	5.

(3)

Each of these examples of "stacks" or "collections" of numbers can be described, respectively, by a column of numbers as follows.

$$\begin{bmatrix} 2 \\ 3 \\ 1 \\ 2 \end{bmatrix}, \quad \begin{bmatrix} 1 \\ 2 \\ 6 \\ 2 \end{bmatrix}, \quad \begin{bmatrix} 39\frac{1}{2} \\ 26 \\ 25 \\ 19\frac{1}{4} \\ 5 \end{bmatrix}. \tag{4}$$

These columns are perfectly meaningful to the reader as long as he or she understands the meaning of each entry or "component" of the column. In the first example, every baseball fan knows that each half-inning is summarized by giving the number of runs, hits, errors, and people left on base in that order. Thus the top component 2 refers to the runs, while the second 3 gives the hits, and so on. In general, mathematicians call a column of numbers a *column vector* and often designate it by a single symbol, say X. Thus,

$$X = \begin{bmatrix} 2 \\ 3 \\ 1 \\ 2 \end{bmatrix} \tag{5}$$

means that X is a symbol for the column vector

$$\begin{bmatrix} 2 \\ 3 \\ 1 \\ 2 \end{bmatrix}.$$

More complicated "stacks" of numbers occur in everyday life as well. For example, the newspaper summary of a baseball game usually lists each player and gives the number of at bats, runs, hits, and runs batted in. An example would be

	AB	*R*	*H*	*RBI*
Deegan	4	1	1	0
Lucas	3	0	2	1
Thrall	4	2	2	1
Perry	2	0	1	2
Packel	3	0	0	0
Brams	3	1	1	0
Heaney	3	0	0	0
Roberts	4	0	1	0
Halmos	3	0	0	0
Total	29	4	8	4

(6)

As another example, consider a factory that produces three types of football equipment: helmets, shoulder pads, and hip pads. In order to produce these items, various amounts of hard plastic, foam plastic, nylon cord, and labor are required and, in order to control and monitor production, the manager may very well be interested in tabulating the data as shown below.

	Product		
Raw material	Helmet	Shoulder pad	Hip pad
hard plastic	4	2	2
foam plastic	1	3	2
nylon cord	1	3	3
labor	3	2	2

(7)

Thus to make one helmet, we need 4 units of hard plastic, 1 unit of foam plastic, 1 unit of nylon cord, and 3 units of labor.

We might denote these more complicated "stacks" of numbers by

$$\begin{bmatrix} 4 & 1 & 1 & 0 \\ 3 & 0 & 2 & 1 \\ 4 & 2 & 2 & 1 \\ 2 & 0 & 1 & 2 \\ 3 & 0 & 0 & 0 \\ 3 & 1 & 1 & 0 \\ 3 & 0 & 0 & 0 \\ 4 & 0 & 1 & 0 \\ 3 & 0 & 0 & 0 \\ 29 & 4 & 8 & 4 \end{bmatrix} \text{ and } \begin{bmatrix} 4 & 2 & 2 \\ 1 & 3 & 2 \\ 1 & 3 & 3 \\ 3 & 2 & 2 \end{bmatrix}, \tag{8}$$

respectively. Each of the stacks of numbers in (8) is called a *matrix*. Note that a matrix is meaningful as long as the reader understands to what the various entries correspond. For example, for the first matrix of (8) to be meaningful, the reader must know the batting order, that is, the order in which the players names appear as well as the order of the headings *ab*, *r*, *h*, *rbi*. Also, observe that each matrix can be considered as a group of column vectors. In the example of the newspaper summary of the baseball game, there are four columns, *ab*, *r*, *h*, *rbi*. Each of these could be listed separately and considered as a column vector.

Of course, one may wish to refer to a matrix by a symbol so it is common to write something like

$$A = \begin{bmatrix} 4 & 2 & 2 \\ 1 & 3 & 2 \\ 1 & 3 & 3 \\ 3 & 2 & 2 \end{bmatrix}, \tag{9}$$

which means that we shall take the symbol A to represent the matrix shown on the right.

Although we chose to use columns to represent our data in (1), (2), and (3), there is no reason why we should not use rows if we want to do so. The data could be given by

$$[2, 3, 1, 2], \quad [1, 2, 6, 2], \quad [39\tfrac{1}{2}, 26, 25, 19\tfrac{1}{4}, 5]. \tag{10}$$

A row of numbers such as those in (10) is often called a *row vector*. If

$$A = \begin{bmatrix} 2 \\ 3 \\ 1 \\ 2 \end{bmatrix} \quad \text{and} \quad B = [2, 3, 1, 2],$$

then we say that B is the *transpose* of A and write

$$B = A^T. \tag{11}$$

In general, if X and Y are matrices, $Y = X^T$ if and only if Y can be obtained from X by interchanging the rows and columns. For example, if A is as given in (9), then

$$A^T = \begin{bmatrix} 4 & 1 & 1 & 3 \\ 2 & 3 & 3 & 2 \\ 2 & 2 & 3 & 2 \end{bmatrix}. \tag{12}$$

Note that the first column of A^T is the transpose of the first row of A, the second column of A^T is the transpose of the second row of A, and so on. In (12), A^T is the matrix that would have resulted if we had tabulated the data on our Factory in the following form.

	Raw materials			
Product	Hard plastic	Foam plastic	Nylon cord	Labor
Helmet	4	1	1	3
Shoulder pad	2	3	3	2
Hip pad	2	2	3	2

(13)

Although we can use either column or row vector to represent data, it is convenient to standardize notation. In accordance with custom we shall use the word "vector" for column vector and all data will be summarized in column form unless otherwise indicated. For example, in (6) each row is a row vector that summarizes the performance of an individual player but we normally use column vectors to show such information. For example, we take

$$D = \begin{bmatrix} 4 \\ 1 \\ 1 \\ 0 \end{bmatrix} \tag{14}$$

as a column vector showing the performance of Deegan. Then

$$D^T = [4, 1, 1, 0] \tag{15}$$

is the first row of (6).

2. Vector Addition, Subtraction, and Multiplication by Scalars

Suppose that two people have shopping lists each containing different amounts of the same items.

$$X = \begin{bmatrix} 2 \\ 3 \\ 1 \\ 2 \end{bmatrix}, \quad Y = \begin{bmatrix} 2 \\ 1 \\ 0 \\ 3 \end{bmatrix}. \tag{16}$$

The two wish to combine their lists so that only one will need to go to the store. An obvious way to accomplish this is simply to add the corresponding components of the columns to get

$$\begin{bmatrix} 4 \\ 4 \\ 1 \\ 5 \end{bmatrix}. \tag{17}$$

This suggests a way in which two vectors of the same size may be combined to produce a new vector. This process is called *vector addition*. We write

$$X + Y = \begin{bmatrix} 2 + 2 \\ 3 + 1 \\ 1 + 0 \\ 2 + 3 \end{bmatrix} = \begin{bmatrix} 4 \\ 4 \\ 1 \\ 5 \end{bmatrix}. \tag{18}$$

Note that in order to add two column vectors, they must be equal in size. In the example (1) of the baseball game, if we let X_1 denote the vector giving the number of runs, hits, errors, and people left on base in inning 1 by the home team, and in general X_i be the vector showing the number of runs, hits, errors, and people left on base for the home team in inning i, then $X_1 + X_2$ gives the total number of runs, hits, errors, and people left on base by the home team after two innings of play. Also $X_1 + X_2 + \cdots + X_9$ would give the same information for a regulation nine-inning game.

More generally, if

$$X = \begin{bmatrix} x_1 \\ x_2 \\ \vdots \\ x_n \end{bmatrix} \quad \text{and} \quad Y = \begin{bmatrix} y_1 \\ y_2 \\ \vdots \\ y_n \end{bmatrix}, \tag{19}$$

then $X + Y$ is the vector

$$X + Y = \begin{bmatrix} x_1 + y_1 \\ x_2 + y_2 \\ \vdots \\ x_n + y_n \end{bmatrix}, \tag{20}$$

Suppose a scorekeeper gave us the vector

$$X = \begin{bmatrix} 5 \\ 7 \\ 2 \\ 4 \end{bmatrix} \tag{21}$$

which shows the total number of runs, hits, errors and people left on base by the home team during a game and we know that Jim Heaney was the visiting team's pitcher for all innings except the last one. If

$$Y = \begin{bmatrix} 1 \\ 2 \\ 0 \\ 1 \end{bmatrix} \tag{22}$$

is the vector showing the runs, hits, errors and people left on by the home team in the ninth inning then

$$Z = \begin{bmatrix} 5 - 1 \\ 7 - 2 \\ 2 - 0 \\ 4 - 1 \end{bmatrix} \tag{23}$$

is a vector which shows the performance of the home team while Jim Heaney was pitching. This suggests another process called *subtraction* in which two vectors of equal size are combined to produce another vector. We call Z in (23) the *difference* between X and Y and we write

$$Z = X - Y. \tag{24}$$

In general, if X and Y are as given in (19) then $X - Y$ is the column vector

$$X - Y = \begin{bmatrix} x_1 - y_1 \\ x_2 - y_2 \\ \vdots \\ x_n - y_n \end{bmatrix}. \tag{25}$$

Once again, it is important to note that subtraction of vectors is meaningless unless the vectors have the same size.

Returning to the shopping list example (2), we may want to double it so as not to buy groceries so often. Thus,

$$2\begin{bmatrix} 1 \\ 2 \\ 6 \\ 3 \end{bmatrix} = \begin{bmatrix} 2 \\ 4 \\ 12 \\ 4 \end{bmatrix}. \tag{26}$$

This suggests still another operation on vectors that is quite different from the first two operations. Instead of combining two vectors to produce a new vector, we have combined a number (sometimes called a *scalar*) and a vector to produce a vector. In general, if c is a scalar (or number) and X is as given in (19), then cX is the vector

$$cX = \begin{bmatrix} cx_1 \\ cx_2 \\ \vdots \\ cx_n \end{bmatrix}, \tag{27}$$

and this operation is called "multiplication of a vector by a scalar."

In example (3), if X is the vector representing costs of five stocks, then $3X$ would be a vector whose entries represent the amount paid for each stock if an investor buys 3 shares of each.

3. Vector Inner Product

Let us return to the shopping list example where we have a vector

$$A = \begin{bmatrix} 1 \\ 2 \\ 6 \\ 2 \end{bmatrix} \tag{28}$$

showing the number of units of bread, coffee, potatoes, and cheese respectively, that we must buy. Suppose, also, a cost vector C is given

$$C = \begin{bmatrix} 0.35 \\ 1.35 \\ 0.20 \\ 0.69 \end{bmatrix}, \tag{29}$$

which shows the cost per unit of bread, coffee, potatoes, and cheese, respectively. The total bill for the purchase may be computed by multiplying each entry in A by the corresponding entry of C and summing.

$$(1)(0.35) + (2)(1.35) + 6(0.20) + 2(0.69) = 5.63. \tag{30}$$

Also, in (3) we have a vector showing the price of certain stocks, say

$$C = \begin{bmatrix} 39\frac{1}{2} \\ 26 \\ 25 \\ 19\frac{1}{4} \\ 5 \end{bmatrix}.$$

Suppose that

$$A = \begin{bmatrix} 100 \\ 50 \\ 100 \\ 200 \\ 50 \end{bmatrix} \tag{31}$$

is a vector showing the number of shares of each stock that an investor buys. Then the amount paid for the stock (not including brokerage fee) is

$$(100)(39\tfrac{1}{2}) + (50)(26) + (100)(25) + (200)(19\tfrac{1}{4}) + (50)(5) = 11{,}850. \tag{32}$$

Both (30) and (32) suggest another operation on vectors in which two vectors are combined to produce a scalar. In general, if X and Y are as in (19), we say that the inner product of X and Y (sometimes called the *dot* product of X and Y) is $X \cdot Y$ where

$$X \cdot Y = x_1 \cdot y_1 + x_2 \cdot y_2 + \cdots + x_n \cdot y_n. \tag{33}$$

Notice that this operation differs from our previous operations in that two vectors are combined and a scalar (number) is produced, whereas the operations of addition, subtraction, and multiplication by a scalar produced vectors as the end result.

In order to be consistent with the definition of multiplication of matrices, which is discussed in the next section, it will be convenient to represent an inner product as the "matrix product" of a row vector and a column vector. Thus with A and C as in (28), and (29), respectively, the inner product of A and C is equal to

$$A^T C = [1, 2, 6, 2]\begin{bmatrix} 0.35 \\ 1.35 \\ 0.20 \\ 0.69 \end{bmatrix} = 5.63. \tag{34}$$

More generally, when X and Y are as in (19) we shall always picture the inner product of X and Y as

$$X^T Y = [x_1, x_2, \cdots, x_n]\begin{bmatrix} y_1 \\ y_2 \\ \vdots \\ y_n \end{bmatrix}, \quad \text{i.e., } X \cdot Y = X^T Y \tag{35}$$

A helpful device for remembering this is to think of the words "Roman Catholic." The initials, R.C., symbolize "row followed by column." We thus speak of the *product* of a row vector and a column vector.

4. Multiplication of a Matrix and a Vector

Consider again the manufacturing process illustrated by the table (7). We form the associated matrix

$$A = \begin{bmatrix} 4 & 2 & 2 \\ 1 & 3 & 2 \\ 1 & 3 & 3 \\ 3 & 2 & 2 \end{bmatrix}. \tag{36}$$

Now suppose an order comes in for 35 helmets, 10 shoulder pads, and 20 hip pads, and the management wants to know how many units of hard plastic, foam plastic, nylon cord, and labor will be required to fill the order. Since 4 units of hard plastic are required for each helmet, 2 units for each shoulder pad, and 2 units for each hip pad, we see that the total number of units of hard plastic needed will be

$$(4)(35) + (2)(10) + (2)(20) = 200 \text{ units}. \tag{37}$$

But now observe that (37) has the same form as the row-by-column product (35), discussed in the previous section. As a matter of fact, if

$$B = \begin{bmatrix} 35 \\ 10 \\ 20 \end{bmatrix} \tag{38}$$

is a vector showing the number of helmets, shoulder pads, and hip pads, respectively, in the order, it is apparent that (37) is simply the product of the first row of A with B. Similarly, observe that the amount of foam plastic needed is

$$(1)(35) + (3)(10) + (2)(20) = 105 \text{ units}, \tag{39}$$

which is simply the product of the second row of A with B. It also follows that the amount of nylon cord needed is

$$(1)(35) + (3)(10) + (3)(20) = 125 \text{ units}, \tag{40}$$

which is the product of row three of A with B. The reader should now verify for himself that the amount of labor required is the product of the fourth row of A with B. In summary, we have seen that if

$$Y = \begin{bmatrix} y_1 \\ y_2 \\ y_3 \\ y_4 \end{bmatrix} \tag{41}$$

is a vector whose components represent the amount of hard plastic, foam plastic, nylon cord, and labor necessary to fill the order, then each y_i is the product of row i of A with the vector B.

The above analysis is suggestive of an operation in which a matrix is combined with a vector to produce another vector. If A is an $n \times m$ matrix (n rows and m columns), and X is a vector of size m (a column vector with m entries), then AX is defined by

$$AX = Y = \begin{bmatrix} y_1 \\ y_2 \\ \vdots \\ y_n \end{bmatrix}, \tag{42}$$

where each y_i is the product of row i of matrix A with the (column) vector X.

Note that for this definition to be meaningful, X must have the same number of entries as A has columns, otherwise the product of a row of A with X is not defined.

To conclude this section, we give one further example to show the usefulness of (42). Suppose airline A has flights between cities x, y, and z as illustrated by the following table.

	x	y	z
x	1	1	2
y	1	0	2
z	2	1	0

(43)

Here each entry indicates the number of daily flights between the city at the left of the row to the city at the top of the column. For example, the 2 in the first row indicates that there are 2 flights daily from x to z. The 1 in the "x, x" position indicates a "sightseeing" flight that circles city x and returns to the airport. Also, there is another airline B, which has daily flights from cities x, y, and z to a fourth city w. The number of daily flights for airline B from x, y, and z to w is summarized in the table below.

	w
x	2
y	4
z	3

(44)

We form the matrix A asociated with (43) and the vector B associated with (44).

$$A = \begin{bmatrix} 1 & 1 & 2 \\ 1 & 0 & 2 \\ 2 & 1 & 0 \end{bmatrix}, \quad B = \begin{bmatrix} 2 \\ 4 \\ 3 \end{bmatrix}. \tag{45}$$

Consider the product of row one of A with the vector B.

$$(1)(2) + (1)(4) + (2)(3) = 12 \tag{46}$$

In the first term, the 1 indicates one flight from x to x (the sightseeing flight), while the 2 indicates two flights from x to w on airline B. Thus the first term of (46) represents the number of "two step" flights from x to w changing planes at city x. Also, in the second term of (46), the 1 indicates a flight on airline A from x to y while the 4 indicates four flights of airline B from y to w. Thus this term, (1)(4), gives the number of "two stage" flights from city x to w changing planes at city y. Similarly, the last term of the left-hand side of (46) gives the number of "two stage" flights from city x to w changing planes at z. Then the entire sum 12 in (46) gives the total number of "two stage" flights from x to w. By similar reasoning the reader should verify that the product of row 2 of A with B gives the number of two stage flights from y to w, and the product of row 3 of A with B gives the number of "two stage" flights from z to w. We have seen then that if A and B are as in (45), AB is a vector whose entries give the number of two stage flights from x, y, and z respectively, to w.

5. Matrix Addition, Subtraction, and Multiplication

Suppose that the manufacturing process of (7) actually consists of two processes. In the first process, the various parts for the helmets, shoulder pads, and hip pads are cut out and then, in process two, they are assembled (mostly by sewing with nylon cord) to make the finished product. Then the first step of the manufacturing processes can be described by the array below.

Raw material	Product Helmet	Shoulder pad	Hip pad
Hard plastic	4	2	2
Foam plastic	1	3	2
Nylon cord	0	0	0
Labor	2.5	1	1

(47)

Notice that no cord is used in this process as indicated by the zeros in row 3. These zeros serve as "placeholders." If we are only concerned with the first step of the manufacturing process, row 3 can be omitted, but nylon cord is used in the assembly process so we include row 3 in our analysis in order for the matrices for each process to have the same row and column associations (or labels).

Now the assembly process can be illustrated by the following array.

Raw material	Product Helmet	Shoulder pad	Hip pad
Hard plastic	0	0	0
Foam plastic	0	0	0
Nylon cord	1	3	3
Labor	0.5	1	1

(48)

Once again, we observe that (48) has two rows of zeros, row one and row two. Since we are interested in combining (48) and (47), it is necessary to include these rows so that the corresponding matrices are the same size.

Now (47) and (48) give rise to the following matrices, respectively.

$$B = \begin{bmatrix} 4 & 2 & 2 \\ 1 & 3 & 2 \\ 0 & 0 & 0 \\ 2.5 & 1 & 1 \end{bmatrix}, \quad C = \begin{bmatrix} 0 & 0 & 0 \\ 0 & 0 & 0 \\ 1 & 3 & 3 \\ 0.5 & 1 & 1 \end{bmatrix}. \tag{49}$$

Note that B and C are the same size and, furthermore, when the corresponding entries of B and C are added, the matrix

$$A = \begin{bmatrix} 4 & 2 & 2 \\ 1 & 3 & 2 \\ 1 & 3 & 3 \\ 3 & 2 & 2 \end{bmatrix} \tag{50}$$

results, which is simply the matrix for (7). It seems natural to say that A is the *sum* of B and C.

Before proceeding, let us introduce a more precise notation to be used with matrices. A small letter with two subscripts will be used to denote each element in a matrix. The first subscript will indicate the row in which the element appears while the second subscript tells the reader the proper column. For example, b_{12} indicates the entry in the first row and second column while b_{34} would denote the entry in the third row and fourth column. In general, b_{ij} denotes the element in the ith row and the jth column. Also, if a capital letter, such as A, is used to denote a matrix, then the small letter a will be used to denote individual elements of the matrix. Thus in (50), $a_{11} = 4$, $a_{12} = 2$, $a_{22} = 3$, and so on.

Now we give a more general definition of matrix addition. If B and C are each matrices having n rows and m columns,

$$B = \begin{bmatrix} b_{11} & b_{12} & \cdots & b_{1m} \\ b_{21} & b_{22} & \cdots & b_{2m} \\ \vdots & & & \\ b_{n1} & b_{n2} & \cdots & b_{nm} \end{bmatrix}, \quad C = \begin{bmatrix} c_{11} & c_{12} & \cdots & c_{1m} \\ c_{21} & c_{22} & \cdots & c_{2m} \\ \vdots & & & \\ c_{n1} & c_{n2} & \cdots & c_{nm} \end{bmatrix} \tag{51}$$

we form the *sum* $B + C$ as follows:

$$B + C = \begin{bmatrix} b_{11} + c_{11} & b_{12} + c_{12} & \cdots & b_{1m} + c_{1m} \\ b_{21} + c_{21} & b_{22} + c_{22} & \cdots & b_{2m} + c_{2m} \\ \vdots & & & \\ b_{n1} + c_{n1} & b_{n2} + c_{n2} & \cdots & b_{nm} + c_{nm} \end{bmatrix}. \tag{52}$$

The sum of two matrices is always the same size as the original two matrices and is obtained by adding the corresponding elements of the original matrices.

Consider now the case in which the president of the firm had the matrix A of (50) and the matrix C of (49). Is there a way he can combine these two to get the matrix B of (49) representing the manufacturing process? Since each entry of A is the sum of the corresponding entries of B and C, it follows that subtracting each entry of C from the corresponding entry in A will yield the entries of B.

$$\begin{bmatrix} 4-0 & 2-0 & 2-0 \\ 1-0 & 3-0 & 2-0 \\ 1-1 & 3-3 & 3-3 \\ 3-0.5 & 2-1 & 2-1 \end{bmatrix} = \begin{bmatrix} 1 & 2 & 2 \\ 1 & 3 & 2 \\ 0 & 0 & 0 \\ 2.5 & 1 & 1 \end{bmatrix}. \tag{53}$$

This suggests the operation, which is called *subtraction*. If B and C are as in (51), then $B - C$ is the *difference* of B and C and is defined by

$$B - C = \begin{bmatrix} b_{11} - c_{11} & b_{12} - c_{12} & \cdots & b_{1m} - c_{1m} \\ b_{21} - c_{21} & b_{22} - c_{22} & \cdots & b_{2m} - c_{2m} \\ \vdots & & & \\ b_{n1} - c_{n1} & b_{n2} - c_{n2} & \cdots & b_{nm} - c_{nm} \end{bmatrix}. \tag{54}$$

Note that $B - C$ will be the same size as B and C and each entry of $B - C$ is obtained by subtracting the corresponding entry of C from that of B.

Before discussing multiplication of matrices, we pause to give another example of the use of addition and subtraction of matrices. Let

$$A = \begin{bmatrix} 1 & 1 & 2 \\ 1 & 0 & 2 \\ 2 & 1 & 0 \end{bmatrix} \tag{55}$$

be the matrix obtained from the airline schedule of (43). Suppose there is another airline C, which services the same cities, and the matrix showing the number of daily flights between the various cities x, y, and z is given by

$$\begin{array}{cccc} & x & y & z \\ x & 0 & 2 & 1 \\ y & 2 & 0 & 0 \\ z & 1 & 0 & 0 \end{array} \tag{56}$$

The matrix associated with (56) is

$$C = \begin{bmatrix} 0 & 2 & 1 \\ 2 & 0 & 0 \\ 1 & 0 & 0 \end{bmatrix}. \tag{57}$$

We now observe that $A + C$ is a matrix showing the total number of flights between the various cities, assuming there is no other airline flying between the cities.

$$A + C = \begin{bmatrix} 1 & 3 & 3 \\ 3 & 0 & 2 \\ 3 & 1 & 0 \end{bmatrix}. \tag{58}$$

Further, if we knew C and the matrix of (58), A could be obtained by subtracting, $(A + C) - C = A$.

Let us now turn our attention to an electronics company that begins with the raw materials, copper, zinc, glass, and plastic and from them produces transistors, resistors, buttons, cases, and computer chips. These latter five products are then combined to produce three types of hand calculators, the T-1, T-2, and T-3. (In an actual company, the list of raw materials, intermediate products, and finished products will be much larger, but to avoid huge matrices we wish to keep the list small.) We form the following array showing the amount of each raw material used in the intermediate products.

	Transistor	Resistor	Button	Case	Computer chip
Copper	2	2	0	0	3
Zinc	1	1	0	0	2
Glass	1	2	0	1	1
Plastic	0	0	1	3	0

(59)

For example, the first entry tells us that 2 units of copper are used in each transistor, and the 3 on the first row tells us that 3 units of copper are used in each computer chip.

The next array shows the number of intermediate products used in each calculator.

	T-1	*T*-2	*T*-3
Transistors	5	6	10
Resistors	7	8	16
Buttons	20	25	45
Cases	1	1	1
Computer chips	4	6	10

(60)

For example, there are five transistors in each *T*-1 calculator and sex in each *T*-2, and so on.

Now (59) and (60) give rise to matrices that we shall call A and B, respectively.

$$A = \begin{bmatrix} 2 & 2 & 0 & 0 & 3 \\ 1 & 1 & 0 & 0 & 2 \\ 1 & 2 & 0 & 1 & 1 \\ 0 & 0 & 1 & 3 & 0 \end{bmatrix}, \quad B = \begin{bmatrix} 5 & 6 & 10 \\ 7 & 8 & 16 \\ 20 & 25 & 45 \\ 1 & 1 & 1 \\ 4 & 6 & 10 \end{bmatrix}. \tag{61}$$

Now to construct the matrix relating the raw materials to the finished calculators, we reason that each *T*-1 takes 5 transistors, 7 resistors, 20 buttons, 1 case, and 4 computer chips (the first column of B), while the amount of copper in a single unit of each of these intermediate products is given by the corresponding entry in the first row of A. Thus,

$$(2)(5) + (2)(7) + (0)(20) + (0)(1) + (3)(4) = 36 \tag{62}$$

represents the amount of copper used in the *T*-1. But (62) is simply the product of row one of A and column one of B. Similarly, to calculate the amount of copper in each *T*-2, one multiplies each entry in row one of A by the corresponding entry of column 2 of B and then sums:

$$(2)(6) + (2)(8) + (0)(25) + (0)(1) + (3)(6) = 46. \tag{63}$$

However, (63) is just the product of row one of A and column two of B. In general, if the matrix showing the number of units of each raw material in each calculator is

$$C = \begin{bmatrix} c_{11} & c_{12} & c_{13} \\ c_{21} & c_{22} & c_{23} \\ c_{31} & c_{32} & c_{33} \\ c_{41} & c_{42} & c_{43} \end{bmatrix}, \tag{64}$$

then c_{ij} is the product or row i of A and column j of B. (The reader should verify this for a few more values of i and j.) Direct calculation gives us

$$C = \begin{bmatrix} 36 & 46 & 82 \\ 20 & 26 & 46 \\ 24 & 29 & 53 \\ 23 & 28 & 48 \end{bmatrix}. \tag{65}$$

Thus the array showing raw materials used in the various calculators is

	Calculators		
Raw material	*T*-1	*T*-2	*T*-3
Copper	36	46	82
Zinc	20	26	46
Glass	24	29	53
Plastic	23	28	48

(66)

In general, if A and B are two matrices and B has the same number of rows that A has columns, we define the *product* AB of A and B to be a matrix AB whose entry in the ith row and jth column is the product of the ith row of A and the jth column of B.

Note that A and B do not have to be the same size but the number of columns in the first factor must be the same as the number of rows in the second factor so that the row-by-column product is defined. If A is a matrix with n rows and m columns and B has m rows and p columns, then the product AB will have n rows and p columns.

As another example of matrix multiplication, take the matrix A associated with the airline schedule of (43) and consider the significance of multiplying A by itself. We usually use A^2 to denote the product AA and it is computed as follows:

$$A^2 = AA = \begin{bmatrix} 1 & 1 & 2 \\ 1 & 0 & 2 \\ 2 & 1 & 0 \end{bmatrix} \begin{bmatrix} 1 & 1 & 2 \\ 1 & 0 & 2 \\ 2 & 1 & 0 \end{bmatrix} = \begin{bmatrix} 6 & 3 & 4 \\ 5 & 3 & 2 \\ 3 & 2 & 6 \end{bmatrix}. \tag{67}$$

The first entry of the product is the inner product of row one with column one.

$$(1)(1) + (1)(1) + (2)(2) = 6. \tag{68}$$

Each "1" in the first term of (68) signifies that there is a flight from x to x. Thus (1)(1) gives the number of "two-stage" flights in which the intermediate stop is at x. The second term (1)(1) arises because there is a flight from x to y and then one from y back to x. Hence, the second term gives the number of "two-stage" flights from x to x by way of y. The third term of (68), (2)(2), arises from the fact that there are two flights from x to z and then two from z back to x. It follows that there are four "two-stage" flights from x to x by way of z. Thus the product (68) gives the total number of "two-stage" flights from x to x via this airline. Similar reasoning will show that the product of row one with column two yields the number of "two-stage" flights from x to y. In general, the matrix A^2 gives the number of possible two-stage flights between the various cities on this airline.

In the airline example (43), if the management decides to double its service, then each entry of the matrix will be multiplied by 2. This suggests an operation in which a scalar is combined with a matrix to produce another matrix.

$$2\begin{bmatrix} 1 & 1 & 2 \\ 1 & 0 & 2 \\ 2 & 1 & 0 \end{bmatrix} = \begin{bmatrix} 2 & 2 & 4 \\ 2 & 0 & 4 \\ 4 & 2 & 0 \end{bmatrix}. \tag{69}$$

In general, if A is a matrix and k is any scalar, then kA is the matrix whose entries are k times the corresponding entry of A. This type of multiplication in which a scalar is combined with a matrix to produce a new matrix is called *multiplication by a scalar*.

6. Properties of Matrix Operations and Special Matrices

So far, we have discussed the following operations on matrices.

(1) Addition—two matrices of equal size are combined to produce a third matrix of the same size.
(2) Subtraction—two matrices of equal size are combined to produce a third matrix of the same size.
(3) Multiplication—two matrices, the first of which has its number of columns equal to the number of rows in the second, are combined to produce a third matrix.
(4) Transposition—one matrix is produced from another.
(5) Multiplication by a scalar—a number and a matrix are combined to produce a new matrix.

By considering a vector as a matrix with one column, these operations are seen to contain the operations on vectors as special cases. For example, the inner product of two vectors yields a number that can be thought of as a 1×1 matrix.

In this section, we shall discuss some properties of the above operations and illustrate each with an example. Then two special matrices with unique properties will be discussed.

The major properties of addition and multiplication of matrices are as follows.

(1) The sum of two matrices will be the same no matter which order is used in adding:

$$A + B = B + A. \tag{70}$$

For example, in (49) we have

$$B + C = C + B = \begin{bmatrix} 4 & 2 & 2 \\ 1 & 3 & 2 \\ 1 & 3 & 3 \\ 3 & 2 & 2 \end{bmatrix}. \tag{71}$$

This property is called the *commutative law* for addition.

Note that there is no commutative law for multiplication of matrices. For example,

$$\begin{bmatrix} 3 & 1 & 0 \\ 1 & 0 & 1 \\ 2 & 1 & 0 \end{bmatrix}\begin{bmatrix} 1 & 5 & 1 \\ 0 & 1 & 0 \\ 1 & 0 & 1 \end{bmatrix} = \begin{bmatrix} 3 & 16 & 3 \\ 2 & 5 & 2 \\ 2 & 11 & 2 \end{bmatrix}, \tag{72}$$

while

$$\begin{bmatrix} 1 & 5 & 1 \\ 0 & 1 & 0 \\ 1 & 0 & 1 \end{bmatrix}\begin{bmatrix} 3 & 1 & 0 \\ 1 & 0 & 1 \\ 2 & 1 & 0 \end{bmatrix} = \begin{bmatrix} 10 & 2 & 5 \\ 1 & 0 & 1 \\ 5 & 2 & 0 \end{bmatrix}. \tag{73}$$

(2) The sum of three or more matrices is the same no matter which order is used in adding:

$$(A + B) + C = A + (B + C). \tag{74}$$

This is called the *associative* law for addition. To illustrate,

$$\begin{aligned} &\left(\begin{bmatrix} 1 & 3 & 1 \\ 0 & 2 & 0 \end{bmatrix} + \begin{bmatrix} 2 & 1 & 3 \\ 1 & 0 & 1 \end{bmatrix}\right) + \begin{bmatrix} 1 & 1 & 1 \\ 1 & 1 & 1 \end{bmatrix} \\ &= \begin{bmatrix} 3 & 4 & 4 \\ 1 & 2 & 1 \end{bmatrix} + \begin{bmatrix} 1 & 1 & 1 \\ 1 & 1 & 1 \end{bmatrix} = \begin{bmatrix} 4 & 5 & 5 \\ 2 & 3 & 2 \end{bmatrix} \end{aligned} \tag{75}$$

and also

$$\begin{bmatrix} 1 & 3 & 1 \\ 0 & 2 & 0 \end{bmatrix} + \left(\begin{bmatrix} 2 & 1 & 3 \\ 1 & 0 & 1 \end{bmatrix} + \begin{bmatrix} 1 & 1 & 1 \\ 1 & 1 & 1 \end{bmatrix} \right)$$
$$= \begin{bmatrix} 1 & 3 & 1 \\ 0 & 2 & 0 \end{bmatrix} + \begin{bmatrix} 3 & 2 & 4 \\ 2 & 1 & 2 \end{bmatrix} = \begin{bmatrix} 4 & 5 & 5 \\ 2 & 3 & 2 \end{bmatrix}. \quad (76)$$

(3) The product of three or more matrices of proper size is the same no matter what grouping is used in the product

$$(AB)C = A(BC). \quad (77)$$

This property is called the *associative* law for multiplication. Note that the factors must be of proper size. For example, if A is 2×2, B is 2×3, and C is 2×3, the product BC is not defined because the number of columns in B is not equal to the number of rows in C. Although the product AB is defined, it produces a 2×3 matrix, which then is not of proper size to multiply with C.

On the other hand,

$$\left(\begin{bmatrix} 2 & 1 \\ 1 & 3 \end{bmatrix} \begin{bmatrix} 1 & 1 & 1 \\ 2 & 0 & 3 \end{bmatrix} \right) \begin{bmatrix} 1 & 2 \\ 1 & 0 \\ 1 & 3 \end{bmatrix} = \begin{bmatrix} 4 & 2 & 5 \\ 7 & 1 & 10 \end{bmatrix} \begin{bmatrix} 1 & 2 \\ 1 & 0 \\ 1 & 3 \end{bmatrix}$$
$$= \begin{bmatrix} 11 & 23 \\ 18 & 44 \end{bmatrix}. \quad (78)$$

Also,

$$\begin{bmatrix} 2 & 1 \\ 1 & 3 \end{bmatrix} \left(\begin{bmatrix} 1 & 1 & 1 \\ 2 & 0 & 3 \end{bmatrix} \begin{bmatrix} 1 & 2 \\ 1 & 0 \\ 1 & 3 \end{bmatrix} \right) = \begin{bmatrix} 2 & 1 \\ 1 & 3 \end{bmatrix} \begin{bmatrix} 3 & 5 \\ 5 & 13 \end{bmatrix}$$
$$= \begin{bmatrix} 11 & 23 \\ 18 & 44 \end{bmatrix}. \quad (79)$$

(4) The product of a matrix and the sum of other matrices (all of appropriate size) is the same as the sum of the products obtained by multiplying each of the matrices by that matrix:

$$A(B + C) = AB + AC, \quad (80)$$

$$(B + C)A = BA + CA. \quad (81)$$

These are called the *distributive laws* for multiplication over addition. Examples to illustrate each of these are given in Exercise 8.

If k and c represent scalars and A and B represent matrices of equal size, then the following illustrate the major properties of scalar multiplication.

$$(c + k)A = cA + kA, \quad (82)$$

$$c(A + B) = cA + cB, \tag{83}$$

$$c(kA) = (ck)A, \tag{84}$$

$$1 \cdot A = A. \tag{85}$$

Examples of each of these properties are given in Exercise 10.

Some major properties of the transpose are

(1) The transpose of the transpose is the original matrix.

$$(A^T)^T = A. \tag{86}$$

For example, let A be as in (9). Then

$$(A^T)^T = \begin{bmatrix} 4 & 1 & 1 & 3 \\ 2 & 3 & 3 & 2 \\ 2 & 2 & 3 & 2 \end{bmatrix}^T = \begin{bmatrix} 4 & 2 & 2 \\ 1 & 3 & 2 \\ 1 & 3 & 3 \\ 3 & 2 & 2 \end{bmatrix} = A.$$

(2) The transpose of a sum is the sum of the transposes.

$$(A + B)^T = A^T + B^T. \tag{87}$$

As an example,

$$\left(\begin{bmatrix} 2 & 1 \\ 1 & 3 \end{bmatrix} + \begin{bmatrix} 1 & 6 \\ 4 & 5 \end{bmatrix}\right)^T = \begin{bmatrix} 3 & 7 \\ 5 & 8 \end{bmatrix}^T = \begin{bmatrix} 3 & 5 \\ 7 & 8 \end{bmatrix}, \tag{88}$$

and also

$$\begin{bmatrix} 2 & 1 \\ 1 & 3 \end{bmatrix}^T + \begin{bmatrix} 1 & 6 \\ 4 & 5 \end{bmatrix}^T = \begin{bmatrix} 2 & 1 \\ 1 & 3 \end{bmatrix} + \begin{bmatrix} 1 & 4 \\ 6 & 5 \end{bmatrix} = \begin{bmatrix} 3 & 5 \\ 7 & 8 \end{bmatrix}. \tag{89}$$

(3) The transpose of a scalar times a matrix is the same as the scalar times the transpose.

$$(cA)^T = cA^T. \tag{90}$$

For example,

$$3\left(\begin{bmatrix} 7 & 1 \\ 2 & 6 \end{bmatrix}\right)^T = \begin{bmatrix} 21 & 3 \\ 6 & 18 \end{bmatrix}^T = \begin{bmatrix} 21 & 6 \\ 3 & 18 \end{bmatrix}, \tag{91}$$

and also

$$3\begin{bmatrix} 7 & 1 \\ 2 & 6 \end{bmatrix}^T = 3\begin{bmatrix} 7 & 2 \\ 1 & 6 \end{bmatrix} = \begin{bmatrix} 21 & 6 \\ 3 & 18 \end{bmatrix}.$$

(4) The transpose of a product is the product of the transposes but in the reverse order.

$$(AB)^T = B^T A^T. \tag{92}$$

Examples to illustrate this property are given in Exercise 11.

The matrix

$$\begin{bmatrix} 1 & 0 & 0 \\ 0 & 1 & 0 \\ 0 & 0 & 1 \end{bmatrix}$$

is a special matrix, for its product with any 3×3 matrix has the following property:

$$\begin{bmatrix} a & b & c \\ d & e & f \\ g & h & i \end{bmatrix}\begin{bmatrix} 1 & 0 & 0 \\ 0 & 1 & 0 \\ 0 & 0 & 1 \end{bmatrix} = \begin{bmatrix} 1 & 0 & 0 \\ 0 & 1 & 0 \\ 0 & 0 & 1 \end{bmatrix}\begin{bmatrix} a & b & c \\ d & e & f \\ g & h & i \end{bmatrix} = \begin{bmatrix} a & b & c \\ d & e & f \\ g & h & 1 \end{bmatrix}. \tag{93}$$

For this reason,

$$\begin{bmatrix} 1 & 0 & 0 \\ 0 & 1 & 0 \\ 0 & 0 & 1 \end{bmatrix},$$

is often called the *identity* 3×3 matrix. Moreover, if I_n denotes the $n \times n$ matrix that has all zeros except for the main diagonal from the upper-left corner to the lower right that consists of all ones and if A is any matrix with n columns and B is any matrix with n rows,

$$AI_n = A, \quad \text{and} \quad I_nB = B. \tag{94}$$

We call I_n the *identity* $n \times n$ matrix because it acts very much like the number one in regular multiplication.

A matrix, all of whose entries are zero, acts very much in the same manner as the number zero under ordinary addition and multiplication.

For example,

$$\begin{bmatrix} 0 & 0 & 0 \\ 0 & 0 & 0 \end{bmatrix} + \begin{bmatrix} a & b & c \\ d & e & f \end{bmatrix} = \begin{bmatrix} a & b & c \\ d & e & f \end{bmatrix}, \tag{95}$$

$$\begin{bmatrix} 0 & 0 & 0 \\ 0 & 0 & 0 \end{bmatrix}\begin{bmatrix} a & b \\ c & d \\ e & f \end{bmatrix} = \begin{bmatrix} 0 & 0 \\ 0 & 0 \end{bmatrix}. \tag{96}$$

If 0_{pm} is used to denote the $p \times m$ matrix consisting of all zeros and A is any $p \times m$ matrix, B has m rows and k columns, and C is any matrix with k rows and p columns,

$$A + 0_{pm} = A, \quad 0_{pm}B = 0_{pk}, \quad C0_{pm} = 0_{kp}. \tag{97}$$

7. Matrices and Profits

Let A be the matrix of the manufacturing process (7), repeated below for convenience.

$$A = \begin{bmatrix} 4 & 2 & 2 \\ 1 & 3 & 2 \\ 1 & 3 & 3 \\ 3 & 2 & 2 \end{bmatrix}. \tag{98}$$

Suppose an order comes in for 35 helmets, 10 shoulder pads, and 20 hip pads, and the manager wishes to know the amount of profit the company will make on this order. He knows the vector P that gives the unit price of each output (helmets, shoulder pads, and hip pads, respectively) and also the cost vector C showing the unit cost of each row material (hard plastic, foam plastic, nylon cord, and labor in this order). For example, let P and C be as follows and let X be the vector showing the order.

$$P = \begin{bmatrix} 30 \\ 25 \\ 25 \end{bmatrix}, \quad C = \begin{bmatrix} 2 \\ 2 \\ 1 \\ 5 \end{bmatrix}, \quad X = \begin{bmatrix} 35 \\ 10 \\ 20 \end{bmatrix}. \tag{99}$$

We observed in (42) that the vector Y showing the amount of each raw material needed to fill the order is given by

$$AX = Y. \tag{100}$$

Now the amount of money brought in from this sale is given by $P^T X$. (Verify this!) Also the amount paid out is given by $C^T Y$. (Verify this!) Thus the profit is given by

$$P^T X - C^T Y. \tag{101}$$

Since $Y = AX$ from (100), we may use the properties of matrix operations developed in Section 6 to simplify (101) as follows:

$$\begin{aligned} P^T X - C^T Y &= P^T X - C^T(AX) \\ &= P^T X - (C^T A)X \\ &= (P^T - C^T A)X. \end{aligned} \tag{102}$$

The student should verify each step of (102), noting the property that was used. Now the vector $P^T - C^T A$ is a row vector whose transpose we denote by F.

$$F = (P^T - C^T A)^T = P - A^T C. \tag{103}$$

The vector F is sometimes called the unit profit vector. In our example,

$$P^T - C^T A = [4, 2, 4]. \quad \text{(Verify!)} \tag{104}$$

Hence the unit profit vector is

$$F = \begin{bmatrix} 4 \\ 2 \\ 4 \end{bmatrix}. \tag{105}$$

The total profit is now calculated as

$$\text{Profit} = F^T X = 240. \tag{106}$$

Other interesting problems arise from Eq. (100) when we consider Y as a vector that gives the amount of each raw material available and ask "How many units of each output can be make?" It may or may not be possible to find exact whole numbers (or even real numbers) as entries for X to make $AX = Y$. Since it is usually not feasible to make fractions of a unit, we may be forced to try to find nonnegative integer entries for the vector X, which makes AX be a vector in which each of the entries is less than or equal to the corresponding entry of Y. In vector terms, we write

$$AX \leq Y. \tag{107}$$

In general, we shall be interested in finding the non negative entries of X that yield the maximum profit from (101). Although we shall not go into such problems here, they are treated as part of a topic called linear programming. (See, for example, Spivey and Thrall [1].)

Exercises

1. Let $X = \begin{bmatrix} 1 \\ 0 \\ 2 \end{bmatrix}$, $Y = \begin{bmatrix} 3 \\ 1 \\ 4 \end{bmatrix}$, $A = \begin{bmatrix} 1 & 7 & 2 \\ 0 & 1 & 4 \end{bmatrix}$. Compute each of the following:

a) $X + Y$
b) $Y - X$
c) $3X$
d) $X^T Y$
e) AX
f) $4X + Y$
g) $2A$

Answers

(a) $\begin{bmatrix} 4 \\ 1 \\ 6 \end{bmatrix}$ (b) $\begin{bmatrix} 2 \\ 1 \\ 2 \end{bmatrix}$

(c) $\begin{bmatrix} 3 \\ 0 \\ 6 \end{bmatrix}$ (d) 11

(e) $\begin{bmatrix} 5 \\ 8 \end{bmatrix}$ (f) $\begin{bmatrix} 7 \\ 1 \\ 12 \end{bmatrix}$

(g) $\begin{bmatrix} 2 & 14 & 4 \\ 0 & 2 & 8 \end{bmatrix}$

2. Let X_1 denote the row vector corresponding to the first row of (6). That is,

$$X_1 = [4, 1, 1, 0].$$

In general, let X_i be the row vector corresponding to the ith row of (6). What can be said about the sum $X_1^T + X_2^T + X_3^T + \cdots + X_9^T$? Compute this sum.

3. Suppose the prices of soap, coffee, tea, and steak are 0.88, 1.35, 0.97 and 1.89, respectively, per unit. Use vector operations to compute the price that a shopper would pay for 2 units of soap, 1 unit coffee, 3 units of tea, and 5 units of steak. (*Answer:* 15.47.)

4. Suppose stocks are priced as shown in (3). Use vector methods to compute the amount (not counting brokerage fee) that an investor pays if he buys 20 shares of American Income, 40 shares of Hammond Corporation, 10 shares of White Eagle, no shares of Turncoat Ind., and no shares of Zefco Products.

5. In example (7), find (by matrix and vector methods) how much of each type of raw material is required to fill an order for 20 helmets, 30 shoulder pads, and 15 hip pads. (*Answer:* 170 units of hard plastic, 140 units of foam plastic, 155 units of nylon cord, and 150 units of labor.)

6. Let A and C be as in (55) and (57), respectively. If A and C represent the flight schedules of two different airline companies between cities x, y, and z, compute AC and explain the meaning of each entry of the resulting matrix. Compute CA and explain the meaning of the entries.

7. Suppose, in a housing project, a sociologist passes out a questionnaire to the residents in which he asks each resident to list the other residents that they consider their best friends. For simplicity, we say that there are only 5 residents and their choices are summarized by the matrix

$$A = \begin{array}{c} \\ x \\ y \\ z \\ w \\ u \end{array} \begin{array}{c} \begin{array}{ccccc} x & y & z & w & u \end{array} \\ \begin{bmatrix} 0 & 1 & 0 & 1 & 0 \\ 1 & 0 & 1 & 0 & 0 \\ 0 & 0 & 0 & 1 & 1 \\ 0 & 0 & 0 & 0 & 1 \\ 1 & 1 & 0 & 1 & 0 \end{bmatrix} \end{array}.$$

The ones in each row indicate the choices of the person to the left of the row. For example, x choses y and w as his best friends while y chooses x and z. Compute the matrix AA^T and explain the meaning of the entries. Compute A^TA and explain the meaning of the entries.

8. Let

$$A = \begin{bmatrix} 1 & 3 & 1 \\ 2 & 1 & 1 \\ 1 & 4 & 6 \end{bmatrix}, \quad B = \begin{bmatrix} 1 & 2 & 1 \\ 0 & 1 & 0 \\ 1 & 3 & 1 \end{bmatrix}, \quad C = \begin{bmatrix} 2 & 3 & 1 \\ 1 & 3 & 1 \\ 4 & 0 & 0 \end{bmatrix}.$$

Verify that (80) and (81) both hold for these matrices.

9. It seems natural in view of our knowledge of arithmetic to define a different type of "multiplication" of matrices in which two matrices A and B of equal size are combined to produce a third matrix C in such a way that each entry of C is the product of the corresponding entries of the factors. Let us agree to call this type of multiplication of matrices the *elementwise product* and denote it by

$$A \times B = C$$

(as compared to $AB = C$ for the multiplication operation defined earlier). Let A be the matrix of Exercise 7. Compute $A \times A^T$ and interpret the meaning of the entries.

10. Let $c = 3$, $k = 5$, $A = \begin{bmatrix} 2 & 1 & 3 \\ 1 & 0 & 2 \end{bmatrix}$, $B = \begin{bmatrix} 1 & 2 & 6 \\ 1 & 1 & 0 \end{bmatrix}$. Show that (82), (83), (84), and (85) hold for these matrices.

11. Let

$$A = \begin{bmatrix} 6 & 7 \\ 1 & 3 \end{bmatrix} \qquad B = \begin{bmatrix} 2 & 1 & 7 \\ 1 & 0 & 2 \end{bmatrix}.$$

Compute $(AB)^T$ and $B^T A^T$. Would $A^T B^T$ be meaningful? Why?

Answer: $(AB)^T = \begin{bmatrix} 26 & 5 \\ 6 & 1 \\ 56 & 13 \end{bmatrix} = B^T A^T$. A^T is 2×2 and B^T is 3×2 so they are not of proper size for multiplication.

12. In (43) use matrix methods to obtain an expression for the number of flights of length 3 or less between cities x, y, and z aboard airline A.

13. Suppose we view the manufacturing process (7) as two distinct procedures, a manufacturing process that we denote by X and an assembly process that is denoted by Y. In X, raw materials are converted into "kits" that contain parts to make helmets, shoulder pads, and hip pads, respectively, with each kit containing all the unassembled pieces. In the assembly process Y, these kits are converted into finished goods. Let the kits for helmets, shoulder pads, and hip pads be denoted, respectively, by H, S, and HP. Since it is desireable to view process X as producing everything needed by process Y, we shall also think of a kit of labor, denoted by L, and a kit of nylon cord, denoted by N, as being "produced" by X. The input–output matrix for X then looks like this.

$X =$

	H	S	HP	N	L
Hard plastic	4	2	2	0	0
Foam plastic	1	3	2	0	0
Nylon cord	0	0	0	1	0
Labor	2.5	1	1	0	1

Thus, nylon cord is regarded as an output whose only input is nylon cord and labor as an output whose only input is labor. Now the second process Y may be symbolized by the following input–output matrix.

$$Y = \begin{array}{c|ccc} & \text{Helmet} & \text{Shoulder pad} & \text{Hip pad} \\ \hline H & 1 & 0 & 0 \\ S & 0 & 1 & 0 \\ HP & 0 & 0 & 1 \\ N & 1 & 3 & 3 \\ L & 0.5 & 1 & 1 \end{array}$$

Thus to assemble a helmet, one needs an "H" kit, 1 unit of nylon cord, and 0.5 units of labor. To assemble a shoulder pad, one requires on "S" kit, 3 units of nylon cord, and 1 unit of labor, and so on.

Verify that $XY = B + C = A$, where A, B, and C are the matrices of (7), (47), and (48), respectively. State (in words) the meaning of the above procedure.

14. a) Let

$$A = \begin{bmatrix} 1 & 0 & 2 \\ 1 & 1 & 3 \end{bmatrix} \quad \text{and} \quad B = \begin{bmatrix} 2 & 1 & 1 \\ 1 & 3 & 4 \end{bmatrix}.$$

If X is the matrix obtained from A by adjoining the identity matrix I_2 to the right side of A, then

$$X = \begin{bmatrix} 1 & 0 & 2 & 1 & 0 \\ 1 & 1 & 3 & 0 & 1 \end{bmatrix}.$$

Also, let Y be obtained from B by adjoining I_3 to the top of B. Then

$$Y = \begin{bmatrix} 1 & 0 & 0 \\ 0 & 1 & 0 \\ 0 & 0 & 1 \\ 2 & 1 & 1 \\ 1 & 3 & 4 \end{bmatrix}.$$

Show that $XY = A + B$.

b) Let A and B be $n \times m$ matrices. Suppose that X is obtained from A by adjoining the $n \times n$ identity I_n to the right side of A, and Y is obtained from B by adjoining the $m \times m$ identity I_m to the top of B. Show that

$$XY = A + B.$$

15. Let A be as in (98) and

$$Y = \begin{bmatrix} 100 \\ 100 \\ 50 \\ 150 \end{bmatrix}.$$

Find a vector X such that

$$AX \leq Y.$$

How many such vectors are there? Find such an X with the largest possible first entry.

Reference

1. Spivey, W. Allen, and Thrall, Robert M. *Linear Optimization.* Holt, Rinehart, and Winston, New York, 1970.

Notes for the Instructor

Objectives. This module can be used in any course that uses matrix operations.

Prerequisites. Arithmetic.

Time. Two class periods.

CHAPTER 7

Sources of Applications of Mathematics in Ecological and Environmental Subject Areas, Suitable for Classroom Use

Homer T. Hayslett, Jr.*

1. Introduction

Mathematics teachers are frequently dissatisfied with their sources of appropriate, realistic examples for classroom use. This paper, which is essentially a review and annotated bibliography (with the annotations appearing in the text itself) of selected articles and books that use mathematics in an ecological or "environmental" context, is a partial remedy for that dissatisfaction, I hope. The variety of mathematics that appears in biological, ecological, environmental, and resource economics literature is amazing—mathematical areas as diverse as Boolean algebra, optimal control theory, and Fourier analysis are used.

Because teachers would ordinarily be searching for examples in a specific area, for example, matrix algebra, each section of this paper is devoted to a particular mathematical area. The references given are not all of uniform difficulty. Some of the articles are readable in their entirety by a student who has the mathematical background necessary to understand the particular mathematical area (e.g., matrix algebra) under which the citation is given. In other articles, the student might understand the particular topic (e.g., matrix algebra) but might not understand all the rest of the mathematics in the article (which might also involve graph theory and probability theory, for instance). And, of course, the ecological subject matter that the mathematics is being used to model might not be completely understandable by the mathematics student. (Incidentally, some of the articles contain a very small ratio of mathematics to ecológical exposition.) The instructor frequently

* Department of Mathematics, Colby College, Waterville, Maine 04901.

will want to discuss in class enough of the ecological background and mathematical argument for an example so that the student understands and appreciates it, and perhaps thereby becomes motivated to explore more on his own.

A word about sources would perhaps be helpful. Anyone who wishes to find additional applications that have an environmental or ecological flavor would find it very fruitful to scan the current issues and back volumes of such journals as *The American Naturalist*, *Mathematical Biosciences*, *Journal of Theoretical Biology*, *Journal of Environmental Economics and Management*, and *The Bulletin of Mathematical Biology*. (Many of the references in this paper come from the first three of these.) Nearly every issue of *The American Naturalist* contains at least one ecological article in which mathematics is used extensively, and the others named have a sprinkling (probably Poisson-distributed!) of such articles in each volume.

Articles about optimal harvesting of resources, the economics of pollution control, and the economics of the exploitation of resources—all of which use mathematics—appear frequently in various economics journals, such as the *Journal of Environmental Economics and Management* (mentioned above), *The Review of Economic Studies*, *The American Economic Review*, and *The Quarterly Journal of Economics*.

More general journals such as *Science*, *American Scientist*, and *Scientific American* also have occasional articles about mathematics applied to ecology, resource, or environmental decisions.

Pielou [115], in her admirable text on mathematical ecology, covers, very carefully and mathematically, population dynamics, spatial patterns in one-species populations, spatial relations of two or more species, and many-species relations. A strong calculus sequence (including differential equations) and a Junior-level probability course are advisable for students tackling this book. Roberts [122], in his excellent book on discrete mathematics and its applications, has some environmentally and ecologically oriented examples, especially graph theory examples dealing with food webs and "energy webs" of industrial society. The middle third of Haberman [56] is an exposition of population dynamics, a very important area in ecological theory. All three of these books are suitable for students who have had a demanding two-year sequence of college mathematics courses. Clark [23] is perhaps a more difficult book: He uses differential equations and optimal control theory heavily, and some knowledge of economics is necessary. This would make a fine text for a course which is team-taught by a biologist, economist, and mathematician.

There are also a number of books that consist of papers, some of which are mathematical, often delivered at conferences or symposia on ecological and environmental areas. Several with which I am familiar and which contain fascinating and useful articles (e.g., [49], [61]) are [18], [19], and [110]. And there are monographs, such as May's [89] on stability and Williamson's [152] on biological population theory.

2. Probability Theory

Probability theory is used a great deal in ecological literature. Articles on optimal foraging, predator–prey relationships, and population growth all make extensive use of probabilistic concepts. Elementary probability formulas are frequently used, of course. The Poisson and binomial probability functions appear frequently. The Poisson is the model that is appropriate when items are randomly scattered in space (for example, the items could be plants, animals, or schools of fish) or time and hence is often applicable. The exponential distribution is encountered frequently, both in its own right and also because of its close relationship with the Poisson. There are many articles in which Markov chains or processes are used. In more theoretical papers, generating functions and stochastic processes, such as birth-and-death processes, are used.

A very nice example of an easy compound probability formula appears in [99, p. 333]:

$$\begin{aligned} P(\text{larval success}) &= P\begin{pmatrix}\text{larva encounters a host and recognizes it as a host} \\ \text{and attaches to the host and succeeds in feeding} \\ \text{from the host}\end{pmatrix} \\ &= p_h p_r p_a p_f, \end{aligned}$$

using obvious symbols.

Saila [126] suggests that Bayes' theorem is a useful tool for making decisions in fisheries science, discusses *a priori* and *a posteriori* probabilities, and gives a hypothetical example that makes use of Bayes' theorem. Bayes' theorem is mentioned by Oster and Heinrich [105] in a discussion of bumblebees' revising, in light of their experience, their perception of which type of flower it is best (most efficient, energetically) for them to forage upon. Bayes' theorem is also mentioned briefly by Felsenstein [45].

The Poisson distribution is a useful, frequently applied probability distribution. There are several reasons why: The assumptions that lead to the Poisson distribution are frequently satisfied in the real world, the Poisson distribution is simple to apply, it has a close relationship with the exponential distribution (which is also simple to apply), and it is the limit of the binomial distribution under certain conditions.

In a very fine short article, Pulliam [116] assumes that the individual members of a flock of finches cock their heads to look for danger a random number of times per minute which has a Poisson distribution with mean λ:

$$f(x) = \frac{\lambda^x e^{-\lambda}}{x!}, \quad x = 0, 1, 2, \cdots. \tag{1}$$

He also assumes that if danger (i.e., a predator) is present, it is necessarily seen by any finch that has cocked its head. After using the fact that if the number of head-cocks is Poisson with a mean rate of λ per minute, then the time T between head-cocks has an exponential distribution with mean $1/\lambda$, that is, the probability density function (p.d.f.) of T is

$$g(t) = \lambda e^{-\lambda t}, \quad \lambda > 0, \quad t > 0, \tag{2}$$

Pulliam obtains

P(at least one finch cocks its head in a fixed time interval of length t)

$= 1 - P$(no finch cocks its head)

$= 1 - [P$(any given finch does not cock its head)$]^n$

$= 1 - (e^{-\lambda t})^n = 1 - e^{-\lambda nt}$,

which is the probability that a predator is observed and the flock flies away. It increases as n increases, and Pulliam concludes that there are advantages to the individual for flocking, at least for finches. (It is generally conceded that flocking confers advantages upon the *group*. But for another view, see [58], a largely discursive paper that treats a difficult problem in geometrical probability.

Namkoong and Roberds [101] assume that the number of "moderate disturbances" to redwood groves (such as fire, flood, insect epidemic) in a 50-yr time period has a Poisson distribution with $\lambda = 2$. They also assume a Poisson distribution for the number of sprouts from a redwood, and for the number of progeny from live trees.

Holgate [62] uses the Poisson distribution as one of the probability distributions for the number of offspring of females, in a study of extinction probabilities for biennials (animals that live just two years, and have offspring each year). He uses the probability generating function for the Poisson, $\psi(s) = e^{\lambda(s-1)}$, to find the generating function of the total contribution of the ith year individual to the next generation. Oster [104], in a fascinating article on the foraging of bumblebees, assumes that the number of flowers, in an area A, of a type upon which the bumblebee will forage has the Poisson probability distribution with $\lambda = \rho A$, where ρ is the density of the flowers in a unit area. If the flowers are not randomly distributed, but instead occur in patches that are Poisson-distributed with parameter λ_1 and within each patch the flowers are Poisson-distributed with parameter λ_2, then we have a compound (Poisson–Poisson) probability distribution.

The Poisson distribution appears in [28], an article on the Birth-Immigration-Death-Emigration (BIDE) model for various kinds of primates. Specifically, Cohen says that if the birth rate is zero and if the population is maintained by a balance of immigration and death or emigration, then the probability that the population contains x individuals after a long time is given by formula (1), with $\lambda = \nu/\mu$, where ν is the immigration rate and μ is the combined death and emigration rate. In [119], the individuals of a species that is the prey of a predator are assumed to be Poisson-distributed. From assumptions about the probability that a female parasite matures in an interval (conditional upon entrance into the host) and the probability distribution of the number of off spring (conditional upon maturation time), the distribution of mature female parasites (and also all females) is seen to be Poisson by recognition of its probability generating function, $e^{\lambda(s-1)}$ [138]. Pella [112], in an article about seining for tuna, assumes that the schools of tuna are Poisson-distributed.

In [15], the number of stationary, signaling females (butterflies are given as an example) that each mobile male inseminates is assumed to follow a Poisson distribution. The Poisson distribution also appears as a limiting form of the binomial distribution in this paper. Straw [135] assumes that the number of visits to any particular flower by some pollinator (out of "many pollinator trips") is a Poisson random variable. Felsenstein [45] discusses a model in which the distribution of the number of offspring is assumed to be Poisson with $\lambda = 1$.

It is well known that the exponential distribution is related to the Poisson distribution in the following way: If the number of events in the time interval from 0 to t has a Poisson probability function with mean λt, then the time between any two successive events has an exponential distribution with mean $1/\lambda$, given by formula (2). For this reason, the Poisson and the exponential distributions frequently occur together in the literature.

The exponential distribution appears in [140] as the probability density function (p.d.f.) of the time between kills of a predator which is searching for prey which occurs in Poisson-distributed groups, and as the p.d.f. of the searching time by a fishing vessel until a Poisson-distributed school of fish is located [112]. Pulliam [117] assumes that the prey items upon which a predator is feeding are Poisson-distributed with mean density λ, and states that the time required to find a prey item is a random variable (r.v.), which has p.d.f. given by (2).

Also, the exponential distribution appears in an excellent article by Moore [153], as the p.d.f. of the distance r from a point selected at random to the nearest plant when the plants are Poisson-distributed with density λ:

$$p(r) = 2r\lambda e^{-r^2\lambda}, \quad \lambda > 0, \quad r > 0. \tag{3}$$

(He gives a very nice probability argument to obtain this formula). He uses the standard change-of-variable technique to find the p.d.f. of r^2. He also finds the p.d.f. of $\overline{r^2}$ (the mean of n independent values of r^2) and estimates λ, using the fact that the distribution of $\overline{r^2}$ has a mean of $1/\pi\lambda$ (biased). The gamma function is used and the chi-squared distribution is mentioned. Oster [104], in his article on bumblebees, states that (3) is the p.d.f. of r, the distance between two randomly selected Poisson-distributed (with density λ) flowers, and uses this p.d.f. to find the average time that the bee spends searching for a flower on which to forage. This distribution also appears in [106, p. 107] and [115, pp. 111–114].

The exponential distribution is also important in its own right, and not simply because of its relation with the Poisson distribution. For example, it is used by Maynard Smith [91]. He considers nonfighting animal contests in which the victory and its associated payoff go to the animal that continues the longest and shows that, if λ is the payoff for winning the contest, the strategy of continuing to play a random time T, which has the p.d.f. (2), is a superior strategy (in a certain precise sense defined in Section 5) to any strategy of continuing for a fixed time. The exponential p.d.f. also appears, in the same context, in [92], [93], and [94].

Besides the Poisson distribution, the discrete distribution that appears most frequently in ecological writings is the binomial distribution. Karlin [71] uses it in a simple genetics context. He says:

> Consider a population of haploid individuals of which i are of type A and $N - i$ of type a. The population reproduces itself in discrete generations. If selection, mutation, and immigration are all absent, then the probabilities of producing A and a alleles for the next generation are, respectively,
>
> $$p = \frac{i}{N} \quad \text{and} \quad 1 - p = \frac{N - i}{N}.$$
>
> The whole of the next generation is formed by N independent repetitions of this sampling with replacement. Thus, the probability that the next generation will contain j members of type A and $N - j$ of type a is
>
> $$p_{ij} = \binom{2N}{j} p^j (1 - p)^{N-j}.$$

The probability that a predator will eat a mix of x and $n - x$ of two kinds of prey on which he is feeding is given by Pulliam [117] to be a binomial distribution. Wilbur [150] says that the number of nests (of a species of bird, for instance) escaping predation is a binomial random variable and uses facts about its mean, np, and variance, npq. The binomial distribution is used by de Jong [36] as a simplified model of competition for food in which each animal tries to get as much food as possible without paying attention to the others (he calls this the "scramble/exploitative situation"). The probability that the animal gets x food particles in t time intervals is given by de Jong to be $\binom{t}{x} p^x (1 - p)^{t-x}$. He uses binomial probabilities throughout the paper and uses the normal approximation to the binomial in the appendix. The binomial distribution appears briefly in [112], in which the random scatter of schools of fish is defined in terms of the binomial distribution, which is promptly approximated by the Poisson distribution.

Other discrete probability distributions, such as the negative binomial, the multinomial, and the geometric, appear occasionally. The negative binomial probability function is mentioned by Cohen [28] in an article on troops of primates. Cohen says that if the birth rate λ is less than the loss rate μ and "if birth, death or emigration, and immigration are all proceeding at strictly positive rates, it may be shown that the probability $p_{NB}(k)$ that the theoretical population contains exactly k individuals after a long time t is independent of time and the initial population size and is given by the negative binomial distribution:

$$p_{NB}(k) = \binom{r + k - 1}{k} p^r q^k, \quad k = 0, 1, 2, \cdots,"$$

where $r = \nu/\lambda$, $q = \lambda/\mu$, and λ denotes the birth rate, ν, the immigration rate, and μ, the combined death and emigration rate. The negative binomial distribution also appears in [30], as the marginal distribution of the number of individuals in each of several groups described by a Markov population process.

In [101], a multinomial distribution is assumed to give the probabilities that a redwood tree will die, will remain in the youth class, or will become mature. The multinomial distribution appears in [103] as the model for the probability that N parasites on a host will be classified into $n + 1$ developmental classes in a particular way. Charnov and Krebs [21] reason that the number of birds in a flock that will give a warning call has a hypergeometric distribution (which they then approximate by the binomial distribution). The geometric distribution is used in [62], a study of biennials (animals that live just two years and have offspring each year), as a probability distribution for the number of offspring of females.

After the exponential distribution, the gamma distribution is probably the most frequently used continuous distribution in ecological research. The property that if $X_1, X_2, \cdots, X_n$ are independent r.v.s. with exponential p.d.f.s, then the r.v. $Y_n = X_1 + X_2 + \cdots + X_n$ has a gamma p.d.f. with parameters n and λ,

$$f(y) = \frac{\lambda^n y^{n-1} e^{-\lambda y}}{\Gamma(n)}, \quad \lambda > 0, \quad y > 0,$$

is applied naturally in the following way: if prey are randomly distributed (i.e., Poisson distributed) with density λ, then the time it takes a predator to find a single prey has an exponential p.d.f. with parameter λ; and the time that it takes a predator to find n prey has a gamma distribution with parameters n and λ (given the first statement, the second statement is easy to prove by means of moment generating functions). Pulliam [117] makes use of this fact to obtain routinely the mean and the variance of the time required by a predator to find n prey: n/λ and n/λ^2. (These follow easily from knowledge of the gamma distribution.)

Other distributions are used infrequently. The Pareto distribution appears in [41]; the beta distribution is used in [51]; the normal distribution appears in [45] and the bivariate normal in [47].

Markov chains are used in various contexts in ecological modeling. Two-state Markov chains are used by Straw [135] in order to describe the moves of a pollinator among two types of flowers (he also gives the transition matrix for three types of flowers); by Oaten and Murdoch [102] to model a predator's feeding [the chain is in state i ($i = 1, 2$) if the predator fed last upon prey i]; by Estabrook and Jespersen [43] as a model for a predator encountering his prey or a mimic of his prey. This last article also contains a six-state Markov chain as a model for predator behavior, and the derivation of closed-form expressions for the probabilities of eating a prey and of eating the mimic of the prey.

Bosso *et al.* [10] use a Markov chain to model sib mating. They use standard Markov chain facts to find the matrix $N = (I - Q)^{-1}$, giving the expected number of times the process is in a given transient state, and the vector giving the expected number of times the process passes through each transient state. Several numerical examples are given. Parks [108] models growth as a Markov process, and Oster [104] uses Markov chains in the modeling and analysis of the foraging behavior of bumblebees.

Transition matrices appear in a treatment of Markovian decision models by Viscusi and Zeckhauser [147]. They apply the Markov model to (1) environmental policies that contain a mix of present-oriented and future-oriented actions (they wish to find the strategy that maximizes the expected discounted rewards); (2) situations in which an action has consequences that are irreversible; and (3) "analyze situations where level of expenditure is a valued output ...." This is an elementary article, primarily expository, and it has a bibliography containing many references on environmental economics.

A Markov chain is used as a model for interspecific interaction in [29], and Markov chains are used in [141], an article on birds' foraging. And in [112], "purse-seining in two-species fishing is viewed as a semi-Markov process" with five states ("searching, successful setting on either species, and unsuccessful setting on either species").

Stochastic processes are used by Levins [77] to estimate "the average fitness of a population that is responding to selection in a fluctuating environment," which "is assumed to be a stationary Markov process of the type described by Uhlenbeck and Ornstein (1930) ...." Holgate [62] uses stochastic branching processes in an investigation of "the effect of different features of the life history of an individual ...." Generating functions, extinction probabilities, the geometric distribution, and the Poisson distribution are all used in this article. Williamson and Charlesworth [151] use a stochastic model, namely, an age classification multitype branching process to answer the question inspired by MacArthur's and Wilson's *The Theory of Island Biogeography:* "How old should the founder (of a newly established colony on an island—author) be if it is desired to maximize the survival probability for the colony?" Generating functions are used in this very mathematical article.

3. Matrix and Linear Algebra

Matrix algebra is applied to a variety of problems in mathematical ecology, and occupies a significant place among the branches of mathematics used in ecological studies. It is used to investigate the stability of interacting species; to describe and analyze food weds (any food web can be thought of as a directed graph and any directed graph has a corresponding matrix); to model flows in the ecosystem—of nutrients, pollutants, or energy; to give probability transition matrices for those system that are always in one of several states and can thus be modeled by Markov chains; and study changes in the age structure of populations. The first and last listed are probably the sorts of applications that are most prevalent in the literature.

An important use of matrix algebra occurs in the determination of whether a set or related species has neighborhood stability (defined below).

Suppose that there are m (I am following the notation and development of May [89]) species in an ecological system and that their rates of change are given by the m functions,

$$\frac{dN_i(t)}{dt} = F_i(N_1, \cdots, N_m), \quad i = 1, 2, \cdots, m.$$

An *equilibrium point* of the system is some point $(N_1^*, \cdots, N_m^*)$ where there is no growth, that is, where

$$\frac{dN_i(t)}{dt} = 0,$$

or, equivalently, where $F_i(N_1^*, \cdots, N_m^*) = 0$. In order to investigate the stability of the system in the neighborhood of an equilibrium point, called *neighborhood stability*, each of the set of m equations is expanded in a Taylor's series about the equilibrium point and quadratic and higher terms are discarded, yielding the m linear differential equations

$$\frac{dx_i(t)}{dt} = \sum_{j=1}^{m} a_{ij}x_j(t), \quad i = 1, 2, \cdots, m,$$

where $x_i(t)$ is a small perturbation of the equilibrium value N_i^* of the ith population and $a_{ij} = (\partial F_i/\partial N_j)^*$ (with the derivative evaluated at the equilibrium point). The system of differential equations can be written in matrix notation:

$$\frac{d\mathbf{x}}{dt} = A\mathbf{x}.$$

The matrix A is called the *community matrix*, and its (i, j)th entry a_{ij} represents the effect of species j on species i near equilibrium.

In order to determine whether there is neighborhood stability, one merely examines the eigenvalues of the matrix A. The criterion for neighborhood stability is that all of the eigenvalues must have negative real parts. See, for example, [88] and [35]; for exposition, see [89, pp. 19–26] or [56, pp. 187–203].

A Leslie matrix (after P. H. Leslie, see [74]), after age-specific fecundity rates and survival rates are given for a population that is divided into classes, gives the way that population changes its structure over time. More accurately, it usually gives the way the population of reproducing members of the population—females, in the case of animals—changes its structure.

However, if the proportion of males and females is equal, then the Leslie matrix describes the changes of the entire population, and variants of the model exist that give the matrix for both males and females.

Suppose that the female members of a population are divided into $k + 1$ classes. A Leslie matrix is of the form

$$L = \begin{pmatrix} F_0 & F_1 & F_2 & \cdots & F_{k-1} & F_k \\ P_0 & 0 & 0 & \cdots & 0 & 0 \\ 0 & P_1 & 0 & \cdots & 0 & 0 \\ \vdots & \vdots & \vdots & & & \\ 0 & 0 & 0 & \cdots & P_{k-1} & 0 \end{pmatrix}.$$

where F_i represents the fecundity of a female in the ith class, and P_i represents the probability that a female in the ith class will survive to become a member of the $(i + 1)$st class. The vector

$$\mathbf{n}_t = \begin{pmatrix} n_{0,t} \\ n_{1,t} \\ \vdots \\ n_{k,t} \end{pmatrix},$$

where $n_{i,t}$ represents the number in the ith class at time t, represents the age structure of the population at time t. Hence, we have the relationship

$$\mathbf{n}_{t+1} = L\mathbf{n}_t,$$

which gives the age structure at time $t + 1$, given the age structure at time t and the Leslie matrix of the age-specific fecundity and survival rates.

The population structure (*not* the total number in the population) is stable when

$$\mathbf{n}_{t+1} = \lambda\mathbf{n}_t;$$

that is, when

$$L\mathbf{n}_t = \lambda\mathbf{n}_t.$$

The Perron–Frobenius theory is applicable here. It says that an irreducible nonnegative matrix (which a Leslie matrix is) always has a positive eigenvalue α, which is a simple root of the characteristic equation; that the moduli of all other eigenvalues do not exceed α; and that there exists an eigenvector with positive entries that correspond to α (see [37]). Once the population has reached the stable structure, then after s periods we have

$$\mathbf{n}_{t+s} = \lambda^s\mathbf{n}_t,$$

which is strongly reminiscent of the exponential law of growth,

$$N = e^{rt}N_0.$$

There are numerous papers that use either the simplest Leslie matrix model or one of its modifications. The seminal paper is [74], although [78] was published three years earlier. An excellent survey article with many examples (and which is readable by students who have had only a little matrix algebra) is [143]. Other articles that are accessible to students are [142], which has a very long example about a Scots pine forest, and [9], which is about redwoods. More advanced articles, suitable for algebraically sophisticated junior or senior students are [37], which also includes some graph theory, and [137], both elegant, short, theoretical articles that apply the Perron–Frobenius theory to Leslie matrices (Sykes calls them "population projection matrices").

There are variations of the basic Leslie matrix model. For example, Pennycuick *et al.* [113] replaced the constant age-specific fecundity and survival values of the basic Leslie matrix model by variable fecundity and survival values that depend upon the total population size. Specifically, they multiplied the constant age-specific fecundity value by $15000/[2500 + N(t)]$ to obtain density-dependent fecundity values. The survival values were multiplied by $1 + \exp\{[N(t)/1389] - 5\}^{-1}$, an inverted logistic function, to give the density-dependent survival factor.

An example of the use of a diagonal matrix is furnished by Beddington and Taylor [4], who use a modified Leslie matrix model to describe the growth of a population that is being harvested:

$$\mathbf{n}_{t+1} = MD\mathbf{n}_t,$$

where M is the usual Leslie matrix, D is a diagonal matrix with diagonal entries $1\text{-}h_i$, and h_i is the proportion harvested of the ith class (so the diagonal matrix accounts for the effect of the harvesting). They assume fixed population size as well as the usual fixed age-specific fecundity and survival rates, and obtain the harvesting strategy that maximizes the yield. They have a very fine short introductory section and references to papers. Caswell [17] also uses a diagonal matrix, in a variation of a lag model of Leslie (see [75]), given by

$$\mathbf{n}_{t+1} = AQ^{-1}\mathbf{n}_t,$$

where A is the usual Leslie matrix model, and

$$Q_t = \begin{pmatrix} q_{0t} & 0 & 0 & \cdots \\ 0 & q_{1t} & 0 & \cdots \\ 0 & 0 & q_{2t} & \cdot \\ \vdots & \vdots & \vdots & \vdots \end{pmatrix},$$

where $q_{it} = 1 + aN(t - i - 1) + bN(t)$. "Thus the growth of each age group is assumed to be affected by the total population size both at the current instant and on the eve of the birth of the age group." For a discussion of lag models, see [56, pp. 162–169].

Doubleday [40] uses much matrix algebra in his paper, which deals with the determination of the maximum possible harvest from populations described by matrix models. He uses linear programming and gives several examples illustrating the theory—a fisheries example, a pest control example, and a whale harvesting example. This is an excellent, readable paper, suitable for seniors, juniors, and bright sophomores.

Matrix theory is used by Bosch [9] in an elementary paper to model the growth of Coast Redwoods (*Sequoia sempervirens*). However, see also the letters by several authors in the October 22, 1971 issue of *Science*, which point out glaring mathematical and environmental inconsistencies in Borch's model.[1] As in the Leslie theory, the eigenvalues play a major role, and Bosch calculates and uses them for a simple 3×3 matrix. There is brief mention of the basis of a vector space.

In [59], matrices and vectors are used to describe energy flows in an ecosystem. There are some simple manipulations, such as $\mathbf{e} = G\mathbf{e} + \mathbf{r} \Rightarrow \mathbf{e} = (I - G)^{-1}\mathbf{r}$. Several special matrices are obtained—a normalized production matrix, a structure matrix, and a special energy flow matrix. A similar article is by Finn [46]. Finn uses matrices to describe and study energy flows in ecosystems. He applies "economic input–output analysis to ecosystem compartment models," and obtains expressions for total system throughflow, average path length of the ith inflow, and for the average path length for an average inflow, mainly by matrix manipulation. (For an example of economic input–output analysis applied to the economics of environmental preservation, see [81].)

Vandermer [144, p. 78] uses the relation $A^{-1} = \operatorname{adj} A/\det A$, where $\operatorname{adj} A$ denotes the adjoint of the matrix A, in proving a criterion for a species to have positive equilibrium density (which means simply that the species is in the ecosystem at equilibrium). Hubbell [64] uses matrix notation, multiplication, adjoint, and determinant in an appendix to a paper that treats two-species food webs as linear dynamic systems of energy filters. Goh [52] uses matrix theory results and reasoning, especially about negative definite matrices and positive definite matrices, in a paper about stability. He also uses the fact that $(AB)^{-1} = B^{-1}A^{-1}$.

Johnson and Brown [69] have a fine example of the calculation of certain genetics parameters, by means of least squares, in a study of the fitness of mice. They write the linear equations in matrix form, and then use matrix addition, multiplication, transposition, and inversion. The matrices are 2×5, 5×2, and 2×2, so the calculation is not overwhelming. Mobley [100] makes use of the concepts of subspace, span, Euclidean norm, matrix inversion and multiplication, and cosine of the angle between two vectors

[1] Brussard, P. F., Levin, S. A., Miller, L. N., and Whittaker, R. H., "Redwoods: A Population Model Debunked." (Technical comment.) *Science*, *174* (1971), 435–436; Diem, J. E., and Mc Gregor, J. L. (1971) *ibid.*; Halbach, K. (1971) *ibid.*; Taibleson, M. Linear Algebra Problem (Letter). (1971) *ibid.*

in the development of an iterative algorithm, which he describes as "computationally simple yet powerful," for the solution of

$$Y = \sum_{p=1}^{m} b_p f_p$$

for the unknown parameters b_p (this is often called "the inverse problem" in ecological literature). He remarks that his iterative solution is valuable because there are computational difficulties with the linear regression solution $B^* = (X^tX)^{-1}(X^tY)$ of the linear model $Y = XB + E$ if X is a large matrix or if the column vectors of X have "near linear dependencies."

An unusual use of a matrix occurs in [68]: A simple covariance matrix

$$S = \begin{pmatrix} s_{xx} & s_{xy} \\ s_{xy} & s_{yy} \end{pmatrix},$$

where s_{xx} is the variance of X, s_{yy} is the variance of Y, and s_{xy} is the covariance of X and Y, is used in the definition of a measure of the home range of an animal, namely, $A = 6\pi|S|^{1/2}$.

In [54] there are necessary and sufficient conditions for the convergence of the age-structure vector to a stable age vector regardless of the initial vector (they are working with Leslie matrices), and the Weak Ergodic Theorem and the Strong Ergodic Theorem of stable population theory are proved. This is a difficult, theoretical paper. Linear operators are used in [80] as a tool to handle mating models. This also is a difficult paper, which contains probability theory as well as linear algebra.

4. Calculus

A wide variety of topics from elementary calculus—derivatives, definite integrals, Maclaurin's and Taylor's series, infinite series of constants, L'Hospital's Rule, and so on—are used in many sorts of ecological and environmental applications. Usually the calculus forms only a small fraction of the article, being embedded either in other kinds of mathematics or in verbiage (not used disparagingly!). Differentiation, integration, and Taylor's series are each used very extensively in ecological writing.

A typical use of the Taylor series is to linearize a system of nonlinear differential equations that describe the interactions of several species in order to investigate neighborhood stability (see Section 2) at the equilibrium points. For example, the first two terms of the Taylor expansion of a system about its equilibrium point is used to linearize the system so that its local stability can be determined [76]. In [114], a system of m nutrients and n primary users of those nutrients is considered, and the Taylor expansion of the net rate of removal of the ith nutrient by each member of a species j of the primary nutrient users about its equilibrium position is employed. A Taylor expansion is used to approximate a system of difference equations in an investigation of local stability of populations [1].

In [111], the Taylor expansion of a vector function of two vector variables is used. This is a fascinating article—one which an instructor trying to impart the importance of linear models and approximations might want to assign to his students. Patten says: "The purpose of this paper is to indicate several lines of consideration for the following propositions: Ecosystems are nominally linear in their large-scale holistic dynamics, and nonlinearity, except where it is useful or can be controlled, is selected against in evolutionary self-design" [111, p. 529].

The Maclaurin's series

$$\psi(Y_n(t)) \cong \psi(0) + \psi'(0)Y_n(t) + \frac{\psi''(0)}{2}Y_n^2(t)$$

is used in [51]. A square root is expanded in a Maclaurin series during the determination of the limiting growth rate of a trophic level in [146]. The expansion of $\log(1 + x)$ in a Maclaurin series is used in [87], an article that explains mathematically the growth and form of the sunflower head.

The integration of the logistic equation

$$\frac{dN}{dt} = (a - bN)N,$$

which is a standard equation for modeling population growth when the population size has an inhibiting effect on the growth rate, furnishes a nice, easy example of the use of partial fractions for integration. (See also [64, p. 106] for the use of partial fractions.) This equation appears in many articles and books, for example, see [148] or [56, pp. 151–160]. Integration by partial fractions is also used in [48], a short article that explores the relationship between the Verhulst–Pearl and Lotka–Volterra population dynamics models. (The logistic equation is also known as the Verhulst–Pearl equation.)

The evaluation of

$$\frac{1}{2}\int_0^1 \sum_{n=1}^{k} (n + 1)p^n = \frac{1}{2}\sum_{n=1}^{k} \int_0^1 (n + 1)p^n\,dp = \frac{k}{2}$$

in [12], which gives the average number of mates obtained in k contests for mates, furnishes an example of the property that the integral of a sum equals the sum of the integrals. This would be a fine example to give very early in a student's study of integration because the integral is so easy and because it illustrates a general theorem. If the instrutor would like to present an explanation of where the integral comes from, it would take only about 10 min—some simple probability theory is involved, but it could be covered intuitively in class.

An excellent example of the ideas behind the use of integration in ecological modeling occurs in Gillespie [51]. He has the integral

$$W_i(n) = \varphi\left\{\int_0^1 g_i(t)\psi_i[Y_n(t)]\,dt\right\}$$

and his explanation of it is worth quoting:

> "ψ_i transforms the state of the environment $Y_n(t)$ into some units of biological function such as the level of activity of a gene. The g_i is a weighting function that weights according to the development time. This allows certain periods in the development to be more or less critical in determining the fitness of the genotype than others. By integrating, we 'add up' the weighted contribution to the total function from each age in the developmental process. Finally, φ transforms the integral into units of fitness."

The integral as a summation is also clearly seen in Kerfoot [72], where an integral represents the total biomass B_T of consuming organisms in a column of water:

$$B_T = N_0 \int_0^\infty 1_x^\ell b_x \, dx,$$

where N_0 is the number of organisms at birth, 1_x^ℓ is the probability that an organism is alive at time x, and b_x is the biomass of any individual at time x. This integral is analogous to the formula, expressed in terms of a summation, which gives the discounted contribution of an individual to future generations (note the idea of "discounting", from economics) and which appears frequently in biological literature (for example, see [139]):

$$\frac{e^{mu}}{\ell(u)} \sum_{k \geq u} e^{-mk} \ell(k) b(k),$$

where $\ell(k)$ is the probability that an individual survives until age k, and $b(k)$ is the birth rate during the kth period of age.

Changes of variable occur in [41] and [153]. The product of the functions

$$f(x) = \frac{1}{v} e^{-x/v} \quad \text{and} \quad g(x) = \begin{cases} x, & x \leq M \\ v_B - M, & x > M \end{cases}$$

is integrated in [93], an article in which game theory is applied to animal conflicts, and furnishes an example of integration by parts and integration of a function which is not defined by a single formula over its entire domain (this sort of function gives difficulties to some students). The integration of the bivariate normal p.d.f. (except for a constant factor) appears in [47].

McLay [95] assumes that stream bed organisms that enter a stream's flow from a disturbed area of the bed settle out at a rate that is proportional to the number remaining, $dN/dx = -rN$, where x is the distance from the disturbed area. Among other calculations, he finds, by integrating the appropriate exponential functions the average distance traveled by an organism and the distance beyond which only a given percentage of the organisms will travel.

Skellam [132] has a triple definite integral that gives the expected number of animals that enters an observer's field of perception (there is excellent explanation of the integral, with a figure) in an article that is about the estimation of animal populations by transect methods. He also uses the Mean Value Theorem, and evaluates the integral

$$\int_0^\infty 2cu^2 e^{-cu^2}\, du$$

(substitution of $x = cu^2$ gives a gamma function).

Mathai and Davis [87], in an article in which they mathematically analyze the growth and form of sunflower heads, give the equation of a logarithmic spiral, $r = e^{a\theta}$, which, for very small a, can be approximated by a spiral of Archimedes, $r = b\theta$. The formula for arc length of a curve expressed in polar coordinates is used.

The geometric series

$$\sum_{x=1}^{\infty} e^{-mx} = \frac{e^{-m}}{1 - e^{-m}}$$

appears in [13] in a discussion of a statement of L. C. Cole, that "for an annual species, the absolute gain in intrinsic growth that could be achieved by changing to the perennial reproductive habit would be exactly equivalent to adding one individual to the average litter size." The geometric series $1 + p^2 + p^4 + \cdots$ and $1 + \left(\frac{p}{\lambda}\right)^2 + \left(\frac{p}{\lambda}\right)^4 + \cdots$ and the manipulation

$$\begin{aligned} 5p^4 + 7p^6 + 9p^8 + \cdots &= \frac{d}{dp}(p^5 + p^7 + p^9 + \cdots) \\ &= \frac{1}{(1-p)^2} - \frac{2p}{(1-p^2)^2} - 1 - 3p^2 \end{aligned}$$

appear in [97], a very interesting article, in a computation of the cohort generation time of the California condor. The geometric series also appears in [132] and in [83], along with the well-known test series $\sum_{n=1}^{\infty} 1/n^p$.

Sequences appear much less frequently. The Fibonacci sequence 1, 1, 2, 3, 5, 8, $\cdots$ appears in [87], an article on sunflower heads.

L'Hospital's rule is used by Rosensweig [124], Abel's Lemma is used by Bryant [13].

5. Differential Equations

A very large proportion of those ecological articles that use any mathematics at all use differential equations. However, there are fewer categories of applications than there are for other areas of mathematics. Although the differential equations used in ecological studies range from very simple logistic equations and linear systems of differential equations to partial differential equations, by far the most widespread use of differential equations is in modeling the interaction and dynamics of two or more species and much of this modeling involves the Lotka–Volterra equations [see Eqs. (4)] or some variant of them. In contrast, the use of probability theory, for example, is not concentrated in any particular area of ecological study, but is used to study optimal foraging, the evolution of species, and conflict behavior, to name but a few areas. And there is a wide variety of probabilistic tools used—the simplest probability formulas, standard probability functions, Markov chains, stochastic processes, and generating functions.

The simplest and most familiar differential equation used to describe an ecological process is undoubtedly the familiar equation describing growth that is not limited by anything, usually called "exponential growth": $dx/dt = \alpha x$ [56, pp. 131–135], [95], [115, p. 8], and [124, p. 282].

The assumption of unrestrained growth, however, is unrealistic in most situations. Two of the factors that limit growth are the size of the population and the carrying capacity of the environment. A model that is closer to reality than the exponential growth model in most situations, and also furnishes a fine example of a useful differential equation which is easy to solve (by separation of variables), is the logistic equation (also called the Pearl–Verhulst equation), one of the forms of which is

$$\frac{dx}{dt} = bx\frac{K - x}{K},$$

in which the rate of change of the population decreases as the size of the population approaches the carrying capacity K of the environment. The logistic equation has variations, which also are not difficult to solve, for example,

$$\frac{dx}{dt} = bx\frac{K - cx}{K}, \quad \text{with solution} \quad x = K/[1 + e^{a-bt}]$$

and

$$\frac{dx}{dt} = bx\frac{K - x^c}{K}, \quad \text{with solution} \quad x = \{K/[1 + e^{a-bct}]\}^{1/c}.$$

These three models appear in [98], in which natural control of insect populations is discussed.

A model is given by Bigger [7] that furnishes a simple example of the solution of a second-order equation. He found that the classical Lotka–Volterra equations [see Eqs. (4)] did not give a very good fit to his data of coffee leaf-miners and their parasites, hence he used the simpler equations

$$\frac{dH}{dt} = mH - nP,$$

$$\frac{dP}{dt} = oH - pP,$$

which gave an excellent fit to his data. From these equations he obtained, after some elementary manipulations, the second-order equation

$$\frac{d^2H}{dt^2} + b\frac{dH}{dt} + cH = 0,$$

which is easily solved for H in the usual way; then P can be found. Second-order equations appear in Clark [25]: After a critique of some commonly used first-order differential equation models for population growth, he presents, in a very well-motivated fashion, some second-order models. Oster [104], after applying the Euler–Lagrange equation of the calculus of variations in order to determine the optimum population trajectory for bumblebee hives, solves the second-order equation

$$\frac{d^2N}{dt^2} + \frac{\alpha}{\beta}N + \frac{\omega - g}{2\beta} = 0.$$

The use of integrating factors occurs in Paltridge and Denholm [107]. They comment that many plants have a rather sharp switch-over point between total concentration on producing green leaves (first stage) and on producing "grain" (second stage). They use the equation

$$\frac{dw}{dt} = k_1 w - S(t)w, \quad 0 \leq t < T_1$$

to describe the net rate of growth of green leaves at time t in the first stage, where k_1 is the constant that gives the rate at which new green leaves are being produced from the existing green leaves, $S(t)$ is the rate at which green leaves are becoming useless for photosynthesis, and T_1 is the switch-over time. This equation has the well-known solution

$$w(t) = w_0 e^{k_1 t} e^{-P(t)},$$

where

$$P(t) = \int_0^t S(u)\,du.$$

For the second stage, they use the equation

$$\frac{dw}{dt} = -S(t)w(t), t \geq T_1$$

which has the solution

$$w(t) = w(T_1)e^{P(T_1)}e^{-P(t)},$$

for the rate of change of green leaf, and the equation $dX/dt = k_2 w(t)$ for the production of grain. Another interesting formula that they obtain is the one for the optimum yield of grain, $X(T) = k_2 w(T_0)/k_1$, where T_0 is the optimum switch time.

A simple linear system appears in [146]. The transfer of nutrients within a single trophic level is described by means of the system

$$\frac{d\mathbf{x}}{dt} = A\mathbf{x},$$

where A is a 2×2 constant matrix. Also, a more complicated set of differential equations is used to describe a four-level trophic system.

The classical Lotka–Volterra equations, which describe the interaction of a predator P, and host (i.e., prey) H, are

$$\begin{aligned} \frac{dH}{dt} &= (a_1 - b_1 P)H, \\ \frac{dP}{dt} &= (-a_2 + b_2 H)P. \end{aligned} \tag{4}$$

For an exposition, see [16], [56, pp. 224–246], [88], [115, pp. 66–70], or [136]. Canale [16] treats the classical Lotka–Volterra equations and two modifications of these—assuming that the prey population is limited by some necessary nutrient, and assuming that both prey and predator populations are limited by a carrying capacity of the environment—and then discusses the phase plane analysis (for an exposition, see [56, pp. 228–239] or [23]) for each of the three models.

Equations (4), which assume that the changes in populations occur instantaneously, can be modified by incorporating a time lag into the model. Ross [125] does this and discusses the nature of the solution (he uses considerable complex analysis here). He also discusses a time lag $du/dt = ku(t - \tau)$ incorporated into the simple deterministic model $du/dt = ku$ for one species using Laplace transforms, the Laplace Inversion Theorem, and the Residue Theorem.

A different kind of modification occurs in Comins and Blatt [32]. Beginning with Eqs. (4), they introduce a term to account for diffusion that is due to an environment that is not homogeneous, and obtain partial differential equations for predator–prey models.

The two-species model is easily generalized to more than two species, of course. Parrish and Saila [109] discuss the Lotka–Volterra equations for one predator and two preys and examine the stability of the system with the aid of a computer. The same one predator–two preys model is discussed by Cramer and May [34]. Barclay and van den Driessche [2] use ten equations of the Lotka–Volterra type to build a model of ten species in four trophic levels:

$$\frac{dN_i}{dt} = \frac{r_i N_i}{K_i}\left(K_i - \sum_{j=1}^{10} \alpha_{ij} N_j\right), \quad i = 1, 2, \cdots, 10,$$

where K_i is the carrying capacity for the ith species, N_i is the population of the ith species, and r_i is the rate of increase of the ith species.

Some authors take a rather general approach. Rapport and Turner [120] express the population dynamics of an ecosystem of m species as

$$\frac{dn_i}{dt} = f_i[\mathbf{n}(t)] - h_i[\mathbf{n}(t)], \quad i = 1, 2, \cdots, m,$$

where $\mathbf{n}(t) = [n_1(t), n_2(t), \cdots, n_m(t)]$ is a vector representing the numbers of the m species at time t, $f_i[\mathbf{n}(t)]$ is the yield function of the ith species, and $h_i[\mathbf{n}(t)]$ is the harvest function. (The harvest–yield model has obvious affinities with economics.) This system of m nonlinear first-order differential equations is more general than the Lotka–Volterra model, which they obtain as a special case. Saunders and Bazin [128] also take a very general approach. They consider a very general model of a nutrient–prey–predator system (three nonlinear first-order differential equations), investigate some special cases of it and their stability, and then generalize to an n-species case.

Many differential equations used in ecological literature are quite difficult. There are complicated differential equations in [17], namely, integro-differential equations due to Volterra (Caswell remarks that this particular work of Volterra is not very well known) and others; in [73], in which stability properties of a plant-pollinator system defined by two nonlinear first-order differential equations are examined; in [70] (Fourier–Kirchoff differential equation of heat flow); in [5], in which the Lotka–Volterra equations are obtained computationally by means of the technique of quasi-linearizations; and in [11], in which a modification of the Lotka–Volterra equations is obtained by assuming that "the rate of change of predators at time, t, $N_2'(t)$, depends on the exposure to prey over an *interval* of time ($[t - T, t]$, $T \geq 0$), rather than simply at the instant t."

6. Game Theory

There are three types of applications of game theory to ecological problems. The first type views the species (in evolutionary theory) or the individual as playing a game against Nature. Articles by Lewontin [79], Oster and Heinrich [105], and Slobodkin and Rapoport [133] take this viewpoint. The second type of application attempts to explain the conflicts or competition of individuals as a game they are playing against each other. The articles by Maynard Smith [91], Maynard Smith and Price [94], and Maynard Smith and Parker [93] are of this sort. The third type of application makes use of game theory to analyze situations in which humans are making decisions (perhaps cooperatively with other individuals or groups) that affect the environment, so that optimal decisions, which are also felt to be fair by all participants, are made (see Heaney and Sheikh [61] and Bird [8]).

Game theory began, as a subject, with von Neumann's and Morgenstern's *Theory of Games and Economic Behavior* in 1944. The first application of game theory to biology (specifically, to evolutionary theory) of which I am aware was made by Lewontin [79], in which he viewed evolution as a game played between a species and Nature. Oster and Heinrich [105] use a decision-theoretic framework to explain the foraging behavior of bumblebees. For the simple case of only two possible types of flowers, they analyze a 2×2 reward matrix and show that if the reward spectrum (the ranking of the flowers in terms of their rewards) is constant in time (or nearly so), then the bumblebee's concentrating on a single type of flower ("majoring," in their terminology) is always better than his playing a mixed strategy. However, in a nonconstant environment, a mixed strategy is best.

Slobodkin and Rapoport [133] also view evolution as a game between the species and Nature. In particular, they draw an analogy between the specific game of Gambler's Ruin (see [44]) and the evolutionary process. They conclude that, since the players (i.e., the species) cannot quit the game and pocket their winnings, the only way they can "win" is to continue playing. Therefore, the optimal strategy for each species is the one which will maximize the duration of the game it is playing against Nature, which is accomplished if the species bets as little as possible on each play. In other words, in response to environmental change, a species should react as little as possible in order to counter that change. There is little explicit mathematics in the article except for the formulas

$$q_z = \begin{cases} 1, & \text{if } p \leq q, \\ \left(\dfrac{q}{p}\right)^z, & \text{if } p > q, \end{cases}$$

which give the probability of ruin for a gambler, beginning with a fortune of z and probability p of winning a unit stake on any play, and playing against an infinitely rich adversary. (This is a random walk beginning at n, with an absorbing barrier at 0. See [44, p. 347].)

The second sort of application views the game as being between individual animals rather than between the animal and Nature. Maynard Smith [91] uses game theory in the study of those conflicts between individual animals that are characterized by display and bluffing rather than by fighting. The winner of such a contest is the individual who perseveres the longest. (Think of a staring contest or of the excellent—from the parents' point of view—children's travel game, "Let's see who can be quiet the longest!" Incidentally, this sort of contest is not exclusively a children's game: Recall the poem "Get up and Bar the Door," in which the first one of an elderly married couple to speak must do just that [84, pp. 315–316].) He defines an evolutionarily stable strategy (ESS) as follows: The strategy I is an ESS if, for all alternative strategies J, either

$$E_I(I) > E_I(J),$$

or

$$E_I(I) = E_I(J), \quad \text{and} \quad E_J(I) > E_J(J),$$

where $E_I(J)$ denotes the expected gain of strategy J played against strategy I. He shows that the strategy of displaying for a random time X, whose probability distribution is given by (2) in Section 1, is an ESS when played against the strategy of displaying for any fixed time (the reward is assumed to equal λ). A proof that an ESS exists under certain conditions is given by Haight in an appendix to [91], and is also published separately in [57].

Maynard Smith and Price [94] consider a population whose individuals have three types of conflict behavior—use of tactics that are not dangerous (display, for example), use of tactics which are dangerous (fight, for example), and retreat. They divide the population into five categories: mouse, hawk, bully, retaliator, and prober–retaliator. The bully, for example, always responds to nondangerous behavior with dangerous behavior, responds to the first instance of dangerous behavior with nondangerous behavior, and retreats if the dangerous behavior is repeated. They simulate each of the $\binom{5}{2}$ possible contests 2000 times with a computer. On the basis of these computer runs they obtain an average payoff for each type of contest (e.g., hawk versus retaliator) with the payoff taken as a measure "of the contributions the contest has made to the reproductive success of the individual." They show these payoffs in a matrix and deduce the ESS. They also consider the type of conflict in which dangerous behavior is impossible and persistence with nondangerous behavior pays off. They show that if the payoff is λ, then the ESS is, once again, a mixed strategy in which an individual persists a random time X with the exponential p.d.f. [See Eq. (2).]

Rapoport [118], in a survey article of the uses of game theory in biology, discusses, among other topics, games against Nature, games against other species, and "quasi-game theoretic models." The paper is quite readable by sophomores. Marchi and Hansell [86] is a very theoretical article, suitable only for advanced undergraduates with much facility with abstract mathematics. The article is primarily about taxonomic theory, but game theory is discussed in the last half of it. An important role in taxonomic theory is played by the concept of a *similarity matrix* whose (i, j)th element is the *taxonomic distance* (calculated according to some definition) between organism i and organism j in the set of organisms under consideration. They use game-theoretic concepts, very abstractly stated, to "derive a restricted set of such possible matrices by applying the concepts of biological competition, thus deriving the framework for a model of evolution."

Heaney and Sheikh [61] consider the following simplified realistic problem: There are several pollution sources (factories and municipalities) in a certain area, and prescribed regional limits on pollution that must be met by a mixture of both on-site and regional off-site pollution control plants. It is required to find the mixture of on-site and off-site (at some central location) disposal for each of the several sources that gives the financially optimal strategy for the region as a whole. They use linear programming to find this optimum. But the optimum strategy thus obtained might not seem fair to all of the polluters, and fairness is important in order to obtain the willing participation of all of the polluters in regional pollution control systems. In order to solve the problem with the condition of fairness in addition to that of optimality, Heaney and Sheikh apply cooperative n-person game theory, making use of the concepts of the core of the game and the Shapley value for the game in order to obtain a solution that is both optimal and fair. This is a fine, readable, relevant article, much of it devoted to a brief exposition of the necessary theory of cooperative n-person game theory and to the working out of a long illustration. Cooperative n-person game theory is also used by Bird [8], in a rather theoretical article in which he uses a weighted Shapley value to obtain a unique allocation of costs for a spanning tree. Possible applications are the computation of charges for electric power or for water.

7. Graph Theory

Graph theory is used frequently in ecological modeling. It is natural to represent the various species in a food web by the nodes of a graph and to direct the edges from predator to prey. There are also environmental applications that deal with efficient transportation networks or municipal services routes (e.g., garbage collection). Graphs can also aid us in understanding the interrelationships between such factors of modern life as power supply, recreational opportunities, gasoline consumption, and the quality of life [123].

Roberts [122] has much material on graph theory in his admirable book and many examples that are environmentally oriented [122, pp. 140–156 (food webs), pp. 156–158 (garbage trucks routing), and pp. 196–203 (energy use)]. Gallopín [49] has written an excellent expository article on graph theory applied to food webs. After a discussion of binary relations and elementary graph theory, he goes on to cover complexity and stability of food webs, the maximum possible number of food chains, trophic distance, and configurations of food webs.

In the context of signed digraphs, Jeffries [66] states a necessary and sufficient condition for qualitative asymptotic stability (see [90] for discussion of qualitative stability) of the community matrix of a food web. This is an excellent, readable article, with some elementary exposition of digraphs (many figures). A sufficient condition for neutral stability (a weaker condition than the asymptotic stability discussed in [66]) appears in [67].

Roberts and Brown [123] wrote an excellent expository article, very suitable for juniors and seniors. After some introductory material on digraphs and weighted digraphs, they discuss pulse processes and stability at some length. Harary [60] shows a community matrix (which he calls an "eating matrix," probably a better term!) for the graph of a food web of 15 species, and calculates (by analogy with concepts used in sociology) the "status," "counterstatus," and "net status" of each animal. This article can be read by beginning mathematics students.

Beltrami and Bodin [6] apply graph theory to the problem of the efficient routing of garbage trucks in New York City. They "describe a set of procedures for routing vehicles through a set of nodes in a network or along its branches": An excellent article. Estabrook [42] develops a mathematical model for biological classification, making use of concepts from graph theory, such as graphs, chains, subgraphs, and maximal connected subgraphs. He also uses the abstract notions of function of two variables, relations, and equivalence relations, and has a flow chart for the classification algorithm.

8. Optimal Control Theory

In the biological, environmental, and economics journals, there is a growing literature on the use of optimal control theory—calculus of variations, dynamic programming, and Pontryagin's maximum principle. The applications of optimal control theory are various, including determination of the best strategies for harvesting resources (such as fish or timber) and controlling pests (such as mosquitoes). Wickwire [149] has a recent paper that surveys the literature of the control of pests and infectious diseases, and contains many examples of optimal control theory applied to those areas.

Calculus of variations is used by Oster [104] to find the optimal (in the sense that the net profit, total productivity less expenditures for living and reproducing, is maximized) population trajectory for a bumblebee hive. This is a long, interesting article with much mathematics: Considerable probability theory is used in the first part of it.

Dynamic programming is applied to maximizing the total profits from the harvesting of natural resources over an N-period time horizon [137]; it is applied to minimizing the cost of agricultural pest control as discussed [129], a readable article with comments about computation and storage requirements; it is applied to maximizing net income from a crop to which pest control is being used [130]; it is briefly discussed as a computational procedure to minimize the cost of "controlling a population in order to steer its distribution toward a desired target at a given time . . . " [50] (this article is quite mathematical with much probability theory—the material on dynamic programming forms only a small part of it); it is used [85] to find the control that will minimize the damage done by pests in an n-period decision process with both linear and nonlinear control costs (Mann also considers the simpler one-period decision process with both linear and nonlinear control costs); it is applied to the problem of maximizing the productivity of a population (described by a stochastic Leslie matrix model) over a stated time horizon [96].

The Pontryagin Maximum Principle is applied to an analysis of the optimal (in the sense of maximizing present value) dynamics of a fishery

[24] (see their appendix); it is applied to the minimization of the cost of a pest control program in a predator–prey system whose dynamic state is given by the Lotka–Volterra equations [53] [a very readable article, in which several strategies of control are considered, among them controls by a pesticide that kills both prey (pests) and their predators, by a pesticide that kills only the predators (!), and by the *release* of prey (! again) and predators)]; it is applied by Litt and Smet [82] to finding the strategy that yields the minimum total discounted cost of pollution over a finite time horizon if some cost is due to cleaning up part of the pollutant at its source and some cost is due to environmental damage from dumping part of the pollutant into a lake; it is used to prove that the sharp division of a plant's growth into a period in which only "green leaf" is produced and a period in which only "grain" is produced is a necessary condition that the yield of the grain be maximized over a given time [39]; it is applied to the problem of harvesting optimally from a population whose growth is described by the Pearl–Verhulst equation (i.e., logistic equation) [26].

9. Miscellaneous

Binomial coefficients appear throughout [49] and are used in [73, p. 270]. The quadratic formula is used in [73, p. 275] (plant–pollinator systems), [1, pp. 322, 323, 330], and [64, p. 103] (food webs). Cartesian products, binary relations, and equivalence relations are used in [49] (food webs). The law of cosines is used in [132, p. 394] (ecological sampling). Cramer's Rule is used in [136, p. 650]. Logarithms are used extensively in various formulas that measure niche breadth in [31]; and logarithmic models of population growth are used in [33].

Elementary analytic geometry is used in [63] to obtain normalized coordinates of predator and prey, in a study of the conditions of speed and manoeverability (i.e., turning radius) for which prey can escape from a predator in full pursuit (this is called the "turning gambit"). This is an interesting article. Howland discusses the practical implications of the theory that he presents and gives several examples (falcons versus pigeons, cheetahs versus gazelles, bats versus moths, and pike versus sunfish). Sneath [134] uses the trignometric formulas

$$\sin\beta = \left[\frac{\tan^2\beta}{1+\tan^2\beta}\right]^{1/2}, \quad \cos\beta = \left[\frac{1}{1+\tan^2\beta}\right]^{1/2},$$

the rotation formulas

$$\begin{aligned} x' &= x\cos\beta + y\sin\beta, \\ y' &= -x\sin\beta + y\cos\beta, \end{aligned}$$

and the formula for the cosine of the angle ψ between two vectors **a** and **b**

$$\cos\psi = \frac{\mathbf{a}\cdot\mathbf{b}}{|\mathbf{a}|\cdot|\mathbf{b}|}.$$

The formula for $\cos\psi$ is also used in (100). The calculation

$$\frac{1}{a+bi} = \frac{a-bi}{(a+bi)(a-bi)} = \frac{a-bi}{a^2+b^2}$$

appears in (100), an article which is concerned with how populations and food webs act as energy filters in the context of a linear differential equation.

The Dirac δ-function is used in [55, p. 242] (air pollution) and in [51, p. 833] (environmental grain); a tensor product is used in [1, pp. 331–332]; an example of a functional is in [51, p. 832]; the Hilbert space ℓ_2 is used in [38, p. 134] (population dynamics); Euclidean hyperspace and Euclidean distance are used in [131] (niche quantification); Parseval's Theorem is applied in [14], an article which applies power spectrum analysis to the study of climatic cycles from observations on the thicknesses of tree rings (interesting observations from a 3000-yr old Sequoia and a 1500-yr old limber pine are given); the Residue Theorem and the Laplace Inversion Theorem are used in [125, p. 481].

Hubbell [64] mentions Euler's formula $e^{i\omega t} = \cos\omega t + i\sin\omega t$ and uses Laplace transforms (p. 101). He has an enlightening comment (p. 101) on the advantage of using Laplace transforms.

References

1. Allen, J. C. "Mathematical Models of Species Interactions in Time and Space," *American Naturalist*, *109* (1975), 319–342.
2. Barclay, H., and van den Driessche, P. "Time Lags in Ecological Systems," *Journal of Theoretical Biology*, 51 (1975), 347–356.
3. Beddington, J. R. "Age Distribution and the Stability of Simple Discrete Time Population Models," *Journal of Theoretical Biology*, *47* (1974), 65–74.
4. Beddington, J. R., and Taylor, D. B. "Optimum Age Specific Harvesting of a Population," *Biometrics*, *29* (1973), 801–809.
5. Bellman, R., Kagiwada, H., and Kalaba, R. "Inverse Problems in Ecology," *Journal Theoretical Biology*, *11* (1966), 164–167.
6. Beltrami, E., and Bodin, L. "Networks and Vehicle Routing for Municipal Waste Collection," *Networks*, *4* (1973), 65–94.
7. Bigger, M. "An Investigation by Fourier Analysis into the Interaction between Coffee Leaf-Miners and Their Larval Parasites," *Journal of Animal Ecology*, *42* (1973), 417–434.
8. Bird, C. G. "On Cost Allocation for a Spanning Tree: A Game-Theoretic Approach," *Networks*, *6* (1976), 335–350.
9. Bosch, C. A. "Redwoods: A Population Model," *Science*, *172* (1971), 345–349.
10. Bosso, J. A., Sorarrain, O. M., and Favret, E. E. A. "Application of Finite Absorbent Markov Chains to Sib Mating Populations with Selection," *Biometrics*, *25* (1969), 17–26.
11. Bownds, J. M., and Cushing, J. M. "On the Behavior of Solutions of Predator–

Prey Equations with Hereditary Terms," *Mathematical Biosciences, 26* (1975), 41–54.
12. Brockelman, W. Y. "Competition, the Fitness of Off-Spring, and Optimal Clutch Size," *American Naturalist, 109* (1975), 677–699.
13. Bryant, E. C. "Life History Consequences of Natural Selection: Cole's Result," *American Naturalist, 105* (1971), 75–77.
14. Bryson, R. A., and Dutton, J. A. "Some Aspects of the Variance Spectra of Tree Rings and Varves," *Annals of the New York Academy of Sciences, 95* (1961), 580–604.
15. Cannings, C., and Cruz Orive, L. M. "On the Adjustment of the Sex Ratio and the Gregarious Behavior of Animal Populations," *Journal of Theoretical Biology, 55* (1975), 115–136.
16. Canale, R. P. "An Analysis of Models Describing Predator–Prey Interaction," *Biotechnology and Bioengineering, 12* (1970), 353–378.
17. Caswell, H. "A Simulation Study of a Time-Lag Population Model," *Journal of Theoretical Biology, 34* (1972), 419–439.
18. Cea, Jean (Editor). *Optimization Techniques: Modeling and Optimization in the Service of Man, Part 1* (Proceedings of the 7th IFIP Conference, Nice, September, 8–12, 1975), Volume 40 in *Lecture Notes in Computer Science* (edited by G. Goos and J. Hartmanis), Springer-Verlag, Berlin, 1976.
19. Charnes, A., and Lynn, W. R. (Editors). *Mathematical Analysis of Decision Problems in Ecology* (Proceedings of the NATO Conference held in Istanbul, Turkey, July 9–13, 1973), Volume 5 in *Lecture Notes in Biomathematics* (Managing Editor, S. Levin), Springer-Verlag, Berlin, 1975.
20. Charnov, E. L. "Optimal Foraging: Attack Strategy of a Mantid," *American Naturalist, 110* (1976), 141–151.
21. Charnov, E. L., and Krebs, J. R. "The Evolution of Alarm Calls: Altruism or Manipulation?" *American Naturalist, 108* (1974) 107–112.
22. Clark, C. W. "Economically Optimal Policies for the Utilization of Biologically Renewable Resources," *Mathematical Biosciences, 12* (1971), 245–260.
23. Clark, C. W. *Mathematical Bioeconomics*, Wiley, New York, 1976.
24. Clark, C. W., Edwards, G., and Friedlaender, M. "Beverton-Holt Model of a Commercial Fishery: Optimal Dynamics," *Journal of Fisheries Research Board of Canada, 30* (1973), 1629–1640.
25. Clark, J. P. "The Second Derivative and Population Modeling," *Ecology, 52* (1971), 606–613.
26. Cliff, E. M., and Vincent, T. L. "An Optimal Policy for a Fish Harvest," *Journal in Optimization Theory and Applications, 12* (1973), 485–496.
27. Cohen, J. E. "Alternate Derivations of a Species-Abundance Relation," *American Naturalist, 102* (1968), 165–172.
28. Cohen, J. E. "Natural Primate Troops and a Stochastic Population Model," *American Naturalist, 103* (1969), 455–477.
29. Cohen, J. E. "A Markov Contingency-Table Model for Replicated Lotka–Volterra Systems Near Equilibrium," *American Naturalist, 104* (1970), 547–560.
30. Cohen, J. E. "Markov Population Processes as Models of Primate Social and Population Dynamics," *Theoretical Population Biology, 3* (1972), 119–134.
31. Colwell, R. K., and Futuyma, D. J. "On the Measurement of Niche Breadth and Overlap," *Ecology, 52* (1951), 567–576.
32. Comins, H. N., and Blatt, D. W. E. "Prey–Predator Models in Spatially Heterogeneous Environments," *Journal of Theoretical Biology, 48* (1974), 75–83.
33. Coutlee, E. L., and Jennrich, R. I. "The Relevance of Logarithmic Models for Population Interaction, *American Naturalist, 102* (1968), 307–321.
34. Cramer, N. F., and May, R. M. "Interspecific Competition, Predation, and Species Diversity: A Comment," *Journal of Theoretical Biology, 34* (1972) 289–293.

35. Deakin, M. A. B. "The Steady States of Ecosystems," *Mathematical Biosciences, 24* (1975), 319–331.
36. de Jong, G. "A Model of Competition for Food," *American Naturalist, 110* (1976), 1013–1027.
37. Demetrius, L. "Primitivity Conditions for Growth Matrices," *Mathematical Biosciences, 12* (1971), 53–58.
38. Demetrius, L. "On an Infinite Population Matrix," *Mathematical Biosciences, 13* (1972), 133–137.
39. Denholm, J. V. "Necessary Conditions for Maximum Yield in a Senescing Two-Phase Plant," *Journal of Theoretical Biology, 52* (1975), 251–254.
40. Doubleday, W. G. "Harvesting in Matrix Population Models," *Biometrics, 31* (1975), 189–200.
41. Eberhardt, L. L. "Similarity, Allometry, and Food Chains," *Journal Theoretical Biology, 24* (1969), 43–55.
42. Estabrook, G. F. "A Mathematical Model in Graph Theory for Biological Classification," *Journal of Theoretical Biology, 12* (1968), 297–310.
43. Estabrook, G. F., and Jespersen, D. C. "Strategy for a Predator Encountering a Model-Mimic System," *American Naturalist, 108* (1974), 443–457.
44. Feller, W. *An Introduction to Probability Theory and Its Applications, Volume 1* (Third Edition), Wiley, New York, 1968.
45. Felsenstein, J. "A Pain in the Torus: Some Difficulties with Models of Isolation by Distance," *American Naturalist, 109* (1975), 359–368.
46. Finn, J. T. "Measures of Ecosystem Structure and Function Derived from Analysis of Flows," *Journal of Theoretical Biology, 56* (1976), 363–380.
47. Fischer, R. A., and Miles, R. E. "The Role of Spatial Pattern in the Competition between Crop Plants and Weeds. A Theoretical Analysis," *Mathematical Biosciences, 18* (1973), 335–350.
48. Gaffney, P. M. "Competition Models," *American Naturalist, 109* (1975), 487–490.
49. Gallopín, G. C. "Structural Properties of Food Webs," in *Systems Analysis and Simulation in Ecology, Vol. II* (B. C. Pattern, Ed.), pp. 241–282. Academic Press, New York, 1972.
50. Getz, W. M. "Optimal Control of a Birth-and-Death Process Population Model," *Mathematical Biosciences, 23* (1975), 87–111.
51. Gillespie, J. "The Role of Environmental Grain in the Maintenance of Genetic Variation, *American Naturalist, 108* (1974), 831–836.
52. Goh, B. S. "Global Stability in Many Species Systems," *American Naturalist, 111* (1977), 135–143.
53. Goh, B. S., Leitmann, G., and Vincent, T. L. "Optimal Control of a Predator–Prey System," *Mathematical Biosciences, 19* (1974), 263–286.
54. Golubitsky, M., Keeler, E. B., and Rothschild, M. Convergence of the Age Structure: Applications of the Projective Metric," *Theoretical Population Biology, 7* (1975), 84–93.
55. Gopalsamy, K. "Urban Air Pollution—A Diffusion Equation Model," *Mathematical Biosciences, 24* (1975), 239–246.
56. Haberman, R. *Mathematical Models: Mechanical Vibrations, Population Dynamics, and Traffic Flow*, Prentice-Hall, Englewood Cliffs, New Jersey, 1977.
57. Haight, J. "Game Theory and Evolution," *Advances in Applied Probability, 7* (1975), 8–11.
58. Hamilton, W. D. "Geometry for the Selfish Herd," *Journal of Theoretical Biology, 31* (1971), 295–311.
59. Hannon, B. "The Structure of Ecosystems," *Journal of Theoretical Biology, 41* (1973), 535–546.
60. Harary, F. "Who Eats Whom," *General Systems, 6* (1961), 41–44.
61. Heaney, J. and Sheikh, H. "Game Theoretic Approach to Equitable Regional

Environmental Quality Management," in *Mathematical Anaylsis of Decision Problems in Ecology* (A. Charnes and W. R. Lynn, eds.), pp. 85–115. Springer-Verlag, Berlin, 1975.
62. Holgate, P. "Population Survival and Life History Phenomena," *Journal of Theoretical Biology, 14* (1967), 1–10.
63. Howland, H. C. "Optimal Strategies for Predator Avoidance: The Relative Importance of Speed and Manoeuverability," *Journal of Theoretical Biology, 47* (1974), 333–350.
64. Hubbell, S. P. "Populations and Simple Food Webs as Energy Filters. I. One-species Systems," *American Naturalist 107* (1973), 94–121. "II. Two-Species Systems," *American Naturalist, 107* (1973), 122–151.
65. Hurlbert, S. H. "The Nonconcept of Species Diversity: A Critique and Alternative Parameters," *Ecology, 52* (1971), 577–586.
66. Jeffries, C. "Qualitative Stability and Digraphs in Model Ecosystems," *Ecology, 55* (1974), 1415–1419.
67. Jeffries, C. "Stability of Ecosystems with Complex Food Webs," *Theoretical Population Biology, 7* (1975), 149–155.
68. Jennrich, R. I., and Turner, F. B. "Measurement of Noncircular Home Range," *Journal of Theoretical Biology, 22* (1969), 227–237.
69. Johnson, P. G. and Brown, G. H. "A Comparison of the Relative Fitness of Genotypes Segregating for the t^{w2} Allele in Laboratory Stock and Its Possible Effect on Gene Frequency," *American Naturalist, 103* (1969), 5–21.
70. Jokl, M. "Some Natural Laws about Harmful Agents in the Human Environment," *Journal of Theoretical Biology, 48* (1974), 1–9.
71. Karlin, S. "Rates of Approach of Homozygosity for Finite Stochastic Models with Variable Population Size," *American Naturalist, 102* (1968), 443–455.
72. Kerfoot, W. B. "Bioenergetics of Vertical Migration," *American Naturalist, 104* (1970), 529–546.
73. King, C. E., Gallaher, E. E., and Levin, D. A. "Equilibrium Diversity in Plant–Pollinator Systems," *Journal of Theoretical Biology, 53* (1975), 262–275.
74. Leslie, P. H. "On the Use of Matrices in Certain Population Mathematics," *Biometrika, 33* (1945), 183–212.
75. Leslie, P. H. "The Properties of a Certain Lag-Type of Population Growth and the Influence of an External Random Factor on a Number of Such Populations," *Physiological Zoology, 32* (1959), 151–159.
76. Levine, S. "Optimal Allocation of Time in Resource Harvesting," *Mathematical Biosciences, 20* (1974), 171–178.
77. Levins, R. "Theory of Fitness in a Heterogeneous Environment, III: The Response to Selection," *Journal of Theoretical Biology, 7* (1964), 224–240.
78. Lewis, E. G. "On the Generation and Growth of a Population," *Sankhya, 6* (1942), 93–96.
79. Lewontin, R. C. "Evolution and the Theory of Games," *Journal of Theoretical Biology, 1* (1961), 382–403.
80. Lillestøl, J. "Pedigree Probability Calculus by Means of Linear Operators," *Theoretical Population Biology, 2* (1971), 328–338.
81. Lipnowski, I. F. "An Input–Output Analysis of Environmental Preservation," *Journal of Environmental Economics and Management, 3* (1976), 205–214.
82. Litt, F. X., and Smet, H. "Optimal Pollution Control of a Lake," in *Optimization Techniques: Modeling and Optimization in the Service of Man, Part 1* (J. Cea, Ed.), pp. 315–330. Springer-Verlag, Berlin, 1976.
83. Longuet-Higgins, M. S. "On the Shannon–Weaver Index of Diversity in Relation to the Distribution of Species in Bird Censuses," *Theoretical Population Biology, 2* (1971), 271–289.
84. MacQueen, J., and Scott, T., Editors, *The Oxford Book of Scottish Verse*,

Clarendon Press, Oxford, 1966.
85. Mann, S. H. "Mathematical Models for the Control of Pest Populations," *Biometrics*, *27* (1971), 357–368.
86. Marchi, E. and Hansell, R. I. "A Framework for Systematic Zoological Studies with Game Theory," *Mathematical Biosciences*, *16* (1973), 31–58.
87. Mathai, A. M., and Davis, T. A. "Constructing the Sunflower Head," *Mathematical Biosciences*, *20* (1974), 117–133.
88. May, R. M. "On Relationships Among Various Types of Population Models," *American Naturalist*, *107* (1973), 46–57.
89. May, R. M. *Stability and Complexity in Model Ecosystems*, Princeton University Press, Princeton, 1973.
90. May, R. M. "Qualitative Stability in Model Ecosystems," *Ecology*, *54* (1973), 638–641.
91. Maynard Smith, J. "The Theory of Games and the Evolution of Animal Conflicts," *Journal of Theoretical Biology*, *47* (1974), 209–221.
92. Maynard Smith, J. "Evolution and the Theory of Games," *American Scientist*, *64* (1976), 41–45.
93. Maynard Smith, J., and Parker, G. A. "The Logic of Asymmetric Contests," *Animal Behavior*, *24* (1976), 159–175.
94. Maynard Smith, J., and Price, G. R. "The Logic of Animal Conflict, *Nature*, *246* (1973), 15–18.
95. McLay, C. "A Theory Concerning the Distance Traveled by Animals Entering the Drift of a Stream," *Journal of Fisheries Research Board of Canada*, *27* (1970), 359–370.
96. Mendelssohn, R. "Optimization Problems Associated with a Leslie Matrix," *American Naturalist*, *110* (1976), 339–349.
97. Mertz, D. B. "The Mathematical Demography of the California Condor Population," *American Naturalist*, *105* (1971), 437–453.
98. Milne, A. "On a Theory of Natural Control of Insect Populations," *Journal of Theoretical Biology*, *3* (1962), 19–50.
99. Mitchell, R. "A Model Accounting for Sympatry in Water Mites," *American Naturalist*, *103* (1969), 331–346.
100. Mobley, C. D. "A Systematic Approach to Ecosystem Analysis," *Journal of Theoretical Biology*, *42* (1973), 119–136.
101. Namkoong, G., and Roberds, J. H. "Extinction Probabilities and the Changing Age Structure of Redwood Forests," *American Naturalist*, *108* (1974), 355–368.
102. Oaten, A., and Murdoch, W. W. "Switching, Functional Response, and Stability in Predator–Prey Systems," *American Naturalist*, *109* (1975), 299–318.
103. O'Callaghan, M., and Fisher, N. I. "A Stochastic Model for the Development and Immunological Control of a Class of Parasites of Sheep," *Mathematical Biosciences*, *19* (1974), 287–297.
104. Oster, G. "Modeling Social Insect Populations. I. Economics of Foraging and Population Growth in Bumblebees," *American Naturalist*, *110* (1976), 215–245.
105. Oster, G., and Heinrich, B. "Why Do Bumblebees Major? A Mathematical Model," *Ecological Monographs*, *46* (1976), 129–133.
106. Paloheimo, J. E. "A Stochastic Theory of Search: Implications for Predator–Prey Situations," *Mathematical Biosciences*, *12* (1971), 105–132.
107. Paltridge, G. W., and Denholm, J. V. "Plant Yield and Switch from Vegetative to Reproductive Growth," *Journal of Theoretical Biology*, *44* (1974), 23–34.
108. Parks, J. R. "A Stochastic Model of Animal Growth," *Journal of Theoretical Biology*, *42* (1973), 505–518.
109. Parrish, J. D., and Saila, S. B. "Interspecific Competition, Predation, and Species Diversity," *Journal of Theoretical Biology*, *27* (1970), 207–220.
110. Pattern, B. C. (Editor). *Systems Analysis and Simulation in Ecology*, *Volume II*,

Academic Press, New York, 1972.

111. Patten, B. C. "Ecosystem Linearization: An Evolutionary Design Problem," *American Naturalist*, *109* (1975), 529–539.
112. Pella, J. J. "A Stochastic Model for Purse Seining in a Two-Species Fishery," *Journal of Theoretical Biology*, *22* (1969), 209–226.
113. Pennycuick, C. J. *et al.* "A Computer Model for Simulating the Growth of a Population, or of Two Interacting Populations," *Journal of Theoretical Biology*, *18* (1968), 316–329.
114. Phillips, O. M. "The Equilibrium and Stability of Simple Marine Biological Systems. I. Primary Nutrient Consumers," *American Naturalist*, *107* (1973), 73–93.
115. Pielou, E. C. *Introduction to Mathematical Ecology*, Wiley-Interscience, New York, 1969.
116. Pulliam, H. R. "On the Advantages of Flocking," *Journal of Theoretical Biology*, *38* (1973), 419–422.
117. Pulliam, H. R. "On the Theory of Optimal Diets," *American Naturalist*, *108* (1974), 59–74.
118. Rapoport, A. "Uses of Game–Theoretic Models in Biology," *General Systems*, *20* (1975), 49–58.
119. Rapport, D. J., and Turner, J. E. "Determination of Predator Food Preferences," *Journal of Theoretical Biology*, *26* (1970), 365–372.
120. Rapport, D. J., and Turner, J. E. "Predator–Prey Interactions in Natural Communities," *Journal of Theoretical Biology*, *51* (1975), 169–180.
121. Rapport, D. J., and Turner, J. E. "Feeding Rates and Population Growth," *Ecology*, *56* (1975), 942–949.
122. Roberts, F. S. *Discrete Mathematical Models: With Applications to Social, Biological, and Environmental Problems*, Prentice-Hall, Englewood Cliffs, New Jersey, 1976.
123. Roberts, F. S., and Brown, T. A. "Signed Digraphs and the Energy Crisis," *American Mathematical Monthly*, *82* (1975), 577–594.
124. Rosensweig, M. L. "Exploitation in Three Trophic Levels," *American Naturalist*, *107* (1973), 275–294.
125. Ross, G. G. "A Difference-Differential Model in Population Dynamics," *Journal of Theoretical Biology*, *37* (1972), 477–492.
126. Saila, S. B. "Systems Analysis Applied to Some Fisheries Problems," in *System Analysis and Simulation in Ecology, Volume II* (B. C. Patten, ed.), pp. 331–372. Academic Press, New York, 1972.
127. Sancho, N. G. F., and Mitchell, C. "Economic Optimization in Controlled Fisheries," *Mathematical Biosciences*, *27* (1975), 1–9.
128. Saunders, P. T., and Bazin, M. J. "On the Stability of Food Chains," *Journal of Theoretical Biology*, *52* (1975), 121–142.
129. Shoemaker, C. "Optimization of Agricultural Pest Management I: Biological and Mathematical Background," *Mathematical Biosciences*, *16* (1973), 143–175.
130. Shoemaker, C. "Optimization of Agricultural Pest Management III: Results and Extensions of a Model," *Mathematical Biosciences*, *18* (1973), 1–22.
131. Shugart, H. H., Jr., and Patten, B. C. "Niche Quantification and the Concept of Niche Pattern," in *Systems Analysis and Simulation in Ecology, Volume II* (B. C. Patten, ed.), pp. 283–327. Academic Press, New York, 1972.
132. Skellam, J. G. "The Mathematical Foundations Underlying the Use of Line Transects in Animal Ecology," *Biometrics*, *14* (1958), 385–400.
133. Slobodkin, L. B., and Rapoport, A. "An Optimal Strategy of Evolution," *Quarterly Review of Biology*, *49* (1974), 179–200.
134. Sneath, P. H. A. "Trend-Surface Analysis of Transportation Grids," *Journal of Zoology*, *151* (1967), 65–122.

135. Straw, R. M. "A Markov Model for Pollinator Constancy and Competition," *American Naturalist*, *106* (1972), 597–620.
136. Strobeck, C. "*n* Species Competition," *Ecology*, *54* (1973), 650–654.
137. Sykes, Z. M. "On Discrete Stable Population Theory," *Biometrics*, *25* (1969), 285–293.
138. Tallis, G. M., and Leyton, M. "A Stochastic Approach to the Study of Parasite Populations," *Journal of Theoretical Biology*, *13* (1966), 251–260.
139. Taylor, H. M. *et al.* "Natural Selection of Life History Attributes," *Theoretical Population Biology*, *5* (1974), 104–122.
140. Taylor, R. J. "Value of Cumping to Prey and the Evolutionary Response of Ambush Predators," *American Naturalist*, *110* (1976), 13–29.
141. Thompson, W. A., and Vertinsky, I. "Application of Markov Chains to an Analysis of a Simulation of Birds' Foraging," *Journal of Theoretical Biology*, *53* (1975), 285–307.
142. Usher, M. B. "A Matrix Approach to the Management of Renewable Resources, with Special Reference to Selection Forests," *Journal of Applied Ecology*, *3* (1966), 355–367.
143. Usher, M. B. "Developments in the Leslie Matrix Model," in *Mathematical Models in Ecology* (J. N. R. Jeffers, ed.), pp. 29–60. Blackwell Scientific Publications, Oxford, 1972.
144. Vandermeer, J. H. "The Community Matrix and the Number of Species in a Community," *American Naturalist*, *104* (1970), 73–83.
145. Vandermeer, J. H. "On the Regional Stabilization of Locally Unstable Predator–Prey Relationships," *Journal of Theoretical Biology*, *41* (1973), 161–170.
146. Verhoff, F. H., and Smith, F. E. "Theoretical Analysis of a Conserved Nutrient Ecosystem," *Journal of Theoretical Biology*, *33* (1971), 131–147.
147. Viscusi, W. K., and Zeckhauser, R. "Environmental Policy Choice under Uncertainty," *Journal of Environmental Economics and Management*, *3* (1976), 97–112.
148. Waldron, M. G. "Competition Models," *American Naturalist*, *109* (1975), 487–489.
149. Wickwire, K. "Mathematical Models for the Control of Pests and Infectious Diseases: A Survey," *Theoretical Population Biology*, *11* (1977), 182–238.
150. Wilbur, H. M. "Propagule Size, Number and Dispersal Pattern in *Ambystoma* and *Asclepias*," *American Naturalist*, *111* (1977), 43–68.
151. Williamson, J. A., and Charlesworth, B. "The Effect of Age of Founder on the Propability of Survival of a Colony," *Journal of Theoretical Biology*, *56* (1976), 175–190.
152. Williamson, M. *The Analysis of Biological Populations*, Edward Arnold Ltd., London, 1972.
153. Moore, P. G. "Spacing in Plant Populations," *Ecology*, *35* (1954), 222–227.

CHAPTER 8

How To Ask Sensitive Questions without Getting Punched in the Nose

John C. Maceli*

1. Introduction

Do you regularly smoke pot? Have you ever had a homosexual experience? Are you a Communist? Do you cheat on your income tax? A "yes" answer to any of the preceding questions may be embarrassing to an individual. In fact, many people would become irate at being asked one of these questions and might well refuse to answer. Some would feel that such matters were personal or confidential and no one's business but their own. However, such questions may be other people's business. For example, consider the case in the armed forces where military officials are interested in estimating the percentage of military men using hard drugs. Based on this estimate they will decide whether or not there is a need to expand the drug rehabilitation program. The officials will need to interview the men about their use of drugs and must be equipped with methods that will elicit truthful answers to sensitive or personal questions about drug use.

All of the classical methods of estimating parameters for human populations are based on the assumption that people will answer the questions asked and also will answer them truthfully. In general, provided the questions deal with nonsensitive or nonembarrassing areas, most people will answer truthfully. But when the questions are of a sensitive or embarrassing type nonresponse is likely.

The randomized response method presents a way to reassure a person being questioned that there is no way the interviewer can figure out what his answer was, although the interviewer can estimate the percentage of

* Department of Mathematics, Ithaca College, Ithaca, New York 14850.

people answering "yes" or falling into a particular category for the population under consideration. Before presenting the method, a few elementary definitions of statistical terms will be given.

2. Definitions

Statistical inference may be defined as a collection of methods by which we make inferences about a population based on information gained from a sample. A *population* is the set of all possible observations of some characteristic of interest. A *sample* is a portion or subset of a population. If a sample of size n is drawn from a population of size N in such a way that every possible sample of size n has the same chance of being selected, the sampling procedure is called *simple random sampling*. The sample thus obtained is called a *simple random sample*. A numerical value that gives some information about a population is called a *population parameter*. For example, suppose one wishes to study the grade point average (GPA) of accounting majors attending a certain college. The set of GPAs for all the accounting majors is the population, and the set of GPAs of all junior accounting majors constitutes a sample. The highest GPA among all accounting majors and the average GPA for all accounting majors are two examples of population parameters.

An important type of problem that statisticians study is the estimation of population parameters based on data gathered from a sample. In the above example we could estimate the average GPA for all accounting majors based on the GPAs of the junior accounting majors. In general, the average GPA for these junior accounting majors will differ from the average GPA for all accounting majors. This is due to the fact that the GPAs of the junior accounting majors represent only a portion of the population. The difference between the average GPA for all junior accounting majors and the average GPA for all accounting majors is an example of a sampling error. Although statisticians are interested in studying ways to reduce sampling errors, we shall not be concerned with sampling errors in this paper. A second kind of problem that arises when one is surveying human populations is that nonsampling errors such as nonresponse and untruthful response also occur. The randomized response method is a way to try to reduce these nonsampling errors.

3. The Randomized Response Method

When an interviewer is conducting a survey dealing with questions of a sensitive nature and meets resistance, he will naturally make an extra effort to gain the confidence of the interviewee. If the questions are not too sensitive, this confidence might increase cooperation. However, there are many subject areas that people are touchy about.

Warner [17] suggests the randomized response method as another method for increasing cooperation. This method is based on the idea that the less revealing answers to questions are, the better the cooperation will be. This is accomplished by having the interviewee respond with answers that furnish information only on a probability basis. Warner applied this method to the estimation of a population proportion.

We now present a more detailed explanation of the randomized response method. Suppose that we wish to estimate the proportion of a population possessing a certain sensitive characteristic. Let us designate those people possessing this characteristic as Group A. Also let π be the proportion of the population belonging to Group A. The objective of the randomized response method is to estimate π without asking a person *directly* whether or not he belongs to Group A. To accomplish this, the interviewer is furnished with a randomization device consisting of a deck of cards that are identical except that a *known* fraction P is marked with the number 1 and the remaining fraction $1 - P$ is marked with the number 2.

The interviewer chooses a simple random sample of size n from the population. The following procedure is repeated with each of the n people chosen in the sample. An interviewee is instructed to choose a card at random from the full deck (which has been well-shuffled) and note the number appearing on the card. The number chosen is *not* shown to the interviewer. The interviewee is now shown the two statements:

Statement 1: I am a member of Group A.

Statement 2: I am not a member of Group A.

He is then asked to respond to the statement that corresponds to the number he has chosen. That is, if the interviewee has chosen a card marked 1, he responds "yes" or "no" to indicate if statement 1 is true or false in his case. Similarly, if the interviewee has chosen a card marked 2, he responds "yes" or "no" to signify whether statement 2 is true or false. Note that the interviewer receives only "yes" and "no" answers; he does not know which statement the interviewee is responding to. However, even while knowing only the number of "yes" answers he can estimate π.

Let us introduce the following notation:

π = proportion of the population belonging to Group A.

$1 - \pi$ = proportion of the population not belonging to Group A.

P = probability that a card with number 1 is chosen.

$1 - P$ = probability that a card with number 2 is chosen.

λ = probability of a "yes" response.

m = number of "yes" responses.

n = size of sample.

Using the addition and multiplication theorems from probability theory, we can write the probability that the interviewer gets a "yes" response in the following way:

$$\begin{aligned} P(\text{“yes” response}) &= P(\text{card marked 1 chosen and “yes” answer reported}) \\ &\quad + P(\text{card marked 2 chosen and “yes” answer reported}) \\ &= P(\text{card marked 1 chosen})P(\text{“yes” answer} \mid \text{card marked 1 chosen}) \\ &\quad + P(\text{card marked 2 chosen})P(\text{“yes” answer} \mid \text{card marked 2 chosen}). \end{aligned}$$

Using the above notation, we have

$$\lambda = P\pi + (1 - P)(1 - \pi). \tag{1}$$

To estimate π, we first estimate λ by the sample proportion of "yes" responses $\hat{\lambda}$. In our case $\hat{\lambda} = m/n$. Substituting $\hat{\lambda}$ for λ and solving for π in Eq. (1) yields the estimate $\hat{\pi}$, where

$$\hat{\pi} = \frac{1}{2P - 1}\left[P - 1 + \frac{m}{n}\right], \quad P \neq \frac{1}{2}. \tag{2}$$

Before listing some properties of the randomized response model we shall consider an example.

Example 1. A study is to be designed to estimate the proportion of seniors in a college who have cheated on a final examination some time during their college careers. It is reasonable to assume that most students would not willingly admit cheating and, therefore, using the randomized response method is appropriate. The interviewer chooses a simple random sample of 200 students from the senior class of a college. The randomization deck is composed of cards 3/4 of which are marked 1 and 1/4 of which are marked 2. Each interviewee is shown the two statements:

Statement 1: I have cheated on a final examination during my college career.

Statement 2: I have not cheated on a final examination during my college career.

The interviewee is then asked to choose a card at random from the deck, read the statement that corresponds to the number he drew, and respond "yes" or "no." Repeating this with each of the 200 seniors in the sample, the interviewer receives a total of 60 "yes" answers. Using Eq. (2), we estimate the proportion of seniors who have cheated on final examinations by

$$\hat{\pi} = \frac{1}{2\left(\frac{3}{4}\right) - 1}\left[\left(\frac{3}{4} - 1\right) + \frac{60}{200}\right]$$
$$= 2[-0.25 + 0.3] = 0.1.$$

So we estimate that 10% of the seniors at the college have cheated on a final examination during their careers.

The randomized response method does not permit interpretation of *individual* responses. In fact, there is no way an interviewer can determine what statement a particular interviewee responded to. Provided the interviewees are convinced of this fact, it follows that cooperation should increase.

The interviewee is not directly asked whether he possesses the sensitive characteristic. He is asked for something less than absolute information. How much he is asked for depends on the value of P in the randomization device. A value of $P = 1/2$ gives no information since Eq. (2) is undefined for this value, whereas a value of $P = 1$ or $P = 0$ gives full information and is equivalent to direct questioning. For P values between 1/2 and 1 (or between 0 and 1/2), the person provides useful but not absolute information as to whether or not he belongs to Group A.

Warner shows that, under the assumption that the "yes" and "no" responses are made truthfully, $\hat{\pi}$ is an unbiased estimate of the true population proportion π. The variance of $\hat{\pi}$ is given by

$$\operatorname{Var}\hat{\pi} = \frac{\pi(1-\pi)}{n} + \frac{P(1-P)}{n(2P-1)^2}. \tag{3}$$

Using these ideas, one can also establish confidence intervals for π. Warner also compares the randomized estimates and direct question estimates under the assumption that the direct question estimates are hampered by less than 100% truthfulness. He shows that the randomized response method is apt to outperform the regular method (direct questioning) in a variety of situations. More precisely, he compares the mean–square errors of the randomized and regular (direct questioning) methods of estimation under the assumption that the interviewed individuals tell the truth in the randomized method but only tell the truth in the regular method with probabilities given by T_1 and T_2. (T_1 = probability that a member of Group A tells the truth in the regular method, and T_2 = probability that a member not in Group A tells the truth in the regular method.) He concluded that for a variety of values of π, P, T_1, and T_2 the mean-square error of the randomized response method was smaller than the mean-square error of the regular method.

4. Unrelated Question Model

Both statements in the Warner method make reference to the sensitive characteristic, a fact which may cause people to be wary of the method and not cooperate as fully as possible. Simmons [10] presents a modification of the Warner method, which he felt would further increase cooperation. This model, called the unrelated question model, is based on the idea that if one of the statements or questions is of an innocuous type people would be more secure in their feeling that they really are not revealing much when they give an answer. That is, a person's confidence in the anonymity of the method would be increased if two unrelated questions were used, one pertaining to the sensitive characteristic and the other to a nonsensitive condition.

In Simmons' model, each interviewee randomly chooses and answers one of the following questions:

Question 1: Are you a member of Group A?

Question 2: Are you a member of Group B?

Group A again represents those people possessing the sensitive characteristic. Group B is chosen in such a way to be *a* nonsensitive or harmless group. Note that membership in Group A does not preclude membership in Group B and vice versa. A person may belong to neither, one, or both groups. Group B should be chosen so that the proportion of the population belonging to it is known. Some possible choices for Question 2 might be:

Question 2a: Were you born in April?

Question 2b: Is the last digit of your ID number odd?

Question 2c: Were you born on one of the following days of the month: 1st, 2nd, 3rd, 4th, 5th, 6th, 7th, 8th, 9th, or 10th?

Each of these questions has the property that either the proportion of the population belonging to Group B is known or else can be estimated before the survey begins. For example, the proportion of people born in April could be estimated from census data; the proportion of people having ID numbers with odd last digits should be one-half.

The unrelated question model proceeds as follows. A simple random sample of size n is chosen from the population. The interviewer has the same randomization device as in the Warner model. Each interviewee chooses a card at random from the full deck (which has been well-shuffled) and responds to the question corresponding to the number he has chosen. Again, the interviewer only receives "yes" and "no" answers. However, he can estimate π using the data.

Once again we can use elementary results from probability theory to write

$$\lambda = P\pi + (1 - P)\pi_B, \tag{4}$$

where λ is the probability of a "yes" response, π is the probability of membership in the Group A, π_B is the probability of membership in Group B, and P is the probability that the sensitive question (i.e., question 1) is chosen. Under the assumption π_B is known we can estimate π. Letting m be the number of "yes" responses in the sample of size n, we can estimate λ by $\hat{\lambda} = m/n$, and solve for π in Eq. (4). This yields the estimate $\hat{\pi}$, where

$$\hat{\pi} = \frac{1}{P}\left[(P - 1)\pi_B + \frac{m}{n}\right], \quad P > 0. \tag{5}$$

We shall first present an example using the unrelated question model and then list some of the properties of this model.

Example 2. We wish to estimate π, the proportion of female students at a college who have had a homosexual experience. Most women would no doubt feel this topic is personal and would be reluctant to answer questions about their sexual activities. Hence, we shall derive an estimate for π using the unrelated question model. The interviewees are presented with the following questions:

Question 1: Have you ever had a homosexual experience?

Question 2: Is the last digit of your ID number even?

The randomization device is again the deck of cards with 3/4 marked 1 and 1/4 marked 2. A simple random sample of size 100 is taken and the interviewer gets 18 "yes" answers. In this case π_B equals 1/2. The estimate π given by Eq. (5) is equal to

$$\frac{1}{3/4}\left[\left(\frac{3}{4} - 1\right)\frac{1}{2} + \frac{18}{100}\right] = 0.073.$$

Therefore, we can estimate that about 7% of the female students at the college have had a homosexual experience.

The unrelated question model is similar to the randomized response model in that it does not permit interpretation of individual responses. However, an estimate of the proportion of population belonging to the sensitive groups can be calculated based on these individual responses. Once again the interviewer is completely ignorant of the question the interviewee has chosen. Therefore, cooperation should increase. We would also expect better cooperation from these people belonging to Group B because Group B is a nonsensitive group and people belonging to this group should be willing to answer truthfully. (This may not be the case in the Warner model where the two groups are complementary.)

We also note that Eq. (5) is defined for $P = 1/2$. Thus we may use randomization devices that lead to each question being chosen with equal probability. The use of $P = 1/2$ would seem to be another way to increase cooperation.

Abernathy *et al.* [1, 2], field tested the unrelated question model in a study of induced abortions in urban North Carolina. Estimates of the proportion of women having an induced abortion during 1968 are given. The authors make some interesting observations about the applicability of the unrelated question model. Along with the questions involving abortions that were handled by the unrelated question model, the women (2800 in number) were asked *directly* the following two questions:

(A) "If an interviewer, like myself, asked one of your friends if she had ever had an abortion, do you think that person would answer truthfully?"

(B) "Do you believe other people will think that there is a trick to the *box* and that we really can figure out which equation they answer?"

(The randomization device consisted of a box containing red and blue balls. The interviewee was asked to shake the box and note the color of the ball appearing in a window in the box. The color appearing determined the question to be answered.) Question (A) was asked before the use of the unrelated question model. Question (B) was asked immediately following its use.

In answer to the preliminary question, 67% reported "no," 17% reported "yes," and 16% were undecided. This indicates that alternate methods are needed for obtaining data in this sensitive area. Regarding the question after the administration, 20% responded "yes," 60% "no," and 20% were still undecided. This shows a remarkable degree of faith in the unrelated question model.

Greenberg *et al.* [9] study the theoretical framework of the unrelated question model. In this paper they show that when π_B is known, Eq. (5) gives an unbiased estimate for π with

$$\operatorname{Var} \hat{\pi} = \frac{\lambda(1 - \lambda)}{nP^2}. \tag{6}$$

Using these ideas one can now calculate confidence intervals for π.

This paper also suggests that the unrelated question model is more efficient than the randomized response method in the sense that the variance of the unrelated question model is smaller than the variance of the randomized response method. Dowling and Shachtman [6] show that this is the case, uniformly in π and π_B, provided P is chosen to be greater than one-third.

It should be noted that it is possible for both models to give estimates that are either negative or greater than one. However, this possibility is small for large samples (Warner [17]). For a discussion on how the estimates may be modified see Devore [5], and Pearl [16].

5. Using the Randomized Response Method and the Unrelated Question Model

The design of sample surveys deals with many different activities. These activities include the preparation needed to start the survey, the administration of the survey, the processing of the data collected, and finally the interpretation of the data. This module is concerned with a small but important part of the design of sample surveys. We have been concerned with methods that will lead to an increase in cooperation on the part of the people interviewed. In this section we shall present a few brief observations on the use of the randomized response method and the unrelated question model in actual surveys.

The first comment deals with the interviewer himself. It is very important that the interviewer fully understands how the method works and is able to explain the rationale behind its use to the interviewee. This understanding should allow the interviewer to instill in the interviewee the feeling that there is no way anyone can figure out what question he answered. This feeling should naturally lead to an increase in cooperation.

The next area concerns the randomization device. The device should be kept as simple as possible. The interviewee should be allowed to inspect the device before the experiment is begun. This inspection should result in two things: one, the interviewee's assurance that there is no trick involved in the device; and two, the interviewer's confidence that the interviewee understands how to use the device.

Another major concern is the wording of the questions. It is very important that the interviewer makes sure the interviewee understands what the questions ask for. As an illustration, consider Example 2 on p. 175. Question 1 deals with homosexuality. What the phrase "had a homosexual experience" means should be made clear to the interviewee. We should also note that illiteracy is a major problem that must be overcome if one wishes to use these methods.

One final comment concerns the choice of the innocuous question in the unrelated question model. Some questions, although innocuous, may not lead to increased cooperation. For example, suppose the choice for the question is "Were you born in New England?" The interviewer may be able to tell by a person's accent whether he belongs to this group. Using this fact and the person's answer to the randomly selected question, the interviewer may be able to tell whether the person belongs to the sensitive group. Thus we are reminded that the innocuous question should be chosen with care.

The final section of this module deals with a few suggestions on how the randomized response can be used in the classroom.

6. Classroom Suggestions

The best way to use this module is to conduct a survey in your class, one that deals with a sensitive subject. Today, there are many such topics of interest to college students. Many get very interested in studying statistics when they find out that statistical methods can allow them to get honest answers to questions dealing with such sensitive topics. The following quote from Campbell and Joiner [4] seems to sum up very well the general attitude of students when they see randomized response methods in action:

> "But Dr. X, how can you tell how many of us smoke pot, without even knowing which of us, if any, answered your question? If statistics can do *that*, I might even get interested enough to learn some statistics for myself!"

Because of this increase in interest, we feel that the survey using the randomized response method should be done during the early part of the term.

The actual survey can be done using very little class time. Class periods do not lend themselves very well to having the instructor privately interview each member of the class. Thus the instructor should choose a randomization device such that all can use it simultaneously. Such devices are easily available to students. For example, most statistics students have a table of random numbers handy and these numbers can be used for the randomization device. The survey can now be performed on the whole class at the same time. The instructor writes the two questions on the board and instructs the students to choose a two-digit random number. Those choosing a number less than 75 answer question 1; otherwise a student answers question 2. The instructor asks all the students who answered "yes" to raise their hands. The estimate can now be calculated based on this hand count. It is useful to see how close the estimate came to the true value. This can be accomplished by having the students answer (in some anonymous way) the sensitive question directly.

Another interesting usage is to have students conduct their own surveys using the randomized response method. In order to do this, the students obviously must understand how the method works. Thus they will have to have a background in basic probability and elementary sampling theory.

Students with more probability background can discuss the models at a higher mathematical level. For example, one may see what happens to these models as n gets large. Also the variances of the estimates can be compared for different values of n, P, π and π_B.

The next section contains some problems relating to these randomized response models. A form that the author has used to conduct a randomized response survey is given in the appendix.

7. Complements and Problems

1. The Alcoholics Anonymous chapter in a large city wishes to determine the proportion of its members who have had at least one alcoholic drink during the past week. Most members would not be willing to admit having had a drink so we decide to use the randomized response method. The randomization device consists of a deck of cards containing 0.8 marked with a 1 and 0.2 marked with a 2. The statements are

   Statement 1: I have had at least one alcoholic drink during the past week.

   Statement 2: I have not had anything alcoholic to drink during the past week.

   Out of a random sample of 100 members the interviewer receives 35 "yes" answers. Using these data, estimate the proportion of the chapter that have had at least one alcoholic drink during the past week.

2. (Continuation of Problem 1.) Find a 95% confidence interval for π, the proportion of members who have had at least one drink during the past week. [Hint: Use the fact that for large n, $\hat{\pi}$ has an approximate normal distribution with mean π and variance given by Eq. (3). Note we can estimate the variance of $\hat{\pi}$ by replacing π by $\hat{\pi}$ in Eq. (3).]

3. The manager of a large department store wishes to estimate the proportion of employees who are unhappy in their job. He decides to employ the unrelated question model using the following questions:

   Question 1: Are you unhappy with your job?

   Question 2: Is the last digit of your Social Security number odd?

   A fair coin is used as a randomization device. The employee tosses the coin and if "heads" is obtained, answers question 1, if the result is "tails", he answers question 2. The manager takes a random sample of size 300 and receives 100 "yes" answers. Estimate the proportion of employees at this department store who are unhappy in their job.

The following problems are more advanced. A calculus-based statistics course is sufficient for their solution.

Both of the models presented in this module can be related to the binomial distribution. If we sample with replacement or assume that the size of the sample is small compared to the size of the population, then we can assume that the number of "yes" answers in the sample of size n has a binomial distribution. More precisely, the number of "yes" answers follows a binomial distribution with parameters n and λ (where λ = probability of a "yes" response). Using this information, we can study the models in more detail.

4. In the Warner model, show that $\hat{\pi}$ is an unbiased estimate of π. That is, show $E(\hat{\pi}) = \pi$. [Hint: $E(\hat{\lambda}) = \lambda$.]

5. (Continuation of Problem 4.) Show that the variance of $\hat{\pi}$ is given by Eq. (3). [Hint: $\text{var}(\hat{\lambda}) = \lambda(1 - \lambda)/n$.]

6. (a) Using the results of Problem 5, show that the variance of $\hat{\pi}$ can be written as the sum of the variance of the direct question model and a term corresponding to the randomization procedure. Note: In the direct question model we estimate π by X/n, where X is the number of "yes" answers and n is the size of the sample. Using the binomial distribution, we find $E(X/n) = \pi$ and $\text{var}(X/n) = \pi(1 - \pi)/n$.
   (b) Explain why we should not use the randomized response method if the direct question model is applicable (i.e., people are willing to answer truthfully).

7. Let $\hat{\theta}$ be an estimate of θ. *Definition.* The error of the estimate $\hat{\theta}$ is given by $2\sqrt{\text{var}\,\hat{\theta}}$. Compare the direct question method and the randomized response method with respect to the sample size needed to ensure a given bound for the error of estimate. Consider the special case where $\pi = 0.5$, $P = 3/4$, and we want our estimate to be within 0.05 of the true value. That is, find the required sample size for the direct question method and for the randomized response method.

8. Show that in the unrelated question model, $\hat{\pi}$ is unbiased.

9. Assuming the binomial model is applicable, one easily can find confidence intervals for λ based on the statistic $\hat{\lambda}$. Since $\hat{\pi}$ is a linear function of $\hat{\lambda}$, one can arrive at confidence interval for π by algebraic manipulation. Find a 95% confidence interval for π, where π = proportion of people unhappy in their job (cf. Problem 3).

Appendix: Randomized Response Survey

Think of the last digit of your Social Security number. (If you do not know or do not have a Social Security number, think of the sixth digit of your home telephone number.) When the question is called for, answer

Question A if your number is 0, 1, 2, 3, 4, 5, or 6

Question B if your number is 7, 8, or 9.

Question A: Have you ever cheated on a college examination?

Question B: Is your number 7 or 8 (as opposed to 9)?

References

1. Abernathy, James R., Greenberg, Bernard G., and Horvitz, Daniel G. "Estimates of Induced Abortion in Urban North Carolina," *Demography*, 7 (1970), 19–29.
2. Abernathy, James R., Greenberg, Bernard G., and Horvitz, Daniel G. "A New Survey Technique and Its Application in the Field of Public Health," *Milbank Memorial Fund Quarterly*, *48*, Part 2 (October 1970), 39–55. These papers discuss the application of the random response technique in the estimation of the proportion of women which have had an abortion.
3. Abul–Ela, Abdel–Latif A., Greenberg, Bernard G., and Horvitz, Daniel G. "A

Multi-Proportions Randomized Response Model," *Journal of the American Statistical Association, 62* (September 1967), 990–1008. This paper extended Warner's model to the trichotomous case designed to estimate the proportions of three related, mutually exclusive groups, one or two of which possessed a sensitive characteristic. The model is further extended to estimate any j proportions ($j > 3$), when all the j group characteristics are mutually exclusive, with at least one and at most $j - 1$ of them sensitive.

4. Campbell, Cathy, and Joiner, Brian L. "How to Get the Answer without Being Sure You've Asked the Question," *The American Statistician, 27* (December 73), 229–231. This paper presents a detailed history of the development of the Randomized Response technique. Some useful teaching suggestions are also presented.
5. Devore, Jay L. "Estimating A Population Proportion Using Randomized Responses," *Mathematics Magazine, 52* (January 79), 38–40. This paper discusses how the Warner estimate can be modified to become a maximum likelihood estimate.
6. Dowling, T., Shachtman, A., and Richard, H. "On the Relative Efficiency of Randomized Response Model," *Journal of the American Statistical Association, 70* (March 75), 84–86.
7. Drogin, R., and Orkin, M. *Vital Statistics*, McGraw-Hill, New York, 1975. An elementary statistics text containing one chapter on randomized response technique.
8. Gerstel, E. K., Moore, Paul, Folsom, R. E., and King, D. A. "Mecklenburg County Drinking-Driving Attitude Survey, 1970," Technical Report prepared under contract No. FH-11-7538 for U.S. Department of Transportation by Research Triangle Institute, Research Triangle Park, North Carolina. This paper uses the random response technique in conducting a drinking-driving attitude survey. Comparisons are made between randomized response and direct question responses.
9. Greenberg, Bernard G., Abul–Ela, Abdel–Latif, A., Simmons, Walt R., and Horvitz, Daniel G. "The Unrelated Question Randomized Response Model: Theoretical Framework," *Journal of the American Statistical Association, 64* (June 1969), 520–539.
10. Horvitz, Daniel G., Shah, B. V., and Simmons, Walt R. "The Unrelated Question Randomized Response Model." *Proceedings of the Social Statistics Section, Washington, DC., American Statistical Association* (1967), 65–72. The papers describe a variation of the Warner technique known as the unrelated question model. The second paper also extends the unrelated question model to the case where there are more than two groups. This paper also discusses a way to build the unrelated question into the randomizing device.
11. Greenberg, Bernard G., Kuebler, Roy R., Jr., Abernathy, James R., and Horvitz, Daniel G. "Application of the Randomized Response Technique in Obtaining Quantitative Data," *Journal of the American Statistical Association, 66* (June 71), 243–250. This paper introduces a method by which the random response technique can be used to obtain quantitative data. These methods were used in the North Carolina abortion study to estimate the mean number of abortions obtained over a lifetime and also to estimate the mean income of heads of households.
12. Lanke, Jan. "On the Choice of the Unrelated Question in Simmons' Version of Raudomized Response," *Journal of the American Statistical Association, 70* (March 75), 80–83.
13. Liu, P. T. and Chow, L. P. "A New Discrete Quantitative Randomized Response Model," *Journal of the American Statistical Association, 71* (March 76), 72–73. This article presents a new model that can be used to obtain quantitative information. It has been shown that the procedures of administering the model are simple and that its efficiency of estimate is higher than the other currently available models.
14. Locander, William, Sudman, Seymour, and Bradburn, Norman. "An Investigation of Interview Method, Threat and Response Distortion," *Journal of the American Statistical Association, 71* (June 76), 269–274. This study examined the joint effects

of question threat and method of administration on response distortion using four interviewing techniques. Randomized response was shown to give the lowest distortion on questions about socially undesirable acts.
15. Mendenhall, W., Ott, L., and Scheaffer, R. *Elementary Survey Sampling*, Duxbury Press, California. A basic book on survey sampling. One section is spent on a discussion of the randomized response technique.
16. Pearl, Robin L., and Federer, Walter T. "Varying Levels of Probability for Selecting Sensitive Questions Using a Randomized Response Technique," *Proceedings of the Social Statistics Section, American Statistical Association*, 1975. This paper presents a discussion of how the estimates may be modified to ensure that the estimates are probabilities.
17. Warner, Stanley L. "Randomized Response: A Survey Technique for Eliminating Evasive Answer Bias," *Journal of the American Statistical Association*, *60* (1965), 63–69. This paper introduces the randomized response technique. Warner finds unbiased estimates and compares their mean-square error with the mean-square errors of conventional estimates under various assumptions about the underlying population.

Notes for the Instructor

Objective. The purpose of this module is to present an interesting method for estimating the proportion of a human population possessing some sensitive characteristic. Although the material is of a statistical nature, I believe it can be used in many basic mathematics courses.

Prerequisites. Elementary probability is needed to understand the development of the method. The required ideas from statistics can be presented along with the module.

Time. The basic material in this module can be covered in one class hour. More time can be spent in an upper level statistics course discussing some of the properties of the estimates.

CHAPTER 9

Measuring Power in Weighted Voting Systems

William F. Lucas*

1. Introduction

1.1. Weighted Voting

There are a large number of voting situations in which some individuals or blocs of voters effectively cast more ballots than others. Such weighted voting systems are found in governmental bodies such as the U.S. Congress, some state legislatures and county boards, in the Electoral College, in voting by stockholders in a corporation, in several university senates, in many other multimember electoral districts in which several representatives are elected at-large from a single district, as well as when strictly disciplined political parties vote as a single bloc.

A prime concern in designing such policy or decision-making assemblies usually is that they are fair and equitable in the sense that they give equal representation to their constituents. There have been many challenges in recent times against existing legislative bodies. There are frequent charges of undemocratic inequity, unfairness, disparities, bias, handicaps, debasement, denying, gross variances, impairment, prohibitions, expediency, malapportionment, disenfranchising, ambiguous and archaic systems, diluting and devaluating the vote, and "stuffing" the ballot boxes. The courts have frequently found deliberative and legislative bodies wanting, and have often

* School of Operations Research and Industrial Engineering, Cornell University. Ithaca, New York 14853.

ruled in favor of impartiality, equal protection, political justice, full participation and representation, the right of suffrage, and the principle of "one man-one vote" for all citizens.

1.2. Voting Power and Its Relation to Weights

Some proponents of weighted voting argue that such systems can be used to adjust for or to cancel out inequalities at another level, such as differences in the populations that various delegates represent. However, the fraction of the total number of votes which a representative possesses, or the number of members in a party is *not* generally synonymous with any meaningful measure of his or its voting power! The ability to cast more ballots does not in itself necessarily increase one's power nor does it do so in a directly proportional way. There may exist major discrepancies between the weights voters have and a good measure of their influences. It is fallacious to expect that one's voting power is directly proportional to the number of votes he can deliver. Yet many attempts to correct inequalities merely assign weights to a delegate proportional to the number of inhabitants he represents, and it is felt that this preserves some equality at the level of the individual citizens. Paradoxically, those who advocate that they are the main beneficiaries of the weighted systems such as the Electoral College are very often the ones most hurt by it in terms of power indices discussed below. The discrepancies between the ratio of weights and the ratio of power will be illustrated by several examples in the following sections. Power is not a trivial function of one's strength as measured by his number of votes. Simple additive or division arguments are not sufficient, but more complicated relations are necessary to understand the real distribution of influence.

1.3. Applications

The power indices discussed below do not constitute an attack on all weighted voting systems per se. Instead, they provide a method for structuring such systems with more understanding, so that certain individual powers can be preserved. Presumably the courts are against indirect or sophisticated discrimination as well as the more obvious types. Weighted voting with periodic adjusting of the weights, when done properly, can perhaps serve as an alternative to creating other inequities, caused by events such as districts of varying size due to shifting populations. It can be used to maintain present advantages or to avoid going through frequent redistricting, reapportionment, realignments, or otherwise disturbing existing constituencies, such as cutting county boundaries to obtain state-wide districts, which in turn may give rise to other potential difficulties such as gerrymandering. Proper weighting can possibly compensate for or offset some other problems or defects that arise when attempting to make all districts "equal."

1.4. Measures for Voting Power

Several examples of weighted voting systems will be scrutinized in what follows in order to gain some insight into the complexities and ramifications inherent in the apportionment of unequal voting strengths. Two of the numerical indices that have been used to measure a subject's share of the power to control or influence outcomes will be discussed. This pinpointing of some of the more formal, technical, and quantifiable aspects of bloc voting should clarify many of the implications and consequences that are built into such divisions of power. From a more complete account and accurate evaluation, one should be able to conclude in a more intelligent manner where the relative power to influence and affect aggregate decisions or laws resides.

These analytical techniques should prove useful in reevaluating some of the existing democratic institutions in terms of fairness, concealed biases, and the degree of protection they provide their constituents. Procedures for adequately modifying, altering, or revising current assemblies to reflect certain changes should be less ambiguous. These methods can be used to evaluate a newly proposed system, or to design a new legislative body from scratch like a college senate (either a hypothetical or proposed one, or to revise an existing one) so as to provide each with the influence he is entitled to. Of course, no scientific theory or mathematical formula will suffice to reveal all of the poorly understood and subtle details, nor the behind-the-scene nuances, which can have significant influence on the outcomes reached by voting in a deliberating or legislative council. Additional comments on the possible inadequacy of such theories are contained in Section 9.

1.5. Outline

Some simple examples of weighted voting systems plus some notations and definitions will be presented in Section 2, and some less trivial examples will be mentioned and evaluated for power ratios in Section 4. The power indices introduced by Shapley and Shubik [78] and by Banzhaf [6] will be discussed in Section 3. Some mini-projects are given in Section 5, and these may be undertaken with or without the suggestions for large size calculations and machine computation described in Section 6. The main project of evaluating the current Electoral College and some of its proposed alternatives is presented in Section 7. Some possible extensions and generalizations for this study and other work on voting appear in Section 8, and some criticisms of this whole approach are mentioned in the final section.

2. Simple Examples

Several simple examples of weighted voting schemes will be considered in this section. We shall first introduce the notation for a *weighted majority game*:

$$[q; w_1, w_2, \cdots, w_n].$$

Here there are *n voters*, or *players*, or *citizens*, denoted by 1, 2, $\cdots$, n; w_i is the voting *weight* of player i and is assumed to be a nonnegative number. Let

$$N = \{1, 2, \cdots, n\}$$

be the set of all n voters, and let S be a typical *coalition* or *bloc* of voters, i.e., a subset of N. A coalition *wins* a vote, or is called *winning*, whenever

$$\sum_{i \in S} w_i \geqq q,$$

where we shall assume that

$$q > \frac{1}{2} \sum_{i \in N} w_i.$$

This q is called the *quota* for the game. In some cases, one also assumes that each $w_i < q$, and one often restricts the w_i and q to integer values.

2.1. Stockholders

The percentage of a company's stock that an investor owns can serve as a weight in a weighted majority game, but it is often not a good measure of his influence or voting power. A man or coalition with over 50% of the stock has full control or has 100% of the voting power whenever decisions are made by a simple majority, i.e., is a *dictator*. A group with exactly 50%, or more, of the stock can *veto* or *block* any such action. In the game [51; 28, 24, 24, 24], the first voter seems to be much stronger than the last three, since he needs only one other to pass an issue whereas the other three must all combine in order to win. In the situation [51; 26, 26, 26, 22], the last player seems powerless since any winning coalition containing him can just as well win without him. The two games [51; 40, 30, 20, 10] and [51; 30, 25, 25, 20] seem identical in terms of voting influence, since the same coalitions are winning in both cases.

2.2. Equal Power

It is clear that in the game $[q; 1, 1, \cdots, 1]$ each player has equal power. Such games arise in pure bargaining situations and in deterrence encounters where each participant has the same amount to lose. However, games such as $[3; 2, 2, 1]$, $[8; 7, 5, 3]$, and $[51; 49, 48, 3]$ are similar to $[2; 1, 1, 1]$ in terms of power, since they give rise to the same collection of winning coalitions. The last of these illustrates the potential value of a small third party such as the Liberal Party in Great Britain. If we add to the game $[3; 2, 1, 1]$ the rule that player 2 can cast an additional vote in the case of a 2 to 2 tie, then it is effectively $[3; 2, 2, 1]$. But if player 1 can cast the tie breaker, then it becomes $[3; 3, 1, 1]$ and he is a dictator. More generally, in the game $[50(n-1)+1; 100, 100, \cdots, 100, 1]$ player n has the same power as the others when n is odd, i.e., the game is similar to one in which all of the players have the same weights or number of votes.

2.3. Dummy Players

A player who has no real voting power is called a *dummy*. Any winning coalition that contains such an impotent voter could win just as well without him. Player 4 in the game $[51; 26, 26, 26, 22]$ is an example. Also, player n in the game $[50(n-1)+1; 100, 100, \cdots, 100, 1]$ is a dummy when n is even. In the game $[16; 12, 6, 6, 4, 3]$, player 5 with 3 votes is a dummy, since no subset of the numbers 12, 6, 6, 4 sums to 13, 14 or 15, and thus player 5 could never be pivotal in the sense that by adding his vote a coalition would just reach or surpass the quota of 16. On the other hand, one can show that player 4 with 4 votes has the same influence in terms of winning coalitions as either player 2 or 3 with 6 votes apiece. This example can be generalized to games like $[268; 48, 36, 30, \cdots, 6, 4, 3]$, where the missing weights are multiples of six. The last three players in the situation $[10; 5, 5, 5, 2, 1, 1]$ are all dummies.

Banzhaf [6] describes a weighted voting system that was used in Nassau County, New York, by the Board of Supervisors in which three of the six municipalities share all of the power equally and three others are dummies in both instances, and this is described in Table 1. Each municipality has one representative whose vote is weighted according to the number of votes listed in the table. Of course, the dummies may be able to influence or sway decisions by their right to debate or in some other way, such as by membership in committees. A more recent revision of this Nassau County example, which avoids dummies, is mentioned in Section 5.6.

The Canadian election in the fall of 1972 gave the results in Table 2, where each of the three listed parties had equal power and those in the "others" category constitute a dummy (individually or as a group). The Liberals later won a majority in the elections of 1974.

Table 1. Nassau County

Municipality	Population 1954	No. of votes 1958	Population 1960	No. of votes 1964
Hempstead, No. 1	618,065	9	728,625	31
Hempstead, No. 2		9		31
North Hempstead	184,060	7	213,225	21
Oyster Bay	164,716	3	285,545	28
Glen Cove	19,296	1	22,752	2
Long Beach	17,999	1	25,654	2
Total	1,004,136	30	1,275,801	115

Table 2. Canada

Party	Leader	No. of seats
Liberals	Pierre E. Trudeau	109
Tories	Robert L. Stanfield	107
New Democrats	David Lewis	31
Others		17

2.4. Veto Power and Dictators

A player or coalition is said to have *veto power* if no coalition is able to win a ballot without his or their consent. A voter is a *dictator* if he controls any vote by himself, i.e., his weight $w_i \geqq q$. There can only be one dictator (recall that we assumed $2q > \Sigma w_i$), and the other players are then all dummies. Player 1 has veto power in the game [51; 50, 49, 1], which is essentially the same as [3; 2, 1, 1]; and if he is a chairman with additional power to break ties, then the game becomes [3; 3, 1, 1] and he is a dictator. Note that the ability of an individual to break tie votes in $[[n/2] + 1; 1, 1, \cdots, 1]$ adds power when n is even and adds nothing when n is odd. This presumes no change in q due to absences or abstentions. Here, $[n/2]$ stands for the greatest integer in $n/2$.

3. Measures in Voting Power

Several quantitative measures for evaluating the abstract power of a voter or coalition have been proposed. The Shapley–Shubik index as well as the Banzhaf index will be introduced in Sections 3.3 and 3.5, respectively. These two value concepts have received the most theoretical attention as well as application to real-world political structures. These indices will be computed for some very simple examples throughout Sections 3 and 4 and applied to some more realistic situations in Sections 5 and 7.

3.1. The Notion of Power

It is clear from our examples that voting power, expressed in some formal or functional sense, is not directly proportional to the number of votes one casts. In fact, an exact proportionality between weights and the power indices defined below seems to be rare in cases other than the one man-one vote situation. We are thus concerned with developing indices that give a reasonable measure of voting power in some technical sense. An individual's index should relate, in a preferably simple way, to one's true ability to affect group decisions by means of casting his weighted vote; and it should hopefully capture and crystallize some of our more intuitive concepts about power, such as why some legislators seem to have a better chance than average of being on the winning side than another. It should indicate one's relative influence, in some numerical way, to bring about the passage or defeat of some bill. It should be based somehow upon the importance of the individual in casting the deciding vote which will guarantee that some issue will carry. It should compare all the opportunities that each voter has to be a sort of critical swing-man in causing a desired outcome. This index should depend upon the number n of players involved, on one's fraction of the total weight, and upon how the remainder of the weight is distributed.

Power depends essentially upon being on the winning side of a division, that is, upon the ability to succeed in joining a winning coalition that supports one's views. Furthermore, it is the possibility of membership in the "minimal" winning coalitions that is sufficient or significant; since any additional votes afterwards become unnecessary and irrelevant, whereas deleting a member beforehand fails to ensure a victory. It is what one brings to a successful alliance that is crucial, and the one who is "last" to join a minimal winning coalition is particularly influential. The possibility of reversing an outcome by changing one's vote on a question is a most important one. The person whose support is necessary for success has a rather strong bargaining position, and one in this uniquely influential marginal or pivotal position is often rewarded handsomely for casting the deciding vote that carries his coalition "over the top." It is assumed for an abstract theory that all theoretically possible voting alignments, or combinations, are equally likely to occur, and thus the scientific measures that are derived below ignore a large number of less technical concepts such as voting in alphabetical order, political ideologies, and many other aspects as will be mentioned in Section 9.

3.2. Terminology

As we mentioned above, a coalition of players that possess enough votes to guarantee passage of an issue is called *winning*. A winning coalition is said to be *minimal winning* if no proper subset of it is winning, and these are the important ones in the following section.

A coalition that is not winning is called *losing*. A subset S of voters is a *blocking* coalition or has *veto* power if its complement $N - S$ is not winning. (Some authors also require that S itself be losing in order to be a blocking coalition.) A player i is a *dictator* if he forms a winning coalition $\{i\}$ by himself. A voter i is a *dummy* if every winning coalition that contains him is also winning without him, that is, he is in no minimal winning coalition.

There are many interrelations and properties for the concepts just defined, especially if additional conditions are assumed, such as our quota q consisting of a simple majority of the total voting weights. In fact, a whole algebra or combinatorial structure of *simple games* can be built up from these ideas as illustrated by Shapley [77] and by later generalizations, but this will not be done here. The interested reader should see p. 87 of Shapley [81] for references on this and some related theories. A good exercise at this point would be to describe which coalitions in the examples of Section 2 are of the various types mentioned in this section. It may prove helpful to actually draw the lattice of all subsets of the set of players for these examples.

3.3. The Shapley–Shubik Index

Shapley and Shubik [78] introduced an index for measuring an individual's voting power, which is a special application of a more general value concept introduced by Shapley [76] in the context of the general von Neumann–Morgenstern [86] theory of multiperson cooperative games. A voter's value is the *a priori* chance that he will be the last member added to turn a losing coalition into a winning one. It thus assigns him the probability of his casting the deciding vote. This expected frequency with which a man is the pivot, over all possible alignments of the voters, appears to be a good indication of his voting power.

More precisely, one looks at all possible orderings of the n players, and considers this as all of the potential ways of building up toward a winning coalition. There are $n!$ such ordered sequences, or permutations, of the n voters. The "!" stands for factorial; $n! = n \times (n - 1) \times \cdots \times 2 \times 1$ and $0! = 1$. For each one of these permutations, some unique player joins and thereby turns a losing coalition into a winning one, and this voter is called the *pivot*. That is, if in the sequence of players $x_1, x_2, \cdots, x_{i-1}, x_i, \cdots, x_n$, $\{x_1, x_2, \cdots, x_{i-1}, x_i\}$ is a winning coalition, but $\{x_1, x_2, \cdots, x_{i-1}\}$ is losing, then i is in the *pivotal position*. Consider the number of permutations of the n voters in which a particular *player* i is the pivot, and then this number divided by the total number of alignments, which is $n!$, is the *Shapley–Shubik* power *index* or voting *value* and is denoted by φ_i:

$$\varphi_i = \text{Number of sequences in which } i \text{ is a pivot} \div n!.$$

Also, let

$$\varphi = (\varphi_1, \varphi_2, \cdots, \varphi_n).$$

We are assuming here that each of the $n!$ alignments is equiprobable. One may consider the random order as a ranking of the voters according to their degree of enthusiasm or intensity of feeling in support of the issue being voted on, and the issue as a random variable. We are not concerned here with the most likely order of voting in some real convention or assembly, such as voting as you enter through some door, or alphabetically, or some other historical or traditional way; nor with developing a realistic theory of how voting coalitions do grow in practical circumstances, even though the formation of a good theory along these lines would be most desirable.

This power index can be expressed by the formula

$$\varphi_i = \sum \frac{(s-1)!(n-s)!}{n!},$$

where

$$s = |S| = \text{number of voters in } S,$$

and where the summation is taken over all winning coalitions S for which $S - \{i\}$ is losing. This follows from the fact that there are $(s-1)!$ orders in which the given $s-1$ players can enter S before i, and there are $(n-s)!$ different orders in which the remaining $n-s$ players can be added to S to form the grand coalition N.

In addition to the probabilistic approach taken above, this same index can be derived by several other approaches: by means of a somewhat dual theory using blocking coalitions instead of winning ones; from a bargaining or fair division scheme suggested by John Harsanyi [37, 38], or from a simple set of axioms (symmetry, additivity, efficiency, and dummies are powerless) given by Shapley [76] for his more general value concept. Shapley's axioms give a *unique* value formula in the more general game theory context, but not when restricted to the class of majority voting games. A variation of his axioms due to Dubey [27] gives a uniqueness result in the case of all "superadditive simple" or "monotone simple" games. In addition to these other approaches, this index has many other nice properties, but we only mention here that the φ_i are nonnegative,

$$\sum_{i \in N} \varphi_i = 1$$

and

$$\sum \frac{(s-1)!(n-s)!}{n!} = \frac{1}{s},$$

where the summation is taken over all coalitions S with a *fixed* number s of players. The reader can verify these.

3.4. An Example

The 24 permutations of the four players 1, 2, 3, and 4 in the weighted majority game [51; 40, 30, 20, 10] are listed below. The "*" indicates which player is pivotal in each *alignment*.

1 2*3 4	2 1*3 4	3 1*2 4	4 1 2*3
1 2*4 3	2 1*4 3	3 1*4 2	4 1 3*2
1 3*2 4	2 3 1*4	3 2 1*4	4 2 1*3
1 3*4 2	2 3 4*1	3 2 4*1	4 2 3*1
1 4 2*3	2 4 1*3	3 4 1*2	4 3 1*2
1 4 3*2	2 4 3*1	3 4 2*1	4 3 2*1

It is clear from this array that

$$\varphi = \frac{(10, 6, 6, 2)}{24}.$$

Or, from the formula we see, for example, that

$$\varphi_1 = 3 \cdot \frac{(3-1)!(4-3)!}{4!} + 2 \cdot \frac{(2-1)!(4-2)!}{4!}$$

since player 1 is pivotal in three *coalitions* consisting of three players and in two coalitions of two players.

3.5. The Banzhaf Index

Another value concept for measuring voting power was introduced by Banzhaf [6]. He is a lawyer, and much of his work has appeared in law journals; and his index, even more so than the one above, has been used in arguments in various legal proceedings. Some of the mathematical experts in this area have presented affidavits in cases before the courts (see Banzhaf [8, p. 306]). Banzhaf's index is also concerned with the fraction of possibilities in which a voter is in the crucial position of being able to change an outcome by switching his vote, that is, being able to alter the whole group's decision by he alone changing. However, he considers all significant *combinations* of "yes" and "no" votes, rather than *permutations* of the players as in the Shapley–Shubik case.

Each voter can vote yea or nay on a particular question; so one can imagine all 2^n possible combinations of such votes by these n players. A player is said to be *marginal*, or a *swing* or *critical*, in a given combination if he can change the outcome, resulting from this combination, from passage to defeat or vice versa by changing just his vote on the issue. Power appears to rest in precisely such marginal situations in which a defection from a bare majority produces a different result or achieves the exactly opposite goal. How often one appears in such a marginal or swing position is taken as the relative index of his influence. The *ratio of voting power* (in the sense of Banzhaf) for player i to that for player j is the number of combinations in which i is marginal divided by the number in which j is marginal. Consider the number b_i of voting combinations in which voter i is marginal. The *Banzhaf power index* or *value* for player i is defined as b_i divided by the sum of all of the b_j taken over the n players. We shall denote player i's Banzhaf value by β_i and let

$$\beta = (\beta_1, \beta_2, \cdots, \beta_n).$$

We again assume that all voting combinations, i.e., divisions into yeas and nays, are equally probable, since one can hardly assert in advance in the case of an abstract theory which possibilities are more likely to occur or prove most significant. We assume that everyone votes on each issue and that no abstentions are allowed.

Note that the Shapley–Shubik index uses *permutations* of the players and is concerned with the order in which winning coalitions are constructed. It assigns importance to the voter who is the last to join a coalition and thus makes it a minimal winning one, whereas the Banzhaf index employs *combinations* and considers just the number of such in which one plays a significant role. It does not look at the chronological order in which the winning coalitions were formed. It is concerned with which *subsets* voted yea or nay, however, and not with the numerical outcome of the vote. Comparing the values φ and β, Riker and Shapley [71, p. 204] state that "Although the numerical values obtained are slightly different, we know of no significant qualitative differences that would arise from defining the power index in this way." Some more recent work however does suggest some differences, and with the recent axiomatization of β by Dubey in Dubey and Shapley [29], these differences should become clear before long. Both value concepts seem to be effective and objective quantitative measures of power, which can be accurately and readily calculated in given cases. They have been accepted by several political scientists and mathematicians as reasonable and believable for understanding the logical structure of many voting problems, and they are not based on any excessive assumption.

Furthermore, both of these value concepts clearly satisfy some of our intuitive feeling toward power expressed earlier; for example, the indices are 1 for dictators and 0 for dummies, and they depend upon winning coalitions and only indirectly upon a voter's numerical weight. By definition, the β_i are nonnegative and

$$\sum_{i \in N} \beta_i = 1.$$

The indices φ and β are symmetric and monotone in the sense that $w_i = w_j$ implies $\varphi_i = \varphi_j$ and $\beta_i = \beta_j$, and $w_i > w_j$ implies $\varphi_i \geqq \varphi_j$ and $\beta_i \geqq \beta_j$. One possible approach to deriving a measure of power is to list desirable conditions like these, and to then search for a function with these properties.

Table 3. Computation of the Banzhaf Index

Players				Pass/Fail		Marginal			
1	2	3	4	*P*	*F*	1	2	3	4
Y	*Y*	*Y*	*Y*	*P*					
Y	*Y*	*Y*	*N*	*P*		*X*			
Y	*Y*	*N*	*Y*	*P*		*X*	*X*		
Y	*N*	*Y*	*Y*	*P*		*X*		*X*	
N	*Y*	*Y*	*Y*	*P*			*X*	*X*	*X*
Y	*Y*	*N*	*N*	*P*		*X*	*X*		
Y	*N*	*Y*	*N*	*P*		*X*		*X*	
N	*Y*	*Y*	*N*		*F*	*X*			*X*
Y	*N*	*N*	*Y*		*F*		*X*	*X*	
N	*Y*	*N*	*Y*		*F*	*X*		*X*	
N	*N*	*Y*	*Y*		*F*	*X*	*X*		
Y	*N*	*N*	*N*		*F*		*X*	*X*	
N	*Y*	*N*	*N*		*F*	*X*			
N	*N*	*Y*	*N*		*F*	*X*			
N	*N*	*N*	*Y*		*F*				
N	*N*	*N*	*N*		*F*				

$24 \times \beta = (10, 6, 6, 2)$

3.6. Computation and Examples

To calculate β for reasonably small examples, one can construct a table that lists the n players on top and the 2^n combinations of "yes" and "no" votes below the players, i.e., all the ways a vote could turn out. Next to each combination one can list whether an issue would pass or fail. Ties are not allowed. A second table aside the first one, also headed by the players, can then be used to record for each player next to each combination whether he was marginal or not. One adds up the number of times a player is marginal and the resulting numbers are proportional to the indices β_i. One could eliminate this second table, of course, by instead underlining or placing a "*" by the marginal voters in the first table.

The example [51; 40, 30, 20, 10] considered above gives rise to Table 3. The resulting indices are $\beta = (10, 6, 6, 2)/24$, which agree in this particular case with φ computed above. In the appendix of Banzhaf [6], there are similar tables for the five-person games [9; 5, 5, 3, 3, 1] and [5; 4, 2, 1, 1, 1], and the results are $7\beta = (2, 2, 1, 1, 1)$ and $11\beta = (7, 1, 1, 1, 1)$, respectively. One should calculate φ for these two cases and compare it with β. A similar exercise is to compute β for [5; 4, 2, 1, 1] and compare it with $\varphi = (9, 1, 1, 1)/12$. In practice, various symmetries allows one to compute β without having to consider the full list of all combinations.

A lattice or geometrical view for the coalitions and swings of an arbitrary

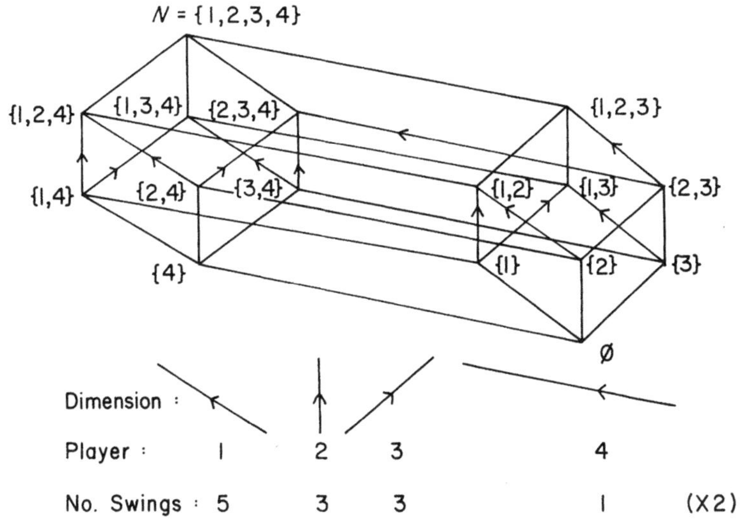

Figure 9.1

four-person voting game can be obtained from Fig. 9.1, which pictures a four-dimensional cube. Coalitions correspond to vertices. Swings of a given player correspond to certain of the edges in the direction of this particular player's dimension, as illustrated by the lines below the hypercube. This figure illustrates swings by means of arrows in the case [51; 40, 30, 20, 10]. To obtain the number of pivots for computing the Shapley–Shubik index φ, one usually needs to count some of the swings more than once.

3.7. Other Value Concepts

Several other value concepts have been suggested for investigating power. The interested reader can consult the references listed by Banzhaf [6, p. 329] and the discussion by Riker [70], as well as the book by Bell *et al.* [10]. A different normalization of the Banzhaf index is used by Coleman [23], whereas Dubey and Shapley [29] concentrate more on the actual probabilities $b_i/2^n$.

4. Additional Examples

Some examples and exercises for voting games that are usually somewhat more complicated than those given in Section 2 are presented in this section, and some of these are taken from real-world situations.

4.1. The United Nations Security Council

The U.N. Security Council consists of the "big five" countries (France, Great Britain, the People's Republic of China, the Soviet Union, and the United States) who are permanent members and each individually has veto power, plus ten "small" countries whose membership rotates. It takes nine votes, the "big five" plus at least four others, to carry an issue. This gives the game [39; 7, 7, 7, 7, 7, 1, 1, 1, 1, 1, 1, 1, 1, 1, 1]. Note that a "small" country i can be *pivotal* in a winning coalition S if and only if S contains exactly nine countries including the five permanent members. There are $9!/3!6!$ such different S that contain i, and the corresponding coefficient in the Shapley–Shubik formula for this 15-person game is $(9 - 1)!(15 - 9)!/15!$. The product of these two numbers gives the power index $\varphi_s = 0.001863$ for any nonpermanent member. A member from the "big-five" has index $\varphi_b = (1 - 10\varphi_s)/5 = 0.1963$. It would be of interest to compute the Banzhaf index for this Council, and to compare these indices with those for the members of the old Security Council before 1963, which was [27; 5, 5, 5, 5, 5, 1, 1, 1, 1, 1, 1] (answer for φ: $6\varphi_s = 1/77$ and $5\varphi_b = 76/77$); or with a potential future Council that adds Japan and/or West Germany as a permanent member, also holding veto power. (The latter two countries now contribute more financially to the U.N. than do Britain or France.) A much more ambitious project is to compute φ or β for the present combined game in the Security Council and the General Assembly, as was done by Brams [16] and Schwödiauer [73] (see Section 4.3).

4.2. Some Other Assemblies

Several other existing assemblies or committees can be found that are weighted voting systems, and it is left as an exercise to express these as weighted majority games and to determine the values for φ and β.

Table 4. New York City Board of Estimates

Member	No. of votes Former system	Present system
Mayor	3	4
Controller	3	4
Council President	3	4
Brooklyn Borough President	2	2
Manhattan Borough President	2	2
Bronx Borough President	1	2
Richmond Borough President	1	2
Queens Borough President	1	2

Table 5. 1965 Israeli Knesset

Party	No. of seats
New Communists	3
Communists	1
Poaelei Aguda	2
Agudat Israel	4
National Religious	11
Mapam	8
The Alignment (Mapai–Ahdut)	49
Haolan Haze	1
Independent Liberals	5
Rafi	10
Gahal	26

Table 6. Tokyo

Party	No. of seats
Liberal-Democrats	51
Komeito	26
Communists	24
Socialists	20
Democratic-Socialists	2
Independents	2

The Board of Estimates for New York City has had eight members with voting strength as indicated in Table 4.

The Israeli Knesset in late 1965 had the division indicated in Table 5, taken from left to right on the political spectrum, as described by Owen [55].

The Tokyo Metropolitan Assembly had elections in 1973 with the results as indicated in Table 6.

The 1973 general elections in Sweden ended in a virtual "tie" with a total of 175 seats between the ruling Social Democrats (157) and Communists (18), as well as for the three opposition parties: Center Party (90), Moderates (51), and Liberals (34).

The State Senate in Hawaii, as reported by Banzhaf [7], had one district in the State with one legislator, one district with two, two districts with three each, and four districts with four legislators from each of them. He also studied the Arkansas House, the Georgia Senate, the Texas House, and the Wyoming Senate. Consider the power of the various districts under the assumption that all delegates from the same district vote the same way on any question. This multimember district situation is studied in more depth in Section 5.3.

4.3. Some Large Games

For the nine-person game [7; 5, 1, 1, 1, 1, 1, 1, 1, 1] with one strong player, one can compute that $\varphi = (10, 1, 1, 1, 1, 1, 1, 1, 1)/18$. More generally, for the n-person game $[q; w_1, 1, 1, \cdots, 1]$, where w_1 is an integer such that $w_1 < q \leqq n - 1$, $\varphi = ((n-1)w_1, n - w_1, n - w_1, \cdots, n - w_1)/n(n-1)$. Note that player 1 occupies each position in a random ordering of the n players with equal probability, and so his value is obtained by merely counting the number of times he is in pivotal position and dividing by n. Note that for small n, $\varphi_1 = w_1/n$ is somewhat larger than the first player's share of the weights, which is $w_1/w = w_1/(w_1 + n - 1)$, where $w = \Sigma_{i \in N} w_i$. But for large n, φ_i approaches player i's share of the weights. Limiting results have been obtained for φ for several classes of games of this sort by Shapley and Shapiro [79], Milnor and Shapley [51], and Shapley [80]; a recent book by Aumann and Shapley [1] describes a whole value theory for various infinite games. Similar types of limiting results have also been obtained by Dubey and Shapley [29] for the Banzhaf index.

In some decision procedures in Australia, each one of the six states has one vote, and the federal government has two votes plus the ability to break ties when a simple majority is necessary to win. This can be expressed as a weighted majority game of the type just mentioned, and its φ and β can be determined. In the U.N. General Assembly with a required two-thirds majority, one has the 138-person game $[98; 3, 1, 1, \cdots, 1]$ since the Soviet Union has three votes.

5. Mini-Projects

This section includes a collection of relatively small projects, any one of which can be undertaken in a class, or by small subgroups of a class, over a period of two or three weeks. These illustrate applications of the power index concept and are suitable for a class that does not have the prerequisites, time, or computer facility in order to pursue the theory or computation required in the next two sections. The calculations for these mini-projects can be done by hand if necessary, and can thus be used as a warm-up or for numerical check against any computer programs developed in the following.

5.1. The Proposed Canadian Constitutional Amendment Scheme

A method for amending the Canadian constitution was proposed in 1971, which involved passage by the federal government as well as a ratifying procedure by the ten provinces. Our immediate objective is to investigate the voting powers exhibited in only this latter ten-person game between the provinces, and to compare the results with the provincial populations.

The winning coalitions or those with veto power can be described as follows. In order for passage, approval is required of

(a) any province that has (or ever had) 25% of the population,
(b) at least two of the four Atlantic provinces, and
(c) at least two of the four western provinces that currently contain together at least 50% of the total western population.

Using current population figures, this means that veto power is held by

(d) Ontario (*O*) and Quebec (*Q*),
(e) any three of the four Atlantic (*A*) provinces (New Brunswick (*NB*), Nova Scotia (*NS*), Prince Edward Island (*PEI*), and Newfoundland (*N*)),
(f) British Columbia (*BC*) plus any one of the three prairie (*P*) provinces [Alberta (*AL*), Saskatchewan (*S*), and Manitoba (*M*)], and
(g) the three prairie provinces taken together.

The various types of winning coalitions are listed in Table 7. Ontario and Quebec are not listed since they are in every winning coalition, but are included in the number s of players in coalition S. The numbers in the last column of Table 7 can be used with the formula for the Shapley value (Section 3.3) to compute φ for each of the provinces as well as regional groups, and these are shown in Table 8. For example,

$$\varphi_O = \frac{[18(5!4!) + 36(6!3!) + 25(7!2!) + 8(8!1!) + 1(9!0!)]}{(10!)} = \frac{53}{168},$$

Table 7. Winning Provincial Coalitions

Type	S	s	No. of such S
1	$1P, 2A, BC$	6	18
2	$2P, 2A, BC$	7	18
3	$3P, 2A$	7	6
4	$1P, 3A, BC$	7	12
5	$3P, 2A, BC$	8	6
6	$2P, 3A, BC$	8	12
7	$3P, 3A$	8	4
8	$1P, 4A, BC$	8	3
9	$3P, 3A, BC$	9	4
10	$2P, 4A, BC$	9	3
11	$3P, 4A,$	9	1
12	$3P, 4A, BC$	10	1
		Total:	88

Table 8. Shapley–Shubik Index for Provinces

Province	φ(in %)	% Population	φ/Population
BC	12.50	9.38	1.334
AL	4.17	7.33	0.570
S	4.17	4.79	0.872
M	4.17	4.82	0.865
(4 Western)	(25.01)	(26.32)	(0.952)
O	31.55	34.85	0.905
Q	31.55	28.94	1.092
NB	2.98	3.09	0.965
NS	2.98	3.79	0.786
PEI	2.98	0.54	5.53
N	2.98	2.47	1.208
(3 Atlantic)	(11.92)	(9.89)	(1.206)

Table 9. Banzhaf Index for Provinces

Province	β(in %)	β/Population
BC	16.34	1.74
AL	5.45	0.74
S	5.45	1.14
M	5.45	1.13
(4 Western)	(32.68)	(1.24)
O	21.78	0.62
Q	21.78	0.75
NB	5.94	1.92
NS	5.94	1.57
PEI	5.94	11.00
N	5.94	2.41
(4 Atlantic)	(23.76)	(2.40)

and

$$\varphi_M = \frac{[6(5!4!) + 10(6!3!) + 5(7!2!) + 1(8!1!)]}{(10!)} = \frac{1}{24}.$$

The calculations for φ described above were made by D. R. Miller [50], and he obtained his population figures for the ten-province area from the *Canadian Almanac and Directory 1972* (Toronto, 1972). There are several extensions of his work that would also be of interest. However, Canada adopted a different constitutional scheme in 1982.

EXERCISES

1. Verify the results for φ, which are given in Tables 7 and 8.

2. Determine the Banzhaf value β for this game between the provinces, and compare it to φ. Also compute the ratios β(in %) ÷ % population. These answers, as computed by Cornell University student Eleanor Walther in May 1974, by D. R. Miller [50] and others are given in Table 9. Note that $\varphi_{AL} > \varphi_{NB}$ but that $\beta_{NB} > \beta_{AL}$, and thus this "simple" game is not a *weighted* majority game.

3. Find φ and β for a revised scheme that gives veto power to $\{BC, AL\}$ and $\{BC, S, M\}$ instead of (f) above, and thus more power to oil-rich Alberta (Miller [50]).

4. Use the "square root" result in Sections 6.2 and 7.3 to determine the relative β for the individual voters (assuming all vote) in the voting game played within their own provinces. Then compute an approximate relative voting power of each citizen in the composed national game by multiplying these latter values by the corresponding φ or β for his province as given in (1) or (2).

The mathematical results leave room for a good deal of discussion. Some have criticized this scheme (before seeing Miller's results) for giving *BC* too much power. Is the low figure for *AL* and the high one for *PEI* justifiable? What are some reasonable alternatives to the proposed scheme? One would wish to avoid making *PEI* a dummy, for example. A brief discussion along these lines is given in Miller's paper.

5.2. Power in a Nine-Man Body

A colleague related to me that he was a member of a nine-man committee on which he and four others formed a coalition. This bloc of five agreed covertly that they would all vote the same way on any issue before the full committee (except for a few deviations for diversionary reasons on minor issues or when others not in their coalition also supported their view), and thus a majority of three or more from this coalition effectively controlled the full committee. So each man in this minimal winning coalition increased his voting power from 1/9th to 1/5th. At the same time, however, my friend was wondering whether three of the other four in his coalition had not formed another secret three-man subcoalition without him, which in turn was controlling the whole committee. It would thus become possible to win on a ballot on which there were really only two favorable votes, and six members would be effectively dummies.

In cases like this, as well as others, it is of interest to investigate the power inherent in the cosets in various partitions of a nine-man body. One might also be concerned with changes in power caused by realigning such blocs, and whether the potential gains to counter-organization come from existing blocs or from the nonaligned individuals. The Shapley values for the various

Table 10. Nine-Man Committee

Partition type	φ
5, 4 (etc.)	(1, 0) (etc.)
4, 4, 1	(1, 1, 1)/3
4, 3, 2	(1, 1, 1)/3
4, 3, 1, 1	(3, 1, 1, 1)/6
4, 2, 2, 1	(3, 1, 1, 1)/6
4, 2, 1, 1, 1	(6, 1, 1, 1, 1)/10
4, 1, 1, 1, 1, 1	(10, 1, 1, 1, 1, 1)/15
3, 3, 3	(1, 1, 1)/3
3, 3, 2, 1	(1, 1, 1, 0)/3
3, 3, 1, 1, 1	(9, 9, 4, 4, 4)/30
3, 2, 2, 2	(3, 1, 1, 1)/6
3, 2, 2, 1, 1	(4, 2, 2, 1, 1)/10
3, 2, 1, 1, 1, 1	(4, 2, 1, 1, 1, 1)/10
3, 1, 1, 1, 1, 1, 1	(9, 2, 2, 2, 2, 2, 2)/21
2, 2, 2, 2, 1	(1, 1, 1, 1, 1)/5
2, 2, 2, 1, 1, 1	(7, 7, 7, 3, 3, 3)/30
2, 2, 1, 1, 1, 1, 1	(25, 25, 11, 11, 11, 11, 11)/105
2, 1, 1, 1, 1, 1, 1, 1	(7, 3, 3, 3, 3, 3, 3, 3)/28
1, 1, 1, 1, 1, 1, 1, 1, 1	(1, 1, 1, 1, 1, 1, 1, 1, 1)/9

sized coalitions in the different types of partitions of a nine-man body have been determined by Krislov [44] and listed in Table 10 for the case of a simple majority quota.

Some similar projects along these lines could be undertaken such as the following exercises.

Exercises

5. Compute the Banzhaf value β for all subsets in all partitions of a nine-man body.
6. Determine φ and β for subsets of committees of sizes different than nine, e.g., of size 5, 7, 8, or 11; and denote the gains in new power ratios which accrue from coalition building.
7. Consider the previous cases for quotas other than a simple majority, e.g., three-fifths or two-thirds.

When one or more individuals defect from a coalition and migrate into another one (perhaps a new singleton), the realigned coalition structure (i.e., partition) will normally exhibit new power indices for the individuals. If "political man" attempts to maximize his voting power as "financial man" attempts to maximize his profits, then one might expect that such changes, e.g., individuals between political parties, might indicate an increase in the migrator's power or the total power of the party he joins, or that migrations are more common among those with little power to begin with. Riker [67] studied these hypotheses in the case of the French National Assembly during the 1950s. During the period he considered, there were many parties, some of which exhibited strict party discipline, as well as frequent migrations. For example, a typical Assembly was a majority game such as

$$[313; 105, 100, 88, 85, 75, 55, 46, 32, 23, 13, 1, 1, 1].$$

Riker developed several formulas to test various power changes before and after migrations. Most of the results were rather ambiguous regarding his hypotheses. It appears that such changes were more for ideological reasons than attempts to gain power, but the situation may have been much too complicated for them to even sense, much less calculate, such indices.

Returning to our nine-man body, we see that several powerful coalitions are quite unstable in the sense that a defector can gain significantly. For example, a partition of type 5, 4 seems highly unstable, since a change to type 4, 4, 1 reduces the power of the five-man coalition from 1 to 1/3 while increasing the swing-man's own share of the power from 1/5 to 1/3.

Some of the notions from Luce's theory of ψ-stability relate to models with changes in partitions. See Chapter 10 by R. D. Luce and H. Raiffa [47].

Investigations into coalition stability and changes in power would be of interest. Brams and Affuso [17] discuss power changes due to additional voters.

EXERCISES

8. Use Table 10, or the results from (5) above, and Riker's paper as an outline to study stability and changes in power to the various individuals and groups in a nine-man committee in which migration is allowed. Similar studies can be done for committees of other sizes, using for example the results in (2).

9. Investigate such changes in power for some real-world body, e.g., some local college committee, or the U.S. Supreme Court where death and new appointments or other reasons bring about changes in the coalition structures as in the case of Justice Rutledge. The reference by Schubert [75] is of some interest here, and the recent paper by Frank and Shapley [31].

5.3. Multimember Districts

In many voting assemblies, such as some state legislatures, the Electoral College, a university senate, etc., the voting representatives often come from districts that differ greatly in the number of citizens they have. It is often thought that any inequity created by differences in population can be balanced by electing different numbers of representatives from the various districts. For example, if one district in a state contains a city and has 4,000,000 people, whereas all other districts have 1,000,000 inhabitants,

Table 11. Some Miniature Districts

District symbol	No. of voters n	No. of combination 2^n	No. Combination Marginal b	% Combination Marginal $100b/2^n$	Individual % Population $100/n$	$100/\sqrt{n}$	$nb/2^n$
A	3	8	4	50.0	33.3	57.7	1.50
B	5	32	12	37.5	20.0	44.7	1.88
C	7	128	40	31.2	14.3	37.7	2.18
D	9	512	140	27.4	11.1	33.3	2.46

then it is viewed as "fair" if the first district elects four times as many representatives *at-large* from its region as does each other district in the state. This seems to assume that the ability of an individual citizen to affect the election of his representatives varies inversely with population. It is shown in the following examples that this is not a valid assumption in terms of the Banzhaf power index. In fact, a citizen-voter's decreasing influence in electing his representatives varies inversely with the *square root* of the increasing population, and this will be demonstrated in general in Section 6.2.

Banzhaf [7] has illustrated how one's influence varies with population for districts with only a few citizens and in the case when the elections are between just two opposing parties, and his example is shown in Table 11. Note there that $b = 2 \times (2m)!/(m!)^2$, where $m = (n - 1)/2$. For example, when $n = 9$, the percentage of voting combinations in which a citizen is marginal (27.4) is closer to $100/\sqrt{n} = 33.3$ than it is to $100/n = 11.1$. For large n, the reciprocal square-root approximation, when properly normalized, is extremely accurate (see Section 6.2). Hence one could argue in the example mentioned above, that the city with 4,000,000 inhabitants should only have twice the number of representatives as a district with 1,000,000 constituents. This type of argument can be made more forcefully when one considers the influence the representatives from large districts have in turn in the state legislature if they vote as an irrevocable bloc. The effect of so "composing" two such voting games is shown in a simple example below, and for the more realistic Electoral College in Section 7.

Consider a small "state" that is divided into seven districts in which the first district has a voting population of nine and each of the other six districts has a voting population of three. Assume that this large district elects three representatives at-large by choosing a group of three people from the same party who then vote the same way on any issue before the state legislature. Each one of the small districts elects one person to the legislature. Furthermore, assume that each representative acts as a true delegate and votes on each question the way in which the majority of his constituents would vote. We see from Table 11 that a citizen-voter from a small district can influence his or her representative's vote in 50% of the voting combinations, whereas the individual in the large district can influence the vote by the party of three legislators in only 27.4% of the combinations in his district's polls. However, in the legislature itself one has the weighted majority game [5; 3, 1, 1, 1, 1, 1, 1]. One can show that the Banzhaf power index for this game is $\beta = (5, 1, 1, 1, 1, 1, 1)/11$. This is close to the Shapley–Shubik index of $\varphi = (9, 2, 2, 2, 2, 2, 2)/21$, which was computed in Section 4 for all such games with one large player. Thus a citizen-voter from the large district can influence his group of three representatives 27.4% (= 140/512) of the time, and they in turn can sway the legislature 78.1% (= 100/128) of the time, for a product of 21.4%. On the other hand, an individual from a small district influences his lone legislator 50% (= 4/8) of the time, and this delegate in turn changes the full legislature 15.6% (= 20/128) of the time, for a product of 7.8%. These products can approximate an individual's power in the "compound" game.

Previous examples had indicated that in a weighted voting situation the "big" players with the most votes often, but *not always*, have somewhat larger indices than their fractions of the total vote would indicate. In this section one observes further that if several delegates are elected at-large from various districts, then the influence of the individual voter in the large districts may be greatly exaggerated relative to the other regions when the number of delegates per district is proportional to its population. Banzhaf [7] actually applied this sort of an analysis to five state legislatures. It would make an interesting project to investigate some additional examples which have such multimember representation, under the assumption of bloc voting behavior.

Exercises

10. Investigate some local or state governmental body, board, agency or convention of citizens that has a multimember representative structure. For example, some school boards have a representation from various constituencies. The school boards in New York City would make an interesting study.

11. A college or university has several schools, divisions or departments of various sizes. Investigate how to construct a representative council for some such structure, for example, a mathematics departmental or divisional executive committee that has "fair" representation from each interest or specialty group.

5.4. Some Current Parliaments

A review of newspapers and newsmagazines will give interesting data concerning various elections and national assemblies, especially in the year 1974, when there were several minority governments in the Western World in which a winning coalition of parties must form in order to obtain a ruling government. Some countries also have five to ten different parties in their

Table 12. Luxembourg

Party	No. of seats Early 1974	Mid 1974
Christian Democrats	21	18
Socialist	12	17
Splinter Socialists	6	5
Liberals	11	14
Communists	6	5
w	56	59
q	29	30

Table 13. Great Britian

Party	No. of seats
Labor	301
Conservatives	296
Liberals	14
Irish Unionists	11
Scottish Nationalists	7
Others	3
Welsh Plaid Cymru	2
Irish Catholics	1
w	635

parliaments, and this requires a reasonably sized computational exercise. Data for four countries are listed below; and one can compute φ and β for these assemblies under the assumption of strict party-line votes. This latter assumption has some validity in at least the formative stages of a government and even at later stages in those countries in which strict party discipline exists.

Tables 12 to 15 are from the spring of 1974, and even this data should be checked further or extended in order to be completely reliable. Such figures are frequently in flux, and one is dealing with rather dynamical situations. For example, some members of the British Parliament soon lost their votes because they had taken leadership roles, etc. The "other" category could also be broken into three singletons. The newspaper reports should be validated. The figures on Denmark do not include a small number of representatives from Greenland and the Faroe Islands. If one wishes to do an accurate investigation, he should first verify and refine the following data. It is also interesting how most election results in the newspapers are reported as the percentage of the popular vote taken by each party (or often just the major parties) rather than the number of seats won, whereas the latter results are the more critical ones, and they are not always easily obtainable from the former percentages.

Table 14. Israel

Party	No. of seats
Labor	51
Likud	39
National Religious	10
Independent Liberals	4
New Communists	4
Orthodox Agudat Israel	3
Agudat Israel Workers	3
Arab Affiliates	3
Civil Rights	2
Moked	1
w	120

Table 15. Denmark

Party	No. of seats	Ordinate[a]
Communists	6	0.00
Socialist Peoples	11	0.18
Social Democrats	46	0.37
Center Democrats	14	0.50
Justice League	5	0.54
Radical Left	20	0.58
Left (Liberals)	22	0.64
Christian Peoples	7	0.79
Conservative Peoples	16	0.84
Progress	28	1.00
w	175	

[a] These ordinates are an estimate of the parties positions on the political spectrum as measured from left to right, and they will be referred to in Section 8.1.

Many coalitional governments also existed in 1981.

Even in countries which have a one-party majority government, one may be able to study the power in various interest groups within this party or the assembly as a whole. See, for example, the study by Lieserson [46] on Japan.

5.5. Cornell University Senate

A broadly representative University Senate had been in operation at Cornell in the early 1970s, and it had significant powers theoretically over events and budgets in important areas such as student life and activities. The size of this Senate as well as of each of its six major groups varied, and these numbers are given in Table 16. The number in the employee's category

Table 16. Cornell Senate

Constituency	1971	φ	β	1972	1974	No.
Students	60	9	4	60	40	15,500
Faculty	60	9	4	60	40	1,550
Employees	5	6	3	13	10	5,000
Alumni	2	2	1	2	1	130,000
Administration	2	2	1	2	2	9
Nonprof. Acad.	3	2	1	3	2	550
w	132	($\div$)	($\div$)	140	95	
q	67	(30)	(14)	71	48	

was increased by eight between 1971 and 1972 for several reasons. Some of these were perhaps more idealistic, such as support for labor in general or because of the large number of members in this class. (At Cornell there are nearly four people in the mostly invisible "supply line" for each professor at the "front.") Other reasons were more practical, such as the fact that the employees were critically involved in the consequences of Senate decisions, and usually it was desirable to have at least one such overworked employee senator on most of the two dozen or so committees and subcommittees. The total size of the Senate was reduced by 1974 in attempts to improve efficiency and because of the large absentee problems. The Shapley–Shubik and Banzhaf values for the 1971 Senate are shown in the table. The correction for the benefit of the employee group in the two later Senates may have been "overdone" however, since the result was three groups of equal power and three *dummies*. [Of course, some students knew right along that the alumni, administration (e.g., the provost and vice presidents) and non professional academics (e.g., librarians, etc.) were "dummies."]

The assumption of bloc voting or "party-line" discipline within the six groups listed in the table is clearly invalid in practice for this particular Senate, as one would expect in most college situations. Extremes of opinion within some of the large groups could be found on almost any issue. On the other hand, there may be specific local issues on which a partitioning of the Senate into various interest groups might make sense. For example, some groups may have strong feelings in favor of or against athletics, whereas different groups may have intense "pro" or "anti" attitudes on Greek living units. Consistent voting patterns might also be discerned on topics such as women or minority students and affirmative action programs. Such data may lead to power analyses and prediction of outcomes on such individual legislation.

There are many interesting projects that one can undertake concerning university, college, school, or departmental senates, and a few of these are suggested below. One could use the data in Table 16, or collect similar figures for his own institution. The numbers for the six constituencies shown in the right-hand column in this table, are for the 1971 Cornell Senate. Except for constitutional amendments and a few procedural matters, a simple majority is used for the quota.

EXERCISES

12. Verify the values of φ and β given in Table 16.

13. Do a "two-level" analysis using the φ and β for Table 16 (or your own college data) plus the "square-root" result in Sections 6.2 and 7.3 to estimate the power of an individual person (not senator) in the six groups.

14. If the committee structure of a senate is known, then one can investigate the power of an individual representative in the sequential process of getting a bill through committee and the senate. For example, as was the case in the first Cornell Senate, an alumnus on the powerful Executive Committee would increase his power as well as that of the alumni group.

15. Given the number of student representatives a senate will have, determine a "fair" allocation of this number among the various colleges in a university, or departments in a college.

16. One can design a senate from scratch by deciding what power the different individuals and/or groups should have and then setting the number of representatives from the various constituencies so as to best achieve this. [See the following section for additional ideas on (15) and (16).]

17. The power of the various committees and/or interest blocs for a university board of trustees or state regents may be of interest, especially in the case of a rather large board as is the case for Cornell University.

5.6. Designing Representative Bodies

In most of the weighted voting problems discussed in this paper, one is given a well-structured problem (i.e., the weights) and is asked to determine the corresponding voting power as measured by the Shapley–Shubik and/or Banzhaf indices. On the other hand, one is often faced with the opposite or reverse problem in practice, i.e., if one is designing a legislature, he is given the size of the districts and he must then determine the weights or number of representatives for each in order to achieve a certain given or desirable measure of power. Exercises 15, and 16 in the previous section are of this type. Most work in this reverse direction uses less elegant or straightforward techniques. One often uses more ad hoc, self-correcting, or guess-and-verify methods. Some approximation algorithms do exist, although they may not always be readily available (without a fee). There are also several substantial and unsolved mathematical problems along these lines, in addition to the practical ones, but the author will not go into further detail here on these more theoretical directions. One should remember, however, that there may be alternate types of solutions to his voting problem, e.g., reapportionment, restricting, or multimember districts, in addition to finding the "correct" (unequal) weights for the lone representative from each district.

Let us return to the voting rules in the Nassau County Board of Supervisors, which is described in Table 1. Recall that the 1958 and 1964 systems each had three dummy municipalities. In 1971 a new scheme was passed which merely changed the quota from a simple majority of 58 to 63 votes in order to pass a bill. [Actually, the County Charter in 1938 allows one vote per 10,000 residents, and thus Hempstead should currently have a weight of 72. However, since no town or city is allowed by this Charter to have more than one-half of the total vote of the board (i.e., 125 ÷ 2), one subtracts ten votes from Hempstead to get 62 and takes w as 115]. There are no dummies in the revised scheme, and the new values of φ and β, as computed by Shigeo Muto with $q = 63$, are shown in Table 17.

Note that the new power indices are not too extreme in comparison with the proportions of the population. Attempts to invalidate this latter scheme via the courts have failed. Related stories appeared in the *New York Times* on May 4, 9, and 12, 1971 and February 2, 1974.

Exercises

18. Verify the values of φ and β given in Table 17.

19. Another problem in the Nassau County scheme is that the two representatives from Hempstead are elected at-large from the full district, which gives rise to questions raised in Sections 6.2 and 7.4. Reconsider this scheme in light of this additional problem. It would also be of interest to study the present situation in Nassau County, since the above system was overturned by a referendum (*New York Times*, November 17, 1974), and additional court rulings followed.

In 1971 a suit was brought against Cortland County, New York, which claimed that its one town-one vote voting scheme was unfair, and the state courts agreed that it was unconstitutional. A proportionately weighted interim scheme was then set up, while the County undertook to devise a new valid apportionment plan. The new system, involving some redistricting,

Table 17. Nassau County Revisited

Municipality	No. of votes	$60\ \varphi_i$	$54\ \beta_i$
Hempstead No. 1	31	17	15
Hempstead No. 2	31	17	15
North Hempstead	21	7	7
Oyster Bay	28	13	11
Glen Cove	2	3	3
Long Beach	2	3	3

Table 18. Cortland County Legislature

District number	Population	% Population	Weights when majority quota is 1/2	3/5	2/3	Case $q = 1/2$ Vote (%)	Power (%)
3	2716	5.918	31	40	38	6.739	5.859
7	2560	5.578	27	35	36	5.870	5.612
13	2517	5.484	26	34	34	5.652	5.482
14	2500	5.447	26	33	34	5.652	5.482
2	2478	5.399	25	33	33	5.435	5.358
8	2467	5.375	25	32	33	5.435	5.358
18	2460	5.360	25	33	33	5.435	5.358
15	2444	5.325	25	32	32	5.435	5.358
16	2442	5.321	25	32	32	5.435	5.358
6	2442	5.321	25	32	32	5.435	5.358
5	2440	5.317	25	32	33	5.435	5.358
19	2434	5.304	24	32	33	5.217	5.238
12	2442	5.277	24	32	32	5.217	5.238
1	2406	5.243	24	31	31	5.217	5.238
17	2402	5.234	24	31	31	5.217	5.238
4	2284	4.977	22	28	29	4.783	4.916
9	2187	4.765	20	26	25	4.348	4.735
10	2153	4.691	19	25	24	4.130	4.727
11	2140	4.663	18	25	23	3.913	4.727
Totals	45894	100.000	460	598	598	100.000	100.000

used the 1970 Decennial Census figures and the Banzhaf index for weighted voting. It has since been accepted by the courts, and took effect on January 1, 1974. The new law for the Cortland County Legislature gives one legislature to each of the 19 districts, and weights his vote as indicated in Table 18. There are different weights necessary for each of three cases, depending upon whether a simple majority, a three-fifths majority, or a two-thirds majority is required to pass an issue. The computation of the desired weights was done by Lee Papayanopoulos, a Rutgers University professor, who has a computer program for obtaining approximate weights to satisfy equity in the sense of the Banzhaf index. (The County paid –2600 for his report, and he later collected \$350 per day for his services in appearing in court.) A study of the table can point out some "discrepancies," which should give rise to further questions. For example, the nine largest districts control 235 votes for more than a simple majority of 231, and yet they have only 49.2% of the population. Note also, for example, that in the two thirds plan, Districts 15, 16, and 6 have one less weight than the slightly smaller Districts 5 and 19. Incidentally, there was some controversy in designing the current scheme about how to count the students at Cortland State.

EXERCISES

20. Consider a corporation in which four stockholders each have 60, 20, 10, and 10% of the stock and for which the company charter calls for all measures to be passed by a simple majority vote of the stock. The directors, knowing that the majority stockholder is a dictator (in our mathematical sense), agree to modify the rules to have "voting power" (say as measured by φ and/or β) approximate the relative stock holdings. Two proposals (or is it three or four?) are put forward:

    A) Majority rules except when all minority stockholders unify against the majority stockholder. (One may question whether this verbal statement means that the minority have merely veto power or are a winning coalition.)
    B) Majority rules except when at least two-thirds of the minority stockholders' *votes* are opposed to the majority stockholder.

21. One might wish to reconsider the projects 15 and 16 in the previous Section 5.5 in light of the discussion in the present section.

22. It would be of interest to undertake a project to redesign some local governmental body. For example, there are still several counties in New York State with unconstitutional systems that are in need of revision. This redesigning has been done for several other counties in New York, and an excellent report on this through 1968 is given in Johnson [42], and a more recent study is presented by Imrie [40] and Walther [87].

5.7. The United States Congress

Several investigations have been made into measures of power for various sorts of legislatures. In a unicameral body in which a winning coalition depends only upon the number of members it contains, each legislator theoretically has equal power. More interesting problems occur in multicameral bodies or "composed" games, in which various majorities in several houses of different size may be required for passage. An interesting case is the U.S. Congress, where a bill requires a majority in the House and the Senate plus the President's signature or a two-thirds majority of both houses in the case of a veto override. Shapley and Shubik [78] have approximated φ as: 5/12 for the House of Representatives as a whole, 5/12 for the Senate, and 1/6 for the President. Several other studies have since been done of the U.S. Congress, and one can refer to Section 12.1 by Luce and Raiffa [47], to Chapters 14 (especially p. 215) and 16 (pp. 245–250) by Rapoport [64], as well as to the references given there for reports on the early work done in this area. Also of interest is Chapter 11 by Luce and Rogow in Shubik [82], and the paper by Riker and Niemi [68]. Several types of similar studies should be of interest.

EXERCISES

23. Investigate the various interest blocs in some legislature like the U.S. Congress, at least for the case of some particular interest area, and then determine the voting power of the various blocs.

24. Do a power analysis for some state legislative system.

25. Consider the "committee system" that exists for some legislative body such as the U.S. Congress or a University Senate, and determine power indices under the assumption that a bill must pass in the committee before it reaches the floor. See the paper by Brams and Papayanopoulos [20] on the Congress.

5.8. Some Mathematical Problems

By now it should be clear to the mathematical reader that there are a great number of mathematical questions and relations that can be pursued, as class projects or basic research, concerning our weighted voting games and power indices. Although our main goal has been to present interesting or relevant applications suitable for mathematical modeling, a few more theoretical sorts of problems are mentioned very briefly in this section. Although there are a host of such interesting questions, only a couple are suggested. No current survey of the state of this field is intended, and no detailed references are given. Although the suggested problems are often very difficult for general n-person voting situations, suitable class projects result if they are restricted to the cases of $n = 3$ or 4.

For an arbitrary n and given q, the set of all possible weighted majority games $[q; w_1, w_2, \cdots, w_n]$ can be considered as the points in an $(n-1)$-dimensional simplex W embedded in n-space. One can normalize the weights so that they sum to $w = 1$. To each game there corresponds a particular collection of winning (or minimal winning) coalitions in the lattice of all subsets 2^N of the voter set $N = \{1, 2, \cdots, n\}$. Each such collection in turn gives rise to a Shapley–Shubik index φ, as well as a Banzhaf index β. Although the set W is infinite, the resulting number of collections of winning coalitions as well as the collections Φ and B of realizable indices φ and β are finite. Since any φ_i can be written as an integer divided by $n!$, and any β_i can, for each particular weight vector, be written as an integer over the total number of marginal situations for all n players, one can investigate how W partitions into equivalent games, i.e., games which give the same φ (or β). One can pick a particular q, or more generally, partition $W \times [0, 1]$ as q varies over the interval 0 to 1 [or just over (1/2, 1) if one wishes to maintain our earlier assumption]. One can see that not all fractions with a denominator of $n!$ can be realized as a φ_i.

It is natural to inquire as to which games have $\varphi = \beta$, and when is φ or β proportional to the weight vector $(w_1, w_2, \cdots, w_n)$. A few examples in the case of φ, are given by Riker and Shapley [71, pp. 208–209].

If an index φ, e.g., $\varphi = (3, 1, 1, 1)/6$, is considered as a weight vector of a new game, then this game will not in turn have the same index φ. Furthermore, not all voting situations (in the sense of minimal winning coalitions) can be represented as weighted majority games. One can consider this question in the case of the Canadian Constitutional Amendment Scheme (Section 5.1); or for the seven-point plane projective geometry discussed by von Neumann and Morgenstern [86, pp. 469–470], i.e., where the minimal winning coalitions consist of the three points (or voters) that lie on a particular one of the seven lines. One interested in mathematical questions about weights should consult Isbell [41] and Lapidot [45] and the references they have.

Various methods for composing or combining games can be introduced. The corresponding power indices do not normally compose in any straightforward manner. For example, consider the situation [3; 2, 1, 1] with $\varphi = (4, 1, 1)/6$, in which the third player is really a group of three players whose vote in turn is determined by majority rule. This "player" really plays the game [2; 1, 1, 1] with $\varphi = (1, 1, 1)/3$ before he votes in the larger situation. We can view this succession of votes as the one game [6; 4, 2, 1, 1, 1], which has $\varphi = (39, 9, 4, 4, 4)/60$ and $\beta = (6, 2, 1, 1, 1)/11$. Hence for example, φ_1 has changed from 2/3 in the original situation to 39/60 in the composite game.

Some results on the average value of φ_i in a given game when the quota q is allowed to vary are discussed by Mann and Shapley [48, e.g., p. 16].

6. Computational Aids

In order to obtain the power indices for games with many players and irregular weights, such as the Electoral College discussed in Section 7, it is rather essential to have some computational devices, as well as machine facilities and programs to implement them. Mann and Shapley [48] used some Monte Carlo techniques to obtain φ for the Electoral College, but greater accuracy was desired. Section 6.1 describes some mathematical tricks, suggested by Mann and Shapley [49], and by David G. Cantor, which simplify the work of calculation, and an actual algorithm for performing this task is referred to. Section 6.2 describes an approximation method using Stirling's formula for computing the number of voting combinations in which an individual voter from a large district is marginal. This technique can be used to compare the relative influences in the sense of Banzhaf of two citizens from different sized districts with equal representation as discussed in Section 5.3, as well as for two individuals from different states in the U.S. Electoral College as is done in Section 7. Section 6.3 mentions an extension of the Shapley value due to G. Owen, which gives a good approximation technique for determining φ and β for some large voting games.

6.1. Computing the Shapley–Shubik Index

The formula developed above for φ was expressed as

$$\varphi_i = \sum \frac{(s-1)!(n-s)!}{n!},$$

where the summation is taken over all coalitions S of s players in which i is pivotal. If one lets

$$c^i_{js} = \text{Number of ways in which } s \text{ players, other than } i, \text{ can have a sum of weights equal to } j,$$

then the formula, in the case of the n-person game $[q; w_1, w_2, \cdots, w_n]$, can be written as

$$\varphi_i = \frac{1}{n}\sum_{s=0}^{n-1}\binom{n-1}{s}^{-1}\sum_{j=q-w_i}^{q-1} c^i_{js},$$

where the numbers

$$\binom{n-1}{s}^{-1} = \frac{s!(n-1-s)!}{(n-1)!}$$

are the binomial coefficients and can be read off the $(n-1)$st row of the Pascal triangle. This latter coefficient, when divided by n, is the number of ways in which the s players in a given coalition S, which join prior to i and the remaining $n-1-s$ players in $N-\{i\}-S$ that follow i, can be ordered. If, and only if, the weights of the s members in S sum to a j in the range $q - w_i \leqq j \leqq q-1$ does player i have enough weight w_i in order to join S and thereby first reach or exceed the quota q. The c^i_{js} then give the number of such distinct coalitions for each j and s. The number of terms in this double summation for φ_i is not excessive for machine calculations, and thus the major task is to determine the values for the c^i_{js}.

As related by Mann and Shapley [49], Cantor's contribution was to point out that the c^i_{js} can be readily obtained from the generating function

$$f_i(x, y) = \Pi(1 + x^{w_k}y),$$

where the product is taken over all $k \in N - \{i\}$, since the desired c^i_{js} are merely the coefficients of the corresponding $x^j y^s$ terms. The proof of this is left as an exercise. For any i, $f_i(x, y)$ can be obtained from the full n-fold product $\Pi(1 + x^{w_k}y)$ divided by $(1 + x^{w_i}y)$.

The c^i_{js} can also be found as the elements of a matrix C^i of integers, and for each player i this matrix can be generated inductively as follows: Define $C^{(0)}$ so that $c^{(0)}_{00} = 1$ and all other $c^{(0)}_{js} = 0$. Then $C^{(r)}$ is obtained from $C^{(r-1)}$ by the relation

$$c^{(r)}_{js} = c^{(r-1)}_{js} + c^{(r-1)}_{j-w_p, s-1},$$

where the last term is taken as 0 when either of its subscripts is negative, and the successive w_p stand for the weights of the distinct players in $N - \{i\}$. After $n-1$ iterations, one gets $C^{(n-1)} = C^i$. One can obtain $C^{(n)}$ by taking all $r \in N$, and then get each C^i by subtracting once, i.e., by reversing our recursive relation above. See also Brams and Affuso [17].

Consider the example $[q; w_1, w_2, w_3, w_4] = [6; 4, 3, 2, 1]$, and compute φ_1. Only the nonzero elements of our matrices will be given. Beginning with $C^{(0)}$ with $c^{(0)}_{00} = 1$, and using

$$c_{js}^{(1)} = c_{js}^{(0)} + c_{j-w_2,s-1}^{(0)},$$

gives $C^{(1)}$ with $c_{00}^{(1)} = c_{31}^{(1)} = 1$. Then

$$c_{js}^{(2)} = c_{js}^{(1)} + c_{j-w_3,s-1}^{(1)}$$

gives $C^{(2)}$ with

$$c_{00}^{(2)} = c_{21}^{(2)} = c_{31}^{(2)} = c_{52}^{(2)} = 1.$$

And

$$c_{js}^{(3)} = c_{js}^{(2)} + c_{j-w_4,s-1}^{(2)}$$

gives $C^{(3)}$ with

$$c_{00}^{(3)} = c_{11}^{(3)} = c_{21}^{(3)} = c_{31}^{(3)} = c_{32}^{(3)} = c_{42}^{(3)} = c_{52}^{(3)} = c_{63}^{(3)} = 1.$$

Our formula restricts j to the range $2 \leqq j \leqq 5$, and gives

$$\varphi_1 = \frac{1!2!}{4!} \cdot 2 + \frac{2!1!}{4!} \cdot 3 = \frac{5}{12}.$$

Not all of the abovementioned matrices need be stored in the computer, and only the ranges $0 \leqq j \leqq q - 1$ and $0 \leqq s \leqq (n-1)/2$ are necessary since $C^{(n-1)}$ is "symmetric" in the sense that $c_{js} = c_{w-w_p-j,n-1-s}$.

A detailed algorithm suitable for computer programming and designed to calculate φ using the approach described above has recently been written by Boyce and Cross [14]. These $c_{js}^{(r)}$ can also prove useful in computing β.

6.2. The Number of Marginal Combinations

Since the number of voting combinations 2^n and the number of marginal combinations, involving factors of the order $n!$, are much too large for even machine calculation, it is necessary to develop simpler approximating devices in order to handle realistically sized voting districts. Assume that a district has n voters where n is taken as *odd*, and that an election is won by a simple majority, that is, by $(n+1)/2$ votes. A particular voter is marginal whenever the other $n-1$ players divide into exactly one half for an issue and the other half against it. The number of such equal divisions or combinations is given by

$$\frac{2(n-1)!}{\left(\frac{n-1}{2}\right)!\left(\frac{n-1}{2}\right)!}$$

where the 2 in the numerator comes from assigning either side in a division the "yes" vote. One can obtain the *relative* influence of each player in the sense of Banzhaf by dividing this fraction by 2^n. Using Stirling's formula (which appears in many advanced calculus texts),

$$m! \approx \sqrt{2\pi m}\, m^m e^{-m},$$

one can reduce this new fraction to

$$\frac{2(n-1)!}{\left[\left(\frac{n-1}{2}\right)!\right]^2} \times \frac{1}{2^n} \approx \frac{2}{\sqrt{2\pi(n-1)}}.$$

If we assume that all voting combinations are equally likely, then this is the fraction of elections in which a particular voter i is decisive, and it varies inversely with the square root of the population. *Note* that since each voter has equal power, one must get $\beta_i = 1/n$; but β_i does *not* give the fraction of elections in which player i is in the critical position.

This result now justifies some of the assertions made in Section 5.3, and will prove useful in Section 7. It shows that the discrimination or the deprivation built into voting districts relates to this square-root factor, if one accepts the Banzhaf analysis. This approximation is a good one for large districts since Stirling's formula is accurate, for example, to one part in one hundred for $m = 100$. Note that this approximation given by Stirling's formula is in the asymptotic sense, i.e., the ratio of the two sides of the equation approaches one for large m; the actual gap between $m!$ and the right-hand side actually increases with m. Another discussion of this "square root effect" is given by Shapley [81, pp. 83–85].

In a few footnotes, Banzhaf [6, p. 335; 8, p. 312] mentions some people who assisted him in calculating β for some of his applications. One computer program by M. Sackson was copyrighted, and leads one to wonder if mathematicians can increase their incomes by copyrighting their important theorems. In Section 5.6, reference was made to Lee Papayanopoulos who assisted Cortland County, New York in designing a weighted voting system using the Banzhaf approach. Johnson [42] also described some of his computer programs for determining proper weights, as did Walther [87].

Another view of marginality is given by Brams and Davis [18, 19].

6.3. A Computation Method for Large Games

Owen [56] introduced a generalization of the Shapley value in the context of general n-person games, and a specific application of his extension is an approximation technique for determining the Shapley–Shubik index. His approach is presented on p. P72–P73 of his paper, and it is quite accurate for games with a large number n of voters if each of the weights w_i is relatively small. It need not be too precise when there is exactly *one* relatively large weight. Owen's method makes use of the normal probability distribution and numerical integration. However, the actual computations are much easier than the exact values as obtained via Section 6.1 in the case of large games such as the Electoral College given in Section 7; Owen [57] has made such calculations for the situation in 1972. Owen's approach is also discussed by Shapley [81, pp. 78–83] along with an application to a proposed New Mexico weighted voting scheme. Owen [58] has also shown how his approach can be used to approximate β.

7. The Electoral College

Previous examples have shown that weighted voting systems occur rather frequently in political situations. This section will be concerned with the familiar process of electing a president of the United States. This is a three-level process in which the citizens in each state vote to determine their choice (the *state game*), who then receives all of that state's weighted vote in the Electoral College (the *national game*). If the latter vote is indecisive, then the final choice is made in Congress (the *Congressional game*). This procedure will be described in more detail in Section 7.1; and the national game, state games, and the combination of these games will be analyzed with respect to voting power in Sections 7.2, 7.3, and 7.4, respectively. Some criticisms of this election process are mentioned in Section 7.5, and some possible alternatives to it are also described there.

The American Electoral College provides a well-known real-world institution that has many nonobvious quantitative aspects despite its apparently transparent structure. It is a topic of at least periodic interest, and major changes in it have frequently been proposed. The mathematical complexity of this election process, and of the proposed alternatives to it, make it appropriate for a classroom project for students with some computing capabilities available.

7.1. Electing a President

Consider the indirect procedure by which an American president is elected. It begins with a national popular vote by all eligible citizens who choose to exercise their right. Each voter picks a particular candidate representing a certain political party. (We are not considering here the preliminary aspects concerning how the candidates survived state primary elections, party conventions, etc.) The candidate who wins the most votes in a given state, no matter how small his margin, will then receive all of that states weighted vote in the Electoral College. This is referred to as the "winner take all" or "unit-vote" rule, which is imposed by state laws. The individual electors who actually cast the votes in the Electoral College are usually mere functionaries. This purely mechanical role is contrary to their view in the Constitution and has had a few defectors in recent years, and the legality of some such state laws may be questionable. In short, the popular vote for the president only determines a group of electors for each state who in turn are pledged to the winning candidate in their state.

The number of electors that each state has in the Electoral College is equal to its number of representatives in both houses of the Congress. Each state has two senators plus one to 47 representatives, where this latter number depends upon its population as determined by the regular decennial census and resulting apportionment (which gives rise to another interesting mathematical problem that will be mentioned again in Section 8). Since there are 100 senators, 435 representatives, plus 3 electors from the District of Columbia, there are a total of 538 seats in the Electoral College. Any candidate who reaches or exceeds the simple majority of 270 votes is declared the new president.

In the event that no one receives a majority in the Electoral College, then the process goes to a third level and the deadlock is resolved in the Congress. This occurred in the elections of 1800 and 1824. The House of Representatives chooses the president from among the top three candidates in the Electoral College. (The Senate picks the vice-president from the top two candidates.) In the House, each state has only a single vote, and a majority of 26 is necessary to win. Note that the small states could have extraordinary power relative to their total population in this Congressional determination. The following mathematical analysis will not be concerned with this third level, or potential "tie-breaking" procedure, in the presidential elections. At this third level some truly bizarre possibilities can occur. For example, at one time before the 1968 election it looked as though the order of finish in the Electoral College could be Nixon–Agnew, Wallace–LeMay, and Humphrey–Muskie with the leading Nixon ticket having less than a majority. This could have resulted in H. H. Humphrey as President and General Curtis LeMay as Vice President. In a fictitious novel, Russell Baker [2] describes how Lindsay, Johnson, and Wallace ran for the Presidency in 1968 with none getting a majority in the Electoral College. As a deadlock developed in the House, the Senate chose R. F. Kennedy as Vice President, who then decided to suspend balloting in the House for President in order to buy time to influence their decision.

Our goal is to investigate some of the mathematical structure of the first two stages in the election of a president, and to analyze how power is distributed between the different states and the individual citizens of these different states. Our previous examples have given reason to believe that such investigations of voting influence can give rise to irregular, surprising, and unpredictable comparisons in terms of a voter's ability to affect the outcome of an election. This quantitative approach will confirm the intuitive and historical evidence to the effect that there is a bias in favor of the large states and their citizens.

There is an excellent source book by Peirce [61] on the Electoral College, which discusses its history, past changes, past and present reform efforts, and potential alternatives. The appendix of this book contains a host of data relevant to any study of this institution.

7.2. The National Game

The Electoral College can be viewed as a 51-person weighted majority game between the states. This assumes that each state (plus the District of Columbia) acts as an independent player, i.e., as a free agent without prior commitments and outside influences. For this game, the sum w of the 51 weights

Table 19. State Electoral Votes

State	1961	1972	State	1961	1972
Alabama	10	9	Montana	4	4
Alaska	3	3	Nebraska	5	5
Arizona	5	6	Nevada	3	3
Arkansas	6	6	New Hampshire	4	4
California	40	45	New Jersey	17	17
Colorado	6	7	New Mexico	4	4
Connecticut	8	9[a]	New York	43	41
Delaware	3	3	North Carolina	13	13
District of Columbia	3	3	North Dakota	4	3
Florida	14	17	Ohio	26	25
Georgia	12	12	Oklahoma	8	7[a]
Hawaii	4	4	Oregon	6	6
Idaho	4	4	Pennsylvania	29	27
Illinois	26	26	Rhode Island	4	4
Indiana	13	13	South Carolina	8	8
Iowa	9	8	South Dakota	4	4
Kansas	7	7	Tennessee	11	10
Kentucky	9	9	Texas	25	26
Louisiana	10	10	Utah	4	4
Maine	4	4	Vermont	3	3
Maryland	10	10	Virginia	12	12
Massachusetts	14	14	Washington	9	9
Michigan	21	21	West Virginia	7	6
Minnesota	10	10	Wisconsin	12	11
Mississippi	7	7	Wyoming	3	3
Missouri	12	12			
			Total	538	538

[a] More recent results give 8 votes to Connecticut and 8 votes to Oklahoma due to a change in how some overseas population is allocated to their home state.

is 538 and the simple majority quota q is 270. The weight w_i for each individual state i is equal to its number of electoral votes, and these are listed in Table 19. We shall treat the District of Columbia throughout as though it were a state. These weights can change every ten years as a result of the national census, and they have occasionally been modified slightly by Congress. So the table lists the weights as they were in 1964 and 1968 elections under the column "1961," and the way they were for the 1972 election under "1972." These are based upon the 1960 and 1970 census figures, respectively, along with the method used to determine the number of seats each state receives in the Congress.

We are interested in determining the voting power for each state in this national game. These results are given in Table 20. The first column lists in descending order the number of electoral votes, or weight w_i, which a

Table 20. Electoral College Power Ratios

Column Number of electoral votes w_i	(A) Number of states i 1961	(B) 1972	(C) Power indices φ_i 1961	(D) 1972	(E) Rescaled indices $538\ \varphi_i$ 1961	(F) 1972	(G) Power ratios $538\ \varphi_i \div w_i$ 1961	(H) 1972
45	0	1	—	0.08830938	—	47.510446	—	1.0557877
43	1	0	0.08406425	—	45.226568	—	1.0517806	—
41	0	1	—	0.07972734	—	42.893309	—	1.0461782
40	1	0	0.07767063	—	41.786804	—	1.0446701	—
29	1	0	0.05500222	—	29.591194	—	1.0203860	—
27	0	1	—	0.05096311	—	27.418153	—	1.0154873
26	2	2	0.04901260	0.04897682	26.368783	26.349529	1.0141839	1.0134433
25	1	1	0.04703309	0.04699893	25.303807	25.285424	1.0121523	1.0114169
21	1	1	0.03919718	0.03916926	21.088085	21.073062	1.0041945	1.0034790
17	1	2	0.03148765	0.03146563	16.940359	16.928509	0.9964917	0.99579468
14	2	1	0.02578474	0.02576694	13.872193	13.862614	0.9908709	0.99018686
13	2	2	0.02389839	0.02388196	12.857334	12.848494	0.9890257	0.98834576
12	4	3	0.02201920	0.02200413	11.846331	11.838222	0.9871943	0.98651844
11	1	1	0.02014710	0.02013337	10.839140	10.831753	0.9853764	0.98470464
10	4	4	0.01828200	0.01826959	9.835718	9.829039	0.9835718	0.98290416
9	3	4*	0.01642383	0.01641273	8.836024	8.830049	0.9817804	0.98111659
8	3	2*	0.01457252	0.01456270	7.840015	7.834733	0.9800019	0.97934191
7	3	4*	0.01272798	0.01271944	6.847652	6.843059	0.9782360	0.97757982
6	3	4	0.01089014	0.01088284	5.858896	5.854968	0.9764827	0.97582844
5	2	1	0.00905894	0.00905301	4.873709	4.870519	0.9747417	0.97410373
4	10	9	0.00723429	0.00722957	3.892051	3.889509	0.9730128	0.97237690
3	6	7	0.00541615	0.00541245	2.913883	2.911898	0.9712958	0.97063223
Totals 538	51	51	0.99999947	0.99999970	537.999790	537.999803	50.2431662	50.2102844

state may have; columns (A) and (B) list the number of such states with the corresponding weights for the years 1961 and 1972, respectively. The power indices, in the sense of Shapley–Shubik, are given in columns (C) and (D) for the two periods being considered. The first of these (C), as well as results for some earlier periods, were reported by Mann and Shapley [49]; the second one (D) was given by Boyce and Cross [14]. Columns (E) and (F) rescale the previous two columns by multiplying by the total weight 538 so that they can be easily compared with the number of electoral votes listed in the first column. Columns (G) and (H) express these comparisons as ratios. It should be noted that the numbers in the table were obtained by decimal calculations on the computer and are rounded off, and are excellent approximations to the exact values that are in fact rational numbers since they have a factor of 51! in the denominator. These results indicate a clear and systematic bias in favor of the large states. However, the total magnitude of the bias is less than 10%, and is thus rather small in the light of the many nonquantifiable aspects in such political institutions. Thus, to a rather good degree of approximation, a state's voting power is proportional to its influence as expressed by its number of electoral votes.

One can design several interesting major classroom projects which are based upon or motivated by the above results, and a few of these are mentioned in what follows.

EXERCISES

26. Determine the power, in the sense of φ or β, for each of the 13 states in the original Electoral College. Power at other historical periods may also be of interest, e.g., at the time of the Civil War.

27. One can attempt to reproduce the results in Table 20 for the year 1972. This would make use of some computational techniques such as those described in Section 6.1 or 6.3, plus the design of a computer program to implement these. A detailed algorithm for doing this is described by Boyce and Cross, but one would still have to program this for his local computing facilities.

28. The data in Table 20 can be analyzed graphically for the 1972 results. One can plot the points (w_i, φ_i) in the plane; find the best fitting straight line, parabola, etc., and test these for goodness of fit. Mann and Shapley [49] illustrate the data graphically for their 1961 results, and report that it has an excellent parabolic fit. Additional statistical analyses of various deviations in the data may be undertaken.

29. One can argue that the states are not independent agents in this national game, but instead that certain states with closely related interests or voting histories combine together and tend to vote alike. One can investigate past voting behavior of states, and aggregate together those who have voted the same way and assume that they are likely to continue to do so in the near future. These new coalitions of states can be treated as the individual players in a new version of the Electoral College game that will now have fewer players but with usually larger weights. This project can be modeled after the recent work by Boyce [13], and there are a host of statistical hypotheses that can be assumed and investigated. For example, Boyce studies the impact of a third-party movement such as the one by George C. Wallace in 1968.

30. An ambitious project would be to investigate the procedures used by the major parties to nominate their presidential candidates at the national conventions, under, say, the somewhat unrealistic assumption that all delegates from a given state vote for the same candidate, i.e., the state is bound by the unit rule. This idealized game is somewhat similar to the Electoral College but the weights and number of states are determined in a slightly different fashion. The reference by David [25], plus some more recent data, may prove useful.

31. Many of the above projects can be undertaken using the 1980 census data.

7.3. The State Game

Consider the game that is played in a particular state. Here the players are the individual voters in the state and a simple majority, or often just a plurality, determines the winner, who will then receive all of this state's votes in the national game discussed in the previous section. It is clear that each individual voter in a given state has equal voting power in his state game, and that his power index is $1/N$, where N is the total number of voters in his state. In the following we shall take N to be the total population of the state and thus assume that such N are proportional to the numbers of voters that the different states have. The number of electoral votes of a state is based on such census figures. We also avoid consideration here of the fact that various numbers of voters may not exercise their right to vote. More important than a player's power index, however, is the chance that he has of being the marginal voter in his state. Conventional wisdom often holds that this probability varies inversely with the population. On the other hand, we saw from the analysis in Section 6.2 that the possibility of being marginal, as determined by Banzhaf, is instead proportional to $1/\sqrt{N}$. This relationship was also discussed in Section 5.3 in connection with representation from multimember districts. For example, the 1960 populations of New York State and the District of Columbia were 16,782,304 and 763,956, respectively. The chance that a voter from New York can sway his state's election compared to that for a voter from the District of Columbia is $1/(16{,}782{,}304)^{1/2}$ to $1/(763{,}956)^{1/2}$, or $(4097)^{-1}$ to $(874)^{-1}$, which gives the ratio 0.2133. In other words a voter from D.C. has 4.687 times the chance of being marginal in his "state" as the voter from New York.

EXERCISE

32. In light of this square-root factor discussed above, what possible types of errors could be introduced into the various analyses in this paper if one uses a state's population figure rather than the number of its citizens who are actually likely to vote?

7.4. The Combined Game

To obtain some measure of the individual voter's total influence in electing a president, one must take into account both the national game and the state games discussed in the last two sections. To better understand this existing system, one must somehow compose the two previous results. We have seen that it is false to presume that each citizen's relative share of power in this two-level game is directly proportional to his state's weight w_i divided by its population N_i. Instead, one can combine the Shapley–Shubik index φ for the national game given in Table 20 with the Banzhaf inverse square-root formula for comparing the different state games in order to get some *approximate* idea of the relative influence of voters from different states. These two measures reflect the power that a given state and an individual within the state have in an election. Consider, for example, a comparison between New York State and the District of Columbia using the 1961 figures in Table 20. Clearly, New York has more power in the national game,

Table 21. Relative Voting Power

State	Population 1960 census	I Present plan	II Proportional plan	III District plan
Alabama	3266740	1.632	1.203	1.302
Alaska	226167	1.838	5.212	3.075
Arizona	1302161	1.281	1.509	1.594
Arkansas	1786272	1.315	1.320	1.459
California	15717204	3.162	1.000	1.004
Colorado	1753947	1.327	1.344	1.472
Connecticut	2535234	1.477	1.240	1.362
Delaware	446292	1.308	2.641	2.189
District of Columbia	763956	1.000	1.543	1.673
Florida	4951560	1.870	1.111	1.197
Georgia	3943116	1.789	1.196	1.267
Hawaii	632772	1.468	2.484	2.092
Idaho	667191	1.429	2.356	2.038
Illinois	10081158	2.491	1.013	1.059
Indiana	4662498	1.786	1.096	1.200
Iowa	2757537	1.596	1.282	1.364
Kansas	2178611	1.392	1.263	1.399
Kentucky	3038156	1.521	1.164	1.299
Louisiana	3257022	1.635	1.206	1.304
Maine	969265	1.186	1.622	1.691
Maryland	3100689	1.675	1.267	1.337
Massachusetts	5148578	1.834	1.068	1.174
Michigan	7823194	2.262	1.055	1.108
Minnesota	3413864	1.597	1.151	1.274
Mississippi	2178141	1.392	1.263	1.399
Missouri	4319813	1.710	1.092	1.211
Montana	674767	1.421	2.329	2.026
Nebraska	1411330	1.231	1.392	1.532
Nevada	285278	1.636	4.132	2.738
New Hampshire	606921	1.499	2.590	2.137
New Jersey	6066782	2.063	1.101	1.162
New Mexico	951023	1.197	1.653	1.707
New York	16782304	3.312	1.007	1.000
North Carolina	4556155	1.807	1.121	1.214
North Dakota	632446	1.468	2.485	2.903
Ohio	9706397	2.539	1.053	1.080
Oklahoma	2328284	1.541	1.350	1.422
Oregon	1768687	1.321	1.333	1.466
Pennsylvania	11319366	2.638	1.007	1.043
Rhode Island	859488	1.259	1.829	1.795
South Carolina	2382594	1.524	1.319	1.405
South Dakota	680514	1.415	2.310	2.018
Tennessee	3567089	1.721	1.212	1.291
Texas	9579677	2.452	1.025	1.070

Table 21. (*continued*)

State	Population 1960 census	I Present plan	II Proportional plan	III District plan
Utah	890627	1.237	1.765	1.764
Vermont	389881	1.400	3.023	2.342
Virginia	3966949	1.784	1.189	1.264
Washington	2853214	1.569	1.239	1.341
West Virginia	1860421	1.506	1.478	1.514
Wisconsin	3951777	1.788	1.193	1.266
Wyoming	330066	1.521	3.571	2.546

and this can be indicated by the ratio of $\varphi_{NY} = 0.084064$ to $\varphi_{DC} = 0.005416$, which is 15.521 and is a little higher than the ratio of weights, i.e., $w_{NY} = 43$ to $w_{DC} = 3$ or 14.333. On the other hand, we saw in the previous section that a voter in N.Y. has only 0.2133 times as much chance of swaying his larger state as a voter from D.C. has of switching his district. Combining these two effects gives $(15.521) \times (0.2133) = 3.311$, which indicates the relative power of an individual in N.Y. to one in D.C. in the two-level election process. Note that we have merely multiplied the results of two separate games here, and that we have taken the φ measure in one case and used the Banzhaf analysis for the state games. We have *not* actually solved the single composed game as we did for one simple example in Section 5.3, because this composition would be a huge game in which some 100,000,000 players participate, and because the behavior of power indices (or more general values in game theory) under various compositions is not completely known. We return to this point in 35 below.

Banzhaf [8, Table I] has compared the ability of a citizen in one state to affect the outcome of a presidential election with the ability of one from another state, and these are shown in column (I) in Table 21. Note that N.Y. and D.C. are the extreme cases. Note also that some states have little more power than D.C., and so the latter is not the only one relatively poor in power. The low value for D.C. is expected since its $w_{DC} = 3$ is assigned in a manner different from the states and is not based so much on population. It is clear from the table that the influence in the various state games greatly exaggerates the small bias in the national game in favor of the larger states. These results do not depend upon some quirk in our definitions of power, but are inherent in the design of the system itself when viewed as an abstract mathematical entity or structure. They surely give rise to some question about whether the "one man-one vote" principle is satisfied in presidential elections. A similar type of conclusion is reached by Brams and Davis (1974).

Some projects parallel to Banzhaf's work can be undertaken.

EXERCISES

33. One can use the 1972 values for w_i and φ_i given in Table 20 along with the 1970 census figures for N_i to obtain an up-dated version of the results in column (I) of our Table 21.

34. One can investigate various statistical deviations indicated in column (I), or its up-dated version mentioned in (33); answer questions about what percentage of the states or people benefit or are disadvantaged by the Electoral College system. Some results of this type are given by Banzhaf [8, Table I].

35. The method of Owen [56, 57] mentioned in Section 6.3 allows one to construct a nonsymmetric value theory for the quotient game that will yield the correct symmetric indices for the *composed* game, and it gives good approximations to the 100,000,000-player national game between all the citizens in the U.S., and it does so with simpler computational problems than those discussed in Section 6.1. Apply Owen's approach to compute the relative voting power of the citizens in the different States in the U.S. Presidential Election.

7.5. Electoral College Reform

The unique Electoral College system was created to serve as a compromise between other possibilities. Yet the difficulties and inequities inherent in it have caused continual criticism over the years. Some changes have been made in the past and many unsuccessful reforms have been attempted. Peirce [61] has an excellent discussion on this. An observation of party campaign strategies or a historical review of close elections confirms, at least empirically, the big state bias in this election process. A good discussion of this is given in an article entitled "The Ox-Cart Way We Pick a Space-Age President" by Hamilton [36]. Some of these close historical results are also mentioned by Banzhaf [8, footnote on pp. 322 and 323] and by Davis [26, p. 135]. Interest in reform tends to peak and wane, but it was particularly intense for a few years around 1968 when Wallace's candidacy raised the serious possibility of a deadlock. Some quantitative considerations of the potential power of certain blocs of states in this third-party movement are discussed by Boyce [13]. Such reform efforts were ultimately defeated by a successful filibuster carried on by Southern and small state senators led by Sam Ervin, and this is reported in the Congressional Quarterly Almanac (Volume 26, 1970, pp. 840–845). Paradoxically, the system was defended by many of those states that fare rather poorly according to our mathematical analyses of power. So we continue with a system that has given rise to two deadlocks (1800 and 1824) and several presidents who received less than a majority of the popular vote (1824, 1844, 1876, 1884, 1888, 1916, 1948, 1960 and 1968). Some presidents received fewer votes than one of their opponents, and a person can theoretically lose an election in which he obtains a majority of the popular vote. Opinion polls also show that the public is in favor of reform. Further discussion on reform is given in the book by Best [11] and in several references in Brams and Davis [19].

Many alternatives to the present Electoral College system have been proposed. One frequently heard suggestion is to abolish this set-up completely and to determine the president directly from the national popular vote. This approach can give rise to some technical difficulties if, for example, we moved toward a system of many parties. But the vote of each individual voter clearly counts the same in this case. However, the plans given serious consideration by Congress recently have usually been variations in the present Electoral College. Two types of these are referred to as the proportional plan and the district plan.

In the proportional plan, a state i with population N_i maintains its electoral vote w_i, but this weight is divided among the candidates in proportion to their statewide popular vote. These numbers need not be restricted to integers. Thus a citizen who changes his vote causes a shift of w_i/N_i electoral votes in the Electoral College. But voters from different states still have different influences under this plan. The relative ability of individuals from different states to affect an election can be easily computed. This was done by Banzhaf [8] using the 1960 population figures and is given in column (II) of Table 21. Since smaller states have more electoral votes per resident than the larger ones, they have more voting power under this plan.

Exercises

36. A simple project is to recompute the numbers in column (II) using the 1972 electoral vote distribution (Table 19) and the 1970 census figures.

37. A more ambitious project would be to investigate a variation of the proportional plan in which votes are distributed to the candidates but not in a directly proportional plan. For example, a candidate who receives 55% of a state's popular vote might be assigned 65% of its electoral vote, or one who receives as much as 65% of the popular vote may get 95% of the electoral vote. In such a system, what sort of curves (popular vote versus electoral votes) would seem appropriate? It would be of interest to pick some trial curves and study what results they would have produced in previous elections. One may wish to limit consideration to only two major candidates, or to design a scheme for multiple parties.

In the district plan for electing the president, the voters in each state elect two electors at-large plus one elector from each congressional district in the state. Each elector then votes for the candidate who obtained the most votes in his district. The inverse square-root formula can be used to determine an individual's relative chance of being marginal in the vote for the two at-large statewide delegates as well as for his own congressional district elector. His power is determined by combining these two possibilities. This case was also calculated using 1960 figures by Banzhaf [8] and is given in column (III) of Table 21. Again, the more populous states are at the disadvantage. On the other hand, the large states have, contrary to their own interests, tended to support such plans as the proportional and district one, while the smaller ones have resisted reform in this direction.

EXERCISES

38. Another project is to calculate the numbers in column (III) using the 1972 data in Table 19 and the 1970 population figures.

39. One can investigate certain statistical deviations in columns (II) and (III), or the new results in (36) or (38), and discuss questions about the numbers of states or individuals who benefit or are disadvantaged by these systems. A few results along these lines are mentioned by Banzhaf [8, Tables II and III].

40. The Behavioral Research Council of Great Barrington, Massachusetts 01230, in their *Bulletin* of January 1974, has proposed a "second revised draft" (a "third" was also planned) of the Constitution of the U.S., which they suggest be used for study purposes in high schools and colleges. Their proposed election procedures have a weighted-voting aspect to them, and it may be of interest to investigate these in light of the power indices discussed above.

41. In a recent book by geographer Pearcy [60], he suggests that the U.S. should be repartitioned into a country with 38 states. He suggests that river valleys, large metropolitian areas, etc., should be part of an individual state rather than serve as boundaries for different states. His states would be more equal in size, and his plan would in theory give significant financial savings. Consider population figures, and design an Electoral College for this new U.S. of 38 states. His plan would also change the apportionment of Congress, another type of voting problem mentioned in Section 8.2.

42. In an editorial in the *New York Times* by Joseph Farkas on March 29, 1974, he suggests: "The principle of one man-one vote should therefore be replaced by a system of proportional representation that would weight each man's vote in proportion to his demonstrated capability to make intelligent choices." Related letters to the editor appeared on April 11. Consider how one might implement this elitist form of democracy in light of the power indices for weighted voting.

8. Additional Voting Problems

Many types of voting situations give rise to problems with a significant mathematical structure. There are several directions in which the weighted voting discussed in this paper can be extended, as well as many other sorts of voting problems, which make use of other mathematical methods. A few of these extensions and alternate approaches will be mentioned in this section. These are included in order to point the interested reader to a few possible directions, and no attempt is made to give any details or to cover all of the possible voting areas. For example, problems involving probabilistic, statistical, clustering, or simulation techniques are not discussed here.

8.1. Affinity of Coalitions

Experience from the real-world indicates that some voting combinations or coalitions of voters are more likely to form than others. This may be caused by personal relations between the players, by closeness of political philosophies, by other ideological grounds, or by common goals or geographical proximity. Owen [55] has developed a modification of the Shapley value, which considers this affinity of certain coalitions, as have Frank and Shapley [31]. The relative position of the voters is described by positioning them on a hypersphere, or else as points in an issue space, and then the likelihood of coalitions depends upon these locations. Owen applied this value to the eleven-party Israeli Knesset in 1965, where the parties were spread from left to right on the political spectrum. It would be an interesting project to apply this to the Israeli Knesset as it existed in 1974 [see Table 14] or 1981, where one would perhaps wish to collect opinions on the orthodox–nonorthodox spread as well as the liberal–conservative spectrum; or to the Danish Parliament in 1974, where some suggested data, taken from four Danish professors, is given in Section 5.4 (iv). The computation of Owen's index is usually *not* extremely difficult. Another view for incorporating "prior position" into the value or power index is given by Shapley [81, pp. 76–78].

8.2. Apportionment of Congress

An important problem in the U.S. and elsewhere, and one with a very interesting history, is how to determine the number of seats that any state will have in the U.S. Congress. It is desirable that any such scheme be fair in the sense that it possesses a certain "consistency" property, that it gives each one of the states nearly its "quota" and that the method has a certain "monotonicity property" (i.e., avoids the "Alabama paradox"). This problem is discussed in Chapter 14 of this volume and in the monograph, *Fair Representation*, by M. L. Balinski and H. P. Young (Yale University Press, 1982).

8.3. Redistricting

Another important political problem is how to partition a region into a certain number of "similar" districts, e.g., dividing a state into Congressional districts. It is desirable, or a legal necessity, that the resulting districts have certain properties, e.g., roughly equal population, contiguity (say convex), compactness (say fat or circular or squarelike rather than thin), etc. One wishes to avoid gerrymandering. Several mathematical methods have been applied to this problem. Garfinkel and Nemhauser [32] developed an algorithm by considering techniques from integer programming. They applied it to 26 census tracts in Sussex County, Delaware, and to 7 districts and 39 counties in the State of Washington. They had difficulty with 55 counties in the State of West Virginia. Other approaches, such as simulation, have also been used on this problem. Several class projects along these lines are possible, e.g., consider how to construct a university senate with constituencies of about equal size, where each senator represents a rather "common" or "homogeneous" group. Redistricting (or *re*apportionment) is usually of keen interest for a year or two following the release of the census data.

8.4. Sequential Voting Strategies

Many common voting procedures have an important strategic aspect to them. In many sequential situations, such as binary voting as is frequently done on a series of proposed amendments, the final outcome may depend upon the order in which the motions are considered. The result may depend upon the information about another's intentions, and thus one may benefit by deceptive, misleading, or diversionary tactics in the earlier stages when there are multiple votes in a sequence. Optimal voting strategies and various equilibria concepts have been studied, e.g., by using the theory of games in extensive (tree) or normal (matrix) forms. Good introductions to some of these situations appear in the excellent little book by Farquharson [30] (including historical examples in his Appendix), and in Chapter 14 (especially Section 14.8) by Luce and Raiffa [47].

8.5. Maps

There has been recent interest in various types of geographical or political maps, called cartograms, which are not drawn in accord with standard map projections. For example, pilots use maps that have a magnification of airport areas, and one can produce highway maps in which cities or complicated interchanges are embedded "continuously" but in a much larger aerial scale. A related theorem in differential geometry appears in Sen [74]; there are potential applications to areas in economics and political science, e.g., see the paper by Tobler (pp. 215–220) in Papayanopoulos [59].

9. Limits of the Mathematical Models

9.1. General Remarks

An important step in the complete model building process is to validate or verify the accuracy and usefulness of the model to the real-world situation. It is not sufficient to work in a mathematical vacuum, for one is required to check whether his conclusions are realistic or whether they must be carefully limited. Awareness of the theoretical or hypothetical nature of the results must be clearly understood when one makes use of his results in practice. This is particularly true in building mathematical models in political science, where it is so easy to be excessively isolated, to discard too many essentials, or to overlook many less quantifiable customs or procedures. In the social sciences, in general, it is most difficult to form complete models that contain all relevant aspects of current reality. After all, the social sciences make a much greater use of adjectives than do the physical sciences or mathematics. In this realm it is usually foolish to claim that one has obtained complete understanding, proofs, full explanation, true meaning, etc. Before employing one's abstract analysis as a true imitation of reality, one normally has to become heavily involved with complicated data and other more empirical activities.

9.2. Additional Considerations

It is clear that our mathematical analysis of certain voting situations is in many ways superficial. It does not include much of the political actuality in the global realm of power, influence, legislation, or elections in our governmental institutions. In the realities of political life there are many alliances, differences, cohesive blocs, discriminations, partisan actions, and additional sources that influence outcomes. One must consider the effects of working behind-the-scene, capabilities in caucus or in the cloakrooms, or other "secondary" considerations, as well as the superimposed or non-elected operating structures or individuals, such as a committee system with a seniority rule of succession to a strong chairman's position. One must also consider the influences of party loyalty, prestige, publicity, bossism, solidarity, persuasion, personal gains, lobbying, fractionalism, bribes, gratuities, patronage, pork barrels, horse trading, campaign financing, and so on. Hopefully, these factors are counter balanced, by or at least not completely divorced from, such elements as honest debate, sincere deliberations, morality, conscience, ethics, reason, fairness, equity, or other rules or "laws" in the game of politics. In extreme cases the whole political structure itself is altered more drastically under coercion, threats, force, wars, coups, or assassinations.

In particular, in many of our examples and suggested projects the assumption that there exists irrevocable blocs of voters is frequently less than realistic. Our applications often discounted effects due to absences, abstentions, tie-breaking rules, using population figures for numbers of voters, and ignored other details of voting procedures. The analysis of the Electoral College in Section 7 clearly overlooks many free-for-all and less-readily-apparent aspects of an actual national convention or political campaign. Some detailed criticisms of Banzhaf's [8] study by a few U.S. Senators and other experts follow his paper, and also appear in the following volume of this same journal (Volume 14, pp. 86–96). However, there is some historical and empirical evidence to support the big-state bias in the Electoral College as is discussed by Peirce [61], Hamilton [36], and Uslander (pp. 61–76 in Papayanopoulos [59]). There is clearly a great deal of material which can be used for classroom discussion or criticism of the previous projects.

At another level of criticism, there is the major question of what is the role of an elected official. Should he serve in the more routine, mechanical, or plebiscitarian role of the true *delegate* or *representative*, who polls, surveys, or in some other way knows the preferences of his citizens, and who merely funnels or transmits this popular opinion to the legislature? Or should he act in a more patrician or *Burkean* mode, where he is more of a free agent or trustee, to whom the voters abdicate power or whose judgment they rely upon? For example, U.S. congressman tend to act in the latter mode on questions about foreign policy or impeachment, whereas they may follow the former role in more local or domestic issues, since their reelection may depend upon it. Additional moral and philosophical concerns about the ends, means, causes, goals, and consequences of power are discussed in some of the writings by Riker.

9.3. Usefulness

It is clear that our weighted voting analysis is only a rather singular, perhaps even trivial, part of the political systems being analyzed. In many cases the weights are not the critical factors, and other practical considerations prove more important. Our conclusions admittedly fall short to the extent that the models are not general enough. However, any model must compromise between excessive complication and incorporation of the total picture. However, one should distinguish between the faults of the analyses, such as erroneous assumptions, incompleteness or incorrect conclusions, on the one hand, as against faults inherent in the actual design or very fabric of the system being modeled, on the other hand, e.g., irrational or illogical behavior, false intuition, or nonlogical structures.

One can nevertheless argue that the power indices are a worthwhile first step in a quantitative investigation of such voting situations. Although limited in scope, such analysis is hardly entirely wanting or completely irrelevant, and there should be little objection to utilizing the results in the limited or spotty context to which they apply. Such studies should be useful in setting up norms, standards, ground rules, or minimal requirements for a voting situation; and they have recently found some implementation and acceptance by the courts in practice. Although fairness or justice are hardly to be found entirely in some simple mathematical formula or symmetry, it would appear that one should attempt to avoid numerical bias, as well as other types, whenever possible. It is hoped that, the power indices surveyed in this paper will have some value as a quantitative aid in judging equality in certain political structures, and they will become part of the conventional wisdom on the subject. Knowledge of power indices might be compared to knowing the odds of obtaining various poker hands; it is rather helpful, but not sufficient in itself to being a good poker player. It is also most likely that once mathematical techniques have successfully entered into political science, they are unlikely to be completely discarded in the future; some recent authors even go so far as to suggest a new field called "governmetrics" analogous to "econometrics."

References

1. Aumann, R. J., and Shapley, L. S. *Values of Non-Atomic Games.* Princeton University Press, Princeton, New Jersey, 1974.
2. Baker, Russell. *Our Next President.* Atheneum, New York, 1968.
3. Balinski, M. L., and Young, H. P. "A New Method for Congressional Apportionment," *Proceedings of the National Academy of Sciences, 71* (November 1974), 4602–4606.
4. Balinski, M. L., and Young, H. P. "The Quota Method of Apportionment," *The American Mathematical Monthly, 82* (August–September 1975).
5. Balinski, M. L., and Young, H. P. "The Webster Method of Apportionment," *Proceedings of the National Academy of Sciences, 77* (January 1980), 1–4.
6. Banzhaf, John F. III. "Weighted Voting Doesn't Work: A Mathematical Analysis," *Rutgers Law Review, 19* (1965), 317–343.
7. Banzhaf, John F. III. "Multi-Member Electoral Districts—Do They Violate the One Man—One Vote Principle," *The Yale Law Journal, 75* (1966), 1309–1338.
8. Banzhaf, John F. III. "One Man, 3.312 Votes: A Mathematical Analysis of the Electoral College," *Villanova Law Review, 13* (Winter 1968), 304–332. Also see comments by Editor (p. 303), Birch Bayh (333–335), Karl E. Mundt (336–337), John J. Sparkman (338–341), Neal R. Peirce (342–346); and in 14 (Fall, 1968) by Editor (86), Albert J. Rosenthal (87–91), and Robert J. Sickels (92–96).
9. Barrett, Carol, and Newcombe, Hanna. "Weighted Voting in International Organizations," *Peace Research Reviews, 2,* Canadian Peace Research Institute, Oakville, Ontario, Canada.
10. Bell, Roderick, Edwards, David, Wagner, V., Harrison, R., (Editors). *Political Power: A Reader in Theory and Research.* The Free Press, New York, 1969.
11. Best, Judith. *The Case Against Direct Election of the President.* Cornell University Press, Ithaca, New York, 1975.
12. Bickel, Alexander M. *Reform and Continuity: The Electoral College, the Convention, and the Party System.* Harper and Row, New York, 1971.
13. Boyce, William M. "A 'Voting Power' Analysis of Recent Coalitions in the Electoral College." Mimeographed paper, 1973.
14. Boyce, William M., and Cross, M-J. "An Algorithm for the Shapley–Shubik Voting Power Index for Weighted Voting." Mimeographed paper, 1973.
15. Bradt, R. N. *et al. Elementary Mathematics of Sets with Applications* (formerly *Universal Mathematics, Part II: Structures in Sets*). Mathematical Association of America, Committee on the Undergraduate Program, Tulane University, New Orleans, Louisiana 1955 and University of Buffalo, Buffalo, New York, 1959; especially Chapter 4.
16. Brams, Steven J. *Game Theory and Politics.* The Free Press, A Division of Macmillan Publishing Co., Inc., New York, 1975.

17. Brams, S. J., and Affuso, Paul J. "Power and Size: A New Paradox." Mimeographed paper, April 1975.
18. Brams, S. J., and Davis, Morton D. "Resource-Allocation Models in Presidential Campaigning: Implications for Democratic Representation," in Papayanopoulos (1973), 105–123.
19. Brams, S. J., and Davis, M. D. "The 3/2's Rule in Presidential Campaigning," *The American Political Science Review*, *68* (March 1974), 113–134.
20. Brams, S. J., and Papayanopoulos, Lee. "Legislative Rules and Legislative Power." Mimeographed paper, June 1974.
21. Brams, Steven J. *Paradoxes in Politics: An Introduction to the Nonobvious in Political Science*. The Free Press, New York, 1976.
22. Brams, Steven J. *The Presidential Election Game*. Yale University Press, New Haven, 1978.
23. Coleman, James S. "Control of Collectivities and the Power of Collectivity to Act," in *Social Choice*, edited by Bernhardt Lieberman. Gordon and Breach, New York, 1971, 269–300.
24. Coleman, J. S. "Loss of Power," *American Sociological Review*, *38* (February 1971), 1–17.
25. David, P. T., Goldman, R. M., and Bain, R. C. *The Politics of National Party Conventions*. Brookings, Washington, D.C., 1960.
26. Davis, Morton D. *Game Theory: A Nontechnical Introduction*. Basic Books, Inc., New York, 1970.
27. Dubey, Pradeep. "On the Uniqueness of the Shapley Value," Technical Report, Applied Mathematics, Cornell University, Ithaca, New York 14853, June 1974.
28. Dubey, Pradeep, "On the Uniqueness of the Shapley Value," *International Journal of Game Theory*, *4* (1975), 131–139.
29. Dubey, Pradeep, and Shapley, Lloyd S. "Mathematical Properties of the Banzhaf Power Index," *Mathematics of Operations Research*, *4* (May 1979), 99–131.
30. Farquharson, Robin. *Theory of Voting*. Yale University Press, New Haven, 1969.
31. Frank, A. Q., and Shapley, L. "The Distribution of Power in the U.S. Supreme Court," A RAND Note, N-1735-NSF, The RAND Corp., Santa Monica, July 1981.
32. Garfinkel, R. S., and Nemhauser, G. L. "Optimal Political Districting by Implicit Enumeration Techniques," *Management Science*, *16* No. 8, (April 1970), B495–B508.
33. Gothman, H. G., and Dougall, H. E. *Corporate Financial Policy*. New York, 1948, 56–61.
34. Groenning, S., Kelley, E. W., and Leiserson, M (Editors), *The Study of Coalitional Behavior*. Holt, Rinehart, and Winston, New York, 1970.
35. Haefele, Edwin T. *Representative Government and Environmental Management*. The Johns Hopkins Press, Baltimore, 1973.
36. Hamilton, John A. "The Ox-Cart Way We Pick a Space-Age President." *New York Times Magazine*, October 20, 1968.
37. Harsanyi, John C. "A Bargaining Model for Cooperative *n*-Person Games," *Contributions to the Theory of Games IV*, *Annals of Mathematics Studies*, No. 40, edited by A. W. Tucker and R. D. Luce, Princeton University Press, Princeton, New Jersey, 1959.
38. Harsanyi, John C. "A Simplified Bargaining Model for the *n*-Person Cooperative Game," *International Economic Review*, *4* (1963), 194–220.
39. Herndon, James F., and Bernd, Joseph L. (Editors). *Mathematical Applications in Political Science*, VI, University of Virginia, Charlottesville, 1972; especially 79–124.
40. Imrie, Robert W. "The Impact of Weighted Vote on Representation in Municipal Governing Bodies of New York State," in Papayanopoulos [59], 192–199.

41. Isbell, John R. "Homogeneous Games III," *Annals of Mathematics Study No. 52, Advances in Game Theory*, edited by M. Dresher, L. S. Shapley, and A. W. Tucker, Princeton University Press, Princeton, New Jersey, 1964, 225–265.
42. Johnson, Ronald E. "An Analysis of Weighted Voting as Used in Reapportionment of County Governments in New York State," *Albany Law Review*, *34*, No. 1 (1969), 1–45.
43. Kemeny, John G., Snell, J. Laurie, and Thompson, Gerald L. *Introduction to Finite Mathematics*, Prentice-Hall, Inc., Englewood Cliffs, NJ, 1957, 74–78 and 108–112; 2nd ed., 1966, 79–83 and 113–116. Also John G. Kemeny, Arthur Schleifer, Jr., Laurie Snell, and Gerald L. Thompson, *Finite Mathematics with Business Applications* (1962), 68–72 and 117–120.
44. Krislov, Samuel. "Power and Coalition in a Nine-Man Body," *The American Behavioral Scientist*, *6* (April 1963), 24–26.
45. Lapidot, E. "The Counting Vector of a Simple Game," *Proceedings of the American Math. Society*, *31* (1972), 228–231.
46. Leiserson, Michael. "Fractions and Coalitions in One-Party Japan: An Interpretation Based on the Theory of Games," *American Political Science Review*, *62* (1968), 770–787.
47. Luce, R. Duncan, and Raiffa, Howard. *Games and Decisions: Introduction and Critical Survey*. John Wiley and Sons, Inc., New York, 1957.
48. Mann, Irwin, and Shapley, L. S. "Values of Large Games, IV: Evaluating the Electoral College by Monte Carlo Techniques," RM 2651, The RAND Corporation, Santa Monica, California, September 1960. Reproduced in part in Shubik [82].
49. Mann, Irwin, and Shapley, L. S. "Value of Large Games, VI: Evaluating the Electoral College Exactly," RM-3158-PR, The RAND Corporation, May 1962. Reprinted in part in Shubik [82].
50. Miller, D. R. "A Shapley Value Analysis of the Proposed Canadian Constitutional Amendment Scheme," *Canadian Journal of Political Science*, *VI* No. 1 (March 1973), 140–143.
51. Milnor, J. W., and Shapley, L. S. "Values of Large Games, II: Oceanic Games," RM-2649, The RAND Corporation, Santa Monica, California, February 1961.
52. Newcombe, Hanna. "If There Had Been Weighted Voting, . . . ," *Peace Research*, *5* (October 1973).
53. Oslen, Marvin E. *Power in Societies*. The Macmillan Company, New York, 1970.
54. Owen, Guillermo. *Game Theory*. W. B. Saunders Company, Philadelphia, Pennsylvania, 1968, especially 179–185.
55. Owen, Guillermo. "Political Games," *Naval Research Logistics Quarterly*, *18* No. 2 (September 1971), 345–355.
56. Owen, Guillermo. "Multilinear Extensions of Games," *Management Science*, *18* No. 5 (January 1972), P64–P79.
57. Owen, Guillermo. "Evaluation of a Presidential Election," *American Political Science Review*, *69* (September 1975).
58. Owen, Guillermo. "Multilinear Extensions and the Banzhaf Value," *Naval Research Logistics Quarterly*, *22* (December 1975).
59. Papayanopoulos, Lee (Editor). *Democratic Representation and Apportionment: Quantitative Methods, Measures, and Criteria*, Annals of the New York Academy of Science, *219* (November 9, 1973).
60. Pearcy, G. Etzel. *A Thirty-Eight State U.S.A.* Plycon Press, 1973.
61. Peirce, Neal R. *The People's President*. Simon and Schuster, New York, 1968.
62. Petersen. *A Statistical History of the American Presidential Elections*. Frederick Ungar Publishing Company, New York, 1963.
63. Polsby, Nelson W., and Wildavsky, Aaron B. *Presidential Election: Strategies of*

American Electoral Politics, 3rd ed. Charles Scribner and Sons, New York, 1971.
64. Rapoport, Anatol. *N-Person Game Theory: Concepts and Applications*. University of Michigan Press, Ann Arbor, 1970.
65. Ratner, David L. "The Government of Business Corporations: Critical Reflections on the Rule of 'One Share, One Vote,'" *Cornell Law Review*, *56* (November 1970), 1–56.
66. Richardson, Moses. *Fundamentals of Mathematics*. Macmillan Company, New York, revised edition, 1958, Sections 64 and 149, pp. 196 and 387; 3rd ed., 1966, Sections 70 and 155, pp. 217 and 431.
67. Riker, William H. "A Test of the Adequacy of the Power Index," *Behavioral Science*, *4* (1959), 120–131.
68. Riker, William H., and Niemi, Donald. "The Stability of Coalitions on Roll Calls in the House of Representatives," *American Political Science Review*, *54* (1962), 58–65.
69. Riker, W. H. *The Theory of Political Coalitions*. Yale University Press, New Haven, 1962.
70. Riker, William H. "Some Ambiguities in the Notion of Power," *American Political Science Review*, *58* (1964), 341–349.
71. Riker, William H., and Shapley, Lloyd S. "Weighted Voting: A Mathematical Analysis for Instrumental Judgment," Chapter 15 in *Representation: Nomos X*, edited by J. Roland Pennock and John W. Chapmen, Atherton Press, Inc., 1968; also as The RAND Corporation paper P-3318, Santa Monica, California, March 1966.
72. Runyon, John H., Verdini, Jennefer, and Runyon, and Sally S. (Editors). *Source Book of American Presidential Campaign and Election Statistics: 1948–1968*. Frederick Ungar Publishing Company, New York, 1971.
73. Schwödiauer, Gerhard. "Calculation of a Priori Power Distribution for the United Nations," Research Memo., No. 24, Institut für Höhere Studien, A-1060, Vienna, Austria, July 1968.
74. Sen, Ashish K. "A Theorem Related to Cartograms," *The American Mathematical Monthly*, *82* (1975), 382–385.
75. Schubert, Glendon A. *Quantitative Analysis of Judicial Behavior*. The Free Press, Glencoe, Illinois, 1959, especially Chapter IV.
76. Shapley, L. S. "A Value for *n*-Person Games," in *Annals of Mathematics Studies*, No. 28, *Contributions to the Theory of Games*, Vol. II, edited by H. W. Kuhn and A. W. Tucker, Princeton University Press, Princeton, New Jersey, (1953), 307–317.
77. Shapley, L. S. "Simple Games: An Outline of the Descriptive Theory," *Behavioral Science*, *7* No. 1 (January 1962), 59–66; also The RAND Corporation, RM-1384, Santa Monica, California, 1954.
78. Shapley, L. S., and Shubik, Martin. "A Method for Evaluating the Distribution of Power in a Committee System," *American Political Science Review*, *48* (September 1954), 787–792. Also Chapter 9 in Shubik [82].
79. Shapley, L. S., and Shapiro, N. Z. "Values of Large Games, I: A Limit Theorem," RM-2648, The RAND Corporation, Santa Monica, California, November 1960, *Mathematics of Operations Research 3* (1978), 1–9.
80. Shapley, L. S. "Values of Large Games, III: A Corporation with Two Large Stockholders," RM-2650-PR, The RAND Corporation, Santa Monica, California, December 1961.
81. Shapley, L. S. Notes entitled "Political Science," pp. 37–92 of *Notes of Lectures on Mathematics in the Behavioral Sciences*, notes by Henry A. Selby, MAA Summer Seminar at Williams College, Mathematical Association of America, 1973.
82. Shubik, Martin (Editor). *Game Theory and Related Approaches to Social Behavior*. John Wiley and Sons, Inc., New York, 1964; especially Part 3: Political Choice, Power, and Voting.

83. Spilerman, Seymour, and Dickins, David. "Who Will Gain and Who Will Lose Influence under Different Electoral Rules?" *American Journal of Sociology, 80* (September 1974), 443–477.
84. Straffin, Philip. D., Jr., *Topics in the Theory of Voting*, UMAP Expository Monograph Series, Birkäuser, 1980.
85. Taylor, Michael. "Proof of a Theorem on Majority Rule," *Behavioral Science, 14* (1969), 228–231.
86. von Neumann, John, and Morgenstern, Oskar. *Theory of Games and Economic Behavior*. Princeton University Press, Princeton, New Jersey, 1944; 2nd ed., 1947, 3rd ed., 1953.
87. Walther, Eleanor A. "An Analysis of Weighted Voting Systems Using the Banzhaf Values," M. S. Thesis, School of O. R. & I. E., Cornell University, Ithaca, 1977.

Notes for the Instructor

This paper describes two numerical indices, due to Shapley and Shubik and to Banzhaf, which are useful for measuring political power in various weighted voting schemes in which some voters effectively cast more or heavier weighted votes than others. A rather detailed review is given of the many uses of these indices in practical situations, as well as some suggestions for potential new applications, research projects, and future directions. It is intended that this presentation serve both as a survey for the interested reader, and as an educational work useful in the college classroom.

There are only a very few simple mathematical concepts among the few formal prerequisites required of the reader. Most of this paper can be followed by one with a familiarity with the most basic concepts from set theory plus a knowledge of permutations and combinations from elementary algebra. Most of the analysis is of a discrete or combinatorial nature. However, some of the arithmetical or computational techniques are fairly complicated in some parts of the later sections, and a higher level of mathematical maturity or sophistication will be required at these points. Nevertheless, some parts of the paper are suitable for use at various levels from secondary school through college and beyond. On the other hand, the material about large-scale computation in Section 6 is somewhat more difficult and presumes some knowledge of more specific college mathematics, the details of which can be seen by skimming through this section. It is most desirable that anyone who will be involved with such calculations have some computer experience beforehand. The user should be alerted to the fact that some part of Section 6 will be necessary for anyone who wishes to go into the detailed computational projects suggested in Section 7. The instructor however should be easily able to fill in most necessary details. Sections 8 and 9 are independent of the earlier sections.

A large number of projects are recommended throughout the paper. These vary in length from routine class exercises (some with answers and some without), to miniprojects that should take a few days to a couple of weeks, to major projects such as in Section 7, which should take from about four to eight weeks, and finally to some suggestions that can develop into long-term original research topics. The miniprojects in Section 5 are often appropriate for student teams of two or three persons, and those in Section 7 could involve up to about six people. The instructor may decide to give none, some, or all of this material to the students as best fits his needs. There may be some advantages in withholding much of this paper in the early stages so that the students can get more practice in the actual model building aspect of research. They may, after examining several examples, be able to derive one of these two power indices, or an alternate one, by themselves. This more undirected approach will of course lead to student doubts and anxieties, and to crises in confidence, and the instructor will continually need to provide guidance and direction and to rekindle enthusiasm by feeding in bits of new information. It is also recommended that the instructor or students make some contact with colleagues in their school's political science or government department. Such "outsiders" may serve in various capacities from mere critics up to members of a team teaching or research endeavor.

The intention was to write this paper so as to be fairly self-contained and to require few, if any, of the works listed in the references. Some of the unpublished reports, RAND memoranda, and papers appearing in law journals might not be readily available to all instructors, and it may take some lead time to acquire them. It will be fairly clear in reading Section 5 as to which references should be available in order to do particular mini-projects. The paper by Banzhaf [6] or Johnson [42] should prove most useful in the latter parts of Section 5. Banzhaf [8], Peirce [61], and perhaps an appropriate reference mentioned in Section 6, would be helpful for doing the projects in Section 7. The books by Farquharson [30], Papayanopoulos [59], Riker [69], and Shubik [82], as well as those containing the papers by Riker and Shapley [71] and Shapley [76] should be available in most school libraries, and can serve as more general reading. Also see the books by Brams [16, 21, 22] and Straffin, and the excellent recent paper by Dubey and Shapley [29].

An incomplete first draft of this paper, dated October 1973, was used in one way or another by about a dozen teachers, including the author, in the spring of 1974. A few of these instructors were part of the official CUPM evaluation, but most of them had contact with the author directly. Preliminary reports indicate a fair amount of success. Incidentally, in at least three of these classes the students arrived at one of these two power indices by themselves—with some hints perhaps. The author is grateful for the comments from Irwin Mann, Joseph Malkevitch, Lloyd Shapley, and Robert Weber who read and made suggestions on the draft version. Except for a few minor changes and additional more recent references, this paper was completed in 1975. An ample number of more current illustrations are readily available for class exercises and projects.

CHAPTER 10

To the (Minimal Winning) Victors Go the (Equally Divided) Spoils: A New Power Index for Simple n-Person Games

John Deegan, Jr.*
Edward W. Packel†

1. Introduction

Our intent in this module is to motivate the development of a new index of power in n-person simple games that models the collective decision-making process of players whose explicit behavioral objective is to *effect* change. Our concern is with games that closely correspond to the character of interpersonal interaction found in organizations, committees, and legislatures; situations in which power and authority, rather than monetary forms of payoff, are the motivating force (i.e., the interaction may be characterized as being "political" in nature).

In order to develop our index of power, we should make certain assumptions about the likelihood of formation of various coalitions of players in a game and the manner in which players in successfully formed *winning* coalitions divide the spoils (i.e., exercise power) in the game. [For readers interested in other power indices motivated by different assumptions about coalition formation and the importance of individual members to such coalitions, see Straffin (Chapter 11, this volume) Dubey [7], Brams [1], Shapley and Shubik [11], Banzhaf [3], and Lucas (Chapter 9, this volume).

To begin with, we assume that all games are *simple*. This essentially means that only winning matters since losers do not participate in the division of the spoils, and that all winning coalitions (and only winning coalitions) receive a positive payoff, which is constant. It will be seen as natural to give these positive payoffs value 1 and all other "payoffs" value 0. We further assume that conflict of interests in dividing the spoils of the

* United States Environmental Protection Agency, Washington, D.C. 20460.

† Mathematics Department, Lake Forest College, Lake Forest, Illinois 60045.

game motivates the behavior of the players, and that all players have *complete* and *perfect* information (which means, respectively, that all players know the "weight" or importance of all other players, and all players know when all other players join a coalition).

As a consequence of these assumptions, players are conceived of as seeking to maximize payoffs against malevolent rather than indifferent opponents. It can also be readily seen that such conflict complicates the maximizing behavior of players by aggrevating problems of alliance (coalitions) formation among the players.

A crucial assumption for what follows is that the only winning coalitions that will actually emerge are the *minimal winning coalitions* (MWCs), those which are *no larger than necessary* to ensure winning. Such an assumption finds justification, in part, from the *size principle* (Riker [9]). "In social situations similar to n-person, zero-sum games with side payments, participants create coalitions just as large as they believe will ensure winning and no larger" (p. 47).

Given our previous assumptions regarding information possessed by the players, our assumption that only *minimal* winning coalitions form seems reasonable for rational players who seek to maximize payoffs. Accordingly, we define a MWC as a winning coalition of players from which the removal of any one member would render it nonwinning.

Formally we define a *simple game* as an ordered pair $(N, \mathscr{W})$, where N is a finite set of n *players* and $\mathscr{W}$ is a collection of all *winning* coalitions (subsets) of N satisfying the following properties.

(i) $\phi \notin \mathscr{W}$ (the empty set is not a winning coalition).
(ii) $\mathscr{W}$ is nonempty (some subset of N is a winning coalition).

In addition, it is sometimes desirable to include a third property, which makes $(N, \mathscr{W})$ a *proper* simple game.

(iii) $S \cap T \neq \phi \forall S, T \in \mathscr{W}$.

Given any such simple game $(N, \mathscr{W})$, we can express it uniquely in terms of the MWCs in $\mathscr{W}$. Thus we can view a simple (proper) game as an ordered pair $(N, \mathscr{M})$ satisfying properties (i), (ii), and (optionally) (iii). The collection $\mathscr{M}$ of MWCs is thus defined by

$$\mathscr{M} = \{S \in \mathscr{W} | S\backslash\{i\} \notin \mathscr{W} \forall i \in N\}.$$

Since our power index will be defined solely in terms of MWCs, we choose to use the $(N, \mathscr{M})$ designation for simple games. Games that fail to satisfy the optional property (iii) are called *improper*, since determination of a winning coalition is in a sense problematical (see Exercise 1). Such games will be necessary, however, for some of the theory that follows.

An important subclass of simple games is the class (mentioned above) known as *weighted voting games*. We use the notation

$$[q; w_1, w_2, \cdots, w_n]$$

to represent a weighted voting game. The w_i symbolizes the voting "weights" of the n players; and q is the *quota* needed to win. Thus $S \subseteq N$ will be a winning coalition if $\sum_{i \in S} w_i \geq q$.

To illustrate simple games and weighted voting games, consider the following two examples. Let $M_3 = (N, \mathcal{M})$ be a simple game with three players $N = \{a, b, c\}$, and $\mathcal{M} = \{\{a, b\}, \{a, c\}, \{b, c\}\}$ (henceforth we omit the inner braces and commas). Equivalently, $\mathcal{M}_3$ can be expressed as the weighted voting game

$$\mathcal{M}_3 = [2; 1, 1, 1],$$

where the players $\{a, b, c\}$ are implicitly identified by their corresponding unit weights. Conversely, consider the weighted voting game

$$\Gamma_2 = [5; 4, 2, 1, 1, 1].$$

If we represent the players with weights 4, 2, 1, 1, 1 by $N = \{a, b, c, d, e\}$, it follows that $\Gamma_2 = (N, \mathcal{M})$, where

$$\mathcal{M} = \{ab, ac, ad, ae, bcde\}.$$

Note that while the simple game $\mathcal{M}_3$ can also be written as a weighted voting game it can be shown that not all simple games can be so represented. On the other hand, it is clear that any weighted voting game can be represented uniquely as a simple game.

The remainder of this paper is organized as follows. In Section 2, we define our index of power and offer a number of worked out examples. In Section 3, we present characterization axioms for our index and provide a uniqueness proof. Section 4 is devoted to applications and limitations of our index. The concluding remarks of Section 5 are followed by a collection of exercises organized by section and graded in difficulty within each section.

2. Power Index Definition and Examples

Let $(N, \mathcal{M})$ be a simple game as defined above. For each player $i \in N$, we define

$$\mathcal{M}(i) = \{S \in \mathcal{M} | i \in S\}.$$

Thus $\mathcal{M}(i)$ is precisely the collection of minimal winning coalitions of which player i is a member.

The power index for player i in the game $(N, \mathcal{M})$ is defined as follows:

$$\rho(i) = \frac{1}{|\mathcal{M}|} \sum_{S \in \mathcal{M}(i)} \frac{1}{|S|}. \tag{1}$$

(Recall that for any finite set U, the symbol $|U|$ denotes cardinality or the number of members belonging to U.)

The rationale for defining ρ in this fashion stems from three fundamental assumptions regarding the behavior of players in simple games.

(1) Only minimal winning coalitions are victorious in simple games.
(2) Players in a victorious MWC divide the payoff equally.
(3) Each MWC has equal probability of forming.

Careful consideration needs to be given to the validity and applicability of each of these assumptions. The first assumption is discussed in Section 1 and will not be further pursued here. The second assumption seems reasonable in a wide variety of game situations (though there are no doubt circumstances in which it may be unrealistic). Some experimental evidence exists in support of this assumption (see Caplow [4], Vinacke and Arkoff [13], Riker [9], and Riker and Ordeshook [10]), but we emphasize that each game needs to be examined individually to estimate the assumption's validity. The third assumption is perhaps the most controversial. While it seems reasonable in certain situations, its appropriateness in any given game should be given careful consideration.

It can be seen that formula (1) for ρ is consistent with and determined by the above three assumptions. Indeed, only *minimal* winning coalitions containing player i appear (assumption 1), and each such coalition is treated consistently in the summation (assumption 3). Furthermore for each $S \in \mathscr{M}(i)$, the $1/|S|$ term indicates that player i shares the spoils equally with the other $|S| - 1$ members of S (assumption 2). The factor $1/|\mathscr{M}|$ serves to normalize the power of the players so that their sum is 1.

We now consider a variety of examples to illustrate the method of computation, properties, and utility of the power index ρ.

Example 1. Let $\Gamma_1 = (N, \mathscr{M})$ with $N = \{a, b, c, d\}$ and $\mathscr{M} = \{ab, bc, acd\}$. Then for player a we have $\mathscr{M}(a) = \{ab, acd\}$, so that

$$\rho(a) = \frac{1}{3}\left(\frac{1}{2} + \frac{1}{3}\right) = \frac{5}{18}.$$

(This results since $|\mathscr{M}| = 3$ and a belongs to minimal coalitions of size 2 and 3.) Similar calculations give

$$\rho(b) = \frac{1}{3}\left(\frac{1}{2} + \frac{1}{2}\right) = \frac{1}{3}, \quad \rho(c) = \frac{5}{18}, \quad \rho(d) = \frac{1}{9}.$$

It is customary to use an n vector to denote the respective powers of the players, so for the game Γ_1, we have $\rho = (5/18, 1/3, 5/18, 1/9)$. Note that the powers of the players do sum to unity, a useful way to check (or to expedite) the calculations.

Clearly our power index can be applied to the subclass of weighted voting games, as we now illustrate.

Example 2. Let $\Gamma_2 = [5; 4, 2, 1, 1, 1]$. Then denoting the players in order by $N = \{a, b, c, d, e\}$, we have $\mathscr{M} = \{ab, ac, ad, ae, bcde\}$. Then,

$$\rho = \frac{1}{5}\left(\frac{1}{2} + \frac{1}{2} + \frac{1}{2} + \frac{1}{2}, \frac{1}{2} + \frac{1}{4}, \frac{1}{2} + \frac{1}{4}, \frac{1}{2} + \frac{1}{4}, \frac{1}{2} + \frac{1}{4}\right)$$
$$= \left(\frac{2}{5}, \frac{3}{20}, \frac{3}{20}, \frac{3}{20}, \frac{3}{20}\right).$$

Note that b has more voting weight than c, but player b's involvement in minimal winning coalitions (and hence his power) is identical to that of c.

Additional elementary examples are supplied in Exercises 7–9. We consider now a more elaborate example to illustrate how judicious counting and use of binomial coefficients facilitates the calculations when several players can be treated symmetrically.

EXAMPLE 3. Consider a simplified legislative system with a president, a three-member house, and a five-member house. Passage of a motion requires the president's vote plus a majority of both houses (all players have just 1 vote). The game is then $\Gamma_3 = (N, \mathscr{M})$, where $N = \{p, s_1, s_2, s_3, r_1, r_2, r_3, r_4, r_5\}$ and $\mathscr{M}$ contains all coalitions of the form pssrrr, where the s's are chosen from s_1, s_2, and s_3 and the r's from r_1, r_2, r_3, r_4, and r_5. Since p must pair up with two "senators" who may be chosen in $\binom{3}{2}$ ways, and with three "representatives" who may be chosen in $\binom{5}{3}$ ways, p belongs to $\binom{3}{2} \times \binom{5}{3} = 3 \times 10 = 30$ minimal winning coalitions, all of size 6. Since these 30 coalitions are the only possible minimal winning ones (why?), we have $\rho(p) = (1/30)(30/6) = 1/6$. Reasoning in a similar fashion for senator s_1, she belongs to $\binom{2}{1} \times \binom{5}{3} = 20$ minimal winning coalitions. Thus $\rho(s_1) = (1/30)(20/6) = 1/9$. We leave to Exercise 4 for section 2 the easy demonstration (in two different ways) that for Γ_3,

$$\rho = \left(\frac{1}{6}, \frac{1}{9}, \frac{1}{9}, \frac{1}{9}, \frac{1}{10}, \frac{1}{10}, \frac{1}{10}, \frac{1}{10}, \frac{1}{10}\right).$$

To increase the realism of this miniature legislature system, we may consider the effect of allowing an override of the president's effective veto power. We leave this as part of Exercise 7(c).

3. Characterization Axioms

We have already mentioned that there exist other power indices that also propose to measure the power of players in a simple game. Since our index was designed to reflect certain assumptions about coalition formation and spoils distribution, it is important to consider whether a variety of power indices might exist, all of which satisfy our assumptions.

One mathematically natural, and cherished, and highly aesthetic approach to such questions is to list a set of axioms embodying the desired properties.

A proof is then sought that at most one structure (here a power index) can satisfy the axioms and that the structure at hand (our index ρ) alone satisfies the axioms. If this approach is successful, what emerges is a uniqueness theorem for the structure in question and a set of characterizing axioms that provide further insight into the nature of the structure.

The astute reader, surmising from the confident philosophical tone of the last paragraph that a set of axioms characterizing ρ is forthcoming, would not be mistaken. Before stating the axioms, we need to define a way of combining certain simple games into a single simple game.

Let $(N_1, \mathcal{M}_1)$ and $(N_2, \mathcal{M}_2)$ be simple games, where N_1 and N_2 are two not necessarily disjoint sets of players. We define the two games to be *mergeable* if

$$\forall S_1 \in \mathcal{M}_1 \quad \text{and} \quad S_2 \in \mathcal{M}_2, S_1 \nsubseteq S_2 \quad \text{and} \quad S_2 \nsubseteq S_1. \tag{2}$$

In this case we define the *merge* $(N, \mathcal{M}) = (N_1, \mathcal{M}_1) \vee (N_2, \mathcal{M}_2)$ to be the game defined by $N = N_1 \cup N_2$ and $\mathcal{M} = \mathcal{M}_1 \cup \mathcal{M}_2$.

The idea behind the mergeability condition (2) is that we want $\mathcal{M}$ to contain only MWC's and $(N, \mathcal{M})$ to itself be a simple game. Thus, we must restrict the pairs of games to be merged. It is readily seen that the merge operation extends to any finite collection of mergeable games and is associative.

We now are prepared to state our power index axioms. Let $\mathcal{G}$ denote the class of all simple games. A *power index* on $\mathcal{G}$ defines for *each* $(N, \mathcal{M}) \in \mathcal{G}$ a function $\Pi: N \to \mathcal{R}$ satisfying:

(i) $\Pi(i) = 0 \Leftrightarrow \mathcal{M}(i) = \phi$.
(ii) Given any permutation $\sigma: N \to N$ with $\sigma(i) = j$ and $S \in \mathcal{M}(i) \Leftrightarrow \sigma(S) \in \mathcal{M}(j)$, then $\Pi(i) = \Pi(j)$.
(iii) $\sum_{i \in N} \Pi(i) = 1$.
(iv) Given $(N, \mathcal{M}) = (N_1, \mathcal{M}_1) \vee (N_2, \mathcal{M}_2)$ with $(N_1, \mathcal{M}_2)$ mergeable, then

$$\Pi(i) = \frac{1}{|\mathcal{M}|}[|\mathcal{M}_1|\Pi_1(i) + |\mathcal{M}_2|\Pi_2(i)] \quad \forall i \in N.$$

The intuitive idea behind these four axioms should be mastered along with their symbolism. Axiom (i) states that players with no power are precisely those who belong to no MWCs (such a player is called a *dummy*).

Axiom (ii), perhaps the hardest to state formally, says something that seems "natural" and indispensible about power indices. Namely, if the names and corresponding MWC membership structure of the players are switched around (the role of the permutation σ), the power of the individuals (regardless of the name changes) remains unchanged. In words, it says that *symmetric* players have equal power.

Axiom (iii) requires the index to be normalized, so that powers can be thought of as percentages or probabilities when appropriate.

Finally, the crucial axiom (iv) states that the power of an individual in a merged game is a weighted mean of the individual's power in the component games, with the number of MWCs in each component game providing the weights. Some thought (perhaps both before and after the proof of the coming theorem) should convince the reader that this axiom embodies the desired properties of equally likely minimal winning coalitions and equally divided spoils (assumptions 1, 2, and 3).

Uniqueness Theorem. *The function* ρ *defined for any simple game by* (1) *satisfies the power index axioms* (i)–(iv). *Furthermore, any index on* $\mathscr{G}$ *satisfying these axioms must be equal to* ρ.

PROOF. We first show that for any simple MWC game $(N, \mathscr{M})$, ρ satisfies axioms (i)–(iv). Recalling that

$$\rho(i) = \frac{1}{|\mathscr{M}|} \sum_{S \in \mathscr{M}(i)} \frac{1}{|S|},$$

axiom (i) follows immediately since $\rho(i) = 0 \Leftrightarrow$ there are no terms in the sum $\Leftrightarrow \mathscr{M}(i) = \phi$. To establish axiom (ii), let $\sigma: N \to N$ satisfy the conditions of (ii). Then,

$$\rho(i) = \frac{1}{|\mathscr{M}|} \sum_{S \in \mathscr{M}(i)} \frac{1}{|S|} = \frac{1}{|\mathscr{M}|} \sum_{\sigma(S) \in \mathscr{M}(j)} \frac{1}{|\sigma(S)|} = \frac{1}{|\mathscr{M}|} \sum_{T \in \mathscr{M}(j)} \frac{1}{|T|} = \sigma(j).$$

Axiom (iii) can be verified as follows: Consider any $S \in \mathscr{M}$ and all the terms in the sum $\sum_{i \in N} \rho(i)$, which result from S. There are precisely $|S|$ such terms (one for each $i \in S$) and each contributes $(1/|\mathscr{M}|)(1/|S|)$. Thus S contributes precisely $1/|\mathscr{M}|$ to the sum. Since there are $|\mathscr{M}|$ such terms in the overall sum (one for each $S \in |\mathscr{M}|$), we have $\sum_{i \in N} \rho(i) = 1$ as desired. For axiom (iv),

$$\rho(i) = \frac{1}{|\mathscr{M}|} \sum_{S \in \mathscr{M}(i)} \frac{1}{|S|} = \frac{1}{|\mathscr{M}|} \left[\sum_{S \in \mathscr{M}_1(i)} \frac{1}{|S|} + \sum_{S \in \mathscr{M}_2(i)} \frac{1}{|S|} \right]$$

$$= \frac{1}{|\mathscr{M}|} [|\mathscr{M}_1| \rho_1(i) + |\mathscr{M}_2| \rho_2(i)].$$

We must now show that any index Π satisfying (i)–(iv) must be equal to ρ. Consider any simple MWC game $(N, \mathscr{M})$ and enumerate the members of $\mathscr{M}$ as $S_1, S_2, \cdots, S_m$ (so $|\mathscr{M}| = m$). Consider the trivial simple games $(N, \mathscr{M}_1), (N, \mathscr{M}_2), \cdots, (N, \mathscr{M}_m)$, where each $\mathscr{M}_k$ is the singleton collection $\{S_k\}$. Then $(N, \mathscr{M}) = (N, \mathscr{M}_1) \vee (N, \mathscr{M}_2) \vee \cdots \vee (N, \mathscr{M}_m)$, since all $\mathscr{M}_k$ are mergeable. For any $i \in N$ and any of the singleton games $(N, \mathscr{M}_k)$, we have

$$\Pi_k(i) = \begin{cases} \dfrac{1}{|S_k|} & \text{if } i \in S_k \\ 0 & \text{otherwise.} \end{cases} \tag{3}$$

The zero values result from axiom (i), while axioms (ii) and (iii) ensure that the other $|S_k|$ symmetric players will each have power $1/|S_k|$. Using axiom (iv) extended inductively to a merge of m rather than 2 games,

$$\begin{aligned}\Pi(i) &= \frac{1}{|\mathcal{M}|}[|\mathcal{M}_1|\Pi_1(i) + |\mathcal{M}_2|\Pi_2(i) + \cdots + |\mathcal{M}_m|\Pi_m(i)] \\ &= \frac{1}{|\mathcal{M}|}\sum_{S\in\mathcal{M}(i)}\frac{1}{|S|} \quad \text{using } |\mathcal{M}_k| = 1 \text{ and (3) for all } k \in N \\ &= \rho(i). \end{aligned}$$

□

We note here that the two well-known power indices of Shapley–Shubik (called ϕ) and Banzhaf (called β) have been characterized by axioms very similar to those above (Dubey [7]). The real difference comes in the critical axiom (iv) where our weighted mean condition is replaced by other additive-type conditions. The proof required for uniqueness of ρ is similar in spirit to those for ϕ and β, but much simpler and more direct. This simplicity carries over to the process of computing values for ρ, but it remains to be seen whether this simplicity of ρ brings with it a lack of realism in the modeling of power in voting situations.

It is also common to interpret the various power indices probabilistically. In this spirit we observe that ρ again has a natural and simple interpretation. Recall that it was assumed that every MWC in a simple game $(N, \mathcal{M})$ has equal probability of forming. Let the "payoff" for participating in a successfully formed $S \in \mathcal{M}$ be $1/|S|$. Then we immediately see that the expectation for player i in such a game is precisely $\rho(i)$. This "expectation" interpretation is, in a sense, the embodiment of our minimal coalition winner/equally divided spoils assumptions.

4. Applications and Limitations

In this section we consider a variety of applications to some real-world and unreal-world situations. The types of games considered here have also been evaluated by means of the Shapley–Shubik index (ϕ) and the Banzaf index (β). By making comparisons among the indices, we can see how the three indices differ and which seem more appropriate in given situations. We also show that various "paradoxes" that have been documented for ϕ and β also arise (with one exception) for ρ. A new and (possibly) controversial paradox will also be exhibited for ρ, which cannot happen with ϕ and β.

Consider the weighted voting game [3; 2, 1, 1]. It is possible to imagine all sorts of experiments and everyday situations that mirror this game with some accuracy. For example, imagine a "divide the dollar" experiment where three players (a, b, c) vote on various motions as to how one dollar should be split among them. Or, imagine a chief navigator a and crew members b

and c, only one of whom is needed to complete a given journey and collect a much desired reward. In each case player a has "veto power," but we shall argue that this does not directly result in any payoff coming his way. To pass a motion (or cross an ocean), player a must enlist the support of b or c. Now, if maximizing immediate profit is the dominant consideration of players in forming effective coalitions (which implies that a will never enlist the support of both b and c), our assumption of only *minimal* winning coalitions forming seems eminently reasonable.

The question of equal division of spoils between minimal coalition members is more delicate and exceedingly elusive. We leave it to the reader to imagine the variety of "rational" approaches that might emerge.

The desired power index values for the game [3; 2, 1, 1] can be shown to be $\rho = (1/2, 1/4, 1/4)$, $\phi = (2/3, 1/6, 1/6)$, and $\beta = (3/5, 1/5, 1/5)$. (See, for example, Straffin, Chapter 11 this volume, for computing ϕ and β). It seems to us that in situations reflecting power to *effect* change (as opposed to preventing it), the ρ values are the most reasonable. It is also pleasant to observe that in this game the powers of the players under ρ are proportional to their weights (one-man, one-vote). However, as Exercise 14 illustrates, this observation may not be so significant.

It is interesting to consider what happens in a simple game when some subset of the players begin to "quarrel" and refuse to participate with each other in winning coalitions. In the case of simple MWC games with two quarrelers this leads to a "smaller" game obtained by deleting any MWCs, which involve both players. Strange things can happen with ρ (also with ϕ and β, see Brams [1]) when quarrels occur.

Consider, for instance, the game with $\mathscr{M} = \{abcde, af, bf\}$. It can be shown (see Exercise 15 for section 4) that if a and b quarrel they both increase their power! Surely this is (at least at first) a nonintuitive result. Indeed, it suggests a basically hostile environment where each player eagerly seeks out quarrels whereby power may be increased. Further thought here, as in many aspects of game theory, leads to more subtle and tentative conclusions. The reader can perhaps contemplate a number of interesting scenarios that illustrate this last point.

It can also be shown (Exercise 15 for this section) that it is possible for quarrelers to lose power, have their power unaffected while affecting others, etc. Finally, it is an immediate consequence of the definition of ρ that quarreling with a dummy cannot affect anyone's power. For the power indices ϕ and β this need not be the case (as Straffin, Chapter 11, this volume, illustrates).

Another interesting paradox occurs for ρ (but not for ϕ or β), which we refer to as a "weighted voting paradox." Simply stated, it is possible for player i to have *more* weight than player j in a weighted MWC game and yet have *less* power. Exercise 16 demonstates this with the game [5; 3, 2, 1, 1, 1]. The impact of this paradox on the worth of ρ in certain political voting situations may be viewed by some as being a serious defect. In the absence of sufficient empirical evidence on the elusive notion of power, however, we believe this issue is still open for discussion. In fact, sociologists have argued that situations where minor players possess greater *potential* for power are not anomalous, but rather frequently occur. If this is true, our index, and ours alone, can reflect this somewhat perplexing character of power.

We now consider a familiar and more complex example that expands upon Example 3, Section 2. The U.S. legislative process involves a president p, 101 senators s (including the vice president, who can break ties), and 435 representatives r. Ignoring veto overrides (which should not be ignored), passage of a motion requires p's vote, 51 s votes, *and* 218 r votes. The number of MWCs is $1 \times \binom{101}{51} \times \binom{435}{218}$ and each MWC has 270 members. Thus p's power is

$$\rho(p) = \frac{1}{\binom{101}{51} \times \binom{435}{218}} \times \frac{\binom{101}{51} \times \binom{435}{218}}{270} = \frac{1}{270}.$$

Each senator is involved in $\binom{100}{50} \times \binom{435}{218}$ MWCs.
Since $\binom{105}{50} = \binom{101}{51} \times 51/101$, we have for each senator s,

$$\rho(s) = \frac{1}{\binom{101}{51} \times \binom{435}{218}} \times \frac{\binom{101}{51} \times \frac{51}{101} \times \binom{435}{218}}{270} = \frac{51}{101} \times \frac{1}{270}.$$

And finally, it can be shown fairly readily that for each representative r,

$$\rho(r) = \frac{218}{435} \times \frac{1}{270}.$$

The above calculations essentially say that the president holds 1/270 of the power in the no-veto override legislative game, and each senator and representative holds about half as much power as the president (senators are very slightly more powerful than representatives). The other indices give the president considerably more power [$\phi(p) \approx 1/2$, $\beta(p) \approx 1/25$], but this has a reasonable explanation. Recall that ρ measures power to *initiate* action (i.e., effect change) and does not include blocking power (or veto power) in its definition or assumptions. The indices ϕ and β weigh power to initiate and power to block equally, so the president with his de facto veto (i.e., he could "abstain") has greatly increased power. The discrepancy between ϕ and β might be seen, in this light, to be much more serious. Coleman [5] has also been sensitive to this dual-faceted aspect of power and has defined separate nonnormalized indices for measuring power to act and power to prevent action.

It is tempting at this stage to sum the powers of individual players in the senate and house in order to get a relative measure of the distribution of power among the various political divisions empowered to initiate and enact legislation. We shall argue that such action, in effect, may go beyond and violate the properties of our model (power is *not* additive). If summation is engaged in, we caution that it should be subjected to careful interpretation.

Our final application is a general one that will address measurement of the power to preserve the status quo (block motions) rather than to effect change (pass motions). Given a simple game $(N, \mathcal{M})$ and subset S of N, we say that S is a *blocking coalition* if its complement $N\backslash S$ contains no MWCs. If in addition S is a minimal (properly contains no others) subset with this property, we call S a *minimal blocking coalition* (MBC). Before treating this formally we consider an example.

The game Γ_4 of Exercise 8 has $N = \{a, b, c, d, e\}$ and $\mathcal{M} = \{ab, acd, ace, ade, bcde\}$. By careful inspection, its MBCs are seen to be $\mathcal{M}^B = \{ab, ac, ad, ae, bcd, bce, bde\}$. Note that $(N, \mathcal{M}^B)$ is by its definition again a simple game, though in this case not a proper one. Calculating the power index for $(N, \mathcal{M}^B)$, we obtain $\rho^B = (12/42, 9/42, 7/42, 7/42, 7/42)$, where the ρ^B notation will be used to define a new power index (the blocking index) on $(N, \mathcal{M})$, the original game. Recall from Exercise 8 that the ρ value for $(N, \mathcal{M})$ was $\rho = (18/60, 9/60, 11/60, 11/60, 11/60)$. We conclude that player b, whose power to effect change is smallest in $(N, \mathcal{M})$ has *relatively* more power to preserve the status quo in $(N, \mathcal{M}^B)$.

Observing that $(N, \mathcal{M})$ is actually the "weighted voting paradox" game $[5; 3, 2, 1, 1, 1]$ in disguise, we see a possible resolution of the paradox if we average the values of ρ and ρ^B. Indeed, we assert that $\rho/2 + \beta/2 = (1/420)(123, 76.5, 73.5, 73.5, 73.5)$. All is not rosy, however, as is shown in Exercise 21.

We are now ready for a concise formal definition of the dual game and the dual index ρ^B. Given $\Gamma = (N, \mathcal{M})$, a simple game, define the dual game $\Gamma^* = (N, \mathcal{M}^B)$, where

$$\mathcal{M}^B = \{T \subseteq N | \bigcup_{i \in T} \mathcal{M}(i) = \mathcal{M} \quad \text{and} \quad \forall S \subsetneq T \bigcup_{i \in S} \mathcal{M}(i) \neq \mathcal{M}\}. \tag{4}$$

We define the *blocking power index* ρ^B on a simple game $\Gamma = (N, \mathcal{M})$ as the result of applying the power index ρ to its dual $\Gamma^* = (N, \mathcal{M}^B)$. The rather imposing definition (4) will be seen, from careful inspection, to say that $T \in \mathcal{M}^B$ if T is blocking $[\bigcup_{i \in T} \mathcal{M}(i) = \mathcal{M}]$ and that no proper subset S of T is also blocking.

The appearance of a distinct second index on simple games suggests a variety of possible questions and ideas. Note that our uniqueness theorem is not violated since ρ^B will not satisfy axiom (iv). In fact, it is not clear at this point what might replace that axiom.

The well-known indices ϕ and β treat blocking and effecting change equally, so for them one obtains $\phi = \phi^B$ and $\beta = \beta^B$. The fact that ρ does not have this property is exciting in the following sense. Given a simple game situation for which we wish to assign power values to the players, we study the psychology and dynamics thoroughly, thereby attaining percentage weights t and $1 - t$ for the extent to which effecting change and blocking should contribute to power. We then define for this game a power index

$$\rho^t = t\rho + (1 - t)\rho^B.$$

(Hence, setting $t = 1/2$, for instance, would weight blocking and effecting change equally.) Thus, we may have at our disposal a continuum of power indices all based upon the *minimal* winning coalition assumption. We leave these ideas afloat for future consideration.

5. Concluding Remarks

One obviously desirable generalization of the index ρ is to the broader class of n-person games in characteristic function form. In Deegan and Packel [6], this development is pursued. Generalization of the index allows removal of the mergeability restrictions appearing in power index axiom (iv) for simple MWC games by means of a natural restatement of the axiom. As a result, the power index ρ is subsequently expressable directly in terms of the characteristic function. This development parallels the recent axiomatization of ϕ and β in Dubey [7] and illuminates the relationship between ρ and the other indices. For example, generalization of ρ reveals that ρ has desired uniqueness properties in all significant subclasses of simple games, unlike certain axiomatic characterizations of the other indices.

On the negative side, it appears that in some games whose MWCs vary dramatically in cardinality, values for ρ may not agree with intuition. In particular, certain degenerate cases of improper games fall into this category. Consider, for example, the dual of the no-veto override U.S. legislature game in Section 4. Attempts by the authors to resolve this difficulty have met with some success, but tend to have a rather ad hoc character.

Another subject for additional consideration is the general tendency of ρ to downgrade the (seemingly) apparent power of higher weighted players and accentuate the (seemingly) apparent lack of power of lower weighted players (in comparison to ϕ and β). Upon reflection, this egalitarian attribution of power (which might be referred to as the "Robin Hood" effect), however, seems neither surprising nor problematical since ρ measures *only* the power to initiate or effect change and not prevent change (as does ρ^B). Investigation of the behavior of ρ in *oceanic* games and *apex* games (see Straffin, Chapter 11, this volume, and Exercise 9 for a discussion of these games) corroborates precisely this feature of the index, as does the President–Senate–House example presented above.

To summarize the main points of this module, we begin by pointing out that the motivation for creating a new power index stems from the concept of simple MWC games. The index ρ, which we define on such games, follows naturally from two simple assumptions; power is the ability of a player to initiate or effect change, and once power is successfully exercised, all players share equally in the spoils.

The index ρ is shown to have both a logical and probabilistic interpretation and a pleasing simple computational form (which neither ϕ nor β possess). We also provide an axiomatic foundation for ρ that characterizes the index uniquely for simple games. A variety of results for ρ from various games are then presented, illustrating both the strengths of the index and its susceptibility to common paradoxes.

Finally, we define a related index ρ^B as a measure of the blocking power of players in simple games. It is offered that this dual notion of power illustrates a potential richness in our index not present in other indices of power.

Exercises

For Section 1:

1. Consider the game $(N, \mathcal{M})$, where $\mathcal{M} = \{abe, bfg, bc, cefg, cdg\}$.
   a) Show that this game is improper.
   b) Discuss what may happen if players a, b, and e favor a certain action while players c, d, and g favor an imcompatible alternative action.
   c) By deleting a single MWC from $\mathcal{M}$, convert $(N, \mathcal{M})$ into a proper game.

2. Dingle Community College has a faculty senate with 4 members, a student senate with 3 members, and an administrative senate with 1 member (the president). Passage of motions requires majority approval (3 or 4 from the faculty) of at least two of the three senates.
   a) Devise an appropriate notation for the players and then list all 19 MWCs for this game.
   b) Do you think the *minimal* winning coalition assumption is appropriate in the context of this game?

3. Prove that a weighted voting game $[q; w_1, w_2, \cdots, w_n]$ is proper if $q > \frac{1}{2}\sum_{i=1}^{n} w_i$, but that the converse does not hold.

For Section 2:

4. Consider the weighted MWC game $[7; 5, 3, 3, 1]$
   a) List the MWCs for the game and compute ρ.
   b) Compare your results with those of Example 1, Section 2, and give an explanation for what you observe.

5. Let $\Gamma = (N, \mathcal{M})$ where $N = \{a, b, c, d\}$ and $\mathcal{M} = \{ab, bc, cd\}$. Compute ρ for the game Γ.

6. Compute ρ for a game with $\mathcal{M} = \{ab, ac, adg, bcd, bdg\}$. Then explain why it is not crucial to have an explicit description of the set N for your computation.

7. Let $\Gamma_3 = (N, \mathcal{M})$ be the simple legislature game of Example 3, Section 2.
   a) Show, using binomial coefficient arguments, that each representative belongs to 18 MWCs and has $\rho(r) = 1/10$.
   b) Argue, using what was done for you in Example 3, that $\rho(r) = 1/10$ without using binomial coefficients or excessive counting arguments.
   c) If we allow a "veto override" whenever 2 senators and 4 representatives join without the president's vote, show that a different game arises that has $\rho(i) = 1/9$ for every player i.

8. Let $\Gamma_4 = (N, \mathcal{M})$ be defined by $N = \{a, b, c, d, e\}$, $\mathcal{M} = \{ab, acd, ace, ade, bcde\}$, and compute ρ for this game.

9. Compute ρ for the general class of *apex* games, which have the form $[l; \underbrace{l-1, 1, 1, \cdots, 1}_{l \text{ players}}]$. Hint: Consider some special cases.

For Section 3:

10. Let $(N_1, \mathcal{M}_1)$ be defined by $\mathcal{M}_1 = \{ab, bcd, acf\}$. Let $(N_2, \mathcal{M}_2)$ be defined by $\mathcal{M}_2 = \{ade, bce\}$.
    a) Argue that $(N_1, \mathcal{M}_1)$, $(N_2, \mathcal{M}_2)$ are mergeable and determine their merge $(N, \mathcal{M})$.
    b) Compute ρ for $(N_1, \mathcal{M}_1)$, $(N_2, \mathcal{M}_2)$, and $(N, \mathcal{M})$ and verify for each player that axiom (iv) holds for this example.

11. Let Γ be the game of Exercise 5, Section 2 and find a permutation $\sigma: N \to N$ with $\sigma(a) = d$ and satisfying the conditions of power index axiom (iii). Prove that there is only one such permutation and explain what the permutation tells you about $\rho(b)$ and $\rho(c)$.

12. Explain how the proof of the Uniqueness Theorem breaks down in the absence of power index axiom (i) (i.e., if dummies are allowed to have positive power). Then reinstate axiom (i) and answer the question with axiom (iii) removed. Hint: Can you think of a trivial assignment of power satisfying axioms (i), (ii), and (iv), but not axiom (iii)?

13. Let $(N, \mathcal{M})$ be a simple game and let $(N, \mathcal{M}_1)$ be the game obtained by deleting a single MWC (call it S) from $\mathcal{M}$ (leaving a collection $\mathcal{M}'$).
    a) Prove that for all $i \notin S$, $\rho_1(i) > \rho(i)$.
    b) Prove that for $i \in S$ we may have $\rho_1(i) > \rho(i)$, $\rho_1(i) = \rho(i)$, or $\rho_1(i) < \rho(i)$ depending on $\mathcal{M}$. Hint: Look at $\mathcal{M} = \{abcde, af\}$.

For Section 4:

14. Consider the games $[101; 100, 99, 1]$ and $[3; 2, 1, 1]$ in terms of the weights of the players and their power as measured by ρ.
    a) Make some conclusions about the significance of the relative values of the weights in weighted voting games.
    b) Do you believe that the "real-world" powers of the second player in each of the two games would differ significantly? Explain.

15. (Quarreling)
    a) Given $(N, \mathcal{M})$ with $\mathcal{M} = \{abcde, af, bf\}$, compute ρ for this game and show

that if a and b quarrel, the ρ values for a and b in the new game both increase. Think about this paradoxical result.

b) By considering $\mathcal{M} = \{abcd, abef, ag, bg\}$ and other games, exhibit separate examples in which 2 player quarrels can
   (i) hurt the quarrelers;
   (ii) hurt one and help the other;
   (iii) leave both quarrelers with unaffected power while affecting other players.

16. (Weighted voting paradoxes.)
   a) Prove that $[5; 3, 2, 1, 1, 1]$ provides an example of a weighted voting paradox as discussed in Section 4.
   b) Consider $[3; 3, 2, 2, 2, 2]$ and show that the player with the most weight has less power than any other player. Then show that this game is an improper one.
   c) (Open question.) Find a *proper* weighted voting game in which the player with the most weight has less power than some other player *or* else prove that this can never happen.

17. (New member and added weight paradoxes.) Consider the following weighted voting games (taken from Brams and Affuso [2]).

$$v_1 = [7; 6, 3, 2, 2]; \qquad v_2 = [8; 6, 3, 2, 2, 1],$$

$$v_3 = [8; 6, 3, 2, 2, 1, 1]; \quad v_4 = [8; 6, 3, 2, 2, 2].$$

By computing ρ_1, ρ_2, ρ_3, and ρ_4 for these games, discover and describe the following "paradoxes."
   a) A new member is added (other weights held fixed) and yet an old member's power is increased. (Quota may and may not stay fixed.)
   b) A member is given increased weight (all other weights held fixed) and yet some other member's power is increased. (See Brams [1] for corresponding paradoxes for ϕ and β.)

18. Consider the U.S. legislative system as described in Section 4.
   a) Allowing for a veto override when 67 of the 100 senators (not the V.P.) *and* 290 of the 435 representatives agree to it (2/3 needed for override), write down (but do not compute) expressions for $\rho(p)$, $\rho(s)$, $\rho(r)$, and $\rho(vp)$.
   b) (Not done to date.) If you have access to a computer or else you love to immerse yourself in computation and approximation, calculate the values for ρ from the expressions obtained in (a). Then comment on to what extent p's power is decreased while s's and r's power are increased by the veto override inclusion.

19. Compute ρ^B for the game $(N, \mathcal{M})$, where $\mathcal{M} = \{abc, ace, ad, afgh\}$. Player a is said to have *veto power* in such a game.

20. Let $\Gamma = \{q; w_1, w_2, \cdots, w_n]$ and define $t = \sum_{i=1}^{n} w_i$.
   a) Prove that the dual game $\Gamma^* = [t - q + 1; w_1, w_2, \cdots, w_n]$.
   b) Prove that $\Gamma = \Gamma^*$ if t is odd and $q = (t + 1)/2$.
   c) Does the converse of (b) hold? Explain.

21. Let $\Gamma = [5; 3, 2, 1, 1, 1, 1]$ and show that

$$\tfrac{1}{2}\rho(b) + \tfrac{1}{2}\rho^B(b) < \tfrac{1}{2}\rho(c) + \tfrac{1}{2}\rho^B(c)$$

even though c has less weight than b.

References

1. Brams, S. J. *Game Theory and Politics*, The Free Press, 1975.
2. Brams, S. J., and Affuso, P. J. "Power and Size: A New Paradox," *Theory and Decision*, 1976.
3. Banzhaf III, J. F. "Weighted Voting Doesn't Work: A Mathematical Analysis," *Rutgers Law Review*, *19* (1965), 317–343.
4. Caplow, T. "A Theory of Coalitions in the Triad," *American Sociological Review*, *21* (1956), 489–493.
5. Coleman, J. S. "Control of Collectivities and the Power of a Collectivity to Act," *Social Choice* (Bernhardt Lieberman, ed.) Gordon and Breach, New York, 1971.
6. Deegan, Jr., J., and Packel, E. W. "A New Index of Power for Simple n-Person Games," *International Journal of Game Theory*, *7* (1978), 113–123.
7. Dubey, P. "Some Results on Values of Finite and Infinite Games," Ph. D. Thesis, Center for Applied Mathematics, Cornell University, 1975.
8. Lucas, W. F. "Measuring Power in Weighted Voting Systems," 1981. Chapter 9 in this volume.
9. Riker, W. H. *The Theory of Political Coalitions*, Yale University Press, New Haven, Connecticut, 1962.
10. Riker, W. H., and Ordeshook, P. C. *An Introduction to Positive Political Theory*, Prentice-Hall, Englewood Cliffs, New Jersey, 1973.
11. Shapley, L. S., and Shubik, M. "A Method for Evaluating the Distribution of Power in a Committee System," *American Political Science Review*, *48* (1954), 787–792.
12. Straffin, Jr., P. D. "Power Indices in Political Science," 1982. Chapter 11 in this volume.
13. Vinacke, W. E., and Arkoff, A. "Experimental Study of Coalitions in the Triad," *American Sociological Review*, *22* (1957), 406–415.

Notes for the Instructor

Objectives.

To define and apply a new notion of power for simple n-person games.

To show how some simple assumptions about coalition formation yield a coherent model for power.

To illustrate the beauty and power of the axiomatic approach in uniqueness proofs.

To discuss the strengths and difficulties of a model for power vis a vis the real world.

To illustrate the utility of binomial coefficients and careful counting in a meaningful way.

Prerequisities.

Elementary set theory and function notation

Summation notation

Binomial coefficients

Remarks. This module is appropriate in finite mathematics, modeling, mathematics for social scientists and game theory courses.

Abstract. A new power index on a class of simple n-person games is proposed, developed, illustrated, and discussed. The assumptions underlying the index are natural and direct, resulting in properties which are concise and convenient both theoretically and computationally. A characterizing set of axioms for the power index leads to a uniqueness theorem on the class of simple n-person games.

This module introduces some new but elementary ideas in the exciting area of power determination in n-person games. Class time needed for the development of the ideas in the module is estimated at 5 hr, although the elementary nature of the material might lower this somewhat if students work independently or have some mathematical sophistication.

The exercises at the end of the module are divided by sections and arranged in estimated order of increasing difficulty within each section. The elusive nature of power and the lack of experimental data on how people interact and exercise power in group situations suggests a variety of class activities or open-ended projects based on "dividing the dollar" in various weighted voting situations. We allude to but do not formally propose such "games" in the module. The instructor should find them received by a class with enthusiasm; the inevitably nonuniform results should shed light upon the difficulty of modeling power and invite the testing of the model developed against "reality." Perhaps the only ironclad conclusion will be that the sponsor of "divide the dollar" games needs solid financial backing.

Several of the topics considered here are parallel with and suggested by the preceding chapter by William F. Lucas and the following chapter by Philip Straffin, Jr. For definitions and results on the Shapley–Shubik and Banzhaf power indices plus a variety of additional topics and exercises, we recommend these modules for additional reading.

CHAPTER 11

Power Indices in Politics

Philip D. Straffin, Jr.*

Introduction

"Political science, as an empirical discipline, is the study of the shaping and sharing of power" (Lasswell and Kaplan in *Power and Society*, 1950).

The study of power is central to the study of political processes. If we can precisely define and measure power, we should be able to say important things about political processes. In general, it is difficult even to define the idea of power precisely (see the first few chapters of Nagel [23] for a discussion of this problem), but for the special case of voting power in decision-making bodies, there are mathematical power indices that have been widely used in recent years. I shall introduce three of these indices in Section 1, after presenting an elementary mathematical formulation of a decision-making body as a so-called "simple game."

Most previous applications of power indices have been to answer questions like "Is this given decision rule fair; does it distribute power equitably?" This kind of question is essentially static. It considers how we should design a decision-making system, but not how members would act in that system. I believe that we can and should use power indices to consider dynamic questions—questions of political processes. Thus Section 2 develops models that use the power indices to study the formation of voting blocs, strategic quarreling, and the bandwagon effect in U.S. presidential nominations. Many of these models are new, and I have tried to point out places where the reader should think critically about them. Enough critical thought might even produce better models.

* Department of Mathematics, Beloit College, Beloit, Wisconsin 53511.

Finally, Section 3 returns to look critically at the original power indices, asking "What do they really measure?" and "When should we use which index?" Ideas developed in that discussion are applied to a current question of constitutional design for Canada.

A healthy selection of exercises comes with each section. They should be used as physical exercises are used—to develop prowess. Most people I know can only learn new ideas thoroughly by using those ideas. The exercises are chances to do that. Solutions to many of them are at the end of the module.

I have three criteria for good mathematical models in the social sciences:

(1) The questions considered should be significant enough, and the results suggestive enough, to interest social scientists.
(2) The ideas involved should be significant enough to interest mathematicians.
(3) The mathematical methods used should be elementary enough to be understood by intelligent people who are not professional mathematicians.

Many mathematicians, by nature fond of deep theorems (as I am), might not agree with (3). My feeling is that much of what mathematics has to offer social science is precise thought about carefully formulated questions, and this does not require advanced methods. In any case, I believe that (2) and (3) are not contradictory.

In fact, I believe that power indices in politics satisfy all three criteria. Whether the models in this module satisfy (1) and (2) is, of course, for readers to decide. One indication that the general subject can be intriguing to both social scientists and mathematicians is another module in this MAA series by John Deegan, a political scientist from the University of Rochester, and Ed Packel, a mathematician from Lake Forest College (Deegan and Packel [11]). Their response to first meeting the subject of power indices was to develop and analyze a new power index, and they had quite a good time doing it.

To be more precise about criterion (3), the only mathematical background needed for this module is strong high school algebra, specifically a good introduction to permutations and combinations and binomial coefficients, and a knowledge of the terminology of set theory. Feeling at home with permutations and combinations will be especially valuable in tackling the exercises. Techniques from calculus are mentioned several times in the module (the idea of a partial derivative in Section 2.3, the idea of an integral in 3.2 and 3.3), but are not necessary to follow the arguments. Elementary ideas from probability are used in Sections 3.2 and 3.3. Willingness to think carefully and critically will, of course, be valuable throughout.

Many people have been kind enough to read this module and offer suggestions for its improvement. It has profited especially from suggestions by Steven Brams, Ed Packel, Peter Rice, Robert Thrall, and Eric Uslaner, to whom I am grateful.

1. Voting Games and Power Indices

1.1. Simple Games

Consider the case of a group of individuals who must collectively decide whether to accept or reject a series of proposals. We may, for instance, think of members of a legislature who must decide to pass or reject a series of bills, or stockholders in a corporation who must accept or reject a series of management proposals. If such a decision-making body is informal, it may not have definite rules for reaching decisions. If it does have definite rules, the effect of the rules should be to specify exactly which coalitions of individual members have the power to ensure acceptance of a proposal. For example, the common example of majority rule specifies that in an n-member decision-making body, a coalition can ensure acceptance of a proposal if and only if it contains more than $n/2$ members. The unanimity rule used in Quaker meetings and most American juries specifies that only the entire group can accept a proposal.

Mathematically, we can represent such a situation as a set N (the members of the decision-making body) together with a collection $\mathscr{W}$ of subsets of N. $\mathscr{W}$ is called the collection of "winning coalitions," and it consists of all coalitions that can ensure acceptance. We can put certain reasonable restrictions on $\mathscr{W}$:

(i) $\varnothing \notin \mathscr{W}$ The empty set of members cannot ensure acceptance.
(ii) $N \in \mathscr{W}$ The entire set of members can ensure acceptance.
(iii) If S and T are subsets of N, with $S \in \mathscr{W}$ and $S \subset T$, then $T \in \mathscr{W}$. If S can ensure acceptance and T contains all the members of S, then T can ensure acceptance.

A pair $(N, \mathscr{W})$ satisfying conditions (i)–(iii) is called a *simple game*, and the members of N are sometimes called *players* in the game. [Some authors call such a pair a *monotonic simple game*, referring to condition (iii).] One interesting class of simple games is the class of *weighted voting games*. Here, each player casts a certain number of votes, which may be different for different players, and a specified quota of votes is necessary to approve. We use the symbol

$$[q; w_1, w_2, \cdots, w_n]$$

to represent a weighted voting game. The numbers w_i are the voting "weights" of the n players, and q is the quota needed to win. In mathematical terms,

$$S \in \mathscr{W} \Leftrightarrow \sum_{i \in S} w_i \geq q.$$

Lucas [18] gives many examples of decision-making bodies that operate as weighted voting games. The n-person majority game and the n-person unanimity game can both be represented as weighted voting games:

$$M_n = \begin{cases} \left[\dfrac{n+1}{2}; \underbrace{1, 1, \cdots, 1}_{n \text{ times}}\right] & (n \text{ odd}) \\ \left[\dfrac{n}{2}+1; \underbrace{1, 1, \cdots, 1}_{n \text{ times}}\right] & (n \text{ even}) \end{cases}$$

$$B_n = [n; \underbrace{1, 1, \cdots, 1}_{n \text{ times}}].$$

(The unanimity game is also called a "pure bargaining game," explaining the use of the letter B.)

There are simple games that cannot be written as weighted voting games. For instance, consider a situation in which a nine-person committee divides itself into three subcommittees, each containing three members. A proposal is to be approved if it is approved by a majority of members in each of a majority of the subcommittees, i.e., at least two members in each of at least two subcommittees. This kind of situation is called a *compound simple game*, and this one is represented by the symbol

$$M_3(M_3, M_3, M_3),$$

which represents the fact that we have a three-person majority game, where the vote of each "player" is determined by the outcome of a separate three-person majority game. This game cannot be represented as a weighted voting game, because the symmetry of the nine players would demand that they all be assigned the same number of votes, yet some four-person coalitions win, and some lose. (Exercise 4b asks you to make this argument more precise.)

Two kinds of compound games are of special importance. If $G_1 = (N_1, \mathscr{W}_1)$ and $G_2 = (N_2, \mathscr{W}_2)$ are simple games with N_1 and N_2 disjoint, we define the *product game* $G_1 \otimes G_2$ to be the game whose set of players is $N_1 \cup N_2$ and in which a coalition is winning if it can win in *both* G_1 and G_2. The *sum game* $G_1 \oplus G_2$ also has $N_1 \cup N_2$ as its set of players, but the winning coalitions are those which can win in *either* G_1 or G_2. A product of games corresponds to a bill needing approval by both of two legislative houses; a sum of games, to a bill needing approval by either of two houses.

Finally, there are simple games that are not even compounds of weighted voting games. These kind of games are probably rare in political situations, but they can be fascinating objects. The simplest example is the four-person game $\Gamma = (N, \mathscr{W})$ with

$$N = \{A, B, C, D\}$$

and

$$\mathscr{W} = \{\{AB\}\{BC\}\{CD\}\{ABC\}\{ABD\}\{ACD\}\{BCD\}\{ABCD\}\}.$$

(See Exercise 6.) One can simplify the description of a game like this by listing only the *minimal* winning coalitions. A set of players is a *minimal winning coalition* if it is winning, and no proper subset of it is winning. The collection of minimal winning coalitions is denoted by $\mathscr{W}^m$. In Γ, $\mathscr{W}^m = \{\{AB\}\{BC\}\{CD\}\}$. Because of the monotonicity condition (iii), $\mathscr{W}$ is completely determined if $\mathscr{W}^m$ is given: the winning coalitions must be exactly those which contain some minimal winning coalition.

There are two interesting things to note about the definition of a simple game. First, consider the situation of a three-person coalition, call it S, in

$$M_6 = [4; 1, 1, 1, 1, 1, 1].$$

Such a coalition is not winning—it cannot ensure acceptance of a proposal—but its complement $N - S$ is also not winning. S is called a *blocking* coalition: it can *prevent* acceptance of a proposal. One interesting way to handle blocking coalitions is discussed in Exercises 8–10.

Second, consider the simple game

$$N = \{A, B, C, D\}$$

$$\mathscr{W} = \{AB, CD, ABC, ABD, ACD, BCD, ABCD\}.$$

(I have suppressed inner brackets for conciseness.) Here the two-person coalition AB can accept a proposal and so can the two-person coalition CD. If these coalitions should accept contradictory proposals, we are clearly in trouble. Simple games which have this property (that there are two disjoint winning coalitions) are called *improper*. Should we consider improper games at all in our subsequent analysis? After all, surely no sensible political system would be designed this way! I think we shall be wise to consider these games, for the simple reason that improper games are present in all societies. The extreme case of an improper game is the game

$$B_n^* = [1; \underbrace{1, 1, \cdots, 1}_{n \text{ times}}]$$

which Douglas Rae [27] calls the "rule of individual initiative." This game abounds in our society, and the fact that it is improper, it might be argued, is the reason we have lawyers and a judicial system. Exercises 11 and 12 have other examples of improper games.

Notes and References. The descriptive theory of simple games is presented in more detail by Shapley [32]. More recent structural results are in Shapley [33]. Lucas' Chapter 9 in this volume is an excellent source on weighted voting games. A complete list of all simple games with four or fewer players is included as an appendix to this module. There are 179 nonequivalent (see Exercise 7) simple games with five players, and the number with six players is unknown.

Exercises

1. Write out all of the winning coalitions and the minimal winning coalitions for each of the following games. Assume the players are denoted by letters of the alphabet in order.

a) $[4; 2, 2, 2, 1]$.
b) $[4; 4, 1, 1, 1]$. (Players here are A, B, C, D.)
c) $[7; 4, 3, 2, 1]$.
d) $M_3(B_1, B_2, B_3)$.
e) $M_3 \otimes M_3$. If you get tired, you might write only the minimal winning coalitions for these
f) $M_3 \oplus M_3$.

2. Give the winning coalitions and the minimal winning coalitions for the simple games representing the following situations. Show a representation of each as a sum or product of weighted voting games.
   a) A committee of four breaks into two subcommittees $\{AB\}$ and $\{CD\}$ and declares that a proposal is approved if it is approved unanimously by one of the subcommittees.
   b) Same split, but now a proposal is approved if it is approved by at least one member of each subcommittee.

3. Represent the following simple games as weighted voting games. That is, give a set of weights and a quota that will produce exactly the winning coalitions shown.
   a) $\mathscr{W} = \{AB, ABC, ABD, ACD, BCD, ABCD\}$.
   b) $\mathscr{W} = \{ABCDEF\}$.
   c) $\mathscr{W} = \{ABCD, ABCDE\}$.
   d) $\mathscr{W} = \{AB, AC, ABC\}$.
   e) $\mathscr{W} = \{A, AB, AC, ABC\}$.
   f) $\mathscr{W} = \{AB, AC, ABC, ABD, ACD, BCD, ABCD\}$.

4. a) Which four-person coalitions in $M_3(M_3, M_3, M_3)$ win, and which lose? (Describe them, do not list them!)
   b) Show more formally than in the text that this game cannot be represented as a weighted voting game by assuming you have such a representation and deriving a contradiction.

5. If there were no possibility of overriding a presidential veto, the U.S. legislative scheme (Congress and the President) could be described as a compound of majority games. Show how to do this.

6. Show that the game Γ cannot be represented as a weighted voting game, using the method of 4b.

7. Two simple games are *equivalent* (or *isomorphic*) if the players can be labeled in such a way that the winning coalitions are exactly the same in both games.
   a) Show that the following three-person games are all equivalent.
      (i) $N = \{A, B, C\}$. Approval is by majority vote, but A has a *veto*.
      (ii) $[3; 2, 1, 1]$.
      (iii) $[5; 3, 2, 2]$.
      (iv) $[17; 16, 1, 1]$.
   b) Divide the following six games into three equivalent pairs
      (i) $[6; 4, 3, 2, 1]$.
      (ii) $[7; 4, 3, 2, 1]$.
      (iii) $[5; 2, 5, 1, 1]$.
      (iv) $[5; 3, 2, 1, 1]$.
      (v) $[5; 2, 2, 3, 1]$.
      (vi) $[40; 1, 20, 15, 66]$.

8. In a simple game $(N, \mathscr{W})$, a coalition S is said to be *blocking* if $N - S \notin \mathscr{W}$ (i.e., the complement of S cannot win). What are all blocking coalitions in
   a) $M_4 = [3; 1, 1, 1, 1]$?
   b) B_3?
   c) Γ?

9. If $G = (N, \mathscr{W})$ is a simple game, the *dual game* is $G^* = (N, \mathscr{W}^*)$, where $S \in \mathscr{W}^*$ if and only if S is blocking in G. So G^* is G with all blocking coalitions made winning. What are the dual games to
   a) B_3?
   b) M_4?
   c) M_5?
   d) $N = \{A, B, C\}$, $\mathscr{W} = \{AB, AC, ABC\}$?

10. If $[q; w_1, w_2, \cdots, w_n]$ is a weighted voting game with $\sum_{i=1}^{n} w_i = w$, show that the dual game is $[w - q + 1; w_1, w_2, \cdots, w_n]$. (The table of four-person games in the Appendix shows dual games.)

11. Show that the following simple games are improper:
    a) The game Γ.
    b) The games in Exercise 2.
    c) Any sum game.

12. The games $M_{n,k}$ are defined by $M_{n,k} = [k; \underbrace{1, 1, \cdots, 1}_{n \text{ times}}]$. For what relation between k and n is $M_{n,k}$ improper?

1.2. The Shapley–Shubik, Banzhaf, and Absolute Banzhaf Power Indices

The information about which coalitions are "winning," which defines a simple game, tells us something about the distribution of *power* in the game. In particular, some coalitions have complete power for approving proposals, and some coalitions have no power for approval. Now consider the situation of an individual player in a game. She may need the answer to a more individualistic question: "How much power do *I* have in this game?" Occasionally, the answer will be clear. Consider, for example, the weighted voting game

$$\begin{array}{c}[5;\ 5,\ 2,\ 1].\\ \quad A\ B\ C\end{array}$$

The winning coalitions in this game are exactly those which contain player A. A proposal will be approved if and only if A approves it. Player A in this case is called a *dictator*, and she clearly has all the power. Players B and C, on the other hand, have no power and are called *dummies*.

If a dictator is present, all other players are dummies, but a player can be a dummy even in the absence of a dictator, as in the game

$$\begin{array}{c}[4:\ 2,\ 2,\ 2,\ 1].\\ \quad A\ B\ C\ D\end{array}$$

In this game, no outcome can be changed by player D's action, because any coalition that could win with D, could also win without him. D has no power and is a dummy. Formally, we call a player a *dummy* if he is a member of no minimal winning coalition.

On the other hand, the general problem of translating information about the power of coalitions into statements about the power of individual players needs ingenuity. Clearly, the power of an individual should depend upon which winning coalitions he is part of. He should "share some of their power." Less obviously, but I think plausibly, we could say that it should depend only upon those winning coalitions to which his presence is *crucial*, i.e., those winning coalitions that would become losing if he defected. After all, if a coalition does not care whether it contains our player or not, can he be said to have power in that coalition? With these ideas in mind, we can write down some general properties we would like an "individual power index" to have:

(i) A power index should be a function K, which assigns to each player i in a simple game a nonnegative real number $K(i) \geq 0$.
(ii) The numbers $K(i)$ should depend only on the collection $\mathscr{W}$ of winning coalitions. In particular, if players i and j have "symmetric" positions with respect to $\mathscr{W}$ (see Exercise 17, then we should have $K(i) = K(j)$.
(iii) $K(i) = 0$ if and only if i is a dummy.
(iv) In a weighted voting game, if $w_i > w_j$, then $K(i) \geq K(j)$.

In addition, if we wish to answer questions like "What fraction of the power in this game do I hold?", we might also like to have a "normalization" condition

(v) $\sum_{i \in N} K(i) = 1.$

Condition (iv) says that in a weighted voting game, having extra votes cannot hurt you. That it need not necessarily help you (hence the "$\geq$" instead of "$>$") is clear from considering

$$\underset{A\ \ B\ \ C}{[4; 3, 2, 2].}$$

Here the winning coalitions are AB, AC, BC, and ABC, and the symmetry part of condition (ii) says that we should assign equal power to each of the players. A's extra vote does not help.

Two major power indices have been proposed and widely accepted by political scientists, mathematical game theorists, and even courts of law. Both of them meet conditions (i)–(v), and both are based on considering to which coalitions the presence of a given player is crucial.

The first such power index was proposed by game theorist Lloyd Shapley and economist Martin Shubik in 1954 in a pioneering article in the *American Political Science Review*. Shapley and Shubik propose that we consider the following scheme:

> There is a group of individuals all willing to vote for some bill. They vote in order. As soon as enough members have voted for it, it is declared passed, and the member who voted last is given credit for having passed it. Let us choose the voting order of the members randomly. Then we may compute how often a given individual is *pivotal*. This latter number serves to give us our index. (Shapley and Shubik, [35].)

This translates into the following procedure. Write down all $n!$ orderings of the n players. In each ordering, underline the player who is *pivotal* in that ordering, whose addition changes the forming coalition from losing to winning. The Shapley–Shubik power index ϕ_i of player i is then simply equal to the fraction of times that i is pivotal:

$$\phi_i = \frac{\text{number of pivots for } i}{\text{total number of orderings}} = \frac{\text{number of pivots for } i}{n!}$$

For example, consider the game Γ of Section 1.1, with $\mathscr{W}^m = \{\{AB\}\{BC\}\{CD\}\}$. There are 24 possible orderings of the players. The pivotal player is underlined in each:

$$\begin{array}{llll}
A\underline{B}CD & B\underline{A}CD & CA\underline{B}D & DA\underline{B}C \\
A\underline{B}DC & B\underline{A}DC & CA\underline{D}B & DA\underline{C}B \\
AC\underline{B}D & B\underline{C}AD & C\underline{B}AD & DB\underline{A}C \\
AC\underline{D}B & B\underline{C}DA & C\underline{B}DA & DB\underline{C}A \\
AD\underline{B}C & BD\underline{A}C & C\underline{D}AB & D\underline{C}AB \\
AD\underline{C}B & BD\underline{C}A & C\underline{D}BA & D\underline{C}BA
\end{array}$$

Hence,

$$\phi_A = \frac{4}{24} = \frac{1}{6}, \; \phi_B = \frac{8}{24} = \frac{1}{3}, \; \phi_C = \frac{8}{24} = \frac{1}{3}, \; \phi_D = \frac{4}{24} = \frac{1}{6}.$$

We often write these together as a vector:

$$\phi = \left(\frac{1}{6}, \frac{1}{3}, \frac{1}{3}, \frac{1}{6}\right).$$

Sometimes symmetry can save us writing out all $n!$ orderings. For example, consider the weighted majority game

$$[5; 3, 2, 1, 1, 1, 1].$$

Since the "1" players are all alike, we need write out only $6 \cdot 5 = 30$ distinct orderings (instead of $6! = 720$):

$$\begin{array}{llllll}
3\underline{2}1111 & 2\underline{3}1111 & 21\underline{3}111 & 211\underline{3}11 & 211\underline{1}31 & 211\underline{1}13 \\
31\underline{2}111 & 13\underline{2}111 & 12\underline{3}111 & 121\underline{3}11 & 121\underline{1}31 & 121\underline{1}13 \\
31\underline{1}211 & 13\underline{1}211 & 11\underline{3}211 & 112\underline{3}11 & 112\underline{1}31 & 112\underline{1}13 \\
31\underline{1}121 & 13\underline{1}121 & 11\underline{3}121 & 111\underline{3}21 & 111\underline{2}31 & 111\underline{2}13 \\
31\underline{1}112 & 13\underline{1}112 & 11\underline{3}112 & 111\underline{3}12 & 1111\underline{3}2 & 1111\underline{2}3
\end{array}$$

Notice that the 1's pivot 12/30 of the time, but since there are four of them, each 1 pivots only 3/30 of the time. We get

$$\phi = \left(\frac{12}{30}, \frac{6}{30}, \frac{3}{30}, \frac{3}{30}, \frac{3}{30}, \frac{3}{30}\right) = (0.4, 0.2, 0.1, 0.1, 0.1, 0.1).$$

Power as measured by the Shapley–Shubik index in a weighted voting game is *not* proportional to the number of votes cast. For instance, the player with $3/9 = 33\frac{1}{3}\%$ of the votes has 40% of the power. If you think of the examples earlier in this section, you can see that no index satisfying conditions (ii) or (iii) could have power proportional to voting weight.

Our second major power index was proposed by a lawyer, John Banzhaf, in 1965:

> The appropriate measure of a legislator's power is simply the number of different situations in which he is able to determine the outcome. More explicitly, in a case in which there are n legislators, each acting independently and each capable of influencing the outcome only by means of his votes, the ratio of the power of legislator X to the power of legislator Y is the same as the ratio of the number of possible voting combinations of the entire legislature in which X can alter the outcome by changing his vote, to the number of combinations in which Y can alter the outcome by changing his vote. (Banzhaf [4, p. 331].)

Operationally, we can calculate the Banzhaf power index as follows. Write down all winning coalitions. In each winning coalition underline the *critical* or *swing* members, those whose defection would cause the coalition to become losing. The power of each player is proportional to the number of times that player appears underlined.

Formally, let $\eta_i =$ the number of winning coalitions to which player i is critical. The Banzhaf power index for player i is given by

$$\beta_i = \frac{\eta_i}{\sum_{i=1}^{n} \eta_i}$$

Dividing by $\sum_{i=1}^{n} \eta_i$ "normalizes" the index, so that it satisfies condition (v).

[η_i counts the number of times player i could change a coalition from winning to losing. Strictly speaking, according to Banzhaf, we should also consider the number of times player i could change a coalition from losing to winning. However, it is not hard to see (Exercise 7) that this number is also equal to η_i, so we need not count it separately.]

As an example, consider the game Γ. Winning coalitions are

$$\begin{array}{llll} \underline{AB} & \underline{CD} & \underline{AB}D & B\underline{C}D \\ \underline{BC} & A\underline{B}C & A\underline{CD} & ABCD \end{array}$$

where the swing members have been underlined. For instance, in the winning coalition ABC, A's defection (or C's) would not be critical, since BC (or AB) is still winning. However, B's defection would be critical, since AC is not winning. Notice that since all three-person coalitions are winning in this game, no players are critical to *ABCD*. We need not even have written *ABCD* down. The numbers of swings are given by

$$\eta = (2, 4, 4, 2).$$

Since $\sum_{i=1}^{4} \eta_i = 12$, the Banzhaf power indices are

$$\beta = \left(\frac{2}{12}, \frac{4}{12}, \frac{4}{12}, \frac{2}{12}\right) = \left(\frac{1}{6}, \frac{1}{3}, \frac{1}{3}, \frac{1}{6}\right).$$

For this game, the Shapley–Shubik and Banzhaf indices agree. We shall see that this is by no means always the case. That it should not always be the case follows from the difference between *permutations* and *combinations*. The Shapley–Shubik reasoning considers the probability that a player will be "pivotal" if all permutations of the players are equally likely. The Banzhaf reasoning considers the probability that a player will be "critical" if all combinations (i.e., coalitions) of the players are equally likely. We shall return to this idea in Section 3.2 after seeing more about how the indices behave in practice.

As a first example of nonagreement, and to see a simplifying calculational technique, let us consider the weighted voting game for which we know the Shapley–Shubik indices:

$$[5; 3, 2, 1, 1, 1, 1].$$

We write down all types of winning coalitions, with swings underlined:

Types of winning coalitions with	Number of ways this can occur	Number of swings for 3	2	1
5 votes: 32	1	1	1	
311	6	6		12
2111	4		4	12
6 votes: 321	4	4	4	
3111	4	4		
21111	1		1	
7 votes: 3211	6	6		
31111	1	1		
		22	10	24

We need not include winning coalitions of 8 or 9 votes, since not even the 3-vote player can be critical to them. The numbers in the second column are from the theory of combinations. For instance, how many ways could you choose 311 from 321111? There is $\binom{1}{1} = 1$ way of choosing the 3-vote player, times $\binom{4}{2} = 6$ ways of choosing the two 1-vote players, giving the answer of 6. We get

$$\eta = (22, 10, 6, 6, 6, 6)$$

and

$$\beta = \left(\frac{22}{56}, \frac{10}{56}, \frac{6}{56}, \frac{6}{56}, \frac{6}{56}, \frac{6}{56}\right) \approx (0.392, 0.178, 0.107, 0.107, 0.107, 0.107).$$

Comparing this with ϕ, we see that the two indices turn out to be quite close in this case, with β giving slightly less power to the two large players and slightly more to the small players. It is possible for the differences to be much more extreme.

In the last few years, game theorists have noted with regret that a certain amount of information is lost when the η_is are normalized to make them add to one. The resulting β_is give an idea of the players' *relative* power, but the η_is also say something about the players' *absolute* power. To keep this information, Dubey and Shapley [14], for example, have proposed considering an *absolute Banzhaf index*

$$\beta_i' = \frac{\text{Total number of swings (positive and negative) for player } i}{\text{Total number of coalitions possible}} = \frac{2\eta_i}{2^n} = \frac{\eta_i}{2^{n-1}}.$$

To see what this does, consider the three-person majority game M_3 and the three-person unanimity game B_3. By symmetry, both of these games will have $\phi = \beta = (1/3, 1/3, 1/3)$. However, it seems intuitively clear that an individual player has more absolute power in M_3 than she does in B_3. For instance, she need convince only one other player to side with her in the majority game but must convince both other players in the unanimity game. Computing β', we get

$$M_3: \underline{AB}\ \underline{AC}\ \underline{BC} \qquad\qquad B_3: \underline{ABC}$$

$$\eta = (2, 2, 2) \qquad\qquad \eta = (1, 1, 1)$$

$$\beta' = \left(\frac{1}{2}, \frac{1}{2}, \frac{1}{2}\right) \qquad\qquad \beta' = \left(\frac{1}{4}, \frac{1}{4}, \frac{1}{4}\right).$$

We would conclude that the individual players are twice as powerful in M_3 as they are in B_3. There are more results along these lines in the exercises. When we consider characterizations of the power indices in Section 3, β' will play a crucial role.

As a final note, recall that in Section 1.1 we mentioned "blocking coalitions," which could prevent a proposal from passing, even though they might not be able themselves to pass a proposal. This would suggest that in addition to studying "approval power," as we have here, we should also study "blocking power." In the terminology of Exercise 9 of Section 1.1, this would involve studying the power indices of the "dual game." Exercise 25 of this section asks you to show that in fact we need not do this: if we apply ϕ or β or β' to measure blocking power, we get exactly the same number as if we use them to measure approval power. The indices ϕ, β, and β' effectively measure *both* kinds of power.

Notes and References. The conditions that a power index should satisfy seem quite natural. For instance, a set almost identical to the ones given here was also recently given by Allingham [1]. Condition (iv), that extra votes cannot hurt you, shows that we are leaving out psychological or sociological considerations. In fact, various authors have argued that in a game with one strong player and two weak players, there will be a tendency for the two weak players to gang up on the strong player (Caplow [9]). A lovely discussion of the Shapley value in game theory, from which the Shapley–Shubik index for simple games comes as a special case, can be found in Luce and Raiffa [19]. Among recent political science books, Riker and Ordeshook [28] discusses the Shapley–Shubik index, and Brams [5] discusses both power indices.

The exercises will give you many examples upon which to practice computations, but more can be found in the Appendix, and in Lucas [18]. Lucas also gives several effective calculational techniques for computing ϕ and β. Shapley and Shubik [35] considered Congress, the United Nations Security Council, and the 1–3–5 legislative scheme of Exercise 22. Banzhaf [4] discussed the Nassau County government, where there were dummies. Several calculational formulas for ϕ appear in Straffin [41].

There are other power indices in use, though they are less well known than Shapley–Shubik and Banzhaf. For instance, James Coleman [10] defines two indices measuring power to initiate action and power to prevent action. These are related to the Banzhaf index, and are discussed by Brams [6]. Deegan and Packel [11] present and analyze a power index based on rewarding only members of minimal winning coalitions. Nagel [23] is a good guide to the literature giving other approaches to questions of precisely defining and measuring power.

Exercises

13. Calculate Shapley–Shubik and Banzhaf indices for
    a) [4; 4, 1, 1, 1].
    b) [7; 4, 3, 2, 1].
    c) [5; 4, 2, 1, 1, 1].
    d) [9; 5, 4, 3, 2, 1].

14. Verify some of the index calculations for four-person games in the Appendix.

15. [7; 5, 3, 3, 1] has an unusual property. Compute ϕ and β and give the property.

16. Calculate ϕ and β for the following games (these games are called "apex games"):
    a) [3; 2, 1, 1, 1].
    b) [4; 3, 1, 1, 1, 1].
    c) $[m; m-1, \underbrace{1, 1, \cdots, 1}_{m \text{ times}}]$, ($\phi$ only).

17. The "symmetry" condition (ii) needs to be made more precise. In a game $(N, \mathscr{W})$ we say that "player i is symmetric to player j" if there is a permutation of N which
 (i) takes i to j.
 (ii) preserves $\mathscr{W}$, i.e., the permutation does not change the winning coalitions.
 a) For the game Γ, check that the permutation

$$\begin{aligned} A &\to D \\ B &\to C \\ C &\to B \\ D &\to A \end{aligned}$$

 preserves $\mathscr{W}$. Which players are symmetric in this game? How is that reflected in the power indices?
 b) (For the mathematically proficient). Check that the relation "i is symmetric to j" defined above is an equivalence relation on the set of players in a simple game.
 c) Find permutations showing that all players are symmetric to each other in the games of Section 1.1, Exercise 2.

18. Check as well as you can that both ϕ and β satisfy conditions (i)–(v).

19. Prove the claim in this section that the number of winning coalitions that would become losing if player i defected is exactly equal to the number of losing coalitions that would become winning if player i joined. (You might consider the pairing of coalitions given by $S \leftrightarrow S - \{i\}$.)

The following three exercises are more difficult.

20. In the present United Nations Security Council (modified since 1954), there are 15 members, and 9 votes are needed for approval. In addition, each of the five major powers has a veto. Interpret this to mean that a winning coalition is one that has at least nine members and includes all of the five major powers. Denote the players by *AAAAAbbbbbbbbbb* and compute power indices. (For Shapley–Shubik, do not work out all $\binom{15}{5} = 3003$ orderings, but think "When would b pivot?"

21. A seven-person legislature has a three-person committee. Approval must be by a majority of *both* the committee and the entire legislature. Denote the members by *AAAbbbb* and compute power indices. What is the ratio of power between a committee member and a noncommittee member?

22. Consider a legislature system with a President and two houses, one of 3 members and one of 5 members. Approval must be by the President and a majority of both houses (so this game is $M_1 \otimes M_3 \otimes M_5$). Denote the players by *abbbccccc*.
 a) Write out which kinds of coalitions are winning in this game.
 b) Calculate the Shapley–Shubik and Banzhaf indices. Check that ϕ makes smaller houses "stronger" (i.e., the president has more power than the sum of the powers of the members of the three-person house, and this sum is larger than the sum of the powers of the members of the five-person house), while β makes larger houses stronger. This result holds in general.
 c) How do indices change if we allow a veto override by a 2/3 vote in both houses (still 2 of 3 in the first house, but 4 of 5 in the second)?

23. Not really an exercise, but a chance for thought. Shapley and Shubik [35] calculate that for the U.S. legislative system without veto override, the President has slightly under 1/2 the power, and the Senate and House each have about 1/4, with the House slightly lower than the Senate (these latter figures are, as in Exercise 22, sums of the power of individual members). With veto override, the figures change to about (1/6, 5/12, 5/12).

    The corresponding Banzhaf figures without veto override are approximately (0.039, 0.313, 0.648). The possibility of veto overrides does *not* change these figures to several decimal places. Which of the two indices, ϕ or β, seems to capture the realities of the situation best?

24. Is it possible for two players i and j to have the same Shapley–Shubik and Banzhaf indices, and *not* be symmetric? Consider the five-person game with $N = \{A, B, C, D, E\}$, $\mathscr{W}^m = \{AB, AC, ADE, BCD, BDE\}$.

25. Show that ϕ, β, and β' are the same for the dual game G^* as they are for G, for all simple games G. (Hence it does not matter if we consider blocking coalitions instead of winning ones. You might like to check this result for games of four or fewer players by consulting the Appendix.)

26. Calculate β' for M_9 and $M_3(M_3, M_3, M_3)$ to see in which game a player has more power.

27. $M_{n,k}$ denotes the game $[k; \underbrace{1, 1, \cdots, 1}_{n \text{ times}}]$. Calculate β' for $M_{5,k}$ for $k = 1, 2, 3, 4, 5$.

    Conclude that for $n = 5$, anyway, majority rule is best among all $M_{n,k}$ in the sense that it maximizes an individual player's absolute power. This result, for all n, appears in Rae [27].

1.3. Power Indices for Infinite Games

Consider a corporation with one major stockholder X who controls 40% of the stock, and suppose the remainder is split evenly among 60 other stockholders, each having 1%. We can use the Shapley–Shubik index to compute the power of the major stockholder. There are 61 players. Since the 60 minor stockholders are symmetric, there are only 61 distinct orderings, depending only on the position of X. Of these 61 orderings, X will pivot if he appears in positions 12–51 inclusive (if we assume that approval must be by an amount just over 50%), i.e., 40/61 of the time.

Now suppose X still controls 40% of the stock, but the remainder is split evenly among 600 other stockholders, each controlling 0.1%. Of the 601 distinct orderings, X will pivot if he appears in positions 102–501, i.e., 400/601 of the time. Clearly, as the number of minor stockholders gets very large, X's share of the power (as measured by Shapley–Shubik index) approaches 2/3.

We can make this idea of a limiting process more precise by formulating the idea of an *oceanic weighted voting game*. Let there be one major player X controlling 40% of the vote, with the remaining 60% held by an infinite "ocean" of minor voters. Think of the minor voters lined up as points in a line segment of length 0.6, as they come to join a coalition in support of some proposal. Voter X can join at any point along this line segment. He will pivot if he joins after 0.1 and before (or at) 0.5. His Shapley–Shubik index is

$$\phi_X = \frac{\text{Length of segment in which } X \text{ pivots}}{\text{Total length of segment}} = \frac{0.5 - 0.1}{0.6} = \frac{2}{3}.$$

This agrees, as it seems clear it should, with the result of the limiting process we first considered.

In a series of RAND reports (Shapley and Shapiro [34], Milnor and Shapley [22]) and a recent, very technical book (Aumann and Shapley [2]), Shapley and others have made this intuitive notion of an oceanic weighted voting game precise. They have also proved limit theorems which say that, in a game with several major players and many minor players, as the number of minor players increases and the share of each one approaches zero in such a way that the total vote held by the minor players remains constant, the Shapley–Shubik indices of the major players approach their value in the appropriate oceanic game. The nice thing is that, as above, the indices in the oceanic game may be easily computable.

To see better how this works, let us look at an example where there are two major voters and an ocean of minor voters. Suppose voter X holds 3/9 of the total vote, and voter Y holds 2/9, with the other 4/9 held by the ocean of minor voters. The minor voters line up along a line segment of length 4/9. X and Y can join at any point along this line segment:

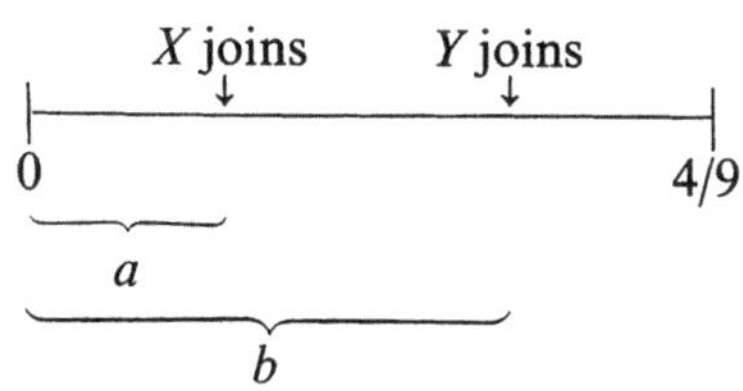

We can represent geometrically the positions at which X and Y join by giving a single point in a square of side 4/9, whose horizontal coordinate is X's position and whose vertical coordinate is Y's:

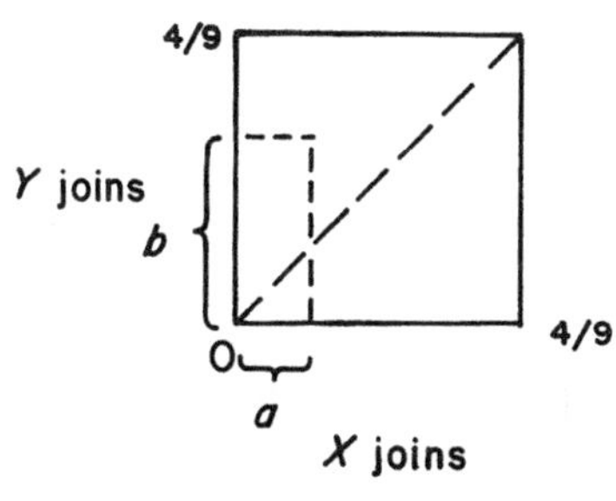

Notice that the point is *above* the diagonal of the square if X joins before Y, and below the diagonal if Y joins before X. Now which points in the square correspond to orderings for which X or Y pivots? With a little careful thought, you can divide the square into regions where X pivots, Y pivots, or voters in the ocean (O) pivot:

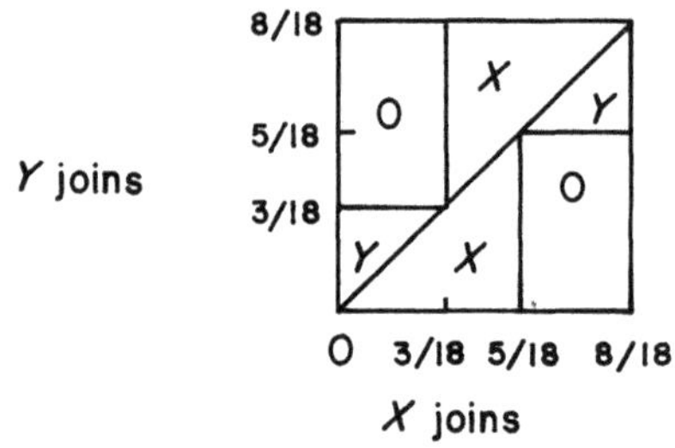

For instance, if X joins before Y (so we are above the diagonal), then X pivots if he joins after $1/2 - 3/9 = 3/18$. On the other hand, if X joins before Y and also before 3/18, then Y pivots if he gets in before 3/18. If he does not, then a voter in the ocean pivots.

Now we can calculate the Shapley–Shubik indices for X or Y by calculating the *area* of the region in which X or Y pivots and dividing by the total area of the square. We get

$$\phi_X = \frac{(5/18)^2}{(4/9)^2} = \frac{25}{64} \approx 0.391$$

$$\phi_Y = \frac{(3/18)^2}{(4/9)^2} = \frac{9}{64} \approx 0.141,$$

with the other 30/64 being shared by the players in the ocean. You should compare these values with the indices for [5; 3, 2, 1, 1, 1, 1], which we calculated in Section 1.2.

If there are three major players in an oceanic game, we represent orderings as points in a cube, and calculate the volumes of the regions where each of the major players pivots. This can be tricky, since it is hard to use a picture as a guide. Beyond three major players and three dimensions, very careful notation of inequalities and the integral calculus, or more sophisticated analysis (Shapley and Shapiro [34, Theorem 1]), are needed. However, we shall see that even oceanic games with two major players can be interesting in political situations.

We have not talked at all about the Banzhaf index for oceanic games. There is a good reason, as you might guess if you look at Exercise 23 in Section 1.2 or Exercise 33 in this section. For many large games, the Banzhaf index just does not give results that seem in reasonable accord with common sense.

For instance, Pradeep Dubey [12] has proved a limit theorem for the Banzhaf index, which says that in a weighted majority game with one major player and a large number of symmetric minor players, the Banzhaf index of the major player approaches 1 as the number of minor players gets large. This explains Exercise 33: in the limit, the major player holds *all* the power.

For two major players, the result is similar. In the limit, the larger of the two major players holds all the power. If the major players are exactly tied, all power resides in the ocean.

In Section 3 we shall talk about ways of comparing ϕ and β, and deciding which to use in what situations. For now, we have one heuristic rule: for games with a few strong players and many weak ones, ϕ may yield more "reasonable" results than β.

Notes and References. In addition to references in the text, Shapley [31] does calculations and drawings for oceanic games with two major players. The complete series of RAND memoranda is available in many large municipal and university libraries.

Exercises

28. Calculate the Shapley–Shubik and Banzhaf indices for the large stockholder with 40% of the shares if the remaining shares are split evenly among
    a) five other stockholders.
    b) seven other stockholders.
    Why is the large stockholder less powerful in (b) than he is in (a)?

29. Show that in an oceanic majority game where there is just one major player X who holds a fraction x of the total vote,

$$\phi_X = \begin{cases} \dfrac{x}{1-x}, & \text{if } x \leq \frac{1}{2}, \\ 1, & \text{if } x \geq \frac{1}{2}. \end{cases}$$

    This relation graphs nicely:

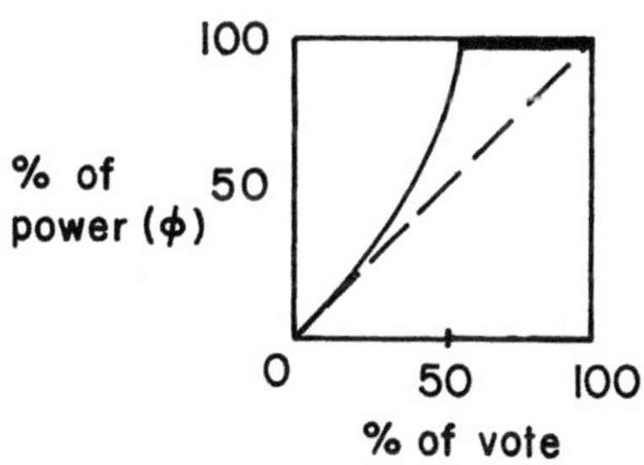

    In particular, the major player's share of the power is always larger than his share of the vote.

30. Calculate the Shapley–Shubik indices of the major players in an oceanic game with two major players in which X holds 25% of the vote and Y holds 15%. You may want to label the following figure.

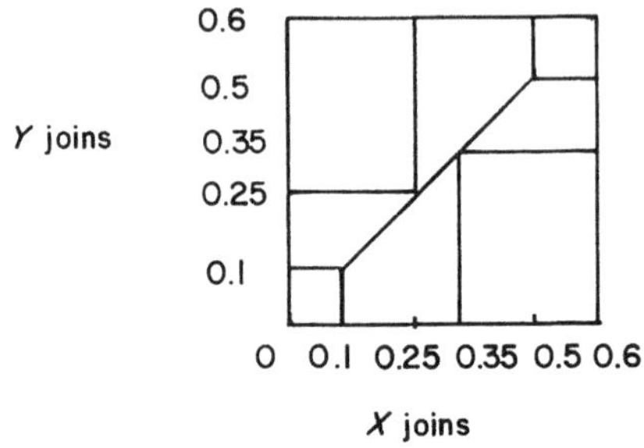

31. For the general oceanic game with two major players, in which X holds a fraction x of the vote and Y holds a fraction y (assume $x < 1/2, y < 1/2$), calculate $\phi_X(x, y)$ and $\phi_Y(x, y)$. As you can see from the text example and Exercise 30, you will get different expressions depending on whether $x + y \geq 1/2$ or $x + y \leq 1/2$.

32. Calculate the Shapley–Shubik indices for the two oceanic games in this section if a 2/3's vote is necessary to win.

33. (If you are good with binomial coefficients.) For the example where X holds 40% of the stock and the remainder is split 60 ways, show that the number of swings for X is given by

$$\sum_{n=11}^{50} \binom{60}{n},$$

whereas the number of swings held by each minor players in $\binom{59}{10} + \binom{59}{50}$. My estimates of these numbers give $\beta_X \approx 0.999995$, with the remaining 0.000005 split 60 ways. Does this seem a reasonable reflection of reality?

2. Using the Power Indices

2.1. The Power of Potential Blocs

In some voting situations, there are "potential blocs"—groups of voters with similar interests and values who might consider joining together and casting their votes in common. One can think of farmers or labor union members as potential blocs in general elections. Political parties are usually only potential blocs in voting in the U.S. Congress; they become actual blocs if party caucuses bind their members to vote together. In the U.S. Electoral College, state delegations are, according to the U.S. Constitution, only potential blocs. In fact, since the beginning of the Republic, state delegations have cast their votes together, as actual blocs, "in an apparent attempt to maximize their voting power" (Brams [6, p. 183]).

Since we now have measures of power, we can analyze the following question: if a potential bloc decides to organize and vote as an actual bloc, does it really gain power? That is, does the bloc really have more power than its individual members originally had? If we are in a majority game where each player has just one vote, the answer is "yes," as you will believe from looking at the graph in Exercise 29 of Section 1.3.

On the other hand, union does not always mean strength in other simple games. For instance, consider the weighted majority game

$$[5; 3, 3, 1, 1, 1].$$

Here $\phi = (9/30, 9/30, 4/30, 4/30, 4/30)$ and $\beta = (2/7, 2/7, 1/7, 1/7, 1/7)$. Now if the three small players unite to form a bloc of three, that bloc will have power 1/3, which is *less* than the total of what the members originally had, measured by either index. Robert Aumann of the Hebrew University in Jerusalem has noted that there is an example of this phenomenon of "in disunity is strength" in the Israeli Knesset. There are three small orthodox religious parties (National Religious, Agudat Israel, and Agudat Israel Workers) with extremely similar political views—a very likely potential bloc. However, these parties have not united to form an actual bloc, and have enjoyed the resulting flexibility to join independently or refrain from joining governing coalitions. Their situation is much like the 1s in our example.

Even in the original case of majority rule with each voter having one vote, the situation may be interesting. As I said above, a potential bloc does gain power by organizing as an actual bloc in that situation, but only as long as no other potential blocs organize. If other potential blocs do organize and become actual blocs, the first bloc may end up with less power than it started with. Perhaps this is best illustrated by an example.

I live and teach in Rock County in Southern Wisconsin. Rock County is dominated by the two cities of Janesville (population 46,000) and Beloit (population 36,000). There is often considerable rivalry between the two cities. The remainder of the county consists of small towns and rural areas. The county is governed by a Board of County Supervisors consisting of 40 members, elected from districts roughly equal in population. Eleven supervisors are from the city of Beloit, 14 are from Janesville, 15 from town and rural areas. Historically, supervisors from the city districts have been quite independent in philosophy and voting behavior. Bloc voting by the supervisors from Beloit or from Janesville has not developed. I do not know about the situation in Janesville, but in Beloit there has been considerable unhappiness among city officials over this lack of cohesiveness. Surely Beloit would wield more influence if its delegation would agree to vote as a bloc.

We can analyze this situation by using the Shapley–Shubik power index to calculate the total power of Beloit's eleven supervisors if they vote independently, and if they organize as a bloc. In the first case, each supervisor will have 1/40 of the total power, and Beloit's eleven together will have 11/40 or $27\frac{1}{2}\%$. In the second case, there are effectively 30 voters: 29 independent supervisors, and the Beloit bloc casting 11 votes. Since 21 votes are needed to pass a measure, Beloit will pivot if it joins a coalition 11th through

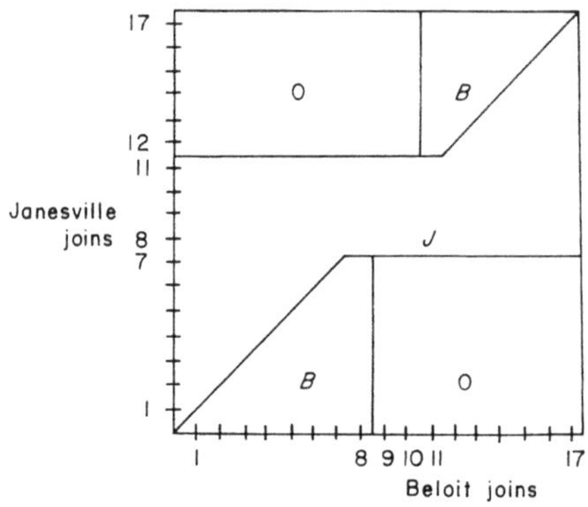

Figure 11.1

21st, i.e., 11/30 of the time. Beloit will have 11/30 or $36\frac{1}{2}\%$ of the power, a considerable increase. Janesville's supervisors, who had $14/40 = 35\%$ of the power before Beloit organized, would have $(14/29)(19/30) = 30\frac{1}{2}\%$ of the power after Beloit organizes.

The problem with this scenario is, of course, that if Beloit's supervisors organize as a bloc, there will be considerable pressure for Janesville's supervisors to organize also. If that happens, we shall have a game of 17 voters: 15 casting a single vote, Beloit casting 11, and Janesville casting 14. We can compute the Shapley–Shubik power indices for this game by counting the lattice points in the regions labeled B, J, and O in Fig. 11.1. We find that Janesville pivots 100/272 of the time, for 37% of the power, while Beloit pivots 49/272 of the time for 18% of the power. In other words, if Janesville also organizes, Beloit is considerably worse off than it was at the beginning.

We can picture these results in the following array, which shows the two strategies available to "Beloit" and "Janesville," together with the percentages of power each would have under the different alternatives:

		Janesville			
		J does not organize		$\bar{J}$ organizes	
Beloit	B does not organize	$27\frac{1}{2}$	35	20	52
	$\bar{B}$ organizes	$36\frac{1}{2}$	$30\frac{1}{2}$	18	37

Notice that Janesville will prefer to organize regardless of what Beloit does, and that once Janesville organizes, Beloit is actually better off *not* organizing. The "natural outcome" seems to be at $B\bar{J}$, with Beloit at a serious disadvantage. As long as the status quo BJ is maintained, Beloit should be very happy

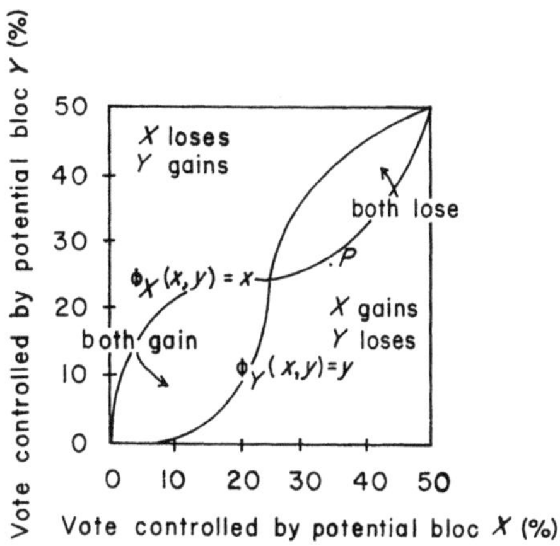

Figure 11.2

not to rock the boat! Perhaps Beloit's supervisors are being canny in their uncooperative behavior, instead of just stubbornly independent. In any case, their independence may be serving Beloit well.

For large games with two potential blocs, we can analyze the power question by using the theory of oceanic games. In Exercise 31 of Section 1.3, you were asked to calculate that if player X controls a fraction x of the vote and player Y controls a fraction y, then

$$\phi_X(x, y) = \begin{cases} \dfrac{(\frac{1}{2} - y)^2}{(1 - x - y)^2}, & \text{if } x + y \geq \dfrac{1}{2} \\[2ex] \dfrac{x(1 - x - 2y)}{(1 - x - y)^2}, & \text{if } x + y \leq \dfrac{1}{2} \end{cases}$$

and of course $\phi_Y(x, y)$ is symmetric to this. Now if two potential blocs X and Y should organize as actual blocs, the power of X would be this $\phi_X(x, y)$. If the members of X and Y vote independently, the members of X will have, by symmetry, power equal to their fraction of the vote, namely x. Thus, the members of X will gain if both X and Y organize precisely when $\phi_X(x, y) > x$ Shapley [31] plots the curves $\phi_X(x, y) = x$ and $\phi_Y(x, y) = y$ to get a picture of what will happen if both X and Y organize (see Fig. 11.2). Two large and evenly matched potential blocs should definitely avoid organizing as actual blocs. The Beloit–Janesville example, or rather its oceanic approximation (Exercise 38), lies at point P Fig. 11.2, with Janesville as X and Beloit as Y.

Notes and References. There is an excellent discussion of the possible loss of power through bloc voting in Section 5.6 of Brams [5]. For data on the Israeli Knesset, see Owen [27] or Lucas, Chapter 9, this volume. The Beloit–

Janesville example appears in Straffin [36]. In thinking about this kind of situation, you should ask in what sense it is meaningful to compare X's power as a bloc with the *sum* of its members' power if they vote independently. In the Shapley–Shubik model, we are comparing the chance that the organized bloc X will pivot against the chance that one of its unorganized members will pivot. But does it mean the same thing for Beloit if the Beloit bloc pivots as it does if some independent Beloit legislator pivots? The original point about the common values of members of potential blocs is important here. In Section 3.3, we shall talk about a way of handling common values.

EXERCISES

34. Check the calculations for ϕ and β in [5; 3, 3, 1, 1, 1].
35. In [5; 4, 3, 1, 1], should the two 1-vote players unite to form a bloc of 2? Use ϕ and β to decide.
36. Check the figures in box $B\bar{J}$ of the example.
37. Calculate the figures that would have appeared in the Beloit–Janesville array if we had used the Banzhaf index instead of the Shapley–Shubik index. Would the subsequent analysis have been different? This is fairly hard.
38. Use Exercise 29 in Section 1.3 and the expressions for $\phi_X(x, y)$ and $\phi_Y(x, y)$ given in this section to calculate the figures for the Beloit–Janesville array if we had approximated the situation by an oceanic game with Beloit (0.275) and Janesville (0.35) as the major players. The idea is to see how good the approximation would have been.
39. The British House of Commons has 635 seats. In the spring of 1974, Labor held 301, Conservatives 296. The remainder were divided among six minor parties. British parties enforce a strict unit rule. Should they? Use the oceanic approximation.

2.2. Quarreling Paradoxes

In our measures of power, we have been assuming that any two members are willing to enter into coalitions with each other. In fact, of course, we have been assuming that all coalitions, or all orders of joining coalitions, are equally likely. This is, of course, an abstraction. There are ways to build ideological differences, for example, into these indices, the best known of which is due to Guillermo Owen [24].

I would like to consider a simpler question than ideological differences: what happens if two players *quarrel*, and refuse to enter into a coalition together? In particular, what effect does quarreling have on the power of the quarrelers, and on the power of innocent bystanders? The first work along these lines was done by Kilgour [16], who used the Shapley–Shubik index. In Kilgour's model, something quite startling happened: in some situations, two players in a simple game could actually *increase* their power by quarreling.

Steven Brams [5, p. 181] showed that a model of quarreling using the Banzhaf index leads to the same conclusion. We normally think that we maximize our power by keeping as many options open as possible, and that restricting our freedom to act lessens our influence. Quarreling, of course, restricts our freedom to act, and hence what Brams calls the "paradox of quarreling members" does seem paradoxical.

Brams' example is the following: Consider the weighted voting game

$$\underset{\textstyle A\ B\ C}{[5; 3, 2, 2]}$$

For this game, $\phi = (2/3, 1/6, 1/6)$ and $\beta = (3/5, 1/5, 1/5)$, as seen by writing out the orderings with the pivots underlined:

$$\begin{array}{ccc} A\underline{B}C & B\underline{A}C & C\underline{A}B \\ A\underline{C}B & {}^*BC\underline{A} & {}^*CB\underline{A} \end{array}$$

and the winning coalitions with the critical defectors underlined:

$$\underline{AB} \quad \underline{AC} \quad {}^*\underline{A}BC.$$

Now suppose members B and C quarrel. What is the effect on the Shapley–Shubik index? In considering the orders in which the players might join a coalition in support of a proposal, we must now rule out those orderings in which B and C join together to help put the coalition over the top, i.e. those orderings in which both B and C join at or before the pivot. There are two orderings in which this happens, marked by an *. In the four other orderings, the coalition becomes winning with the help of only one of B or C. Since by our original Shapley–Shubik assumption these four are equally likely, we get a *Shapley–Shubik index with quarreling* of

$$\phi_{BC}^{Q} = \left(\frac{1}{2}, \frac{1}{4}, \frac{1}{4}\right).$$

The Banzhaf model for quarreling is even simpler. We merely eliminate from consideration those winning coalitions containing both B and C (just ABC above) and compute proportions of critical defections in the remaining winning coalitions. We get

$$\beta_{BC}^{Q} = \left(\frac{1}{2}, \frac{1}{4}, \frac{1}{4}\right)$$

with the same qualitative effect of an increase in B and C's share of the power at the expense of A. We have:

(1) If two members quarrel, they may both gain power (as measured by ϕ or β).

If you let A and B quarrel in the above game, you can see that

(2) If two members quarrel, they may both lose power.

This, of course, seems much more natural than (1). However, if we use our models of quarreling to look at other examples, we find other strange things happening:

(3) If two members quarrel, one may gain power while the other loses power. (*A* quarrel might hurt you while helping your opponent, or visa versa ....)
Example: A and D quarrel in $[5; \underset{A}{3}, \underset{B}{2}, \underset{C}{2}, \underset{D}{1}]$

$$\phi = \beta = \left(\frac{5}{12}, \frac{1}{4}, \frac{1}{4}, \frac{1}{12}\right)$$

$$\phi_{AD}^{Q} = \beta_{AD}^{Q} = \left(\frac{3}{8}, \frac{1}{4}, \frac{1}{4}, \frac{1}{8}\right)$$

(4) A quarrel may not affect the power of the quarrelers at all, but change the power of innocent bystanders.
Example: B and C quarrel in the game of the last example.

$$\phi_{BC}^{Q} = \beta_{BC}^{Q} = \left(\frac{1}{2}, \frac{1}{4}, \frac{1}{4}, 0\right)$$

Poor D, whose only chance to become part of a minimal winning coalition was with BC, has become a dummy.

(5) Quarreling with a dummy can hurt you. (It may be worthwhile staying on friendly terms even with those who have no power.)
Example: A quarrels with D in $[4; 2, 2, 2, 1]$.

$$\phi = \beta = \left(\frac{1}{3}, \frac{1}{3}, \frac{1}{3}, 0\right)$$

$$\phi_{AD}^{Q} = \beta_{AD}^{Q} = \left(\frac{1}{4}, \frac{3}{8}, \frac{3}{8}, 0\right)$$

Finally, in the Shapley–Shubik model (although not in the Banzhaf model) we can study the effect of *one-way* or *nonreciprocated* quarrels.

Suppose that, in the weighted voting game $[7; \underset{A}{4}, \underset{B}{3}, \underset{C}{2}, \underset{D}{1}]$ player B hates player C and refuses to join any coalition in support of a proposal that C has already joined. Player C has no such hostile feelings about B. What is the effect upon the power of B and C? Orderings and pivots are

$A\underline{B}CD$	$B\underline{A}CD$	$^{*}CA\underline{B}D$	$DA\underline{B}C$
$A\underline{B}DC$	$B\underline{A}DC$	$CA\underline{D}B$	$DA\underline{C}B$
$^{*}AC\underline{B}D$	$^{+}BC\underline{A}D$	$^{*}CB\underline{A}D$	$DB\underline{A}C$
$AC\underline{D}B$	$^{+}BCD\underline{A}$	$^{*}CBD\underline{A}$	$^{+}DBC\underline{A}$
$AD\underline{B}C$	$BD\underline{A}C$	$CD\underline{A}B$	$DC\underline{A}B$
$AD\underline{C}B$	$^{+}BDC\underline{A}$	$^{*}CDB\underline{A}$	$^{*}DCB\underline{A}$

With no quarreling, we have

$$\phi = \left(\frac{14}{24}, \frac{6}{24}, \frac{2}{24}, \frac{2}{24}\right) \approx (0.58, 0.25, 0.08, 0.08).$$

B's hostility to C rules out orderings marked by *, giving

$$\phi^{Q}_{B \to C} = \left(\frac{10}{18}, \frac{4}{18}, \frac{2}{18}, \frac{2}{18}\right) \approx (0.56, 0.22, 0.11, 0.11).$$

B has hurt himself and helped his victim.

If we reversed the situation and had C hating B, the orderings marked by^{+} would be ruled out, giving

$$\phi^{Q}_{C \to B}\left(\frac{10}{20}, \frac{6}{20}, \frac{2}{20}, \frac{2}{20}\right) = (0.50, 0.30, 0.10, 0.10)$$

C would help B, and also help herself!

The general result on one-way quarreling is

(6) A one-way quarreler can only help his victim, but he may either help or hurt himself.

Looking at the above examples and others you may wish to (Exercise 43), can you see why the victim cannot be hurt?

I find these kinds of results fascinating and suggestive, but I would warn you to look at them critically. If we conclude from our models of quarreling, using the Shapley–Shubik and Banzhaf power indices, that two players in a simple game can increase their share of the power by quarreling, this could mean one of three things:

(i) The conclusion is true, a subtlety of political situations that precise analysis has thrown light upon.
(ii) The conclusion is a peculiarity of the power indices, showing that they have strange properties that should make us wary of where and how we use them.
(iii) The conclusion is a peculiarity not of the indices but of the model of quarreling we made using the indices. The model does not adequately reflect properties of real world quarrels.

My feeling is that the answer is probably (i) or (iii), but I have not been able to decide which. When you think about this, you might look carefully at the original example of [5; 3, 2, 2], say in the Shapley–Shubik model. Before the quarrel, A had the rosy prospect of one third of the time, B and C getting together and coming to her to plead for her support. After the quarrel, she knows that this will never happen. Does this change really mean that A has a smaller share of the power, and B and C have larger shares?

Notes and References. Kilgour's article [16] is in the general language of mathematical game theory, and hard to read. Brams' [6] Section 7.10 on quarreling is brief and readable. Owen's article [24] on incorporating ideological differences into the Shapley–Shubik index requires a little n-dimensional geometry, and one should look at the Israeli Knesset example at the end of the article to see clearly what is involved. In the late 1950s, Thomas Schelling [30] and Daniel Ellsberg [15] gave many lovely examples to show that, in negotiation situations, one may benefit by restricting one's freedom of action. The quarreling paradoxes might be looked at in that tradition.

Exercises

40. Check the calculations for at least two of the examples on p. 280.

41. Analyze the effect of quarrels in
    a) $[4; \underset{A}{3}, \underset{B}{1}, \underset{C}{1}, \underset{D}{1}]$.
    b) The game Γ of Section 1.

42. ϕ and β need not agree about the effect of quarreling. Show this by considering a BC quarrel in $[5; \underset{A}{3}, \underset{B}{2}, \underset{C}{1}, \underset{D}{1}]$.

43. In $[7; \underset{A}{4}, \underset{B}{3}, \underset{C}{2}, \underset{D}{1}]$, consider the effect of one-way quarrels involving A and C, or A and B. For each case you consider, note carefully who is helped and who is hurt.

44. Prove the general result (6) about one-way quarrels.

45. In light of the examples of this section, and other examples you have looked at, what would you think of the following general statement: "In general, quarreling hurts the strong, but may help the weak." Could you make it more precise? I think there might be some interesting results possible here.

46. In Chapter 7 of Brams [6], there is a discussion of another paradox involving power. Brams calls it the "paradox of new members." Calculate the Banzhaf indices for the following weighted majority games:
    a) $[7; 6, 3, 2, 2]$.
    b) $[8; 6, 3, 2, 2, 1]$.
    c) $[8; 6, 3, 2, 2, 1, 1]$.
    d) $[8; 6, 3, 2, 2, 2]$.
    Notice that the decision rule remains majority-rule, so the quota goes up as new members are added. The paradoxical thing is that adding new members *increases* the power of the 6-vote player here. His power is higher in all of (b), (c), and (d) than it is in (a). Brams gives other examples of this paradox.

2.3. The Bandwagon Effect

Consider a political situation in which two opposing blocs vie for the support of uncommitted voters in an attempt to achieve winning size. The examples we shall look at later in this section concern U.S. Presidential nominating conventions, with candidates vying for the support of uncommitted delegates, but of course there are many similar situations in politics. As the two blocs grow, at some point a "bandwagon effect" often becomes noticeable. Uncommitted voters suddenly find it advantageous to begin committing themselves to the larger bloc, quickly enlarging it to winning size.

Can we use measurements of power to analyze this kind of situation? Yes, if we take our clue from the phrase "suddenly find it advantageous": when would commitment suddenly become advantageous? I am going to propose a model that will try to answer that question, but perhaps we should first note that one kind of interpretation says that calculations of advantage are *not* what happens as a bandwagon begins to roll. Here is Ralph Martin describing a bandwagon at a Presidential nominating convention:

> The bandwagon is a fever that takes statistics out of the definition of politics. It's a thing of chemistry that boils blood, jumps feet, waves hands, shouts voices, bangs fists, and heightens hangovers. It parts from reason in the same way that love does or hate does. It is a mass orgy of feeling that sweeps with the fervor of a religious revival. It is the Fourth of July on Christmas morning. (Martin [20], p. 444].)

On the other hand, here is Nelson Polsby on the same situation:

> Delegates to the national conventions are expected to behave in a way that will maximize their political power; that is, they are politicians. (Polsby [26, p. 609].)

If Polsby is correct, perhaps rational decision making plays an important part at least in getting a bandwagon going, before the "mass orgy of feeling" begins.

Now for the model. The original idea can be found in Brams and Riker [7]. There are two opposing blocs, call them X and Y, and a collection of uncommitted voters U. Using the Shapley–Shubik index, we could calculate the power of X, the power of Y, and the power of a single voter in U. However, if X and Y are indeed opposing, it seems reasonable that in our calculations we should rule out orderings in which they join together to win (i.e., we should consider them as quarreling, in the sense of Section 2.2). In fact, Brams and Riker suggest that we should consider only orderings in which *exactly one* of X or Y is present when the coalition first becomes winning. In other words, they also rule out the possibility of uncommitted voters uniting to win without either X or Y.

For a simple example, consider $[5; \underset{X}{3}, \underset{Y}{2}, \underbrace{1, 1, 1, 1}_{U}]$. We wrote out the orderings and pivots for this game in Section 1.2. Of the 30 orderings, 9 are ruled out by the restriction that exactly one of the "3" or "2" should appear at or before the pivot:

$$
\begin{array}{cccc}
3\underline{2}1111 & 2\underline{3}1111 & 21\underline{3}111 & 211\underline{3}11 \\
31\underline{2}111 & 13\underline{2}111 & 12\underline{3}111 & 121\underline{3}11 \\
 & & & 112\underline{3}11
\end{array}
$$

If we use the remaining 21 orderings to calculate a modified Shapley–Shubik index, we get

$$\left(\frac{6}{21}, \frac{3}{21}, \frac{3}{21}, \frac{3}{21}, \frac{3}{21}, \frac{3}{21}\right) \approx (0.286, 0.143, 0.143, 0.143, 0.143, 0.143).$$

If you compare these figures with those on p. 265, you will see that X and Y have been hurt by their "quarrel."

Now we want to know if we should expect a bandwagon to start, presumably for X, in this situation. To that end, we should look at one of the uncommitted voters trying to decide if he should commit his support to X, or remain uncommitted. If he joins X, he will increase X's power by some amount, and we might think of this amount of increase as measuring the amount of reward, or concessions, which our voter could extract from X as the price for his support. The idea is that an uncommitted voter should commit to X if the increment of power he will add to X is larger than the power he would have if he remains uncommitted. Since the situation is the same for all uncommitted voters, the bandwagon effect should occur precisely when an uncommitted voter can add more power to X by joining X, than he has while uncommitted.

In our example, if an uncommitted voter commits to X, the new game will be

$$\begin{bmatrix} 5; 4, 2, 1, 1, 1 \\ \quad X\ Y\ \ \ U \end{bmatrix}.$$

You should try writing down the 20 possible orderings for this game, underlining the pivots, crossing out the 7 "illegal" orderings, and calculating the modified Shapley–Shubik index to be

$$\left(\frac{6}{13}, \frac{1}{13}, \frac{2}{13}, \frac{2}{13}, \frac{2}{13}\right) \approx (0.462, 0.077, 0.154, 0.154, 0.154).$$

Our uncommitted voter would raise the power of X from 0.286 to 0.462, an increment of 0.176, which is more than the 0.143 he would have by remaining uncommitted. He should join X, and we are in the region of the bandwagon effect. (Exercise 48 asks you to check that an uncommitted voter would be ill-advised to join Y. He would contribute an increment of only 0.071, considerably less than even the 0.143 he would have by remaining uncommitted.)

Most games for which we want to study the bandwagon effect are large games, and we can use the idea of an oceanic game to approximate these games. This explains why I concentrated on the Shapley–Shubik index above. You can use the Banzhaf index to study bandwagons for small games (see Exercise 49), but for large games it is useless for this purpose, because of Dubey's result [12, 14].

Let x be the fraction of votes controlled by bloc X, y the fraction controlled by bloc Y, and $u = 1 - x - y$ the fraction held by an ocean of uncommitted voters. We shall assume majority rule and that x and y are both $< \frac{1}{2}$, or one bloc would already have won. To calculate modified Shapley–Shubik power

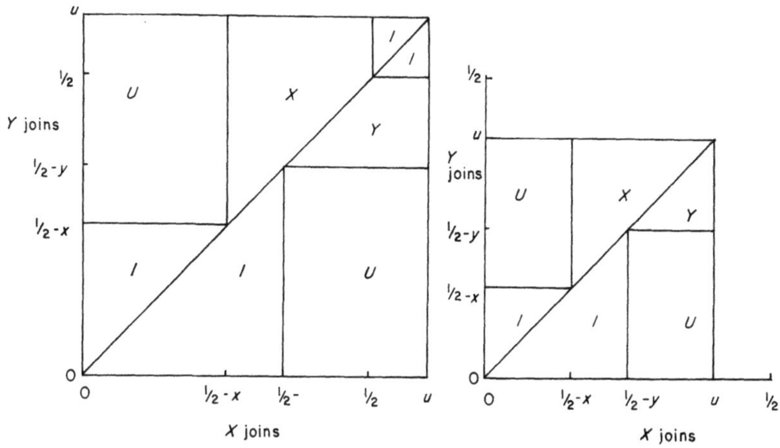

Figure 11.3. (a) $x + y \leq \frac{1}{2}$ $u \geq \frac{1}{2}$. (b) $x + y \geq 1/2(u \leq 1/2)$. X means X pivots; Y means Y pivots; U means an uncommitted voter pivots; I means an illegal ordering.

indices for X and Y, we use the same kind of pictures as in Section 1.3 (you may have drawn them for Exercise 31 in that section). (See Fig. 11.3.) Note that orderings represented by points in the lower left-hand corners and the upper right-hand corner of Fig. 11.3(a) are ruled out by our condition that exactly one of X or Y should appear at or before the pivot. You can try calculating, if you wish, to get

$$\phi_X(x, y) = \begin{cases} \dfrac{x(1 - x - 2y)}{1 - x - y - x^2 - y^2}, & \text{if } x + y \leq \frac{1}{2} \\[2ex] \dfrac{(\frac{1}{2} - y)^2}{(1 - x - y)^2 + 2(\frac{1}{2} - x)(\frac{1}{2} - y)}, & \text{if } x + y \geq \frac{1}{2}. \end{cases}$$

The formulas for ϕ_Y are symmetric to this. One can also calculate the total power of the uncommitted voters:

$$\phi_U(x, y) = \begin{cases} \dfrac{(1 - 2x)(1 - 2y)}{1 - x - y - x^2 - y^2}, & \text{if } x + y \leq \frac{1}{2}, \\[2ex] \dfrac{(1 - 2x)(1 - 2y)}{(1 - x - y)^2 + 2(\frac{1}{2} - x)(\frac{1}{2} - y)}, & \text{if } x + y \geq \frac{1}{2}. \end{cases}$$

Now consider a small bloc of uncommitted voters, comprising a fraction Δx of the total vote, considering whether to join X. If they do, the power increment they will contribute is $\phi_X(x + \Delta x, y) - \phi_X(x, y)$. If they remain uncommitted, their total power will be $(\Delta x/u)\phi_U(x, y)$. Hence they should join X if

$$\phi_X(x + \Delta x, y) - \phi_X(x, y) > \frac{\Delta x}{u}\phi_U(x, y),$$

i.e., if

$$\frac{\phi_X(x + \Delta x, y) - \phi_X(x, y)}{\Delta x} > \frac{\phi_U(x, y)}{u}.$$

In the limit as $\Delta x \to 0$, the left-hand side of this inequality becomes a quantity familiar in calculus, the partial derivative of ϕ_X with respect to x. Hence we conclude that the bandwagon effect occurs for bloc X when

$$\frac{\partial \phi_X}{\partial x} > \frac{\phi_U}{u}.$$

If you know how to take partial derivatives, you can actually calculate the equations for the curve where $\partial\phi_X/\partial x = \phi_U/u$ (Exercise 53). If you do not know how, the results are as follows. When $x + y \geq \frac{1}{2}$, the curve where $\partial\phi_X/\partial x = \phi_U/u$ is a straight line $(\frac{1}{2} - y) = a(\frac{1}{2} - x)$, where $a \approx 1.78$. When $x + y \leq \frac{1}{2}$, the less tractable denominator of ϕ_X and ϕ_U produces a more complicated curve. Both curves together make up what we might call the "bandwagon curve" for X, which divides the region in which uncommitted voters should commit to X from the region in which uncommitted voters

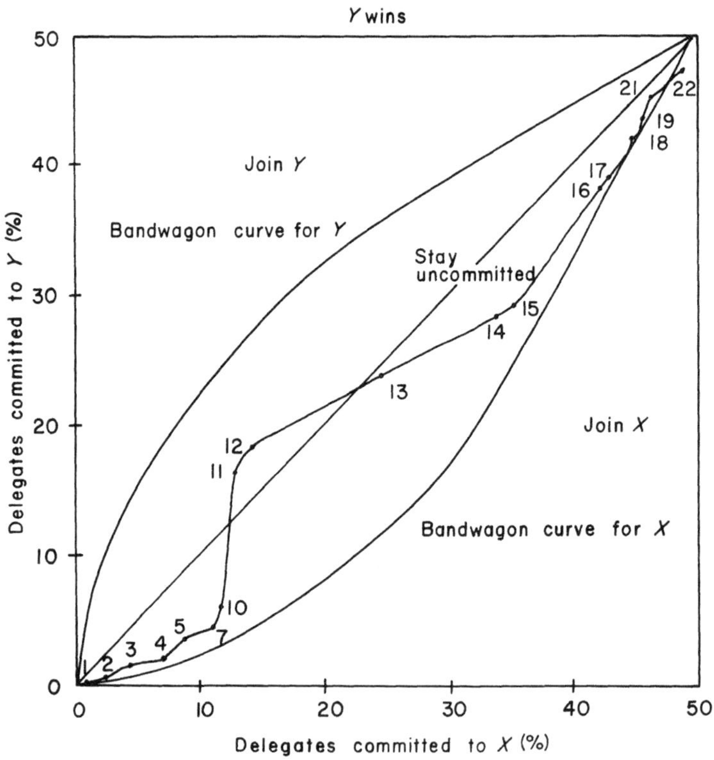

Figure 11.4

should stay uncommitted. The bandwagon curves for both X and Y, and the appropriate advice for uncommitted voters, are shown in Fig. 11.4.

If $x + y \geq \frac{1}{2}$, it is easy to tell when you are in the bandwagon region for X: you are there when $(\frac{1}{2} - y)/(\frac{1}{2} - x) > 1.78$, i.e., when Y must gain more than 1.78 times as many votes as X must gain to win. When $x + y < \frac{1}{2}$, one has to do a harder calculation. A rough guideline is the following tabulation.

Total voters committed to both blocs (%)	Split necessary to start a bandwagon for the stronger bloc
10	8 to 2
20	15 to 5
30	21 to 9
40	27 to 13
50	32 to 18

The zigzag line in Fig. 11.4 is a plot of the percentages of total delegates committed to candidates X (Ford) and Y (Reagan) in the 1976 contest for the Republican Presidential nomination, as the percentages changed between March and July 1976. The small numerals represent time in weeks from the beginning of the Presidential primaries in New Hampshire. The data are from the *Congressional Quarterly* and the *New York Times*. Notice the path stays in the neutral region until the end. It does approach the bandwagon curves several times. The closest early approach for Ford was in week No. 4 after the Illinois primary. The closest approach for Reagan was in weeks Nos. 11 and 12 after the Texas and Indiana primaries. At both these points, there was considerable speculation in the media about the bandwagon effect. Our analysis would suggest that such speculation was premature, as of course was the case.

The path entered the bandwagon region for Ford in week No. 22—more precisely, on July 17 (Exercise 52) when the Connecticut delegation gave Ford 35 votes. On July 19, the *Washington Post* headlined "Privately, Some Aides See Reagan at End of Trail," and the story was picked up across the country. The same day, the *Los Angeles Times* reported a change in tactics by Ford delegate hunters: "The message Ford people are now sending to uncommitted delegates is simple and direct: you had better get aboard—the train is about to leave without you."

When the figures are bandwagon-starting, there are two obvious strategies available to the minority candidate. The first is to muddy the figures. On July 20, Reagan's campaign manager announced 1140 delegates committed to Reagan (1130 needed for nomination) and stoutly maintained that figure over the next few weeks in spite of considerable incredulity from objective observers. The second strategy is to do something to draw attention away from the figures altogether. On July 26, Reagan announced his selection of

Senator Richard Schweiker as his candidate for Vice-President. After the initial furor died down, the *New York Times* analyzed the situation:

> Ronald Reagan's big gamble ... has achieved what Mr. Reagan probably hoped it would: he has probably eliminated the possibility that he will lose the Presidential nomination to Gerald Ford before the Republican convention begins. (*N.Y. Times*, August 8, 1976.)

Regardless of the subsequent outcome, the bandwagon curve analysis gives a context in which to understand these remarkable events.

It is also possible to use this kind of bandwagon model to calculate when the bandwagon effect should occur if there are more than two major blocs. The principal difference is that one must allow for the possibility that some of the blocs may form alliances and pool their support, while other blocs may be unable or unwilling to form alliances. In the case of two blocs X and Y, we argued that X and Y would not form an alliance. If there are three or more blocs, we must decide which alliances are possible and which are not.

As an example of how the method might work for three blocs, consider the interesting case of the 1956 Democratic Vice-Presidential nomination. After his nomination for the Presidency, Adlai Stevenson unexpectedly threw the nomination for Vice-President open to the convention. A spirited race arose among Estes Kefauver, whom Stevenson had just defeated for the Presidential nomination, a young Senator from Massachusetts named Jack Kennedy, Albert Gore of Tennessee, and Hubert Humphrey of Minnesota. Humphrey faded quickly. The second ballot tally was

Jack Kennedy	618	45%
Estes Kefauver	$551\frac{1}{2}$	40%
Gore	$110\frac{1}{2}$	8%
Others	92	7%
Total	1372	(687 needed to nominate)

First of all, notice that if Gore's votes were counted as individual uncommitted votes, Kennedy would be in the bandwagon region:

$$\frac{50 - 40}{50 - 45} = 2 > 1.78.$$

In fact, Kefauver went on to win the nomination. The existence of the Gore bloc blunted the bandwagon. Let us see how.

As a model, let us consider the weighted voting game

$$[50;\ \underset{J}{45},\ \underset{E}{40},\ \underset{G}{8},\ \underbrace{1, 1, 1, 1, 1, 1, 1}_{\text{uncommitted}}].$$

(Alternatively, one might use an oceanic model, but with three major players we know that would involve hard work.) We need alliance assumptions. Clearly, JE should be ruled out. Albert Gore was friendly with Kennedy, but he was the junior Senator from Tennessee, where Kefauver was the senior

Senator. The Tennessee delegation was the heart of Gore's support, and it would not follow him to Kennedy. In fact, Gore was under strong constant pressure to withdraw in favor of Kefauver. For the model, we shall rule out JG and allow EG.

Under these alliance conditions, 408 of the $10 \cdot 9 \cdot 8 = 720$ possible orderings are ruled out. For example, 41 1 1 $\underline{45}$ 1 1 7 1 1 1 and 1 7 41 $\underline{45}$ 1 1 1 1 1 1 would both be ruled out. Of the 312 remaining orderings, you can check that J has 20 pivots, E and G both have 98, and uncommitted delegates have 96, giving modified Shapley–Shubik indices of

$$(0.064, 0.314, 0.314, 0.043, 0.043, 0.043, 0.043, 0.043, 0.043, 0.043).$$

Notice how strongly Kennedy is disadvantaged by not being able to form an alliance with Gore. Now consider these possible changes:

(1) G joins E, giving $[50; 45, 48, 1, 1, 1, 1, 1, 1, 1]$.
New power indices turn out to be

$$(0.111, 0.389, 0.071, 0.071, 0.071, 0.071, 0.071, 0.071, 0.071).$$

G can contribute only 0.075 to E, much less than he has by not joining E. Gore was *very* reluctant to endorse Kefauver.

(2) An uncommitted delegate joins J, giving $[50; 46, 40, 8, 1, 1, 1, 1, 1, 1]$, with power indices

$$(0.088, 0.285, 0.285, 0.057, 0.057, 0.057, 0.057, 0.057, 0.057).$$

She has contributed only 0.024 to J, less than she had while uncommitted.

(3) An uncommitted delegate joins E, giving

$$[50; 45, 41, 8, 1, 1, 1, 1, 1, 1]$$

with power indices

$$(0.039, 0.377, 0.377, 0.034, 0.034, 0.034, 0.034, 0.034, 0.034).$$

She has contributed 0.063 to E, *more* than the 0.043 she had while uncommitted.

We would predict a bandwagon effect for Kefauver. If you would like to compare this prediction to what actually happened, see, e.g., Martin [20].

Notes and References. Brams and Riker [7] present three different bandwagon models and analyze how bandwagons might form in a 10-member voting body. One model is the Shapley–Shubik index model we have been talking about, and we have seen that it generalizes nicely to large voting bodies. They also use a Banzhaf index model (Exercise 49), which we know does not work well for large games. The third kind of model is based on notions of an uncommitted member contributing to X an increase in X's probability of winning, and calculations of that uncommitted member's "expected share of the spoils."

The bandwagon curve presented here also appears in Straffin [38]. Ralph Martin's [20] account of the 1956 Democratic Vice-Presidential nomination is wonderful. Numerical data for the nominating conventions of both parties can be found in Bain and Parris [3]. In 1980, I regret to say, neither George Bush nor Ted Kennedy allowed the bandwagon curve to guide their behavior.

Exercises

47. Check the calculation of modified Shapley–Shubik indices for [5; 4, 2, 1, 1, 1] on p. 284.

48. Check, as mentioned on p. 283, that in $[5; \underset{X}{3}, \underset{Y}{2}, 1, 1, 1, 1]$ an uncommitted delegate would be ill-advised to join Y.

49. Analyze the possibility of a bandwagon effect in $[5; \underset{X}{3}, \underset{Y}{2}, 1, 1, 1, 1]$ using the Banzhaf index instead of the Shapley–Shubik index. Recall that X and Y should not be allowed to appear together in a winning coalition.

50. Using the Shapley–Shubik index model, should there be a bandwagon effect in $[6; \underset{X}{4}, \underset{Y}{3}, 1, 1, 1, 1]$?

51. The oceanic approximation to [5; 3, 2, 1, 1, 1, 1] would have X with 33% of the vote, Y with 22%. Plot this point in Fig. 11.4 to see if the oceanic approximation would show a bandwagon effect for X.

52. Use the $(1/2 - y)/(1/2 - x) > 1.78$ criterion to decide if the leading candidate was in the bandwagon region in the following examples:
    a) *N.Y. Times* count, July 17, 1976:
       Ford 1067
       Reagan 1043
       (Total number of delegates: 2259)
    b) *N.Y. Times* count, July 19, 1976:
       Ford 1102
       Reagan 1063
    c) *Associated Press* count, July 17:
       Ford 1031
       Reagan 1000
    d) *Associated Press* count, July 19:
       Ford 1066
       Reagan 1020
    e) *Associated Press* count, July 20:
       Ford 1081
       Reagan 1023
    f) 1940 Republican Presidential nomination, 5th ballot:
       Willkie 429
       Taft 377
       (Total: 1000)
       (Willkie won on the next ballot.)

g) 1920 Republican Presidential nomination, 9th ballot:
   Harding $374\frac{1}{2}$
   Wood 249
   (Total: 984)
   (Harding won on the next ballot.)

53. If you like the bandwagon curve, you might like to check some of its derivation:
   a) Check the derivation of the expressions for ϕ_X and ϕ_U from Fig. 11.3 (Remember that $u = 1 - x - y$.)
   b) The formulas given for ϕ_X and ϕ_U, at least in the region $x + y \geq 1/2$, can be made much simpler by substituting $v = 1/2 - x$, and $w = 1/2 - y$. (Note that then $u = v + w$.) Show that we then get

$$\phi_X(v, w) = \frac{w^2}{v^2 + 4vw + w^2}, \qquad (x + y \geq 1/2)$$
$$\phi_U(v, w) = \frac{4vw}{v^2 + 4vw + w^2}.$$

   c) If you can compute partial derivatives, check that

$$\frac{\partial \phi_X}{\partial x} = -\frac{\partial \phi_X}{\partial v} = \frac{w^2(2v + 4w)}{(v^2 + 4vw + w^2)^2},$$

   and hence that the condition $\partial \phi_X/\partial x = \phi_U/u$ becomes

$$\frac{w(2v + 4w)}{v^2 + 4vw + w^2} = \frac{4v}{v + w},$$

   which reduces to $2w^3 + w^2v - 7wv^2 - 2v^3 = 0$.

   d) Divide by v^3 and set $z = w/v$ to get a cubic polynomial equation in z. Check that 1.78 is an approximate root of this equation. Hence, when $x + y \geq 1/2$, $\partial \phi_X/\partial x = \phi_U/u$ precisely when $1.78 \approx w/v = (1/2 - y)/(1/2 - x)$.

54. Check at least one of the index calculations in the Kennedy–Kefauver–Gore example.

55. Analyze for possible bandwagon effects the following approximation to the 1976 Democratic Presidential nomination contest after the Pennsylvania primary and Scoop Jackson's effective withdrawal:

$$[10;\ 7,\ 3,\ 2,\ 1,\ 1,\ 1,\ 1,\ 1,\ 1,\ 1]$$
$$C\ M\ W \quad \text{uncommitted}$$

The players are Jimmy Carter (C), Mo Udall (M), and George Wallace (W). Assume alliances CW and CM are possible, but MW is not.

3. Characterizing the Power Indices

3.1. Axiomatic Characterizations

We have seen that the Shapley–Shubik index ϕ and the Banzhaf index β do not agree for most simple games, and that the degree of disagreement can be quite startling for some games. In Section 3.3 we shall examine a serious disagreement between ϕ and β in analyzing a proposed constitutional amendment scheme in Canada. The natural question in this context is, "Which index is correct?" A less absolutist phrasing of the same question might be, "Which index should be used in a given situation?"—for it might be the case that ϕ is more applicable (more "correct") for some situations, and β is more applicable in others. We must give serious consideration to this kind of question if we plan to use the two indices as we have in Section 2 to gain insight into interesting political situations.

There are several simple observations we can make about ϕ and β. One is that they seem to be based on emphasizing different parts of the political process. The Shapley–Shubik index focuses on the *order* in which a winning coalition forms, and defines the power of a player to be proportional to the number of orderings in which she is pivotal. The Banzhaf index ignores questions of ordering and looks only at the final coalition which forms in support of some proposal. The power of a player is defined to be proportional to the number of coalitions to which she is crucial—which are winning but would become losing if she left, or visa versa.

One might argue that we should judge ϕ and β by these interpretations: if politicians think more about the order in which players join a coalition in support of a proposal, use ϕ. If they think more in terms of what effect an individual could have once a coalition has formed, use β. One problem with this approach is that, perhaps surprisingly, there are other ways of arriving at the same indices, ϕ and β, which make no reference to orderings or to swing voters. In fact, in this section and the next, I want to look carefully at two such alternate derivations. We cannot accept or reject an index on the basis of one derivation of it, if there are other equally good derivations.

Another observation we can make is that ϕ and β behave qualitatively differently in near-oceanic games, ones with several major players and many minor ones. I have suggested that β seems intuitively unreasonable in many of these situations. For instance, does the U.S. President have less than 4% of legislative power? Or, if two stockholders have 31% and 30% of the shares of a large corporation with other shares divided among many small stockholders, does the 31% stockholder have nearly all the power? The possible pitfall here is the phrase "intuitively unreasonable." To judge carefully between ϕ and β, we would like to highlight reason and use intuition sparingly.

We began our presentation of the power indices in Section 1.2 with a different kind of approach, one very characteristic of mathematics. To highlight the role of reason in judging a power index, write down as many properties as you can which you believe a reasonable power index should have. Three things can then happen:

(1) There is no possible power index that satisfies all your properties. You may then give up, or you may weaken, or omit some of your desired properties and try again.
(2) There may be several or many different power indices that satisfy your properties. You may then investigate further and discover new desirable properties to add.
(3) There may be one and only one possible index that satisfies all your properties.

A mathematician calls the properties you write down *axioms*, and in the golden situation of (3), he would say you have an *axiomatic characterization* of the resulting index.

Recalling that ϕ and β both satisfy properties (i)–(v) in Section 1.2, we are in the more ambiguous situation (2). In this section, I want to discuss two ways of adding axioms. One way will lead to an axiomatic characterization of ϕ, the other to an axiomatic characterization of β. How then do we judge between ϕ and β? The interesting answer is that we can now go back and look at the axioms that characterize ϕ and β. If the axioms that characterize ϕ, say, seem more descriptive of some given political situation than those which characterize β, use ϕ for that situation.

The axiomatic characterizations I have in mind are due basically to Pradeep Dubey ([12, 13]). We begin by noticing that we may as well work with the absolute Banzhaf index β' instead of β. It turns out to be easier and it differs from β only in not being normalized: β' and β give the same *ratios* of power between two players. Dubey's principal additional axiom involves the way a power index behaves when we take products and sums of games. Actually, he needs a slight generalization of products and sums. In our definition in Section 1.1 of the product and sum of $G_1 = (N_1, \mathscr{W}_1)$ and $G_2 = (N_2, \mathscr{W}_2)$, we required N_1 and N_2 to be disjoint—the games were to have no players in common. The same idea can be used if N_1 and N_2 overlap, but we use a different notation. For any simple games $G_1 = (N_1, \mathscr{W}_1)$ and $G_2 = (N_2, \mathscr{W}_2)$, define

$G_1 \wedge G_2$ to be the game with player set $N = N_1 \cup N_2$, where a coalition is winning if it wins in both G_1 and G_2,

$G_1 \vee G_2$ to be the game with player set $N = N_1 \cup N_2$, where a coalition is winning if it wins in either G_1 or G_2.

Of course, if N_1 and N_2 are disjoint, we just have $G_1 \wedge G_2 = G_1 \otimes G_2$ and $G_1 \vee G_2 = G_1 \oplus G_2$. To help with bookkeeping (as below) we can consider the original games G_1 and G_2 to be played by player set N by just adjoining the additional players as dummies.

Dubey's composition axiom is

(vi) $K_i(G_1) + K_i(G_2) = K_i(G_1 \wedge G_2) + K_i(G_1 \vee G_2)$.

[Here, as in axioms (i)–(v) in Section 1.2, K refers to some general power index we are studying, which might be ϕ or β' or some other index.] In words, the sum of player i's power in G_1 and G_2 should be equal to the sum of his power in $G_1 \wedge G_2$ and $G_1 \vee G_2$.

It is remarkable that both ϕ and β' satisfy axiom (vi). For example, suppose $N = \{A, B, C, D\}$,

$$G_1 = \underset{\textstyle\ \ A\ B\ C\ D}{[2; 1, 1, 1, 0]} \qquad G_2 = \underset{\textstyle\ \ A\ B\ C\ D}{[3; 0, 2, 1, 1]}.$$

G_1 is really M_3, with players A, B, C, but D has been added as a dummy. G_2 really involves only B, C, D but A has been added as a dummy. You can check that

$$\beta'(G_1) = \left(\frac{4}{8}, \frac{4}{8}, \frac{4}{8}, 0\right), \quad \text{and} \quad \beta'(G_2) = \left(0, \frac{6}{8}, \frac{2}{8}, \frac{2}{8}\right).$$

Now the winning coalitions in $G_1 \wedge G_2$ are (swings underlined)

$$\underline{BC} \quad A\underline{BC} \quad \underline{ABD} \quad \underline{BC}D \quad A\underline{B}CD$$

so $\beta'(G_1 \wedge G_2) = (1/8, 5/8, 3/8, 1/8)$. Winning coalitions in $G_1 \vee G_2$ are

$$\begin{matrix} \underline{AB} & \underline{BC} & ABC & \underline{AC}D & ABCD \\ \underline{AC} & \underline{BD} & A\underline{B}D & \underline{B}CD & \end{matrix}$$

so $\beta'(G_1 \vee G_2) = (3/8, 5/8, 3/8, 1/8)$. If we add appropriately, we do indeed get $\beta'(G_1) + \beta'(G_2) = \beta'(G_1 \wedge G_2) + \beta'(G_1 \vee G_2)$.

The Shapley–Shubik index works just as nicely. You should check (Exercise 56) that

$$\phi(G_1) = \left(\frac{8}{24}, \frac{8}{24}, \frac{8}{24}, 0\right),$$

$$\phi(G_2) = \left(0, \frac{16}{24}, \frac{4}{24}, \frac{4}{24}\right),$$

$$\phi(G_1 \wedge G_2) = \left(\frac{2}{24}, \frac{14}{24}, \frac{6}{24}, \frac{2}{24}\right),$$

$$\phi(G_1 \vee G_2) = \left(\frac{6}{24}, \frac{10}{24}, \frac{6}{24}, \frac{2}{24}\right).$$

For a last axiom, recall that B_r denotes the unanimity game with r players.

(vii) If i is a player in B_r, then $K_i = 1/r$.

Theorem 1. (Dubey [12, 13]). *The Shapley–Shubik index* ϕ *is the one and only power index which satisfies* (i), (iii), (vi), *and* (vii) (*see Section 1.2*). [*It also, of course, satisfies* (ii), (iv), *and* (v), *but these are not necessary to characterize it.*]

In other words, if we want an index that satisfies our obvious axioms (i)–(iv), composes nicely as in (vi), and gives each player in an r-person unanimity game power equal to $1/r$, ϕ is our *only* choice. For β', we have:

(vii′) If i is a player in B_r, then $K_i = 1/(2^{r-1})$.

Theorem 2. *The absolute Banzhaf index* β' *is the one and only power index which satisfies* (i), (iii), (vi), *and* (vii′). [*It also satisfies* (ii) *and* (iv), *but these are not necessary to characterize it.*]

If we want to keep (i), (iii), and (vi), but think that a player in an r-person unanimity game should have power equal to only $1/2^{r-1}$, β' is our only choice.

How shall we think of the difference between (vii) and (vii′)? Alvin Roth [29] suggests we think of these conditions as expressing different attitudes of the players toward what he calls "strategic risk." Suppose you are trying to decide which of two decision-making situations will give you the most power:

Alternative I is to be a player in B_r. A decision will be made unanimously by a committee of r members of which you are one member.

Alternative II is a lottery that gives you a probability $1/r$ of being a dictator (making the decision by yourself), and a probability $1 - (1/r)$ of being a dummy (having no say in the decision).

If you think alternatives I and II give you equal power, you should accept axiom (vii). If you think alternative II gives you more power than alternative I, but would be indifferent between alternative I and

Alternative III a lottery with probability $1/2^{r-1}$ of being a dictator, probability $1 - (1/2^{r-1})$ of being a dummy, then you should accept axiom (vii′). The probabilities in alternatives II and III are quite different for all but very small values of r. For instance, if $r = 6$, alternative II gives you probability 1/6 of being a dictator, while alternative III gives you probability only 1/32 of being a dictator.

Axiom (vii) seems to say, "Well, I have as much chance of persuading the group to agree with me as anyone else does of persuading the group to agree with him." Axiom (vii′) seems to say, "It is in fact very hard for *anyone* to persuade *everyone* in a reasonably large body to agree with him." Axiom (vii′) is very pessimistic about unanimous decision making. In a situation in which people have little chance or ability to convince other people of their point of view, perhaps (vii′) is more applicable and the Banzhaf index gives a better idea of the players' relative power. Where people have a good chance of convincing each other, the Shapley–Shubik index might be better.

The problem with this analysis is that axiom (vi), as well as (vii) and (vii′), is crucial to the Dubey characterization. Unless we believe that axiom (vi) should hold for power indices, we should not be content with using the Dubey characterization to discriminate between ϕ and β' on the basis of axioms (vii) and (vii′). Now, to a mathematician axiom (vi) is beautiful—it has a lovely symmetry about it—and Dubey's theorems are certainly beautiful mathematics. On the other hand, if we try to think of how to interpret axiom (vi) as a statement about power in political situations, I think the best we can say is that it appears "somewhat opaque" (Roth [29]). You should definitely think about interpreting axiom (vi) (Exercise 61), and you may be more successful in convincing yourself of its inherent reasonableness than I have felt. In any case, I think it makes sense to examine another kind of approach to distinguishing between ϕ and β. In the next section we shall look at how these indices can be given probabilistic interpretations.

Notes and References. A careful discussion comparing ϕ and β in terms of their definitions can be found in Section 5.4 of Brams [5]. Dubey's proof of his theorems (Dubey [12, 13]; Roth [29]) is very mathematically appealing. One major idea of the proof is discussed in Exercise 60. To follow the entire proof, you do not need advanced mathematical techniques, but you do need ability to follow a very careful argument and familiarity with proofs by "mathematical induction."

Exercises

56. Check the calculations for ϕ in the example in this section.

57. Show that β does *not* satisfy axiom (vi), by considering the example in this section.

58. Check that β' satisfies axiom (vii′).

59. Verify that β' and ϕ satisfy axiom (vi) in the following two examples. Begin, of course, by saying what $G_1 \wedge G_2$ and $G_1 \vee G_2$ are, say by giving their winning coalitions.

a) $G_1 = \underset{A\ B}{[2;\ 1,\ 1]}$, $G_2 = \underset{C\ D}{[1;\ 1,\ 1]}$

b) $G_1 = \underset{A\ B\ C\ D}{[5;\ 3,\ 2,\ 1,\ 1]}$, $G_2 = \underset{A\ B\ C\ D}{[5;\ 1,\ 2,\ 2,\ 3]}$

60. Consider the simple game G with player set $N = \{A, B, C, D\}$ and $\mathscr{W}^m = \{AB, ACD\}$. Let G_1 be the two-person unanimity game with players A, B. Let G_2 be the three-person unanimity game with players A, C, D.

a) Show that $G = G_1 \vee G_2$.
b) Show that $G_1 \wedge G_2$ is also an unanimity game.
c) If K is a power index satifying axioms (iii), (vi) and (vii), calculate $K(G)$ by using that axiom (vii) determines K for unanimity games, while axiom (vi) says

$$K(G) = K(G_1 \vee G_2) = K(G_1) + K(G_2) - K(G_1 \wedge G_2)$$

and all the games on the right are unanimity games. Check, using the table in the Appendix, that $K(G) = \phi(G)$.
d) Similarly, calculate $K(G)$ if K is a power index satisfying axioms (iii), (vi) and (vii′), and check that $K(G) = \beta'(G)$.

One can use this kind of reasoning to prove Dubey's theorems. Axiom (vii) [or (vii′)] says that K must agree with ϕ (or β') for games with only *one* minimal winning coalition (unanimity games). This kind of reasoning then shows that K must agree with ϕ (or β') for games with exactly *two* minimal coalitions. You continue working up, or use the general principle of "mathematical induction."

61. One can restate axiom (vi) as

$$\frac{K_i(G_1) + K_i(G_2)}{2} = \frac{K_i(G_1 \wedge G_2) + K_i(G_1 \vee G_2)}{2}$$

and think of the expressions on the left and right as the *average* power of player i in two situations. Give a "justification" for axiom (vi) using a hypothetical legislator trying to decide between two proposed alternatives:
(1) Flip a coin to decide whether a proposal should be acted on by committee 1 or committee 2.
(2) Send the proposal to *both* committees, but then flip a coin to decide if approval shall be required by both committees, or just by one of them.

Our hypothetical legislator might be a member of both committees, but have more power in one committee than in the other.

3.2. Probabilistic Characterizations

There are two questions of probability that are important to members of a decision-making body. Let me write them both, although we shall be dealing mostly with the first:

Question of Individual Effect. *What is the probability that my vote will make a difference, that is, that a proposal will pass if I vote for it, but fail if I vote against it?*

Question of Individual-Group Agreement. *What is the probability that the group decision will agree with my decision on a proposal?*

The answers to these questions will depend on both the decision rule of the body, and the probabilities that the various members will vote for or against a proposal. In our context, the decision rule is given as a simple game. In some particular political example, we might also be able to estimate voting probabilities of the players for some particular proposal or class of proposals. On the other hand, if we are interested in general theoretical questions of power, we cannot reasonably assume particular knowledge about individual players or proposals. Hence we should only make assumptions about voting probabilities which do not discriminate among the players. You can probably think of many assumptions we might make, but here are two interesting ones:

Homogeneity Assumption. *Every proposal to come before the decision-making body has a certain probability p of appealing to* each *member of the body. For various proposals, p varies uniformly between* 0 *and* 1. (*The homogeneity is among members: they all have the same probability p of voting for a given proposal, but p varies from proposal to proposal.*)

or

Independence Assumption. *Every proposal has a probability p_i of appealing to the ith member. Each of the p_is is chosen uniformly and independently from the interval* $[0, 1]$. (*Here how one member feels about a proposal has nothing to do with how any other member feels.*)

Notice that the homogeneity assumption does not assume that members will all vote the same way, but it does say something about their similar criteria for evaluating proposals. For instance, some bills that came before a legislature seem to have a high probability of appealing to all members, and pass by large margins: those have high ps. Others are overwhelmingly defeated (low ps) or controversial (ps near 1/2).

If we consider the question of individual effect with either of the above assumptions about voting probabilities, we get interesting results:

Theorem 1. *The Shapley–Shubik index ϕ gives the answer to the question of individual effect under the homogeneity assumption about voting probabilities.*

The proof of this theorem is a little tricky, and I will illustrate it but not prove it here. See Notes and References.

Theorem 2. *The absolute Banzhaf index β' gives the answer to the question of individual effect under the independence assumption about voting probabilities.*

This result is a little easier to see. First notice that if player i's probability of voting for a given proposal varies uniformly between 0 and 1 for different proposals, the net effect is that she will vote for 1/2 of the proposals and against 1/2. Her behavior over a long series of proposals is exactly the same as if she had probability 1/2 of voting for each one. If each player can be thought of as having probability 1/2 of voting for any given proposal, then we can think of all coalitions as being equally likely to be the coalition that supports a proposal (since each player is equally likely to be in the supporting coalition or not in it). Clearly, a player's vote "makes a difference" if and only if she is a swing voter for the coalition which forms in support of a proposal. So the probability of player i's vote making a difference is exactly the probability that player i will be a swing voter, given that all coalitions are equally likely to form, and of course this is exactly β_i'. Hence Theorem 2.

Let us look at an example of how these results work. Consider $[3; \underset{A}{2}, \underset{B}{1}, \underset{C}{1}]$.
Suppose temporarily that each voter will vote for a proposal with probability p. What is the probability that A's vote will make a difference between approval and rejection? If both B and C vote against the proposal, A's vote will *not* make a difference, since the proposal will fail regardless of what he does. On the other hand, if B or C or both vote for the proposal, A's vote will decide between approval and rejection. Hence the probability that A's vote will make a difference is given by

$$\pi_A(p) = \underset{B\text{ for, }C\text{ against}}{p(1-p)} + \underset{B\text{ against, }C\text{ for}}{(1-p)p} + \underset{\text{both for}}{p^2} = 2p - p^2.$$

Similarly, B's vote will make a difference only if A votes for, and C votes against. (If they both voted for, the proposal would pass regardless of what B did.)

$$\pi_B(p) = \underset{A\text{ for, }C\text{ against}}{p(1-p)} = p - p^2.$$

By symmetry, we also have

$$\pi_C(p) = p - p^2.$$

Now look at the two voting assumptions. The homogeneity assumption says we must average the probability of making a difference $\pi_A(p)$, say, over all p between 0 and 1. This is done by a technique from elementary calculus called "integrating between 0 and 1."

What you need to know about this is that "$\int_0^1 p^m\,dp$" means the average value of p^m as p varies uniformly between 0 and 1, and that this average value is $1/(m+1)$.

So under the homogeneity assumption, the answer to the question of individual effect is

$$\text{for } A\text{:}\quad \int_0^1 \pi_A(p)\,dp = \int_0^1 (2p - p^2)\,dp = \frac{2}{2} - \frac{1}{3} = \frac{2}{3},$$

$$\text{for } B\text{:}\quad \int_0^1 \pi_B(p)\,dp = \int_0^1 (p - p^2)\,dp = \frac{1}{2} - \frac{1}{3} = \frac{1}{6},$$

$$\text{for } C\text{:}\quad \int_0^1 \pi_C(p)\,dp = \int_0^1 (p - p^2)\,dp = \frac{1}{2} - \frac{1}{3} = \frac{1}{6}.$$

If you check the Appendix, or work it out directly, you will see that these numbers are exactly ϕ_A, ϕ_B, ϕ_C, thus verifying Theorem 1 for this example.

The other voting assumption, the independence assumption, is equivalent, as we noted in justifying Theorem 2, to assuming that all players vote with probability 1/2 for or against a proposal. Hence, we can answer the question of individual effect under the independence assumption by simply setting $p = 1/2$:

$$\text{for } A\colon \quad \pi_A\left(\frac{1}{2}\right) = 2\left(\frac{1}{2}\right) - \left(\frac{1}{2}\right)^2 = \frac{3}{4},$$

$$\text{for } B\colon \quad \pi_B\left(\frac{1}{2}\right) = \left(\frac{1}{2}\right) - \left(\frac{1}{2}\right)^2 = \frac{1}{4},$$

$$\text{for } C\colon \quad \pi_C\left(\frac{1}{2}\right) = \left(\frac{1}{2}\right) - \left(\frac{1}{2}\right)^2 = \frac{1}{4}.$$

Again, you should check that these numbers are exactly β'_A, β'_B, and β'_C, thus verifying Theorem 2 for this example.

In general, it is quite a joy to do these calculations and verify that you always get ϕ and β' from them. You should definitely try the exercises. In fact, once you get used to writing down the functions $\pi_i(p)$, you may find it easier to calculate ϕ_i and β'_i by this means than to do it directly by the means of Section 1. The polynomials $\pi_i(p)$ for simple games with four or fewer players are included in the Appendix.

How do Theorems 1 and 2 help us think about ϕ and β' (or its normalized version β)? First, they show us again that orderings and pivots, or swings, are not crucial to the definitions of these power indices. The indices arise as answers to a very natural probabilistic question under fairly natural symmetric assumptions about voting behavior. Second, they offer what I think is the most natural way to distinguish between ϕ and β. If voters in some political situation behave completely independently, β is the most appropriate index. If voters have a certain degree of homogeneity, ϕ is most appropriate.

This formulation also throws light on some of the tentative conclusions we have already come to. Why does β seem so counterintuitive for certain large games? Perhaps because we are not familiar with many large groups where members behave completely independently. For large groups, the homogeneity assumption may be more reasonable. Why do ϕ and β seem to be associated with a higher or lower ability to influence other voters? Perhaps because homogeneous groups are more manipulable than groups whose members behave completely independently. You might like to think more carefully about these kinds of connections.

I have not yet said anything about the question of individual–group agreement, yet this question is clearly important. It would be especially important to a voter who is "issue oriented"—who is interested in having the group decision agree with his preference whether or not his vote is crucial to the outcome. It is pleasing that one of the power indices also has something to say about this question:

Theorem 3. *The answer to player i's question of individual–group agreement, under the independence assumption about voting probabilities, is given by* $(1 + \beta_i')/2$.

To prove this theorem, use Theorem 2, which says that β_i' gives the probability that player i's vote will make the difference between approval and rejection. Since his vote makes the difference, in this situation the group decision will always agree with his. On the other hand, with probability $1 - \beta_i'$ player i's vote will *not* make a difference, but in this case the group will still agree with him, by chance, half the time. Hence the total probability that the group decision will agree with player i's decision is

$$(\beta_i')(1) + (1 - \beta_i')\left(\frac{1}{2}\right) = \frac{1 + \beta_i'}{2}.$$

For an example, let us look again at $[3; \underset{A}{2}, \underset{B}{1}, \underset{C}{1}]$. What is the probability that, under the independence assumption, the group decision will agree with A's preference? With probability 1/2, A will support a proposal. It will then pass *unless* B and C both oppose it, which will happen with probability 1/4. If A opposes the proposal (probability 1/2), it will always fail. The probability of agreement with A is thus

$$\frac{1}{2}\left(1 - \frac{1}{4}\right) + \frac{1}{2}(1) = \frac{7}{8} = \frac{1 + \frac{3}{4}}{2} = \frac{1 + \beta_A'}{2}.$$

Similarly, if B supports a proposal (probability 1/2), it will pass if and only if A supports it (probability 1/2). If B opposes the proposal (probability 1/2), it will fail unless both A and C support it (probability 1/4):

$$\frac{1}{2}\left(\frac{1}{2}\right) + \frac{1}{2}\left(1 - \frac{1}{4}\right) = \frac{5}{8} = \frac{1 + \frac{1}{4}}{2} = \frac{1 + \beta_B'}{2}.$$

Theorem 3 is thus verified for this example. You can try another example in Exercise 66.

Finally, what about the question of individual–group agreement under the homogeneity assumption? Unfortunately, the answer is given not by ϕ, but by a new power index, which I am tempted to denote σ and call the Straffin index. Knowing that the world probably does not need a new power index, I shall consign σ to an exercise.

Notes and References. The probability interpretations of this section have been in the air and known to mathematical game theorists for some time.

The interpretation of ϕ has been known at least since Owen [25], where you can find a proof of Theorem 1. Owen did not think of his result in the way I have presented it here, and much of my thinking on this question was clarified in talks with David Heath of Cornell. Further material on the ideas in this section can be found in Straffin [37], [39], and [40].

Exercises

62. Consider $[5;\ \underset{A}{3},\ \underset{B}{2},\ \underset{C}{1},\ \underset{D}{1}]$.

    Show that

$$\pi_A(p) = \underbrace{p}_{B\text{ for}} + \underbrace{(1-p)p^2}_{B\text{ against, }C\text{ and }D\text{ for}} = p + p^2 - p^3$$

$$\pi_B(p) = \underbrace{p(1-p^2)}_{A\text{ for, not both }C\text{ and }D\text{ for}} = p - p^3$$

$$\pi_C(p) = \underbrace{p(1-p)p}_{A\text{ for, }B\text{ against, }D\text{ for}} = p^2 - p^3.$$

    Hence check that

$$\beta' = (\tfrac{5}{8}, \tfrac{3}{8}, \tfrac{1}{8}, \tfrac{1}{8})$$

$$\phi = (\tfrac{7}{12}, \tfrac{3}{12}, \tfrac{1}{12}, \tfrac{1}{12})$$

    by the method of this section.

63. Calculate the "power polynomials" $\pi_i(p)$, and the resulting ϕ_i and β_i' for players in the following games:
    a) $[4; 3, 1, 1, 1]$.
    b) $[5; 2, 2, 1, 1]$.
    c) The game Γ of Section 1.

    Check your results with the Appendix.

64. Explain why
    a) $\pi_i(0) = 0$, unless player i can approve a proposal by himself.
    b) $\pi_i(1) = 0$, unless player i can block a proposal by himself (i.e., has a veto).
    c) $\pi_i(p) = 0$, for all p if and only if player i is a dummy.
    d) $\pi_i(p) = 1$, for all p if and only if player i is a dictator.

65. If i is a player in B_n, what is $\pi_i(p)$? Check that the resulting ϕ_i and β_i' are what they should be.

66. Consider $[5;\ \underset{A}{3},\ \underset{B}{2},\ \underset{C}{1},\ \underset{D}{1}]$. Let $\rho_i(p)$ be the probability that the group decision agrees with player i's decision, given that all players (including i) vote for a proposal with probability p.
    a) Show that

$$\rho_A(p) = \underbrace{p}_{A\text{ yes}}\ [\underbrace{p}_{B\text{ yes}} + \underbrace{(1-p)p^2}_{B\text{ no, }C+D\text{ yes}}] + \underbrace{(1-p)(1)}_{A\text{ no}} = 1 - p + p^2 + p^3 - p^4$$

$$\rho_B(p) = \underset{B\text{ yes}}{p}\;\underset{A\text{ yes}}{(p)} + \underset{B\text{ no}}{(1-p)}\underset{\substack{\text{not all of}\\ A,\,C,\,D\text{ yes}}}{(1-p^3)} = 1 - p + p^2 - p^3 + p^4$$

$$\begin{aligned}\rho_C(p) &= \underset{C\text{ yes}}{p}\;\underset{A\text{ yes}}{[p}\;\underset{B\text{ yes}}{(p} + \underset{B\text{ no},\,D\text{ yes}}{(1-p)p)]} + \underset{C\text{ no}}{(1-p)}[\underset{A\text{ no}}{(1-p)} + \underset{A\text{ yes},\,B\text{ no}}{p(1-p)}]\\ &= 1 - p - p^2 + 3p^3 - p^4.\end{aligned}$$

b) Now calculate $\rho_A(1/2)$, $\rho_B(1/2)$, and $\rho_C(1/2)$ and show that these are $(1 + \beta'_A)/2$, $(1 + \beta'_B)/2$, and $(1 + \beta'_C)/2$, thus verifying Theorem 3 for this case. (You calculated β'_A, β'_B, β'_C in Exercise 62.)

67. Define a new index as follows. You are given a simple game with n players. Write down all orderings of the players and underline pivots. For example, in $[5; 3, 2, 1, 1]$:
$A\ B\ C\ D$

$A\underline{B}CD$	$B\underline{A}CD$	$CA\underline{B}D$	$DA\underline{B}C$
$A\underline{B}DC$	$B\underline{A}DC$	$CA\underline{D}B$	$DA\underline{C}B$
$AC\underline{B}D$	$BC\underline{A}D$	$CB\underline{A}D$	$DB\underline{A}C$
$AC\underline{D}B$	$BCD\underline{A}$	$CBD\underline{A}$	$DBC\underline{A}$
$AD\underline{B}C$	$BD\underline{A}C$	$CD\underline{A}B$	$DC\underline{A}B$
$AD\underline{C}B$	$BDC\underline{A}$	$CDB\underline{A}$	$DCB\underline{A}$

Award a player 1 if he is the pivot, $1 - 1/(n + 1)$ if he misses being the pivot by one position (on either side), $1 - 2/(n + 1)$ if he misses being the pivot by two positions, etc. Define σ_i = the average award to player i, over all orderings.

a) Check that for the example above

$$\sigma_A = \tfrac{1}{24}[14 \cdot 1 + 6 \cdot \tfrac{4}{5} + 4 \cdot \tfrac{3}{5}] = \tfrac{53}{60}.$$

b) Calculate that $\sigma_B = 47/60$ and $\sigma_C = \sigma_D = 43/60$.
The answer to player i's question of individual–group agreement under the homogeneity assumption is given by $\int_0^1 \rho_i(p)dp$, where $\rho_i(p)$ is as in Exercise 66. I claim that this is always equal to σ_i:

c) Use the results of Exercises 66 and 67a, b to show that, yes indeed,

$$\int_0^1 \rho_i(p)dp = \sigma_i \quad \text{for the players in } [5; 3, 2, 1, 1].$$

68. The power index σ does not satisfy two of axioms (i)–(v) in Section 1.2. Which are the two axioms?

3.3. A Proposed Canadian Constitutional Amendment Scheme

The Constitution of Canada is contained in the British North America Act of 1867, the act of the British Parliament which first granted self-government to Canada. This is a strange situation—for the Constitution of one country to be embodied in legislation of another country. Particularly awkward is the fact that in order to amend important provisions in the Constitution, Canada must request the British Parliament to enact the desired amendment. This has actually been done twelve times, and the British Parliament has always graciously agreed. Still, "patriation of the Canadian Constitution" is an issue of at least symbolic importance for Canadians.

The British government has been willing for many years to turn the Canadian Constitution over to Canada. The major legal hurdle is that the Canadian national government and the Canadian Provinces must first agree on a procedure for amending the Constitution in Canada. Which provinces shall have how much say in approving Constitutional amendments? The question is delicate because of the extreme disparity in size among the ten Canadian provinces—from Ontario and Quebec, with almost one third of the Canadian population each, to Prince Edward Island with less than 1% of the Canadian population. In fact, the question is so delicate, and so complicated by the cultural concerns of Quebec, and the small provinces' fear of domination by Ontario and Quebec, that Federal–Provincial conferences failed in 1927, 1935, 1950, 1960, and 1964 to agree on an all-Canadian Constitutional amendment scheme.

The most recent Constitutional Conference was held in Victoria in 1971. The Victoria Conference produced a draft of a Canadian Constitutional Charter, which was immediately approved by eight of the ten provinces (Saskatchewan made no decision), and disapproved by Quebec, which held out for more cultural guarantees. The Constitutional amendment scheme in the Victoria Charter was ingenious.

It would require a Constitutional amendment to be approved by

(1) Quebec **and**
(2) Ontario **and**
(3) Two of the four Atlantic provinces (New Brunswick, Nova Scotia, Prince Edward Island, and Newfoundland) **and**
(4) British Columbia and one Central province (Alberta, Saskatchewan, Manitoba) *or* all three Central provinces (Canada, 1971).

This scheme can be represented as a simple game:

$$\underset{\text{Quebec}}{B_1} \otimes \underset{\text{Ontario}}{B_1} \otimes \underset{\text{Atlantic}}{M_{4,2}} \otimes \underset{\text{British Columbia and Central.}}{[3; 2, 1, 1, 1]}$$

Several years ago, D. R. Miller [21] published a Shapley–Shubik index analysis of this scheme, in which he concluded that the scheme "produces a distribution of power that, according to one standard measurement scheme at least, matches the distribution of population surprisingly well." Miller did not publish a Banzhaf index analysis of the amendment scheme, which, however, can be found in Lucas (Chapter 9, this volume). The results of both analyses are shown in Table 1.

Notice that the conclusion of the Banzhaf analysis would be quite different. The scheme would *not* be satisfactory; it would seriously underrepresent

Table 1. Analyses of the Proposed Canadian Constitutional Amendment Scheme.

Province	Percentage of power: Shapley–Shubik index	Percentage of power: Banzhaf index	Percentage of population	
Ontario	31.55	21.78	34.85	average 31.90
Quebec	31.55	21.78	28.94	
British Columbia	12.50	16.34	9.38	
Central				
Alberta	4.17	5.45	7.33	average 5.65
Saskatchewan	4.17	5.45	4.79	
Manitoba	4.17	5.45	4.82	
Atlantic				
New Brunswick	2.98	5.94	3.09	average 2.47
Nova Scotia	2.98	5.94	3.79	
P.E.I.	2.98	5.94	0.54	
Newfoundland	2.98	5.94	2.47	

Ontario and Quebec, and seriously overrepresent British Columbia and the Atlantic provinces. (How could provinces with a veto be underrepresented? The intuitive answer is that the other provinces have "too much of a veto," so that Ontario and Quebec would not have as good a chance as they should to have an amendment they favor adopted.) Particularly striking is the fact that the two power indices actually give different *orders* for the power of the players. ϕ says the Central Provinces are more powerful than the Atlantic provinces, and β says the opposite!

The obvious question is which index is more applicable, which one should we believe? From the considerations of Section 3.2, we should use ϕ if we believe there is a certain kind of homogeneity among the provinces, β if we believe they are more likely to act independently of each other. The problem is that neither assumption seems completely reasonable. Quebec and British Columbia, for example, would seem quite likely to behave independently. The four Atlantic provinces, on the other hand, have common interests and would seem more likely to satisfy the homogeneity assumption. The natural thing to do would be to think of some groups of provinces as being homogeneous among themselves, but behaving independently of other provinces or groups of provinces. This can easily be handled in the probability interpretation of Section 3.2. If a group of provinces is homogeneous, assign the members of that group the same p, which varies between 0 and 1 independently of the ps assigned to other provinces or groups of provinces. If we then ask the question of individual effect, we shall get an answer that is neither ϕ nor β', but a kind of hybrid of the two that may reflect reality better than either pure index.

Let us see how this would work. Assume that the four Atlantic provinces are homogeneous among themselves and assign them p_A. Also assume that

Table 2

Provinces	All homogeneous (ϕ)	*A*s homogeneous *C*s and *B* homogeneous	*A*s homogeneous *C*s homogeneous	All independent (β)	Average % of population
Quebec or Ontario	31.55	26.09	23.08	21.78	31.90
British Columbia	12.50	13.04	11.54	16.34	9.38
Central province	4.17	4.35	7.69	5.45	5.65
Atlantic province	2.98	5.43	4.81	5.94	2.47

the Central provinces are homogeneous among themselves, and assign them p_C. Quebec (p_Q), Ontario (p_O), and British Columbia (p_B) behave independently. Now calculate the probability that Quebec's vote, say, will make a difference:

$$\underset{O\text{ yes}}{\pi_Q = p_O}\underset{2\text{ or more }A\text{'s yes}}{[6p_A^2(1-p_A)^2 + 4p_A^3(1-p_A) + p_A^4]}$$

$$\cdot\underset{B\text{ yes}\quad\text{and}\quad 1\text{ or }2C\text{'s yes or}\qquad\qquad 3C\text{'s yes}}{[p_B(3p_C(1-p_C)^2 + 3p_C^2(1-p_C)) + p_C^3]}$$

We now take the average as p_O, p_A, p_B, and p_C vary independently between 0 and 1. Technically, that involves a "fourfold multiple integral," and I shall just give the result for π_Q and the others:

$$\pi_Q = \pi_O = \frac{24}{160}, \quad \pi_C = \frac{8}{160},$$

$$\pi_B = \frac{12}{160}, \quad \pi_A = \frac{5}{160}.$$

We must normalize these numbers in order to compare them to ϕ and β and the percentage of population held by each province. Recalling that there are $3C$s and $4A$s, the π_is sum to 104/160, so we normalize by multiplying by 160/104. Table 2 shows the normalized results for this case, and also for the case where we consider British Columbia homogeneous with the Central provinces. If we believe that one of our intermediate homogeneity assumptions is more realistic than either complete homogeneity or complete independence, we would advise the Canadian government that the proposed scheme is not as good as ϕ would indicate, but not quite as bad as β would indicate.

Finally, consider the amendment scheme from Quebec's point of view. Recall that Quebec refused to approve the Victoria Charter because it wanted more guarantees of cultural sovereignty. Quebec seems often to consider itself an island of French culture in the sea of English Canada. We could reflect this by treating all nine other provinces as homogeneous among themselves, and Quebec as independent. If we do this, we get the interesting result:

Quebec: 38.69	British Columbia: 11.61
Ontario: 25.84	Central province: 3.87
	Atlantic province: 3.07

From this point of view, Quebec's veto gives it considerable power.

In general, I believe that many applications of power indices may call for these kinds of intermediate homogeneity assumptions, and that we should think carefully before we rush in with either ϕ or β as the sole answer.

Note that the effect of homogeneous behavior in certain groups leads to nonintuitive variations in power, at least in complicated games like the Canadian Constitution game. For instance, consider the effect of British Columbia's possible homogeneity with the Central provinces. Is it obvious that such homogeneity should give Quebec and Ontario more power?

On the other hand, in easy games this partial-homogeneity effect seems to be in good accord with common sense. As an example, consider

$$M_3 = \underset{A\ B\ C}{[2;\ 1,\ 1,\ 1].}$$

Let p_A, p_B, and p_C be the probabilities that A, B, and C will vote for a proposal. We can easily calculate the probabilities of a player's vote making a difference:

$$\pi_A = p_B(1 - p_C) + (1 - p_B)p_C,$$
$$\pi_B = p_A(1 - p_C) + (1 - p_A)p_C,$$
$$\pi_C = p_A(1 - p_B) + (1 - p_A)p_B.$$

If the p_is are all independent (β') or all equal (ϕ) as they vary between 0 and 1, we shall find, of course, that the players have equal power. But suppose B and C are homogeneous ($p_B = p_C$), but A is independent. Then the answers to the question of individual effect are

$$\text{for } A: \quad \int_0^1 2p_B(1 - p_B)\,dp_B = \frac{1}{3}$$

$$\text{for } B \text{ or } C: \quad \left(\int_0^1 p_A\,dp_A\right)\left(\int_0^1 (1 - p_B)\,dp_B\right) + \left(\int_0^1 (1 - p_A)\,dp_A\right)\left(\int_0^1 p_B\,dp_B\right)$$
$$= \frac{1}{2}\cdot\frac{1}{2} + \frac{1}{2}\cdot\frac{1}{2} = \frac{1}{2}.$$

B and C both have more power than A. In particular, we could normalize (1/3, 1/2, 1/2) to (1/4, 3/8, 3/8) and compare that to (1/3, 1/3, 1/3). Homogeneity helps you in M_3, which seems quite reasonable.

Now do the same kind of analysis for the three-person unanimity game B_3, again assuming that players B and C are homogeneous, and A is independent. You should get figures of (1/3, 1/4, 1/4), which normalizes to (4/10, 3/10, 3/10). Here it is the odd man out who gains power, and I think that is also reasonable.

The general question of who gains and who loses under various assumptions of partial homogeneity looks like an interesting field for investigation.

Notes and References. Some of the material in this section appears in Straffin [37]. A recent application of partial homogeneity can be found in Kleiner [17]. *Added in proof*: the Canadian constitution was finally patriated in 1982, with an amendment scheme much less satisfactory, from a power analysis point of view, than the Victoria scheme.

EXERCISES

69. Show that ϕ and β give different power orders among the players for the slightly easier game $M_{4,2} \otimes [3; 2, 1, 1, 1]$. (As recently as 1975, Allingham [1] thought that there was no example known where ϕ and β give different orders. I believe that this eight-person game is probably the easiest example of this phenomenon.)

70. Check the above figures for a partial homogeneity assumption on B_3.

71. Calculate the results of the two different kinds of partial homogeneity assumption on $[3; \underset{A}{2}, \underset{B}{1}, \underset{C}{1}]$. Who gains and who loses [as compared to complete homogeneity (ϕ) or complete independence (β)]?

72. If you can do multiple integrals, or if you can see some of the good simplifying tricks, you might like to try checking my figures for partial homogeneity assumptions in the Canadian Constitutional amendment scheme.

73. Premier Lougheed of Alberta protested in April 10, 1976, that Alberta was under-represented in the proposed Constitutional Amendment Scheme. He suggested that *any two* Western provinces (British Columbia, Alberta, Saskatchewan, Manitoba) be sufficient to approve an amendment, instead of the present provision 4). Do you think this would increase Alberta's power? Try a Shapley–Shubik index calculation to see.

74. If you had to advise the Canadian government on the proposed scheme's fairness, what (given the results of Tables 1 and 2 and the Quebec calculation) would you honestly say?

Appendix

The table on the following pages contains all essentially distinct (Section 1.1, Exercise 7), simple games of four or fewer players that do not contain dummies. Of course, you can add a dummy to a three-person game to get a four-person game, etc. The reference letters in the first column are the letters used by Shapley [32]. The weighted voting representations given in column 4 are the simplest ones, but of course there are many other equivalent representations. The "power polynomials" $\pi_i(p)$ in column 8 are listed for the players in order of decreasing power. For example, in game (j) we have $\pi_A(p) = p + p^2 - p^3$, $\pi_B(p) = p - p^3$, and $\pi_C(p) = \pi_D(p) = p^2 - p^3$. You might like to check that $\int_0^1 \pi_i(p)\,dp = \phi_i$ and $\pi_i(1/2) = \beta_i'$, as stated in Section 3.2. I think the remarks in column 9 should be clear from the text, except that "veto" refers to the existence in the game of a veto player (Section 3.2, Exercise 64).

Several relationships between a game G and its dual game G^* (Section 1.1, Exercise 9) are clear in the table. For instance, G and G^* have the same ϕ, β, and β' (Section 1.2, Exercise 25). The weighted voting representations are closely related (Section 1.1, Exercise 10). If G is a compound game, there is a

Table 3

Reference letter	Number of players	$\mathscr{W}^m$	Weighted voting representation	ϕ	β	β'	$\pi_i(p)$'s	Remarks
(a)	1	A	[1; 1]	(1)	(1)	(1)	1	B_1, M_1, dictator, self-dual.
(b)	2	AB	[2; 1, 1]	$\left(\frac{1}{2}, \frac{1}{2}\right)$	$\left(\frac{1}{2}, \frac{1}{2}\right)$	$\left(\frac{1}{2}, \frac{1}{2}\right)$	p	B_2, M_2, vetos
(b*)	2	A, B	[1; 1, 1]	$\left(\frac{1}{2}, \frac{1}{2}\right)$	$\left(\frac{1}{2}, \frac{1}{2}\right)$	$\left(\frac{1}{2}, \frac{1}{2}\right)$	$1 - p$	B_2^*, improper
(c)	3	ABC	[3; 1, 1, 1]	$\left(\frac{1}{3}, \frac{1}{3}, \frac{1}{3}\right)$	$\left(\frac{1}{3}, \frac{1}{3}, \frac{1}{3}\right)$	$\left(\frac{1}{4}, \frac{1}{4}, \frac{1}{4}\right)$	p^2	B_3, vetos
(c*)	3	A, B, C	[1; 1, 1, 1]	$\left(\frac{1}{3}, \frac{1}{3}, \frac{1}{3}\right)$	$\left(\frac{1}{3}, \frac{1}{3}, \frac{1}{3}\right)$	$\left(\frac{1}{4}, \frac{1}{4}, \frac{1}{4}\right)$	$1 - 2p + p^2$	B_3^*, improper
(d)	3	AB, AC	[3; 2, 1, 1]	$\left(\frac{2}{3}, \frac{1}{6}, \frac{1}{6}\right)$	$\left(\frac{3}{5}, \frac{1}{5}, \frac{1}{5}\right)$	$\left(\frac{3}{4}, \frac{1}{4}, \frac{1}{4}\right)$	$2p - p^2$ $p - p^2$	$B_1 \otimes B_2^*$, veto
(d*)	3	A, BC	[2; 2, 1, 1]	$\left(\frac{2}{3}, \frac{1}{6}, \frac{1}{6}\right)$	$\left(\frac{3}{5}, \frac{1}{5}, \frac{1}{5}\right)$	$\left(\frac{3}{4}, \frac{1}{4}, \frac{1}{4}\right)$	$1 - p^2$ $p - p^2$	$B_1 \oplus B_2$, improper
(e)	3	AB, AC, BC	[2; 1, 1, 1]	$\left(\frac{1}{3}, \frac{1}{3}, \frac{1}{3}\right)$	$\left(\frac{1}{3}, \frac{1}{3}, \frac{1}{3}\right)$	$\left(\frac{1}{2}, \frac{1}{2}, \frac{1}{2}\right)$	$2p - 2p^2$	M_3, self-dual
(f)	4	$ABCD$	[4; 1, 1, 1, 1]	$\left(\frac{1}{4}, \frac{1}{4}, \frac{1}{4}, \frac{1}{4}\right)$	$\left(\frac{1}{4}, \frac{1}{4}, \frac{1}{4}, \frac{1}{4}\right)$	$\left(\frac{1}{8}, \frac{1}{8}, \frac{1}{8}, \frac{1}{8}\right)$	p^3	B_4, vetos
(f*)	4	A, B, C, D	[1; 1, 1, 1, 1]	$\left(\frac{1}{4}, \frac{1}{4}, \frac{1}{4}, \frac{1}{4}\right)$	$\left(\frac{1}{4}, \frac{1}{4}, \frac{1}{4}, \frac{1}{4}\right)$	$\left(\frac{1}{8}, \frac{1}{8}, \frac{1}{8}, \frac{1}{8}\right)$	$1 - 3p + 3p^2 - p^3$	B_4^*, improper
(g)	4	ABC, ABD	[5; 2, 2, 1, 1]	$\left(\frac{5}{12}, \frac{5}{12}, \frac{1}{12}, \frac{1}{12}\right)$	$\left(\frac{3}{8}, \frac{3}{8}, \frac{1}{8}, \frac{1}{8}\right)$	$\left(\frac{3}{8}, \frac{3}{8}, \frac{1}{8}, \frac{1}{8}\right)$	$2p^2 - p^3$ $p^2 - p^3$	$B_2 \otimes B_2^*$, vetos
(g*)	4	A, B, CD	[2; 2, 2, 1, 1]	$\left(\frac{5}{12}, \frac{5}{12}, \frac{1}{12}, \frac{1}{12}\right)$	$\left(\frac{3}{8}, \frac{3}{8}, \frac{1}{8}, \frac{1}{8}\right)$	$\left(\frac{3}{8}, \frac{3}{8}, \frac{1}{8}, \frac{1}{8}\right)$	$1 - p - p^2 + p^3$ $p - 2p^2 + p^3$	$B_2^* \oplus B_2$, improper
(h)	4	ABC, ABD, ACD	[4; 2, 1, 1, 1]	$\left(\frac{1}{2}, \frac{1}{6}, \frac{1}{6}, \frac{1}{6}\right)$	$\left(\frac{2}{5}, \frac{1}{5}, \frac{1}{5}, \frac{1}{5}\right)$	$\left(\frac{1}{2}, \frac{1}{4}, \frac{1}{4}, \frac{1}{4}\right)$	$3p^2 - 2p^3$ $2p^2 - 2p^3$	$B_1 \otimes M_3$, veto

Table 3 (*continued*)

Reference letter	Number of players	$\mathscr{W}^m$	Weighted voting representation	ϕ	β	β'	$\pi_i(p)$'s	Remarks
(h*)	4	A, BC, BD, CD	[2; 2, 1, 1, 1]	$\left(\frac{1}{2}, \frac{1}{6}, \frac{1}{6}, \frac{1}{6}\right)$	$\left(\frac{2}{5}, \frac{1}{5}, \frac{1}{5}, \frac{1}{5}\right)$	$\left(\frac{1}{2}, \frac{1}{4}, \frac{1}{4}, \frac{1}{4}\right)$	$1 - 3p^2 + 2p^3$ $2p - 4p^2 + 2p^3$	$B_1 \oplus M_3$, improper
(i)	4	ABC, ABD, ACD, BCD	[3; 1, 1, 1, 1]	$\left(\frac{1}{4}, \frac{1}{4}, \frac{1}{4}, \frac{1}{4}\right)$	$\left(\frac{1}{4}, \frac{1}{4}, \frac{1}{4}, \frac{1}{4}\right)$	$\left(\frac{3}{8}, \frac{3}{8}, \frac{3}{8}, \frac{3}{8}\right)$	$3p^2 - 3p^3$	M_4
(i*)	4	AB, AC, AD, BC, BD, CD	[2; 1, 1, 1, 1]	$\left(\frac{1}{4}, \frac{1}{4}, \frac{1}{4}, \frac{1}{4}\right)$	$\left(\frac{1}{4}, \frac{1}{4}, \frac{1}{4}, \frac{1}{4}\right)$	$\left(\frac{3}{8}, \frac{3}{8}, \frac{3}{8}, \frac{3}{8}\right)$	$3p - 6p^2 + 3p^3$	$M_{4,2}$, improper
(j)	4	AB, ACD	[5; 3, 2, 1, 1]	$\left(\frac{7}{12}, \frac{3}{12}, \frac{1}{12}, \frac{1}{12}\right)$	$\left(\frac{5}{10}, \frac{3}{10}, \frac{1}{10}, \frac{1}{10}\right)$	$\left(\frac{5}{8}, \frac{3}{8}, \frac{1}{8}, \frac{1}{8}\right)$	$p + p^2 - p^3$ $p - p^3$ $p^2 - p^3$	$B_1 \otimes (B_1 \oplus B_2)$, veto
(j*)	4	A, BC, BD	[3; 3, 2, 1, 1]	$\left(\frac{7}{12}, \frac{3}{12}, \frac{1}{12}, \frac{1}{12}\right)$	$\left(\frac{5}{10}, \frac{3}{10}, \frac{1}{10}, \frac{1}{10}\right)$	$\left(\frac{5}{8}, \frac{3}{8}, \frac{1}{8}, \frac{1}{8}\right)$	$1 - 2p^2 + p^3$ $2p - 3p^2 + p^3$ $p - 2p^2 + p^3$	$B_1 \oplus (B_1 \otimes B_2^*)$, improper
(k)	4	AB, ACD, BCD	[4; 2, 2, 1, 1]	$\left(\frac{1}{3}, \frac{1}{3}, \frac{1}{6}, \frac{1}{6}\right)$	$\left(\frac{1}{3}, \frac{1}{3}, \frac{1}{6}, \frac{1}{6}\right)$	$\left(\frac{1}{2}, \frac{1}{2}, \frac{1}{4}, \frac{1}{4}\right)$	$p + p^2 - 2p^3$ $2p^2 - 2p^3$	$M_3(B_1, B_1, B_2)$
(k*)	4	AB, AC, AD, BC, BD	[3; 2, 2, 1, 1]	$\left(\frac{1}{3}, \frac{1}{3}, \frac{1}{6}, \frac{1}{6}\right)$	$\left(\frac{1}{3}, \frac{1}{3}, \frac{1}{6}, \frac{1}{6}\right)$	$\left(\frac{1}{2}, \frac{1}{2}, \frac{1}{4}, \frac{1}{4}\right)$	$3p - 5p^2 + 2p^3$ $2p - 4p^2 + 2p^3$	$M_3(B_1, B_1, B_2^*)$, improper
(l)	4	AB, AC, BCD	[5; 3, 2, 2, 1]	$\left(\frac{5}{12}, \frac{3}{12}, \frac{3}{12}, \frac{1}{12}\right)$	$\left(\frac{5}{12}, \frac{3}{12}, \frac{3}{12}, \frac{1}{12}\right)$	$\left(\frac{5}{8}, \frac{3}{8}, \frac{3}{8}, \frac{1}{8}\right)$	$2p - p^2 - p^3$ $p - p^3$ $p^2 - p^3$	
(l*)	4	AB, AC, AD, BC	[4; 3, 2, 2, 1]	$\left(\frac{5}{12}, \frac{3}{12}, \frac{3}{12}, \frac{1}{12}\right)$	$\left(\frac{5}{12}, \frac{3}{12}, \frac{3}{12}, \frac{1}{12}\right)$	$\left(\frac{5}{8}, \frac{3}{8}, \frac{3}{8}, \frac{1}{8}\right)$	$3p - 4p^2 + p^3$ $2p - 3p^2 + p^3$ $p - 2p^2 + p^3$	improper
(m)	4	AB, AC, AD	[4; 3, 1, 1, 1]	$\left(\frac{9}{12}, \frac{1}{12}, \frac{1}{12}, \frac{1}{12}\right)$	$\left(\frac{7}{10}, \frac{1}{10}, \frac{1}{10}, \frac{1}{10}\right)$	$\left(\frac{7}{8}, \frac{1}{8}, \frac{1}{8}, \frac{1}{8}\right)$	$3p - 3p^2 + p^3$ $p - 2p^2 + p^3$	$B_1 \otimes B_3^*$, veto
(m*)	4	A, BCD	[3; 3, 1, 1, 1]	$\left(\frac{9}{12}, \frac{1}{12}, \frac{1}{12}, \frac{1}{12}\right)$	$\left(\frac{7}{10}, \frac{1}{10}, \frac{1}{10}, \frac{1}{10}\right)$	$\left(\frac{7}{8}, \frac{1}{8}, \frac{1}{8}, \frac{1}{8}\right)$	$1 - p^3$ $p^2 - p^3$	$B_1 \oplus B_3$, improper

Table 3 (*continued*)

Reference letter	Number of players	$\mathscr{W}^m$	Weighted voting representation	ϕ	β	β'	$\pi_i(p)$'s	Remarks
(n)	4	AB, AC, AD, BCD	[3; 2, 1, 1, 1]	$\left(\frac{1}{2}, \frac{1}{6}, \frac{1}{6}, \frac{1}{6}\right)$	$\left(\frac{1}{2}, \frac{1}{6}, \frac{1}{6}, \frac{1}{6}\right)$	$\left(\frac{3}{4}, \frac{1}{4}, \frac{1}{4}, \frac{1}{4}\right)$	$3p - 3p^2$ $p - p^2$	self-dual, apex game
(o)	4	AB, CD	none	$\left(\frac{1}{4}, \frac{1}{4}, \frac{1}{4}, \frac{1}{4}\right)$	$\left(\frac{1}{4}, \frac{1}{4}, \frac{1}{4}, \frac{1}{4}\right)$.	$\left(\frac{3}{8}, \frac{3}{8}, \frac{3}{8}, \frac{3}{8}\right)$	$p - p^3$	$B_2 \oplus B_2$, improper
(o*)	4	AC, AD, BC, BD	none	$\left(\frac{1}{4}, \frac{1}{4}, \frac{1}{4}, \frac{1}{4}\right)$	$\left(\frac{1}{4}, \frac{1}{4}, \frac{1}{4}, \frac{1}{4}\right)$	$\left(\frac{3}{8}, \frac{3}{8}, \frac{3}{8}, \frac{3}{8}\right)$	$2p - 3p^2 + p^3$	$B_2^* \otimes B_2^*$, improper
(p)	4	AB, BC, CD	none	$\left(\frac{1}{6}, \frac{1}{3}, \frac{1}{3}, \frac{1}{6}\right)$	$\left(\frac{1}{6}, \frac{1}{3}, \frac{1}{3}, \frac{1}{6}\right)$	$\left(\frac{1}{4}, \frac{1}{2}, \frac{1}{2}, \frac{1}{4}\right)$	$2p - 2p^2$ $p - p^2$	Γ, improper equivalent to its dual

Reference letter	Number of players	$\mathscr{W}^m$	Weighted Voting Representation	ϕ	β	β'	$\pi_i(p)$'s	Remarks

nice relation between the compound representations of G and G^*, as seen in (j) and (j*), or (k) and (k*). Finally, you might like to check that if $\pi_i(p)$ is the power polynomial for player i in G, then the power polynomial for i in G^* is equal to $\pi_i(1 - p)$.

Solutions to Selected Exercises

Section 1.1

1. a) $\mathscr{W} = \{AB, AC, BC, ABC, ABD, ACD, BCD, ABCD\}$
   $\mathscr{W}^m = \{AB, AC, BC\}$
   b) $\mathscr{W}^m = \{A\}$
   c) $\mathscr{W} = \{AB, ABC, ABD, ACD, ABCD\}$
   $\mathscr{W}^m = \{AB, ACD\}$
   d) $\mathscr{W}^m = \{ABC, ADEF, BCDEF\}$
   e) $\mathscr{W}^m = \{ABDE, ABDF, ABEF, ACDE, ACDF, ACEF, BCDE, BCDF, BCEF\}$
   f) $\mathscr{W}^m = \{AB, AC, BC, DE, DF, EF\}$

2. a) $B_2 \oplus B_2$ b) $[1; 1, 1] \otimes [1; 1, 1]$. See Appendix

3. a) $[4; 2, 2, 1, 1]$ b) $[6; 1, 1, 1, 1, 1, 1]$ c) $[8; 2, 2, 2, 2, 1]$
   d) See Exercise 7 e) $[3; 3, 1, 1]$ f) $[5; 3, 2, 2, 1]$

4. a) A four-person coalition wins if it is split among the three subgames as $2 - 2 - 0$, loses if it is split $3 - 1 - 0$ or $2 - 1 - 1$.

5. $M_1 \otimes M_{101} \otimes M_{435}$. The "101" is because of the Vice-President.

7. a) Note that in the game (i) the only winning coalitions are AB, AC, ABC.
   b) (iii) is equivalent to (vi): "B" in (iii) corresponds to "D" in (vi).
   (ii) is equivalent to (iv).
   (i) is equivalent to (v): "A" in (i) corresponds to "C" in (v).

8. a) All coalitions of two or more players.
   b) Any nonempty coalition.
   c) AC, BD, BC, etc.

9. c) M_5 For others, see Appendix.

11. Find disjoint winning coalitions.

12. $k \le \frac{n}{2}$.

Section 1.2

13. a) $\phi = (1, 0, 0, 0) = \beta$
    b) This is game (j) in the Appendix.
    c) $4\underline{2}111$ $2\underline{4}111$ $21\underline{4}11$ $211\underline{4}1$ $211\underline{1}4$
    $4\underline{1}211$ $1\underline{4}211$ $12\underline{4}11$ $121\underline{4}1$ $121\underline{1}4$
    $4\underline{1}121$ $1\underline{4}121$ $11\underline{4}21$ $112\underline{4}1$ $112\underline{1}4$
    $4\underline{1}112$ $1\underline{4}112$ $11\underline{4}12$ $111\underline{4}2$ $111\underline{2}4$
    $\phi = (\frac{6}{10}, \frac{1}{10}, \frac{1}{10}, \frac{1}{10}, \frac{1}{10})$

Types of winning coalition	Number of ways	Number of swings for 4	2	1
$\underline{42}$	1	1	1	
$\underline{41}$	3	3		3
$\underline{4}21$	3	3		
$\underline{4}11$	3	3		
$\underline{4}211$	3	3		
$\underline{4}111$	1	1		
$\underline{2111}$	1		1	3
42111	1			
		14	2	6

$\beta = (\frac{7}{11}, \frac{1}{11}, \frac{1}{11}, \frac{1}{11}, \frac{1}{11})$

d) $\phi = (\frac{22}{60}, \frac{17}{60}, \frac{12}{60}, \frac{7}{60}, \frac{2}{60})$, $\beta = (\frac{9}{25}, \frac{7}{25}, \frac{5}{25}, \frac{3}{25}, \frac{1}{25})$
This one takes a while.

15. ϕ and β are equal, and in the same proportion as the players' weights.

16. a) $\phi = (\frac{1}{2}, \frac{1}{6}, \frac{1}{6}, \frac{1}{6}) = \beta$
b) This game is equivalent to 13c
c) ϕ gives $\frac{m-1}{m+1}$ to the apex player, $\frac{2}{m(m+1)}$ to each minor player.
β is harder.

17. c) For the game in Section 1.1, Exercise 2a, the winning coalitions remain invariant under each of the permutations

$$\begin{array}{lll} A \to B & A \to C & A \to D \\ B \to A & B \to D & B \to C \\ C \to D & C \to A & C \to B \\ D \to C & D \to B & D \to A \end{array}$$

The same permutations work for 2b.

18. (i) and (v) are clear. For (iii) note that i is a dummy if and only if he never pivots or swings. For (iv) note that if $w_i > w_j$, then i will pivot or swing in any situation in which j would, and maybe a few more. (ii) seems clear, but needs care if you want to write it out formally.

20. For ϕ, note that a "b" can pivot only if he is preceded by all 5As and exactly 3bs. This can happen in $\binom{8}{3} = \frac{8 \cdot 7 \cdot 6}{3 \cdot 2 \cdot 1} = 56$ ways. For all other $3003 - 56 = 2947$ orderings, it is an A who pivots. ϕ gives each A approximately 0.196, each b approximately 0.002.

For β, the winning coalitions look like

$$\underline{A}\ \underline{A}\ \underline{A}\ \underline{A}\ \underline{A}\ \underline{b}\ \underline{b}\ \underline{b}\ \underline{b}$$
$$\underline{A}\ \underline{A}\ \underline{A}\ \underline{A}\ \underline{A}\ b\ b\ b\ b\ b$$
$$\cdots$$
$$\underline{A}\ \underline{A}\ \underline{A}\ \underline{A}\ \underline{A}\ b\ b\ b\ b\ b\ b\ b\ b\ b\ b.$$

The As swing $5[\binom{10}{4} + \binom{10}{5} + \binom{10}{6} + \cdots + \binom{10}{10}] = 4240$ times.
The bs swing $4[\binom{10}{4}] = 840$ times.
β gives each A approximately 0.167, each b approximately 0.017. In other words, β gives the nonpermanent members *eight times* as much power as ϕ gives them.

21. β: The only winning coalitions with swings are

$\underline{AAbb}$	$3 \cdot 6 = 18$ ways	As have 78 swings
$\underline{AAAb}$	$1 \cdot 4 = 4$ ways	bs have 40 swings
$\underline{AA}bbb$	$3 \cdot 4 = 12$ ways	Each A has 26 swings
$\underline{AA}bbbb$	$3 \cdot 1 = 3$ ways	Each b has 10 swings
		Ratio is $26 : 10$ or $2.60 : 1$.

ϕ: of the 35 district orderings, As pivot in 25, bs in 10.
Ratio is $\frac{25}{3} : \frac{10}{4}$ or $3.33 : 1$.

22. a) $\underline{a}\,\underline{b}\,\underline{b}\,\underline{c}\,\underline{c}\,\underline{c}$ $\quad \underline{a}\,\underline{b}\,\underline{b}\,c\,c\,c\,c\,c$ $\quad \underline{a}\,b\,b\,b\,c\,c\,c\,c$
$\underline{a}\,\underline{b}\,\underline{b}\,c\,c\,c\,c$ $\quad \underline{a}\,b\,b\,b\,\underline{c}\,\underline{c}\,\underline{c}$ $\quad \underline{a}\,b\,b\,b\,c\,c\,c\,c\,c$

b) For β, the swings are underlined above. You just need to write down in how many ways each kind of winning coalition can be formed. For example, the first kind can be formed in

$$\binom{1}{1}\binom{3}{2}\binom{5}{3} = 1 \cdot 3 \cdot 10 = 30 \text{ ways.}$$

You should find that a has 64 swings, the bs have 96, the cs have 120.
For ϕ, Shapley and Shubik [35] show that a has 192 pivots, bs have 162, cs have 150 (of the total 504 distinct orderings).

c) Winning coalitions are now of the form

$$\underline{a}\,\underline{b}\,\underline{b}\,\underline{c}\,\underline{c}\,\underline{c}\,\underline{c} \quad \underline{a}\,\underline{b}\,\underline{b}\,c\,c\,c\,c\,c \quad \underline{a}\,b\,b\,b\,\underline{c}\,\underline{c}\,\underline{c}\,\underline{c} \quad \underline{a}\,b\,b\,b\,c\,c\,c\,c\,c$$

I get that the swings are now 24, 36, 80 for a, bs, cs.
Pivots are now 142, 102, 260, for a, bs, cs.
The cs have profited.

24.
$$\phi = \left(\tfrac{24}{60}, \tfrac{14}{60}, \tfrac{9}{60}, \tfrac{9}{60}, \tfrac{4}{60}\right), \quad \beta = \left(\tfrac{5}{13}, \tfrac{3}{13}, \tfrac{2}{13}, \tfrac{2}{13}, \tfrac{1}{13}\right).$$

Yet C and D are not symmetric, since C is in a two-person winning coalition and D is not.

25. To calculate ϕ for G^*, write down the same orderings and underline the same pivots as for G, but now think of players joining a coalition starting from the *end* of the ordering and reading *backwards*. Clearly each player has the same number of pivots.
β and β' are harder.
S gives a swing for i in G if $i \in S, S \in \mathscr{W}, S - \{i\} \notin \mathscr{W}$.
T gives a swing for i in G^* if $i \in T, T \in \mathscr{W}^*, T - \{i\} \notin \mathscr{W}^*$
i.e., $i \in T, N - T \notin \mathscr{W}, N - (T - \{i\}) \in \mathscr{W}$.
Now consider the one-to-one correspondence $S \leftrightarrow N - (T - \{i\})(i \in S, i \in T)$.

26. For M_9,

$$\beta_i' = \frac{1}{2^8}\binom{8}{4} = \frac{70}{256}.$$

For $M_3(M_3, M_3, M_3)$, $\beta_i' = 64/256$.

27. When $k = 1$ or 5, $\beta_i' = 1/16$. When $k = 2$ or 4, $\beta_i' = 4/16$. When $k = 3$, $\beta_i' = 6/16$. For general n, k it's not hard to show that

$$\beta_i' = \frac{1}{2^{n-1}}\binom{n-1}{k-1}.$$

Section 1.3

28. a) $\phi_X = \frac{2}{3}$, $\beta_X = \frac{3}{4}$
b) $\phi_X = \frac{1}{2}$, $\beta_X = \frac{4}{7}$.
In (b) the large stockholder needs two small stockholders in order to win, whereas in (a) he only needs 1. Notice that he should *oppose* the dilution of stock from (a) to (b) if it should be proposed.

29. The interval of oceanic players has length $1 - x$. X will pivot if he joins between $1/2 - x$ and $1/2$, if $x < 1/2$.

30. Labels are

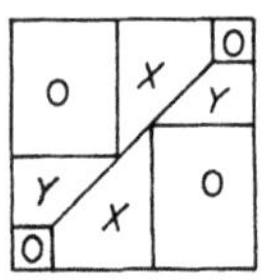

$\phi_X = 0.1125/0.36 = 0.3125$
$\phi_Y = 0.0525/0.36 = 0.146$

31. See Section 2.1.

32. a) X holds 4/10 of vote, 6/10 in ocean.
X will pivot if joins from $2/3 - 4/10$ to $6/10$, i.e., $8/30$ to $18/30$.
Hence, $\phi_X = \dfrac{(18/30 - 8/30)}{6/10} = 5/9$.
b) X holds 3/9, Y holds 2/9, ocean holds 4/9.
$\phi_X = \frac{1}{2}$; $\phi_Y = \frac{1}{4}$.

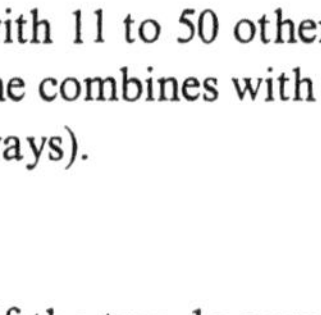

33. X swings when he combines with 11 to 50 others.
A minor player swings when he combines with x and 10 others ($\binom{59}{10}$ ways) or with 50 other minor players ($\binom{59}{50}$ ways).

Section 2.1

35. $\phi = (1/2, 1/6, 1/6, 1/6) = \beta$. If the two 1s combined, together they would get 1/3, which is no gain and no loss.

37.

	J	$\bar{J}$
B	$27\frac{1}{2}$, 35	4, 91
$\bar{B}$	45, 27	11, 36

Beloit would now organize if Janesville did, but at a serious loss of power.

38.

	J	$\bar{J}$
B	$27\frac{1}{2}$, 35	$19\frac{1}{2}$, 54
$\bar{B}$	38, 30	16, 36

The approximation is pretty good, I think.

39. Labor held 0.474 of the vote, Conservatives 0.466. If they form blocs, and we use the oceanic approximation, we get that $\phi_L = 0.321$ and $\phi_C = 0.188$. They are both hurt badly.

Section 2.2

41. a) Without quarreling, $\phi = (9/12, 1/12, 1/12, 1/12)$ and $\beta = (7/10, 1/10, 1/10, 1/10)$.
If A and B quarrel, $\phi^Q_{AB} = (3/5, 0, 1/5, 1/5)$ and $\beta^Q_{AB} = (6/10, 0, 2/10, 2/10)$, hurting A and B both.
If B and C quarrel, $\phi^Q_{BC} = (5/8, 1/8, 1/8, 1/8)$ and $\beta^Q_{BC} = (5/8, 1/8, 1/8, 1/8)$, helping B and C both.
b) $\phi = (1/6, 1/3, 1/3, 1/6) = \beta$, $\phi^Q_{BC} = (1/4, 1/4, 1/4, 1/4) = \beta^Q_{BC}$, $\phi^Q_{AB} = (0, 1/7, 4/7, 2/7) = \beta^Q_{AB}$, $\phi^Q_{BD} = (1/9, 1/3, 1/3, 2/9) = \beta^Q_{BD}$, $\phi^Q_{AD} = (1/8, 3/8, 3/8, 1/8) = \beta^Q_{AD}$.
Quarrelers get hurt except for B and D, where D gains and B remains the same.

42. $\phi = (7/12, 3/12, 1/12, 1/12)$, $\beta = (5/10, 3/10, 1/10, 1/10)$, $\phi^Q_{BC} = (3/7, 2/7, 1/7, 1/7)$, $\beta^Q_{BC} = (3/7, 2/7, 1/7, 1/7)$.

43. $\phi = (7/12, 3/12, 1/12, 1/12)$
$\phi^Q_{A\to C} = (4/12, 5/12, 2/12, 1/12)$, helps victim.
$\phi^Q_{C\to A} = (14/20, 5/20, 0, 1/20)$, helps victim.
$\phi^Q_{A\to B} = (2/7, 3/7, 1/7, 1/7)$, helps victim.
$\phi^Q_{B\to A} = (7/9, 0, 1/9, 1/9)$, helps victim.

44. The victim cannot lose any pivots.

46. See Brams [6, p. 182].

Section 2.3

49.

Swings in winning coalitions	Number of ways	Swings for 3	2	1
$\underline{3}\ \underline{2}$	X			
$\underline{3}\ \underline{1}\ \underline{1}$	6	6		12
$\underline{2}\ \underline{1}\ \underline{1}\ \underline{1}$	4		4	12
$\underline{3}\ \underline{2}\ 1$	X			
$\underline{3}\ 1\ 1\ 1$	4	4		
$\underline{2}\ 1\ 1\ 1\ 1$	1		1	
$\underline{3}\ 2\ 1\ 1$	X			
$\underline{3}\ 1\ 1\ 1\ 1$	1	1		
		11	5	24

Modified $\beta = (11/40, 5/40, 6/40, 6/40, 6/40, 6/40) = (0.275, 0.125, 0.150, 0.150, 0.150, 0.150)$. If an uncommitted voter joins X, we shall have $[5; 4, 2, 1, 1, 1]$. For this, one calculates a modified $\beta = (7/14, 1/14, 2/14, 2/14, 2/14) \approx (0.500, 0.071, 0.143, 0.143, 0.143)$. Our uncommitted voter would contribute 0.225 to X, which is more than 0.150, so β also tells us we should have a bandwagon effect.

50. You will find the figures here to be exactly the same as the text figures for $[5; 3, 2, 1, 1, 1, 1]$. Can you see why?

51. It is slightly in the stay uncommitted region, due to the inexactitude of the approximation.

52. a) $\dfrac{\frac{1}{2}(2259) - 1043}{\frac{1}{2}(2259) - 1067} = \dfrac{86.5}{62.5} \approx 1.38 < 1.78$. No bandwagon.

f) $\dfrac{\frac{1}{2}(1000) - 377}{\frac{1}{2}(1000) - 429} = \dfrac{123}{71} \approx 1.73$. No bandwagon, but close. The fact that there *was* means delegates could not sense the second decimal place!

55. There are $10 \cdot 9 \cdot 8 = 720$ possible orderings. The alliance hypotheses rule out 234 of them. Of the remaining 486 orderings, C has 294 pivotes, M has 42, W has 32, uncommitted voters 118, giving modified Shapley–Shubik indices

$$(0.605, 0.086, 0.066, 0.035, 0.035, 0.035, 0.035, 0.035, 0.035, 0.035).$$

If an uncommitted voter joined C we would have

$$[10; 8, 3, 2, 1, 1, 1, 1, 1, 1].$$

With the same alliance assumptions, the modified ϕ is now

$$(0.708, 0.057, 0.057, 0.030, 0.030, 0.030, 0.030, 0.030, 0.030).$$

Since $0.708 - 0.605 > 0.035$, C has a bandwagon.

Section 3.1

59. a) $G_1 \wedge G_2$ is game (g) in the Appendix.
$G_1 \vee G_2$ is game (g*) with AB and CD interchanged, so that $\phi = (1/12, 1/12, 5/12, 5/12)$ and $\beta' = (1/8, 1/8, 3/8, 3/8)$.
b) $G_1 \wedge G_2$ is game (h) in the Appendix.
$G_1 \vee G_2$ is a permuted version of Γ, game (p) in the Appendix, with $\phi = (1/6, 1/3, 1/6, 1/3)$ and $\beta' = (1/4, 1/2, 1/4, 1/2)$.

60. b) $G_1 \wedge G_2 = B_4$.
c) Since K satisfies axiom (vii), we must have $K(G_1) = (1/2, 1/2, 0, 0)$,

$$K(G_2) = (1/3, 0, 1/3, 1/3), \quad K(G_1 \wedge G_2) = (1/4, 1/4, 1/4, 1/4).$$

Hence

$$K(G) = K(G_1 \vee G_2) = (1/2, 1/2, 0, 0) + (1/3, 0, 1/3, 1/3) - (1/4, 1/4, 1/4, 1/4)$$
$$= (7/12, 3/12, 1/12, 1/12), \text{ which checks with } \phi.$$

d) Same kind of calculation, except now $K(G_1) = (1/2, 1/2, 0, 0)$, $K(G_2) = (1/4, 0, 1/4, 1/4)$, $K(G_1 \wedge G_2) = (1/8, 1/8, 1/8, 1/8)$.

Section 3.2

62. $\phi_A = \int_0^1 \pi_A(p)\,dp = \int_0^1 (p + p^2 - p^3)\,dp = 1/2 + 1/3 - 1/4 = 7/12$
$\beta'_A = \pi_A(1/2) = (1/2) + (1/2)^2 - (1/2)^3 = 5/8$, etc.

65. For a player in B_n, his vote makes a difference only if all other players vote yes, and this happens with probability p^{n-1}. So $\pi_i(p) = p^{n-1}$. Hence, $\phi_i = \int_0^1 p^{n-1}\,dp = 1/n$ and $\beta'_i = (1/2)^{n-1} = 1/2^{n-1}$ as they should be.

66. a) The probability that the group decision agrees with A is equal to Prob (A votes yes) · Prob (Group decides yes given that A votes yes) + Prob (A votes no) · Prob (Group decides no given that A votes no).
The last probability is 1, since without A the group cannot approve. The second probability is as in the square brackets of the expression for $\rho_A(p)$.

67. c) $\int_0^1 \rho_A(p)\,dp = \int_0^1 (1 - p + p^2 + p^3 - p^4)\,dp$
$= 1 - 1/2 + 1/3 + 1/4 - 1/5 = 53/60.$

68. It does not satisfy (v) and it also does not satisfy (iii), since even a dummy has a nonzero probability of the group agreeing with her.

Section 3.3

69. Call the players *aaaabccc*.

Then $\beta_a = 12/114$, $\beta_c = 11/114$, but $\phi_a = 39/420$, $\phi_c = 44/420$.

70. For A: $\int_0^1 p_B^2\,dp_B = 1/3$. For B or C: $(\int_0^1 p_A\,dp_A)(\int_0^1 p_B\,dp_B) = 1/2 \cdot 1/2 = 1/4$.

71. If A and B are homogeneous with C independent, one gets (3/4, 1/4, 1/6), which normalizes to (9/14, 3/14, 2/14). If you compare these carefully to ϕ and β for game (d) in the Appendix, you will find that the odd man out is hurt. Result is similar if B and C are homogeneous.

73. This would not be wise, for it would reduce the Western provinces' power to that of the Atlantic provinces. Specifically, ϕ would become 35.24% for Quebec and Ontario, and 3.69% for all other provinces. Alberta's power would *decline* from 4.17% to 3.69%.

References

1. Allingham, M. G. "Economic Power and the Values of Games," *Zeitschrift für Nationalökonomie*, *35* (1975), 293–299.
2. Aumann, R. J., and Shapley, L. S. *Values of Non-Atomic Games*, Princeton University Press, Princeton, New Jersey, 1974.
3. Bain, Richard, and Parris, Judith. *Convention Decisions and Voting Records*, Brookings Institution, Washington, D.C., 1973.
4. Banzhaf, J. F. "Weighted Voting Doesn't Work: A Mathematical Analysis," *Rutgers Law Review*, *19* (1965), 317–343.
5. Brams, S. J. *Game Theory and Politics*, Free Press, 1975.
6. Brams, S. J. *Paradoxes in Politics*, Free Press, 1976.

7. Brams, S. J., and Riker, W. H. "Models of Coalition Formation in Voting Bodies," *Mathematical Applications in Political Science VI* (Herndon and Bernd, eds.), pp. 79–124. University of Virginia Press, Charlottesville, 1972.
8. Canada, Constitutional Conference Proceedings, Victoria, B. C. June 14, 1971, Information Canada, Ottawa.
9. Caplow, Theodore, *Two Against One: Coalitions in Triads*, Prentice-Hall, Englewood Cliffs, New Jersey, 1968.
10. Coleman, James "Control of Collectivities and the Power of a Collectivity to Act," *Social Choice*, (Lieberman, ed.), pp. 277–287. Gordon and Breach, 1971.
11. Deegan, J., and Packel, E. "To the (Minimal) Victors Go the (Equally Divided) Spoils: a New Power Index," 1982. Chapter 10 in this volume.
12. Dubey, Pradeep. "Some Results on Values of Finite and Infinite Games," Technical Report, Center for Applied Mathematics, Cornell University, Ithaca, New York 14853, 1975.
13. Dubey, Pradeep. "On the Uniqueness of the Shapley Value," *International Journal of Game Theory*, *4* (1975), 131–140.
14. Dubey, P., and Shapley, L. S. "Mathematical Properties of the Banzhaf Power Index," *Mathematics of Operations Research*, *4* (1979), 99–131.
15. Ellsberg, Daniel. "The Theory and Practice of Blackmail," Rand Corporation, Santa Monica, 1959.
16. Kilgour, D. M. "A Shapley Value for Cooperative Games with Quarreling," *Game Theory as a Theory of Conflict Resolution* (Rapoport, ed.), pp. 193–206. D. Reidel, Boston, 1974.
17. Kleiner, Alex. "A Weighted Voting Model," *Mathematics Magazine*, *53* (1980), 28–32.
18. Lucas, W. F. "Measuring Power in Weighted Voting Systems," 1982. Chapter 9 in this volume.
19. Luce, R. D., and Raiffa, H. *Games and Decisions*, Wiley, New York, 1957.
20. Martin, Ralph G. *Ballots and Bandwagons*, Rand McNally, New York, 1964.
21. Miller, D. R. "A Shapley Value Analysis of the Proposed Canadian Constitutional Amendment Scheme," *Canadian Journal of Political Science*, *6* (1973), 140–143.
22. Milnor, J. W., and Shapley, L. S. "Values of Large Games II: Oceanic Games" RM2649, Rand Corporation, 1961. Reprinted in *Mathematics of Operations Research*, *3* (1978), 290–307.
23. Nagel, Jack. *The Descriptive Analysis of Power*, Yale University Press, New Haven, Connecticut, 1975.
24. Owen, Guillermo. "Political Games," *Naval Research Logistics Quarterly*, *18* (1971), 345–355.
25. Owen Guillermo. "Multilinear Extensions of Games," *Management Science*, *Series A*, *18* (1972), P64–P79.
26. Polsby, Nelson. "Decision-making at the National Conventions," *Western Political Quarterly*, *13* (1960), 609–619.
27. Rae, Douglas. "Decision Rules and Individual Values in Constitutional Choice," *American Political Science Review*, *63* (1969), 40–56.
28. Riker, W. H., and Ordeshook, P. *An Introduction to Positive Political Theory*, Prentice-Hall, Englewood Cliffs, New Jersey, 1973.
29. Roth, Alvin. "Utility Functions for Simple Games," *Journal of Economic Theory*, *16* (1977).
30. Schelling, Thomas. *The Strategy of Conflict*, Harvard University Press, Cambridge, Massachusetts, 1960.
31. Shapley, L. S. "Values of Large Games III: A Corporation with Two Large Stockholders," RM-2650-PR, Rand Corporation, 1961. Reprinted as part of Milnor and Shapley in *Mathematics of Operations Research*, *3* (1978), 290–307.

32. Shapley, L. S. "Simple Games: An Outline of the Descriptive Theory," *Behavioral Science*, *7* (1962), 59–66.
33. Shapley, L. S. "Compound Simple Games III: On Committees," RM-5438-PR, Rand Corporation, 1967.
34. Shapley, L. S., and Shapiro, N. Z. "Values of Large Games I: A Limit Theorem" RM-2648, Rand Corporation, 1960. Reprinted in *Mathematics of Operations Research*, *3* (1978), 1–9.
35. Shapley, L. S., and Shubik, M. "A Method for Evaluating the Distribution of Power in a Committee System," *American Political Science Review*, *48* (1954), 787–792.
36. Straffin, P. D. "The Power of Voting Blocs: An Example," *Mathematics Magazine*, *50* (1977), 22–24.
37. Straffin, P. D. "Homogeneity, Independence, and Power Indices," *Public Choice*, *30* (1977), 107–118.
38. Straffin, P. D. "The Bandwagon Curve," *American Journal of Political Science 21* (1977), 695–709.
39. Straffin, P. D. "Probability Models for Power Indices," *Game Theory and Political Science* (P. C. Ordeshook, ed.), pp. 477–510. New York University Press, 1978.
40. Straffin, P. D. "Using Integrals to Evaluate Voting Power," *The Two-Year College Mathematics Journal*, *10* (1979), 179–181.
41. Straffin, P. D. *Topics in the Theory of Voting*, Birkhauser, Boston, 1980. Chapter one.

Notes for the Instructor

Objectives. This module is appropriate for courses in finite mathematics, mathematical models in social science, quantitative political science, or game theory.

Prerequisites. Precalculus algebra, including a strong introduction to permutations, combinations, and binomial coefficients. The notation of set theory. Elementary probability in Sections 3.2 and 3.3.

Time. Four to six weeks. A shorter unit could be made of Sections 1.1, 1.2, all but the last part of Sections 2.1, 2.2, and just the first part of Section 2.3.

CHAPTER 12

Committee Decision Making

Peter Rice*

1. Introduction

This teaching module develops a normative spatial model of the committee decision-making process. Meant for use in the undergraduate classroom, it develops the requisite notions from Political Science from the beginning and uses only basic mathematics (cf. Appendix II). Three different suggestions for models are explained instead of presenting only one model. It is recommended that the students write a paper at the end of the module in which they describe, support, and criticize one of these models, or one of their own construction.

The module is designed to be used in a freshman mathematics course for liberal arts majors. In such a situation, the requisite mathematics (described in Appendix II) would have to be developed. The whole module, models plus mathematics, requires a full semester, but if used in mathematics modeling classes at an advanced level, less time is required. By skipping Section 9 and the concluding section, and presenting no background mathematics, the basic module can be completed in about seven class hours.

The only exercises included in the module are directly related to the models. Additional exercises on the mathematics that is presented should also be included. There are suggestions for extensive class discussion, and it has been found to be useful to promote such discussion. Modeling in the social sciences is not as cut and dried as in the physical sciences, and the discussion tends to illustrate the difficulties.

* Department of Mathematics, University of Georgia, Athens, Georgia 30601.

A novel aspect of this module is that it begins with an experiment, and the data from the experiment are used to motivate and test the module. It also forms the basis for a discussion of statistical testing and the role of the normative model.

2. Committee Decision-Making Experiment

A model in Political Science, like models in other areas, is based on situations that actually occur, and it is usually of great help to the modeler to have personal experience of such occurrences to develop his intuition. For this reason, and to provide data for testing the model we shall develop, this course begins with an experiment.

Experiments in the social sciences are generally much more difficult to design than experiments in the physical sciences because human beings are not consistent and are subject to many distracting influences, and human response is the subject of the social sciences. The experiment described here has several defects that will be discussed later. It is our experience that detailed discussion of experimental design can lead one to the conclusion that a good experiment is virtually impossible. Avoiding this problem, we plunge ahead.

The instructor will design a committee decision problem dealing with a budget based on real situations that have recently occurred locally. This is a good way of avoiding lack of interest or misunderstanding of the problem by the subjects. Ideally, the problem will deal with the allocation of all of a fixed amount of money to three agencies, projects, divisions of government, etc. The committee that will decide on the allocation will have four to six members (five is a good number) and each of the committee members will have a constituency (see Appendix I for an example) to which he is assumed to be responsible. Thus he has a framework within which to forge his attitudes. Without this framework, there is the danger that subjects will not hold to and argue from a specific position.

After studying the issues and constituency description, each subject will choose an allocation of the total budget to the three issues that he or she feels is ideal. The subjects are divided into separate committees and the committee session begins with the recording of these ideal allocations. After discussing the issues and various possible allocations, the committee decides on one allocation, which is also recorded.

Discussion. Is it more realistic to require a unanimous vote or a majority vote, or is it better to leave the decision rule unspecified?

Immediately after the committee has ended its work, each subject is required to evaluate a list of allocations, listing them in order from best to

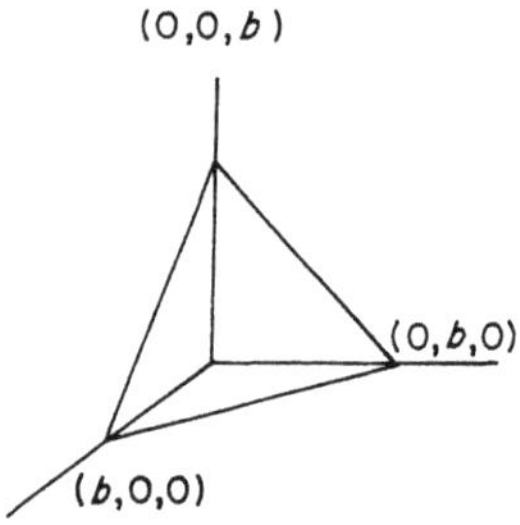

Figure 12.1

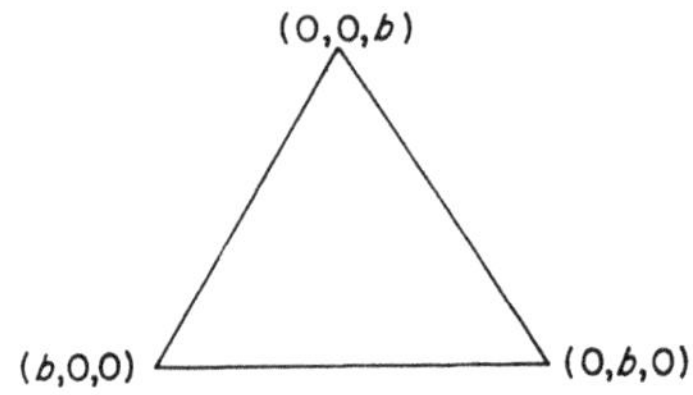

Figure 12.2

worst in the opinion of the individual, ties allowed. This list, made up by the instructor, should be representative of all possible allocations, both reasonable and unreasonable. (See Appendix I for an example.) The instructor will collect and tabulate all data for distribution to the class.

3. Geometric Representation of the Situation

If the issues are numbered 1, 2, and 3, then an allocation is a vector (x_1, x_2, x_3), where x_i is the dollar amount allocated to issue i. The space of such vectors is called the issue space. If the total budget is b, the budget constraint

$$x_1 + x_2 + x_3 = b$$

and the natural constraints $x_1, x_2, x_3 \geq 0$ define a triangular region in the issue space (Fig. 12.1). Thus, every feasible allocation is a point of this triangle (Fig. 12.2). It is easy to locate points in this triangle. The line l parallel to the side S opposite $(b, 0, 0)$, which has the property that the ratio of the distance between S and l to the distance between S and $(b, 0, 0,)$ is a/b, is the set of all points in the triangle with first coordinate a. Thus the point $(b/3, b/3, b/3)$ is located one third of the way up from each side (see Fig. 12.3). Each individual's ideal allocation is a point in this triangle, and the committee outcome is a point as well. This geometric representation is a helpful intuitive device, as well as being the basis for the model to be developed later. Such models are called *spatial* models.

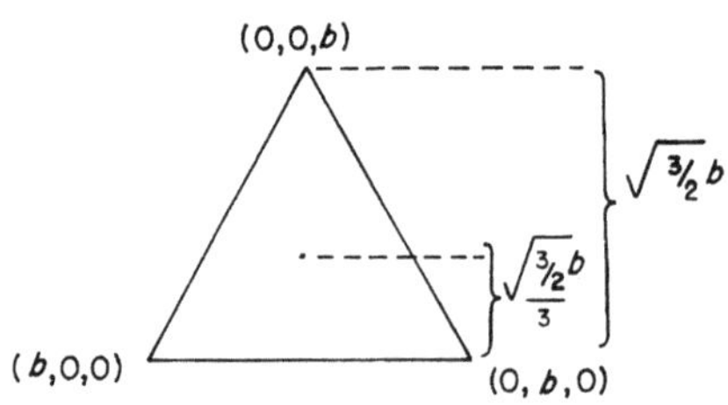

Figure 12.3

EXERCISE

1. For each committee that was formed in the experiment, plot the triangle, the ideal allocations, and the outcome.

Discussion. Are there any matters which influenced the committee outcome and cannot be represented geometrically?

4. Utility

Suppose that there are a list of alternatives $a_1, a_2, \cdots, a_n$ and an individual i must decide his preferences among them. We suppose it possible for individual i to decide between any two of them, thus being able to write down

$$a_j P_i a_k \quad (i \text{ prefers } a_j \text{ over } a_k)$$

$$a_j I_i a_k \quad (i \text{ is indifferent between } a_j \text{ and } a_k)$$

for every pair (a_j, a_k). Keep in mind, as an example, the list of allocations that were evaluated after the committee experiments.

We shall rewrite individual i's preferences using the symbol R_i meaning "not worse than." Thus,

$$a_j P_i a_k \quad \text{becomes} \quad a_j R_i a_k \quad \text{and not} \quad a_k R_i a_j,$$

$$a_j I_i a_k \quad \text{becomes} \quad a_j R_i a_k \quad \text{and} \quad a_k R_i a_j.$$

For the sake of intuition, you may think of P_i as $>$, I_i as $=$ and R_i as $\geq$.

It would be indeed strange if this individual wrote $a_j R_i a_k$, $a_k R_i a_l$, and $a_l R_i a_j$, unless he meant that he were indifferent between all of them, so we shall assume just that:

$$a_j R_i a_k,\ a_k R_i a_l,\ a_l R_i a_j \quad \text{implies} \quad a_j I_i a_k I_i a_l.$$

That is, we assume that strictly cyclic preferences do not exist. Then it is possible to arrange the alternatives in a sequence as they are preferred by individual i:

$$a_3 R_i a_{14} R_i a_7 R_i \cdots, \text{etc.}$$

EXERCISES

2. Prove that this sequential arrangement is always possible.

3. Give examples in another context of alternatives between which it is not possible to give a preference, even one of indifference.

Given a set of alternatives in the sequential order that individual i determines, attach a real number to each alternative, starting with the largest number at one end and using progressively smaller numbers, making sure that alternatives between which he is indifferent receive equal numbers. For example,

$$\begin{array}{c} a_4 R_i a_1 R_i a_2 R_i a_3 \quad \text{with} \quad a_1 I_i a_2 \\ \downarrow \quad \downarrow \quad \downarrow \quad \downarrow \\ -1 < 0 = 0 < \pi \end{array}$$

The numbers represent his preferences via the relationship

$$a_j R_i a_k \quad \text{if and only if (the number attached to } a_j) \leq \text{(the number attached to } a_k).$$

In choosing to use lower numbers to refer to higher preferences, we have made a purely arbitrary choice, which will be useful in this model. We will call this number the *loss* of the alternative. (If we had used larger numbers for higher preferences, we would call the number the *utility* of the alternative.)

The relationship between the alternatives and their losses can be expressed as a function, the *loss function* f_i:

$$f_i(a_1) = 0$$

$$f_i(a_2) = 0$$

$$f_i(a_3) = \pi$$

$$f_i(a_4) = -1$$

Returning to the list of allocations that were evaluated after the committee experiments, we choose one individual and suppose he ranked ten alternatives $a_1 R_i a_2 R_i \cdots R_i a_{10}$. We can form a loss function for this individual in many ways. (The reader will have noticed that the absolute size of the first number and the distance between adjacent numbers can be chosen freely.)

Hypothesis. *The function $d_i(a_j)$ = (Euclidian distance between a_j and i's ideal allocation in the issue space) is a loss function.*

This is an hypothesis because it may turn out to be supported or rejected by the data, the actual rankings by individuals in the experiment.

EXERCISE

4. For each individual i that participated in the experiment and each allocation a_j on the list that he evaluated, calculate $d_i(a_j)$.

To test the hypothesis, it is sufficient to compare the ranking of alternative allocations given by individual i with the ranking implied by the function d_i

for each individual. Most probably, most individual rankings will not agree with the hypothesis, and the hypothesis must be rejected. However, most probably the difference between the actual ranking and the distance ranking is small, so we would like to rescue the hypothesis.

The hypothesis is defective because it does not allow for human errors. It says that if $d_i(a_1) > d_i(a_2)$, then individual i will rank a_2 above a_1 *without fail*. But, if $d_i(a_1)$ and $d_i(a_2)$ are almost equal, it is easy to make a mistake and choose $a_1 P_i a_2$ or $a_1 I_i a_2$. What we need to do is understand how human error can be introduced into the ranking process, assume some error is normal, and compare the expected result with actual rankings. This is the general method of statistical testing.

It is easy to describe a method for ranking m alternatives. (Exercise: Do this.) We could assume that there is a small probability of making an error on each comparison of two alternatives and use the ranking method to count the probabilities of various mistakes. However, there is a problem in taking this approach: Not everyone can be expected to use the same method of ranking. What we need, and probably will not be able to find, is a process through which *everyone* goes in producing a final ranking. This problem faces everyone who attempts to produce mathematical models about human beings, and the usual solution is to make a reasonable approximation to the desired result and be satisfied with a greater margin of error. We shall do this by assuming that everyone checks their final ranking by running down the list, comparing each item to the one below it. When all comparisons check, the list is in final form. If the list contains m alternatives, then $M = m - 1$ comparison are made.

Hypothesis H_p. *In comparing two allocations, an individual will give the higher ranking to the allocation closer to his ideal allocation with probability p.*

The probability of making c "mistakes" is

$$B(M - c\colon M, p) = \binom{M}{M - c} p^{M-c}(1 - p)^c.$$

To count the number of "mistakes," we assume the ranking according to distance is correct. The number of "mistakes" in a ranking produced by an individual is the number of adjacent pairs on his list that are "out of order" according to the distance ranking.

EXERCISE

5. Count the number of mistakes made by each individual in the ranking experiment.

It remains to use the data to test H_p for some p. There is no good rule for choosing p, since it is the measure of human error in some situations, and different situations call for different errors. However, if the allocations that were ranked are well-spread out, $p = 0.9$ would be a high degree of accuracy and $p = 0.75$ would be reasonable. Remember that the individuals doing the ranking were not looking at the geometric representation, so geometric distance perception did not come into play. To accept H_p at a confidence level of 90% (a standard confidence level for experiments with human beings), each individual would have to have no more than D mistakes, where D is the largest number such that

$$\sum_{c=0}^{D} B(M - c\colon M, p) \leq 0.9.$$

EXERCISE

6. Calculate D for several values of p, finding a p for which H_p is confirmed at the 90% confidence level.

There are occasions when it is desirable to have a value of p, which measures the probability that individuals in this situation will use distance to measure loss, when comparing two allocations. We can either choose p ad hoc and confirm H_p with the data, or assume H_p is true for some p and use the data to calculate p, but the single body of data we have will not allow us to do both. Ideally, we should perform a separate experiment to calculate p, then accept to or reject H_p.

Discussion. If $d_i(a_1)$ are close together, the probability of a mistake is larger than if they are farther apart. Also, as a_1 and a_2 get farther away from the ideal allocation, the probability of mistake increases. Can these two ideas be used to design a better hypothesis? How would such an hypothesis be tested? How could an experiment to measure p directly be designed? If an individual feels more strongly on one issue than on the others, his sense of loss for divergence on that issue would be more than for others, and d_i would not measure loss. How could this be tested? It may be that the role an individual plays affects his evaluation of allocations in ways other than setting the ideal point. Is there such a bias in the data? How would one test for it?

5. Remarks on Models in Political Science

A model is any mechanism which, given input data, generates an outcome of some sort. We are working on the problem of designing a model that generates the outcome of committee deliberations when the ideal allocations of the committee members are given. It is appropriate to ask what such a model is good for, as the answer may well help form the model itself. A *predictive* model, as the name implies, predicts actual outcomes. Such a model stands or falls on its statistical reliability. A *normative* model generates the outcome that ought to occur, for whatever reasons, and is judged by its acceptability. For example, consider the housewife's regular trips to the grocer. A predictive model would generate a schedule of times for these trips based on such information as the number of consumers of food in the home, the weather, the prices of food on given days, etc. A normative model would use the same information to tell the housewife when she should go to the grocer. The predictive model is accurate or it is not, while accuracy has nothing to do with the normative model. The latter, however, is good or bad depending on whether the average housewife would agree with its outcome, were she fully informed on the problem.

Predictive mathematical models in the social sciences are difficult to build, but there are many normative models. We should find it difficult indeed to construct a predictive model of the committee decision process, so we shall work on a normative model. The criterion for acceptance of a normative model given above requires us to give careful consideration to several factors. First, the internal machinery that computes the outcome must conform to our idea of the way outcomes "should" be computed. This rules out such things as black boxes, astrology, dictatorship, and the like. It also recognizes that human beings have generally agreed on some aspects of decision making, and these must be ingredients of any successful model. Second, the model must employ the actual preferences of individuals involved in the committee, and not assume that they have some common ideal loss function, for it is the clash of actual preferences that defines the problem. Third, the model, since it deals with actually occurring situations, should predict actual outcomes in sufficiently many cases to convince the critical reader that it does not vary greatly from reality. This is not a statistical test, but a recognition of the fact that human beings consider what they do to be substantially correct, subject only to momentary irrationalities and occasional misunderstandings. To pass the acceptability test, the normative model must acknowledge this attitude.

In the end, we should recognize that the real value of a normative model is that, once a successful model exists, we shall understand much better the committee decision process. We hardly expect our model to replace committees.

We describe below three models, and it is the job of the class to choose one, combine them in some way, or construct an entirely different model, then use the data collected in the experiment to evaluate it.

6. The Barycenter Model

There are n issues to which allocations are to be made, so an allocation is a vector $P = (x_1, \cdots, x_n)$. There are m individuals on the committee with

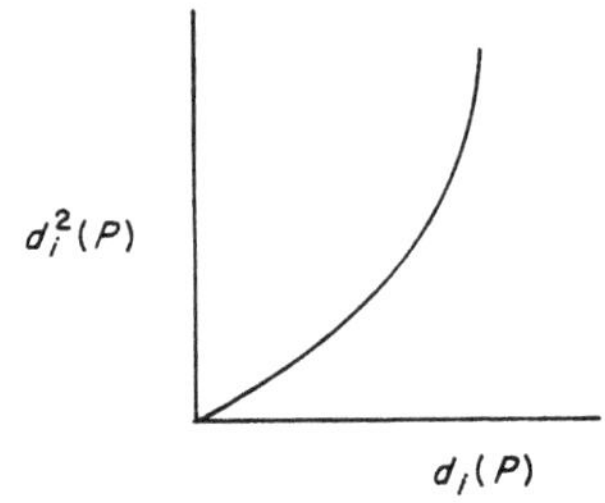

Figure 12.4

corresponding ideal allocations $P_i = (a_{i1}, \cdots, a_{in})$, $i = 1, \cdots, m$. Assuming H_p is true, each individual measures loss with the distance function

$$d_i(P) = \sqrt{(x_1 - a_{i1})^2 + (x_2 - a_{i2})^2 + \cdots + (x_n - a_{in})^2}.$$

We form the committee loss function

$$f(P) = d_1^2(P) + d_2^2(P) + \cdots + d_m^2(P).$$

This function measures the total dissatisfaction of the committee with the allocation P. Each individual is represented with equal weight in the function, so it is fair, and $d_i(P)$ is the actual loss function of individual i. In using $d_i^2(P)$ instead of $d_i(P)$, we introduce the idea that an individual's rate of increase of loss increases with distance (see Fig. 12.4). Up to this point, the actual value of the loss function has no meaning, but the function f adds the values of the individual loss functions d_i^2, and thereby compares the actual values. Thus, the values of the d_i^2 take on interpersonal meanings. For example, consider $m = 2$ and a point P, which is nearer to P_1 than P_2. A small change in P makes a smaller change in $d_1^2(P)$ than it does in $d_2^2(P)$, signifying that individual 2 is more sensitive to small changes of P than is individual 1. The attitudes of these two individuals are compared in the sum $f(P) = d_1^2(P) + d_2^2(P)$. This *interpersonal comparison of utility* is considered problematic by many people.

As long as each individual is fairly represented in f, it represents the attitude of the committee as a whole toward P, and it is reasonable to assume that the committee would choose the allocation P, which minimizes it.

We calculate the partials of f with respect to the variables x_j and set them equal to zero. Since f is differentiable and nonnegative on the feasible set, it must have a minimum value at the point which satisfies those equations.

$$\frac{\partial f}{\partial x_j} = 2(x_j - a_{1j}) + 2(x_j - a_{2j}) + \cdots + 2(x_j - a_{mj}) = 0,$$

$$mx_j = a_{1j} + a_{2j} + \cdots + a_{mj},$$

$$x_j = \frac{1}{m}\sum_{i=1}^{m} a_{ij},$$

$$\bar{P} = (x_1, \cdots, x_j) = \frac{1}{m}\sum_{i=1}^{m}(a_{i1}, \cdots, a_{in}) = \frac{1}{m}\sum_{i=1}^{m} P_i.$$

Note that if $P_1, \cdots, P_m$ satisfy the budget constraint $a_{i1} + \cdots + a_{in} = b$, then so does $\bar{P}$. The point $\bar{P}$, at which f has its minimum value, is called the *barycenter* (center of mass) of the set $\{P_1, \cdots, P_m\}$. The barycenter model selects $\bar{P}$ as the outcome allocation of the committee deliberations.

The barycenter may be justified on other grounds as well. $\bar{P} = [\sum_{i=1}^{m} P_i]/m$ is the average of the ideal allocations. When two people decide on a division of money, there is a strong tendency to split it equally. When finding a compromise between conflicting claims or desires, it is common to "split the difference." In both of these cases, the average of the two ideal positions is the compromise. Conceivably, this tendency to view the average as a fair compromise could be extended to situations where more than two people are involved. However, interpersonal comparisons of utility is still involved in this analysis, in as much as it is assumed that the dollar figures of the ideal allocations represent personal utility on an issue, and these are added.

EXERCISE

7. Calculate the barycenters for the experimental data.

Discussion. How does the barycenter fit the data? How should it fit the data to be acceptable? How well does this model reflect the actual working of a committee? Is the interpersonal comparison of utility justifiable?

7. The Pareto Model

Let $P_1, \cdots, P_m$ be the ideal points as before. A point P is *Pareto optimal* if there does not exist a point Q such that QR_iP for all $i = 1, \cdots, m$ and QR_iP for at least one i. Thus, P is Pareto optimal if there is no point that is "better" for at least one individual and is "worse" for none.

Theorem. *If loss is measured by distance, then the set of Pareto optimal points is the convex hull of* $P_1, \cdots, P_m$.

PROOF. Let H be the convex hull and let $P \notin H$. Let Q be the point on the boundary of H, which is closest to P, and let T be the hyperplane perpendicular to PQ at Q. It is easy to see that H lies on one side of T and P lies on the other. For, if $R \in H$ lies on the same side of T as P, there must be a point R' on the line joining Q and R which is closer to P than Q, and $R' \in H$

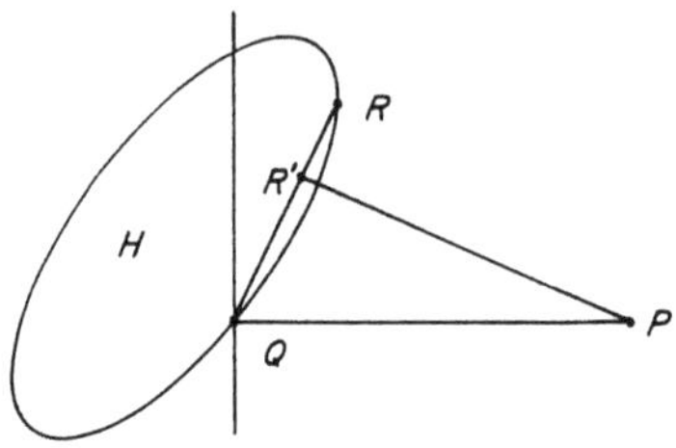

Figure 12.5

because H is convex. Figure 12.5 shows this situation for $n = 2$, and this picture is valid for any n. It follows that Q is closer to P_i than P for each i, so P is not Pareto optimal. Conversely, suppose P is not Pareto optimal. Then there is a point Q, which is at least as close as P to P_i, $i = 1, \cdots, m$ and closer to at least one P_i. Let T be the hyperplane, which is the perpendicular bisector of PQ. All points of H must lie on the same side of T as Q, while P is on the other side, so $P \notin H$. □

The Pareto model demands that the outcome be Pareto optimal. Unfortunately, there are many such points and the model does not distinguish between them. On the other hand, this model does not require any interpersonal comparison of utility. Also, this model extends the idea of the average. The points in the convex hull H of the points $P_1, \cdots, P_m$ are the weighted averages (convex combinations) of the points $P_1, \cdots, P_n$: $P \in H$ if and only if

$$P = \mu_1 P_1 + \mu_2 P_2 + \cdots + \mu_m P_m, \mu_1 + \cdots + \mu_m = 1, \mu_i \geq 0.$$

This means that the barycenter is Pareto optimal, and also shows that each Pareto optimal point satisfies the budget constraint if $P_1, \cdots, P_m$ do.

EXERCISE

8. Were the experimental outcomes Pareto optimal?

Discussion. Discuss and evaluate this model.

8. The Core Model

The core is a concept from game theory. Interpreted in the context of the committee decision problem, it is the set of points that have the property that no effective coalition can do better for each of its members. To be exact, let $P_1, \cdots, P_m$ be the ideal allocations. An effective coalition is any set of r of these points, $m/2 < r \leq m$. When r is as small as possible in this range, it is a simple majority S of m. When $r = m$, the only effective coalition is the whole committee. A point is in the *r-core* if it is Pareto optimal for each effective coalition of size r, loss being measured by distance. Let $C(r)$ be the r-core. Some theorems that are left for the student to prove are the following.

Theorem. $C(r) \subset C(r + 1)$ *for all* $r \leq m - 1$.

Theorem. $C(r)$ *may be empty.*

Theorem. *For four points in the plane* ($m = 4$, $n = 3$ *with budget constraint*) $C(3)$ *is always nonempty.*

The student may be interested in developing other theorems.

In this model, the outcome is a point in $C(s)$, where s is a simple majority of m. If $C(s)$ is empty, then it is in $C(s + 1)$, etc.

EXERCISE

9. Compare this model against the data.

Discussion. Does this model involve interpersonal comparison of utility? How does its acceptability compare with the other two models?

9. General Discussion

At this point the class should discuss the three models and choose one that seems best, or develop one of their own. It is advisable to require each one to write a paper in which the chosen model is explained, its acceptability argued, and its shortcomings pointed out.

This is also a good time to discuss the experiment in detail, pointing out its faults and attempting to design a better one. For example, the idea of a simulation experiment, where subjects play roles, should be compared with a simple money payoff experiment where the subject receives a sum of money equal to his loss (measured by distance). Which one would be more faithful to a real committee situation? Also, time restrictions, the possibility of making deals outside of the committee, effects of the classroom situation on individual behavior, and whether it would be wise to repeat the experiment after building the model should be discussed.

10. The Arrow Theorem

Given a society of m individuals, a list of independent alternatives $a_1, \cdots, a_n$, and a preference ranking R_i for each individual, we ask if there is any method of determining a preference ranking R over the alternatives for the whole society. Of course there are such rankings, such as allowing $R = R_1$, which makes individual 1 a dictator. More to the point, we would like to know if there is a "fair" way of choosing R.

One possibility would be to let the whole society sit as a committee and choose one, say a_1, as the best. Then, discarding a_1 from the list, they could choose the second best, say a_2, and proceeding in this fashion, make a list

$$a_1, a_2, a_3, \cdots, a_n,$$

which would define R:

$$a_1 R a_2 R a_3 \cdots R a_n.$$

With a good model of the committee at hand, we could save them the trouble of sitting in the committee, as our model would tell us how to compute R directly from $R_1, R_2, \cdots, R_n$. The question still remains, is this R "fair"?

To answer this question, we pose some conditions, which any good R should satisfy. Let X be the set of alternatives

$$X = \{a_1, a_2, \cdots, a_n\},$$

and let $\mathscr{R}$ be the set of all preference relations on X, and $\mathscr{R}^n = \mathscr{R} x \mathscr{R} x \cdots x \mathscr{R}$. A function

$$f: \mathscr{R}^n \to \mathscr{R}$$

is an *Arrowian social welfare function* if it satisfies these three conditions.

The Pareto Principal. Let $f(R_1, \cdots, R_n) = R$. For any $x, y \in X$, if $x R_i y$ for each i, then $x R y$.

Independence of Irrelevant Alternatives. Let $f(R_1, \cdots, R_n) = R, f(R'_1, \cdots, R'_n) = R'$, and let S be any subset of X. If R_i and R'_i agree on S for all i ($x R_i y$ iff $x R'_i y$ for all $x, y \in S$, all i), then R and R' agree on S.

Nondictatorship. There does not exist an i such that for all $(R_1, \cdots, R_n)$, if xR_iy, then xRy.

One other axiom that is implicit here but is usually stated separately is that f must be defined on all of $\mathscr{R}^n$.

The Pareto principal says that if each individual agrees that x is not worse than y, then the social welfare function must respect this unanimity. To exemplify the axiom of independence of irrelevant alternatives, let a group be considering the altenatives a, b, c, and d. Suppose that each individual has ranked these alternatives with R_i, and the social welfare function, putting these rankings together, says that aRb. If now some of the individuals change their minds, getting new preferences R_i', but their attitude to the pair a and b do not change, then the axiom says that the social welfare function gives $aR'b$, even though it may have changed on other pairs. Nondictatorship says that there is no dictator. There is a dictator if there is one individual whose preference is always adopted as the social preference rankings, regardless of how the situation might change. Arrow's general possibility theorem says that if there are at least two individuals and at least three alternatives, then there does not exist an Arrowian social welfare function. This means that, no matter how fair the committee precedure is, it must violate one of these axioms.

Discussion. Give concrete examples in which the axioms have simple meanings and discuss their desirability. What implications does this theorem have for the committee decision process?
(Note to the teacher: The proof of the theorem may be presented here if time allows. The requisite mathematical background has already been assumed. Three references to the proof are given in the notes.)

NOTE. Utility theory and Arrow's theorem are explained clearly and in detail in A. K. Sen., *Collective Choice and Social Welfare*, Holden-Day, 1970, in Peter C. Fishburn, *The Theory of Social Choice*, Princeton University Press, New Jersey, 1973, and in Jerome Rothenberg, *The Measurement of Social Welfare*, Prentice-Hall, Englewood Cliffs, 1961. The barycenter model is part of the folklore of Political Science and the core model is essentially the model developed by Charles R. Plott in *A Notion of Equilibrium and its Possibility under Majority Rule, American Economic Review*, 57 (1967), 787–806. For further reading in the general area, see Morris P. Fiorina, *Representatives, Roll Calls and Constituencies*, Lexington, D.C. Heath, 1974; James Buchanan and Gordon Tullock, *The Calculus of Consent*, University of Michigan Press, Ann Arbor, 1962; Albert Breton, *The Economic Theory of Representative Government*, Aldine, Chicago, 1973.

Appendix I: An Example of an Experiment

The City Council has established a committee consisting of five of its members to recommend the dispersal of $35,000 revenue-sharing funds. The council has received three requests totaling $130,000, which have been discussed in open meetings and in the newspapers.

Proposal 1. The city Bicycle Club proposes the construction of bicycle paths. It costs about $1000 per mile for bike paths and matching funds are available from the federal government, so $1000 buys two miles of paths. An 80-mile system would be ideal.

Pro. Because the city has so many narow streets, the paths are needed to get the cyclists off the street to relieve congestion and for safety. (Students, professors, and school children make up the bicycling community.) Present efforts to build paths are too little and too slow. We need them now.

Con. The need is obvious, but the Planning and Development Commission is applying for a federal grant that would pay for a system for the whole county. Since bike routes for school children have already been built near schools, the situation does not call for immediate action, and we should wait on the outcome of the grant application.

Proposal 2. Hope Haven, the city's only school for retarded children wants $50,000 to expand.

Pro. Hope Haven is financed by state, county, and city grants as well as by churches and the Community Chest. It offers education to mentally retarded children (mostly white) of parents who cannot afford private schools. There are children waiting to get in, and the school takes pride in its past record of success. The money requested would allow expansion to meet all present needs and prepare for future needs.

Con. If this money is given to Hope Haven now, it would have to be followed by equivalent sums each year since most of it would go for salaries. They should be approaching the agencies now providing support with a request of long-term funding, instead of the one-shot money revenue sharing can offer.

Proposal 3. The Kiddie Klub day care center requests $40,000 to improve facilities.

Pro. Mrs. Smith and Mrs. Jones have given of themselves without thought of profit to provide day care for children of working mothers who cannot afford the more expensive day care offered by other centers. However, they are in violation of state laws because of crowded conditions and improper facilities. If they do not correct these conditions soon, they will be forced to close.

Con. This appeal has been made to church groups and they have already responded with some help. It is likely that more help could be found without much trouble. Moreover, the ladies have not explored other sources of funding. For example, if parents are on welfare or in state job-training programs, the state will help to pay day-care costs for their children. Also, should tax money be used to support a private enterprise?

The Committee. Five city council members were appointed to the committee. Although a councilman is concerned with all matters affecting the city, he is particularly interested in the issues that affect his constituents.

Councilman	Age	Party	Constituency
1	32	Rep.	Middle and upper class older residential area.
2	45	Dem.	Predominantly black urban area.
3	58	Dem.	Middle and working class residential area and downtown business district.
4	56	Dem.	Middle class suburban area and student dormitories. (Students have a vote in local elections.)
5	68	Dem.	White working class residential area including rental apartments and factories

Allocation Evaluation

Name:
Ideal allocation: 1 2 3
Councilman: Committee:

Evaluate each of the following allocations, using the numbers from 1 = best possible to 10 = worst possible. If two allocations appear equally good (or bad), use the same number for both.

1	2	3	Rating
0	0	35,000	
5,000	20,000	10,000	
10,000	10,000	15,000	
25,000	5,000	5,000	
15,000	0	20,000	
5,000	10,000	20,000	
5,000	30,000	0	
15,000	15,000	5,000	
20,000	15,000	0	
20,000	5,000	10,000	

Committee Report

Committee:
Ideal allocations

	Allocation		
Councilman	1	2	3
1			
2			
3			
4			
5			
Agreed on allocation:	1	2	3

Appendix II: Mathematical Notes

The mathematics required in Section 2 is the basic geometry of R^n. Topics include representation of points by vectors, the representation of hyperplanes by linear equations, and the euclidian distance function. This may be restricted to R^3, if desired.

Section 3 requires background in several topics. The first is the idea of a partial order on a finite set. The understanding of the distance function in R^n (or R^3 if desired) comes next. Finally, statistics is used. For this, a knowledge of basic combinatorics, the binomial distribution and single tail hypothesis testing with confidence intervals, is sufficient.

The barycenter model in Section 5 uses calculus to find the minimum value of a differentiable function of several variables. If the students have no background in calculus and it is not desirable to introduce it, the proof may be skipped. A few pictures can convince the student of the idea of the theorem. This section also used the idea of a convex combination of a finite set of points. It is a good idea to discuss this in general, using it to coordinate the triangle $(b, 0, 0)$, $(0, b, 0)$, $(0, 0, b)$ introduced in Section 2.

In Section 6, the concept of a convex polytope is used. This may be developed in R^3, if desired. It is a good idea to develop the basic theory of convex polytopes before beginning Section 5.

Section 9 uses only basic set theory, including the cartesian product.

Notes for the Instructor

Objectives. To be used in a freshman "mathematics for liberal arts" course. Also suitable for part of a course on mathematical models in the social sciences.

Prerequisites. When used for freshmen, all requisite mathematics can be developed with a background of high school mathematics. See also Appendix I.

Remarks. Time required for total module and presentation of background mathematics: 30 h. Time required for shortened module without mathematics instructions: 7 h.

CHAPTER 13

Stochastic Difference Equations with Sociological Applications

Loren Cobb*

1. Difference Equation Models

For the sake of simplicity, all the variables in all of the examples given in these notes will refer to "the number of people of a certain type in a population with stationary age structure." Variables (e.g., X_5, Y_0, Z_t) will be written in capitals with a subscript indicating time (measured in years), and constants (e.g., a, b, v) will be written in lower case letters.

Suppose A_t = "the number of people in a particular age group of the population at time t." The condition stated above that the age structure be stationary means that:

$$A_{t+1} = A_t, \quad \text{for all } t.$$

That is, the total number of people in this age group does not change, although people move into and out of the age group every year. Stationarity for the entire age structure means that the size of each age category does not change over time.

Now suppose that R_t stands for the size of a (small) religious sect at time t. How can it grow? The results of an active missionary program in which a certain proportion (say "a") of the membership is successful in its recruiting a quota of one new member every year are described by the following equation (called a difference equation):

$$R_{t+1} = R_t + aR_t, \quad \text{for every year } t. \tag{1}$$

* Department of Biometry, Medical University of South Carolina, Charleston, South Carolina 29425.

Exercise

1. Assume that this sect was founded by 12 persons in year zero (i.e., that $R_0 = 12$). On a sheet of graph paper label time on the horizontal axis (from 0 to 20) and size on the vertical axis (0 to 1000). Use your calculator to compute R_t from Eq. (1) using $a = 0.15$ and $t = 0$–20. Graph those values on the graph paper. Repeat using $a = 0.2$ and $a = 0.25$.

Equation (1) describes the growth of R only in terms of the previous size of R, not directly in terms of time. In other words, one cannot calculate the values of R_t without first having calculated R_{t-1}, whose value itself cannot be calculated without R_{t-2}, etc., extending back in a long chain of calculations to R_0. In this case, however, it is possible to deduce an equation which eliminates the need for such a chain of calculations, as follows:

If Eq. (1) is correct, then

$$R_1 = (1 + a)R_0,$$

$$R_2 = (1 + a)R_1 = (1 + a)(1 + a)R_0 = (1 + a)^2 R_0.$$

Similarly,

$$R_3 = (1 + a)R_2 = (1 + a)(1 + a)^2 R_0 = (1 + a)^3 R_0.$$

Generalizing to an arbitrary time t, we have

Theorem 1. *If for all t, $R_{t+1} = R_t + aR_t$, then $R_t = (1 + a)^t R_0$.*

Theorem 1 provides an equation in closed form, as distinguished from the open form of Eq. (1), which describes the same growth process. Closed form equations for a surprisingly large array of dynamic processes can be found by first reducing their open-form equation to a variation on the theme of (1), which permits passage to the closed form. Even those complex processes that do not have a closed form can be studied with the technique used in Exercise 1.

Exercises

2. Verify that Theorem 1 works for any three points of the graph that you created for Exercise 1.

3. Now suppose that our little religious sect also suffers attrition, in that a constant proportion (say "b") of the total membership abandons their faith every year. Write down an appropriately modified version of Eq. (1), and deduce its closed form. What would the growth curve of R look like if b were greater than a? Make an illustrative graph with several values of a and b represented.

Let us now turn to an elementary model of crime, or more exactly, the number of criminals found in society, a variable we shall call C_t. Generalizing wildly, we note that the vast majority of new criminals are adolescent, and that the rate of attrition from the ranks of criminals is steady and relatively independent of the age of the criminal, with the result that there are very few elderly criminals. Therefore, let us say that every year a constant number of adolescents (say "a") embark on a career of crime, while at the same time a constant proportion (say "b") of all criminals adopt a more legal means of livelihood. The open equation for criminality is

$$C_{t+1} = C_t + a - bC_t, \quad \text{for all } t. \tag{2}$$

In the following paragraphs, we shall see that this model can be used to find answers to the following questions:

(1) When is the number of criminals constant?
(2) What is the effect on C_t of changes in a or b?

EXERCISE

4. Calculate and graph the process described by Eq. (2) for $t = 0$–10, using $a = 100$, $b = 0.2$, and $C_0 = 1000$. Repeat with $C_0 = 0$. What do you conclude about the behavior of C?

The apparent existence of a stationary point toward which the model of Eq. (2) moves regardless of its initial value can be confirmed analytically with ease. Recall that stationarity implies $C_{t+1} = C_t$. This condition is possible only if the net change in C_t is zero, that is $a\text{-}bC_t = 0$. But this equation is true only if $C_t = a/b$. Denoting this value with an asterisk, we conclude:

$$C^* = a/b \text{ is a stationary point for Eq. (2).}$$

Thus we see that the total number of criminals will remain constant only if it is exactly $C^* = a/b$, the ratio of the annual number of adolescents who become criminals to the annual rate of reformation of criminals.

Our next task in this section is to show that while the model of Eq. (2) superficially appears to differ from the model of Eq. (1) (the religious sect), they are actually of the same generic type. This fact will enable the deduction of a closed form for our little theory of crime.

The key step in this procedure is to examine the difference between C_t and its stationary point C^*. Let us denote this difference by X_t, so that

$$X_t = C_t - C^*, \quad \text{or} \quad C_t = X_t + C^*.$$

Substituting this last equality into Eq. (2), we find the following:

$$\begin{aligned} C_{t+1} &= C_t + a - bC_t, \\ (X_{t+1} + C^*) &= (X_t + C^*) + a - b(X_t + C^*), \\ X_{t+1} &= X_t + a - b(X_t + a/b), \quad (\text{recall: } C^* = a/b) \\ X_{t+1} &= X_t - bX_t. \end{aligned}$$

Observe that X_t follows an open equation of the type seen in Eq. (1). Therefore, we can use Theorem 1 to write down the appropriate closed form equation for X:

$$X_t = (1 - b)^t X_0.$$

Lastly, we convert this equation back into terms that refer to C_t:

$$\begin{aligned} X_t &= (1 - b)^t X_0, \\ C_t - C^* &= (1 - b)^t (C_0 - C^*), \\ C_t &= C^* - (1 - b)^t C^* + (1 - b)^t C_0, \\ C_t &= (1 - (1 - b)^t) C^* + (1 - b)^t C_0. \end{aligned}$$

Gathering all these calculations together, we can state the following theorem:

Theorem 2. *If for all t, $C_{t+1} = C_t + a - bC_t$, then $C^* = a/b$ is the stationary point for C, and $C_t = (1 - (1 - b)^t)C^* + (1 - b)^t C_0$.*

EXERCISE

5. Verify the preceding result on any three adjacent points of the graph that you constructed for Exercise 4.

The behavior of the variable C in Theorem 2 can be made plain by rewriting its open equation in this equivalent form:

$$C_{t+1} = C_t + b(C^* - C_t).$$

This equation reveals the different types of behavior that can be exhibited by C, depending on the value of b. It can be seen immediately, for example, that C increases when it is less than C^* only if $b > 0$. Thus a necessary condition for $C_t \to C^*$ as $t \to \infty$ is that $b > 0$. But is this condition sufficient? That is the subject of the next exercise.

EXERCISES

Deduce and describe the behavior of C under these seven conditions:

6. $b < 0$,
7. $b = 0$,
8. $0 < b < 1$,
9. $b = 1$,
10. $1 < b < 2$,
11. $b = 2$,
12. $b > 2$.

(Hint: If deduction fails, try a graphical approach with the parameters of Exercise 4). Under which of these conditions does C approach C^*?

In terms of our theory of crime, b is the annual proportion of criminals who adopt a more legal means of livelihood. For this theory, therefore, $0 < b < 1$, and the behavior of C_t is described by the answer to Exercise 8 above.

Our last task in this section is to consider social systems whose growth is largely controlled by external forces. Take, for example, the population of a frontier town in the nineteenth century. The mortality rate in these towns was quite high, especially the infant mortality rate, and most growth occurred as a result of immigration from the East. The number of people moving in had little to do with the size of the town: They were primarily determined by economic and social conditions in the East. Thus a reasonable model for the growth of a frontier town's population P_t, in terms of its mortality rate m and amount of immigration I_t, is this:

$$P_{t+1} = P_t - mP_t + I_t. \tag{3}$$

Note that because input in the form of immigration (I) is unspecified, it is impossible to obtain a closed form solution to Eq. (3). By following the same procedure as we did for Eq. (1), however, it is possible to achieve a useful statement.

If Eq. (3) is correct, then:

$$\begin{aligned} P_1 &= (1 - m)P_0 + I_0, \quad \text{and} \\ P_2 &= (1 - m)P_1 + I_1 \\ &= (1 - m)\{(1 - m)P_0 + I_0\} + I_1 \\ &= (1 - m)^2 P_0 + (1 - m)I_0 + I_1. \end{aligned}$$

Similarly,

$$\begin{aligned} P_3 &= (1 - m)P_2 + I_2 \\ &= (1 - m)\{(1 - m)^2 P_0 + (1 - m)I_0 + I_1\} + I_2 \\ &= (1 - m)^3 P_0 + (1 - m)^2 I_0 + (1 - m)^1 I_1 + (1 - m)^0 I_2. \end{aligned}$$

Generalizing to an arbitrary time t:

$$P_t = (1 - m)^t P_0 + \sum_{j=0}^{t-1} (1 - m)^{t-j-1} I_j.$$

If we substitute $k = t - j$, then we obtain

$$P_t = (1 - m)^t P_0 + \sum_{k=1}^{t} (1 - m)^{k-1} I_{t-k}.$$

Theorem 3. *If for all t, $P_{t+1} = P_t - mP_t + I_t$, then*

$$P_t = \sum_{k=1}^{t} h_k I_{t-k} + (1 - m)^t P_0,$$

where $h_k = (1 - m)^{k-1}$.

Theorem 3 is as near as we can come to a closed form solution for the growth of our frontier town. The sum in this equation is known as a *convolution*. Theorem 3 expresses the idea that the present size of the town is a convolution of the immigration history, with weight h_k applied to immigration k years ago. A very broad class of social phenomena can be described by this kind of equation.

EXERCISES

13. Show that

$$\sum_{k=0}^{t-1} x^k = \frac{(1 - x^t)}{(1 - x)}.$$

Hint: Let S represent the sum on the left. First show that $xS = S - 1 + x^t$, then solve for S.

14. Suppose $I_t = a$ for all t (i.e., that immigration is constant). Show, using the previous exercise with $x = 1 - m$, that Theorem 3 reduces to Theorem 2, with stationary value $P^* = a/m$.

2. Review of Probability and Statistics

The variables of the preceding section were all "deterministic," meaning that at each point in time they have a definite, or determined, value. In many cases, however, it is unrealistic to presume that enough information about a variable is available to identify the complete equation that would determine its future values exactly, or even to presume that such an equation exists at all. In these situations it is appropriate to use so-called "random" variables. A random variable has an uncertain value, in the sense that we can associate a probability of occurrence with each of the values in its range. The usefulness of random variables lies in the fact that it is frequently possible to make exact statements about these probabilities even though it is impossible to specify the variable's value exactly. In all that follows capital letters will be used to represent random variables, whereas lower case letters will represent specific quantities or constants. The event in which a random variable X has the value v will be denoted by $\{X = v\}$, and its probability will be denoted by $f(v)$, so that

$$f(v) = \text{Prob}\{X = v\}.$$

There is a definite probability associated with each value in the range of a random variable. The set of these probabilities forms the probability distribution of the random variable. In most of the material to follow we shall be concerned only with random variables whose range is the nonnegative integers, and therefore their probability distributions will be defined only on these points. With this in mind, two of the fundamental properties of a probability distribution can be stated as:

(1) $0 \le f(v) \le 1$, for all v,
(2) $\sum_v f(v) = 1$.

The summation in the latter equation is carried out across all values in the range of the random variable X. If the range of X is the real number line, then the distribution $f(v)$ is called a probability density function, and the summation must be replaced with an integral. We shall avoid the niceties of mathematical rigor in these circumstances by assuming the approximation:

$$f(v) = \text{Prob}\{v - 0.5 \le X < v + 0.5\}.$$

All of the "proofs" that follow in this section ignore the minor difficulties introduced by this approximation. Their logic, however, is the same as would be used at any level of rigor, and from this logic much can be learned.

Probability distributions serve the same purpose for random variables as values do for deterministic variables. The graph of a probability distribution conveys roughly the same information, in the sense that from it one can tell which values are likely and which are not likely, etc. The following examples suggest some of the variety of shapes that probability distributions can assume (see Fig. 13.1).

Random variables can seldom be studied in isolation from other variables. Pairs of random variables have two-dimensional probability distributions, which assign probabilities to the simultaneous event $\{X = u$ and $Y = v\}$:

$$p(u, v) = \text{Prob}\{X = u \text{ and } Y = v\}.$$

Note that, as before, $0 \le p(u, v) \le 1$, and $\sum_u \sum_v p(u, v) = 1$. The distributions of either X or Y alone can be derived from the two-dimensional probability distribution as follows:

$$f(u) = \text{Prob}\{X = u\} = \sum_v p(u, v),$$

$$g(v) = \text{Prob}\{Y = v\} = \sum_u p(u, v).$$

Definition. Two random variables are independent if: $\text{Prob}\{X = u$ and $Y = v\} = \text{Prob}\{X = u\}\,\text{Prob}\{Y = v\}$ for every u, v pair.

Intuitively, independence means that the probability that X has value u does not depend on the value of Y. Stated differently, $f(u) = p(u, v)/g(v)$ for any v (unless $g(v) = 0$). Independence is a very strong condition—it holds only between variables that are completely unrelated.

Definition. The expectation of a random variable is

$$E[X] = \sum_v v f(v).$$

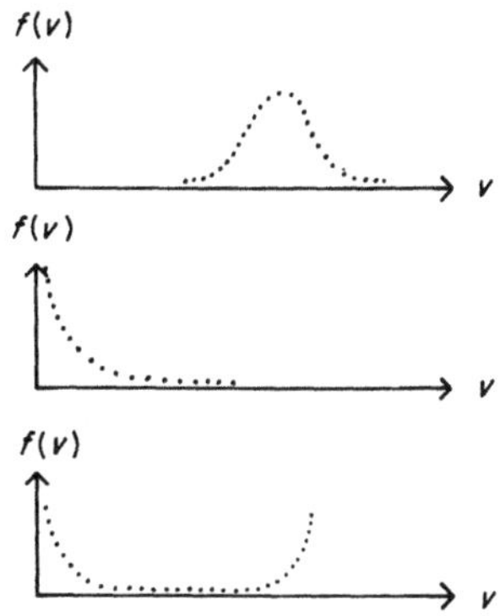

Figure 13.1

Notice that if X definitely has some specific value, say x, then $f(x) = 1$ and $f(v) = 0$ for all $v \neq x$. Thus in this case,

$$E[X] = \sum_{v} vf(v) = xf(x) = x.$$

By convention, therefore, the expectation of a constant is just the constant itself:

$$E[a] = a, \quad \text{for any constant } a.$$

The expectation of a random variable is a statistic that may be referred to as its expected value, its arithmetic mean, its first moment, or its average. In most of the material to follow, we shall study random variables in terms of (among other things) their expected values.

The expectation operator $E[\ \ ]$ is an extremely useful tool. Its definition is readily extendable to any function of random variables. In the case of a function $h(X)$ of a random variable, for instance,

$$E[h(X)] = \sum_{u} h(u)f(u);$$

and in the two-variable case,

$$E[h(X, Y)] = \sum_{u}\sum_{v} h(u, v)p(u, v).$$

EXAMPLES

1. $E[aX] = \sum_u auf(u)$
2. $E[X^2] = \sum_u u^2 f(u)$
3. $E[X^k] = \sum_u u^k f(u)$
4. $E[XY] = \sum_u \sum_v uvp(u, v)$
5. $E[X + Y] = \sum_u \sum_v (u + v)p(u, v)$
6. $E[X^k Y^j] = \sum_u \sum_v u^k v^j p(u, v)$

These features of the expectation operator permit the deduction of its algebraic properties. First, it can be shown that

$$E[aX] = aE[X].$$

PROOF.

$$E[aX] = \sum_v avf(v) = a\sum_v vf(v) = aE[X].$$

Second, the expectation of a sum of random variables is just the sum of their expectations:

$$E[X + Y] = E[X] + E[Y], \text{ for any } X, Y.$$

Again, the proof is simple:

$$\begin{aligned} E[X + Y] &= \sum_u \sum_v (u + v)p(u, v) \\ &= \sum_u u \sum_v p(u, v) + \sum_v v \sum_u p(u, v) \\ &= \sum_u uf(u) + \sum_v vg(v) \\ &= E[X] + E[Y]. \end{aligned}$$

□

The foregoing properties of the expectation operator establish its linearity. The linearity of the expectation operator is of fundamental importance and will prove useful in all that follows. It can be summarized in one statement in this way:

Theorem 4. $E[aX + bY] = aE[X] + bE[Y]$, *for any a, b.*

Recall that $E[X]$ is sometimes referred to as the "first moment" of the random variable X. The kth moment of X is a statistic given by $E[X^k]$, which is *not* in general equal to $(E[X])^k$. The moments of a random variable (when they exist as finite numbers) can provide information about the shape of its probability distribution if properly interpreted. For example, the difference between $E[X^2]$ and $(E[X])^2$ is a statistic referred to as the "variance" of the random variable X. This statistic measures the amount of variation in the random variable:

Definition. $V[X] = E[X^2] - (E[X])^2.$

The variance measures variation in the sense that it can be interpreted as the "expected squared deviation of the random variable from its expected value." This interpretation follows from this line of reasoning:

$$E[(X - E[X])^2] = E[X^2 - 2XE[X] + (E[X])^2]$$

$$= E[X^2] - E[2XE[X]] + E[(E[X])^2]$$
$$= E[X^2] - 2E[X]E[X] + (E[X])^2$$
$$= E[X^2] - (E[X])^2$$
$$= V[X].$$

This interpretation reveals that $V[X]$ is always nonnegative, and that $V[X] = 0$ only if X is a constant (i.e., not random). The usefulness of the variance as a measure of the spread, or dispersion, of a probability distribution will gradually become apparent. A physical interpretation of the expectation and variance statistics may help at this point. Consider a material X of unit mass spread out on a line so that the amount of mass concentrated at each point v is $f(v)$. Then the expectation of X is its "center of gravity," and the variance of X is its "moment of inertia."

The variance can be used to calculate an upper bound to the probability that a random variable may deviate from its expected value by more than a specified amount. This is Chebyshev's theorem:

Theorem 5. $$\text{Prob}\{|X - E[X]| \geq k\} \leq V[X]/k^2.$$

PROOF. We show first that $\text{Prob}\{|X| \geq k\} \leq E[X^2]/k^2$:

$$\text{Prob}\{|X| \geq k\} = \sum_{|v| \geq k} f(v) \leq \sum_{|v| \geq k} v^2 f(v)/k^2 \leq E[X^2]/k^2.$$

Application of this result to $X - E[X]$ yields Theorem 5. □

An interesting alternate form of Chebyshev's theorem can be obtained from the substitution $k = z(V[X])^{1/2}$:

$$\text{Prob}\{|X - E[X]| \geq z\sqrt{V[X]}\} \leq 1/z^2.$$

This statement suggests that the quantity $(V[X])^{1/2}$ forms a "natural" unit for measuring the probable deviation of X from its expected value. For example, the probability of a deviation greater than two of these units is less than 25%, and the probability of a deviation greater than three of these units is less than 11.1%, etc. For this purpose the so-called standard deviation statistic is defined as:

Definition. $$D[X] = +\sqrt{V[X]}.$$

The degree of statistical dependence between two random variables is conveniently measured by their "covariance," a statistic which we develop next. Recall that two random variables X and Y are by definition independent if $p(u, v) = f(u)g(v)$ for every u, v pair. It is also true that

Theorem 6. $E[XY] = E[X]E[Y]$ *if* X *and* Y *are independent.*

PROOF.
$$E[XY] = \sum_u \sum_v uvp(u, v) = \sum_u \sum_v uvf(u)g(v)$$
$$= \left(\sum_u uf(u)\right)\left(\sum_v vg(v)\right) = E[X]E[Y]. \qquad \square$$

It is important to note that the converse of Theorem 6 is NOT necessarily true. However, if $E[XY] \neq E[X]E[Y]$, then X and Y are surely dependent. The difference between $E[XY]$ and $E[X]E[Y]$ is frequently used as a statistic to measure the degree of statistical dependence between X and Y. It is called the covariance:

Definition.
$$C[X, Y] = E[XY] - E[X]E[Y].$$

Notice that the covariance of a variable with itself is its variance: $C[X, X] = V[X]$. Just as with the variance, there is an alternate formula for the covariance:

$$C[X, Y] = E[(X - E[X])(Y - E[Y])].$$

From this formula it can be seen that the covariance of X and Y is positive if it is likely that both variables are either both greater than their expected values or both less than their expected values. Contrariwise, the covariance will be negative if it is likely that a greater than expected value for either variable coincides with a less than expected value for the other. The covariance of two variables is thus positive if they vary positively with each other, and negative if they vary negatively with each other.

The covariance operator has algebraic properties that are derived from those of the expectation operator:

Theorem 7. *For any random variables X, Y, and Z:*
(1) $C[a, X] = 0$ *for any constant* a;
(2) $C[X, X] = V[X]$;
(3) $C[X, Y] = C[Y, X]$;
(4) $C[aX + bY, Z] = aC[X, Z] + bC[Y, Z]$ *for any* a, b;
(5) $|C[X, Y]| \leq D[X]D[Y]$.

PROOF. (#1, 2, and 3 are trivial). For #4:

$$\begin{aligned}
C[aX + bY, Z] &= E[(aX + bY)Z] - E[aX + bY]E[Z] \\
&= E[aXZ + bYZ] - (aE[X] + bE[Y])E[Z] \\
&= aE[XZ] + bE[YZ] - aE[X]E[Z] - bE[Y]E[Z] \\
&= a(E[XZ] - E[X]E[Z]) + b(E[YZ] - E[Y]E[Z]) \\
&= aC[X, Z] + bC[Y, Z]. \qquad \square
\end{aligned}$$

Proof of #5 is left for Exercise 17.

The variance operator has a similar list of algebraic properties, all of which will prove useful.

Theorem. *For any random variables X and Y:*
(1) $V[a] = 0$ *for any constant a;*
(2) $V[X] \geq 0$*;*
(3) $V[X + Y] = V[X] + 2C[X, Y] + V[Y]$*;*
(4) $V[a + bX] = b^2 V[X]$ *for any a, b;*
(5) $V[aX + bY] = a^2 V[X] + 2abC[X, Y] + b^2 V[X]$ *for any a, b;*

PROOF OF #3.

$$\begin{aligned} V[X + Y] &= C[X + Y, X + Y] \\ &= C[X, X] + C[X, Y] + C[Y, X] + C[Y, Y] \\ &= V[X] + 2C[X, Y] + V[Y]. \end{aligned}$$ □

Proofs of #4 and #5 follow easily.

EXERCISES

15. Show that the standard deviation operator has these algebraic properties for any random variables X and Y:
 a) $D[a] = 0$ for any constant a;
 b) $D[X] \geq 0$;
 c) $D[aX] = |a|D[X]$;
 d) $D[X + Y] \leq D[X] + D[Y]$ (the triangle inequality).
16. Show that $V[X - Y] = V[X] - 2C[X, Y] + V[Y]$.
17. Prove the Cauchy–Schwartz Inequality, Theorem 7(5). Hint: Let $Z = Y - bX$, where $b = C[X, Y]/V[X]$. The inequality follows from the observation that $V[Z] \geq 0$.
18. Define the correlation operator as
$$R[X, Y] = C[X, Y]/(D[X]D[Y]).$$
 Show that it has the following properties:
 a) $-1 \leq R[X, Y] \leq 1$;
 b) $R[X, Y] = 0$, if X and Y are independent;
 c) $R[a + bX, Y] = R[X, Y]$;
 d) $R[X, Y] = +1$, if $Y = a + bX$ and $b > 0$.
19. *Standardization* of a random variable is accomplished by the transformation $Z_X = (X - E[X])/D[X]$. Show that
 a) $E[Z_X] = 0$;
 b) $D[Z_X] = 1$;
 c) $E[Z_X Z_Y] = R[X, Y]$;
 d) $\text{Prob}\{|Z_X| \geq z\} \leq 1/z^2$.

20. Suppose that we believe that $Y = a + bX + U$, although we do not know the exact values of a and b. Assuming only that $E[U] = 0$ and $C[X, U] = 0$, show that a and b can be calculated from the statistics of X and Y as follows:
   a) $b = C[Y, X]/V[X]$;
   b) $a = E[Y] - bE[X]$.

   This technique is called "linear regression." If X and Y are standardized variables, show that:

   c) $b = R[X, Y]$;
   d) $a = 0$.

3. Stochastic Difference Equations

In this section we show how the theory of probability distributions and their associated statistics can be applied to the previously developed difference equation models to yield a technique of social theory construction that is more powerful than either of its two components. The adjective "stochastic" is derived from the Greek word for "guess," and its use suggests the fact that some of the variables in a difference equation may be uncertain: we may know only their probability distributions, or indeed, only some of their statistics. This uncertainty changes through time as the system evolves, and the value of the theory of stochastic difference equations lies in its ability to describe this evolution.

There are three ways in which stochastic elements may enter into difference equations:

(1) The initial value may be random;
(2) The external input variables may be random;
(3) The coefficients themselves may be random.

Of these the first presents no difficulties or surprises, while the last requires techniques that exceed the scope of this section. We shall focus primarily upon the second case.

The case in which the initial value of a variable controlled by a difference equation is random is straightforward. Consider the religious sect example of Section 1 [Eq. (1)]: we can "unwind" the process by the following argument. If $R_t = v$, then it must have been the case that $R_{t-1} = (1 + a)^{-1}v$, and so,

$$\text{Prob}\{R_t = v\} = \text{Prob}\{R_{t-1} = (1 + a)^{-1}v\},$$

and from this comes the general case

$$\text{Prob}\{R_t = v\} = \text{Prob}\{R_0 = (1 + a)^{-t}v\}.$$

Thus we can relate the probability distribution of the size of the sect at time t directly back to its initial distribution.

The statistical dynamics of the distribution of R are more clearly revealed through the use of the statistical operators developed in Section 2. If the expectation operator is used on both sides of Eq. (1), we obtain

$$\begin{aligned} E[R_{t+1}] &= E[R_t + aR_t] \\ &= E[R_t] + aE[R_t], \end{aligned}$$

which is recognizably a difference equation for the expected value, $E[R_t]$. So, by Theorem 1, $E[R_t] = (1 + a)^t E[R_0]$. Thus we have seen that the expected value of R_t evolves along the same trajectory that R_t would have if it were not stochastic. But what about the standard deviation of R_t? Because the standard deviation is the positive square root of the variance, it is convenient to start by searching for a difference equation for $V[R_t]$. As before, we use the variance operator on both sides of Eq. (1):

$$\begin{aligned} V[R_{t+1}] &= V[R_t + aR_t] \\ &= V[R_t] + 2C[R_t, aR_t] + V[aR_t] \\ &= V[R_t] + 2aC[R_t, R_t] + a^2 V[R_t] \\ &= V[R_t] + (2a + a^2) V[R_t]. \end{aligned}$$

This is the desired difference equation. It will be useful later. Now, by Theorem 1, we deduce that

$$\begin{aligned} V[R_t] &= (1 + 2a + a^2)^t V[R_0] \\ &= (1 + a)^{2t} V[R_0]. \end{aligned}$$

To obtain $D[R_t]$, we have but to take a square root:

$$D[R_t] = |1 + a|^t D[R_0].$$

Gathering all these calculations together, we can state the stochastic form of Theorem 1:

Theorem 9. *If for all t, $R_{t+1} = R_t + aR_t$, (R_0 random) then*

$$\text{Prob}\{R_t = v\} = \text{Prob}\{R_0 = (1 + a)^{-t} v\},$$

$$E[R_t] = (1 + a)^t E[R_0], \quad \text{and} \quad D[R_t] = |1 + a|^t D[R_0].$$

Notice that in the example of the religious sect the growth coefficient a is positive. Therefore, by Theorem 9, not only does the expected size of the sect grow geometrically with time, but so also does the standard deviation. Intuitively, the growth process affects equally the size of the sect and the degree of our uncertainty about its true size. Any initial uncertainty is magnified at the same rate as the size of the sect itself.

EXERCISES

21. Assume that $a = 0.2$, $E[R_0] = 12$, $D[R_0] = 1$. Plot both $E[R_t] + 2D[R_t]$ and $E[R_t] - 2D[R_t]$ for $t = 0$–20. The probability that R_t runs outside these bounds is less than what value? (Use Chebyshev's theorem.)

22. What would happen to $D[R_t]$ for a sect that is suffering a net loss of membership ($a < 0$)? Assume that $E[R_0] = 800$, $D[R_0] = 100$, $a = -0.2$, and create the corresponding plot.

23. Derive the following theorem from Theorem 9, just as Theorem 5 was derived from Theorem 1.

Theorem 10. *If for all t,* $X_{t+1} = X_t + a - bX_t$ *(*X_0 *random), then* $X^* = a/b$ *is the stationary point for* X*, and* $E[X_t] = (1 - (1 - b)^t)X^* + (1 - b)^t E[X_0]$*, while* $D[X_t] = |1 - b|^t D[X_0]$.

Theorem 10 can be applied to the mini-theory of crime in Section 1. If at time zero the number of criminals (C_0) is uncertain, then Theorem 10 states that as time passes, C_t will approach $C^* = a/b$ (assuming, of course, that $0 < b < 1$). In fact, the number of criminals will approach C^* no matter what C_0 was, with complete certainty.

Turning now to the major topic of this section, we develop the stochastic theory of populations whose growth is affected by both mortality and random immigration. Henceforth we shall assume that the initial size of these populations is *not* stochastic (i.e., the initial variance is zero).

Recall our nineteenth century frontier town, whose population P_t suffers from a constant mortality rate m and enjoys an annual amount of immigration I_t (which is now a random variable):

$$P_{t+1} = P_t - mP_t + I_t \quad \text{[cf. Eq. (1.3)]}$$

Not surprisingly, the stochastic evolution of P_t is heavily dependent upon the nature of the random input history $I_0, I_1, I_2, \cdots, I_{t-1}$. To start, we shall make some simplifying assumptions about this history:

(1) The probability distribution of immigration is stationary, that is, it does not change throughout the history of I.
(2) In each year, the amount of immigration is statistically independent of the size of the frontier town.

Neither of these assumptions is critical to what follows, but they serve to clarify the main lines of the development. Their practical effect can be summarized in this way:

(1) $E[I_t] = E[I]$, for any t.
(2) $V[I_t] = V[I]$, for any t.
(3) $C[I_t, P_t] = 0$, for any t.

Now we proceed exactly as we did in the case of random initial values, by looking for difference equations for the statistics of P. First, for $E[P_t]$, we use the expectation operator on both sides of Eq. (3):

$$\begin{aligned} E[P_{t+1}] &= E[P_t - mP_t + I_t] \\ &= E[P_t] - E[mP_t] + E[I_t] \\ &= E[P_t] - mE[P_t] + E[I]. \end{aligned}$$

This is the desired difference equation. Note that it resembles Eq. (2). Therefore, by Theorem 2, the expected population size $E[P_t]$ has a stationary value $E[P^*] = E[I]/m$. Further, since $E[P_0] = P_0$,

$$E[P_t] = (1 - (1 - m)^t)E[P^*] + (1 - m)^t P_0.$$

Thus we have found a closed form equation for the expected population size.

The second step of the stochastic analysis is, as before, to look for a difference equation for $V[P_t]$, the variance of the population size. Using the variance operator on both sides of Equation (3):

$$\begin{aligned} V[P_{t+1}] &= V[P_t - mP_t + I_t] \\ &= V[P_t - mP_t] + 2C[P_t - mP_t, I_t] + V[I_t] \\ &= V[P_t] - 2mC[P_t, P_t] + (-m)^2 V[P_t] + V[I] \\ &= V[P_t] - (2m - m^2)V[P_t] + V[I]. \end{aligned}$$

Note that we have used the independence of I_t and P_t in this derivation. The result is again a difference equation that resembles Equation (3). Therefore, by Theorem 3 again, the variance of the population size has a stationary value $V[P^*] = V[I]/(2m - m^2)$, and, since $V[P_0] = 0$,

$$\begin{aligned} V[P_t] &= (1 - (1 - 2m + m^2)^t)V[P^*] + (1 - 2m + m^2)^t V[P_0] \\ &= (1 - (1 - m)^{2t})V[P^*]. \end{aligned}$$

Expressing this result in terms of standard deviations, we find that $D[P_t]$ has a stationary value $D[P^*] = D[I]/[m(2 - m)]^{1/2}$, and that

$$D[P_t] = [1 - (1 - m)^{2t}]^{1/2} D[P^*].$$

Our final theorem can be stated as follows:

Theorem 11. *If for all t, $P_{t+1} = P_t - mP_t + I_t$ (I random), where I_t is stationary and independent of P_t, then for $0 < m < 2$, $E[P_t]$ and $D[P_t]$ converge to the stationary values $E[P^*] = E[I]/m$, and $D[P^*] = D[I]/[m(2 - m)]^{1/2}$. Further, the statistical dynamics of P_t are $E[P_t] = (1 - (1 - m)^t)E[P^*] + (1 - m)^t P_0$, and $D[P_t] = [1 - (1 - m)^{2t}]^{1/2} D[P^*]$.*

Thus the probability distribution of the population of our little frontier town converges to a shape that depends upon $E[I]$ and $D[I]$, the stationary statistics of the random immigration input and upon the mortality rate m. As an example, if $E[I] = 100$ persons per year, while $D[I] = 30$ persons per year, then by Chebyshev's theorem the probability that the immigration is any one year is outside the range 40–160 persons is less than 25%. If the frontier mortality rate is 2% ($m = 0.02$) per year, then the ultimate expected size of the town is $100/0.02 = 5000$ persons, with a standard deviation of $30/[0.2(2 - 0.2)]^{1/2} = 50$ persons. *Notice that the relative uncertainty of the ultimate size is much less than the relative uncertainty of the annual immigration.*

The use of statistical operators, together with the assumption of stationarity of the immigration and its independence from the size of the town have enabled us to find closed form equations for the statistical dynamics of the population, even though they were not available for the nonstochastic process. This is an illustration of the power of stochastic difference equations.

Exercises

In the preceding material we have ignored the dynamics of the dependence of P_t on its own previous values. This dependence, called "autocorrelation," plays a central role in the statistical analysis of time series. Using the same assumptions as in Theorem 11, derive the following results:

24. $C[I_{t+k}, I_t] = 0 \quad \text{for } k > 0$.
25. $C[P_{t+1}, P_t] = (1 - m)V[P_t]$.
26. $C[P_{t+k}, P_t] = (1 - m)^k V[P_t]$.
27. $R[P_{t+k}, P_t] = (1 - m)^k D[P_t]/D[P_{t+k}]$.
28. $R[P_{t+k}, P_t] = (1 - m)^k$, if P has reached its stationary equilibrium distribution by time t.
29. Although all of the variables described in these models measured numbers of persons, there is no special reason (beyond mere convenience) why this should be so. Similar models can be developed with variables that measure such quantities as income, social status, and political orientation, etc. Choose a sociological variable and use the theory of stochastic difference equations to deduce its statistical dynamics.

Notes for the Instructor

Objectives.

(1) To demonstrate the use of linear difference equations in the construction of social theories.

(2) To show how to convert a deterministic theory into a stochastic theory through the use of random variables and their statistics.

(3) To introduce the fundamental concepts of statistical dynamics in relation to social theory.

Prerequisites. High School algebra and one course in probability or statistics. A single course in finite mathematics might suffice.

Time. Two to four weeks.

CHAPTER 14

The Apportionment Problem

William F. Lucas*

1. The Basic Problem

1.1. Introduction

One of the first equity problems that arises in the distribution of resources is the apportionment problem. It is concerned with distributing available personnel or other resources in "*integral* parts" to different subdivisions or tasks. One may be distributing seats in a legislature among different political constituencies, allocating the number of available teachers for a high school or college to the different departments, or determining the number of ships to be assigned to the different fleets in the Navy given certain priorities and goals. In practice this problem frequently arises even before one considers the classical assignment problem that is concerned with the existence of feasible and *efficient* assignments of resources to various units, such as assigning particular individuals to certain jobs. Several different methods for solving the apportionment problem as well as many of the relevant properties of the various methods will be presented in this chapter, along with examples that indicate a few of the more obvious applications.

The apportionment problem is concerned with partitioning a given positive integer h into nonnegative integral parts $a_1, a_2, \cdots, a_s$ such that their sum $a_1 + a_2 + \cdots + a_s = h$, and such that these parts are as "near as possible" proportional, respectively, to a set of given nonnegative integers

* School of Operations Research and Industrial Engineering, Cornell University, Ithaca, New York 14853.

$p_1, p_2, \cdots, p_s$. If the resulting *exact quotas* $q_i = hp_i/(p_1 + p_2 + \cdots + p_s)$ were to be integers for all $i = 1, 2, \cdots, s$, then an "exact" or "perfect" apportionment would be obtained by setting each $a_i = q_i$. This ideal case of integral q_i is, however, an extremely rare occurrence. The problem thus arises in rounding the fractions q_i to "nearby" integral values a_i. In applications this rounding process introduces inequities between the different units or communities. Thus it is important to choose the values a_i in a "fair" or "just" manner, i.e., one wishes to "minimize" the resulting inequities between the various groups or tasks. However, "minimizing inequity" or "as nearly as possible" can be, and actually have been, given different mathematical interpretations.

The stated problem appears to be a rather simple "approximation" problem that should be easy to solve in the general case. It may seem as though some obvious process for rounding fractions or that some best scheme for minimizing some natural measure of inequality would provide one with a straightforward answer. However, this is not the case. An historical example to illustrate the nonobviousness of any one solution is the fact that the Congress of the United States has used *four* such schemes to apportion the seats in the House of Representatives among the various states over the past 200 yr, and they have on many occasions (beginning in 1790) held lengthy debates on this issue. A superb exposition of apportionment in the U.S. Congress is included in an important and award-winning exposition by Balinski and Young [3], in the articles by Chafee [16] and Willcox [36], and in particular in the interesting monograph by Balinski and Young [12].

For any apportionment method there are certain desirable properties that one normally wishes to be satisfied. What happens, however, is that a few of these very natural "requirements" are inconsistent, that is, no method is able to satisfy them simultaneously in the general case. So the apparent but misleading simplicity of this problem makes it an intriguing and nontrivial one for the mathematical scientist, and one that should be addressed with more care in those applications in which such "fair divisions" are important. Recent research has established the existence of a dilemma that is a little reminiscent of the famous "impossibility" discoveries of Heisenberg in physics, Gödel in logic, and Arrow in social choice theory. No matter which particular scheme one chooses to use, it will possess certain "flaws," which leave it open for criticism. In practice, one should normally decide in advance as to which principles or properties must be present in the method employed, as well as which of the corresponding resulting "faults" are acceptable. Otherwise, one apportioning employees could be confronted with some surprising and embarrassing "paradoxes." For example, a local high school is able to add one extra teacher at the last minute, and the mathematics department is then informed that they must cut one of the teachers they were formally allocated.

1.2. Illustrations

The apportionment problem arises in many structures and institutions in society. Most of the literature on this problem describe it in the political context. The classical example is to determine how the given number of seats in a representative assembly should be allocated to the different constituent units. The most discussed case in the United States concerns the assignment of the 435 seats in the U.S. House of Representatives to the 50 states according to their populations. The U.S. Constitution requires that the number of seats per state be "according to their respective numbers" (normally interpreted as direct proportionality), that each state have at least one seat, and that "the number of representatives shall not exceed one for every thirty thousand" people. The U.S. Constitution did not provide a specific method, however. Also, they had different ways of counting "people" and for determining eligible voters at the time. Furthermore, the latter stated "maximum" requirement is now obsolete in practice. This Congressional case is discussed in detail in Balinski and Young [3, 12] as well as in many of the other references for this chapter. Many other countries, international assemblies, and more local governments and organizations have a similar apportionment problem.

In many countries the number of seats that a party is allowed in its national parliament is proportional to the percentage of votes it obtained in an election. The same is often true in many local governmental bodies in these countries. The particular apportionment method so employed can change the number of seats a party obtains and can thus be a major political issue, as occurred in Israel in recent years. One scheme may "favor" large parties, whereas another is generally advantageous to smaller parties.

A large number of different apportionment problems routinely arise in a typical school district. For example, consider a small city school district such as the Ithaca City School District, which includes surrounding urban and rural areas as well as the city itself. The district has one high school, and two junior high schools (grades 7 to 9), and had 13 elementary schools. It also has had decreasing enrollments, many empty classrooms, and is losing teachers. The School Board and the Administration have tighter budgets and the unpleasant task of implementing the "management of decline" or of undertaking "retrenchment." They must decide whether to close one of the junior highs and/or a few of the elementary schools (and which ones), whether to change from a (K–6, 7–9, 10–12) system to another one such as (K–5, 6–8, 9–12), where to cut the teachers and staff, and what academic programs to reduce. Clearly, many apportionment problems are present. How to distribute the elementary school teachers among the schools, and how to distribute high school teachers among the departments in light of certain student–teacher ratios? (Since teachers can be split between departments or be part-time, one may wish to use *one class* as the basic integral unit.) Which system for dividing the grades into three levels will best fit the existing facilities? How to split students among the various tenth grade mathematics courses and sections? How many classes should there be for a given grade at a particular school (or how best to mix such grade levels into single classrooms if such is necessary or is the school's policy)? In many cases, such apportionment decisions have been made in an ad hoc manner by some vice-principal or unknown central administrator. Although such approaches may have been tolerated in a period of expansion, they will frequently be challenged in a period of declining growth when people are losing their jobs.

The reader should be able to think of some apportionment problems that exist in his or her own institution. In an academic department, it may be the number of people in each speciality in order to cover the corresponding classes or at least the advanced classes. Or perhaps this should depend upon the amount of research funds accrued, the interest of the graduate students, the areas in which jobs are available, or some other considerations.

A branch of the armed services may have a large number of various types of units that have different goals, priorities, and requirements, including manpower. The service in turn has a certain number of people of various ranks (grades) and qualifications (ratings) that must be allocated among the different units to meet present or forecasted needs. Each unit may have an authorized number of people at each grade and rating, and may have absolute minimum or maximum requirements as well. However, the total available personnel cannot be expected to match the sum of the various unit authorizations. Certain shortfalls in staffing and various substitutions in grades and rating must necessarily occur. How should the armed services respond to this problem in the light of its goals and priorities? John P. Mayberry [27] has investigated this problem in the case of all enlisted personnel in the U.S. Navy. The U.S. Navy also has many apportionment problems in areas other than manpower. As mentioned above, it must distribute its active ships among it various fleets and commands, and items such as aircraft carriers clearly come in integral numbers.

Apportionment problems can also arise within mathematics itself. For example, in numerical analysis or approximation theory, one may wish to approximate a continuous function by the "best-fitting" (i.e., in some sense such as the area under the curve) integral-valued step function with steps of integral length. One can replace integers here by rational numbers that are multiples of some smallest one. Most modern techniques in numerical analysis do not require equal step sizes, however.

1.3. The Problem

Some notation and terminology will be introduced before stating the problem more precisely. As with most publications in this area, the terms that naturally appear in the application of apportionment to political assemblies will be used. Let N be the set of natural numbers $\{0, 1, 2, \cdots, n, \cdots\}$ (including zero), and let

$$N_s = \{1, 2, \cdots, s\}$$

represent a given set of s *states* denoted by $1, 2, \cdots, s$. Assume that the s states have the respective *populations*

$$p_1, p_2, \cdots, p_s,$$

and that the total number of seats in the assembly, which will be called the *house size*, is h. For given populations $p_1, p_2, \cdots, p_s$ and house size h, our problem is to determine an *apportionment*

$$a_1, a_2, \cdots, a_s$$

for which $\Sigma_{i=1}^s a_i = h$, and each a_i is a nonnegative integer. Introduce the vectors

$$p = (p_1, p_2, \cdots, p_s)$$

and

$$a = (a_1, a_2, \cdots, a_s),$$

and express the *total population* by $P = \Sigma_{i=1}^s p_i$. In the remainder of this chapter, the range of the summation indices will normally not appear, since it will be understood that

$$\sum = \sum_{i=1}^{s}.$$

An *apportionment solution* is a function f, which assigns an apportionment vector a to any given population vector p and fixed house size h, i.e.,

$$f\colon \{p\} \times N \to \{a\}.$$

Since ties can occur, one does not always wish to have a specified uniquely. Thus, one usually talks instead about an *apportionment method* M, which is a nonempty set of apportionment solutions.

The total number of representatives h will be assumed as fixed for any given problem. In practice this choice may be determined by the seating capacity of the assembly, in order to be of a manageable size, by limiting the total number of legislators so as to avoid diluting their power and causing apathy or for various other reasons. In many real instances, however, the value of h is allowed to vary until after various resulting as have been examined and one particular a is selected, which in turn determines h. The U.S. Congress did not fix its value of h until after the census in 1910.

For each state i, define its (*exact*) *quota* as

$$q_i = q_i(p, h) = hp_i/P,$$

and let

$$q = q(p, h) = (q_1, q_2, \cdots, q_s).$$

This vector would be an "ideal" apportionment if it had integer components. However, one almost always has to round the values q_i to nearby integers. Define the *lower quota* for state i to be the largest integer in q_i and denote this by

$$\lfloor q_i \rfloor = [q_i],$$

where [ ] denotes the "greatest integer" function. Similarly, define the *upper quota* for state i as the smallest integer greater or equal to q_i and denote it by

$$\lceil q_i \rceil = -[-q_i].$$

If q_i is noninteger, $\lceil q_i \rceil = \lfloor q_i \rfloor + 1$. Also let

$$\lfloor q \rfloor = (\lfloor q_1 \rfloor, \lfloor q_2 \rfloor, \cdots, \lfloor q_s \rfloor)$$

and

$$\lceil q \rceil = (\lceil q_1 \rceil, \lceil q_2 \rceil, \cdots, \lceil q_s \rceil).$$

In many applications there is a *minimum requirement*

$$r = (r_1, r_2, \cdots, r_s)$$

and/or a *maximum requirement*

$$b = (b_1, b_2, \cdots, b_s),$$

which must be satisfied, i.e., $r \leq a \leq b$. For the U.S. House of Representatives, the minimum requirement is

$$r = e \equiv (1, 1, \cdots, 1)$$

and the minimal size of 30,000 for a congressional district implies an (obsolete) maximum requirement. A branch of the military may have a minimum requirement of e (or else the unit exists only on paper in terms of manpower) and may also have some high-priority units whose specified authorizations absolutely must be met. Certain academic units must also maintain certain minimum levels of staffing or else risk losing their accreditation.

If an apportionment problem also has a minimum or maximum condition, then it will be referred to as the *general apportionment problem.* In this case one can introduce different definitions for generalized (exact) quota, lower quota, and upper quota. However, these will not be defined here; they will be presented in Section 5.

1.4. A Geometric View

A geometric description of the apportionment problem for the case $s = 3$ is presented in Fig. 14.1. For any total population P, there is a *population "simplex"* (integer points on an equilateral triangle):

$$\mathscr{P} = \{p : p_1 + p_2 + \cdots + p_s = P \text{ and each } p_i \in N\},$$

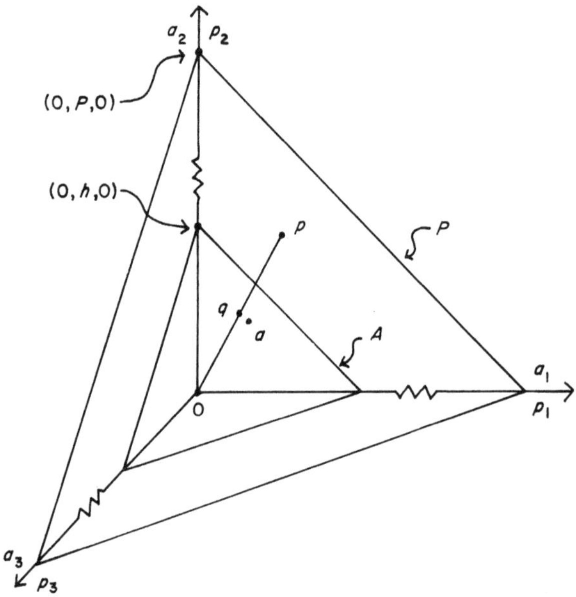

Figure 14.1. The Apportionment Problem for $s = 3$

and for any house size h, there is an *apportionment "simplex"*:

$$\mathscr{A} = \{a\colon a_1 + a_2 + \cdots + a_s = h \text{ and each } a_i \in N\}.$$

If a particular population vector p is projected to the origin 0, it will intersect the $s - 1$ dimensional hyperplane containing $\mathscr{A}$ at the quota vector q. The problem is to choose an integral valued apportionment vector a on the simplex $\mathscr{A}$ which is in some sense "close" to q.

The triangles embedded in 3-space can also be viewed in two dimensions as in Fig. 14.2. The coordinate value of p_i is the distance from p to the side opposite the vertex p^i, where $i = 1, 2,$ or 3. One knows from Viviani's lemma that for *any* point p on $\mathscr{P}$ the three perpendicular projections to the three sides of $\mathscr{P}$ sum to the same constant. (One could introduce barycentric coordinates and describe the points in $\mathscr{P}$ or $\mathscr{A}$ by a pair of numbers.) An apportionment solution is then a function f, which maps $\mathscr{P}$ into $\mathscr{A}$. Since the point $a = f(p, h)$ should be "close to" $q = q(p, h)$, one can think of f as partitioning the "solid" simplex (of nonintegral, but still rational points)

$$\overline{\mathscr{A}} = \{x = (x_1, x_2, x_3)\colon x_1 + x_2 + x_3 = h \text{ and each } x_i \geq 0\}$$

into regions "about" each integer vector $a \in \mathscr{A}$, such that if q falls into such a region, then it is rounded to the corresponding a. For example, if one specifies an apportionment method M by taking "close to" to mean that one picks a to be the integer point nearest to q in the sense of the ordinary Euclidean distance, then one obtains the partitioning of $\overline{\mathscr{A}}$ illustrated in

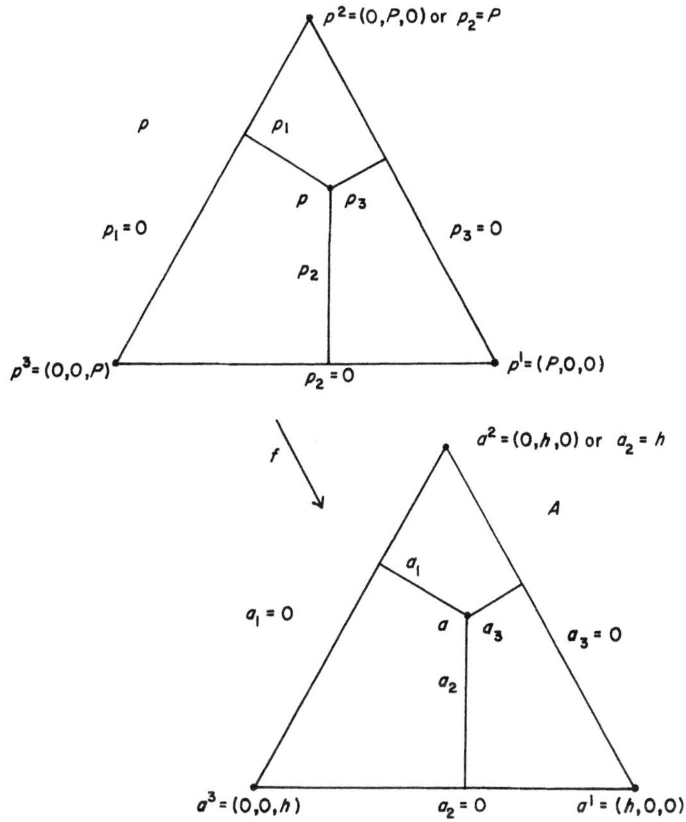

Figure 14.2. A Geometric View in Dimension $s - 1$

Fig. 14.3 for the case where $h = 5$. Note that this specifies a method M and not a particular solution f, since ties occur when q falls on a boundary line between hexagons.

A similar geometry exists in higher dimensions when $s > 3$. Different apportionment methods correspond to alternate ways of partitioning the "solid" apportionment simplex $\overline{\mathscr{A}}$ into "regions."

EXERCISES

1. What would the apportionment regions look like in Fig. 14.3 if one superimposed the minimum condition $a \geq e = (1, 1, 1)$.

2. Describe the geometric model for the apportionment problem in the case $s = 4$.

*3.[1] Describe the geometric nature of the apportionment regions in Exercise 2 where $s = 4$ when the apportionment method uses the Euclidean distance, as was done in Fig. 14.3 for the case $s = 3$.

[1] A somewhat more difficult exercise is denoted by an asterisk (*).

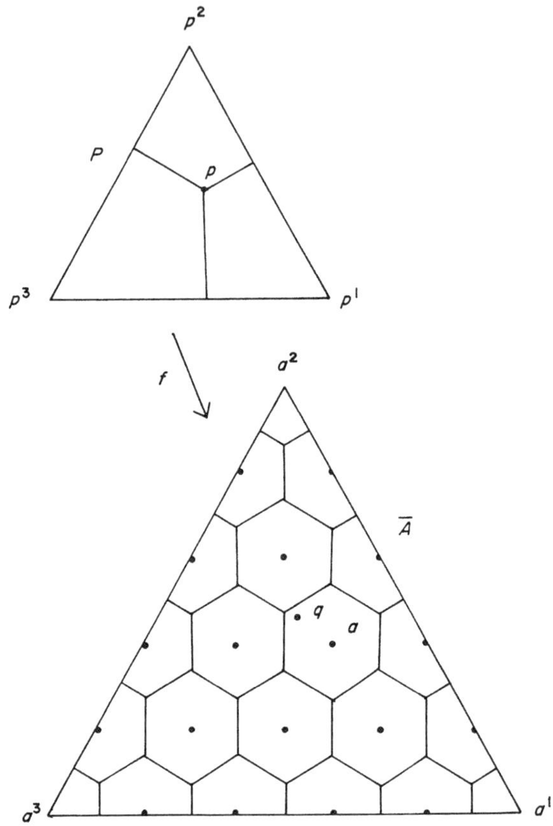

Figure 14.3. The LF Method for $s = 3$ and $h = 5$

1.5. Alternate Approaches

The apportionment problem arises because the exact proportions, or quotas, q_i are usually fractions that deviate from the ultimate integer allotments a_i. If one is allocating human beings or other indivisible objects, then the a_i are necessarily integers. In the political and manpower cases, it is usually individual people who are involved. Whereas, in collecting taxes, the fractional values can be used. In some cases, however, one may wish to avoid the apportionment problem altogether, and this can often be done by either altering the original problem somehow or by coming up with some way of actually implementing the fractional values q_i. For example, one could allow fractional legislative districts whose representatives carry a fraction of a vote. Or one assembly seat may be split over time between two districts. Or the representative from a partial district may be allowed to vote only some of the time as determined by a probabilistic device. (Merrill M. Flood has in recent years investigated certain probabilistic schemes for voting and selecting representatives.) On the other hand, it is well known that in weighted voting systems one's voting power is not proportional to his or her weighted vote; see, e.g., Chapters 9, 10, and 11, this volume. In the case of allocating manpower, there may be no serious difficulty in dividing a person's efforts between two units or employing someone part-time.

In some instances the ultimate value h is allowed to vary (which will not be the approach taken in this chapter). The group proceeds to examine the resulting values of $a_i(p, h)$ for a given method M, and selects the particular h that produces an apportionment a, which the group is satisfied with. This was the case with the U.S. Congress before the census of 1910.

Another way of avoiding the apportionment problem is instead to tackle the *re*apportionment problem (or districting problem) in which your goal is to make all districts so that they have nearly the same population. In a case like the U.S. House of Representatives, this would cause some alteration such as changing state boundaries. (Pearcy [31] has recently suggested that in hindsight it is clear that the U.S. state boundaries should have been drawn differently.)

Of course, in the political arena there may be overriding issues of a non-technical nature that will determine which apportionment method will be employed. The current law determining apportionment for the U.S. House of Representatives was passed after the 1940 census and was chosen over a competing method used from 1910 through 1930, which in turn was also somewhat similar to the method used in 1840. A Democratic Congress chose the former method that gave the "extra" seat to Arkansas (likely for a Democrat) over the latter method that would have given the additional seat to Michigan (likely for a Republican). Naturally, arguments of a mathematical nature were presented for making this essentially political choice.

In the remainder of this chapter several different apportionment methods that have been employed or proposed will be discussed, as well as some of the undesireable properties that they possess. The main point is that there is really no method that proves to be completely satisfactory.

2. Some Traditional Methods

2.1. An Obvious Method

A person considering the apportionment problem for the first time might very well come up with a common scheme that is called the *Method of Largest Fractions*, which we shall denote by *LF*. This is also referred to as the *Method of Greatest Remainders* or as the *Hare Quota Method*, as well as the *Method of Computed Ratios*. It has also been named after Alexander

Hamilton, who suggested its use for the U.S. Congress in 1791, but the related bill was vetoed by President Washington who preferred a method recommended by Thomas Jefferson and others instead. This method was used for the Congress from 1851 up until 1910, and at that time named after Congressman S. F. *Vinton*.

Method LF. Given a population vector $p = (p_1, p_2, \cdots, p_s)$, a house size h, and the resulting quota vector $q = (q_1, q_2, \cdots, q_s)$. Then *LF* first assigns each state $i \in N_s$ its lower quota $\lfloor q_i \rfloor$. Next, it orders the fractions $q_i - \lfloor q_i \rfloor$ in decreasing numerical order and assigns one additional seat to the first $h - \Sigma \lfloor q_i \rfloor$ states in this orderings. (Recall that i ranges from 1 to s in this sum.)

It turns out that there are several other natural ways to arrive at an apportionment method that turns out to be equivalent to *LF*. Some such approaches that attempt to minimize some global or local measure of inequity are indicated below.

Exercises

4. Prove that *LF* corresponds to the solutions of the following optimization problems in which a has *integer* components that sum to h.

   (i) $\min_a \Sigma |a_i - q_i|$. (Recall: $\Sigma = \Sigma_{i=1}^s$.)

   (ii) $\min_a \Sigma (a_i - q_i)^2$.

   (iii)* $\min_a \|a - q\|$ over any l_p norm $\|\ \|$. (Here $p \neq$ population.)

5. Prove that *LF* minimizes the largest "inequity" to any individual state, i.e., *LF* solves

$$\min_a \max_i |a_i - q_i| \quad \text{for} \quad i \in N_s.$$

6. Show that *LF* is characterized by the property of "binary fairness," i.e., one cannot for an *LF* solution a switch a seat from any state i to any other state j and reduce the expression

$$|a_i - q_i| + |a_j - q_j|.$$

   LF also satisfies "binary consistency," i.e., such a switch of a seat cannot reduce the values of *both* $|a_i - q_i|$ and $|a_j - q_j|$.

A geometric view of *LF* for the case $s = 3$ and $h = 5$ was given in Fig. 14.3. Figure 14.4 illustrates the geometry of *LF* for the case $s = 2$. There is a solid unit square, or *box* $\mathscr{B}$, that contains q and has integral valued vertices; and the resulting apportionment a is a vertex from $\mathscr{A} \cap \mathscr{B}$ depending upon the projections of q on the induced coordinate axis of this unit square. In higher dimensions, $\mathscr{B}$ is replaced by a unit hypercube or box called the *quota hypercube* of s dimensions.

The computations that arise in using *LF* are trivial ones.

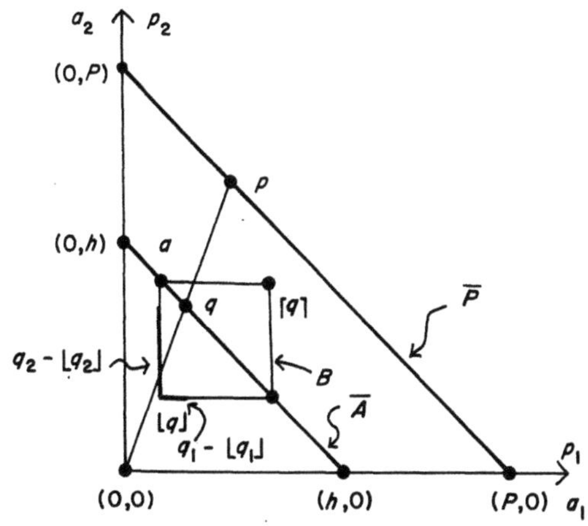

Figure 14.4. The *LF* Method for $s = 2$

2.2. Desirable Properties

There are several natural properties that one may wish to have in the particular apportionment method he or she employs. A few of these will be described in this section.

Property O. For a given value of h, a method M is called *quota monotone* if an increase in q_i (due to a change in p) will never cause a decrease in a_i for any $i \in N_s$.

Tables 1 and 2 below (see Steinhaus [33, pp. 72–75]) show that *LF* does not possess this property. In these illustrations, $h = 5$.

Table 1. An Example Using Method *LF*

i	p_i	q_i	$\lfloor q_i \rfloor$	a_i
1	435	1.45	1	2
2	690	2.30	2	2
3	375	1.25	1	1
Σ	1500	5	4	5

Table 2. Illustrating the Failure of Property *O*

i	p_i	q_i	$\lfloor q_i \rfloor$	a_i
1	465	1.55	1	1
2	555	1.85	1	2
3	480	1.60	1	2
Σ	1500	5	3	5

Exercise

7. Describe why no "natural" or "reasonable" apportionment method could in general be expected to be quota monotone. For example, consider the case $s = 3$ and the shape of the regions in $\overline{\mathscr{A}}$, which would be necessary in order to have this property. Can you describe some "unreasonable" apportionment methods that have property O? (Hint: The U.S. Senate.)

Property Q. An apportionment method M is said to *satisfy (exact) quota* if for every apportionment solution f in M and any p or h, the resulting apportionment $a = f(p, h)$ satisfies

$$\lfloor q_i \rfloor \leq a_i \leq \lceil q_i \rceil \quad \text{for all } i \in N_s.$$

Property LQ. M satisfies lower quota if for every p, h, and $f \in M$,

$$\lfloor q \rfloor \leq a.$$

Property UQ. M satisfies upper quota if for every p, h, and $f \in M$,

$$a \leq \lceil q \rceil.$$

Exercise

8. Show that *LF satisfies quota*, i.e., property Q.

Property H. An apportionment method M is called *house monotone* if for every $f \in M$,

$$f(p, h) \leq f(p, h + 1),$$

i.e., if the legislature increases its size, then no state will lose a former seat using this same method M.

The major difficulty with the LF methods is that it violates house monotonicity as can be seen from Huntington [23]; his example No. 8 is given in Table 3. This fact caused great debate in the U.S. Congress when it actually affected the States of Alabama, Maine, and Colorado in some of the

Table 3. The Alabama Paradox

		$h = 100$			$h = 101$		
i	p_i	q_i	$\lfloor q_i \rfloor$	a_i	q_i	$\lfloor q_i \rfloor$	a_i
1	453	45.3	45	45	45.753	45	46
2	442	44.2	44	44	44.642	44	45
3	105	10.5	10	11	10.605	10	10
$\sum$	1000	100	99	100	101	99	101

apportionments considered after the censuses taken in 1880, 1890, and 1900, respectively. In U.S. history the violation of house monotonicity is often referred to as the *Alabama paradox*. (The word "paradox," as often used in the political science literature, may sound too strong to the mathematical scientist, at least after he understands why it can occur.)

EXERCISES

9. Using the *LF* method, sketch the apportionment regions (hexagons) for the cases $s = 3$ and $h = 3$, 4, and 5. (The case $h = 5$ was done in Fig. 14.3.) If you sketch each case on an equilateral triangle of the same size, then you can compare these figures to see which values of q can give rise to the Alabama paradox.
10. Can you discover an example in which an increase in house size h can cause a state to lose more than one seat using the method *LF*?

Some variations in the method *LF* have also been proposed. One of these assigns each state its lower quota $\lfloor q_i \rfloor$ and then assigns any remaining seats, one each, to the largest fractions $(q_i - \lfloor q_i \rfloor)/p_i$.

EXERCISE

11. Find an example that illustrates that this modified method of largest fractions can exhibit the Alabama paradox.

Property P. An apportionment method M is called *population monotone* if an increase in population of just state will never cause that state to lose a seat, where the value of h and the populations of the other states are assumed to remain unchanged. In other words, if $p_i < p_i'$ and $p_j = p_j'$ for all $j \in N - \{i\}$, then for each $f \in M$

$$a_i = f_i(p, h) \leq f_i(p', h) = a_i'.$$

(Population monotone has also been defined in other ways, e.g., see Section 4.4.)

It would be most undesirable if this property did not hold. A state may find itself in a position where it could increase its representation by understating its true population. Or a high school mathematics department may be the *only* department to gain students, only to lose one of their teachers while the total number of teachers in the school remained constant.

2.3. The Jefferson Method

Following the 1790 census and a 1792 congressional bill (later vetoed) in favor of *LF*, Thomas Jefferson recommended an apportionment method for the 15 states in the U.S., which was finally adopted with the value $h =$

105. It will be referred to here as the *Method of Greatest Divisors* and denoted by *GD*. In addition, it has been named after C. W. *Seaton* (who suggested it in 1881) and V. *d'Hondt* [19], a Belgium mathematician, and referred to as the Method of *Rejected Fractions* as well as *Assumed Ratios*; it also turns out to be one of the five methods later studied by Huntington from a different point of view. It is interesting to note that *GD* tends to "favor" larger states and, in 1792, for $h = 105$ *GD* gave Virginia (the largest state) one more seat than *LF* would have, causing Delaware (the smallest state) to lose one. (The Congressional bill for *LF*, however, had $h = 120$ rather than $h = 105$.) *GD* was used in the U.S. Congress from 1792 to 1830.

The value, or "common ratio," $\bar{\lambda} = P/h$ is the average size of a representative district over a whole country. In the "ideal" case in which each $p_i/\bar{\lambda}$ is an integer, then the "perfect" apportionment is $a_i = p_i/\bar{\lambda}$ for each $i \in N_s$. Recall that we are assuming that p and h are given, which in turn determines P and q.

Method GD. Determine a value of λ such that $\Sigma \lfloor p_i/\lambda \rfloor = h$. *GD* then assigns the values $a_i = \lfloor p_i/\lambda \rfloor$ for each state $i \in N_s$. In the unlikely event of a tie, one will obtain $\Sigma \lfloor p_i/\lambda \rfloor = h' > h$ (or $<h$) for all λ. In this case there is a maximal value λ_0 at which the above sum just obtains the *first* value $h' > h$, and for which two or more of the terms p_i/λ_0 are integer valued. One must then use some ad hoc rule to decide which states ($h' - h$ in number) must lose a seat, i.e., obtain the apportionment $a_i = (p_i/\lambda_0) - 1$.

Actually, Jefferson referred to the "nearest" value of λ. So he was solving the integer linear programming problem: find the maximum $\lambda(= \lambda_0)$ so that $\Sigma \lfloor p_i/\lambda \rfloor \geq h$.

The apportionments resulting from the three methods, *LF*, *GD*, and *MF* (which is discussed in the next section), appear in Table 4, for example

Table 4. *GD* Violates Upper Quota

State i	$p_i = 100q_i$	$\lfloor q_i \rfloor$	$\lceil q_i \rceil$	*LF* a_i	*GD* a_i	*MF* a_i
1	8785	87	88	88	90	90
2	126	1	2	2	1	1
3	125	1	2	2	1	1
4	124	1	2	1	1	1
5	123	1	2	1	1	1
6	122	1	2	1	1	1
7	121	1	2	1	1	1
8	120	1	2	1	1	1
9	119	1	2	1	1	1
10	118	1	2	1	1	1
11	117	1	2	1	1	1
Σ	10,000	97	108	100	100	100

No. 3, with $h = 100$, from Huntington's classical paper [23]. It is clear that the GD method can violate property UQ, i.e., some states may receive an $a_i > \lceil q_i \rceil$. This was an issue in the U.S. Congress after the census of 1830 when New York received more than its upper quota (using a variant of the GD method presented in the next section).

Note that if the ratio λ_0 is "fixed," then state i's apportionment a_i depends upon p_i and not upon P or the other p_j for $j \neq i$.

Exercises

12. Verify the GD apportionment in Table 4.
13. Prove that a (unique) optimal value for λ_0, as defined above, always exists.
14. Show that the GD method always satisfies properties LQ, H, and P.
15. If $h \geq s$, does it follow that GD will always satisfy the minimum requirement $a \geq e = (1, 1, \cdots, 1)$?

A geometric view of GD in the simple case $s = 2$ is presented in Fig. 14.5. Recall that $\mathscr{B}$ is the solid unit square containing q. GD selects a vertex from $\mathscr{B} \cap \mathscr{A}$ according to which "upper" face (side) of $\mathscr{B}$ is penetrated by the line joining point p to the origin 0. Ties can occur only when this penetration is at the intersection of two or more *full* dimension faces of $\mathscr{B}$, i.e., on some *lower* dimensional boundary "face" of $\mathscr{B}$. For example, when $s = 2$, ties occur when $p_i/\lambda_0 = \lceil q \rceil$. Note that one can view $\Sigma \lfloor p_i/\lambda \rfloor$ as a nonincreasing step function over the ray from 0 through p. A similar geometry holds in

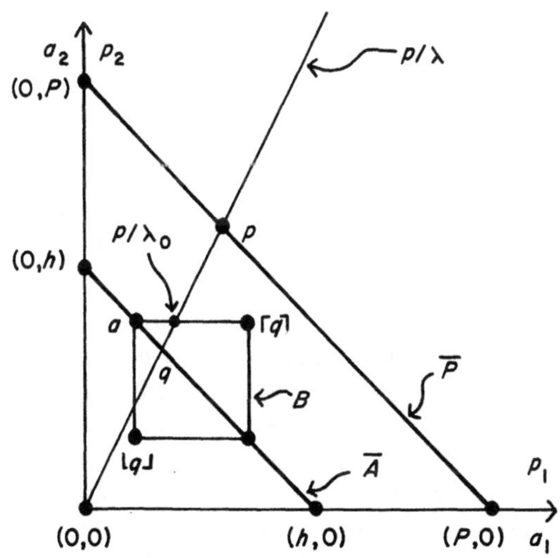

Figure 14.5. The GD Method for $s = 2$

higher dimensions when $s > 2$, except that p/λ_0 may be on a face of a unit cube other than $\mathscr{B}$.

Exercises

16. For the case $s = 2$ and $h = 4$, describe how GD partitions $\overline{\mathscr{A}}$ into regions (line segments) which give rise to the same apportionment vectors a. Are these five line segments of equal length?

17. For the cases $s = 3$ and $h = 3, 4$ and 5 sketch the shape of the planar apportionment regions which form a partition of $\overline{\mathscr{A}}$ using the GD method. This was done in Exercise 9 as well as in Fig. 14.3 for the LF method, and the resulting regions in that case were regular hexagons. Observe in the resulting figures which values of q result in a violation of the upper quota property.

2.4. Major Fractions

The previous section described the GD method that rounded the fractions p_i/λ_0 *down* to the nearest integer. One could also develop a dual approach that rounds such fractions *upward*. This relates to another rather natural method SD called "smallest divisors," which will be discussed briefly in Sections 3.4 and 4.3. Another approach is to attempt to round up or down from the values halfway between the integers, i.e., round each q_i to the nearest integer. It seems reasonable to try to avoid cases where $q_i - 1/2 > a_i$. However, it is not always possible to accomplish this. Consider the case of three states with equal population and $h = 5$: not all three states can be rounded from their quota 5/3 to their reasonable claim of two seats. This could only be done in general if one changed the definition of "quota" or altered the value of h, and such "pseudo-quotas" have been proposed. These ideas naturally lead to consideration of the *Method of Major Fractions*, which will be denoted by MF. This approach was advocated by Daniel *Webster* in 1832, and by Walter F. *Willcox* in 1910, an economist and statistician from Cornell University who also held degrees in law as well as a Ph.D. degree. It is also called the method of *Arithmetic Mean* and, like GD and SD, was later arrived at by Huntington through a different approach.

Method MF. For a given p and h, determine a value of λ such that $\Sigma \lfloor (p_i/\lambda) + (1/2) \rfloor = h$. MF then assigns these values $\lfloor p_i/\lambda + 1/2 \rfloor = a_i$ for each state $i \in N_s$. In the rare case of a tie, one may have this sum greater or less than h for all λ. One then takes the largest $\lambda = \lambda_0$, which brings this sum to the first integer $h' > h$. Some of the two or more states with integer values $p_i/\lambda_0 + 1/2$ must receive only $a_i = p_i/\lambda_0 - 1/2$, using some ad hoc tie-breaking rule. The apportionments resulting from the three methods LF, GD, and MF are shown in Table 5 for example No. 2 in Huntington [23], where $h = 100$. It is clear that MF violates property LQ. It may also violate UQ.

Table 5. *MF* Violates Lower Quota

State i	$p_i = 100q_i$	$\lfloor q_i \rfloor$	$\lceil q_i \rceil$	*LF* a_i	*GD* a_i	*MF* a_i
1	9215	92	93	92	95	90
2	159	1	2	2	1	2
3	158	1	2	2	1	2
4	157	1	2	2	1	2
5	156	1	2	1	1	2
6	155	1	2	1	1	2
$\sum$	10,000	97	103	100	100	100

EXERCISE

18. Verify the values for a_i in Table 5.

The difference between *GD* and *MF* is analogous to stating one's age. Whereas one normally states his age as that obtained on his or her last birthday, an insurance company will round to the age at one's *nearest birthday*.

EXERCISES

19. Show that *MF* always satisfies properties *H* and *P*.

20–23. Do Exercises 12, 13, 15, and 16 in Section 2.3 for the method *MF* presented above, instead of for the *GD* method presented in the previous section.

*24. Prove that *MF* corresponds to the solutions of the following optimization problems in which a has integer components that sum to h.
(i) $\min_a \Sigma\, q_i(a_i/q_i - 1)^2$.
(ii) $\min_a \Sigma\, (a_i - q_i)^2/q_i$.
(iii) $\min_a \Sigma\, a_i(a_i - q_i)^2/(a_i q_i)^{1/2}$.

3. Local Measures of Inequity

3.1. Introduction

In the early 1920s, E. V. Huntington, a mathematician at Harvard University, proposed and analyzed some new approaches to the apportionment problem. He focused his attention on "local" measures of inequity between *pairs* of states. His goal in some sense was to "minimize" simultaneously all such pairwise inequities over the set of s states. This may initially appear as an enormous task, since $s(s - 1)/2$ comparisons are involved, and there seems to be no guarantee beforehand that such a minimum even exists. In addition, several natural ways to measure inequity between a pair of states suggest themselves, and not all of these give rise to the same result. On the other hand, many of his different, yet rather obvious, measures of inequity do give rise to the *same* workable apportionment method, and this resulting scheme is in a "symmetrical" position relative to the five separate methods arrived at through the Huntington approach. This one particular method recommended by Huntington is referred to as the method of *Equal Proportions*, the method of the *Geometric Mean*, or the *Main Huntington* method. Since 1941, this method has been the one used to apportion the U.S. House of Representatives.

Huntington's approach considers ratios such as p_i/a_i (the average district size in state i) and a_i/p_i (the average individual's share of a representative in state i), and attempts to make these as nearly equal as possible over all s states. The ideal case would be when all p_i/a_i were the same. To say that two such terms are "nearly equal" may mean their *difference* is near zero, or that their *ratio* is close to one. And the pertinent difference between numbers x and y may refer to the *absolute difference* $x - y > 0$, or to the *relative difference* $(x - y)/\min\{x, y\}$. Huntington considered 64 cases involving the relative and absolute differences and ratios involving the four parameters p_i, a_i, p_j, and a_j for a pair of states i and j. As a result he arrived at five different apportionment schemes (of which three were new ones), as well as some "unworkable" schemes for which the pairwise comparison approach would not in general converge to an overall minimum, i.e., successive pairwise improvements could lead to cycling. Of these five methods, Huntington recommended the *unique* one resulting from taking *relative* differences and the one that appeared in the most "prominent" position among the five.

3.2. Global versus Local Measures of Inequity

In the physical and engineering sciences, as well as in much of classical statistics, one is frequently concerned with the total or average error involved, which is considered here as a "global" measure. If one is constructing a reflecting radio telescope or a solar heat collector (or a solar device for burning the sails off the enemies' ships as suggested of Archimedes), then he or she might be concerned with how much their device varies from a perfect spherical (or conical) section and might use the root mean square as an appropriate measure of error. The goal for a very large radio telescope dish may be to have an "average" error of a few millimeters, whereas there may be some individual spots where the error is a few centimeters.

On the other hand, in many societal considerations one is often more concerned with more "local" measures of error or inequity. One's goal may be to minimize inequity between individuals or units, or to minimize the largest inequity. A country can have a fairly large median family income and yet have gross individual differences. Average salaries might be high while large discrepancies exist between different labor units or individuals in a department. In the social sciences, such pairwise comparisons or other "local" measure often seem more appropriate if one is seeking to arrive at a fair or just outcome. The Huntington approach to the apportionment problem makes use of this latter philosophy.

EXERCISES

25. Determine the absolute and relative differences between the numbers (i) 10 and 15; and (ii) 1,000 and 1,005.

26. Determine how much the following ratios differ from 1: (i) 10/15; (ii) 15/10; (iii) 1,005/1,000; and (iv) 1,000/1,005.

3.3. Equal Proportions

The main method of Huntington [21, 23] is called *Equal Proportions* and will be denoted by *EP*. It selects any one of the several natural *relative* differences as the measure of inequity. His rule is to minimize this inequity between pairs of states. The "best" apportionment is then obtained when no switching of seats between states can improve any such pairwise comparison.

Method EP. To be specific, take as the measure of *inequity* between two states i and j the relative difference between the average district sizes in these two states, i.e., consider the quantity

$$\left|\frac{p_i}{a_i} - \frac{p_j}{a_j}\right| \div \min\left\{\frac{p_i}{a_i}, \frac{p_j}{a_j}\right\}.$$

Then apply *Huntington's rule*: If the measure of inequity between two states i and j can be reduced by transfering a seat from the more "favored" state i to the less favored state j, then this transfer should be made. When one continues to apply Huntington's rule to the measure of inequity mentioned above, he or she will eventually arrive at a point where no additional transfers will reduce an equity between any pair of states. The resulting "optimal" apportionment vector a corresponds to the *EP* method.

Huntington [23] shows that when his rule is applied to several other (but not all) measures of inequity, the process will also converge and to the same *EP* result.

Assuming for the moment that this procedure for *EP* does converge, it would appear as though a very involved computational process or lengthy algorithm would be required for large values of s. For example, when $s = 50$, $s(s - 1)/2 = 1{,}225$ is the number of pairs of states, and any pair may be considered several times. It turns out, however, that there is an alternate approach to the *EP* method, which makes use of the *rank function*

$$\frac{1}{[n(n+1)]^{1/2}} \quad \text{for } n \in N,$$

which leads to very simple computations for determining an *EP* apportionment. This equivalence is a consequence of the following result for determining whether or not it is better (in the sense of lessening pairwise inequity) to switch a seat between two particular states.

Lemma. *Between two states i and j, respectively,*

(i) $$a_i + 1, \quad a_j$$

is a better assignment than

(ii) $$a_i, \quad a_j + 1$$

if and only if

$$\frac{p_i}{[a_i(a_i+1)]^{1/2}} > \frac{p_j}{[a_j(a_j+1)]^{1/2}}.$$

PROOF. Let us assume that i is the more favored state in assignment (i). If i is still the more favored state in assignment (ii), then clearly a transfer of a seat from i to j is called for, (ii) is the better apportionment, and one must consider whether additional seats should be transferred from i to j. So the crucial part of the proof is to verify the lemma when i is the more favored state in assignment (i) and j is the more favored state in (ii), i.e., when $(p_j/a_j) - [p_i/(a_i+1)] > 0$ and $(p_i/a_i) - [p_j/(a_j+1)] > 0$. It follows from our measure of inequity that (i) is a better assignment than (ii), if and only if

$$\frac{(p_j/a_j) - [p_i/(a_i+1)]}{p_i/(a_i+1)} < \frac{(p_i/a_i) - [p_j/(a_j+1)]}{p_j/(a_j+1)},$$

if and only if

$$\frac{p_j(a_i+1) - p_i a_j}{p_i a_j} < \frac{p_i(a_j+1) - p_j a_i}{p_j a_i},$$

if and only if

$$\frac{p_j^2}{a_j(a_j+1)} < \frac{p_i^2}{a_i(a_i+1)}. \qquad \square$$

As a result of this lemma, one arrives at a simple working rule for determining an *EP* apportionment a. One merely computes the numbers $p_i/[n(n+1)]^{1/2}$ for all $i \in N_s$ and some integers $n \in N$, and then just assigns the seats in turn to the largest such numbers. This lemma also indicates that the Huntington rule for switching seats between states will eventually converge to a "stable" or "optimal" outcome at which no transfer of a seat can improve the result.

Note that the rank function $1/[n(n+1)]^{1/2}$ takes on the value ∞ for $n = 0$, and thus the *EP* method automatically gives each state at least one seat if $h \geq s$, i.e., *EP* satisfies the minimum requirement $r = e = (1, 1, \cdots, 1)$. The denominator of this rank function is the "geometric mean" of the numbers n and $n + 1$.

In solving the apportionment problem, ties (for who gets the "last" seats) are quite infrequent in practice. But they can occur, e.g., if two states have the same population. If a tie occurs between states with unequal populations, Huntington suggests that it be broken in favor of the larger state. In case of equal populations, some other ad hoc rule can be used. Note, however, that ties should be most rare when using the *EP* method since its rank function gives rise to irrational numbers for most values of n.

Since *EP* is the current law-of-the-land for the U.S. House of Representatives, it is of particular interest as to which of the desirable properties mentioned in Section 2.2 it satisfies. The primary fault with *EP* is that it does not satisfy the quota property Q, and it can violate both lower and upper quota.

Exercises

27. Determine the apportionment a using the *EP* method for the problems given in Tables 4 and 5, and thus verify that *EP* violates properties *UQ* and *LQ*.

28. Show that *EP* satisfies properties *H* and *P*.

The fact that *EP* can violate upper and lower quota, and that it is based on a somewhat "arbitrary" or "ad hoc" measure of inequity has lead to some criticism of this approach, as indicated in the references by Balinski and Young. For example, on page 711 of one paper [3], they also mention an example for which *EP* seems "unstable" in the sense that a small change in the population of one state (along with changes in other states) may lead to a substantial change in the number of seats this state obtains using *EP*.

Nevertheless, Huntington [23] also demonstrated that several other natural measures of inequity that make use of the *relative* differences also give rise to the same *EP* method. *EP* also results when one minimizes via pairwise comparisons the *absolute* differences $[(a_i/p_i)/(a_j/p_j)] - 1 > 0$ (the "ratio surplus") and $1 - [(a_i/p_i)/(a_j/p_j)] > 0$ (the "ratio deficiency"). *EP* can also be obtained by minimizing certain "global" measures of inequity.

Exercise

*29. Show that *EP* is the solution to

$$\min_a \sum \left[\frac{(a_i - q_i)^2}{a_i}\right].$$

3.4. Other Huntington Methods

It is true that several different but natural measures of inequity lead to *EP* using Huntington's rule of pairwise comparisons. However, there are some other rather natural measures that do not lead to *EP* using his approach. Four additional methods that do arise will be described briefly in this section.

If one chooses to minimize the *absolute* (rather than relative) difference (called "representative deficiency")

$$\frac{a_i p_j}{p_i} - a_j > 0$$

between pairs of states i and j, where i is the more favored state, then the resulting apportionment turns out to be the *GD* method presented in Section 2.3.

Exercises

30. Show that this Huntington method just described has rank function

$$\frac{1}{n+1}.$$

Hint: The proof is similar to that for the lemma in the previous section.

31. Show that this particular Huntington method is equivalent to *GD*.

If one instead minimizes pairwise the *absolute* difference (called "difference in representative share")

$$\frac{a_i}{p_i} - \frac{a_j}{p_j} > 0,$$

then the resulting apportionment is again the *MF* method discussed in Section 2.4.

Exercises

32. Show that this Huntington method has rank function

$$\frac{1}{n+1/2}.$$

Note that the reciprocal of this rank function is $[n + (n + 1)]/2$, i.e., the "arithmetic mean" of the two successive integers n and $n + 1$.

33. Show that this latest method is equivalent to *MF*.

Method HM. If one selects to minimize pairwise the inequity measure, which is the *absolute* (not relative) difference,

$$\frac{p_j}{a_j} - \frac{p_i}{a_i} > 0,$$

where i is the more favored state, then one obtains a new apportionment method due to Huntington called the method of the *Harmonic Mean* and denoted by *HM*. Its rank function is

$$\frac{2n + 1}{n(n + 1)} = 1 \div \frac{n(n + 1)}{n + (n + 1)},$$

where the latter denominator is the "harmonic mean" of the two numbers n and $n + 1$. This is also called the method of James *Dean*.

Method SD. If one decides to minimize the *absolute* (not relative) difference (called "representative surplus")

$$a_i - \left(\frac{p_i}{p_j}\right) a_j > 0$$

between pairs of states i and j, where i is the more favored state, then one obtains another new Huntington method called *Smallest Divisors* and denoted by *SD*. This method has the rather natural rank function:

$$\frac{1}{n}.$$

SD is also called the method of John *Q. Adams*.

In total, Huntington [23] examined 64 different measures of inequity (see p. 107), 32 relative differences, and 32 absolute differences. All of the relative differences and two of the absolute differences lead to *EP*. Various absolute differences gave rise to the other four methods described in this section. And twelve of his absolute differences turn out to be unworkable, i.e., the attempt to arrive at an optimal solution by pairwise comparisons will not converge in general and one can cycle indefinitely. An example of such an unworkable measure is the absolute difference

$$\frac{a_i}{a_j} - \frac{p_i}{p_j} > 0.$$

Huntington [23] provides counterexamples to illustrate cycling for these twelve unworkable measures of inequity. In these examples one never arrives at a "stable" apportionment a for which no switch of a seat between two states will improve (i.e., lessen) their measure of inequity. That is, there will always be a pair of states for which a switch of a seat will lessen the inequity between them.

Exercise

34. Show that the unworkable measure mentioned will cycle when applied to the apportionment problem with $p = (762, 534, 304)$ and $h = 16$, which is Huntington's example No. 13.

The computations necessary to find an apportionment a for any of the five workable Huntington methods are quite simple. One merely multiplies the populations p_i for all $i \in N_s$ by the corresponding rank function evaluated for some nonnegative integers $n = 0, 1, 2, \cdots, m(\leq h)$. The corresponding numbers provide a priority list, and one assigns the seats in order (or inductively) to the states that correspond to the successive highest numbers.

EXERCISE

35. Compare the five rank functions for the different Huntington methods, and verify that these methods will favor large states over smaller states in the order

$$GD, MF, EP, HM, SD.$$

Note that EP occupies the middle or symmetrical position with respect to a bias toward large or small states.

A main criticism of the five Huntington methods is that they all fail in general to satisfy the quota condition Q, a fact not stressed or even mentioned in many papers on these methods. However GD does satisfy LQ, and SD satisfies UQ.

In addition, the Huntington methods do use a multiplicity of "arbitrary" measures of inequity, and it is not clear as to what criteria should be used to select any one over another upon this basis.

EXERCISES

36. Verify that the following example by Balinski and Young [3, p. 723] illustrates how all five of the Huntington methods may violate the quota condition Q simultaneously: $p = (5117, 4400, 162, 161, 160)$ and $h = 100$.
37. Examine the rank functions for the Huntington methods when $n = 0$, and determine which of these five methods automatically satisfy the minimum requirement $a \geq r = (1, 1, \cdots, 1)$ when $h > s$.

Finally, it should be noted that each of the Huntington methods can also be defined in terms of a "sliding divisor" λ, which was used to characterize the GD and MF methods in Sections 2.3 and 2.4. For more on this approach for the method EP, see Balinski and Young [3, pp. 706–707].

EXERCISES

38. Verify that the following example by Balinski and Young [3, p. 708] gives rise to a different apportionment a for all five of the Huntington methods: $p = (9061, 7179, 5259, 3319, 1182)$ and $h = 26$.
39. Show that all five Huntington methods always satisfy the monotonicity properties H and P.

3.5. General Huntington Methods

Each of the five Huntington methods was defined in terms of some measures of inequity. Nevertheless, each of these five methods was also characterized by a resulting rank function. Using this latter approach, one can clearly introduce a great variety of different apportionment methods by merely creating an unlimited number of different rank functions, subject only to their being "appropriate" functions for the problem at hand. Additional discussions on this approach appear in the papers by Balinski and Young.

4. The Axiomatic Approach

4.1. The Role of Axioms

The use of axioms often plays an important role in present-day mathematical modeling in the social sciences, and they often enter at an earlier stage of the analysis than is the case for other areas of applied mathematics. Modeling in the social sciences often begins by listing fundamental principles, desirable properties, or basic goals, which must be present in the system under investigation. Such ingredients may arise from a variety of considerations such as common sense, empirical data, essential standards, necessary constraints, political acceptability, equity considerations, etc. And it is normally preferable to list and evaluate such desirable properties before performing the detailed mathematical analysis, rather than arguing after-the-fact and in light of the nature of the various mathematical models employed as to which of the desirable properties is more or less essential. The preferred properties can be taken as the axioms or postulates that the resulting models must satisfy. The major part of the mathematical analysis may then be to identify which mathematical structures or what appropriate functions or relations satisfy the given axioms.

In some cases there will be no mathematical system that is consistent with the axioms, and one then faces the problem of weakening the axioms, i.e., of dropping some of the preferred social goals. However, a model that can violate the axioms in theory, but will likely do so only rarely in practice, might prove to be acceptable in many societal contexts. A well-known case of nonexistence appeared in the initial work by Arrow [1] on social choice theory, and his rather surprising result greatly influenced the mathematical approach and standards of rigor used in modeling in the social sciences. On the other hand, there may be a multiplicity of different models or relations that satisfy the axioms. In this case one may, or may not, want to introduce additional axioms or use other criteria to select one from the competing systems. In many social science models, uniqueness is a most desirable result. In the field of game theory, the Nash bargaining solution for noncooperative games and the Shapley value for cooperative games give unique results satisfying the corresponding axioms; this could prove of some comfort to an arbitrator or judge who wished to employ such solution concepts to settle a real-world problem concerned with fairness.

The use of axioms at an early stage in social science modeling can often be contrasted with the role of axioms in the physical sciences or in other areas. Theoretical discoveries in the physical sciences often use experimental data and intuition and frequently result from a variety of analytical techniques making use of successively better mathematical approximations or even "hit-and-miss" trials. Although a detailed listing of assumptions may be involved throughout, a precise axiomatization of a physical theory often comes at a later stage of its development. Such "cleaning up," or placing of the theory in a concise and rigorous framework, is most desirable. Nevertheless, the teaching of such theories in this compact axiomatic way is of concern to some applied mathematicians, since the intuitive concepts underlying the discovery may not be sufficiently covered (see Woods [37]).

In the mid-1970s M. L. Balinski and H. P. Young brought the axiomatic approach to the study of the apportionment problem. Some desirable properties such as Q, H, and P in Section 2.2, as well as others, became possible axioms, and the goal was to construct apportionment schemes that satisfy certain subsets of these reasonable conditions. Willcox, Huntington, and several other mathematical scientists who studied the apportionment problem were, of course, very much aware of the axiomatic method and even labeled some of their basic assumptions as postulates. But they usually focused their initial attention more upon measures of inequity, biases, and rank functions, rather than upon the resulting general properties of their methods. So the approach taken by Balinski and Young seems like a most appropriate one, and it ultimately led to the discovery that a few of the most desirable properties for an apportionment method are in fact inconsistent, i.e., any scheme must in some instances violate one or more of the properties. This clarification will be most useful in further studies as well as in making recommendations to groups dealing with apportionment problems.

4.2. The Quota Method

None of the apportionment methods presented so far satisfy both the quota condition (Property Q) and the condition of house monotonicity, i.e., avoids the Alabama paradox (property H); and both of these have been the subject of serious debate in the U.S. Congress. In 1974, Balinski and Young [2] presented a scheme, called the *Quota Method* and denoted here by QM, which always satisfies properties Q and H. Furthermore, they proved that their method was the *unique* one satisfying conditions Q and H plus a third rather "reasonable" axiom, which they called "consistency."

The quota method assigns seats to states in an inductive way and merely checks at each step to see that Q is not violated. It uses the same rule as in the GD method to determine which state receives the next seat, but rules this state ineligible if it will violate UQ as a result of its obtaining this additional seat. So each successive seat is assigned to the state with the highest priority that is *eligible* to receive it. Recall that the GD method satisfies properties H and LQ, and thus QM will hopefully have properties H and Q. QM satisfies UQ by definition, and it only remains to show that the nonassignment of seats to ineligible states will not cause LQ or H to be violated. It is important to emphasize that the seats are assigned recursively in QM. If an apportionment a is arrived at by the GD method and also satisfies UQ, it need not be the same result as obtained for the identical problem using QM. The geometric shape of the apportionment regions for QM are not merely the same as those for GD appropriately truncated to satisfy UQ.

A more precise description of QM follows the definition of "eligibility." If f is an apportionment solution and $f_i(p, h) = a_i$, then state i is *eligible at* $h + 1$ *for* its $(a_i + 1)$st seat if $a_i < q_i(p, h + 1) = (h + 1)p_i/p$. That is, i does not violate UQ at $h + 1$ when i has $a_i + 1$ seats. Let

$$E(a, h + 1) = \{i \in N_s\colon i \text{ is eligible for } a_i + 1 \text{ at } h + 1\}.$$

The quota method can now be defined via induction on the house size h.

Method QM. The quota method consists of all apportionment solutions $f(p, h)$ such that

$$f(p, 0) = 0 \quad \text{for all } i \in N_s,$$

and if $k \in E(a, h + 1)$ and

$$\frac{p_k}{(a_k + 1)} \geq \frac{p_j}{(a_j + 1)} \quad \text{for all } j \in E(a, h + 1),$$

then

$$f_k(p, h + 1) = a_k + 1, \quad \text{for one such } k, \text{ and}$$
$$f_i(p, h + 1) = a_i, \quad \text{for all } i \in N_s - \{k\}.$$

Exercises

40. Compute the apportionment a using QM for the problems in Table 4, Table 5, Exercise 36, and Exercise 38.

41. Check that QM satisfies property H.

42. Show that QM need not automatically satisfy the minimum requirement $r = e = (1, 1, \cdots, 1)$, when $h \geq s$.

43. Use QM to find an apportionment a for the problem with $p = (10, 10, 55)$ and $h = 1, 2, \cdots, 10$. Are there some such values of h that could cause controversy?

Table 6(a) *QM* Violates Population Monotonicity

State	Pop.	a_i using *QM* for h =					
i	p_i	1	2	3	4	5	6
1	122	1	2	2	3	4	4
2	17	0	0	0	0	0	0
3	35	0	0	1	1	1	2
4	16	0	0	0	0	0	0
5	10	0	0	0	0	0	0
$\sum$	200	1	2	3	4	5	6

Table 6(b) *QM* Violates Population Monotonicity

State	Pop.	a_i using *QM* for h =					
i	p_i	1	2	3	4	5	6
1	122	1	2	2	3	3	4
2	17	0	0	0	0	1	1
3	39	0	0	1	1	1	1
4	16	0	0	0	0	0	0
5	10	0	0	0	0	0	0
$\sum$	204	1	2	3	4	5	6

44. Find an apportionment a for the problem with $s = 6$, $p = (27744, 25178, 19947, 14614, 9225, 3292)$, and $h = 36$ for *all seven* of the apportionment methods presented in this chapter, i.e., *LF*, *GD*, *MF*, *EP*, *HM*, *SD*, and *QM*.
45. Verify the *QM* apportionment a given in Table 6(a) and 6(b) for $h = 1, 2, 3, 4, 5, 6$.

The difficulty with method *QM* is that it may not satisfy the very desirable property *P*, i.e., population montonicity, when $s \geq 5$ as is illustrated in Table 6. The discovery of this fact in 1978 by Balinski and Young surely eliminates this method as a serious contender for use in real-world applications, especially when the total population *P* can vary.

It was mentioned above that *QM* was characterized *uniquely* by properties *Q* and *H* plus a third property called "consistency." Roughly speaking, an apportionment method is *consistent* if it treats "tied" states, say i and j, in an equal manner depending only upon a_i, p_i, a_j, and p_j, i.e., there are "appropriate" extensions or truncations of the resulting apportionment solutions. Consistency is like an "independence of irrelevant alternatives" condition in social choice theory. (See Saari [32] and Arrow [1].) Since a precise definition of this term is rather lengthy, it will not be presented here.

The five Huntington methods possess this property, but *LF* does not have it. Balinski and Young have used this term in more than one way in their papers, and Still [34] specifies three forms of "consistency" that could be considered. The interested reader should consult these papers for more details concerning this concept.

The method *QM* seems to favor large states (as did *GD*), but *QM* does not have a rank function and cannot be compared directly with the five Huntington methods or with *LF*.

4.3. Axioms for Other Methods

One can follow the axiomatic approach of Balinski and Young and use it to characterize some of the other apportionment methods discussed in this chapter as well as to discover many additional ones. This approach has since given rise to several huge classes of known apportionment schemes that have recently been described and characterized.

Balinski and Young [4, 10] characterized the *GD* method uniquely as the one satisfying properties *LQ* and *H* plus a "consistency" condition. And in [4] they also show that *SD* is similarly determined by *UQ*, *H*, and "consistency." In [7] they demonstrate that *MF* is uniquely described by property *H*, "consistency," and a property called "relatively well rounded." The latter concept relates to "binary consistency" mentioned in Exercise 6. In [7] and [8], they characterize a class of *general* Huntington methods (recall Section 3.5) as those satisfying property *H* and "consistency" (or "uniformity"). Balinski and Young [7] also describe a class of generalized Hamiltonian methods, which includes *LF*, using "binary fairness" mentioned in Exercise 6, but this whole family of methods violates property *H*.

Still [34], as well as Balinski and Young [9], characterized the class of all "quotatone" methods of apportionment, i.e., those satisfying both properties *Q* and *H*. Still also gives a lucid discussion on different types of consistency and suggests ways to "modify" classical methods, such as *LF* and the Huntington methods, to have them satisfy additional desirable properties such as *H* or *Q*. Mayberry [28] and Lawrence R. Ernst (at the U.S. Bureau of the Census) describe large classes of methods with properties *H* and *Q*. Mayberry [26] concentrated on a *Dual Quota Method*, denoted *DQM*, which is analogous to Balinski and Young's *QM*. Mayberry was more concerned with upper bounds (or maximum) requirements, as a result of an application on apportioning manpower. So his method is based on the selection rules in *SD*, uses a "downward" induction, and requires that *LQ* be satisfied at each step. The result is a unique method that satisfies *H*, *Q*, and "dual consistency," and it is "symmetrical" or "dual" to *QM*.

Questions related to "stability" of apportionment systems and to the idea of states forming coalitions (or parties merging) are considered by Balinski and Young [10].

Unfortunately, it is now conjectured that all apportionment methods with properties Q and H must violate property P, which is a most desirable property. So most of the many new methods referred to in this section possess a most unacceptable property. The known incompatibility of Q, H, and a variant of P (denoted SP and defined in the next section) was an unexpected and disturbing result, but one that must be faced up to by those making apportionments.

4.4. Additional Axioms

Many other basic properties of apportionment methods have been recognized, defined, and studied. These can also be taken as desirable criteria or basic axioms for possible apportionment schemes. Balinski and Young [11] discuss the properties called homogeneity, proportionality, symmetry, completeness, uniformity, and near-quota (or binary consistency or relatively well rounded) and demonstrate some of the relationship between these as well as some of our previously listed properties. Uniformity "preserves" apportionments when restricted to any subset of the states under consideration. Different forms of population monotonicity have also been defined in addition to the property P introduced in Section 2.2. Balinski and Young [11] define population monotonicity in the particular case where the house size h and the number of states s is fixed (which we call *strong population monotonicity* and denote by SP) as follows.

Property SP. Given the fixed values h and s. If the population p changes, then the resulting apportionment a should not change so as to give more seats to a state with relatively smaller population and less seats to a state with relatively greater population (except in the case of a "tie").

Balinski and Young [11] show that uniformity implies property H, and that it necessitates a general Huntington method. They also show that for a fixed $s > 3$ and a fixed $h \geq s$, that property SP is equivalent to having a general Huntington (or divisor) method possessing a rank function. In addition, they prove that no uniform method satisfies the quota property Q in general, and that for fixed $s > 3$ and fixed $h \geq s + 3$, there is no method with property SP that satisfies property Q. That is, property Q is incompatible with some other fundamental and desirable properties. The "discrete" nature of this quota property is inconsistent with some more "continuous" type of properties such as SP. Some would thus argue that property Q is the constraint that should be dropped from the basic axioms for apportionment schemes. The apportionment method MF is the only one of the five Huntington methods that always satisfies property Q in the special case $s = 3$, as well as the property called "near-quota" for any s.

4.5. Bias

Some apportionment schemes tend to favor larger states, whereas others more often favor smaller states. The "rounding down" in the *GD* method of Jefferson hurts large states relatively less than small states, and the "rounding up" in the *SD* method of Adams benefits small states. A comparison of rank functions for different general Huntington methods will indicate which ones are more beneficial to large states over small states. It is interesting to note that Thomas Jefferson was from Virginia, the largest state at the time, and that John *Q*. Adams was attempting to preserve Congressional seats for his state of Massachusetts and the smaller New England states in general.

One can introduce the statistical notion of bias and compare different apportionment methods with respect to this property. There are, however, several rather straightforward ways to define bias, some between states pairwise and others more global in nature. Balinski and Young have analyzed several such bias concepts for apportionment methods. These are discussed briefly in their recent paper [11] and in greater detail in their book [12]. Their main conclusion is that the method *MF* of Daniel Webster is the only one of the five main Huntington methods that is unbiased. *GD* favors large states, whereas *EP*, *HM*, and *SD* all favor smaller-sized states to an increasing degree.

One can also use statistical arguments, or make simulations studies, to show that the *MF* method does not frequently violate the quota property *Q*, and recall that at least one such desirable property must fail.

On the basis of its unbiasness regarding relative state size as well as its axiomatic properties referred to in Section 4.4, Balinski and Young currently support the method *MF* as the one most appropriate for legislative apportionment, such as for the U.S. House of Representatives. Thus they strongly reinforce the position presented by Webster some 150 yr ago and advocated by Walter F. Willcox [35, 36] throughout the first half of the twentieth century.

5. The General Apportionment Problem

5.1. Minimum and Maximum Requirements

As mentioned previously, in many apportionment situations there is a *minimum requirement* $r = (r_1, r_2, \cdots, r_s)$, such that any final apportionment $a = f(p, r, h)$ must have $a \geq r$. There also may exist an *upper bound or maximum requirement*

$$b = (b_1, b_2, \cdots, b_s),$$

such that $a = f(p, b, h)$ or $f(p, r, b, h)$ must have $a \leq b$. Many legislative assemblies such as the U.S. House of Representatives have a minimum requirement of $r = e = (1, 1, \cdots, 1,)$. The number of deputies per department in France must be at least two, i.e., $r = 2e$. The U.S. House of Representatives also has an indirect maximum requirement on representatives per state, which follows from the constitutional mandate that there "... be not more than one per thirty thousand ..." persons. Currently, congressional districts are so large that this bound is of no real concern, but it was an important consideration, and might not have always been satisfied by some apportionment methods and values of h proposed, in the early years of the United States. Some representative systems allow minimum requirements that exceed quota for certain minority or special interests groups from which guaranteed representation is desired or just. In manpower allocations, minimum requirements may be necessary because of high-priority units that must be manned to certain levels at all times regardless of costs. The lack of available or sufficiently qualified personnel may force upper bounds on the numbers assigned to some work units. There may also be maximum requirements, which cannot be exceeded (e.g., caused by a tax payer's revolt), independent of whether or not they meet or exceed lower quotas. A federally funded school program may have prescribed student–teacher ratios less than the school districts in general, and thus result in more teachers for some programs than others of similar size. An apportionment problem with such over-riding requirements r and b will be called a *general apportionment problem*. The previous case with $r = 0$ and $b \geq he = (h, h, \cdots, h)$ will, from hereon, be referred to as the *pure* apportionment problem whenever such a distinction is necessary.

If the requirements r and b are incompatible or too restrictive, then it may be impossible to obtain a suitable apportionment a, e.g., if $r \nleq b$ or if $h < \sum r_i$. And relatively high values for some r_i or low values of h might force one into an undesirable result; e.g., if the U.S. House had $h = 50$ and $r = e$, then each state would get only one representative, which seems unfair to large states such as California and New York. And the minimum and maximum requirements may very well make it impossible to meet quota, i.e., to satisfy property Q. An alteration in this condition will then be necessary.

5.2. Generalized Quota

For the general apportionment problem, it is appropriate to modify the definitions for quota (lower, upper, and exact) and to relax property Q. After allocating the minimum requirements r_i, there may not be enough seats left to satisfy LQ for states with $r_i < \lfloor q_i \rfloor$. Balinski and Young [2, 3], who considered r but not b, defined *generalized upper quota* to be

$$u_i = \max_i \{r_i, \lceil q_i \rceil\},$$

and they defined *generalized lower quota* l_i inductively as follows. Let

$$J_0 = N_s = \{1, 2, \cdots, i, \cdots, s\} \quad \text{and} \quad h_0 = h,$$

$$J_1 = \left\{ i \in J_0 : q_i = \frac{h_0 p_i}{\sum_{j \in J_0} p_j} > r_i \right\}$$

$$\text{and} \quad h_1 = h_0 - \sum_{i \in J_0 - J_1} r_i,$$

$$\cdots$$

$$J_m = \left\{ i \in J_{m-1} : \frac{h_{m-1} p_i}{\sum_{j \in J_{m-1}} p_j} > r_i \right\}$$

$$\text{and} \quad h_m = h_{m-1} - \sum_{i \in J_{m-1} - J_m} r_i.$$

Then

$$l_i = \left\lfloor \frac{p_i \left(h - \sum_{i \notin J_m} r_i \right)}{\sum_{j \in J_m} p_j} \right\rfloor \qquad \text{if } i \in J_m,$$

and

$$l_i = r_i \qquad \text{if } i \notin J_m.$$

Note that $J_0 \supset J_1 \supset \cdots \supset J_m$ for some finite m. Also introduce the vectors

$$u = u(p, r, h) = (u_1, u_2, \cdots, u_s)$$

and

$$l = l(p, r, h) = (l_1, l_2, \cdots, l_s).$$

Exercise

46. Find q, u, and l for the problem with $p = (54, 48, 32, 21, 19, 18, 8)$, $h = 20$, and $r = (3, 2, 4, 2, 2, 2, 2)$.

47. Find $\lfloor q \rfloor$, u, and l for the problem (given in Still [34]) with $p = (41000, 31000, 15000, 13000)$, $h = 10$, and $r = (2, 2, 2, 1)$. Are you satisfied with the comparison of l with $\lfloor q \rfloor$?

One could object to the above definition of l_i on grounds that it may reduce $\lfloor q_i \rfloor$ to a lower value l_i when this is not necessary, as in Exercise 47. It is also possible to obtain the result $u_i - l_i > 1$ in some cases, as for states $i = 1$ and 2 in Exercise 46. So Still [34] varied the definition of *generalized lower quota* to get

$$l_i' = \max\{\lfloor q_i \rfloor, r_i\} \quad \text{when } \sum \max\{l_i, r_i\} \le h$$

and

$$l_i' = l_i \qquad \text{when } \sum \max\{l_i, r_i\} > h,$$

where l_i is as defined above. That is, one does not reduce $\lfloor q_i \rfloor$ unless there are not enough seats to meet both r and $\lfloor q \rfloor$.

Mayberry [28], who was concerned with maximum requirements b as well as u, introduced a *generalized exact quota* defined by

$$q_i'' = \max\{r_i, \min\{b_i, \lambda p_i\}\},$$

where λ is chosen so that $\sum q_i'' = h$.

EXERCISE

48. Show that such a λ does exist, and that the λ and q_i'' are well defined.

Generalized lower and *upper quota*, respectively, then become

$$l_i'' = \lfloor q_i'' \rfloor \quad \text{and} \quad u_i'' = \lceil q_i'' \rceil.$$

For the general apportionment problem, it seems natural to replace the quota condition, i.e., property Q, by the following *generalized quota* condition.

Property $Q(r, b)$. $l'' \leq a = f(p, r, b, h) \leq u''$.

One may, however, prefer to use l or l' in place of l'' in this condition. These generalized lower and upper quotas are also functions of p, r, b, and h as indicated above. If a problem has no constraint b, one can denote property $Q(r, b)$ by $Q(r)$.

Properties such as H and P do not change for the *general* apportionment problem.

5.3. General Apportionment Methods

It is necessary to have *general* apportionment *methods* to handle this general apportionment problem, which has minimum and/or maximum requirements r or b. In many problems, it is not clear as to how the minimum requirement r (or the maximum requirement b) is to be implemented. Should each state i be given r_i seats to begin with, and then apportion the remaining $h - \sum r_i$ seats according to the *original* populations p_i? This is like giving each state two seats in the U.S. Senate, and then apportioning the seats in the House according to populations. Or is the goal instead to arrive at a "good" apportionment based initially on the population figures and to then make sure it satisfies $a \geq r$, or instead to modify a if necessary? Usually the latter is the one taken in this article.

The axiomatic approach of Balinski and Young has been extended to obtain *general* approtionment methods that possess certain desirable properties. In their original papers, Balinski and Young [2, 3] described a *Quota Method with Minimum Requirement*, denoted $QM(r)$, which is characterized uniquely by the properties $Q(r)$ (using l), H, and "consistency," if it has an *unbiased minimum requirement*, i.e.,

$$\frac{p_i}{r_i} \geq \frac{p_j}{r_j}, \quad \text{whenever} \quad p_i \geq p_j \quad \text{for all} \quad i, j \in N_s.$$

The method is quite similar to QM and will not be described here. Still [34] also described the class of general apportionment methods that satisfies $Q(r)$, and H. Mayberry [26, 28] introduced the concept of a maximum requirement b and described methods satisfying $r \leq l'' \leq a \leq l'' \leq u$. In particular, he uniquely characterized a *General Dual Quota Method*, denoted by $DQM(r, b)$, which is also based on the SD approach. He refers to QM as the *primal* quota method.

However, the general apportionment methods normally generalize the results obtained for *pure* apportionment problems, i.e., the former reduce to the latter when $r = 0$ and b is large, e.g., $b \geq he$. So the general apportionment methods that do satisfy properties H and $Q(r, b)$ will likely also, unfortunately, *fail* to satisfy the fundamental property P on population monotonicity. So the same difficulties that arise in the pure case are still presented in the more general problem.

6. Conclusions

6.1. Summary

One of the first problems concerned with equity that arises in politics, operations research, and elsewhere is the apportionment problem. It initially appears to be a trivial mathematical problem, and it is routinely solved by elementary ad hoc methods, usually without much serious thought given to it. A closer examination shows that this deceptively simple problem regularly gives rise to many politically or socially unacceptable results. All of the known traditional apportionment schemes possess some undesirable properties. And any manager concerned with such allocations should be informed of the corresponding faults associated with the various schemes. Several of the classical apportionment methods and their undesirable properties were described in this chapter. However, not all of the known methods were included. Furthermore, very little new mathematical knowledge has been added to this area between the 1920s and a few years ago.

In the 1970s Balinski and Young employed the axiomatic approach on this problem. They listed desirable properties and then they, and later others, were successful in finding apportionment methods satisfying these properties. However, they then discovered additional undesirable properties for these new methods. New insights also indicate that these old and new faults are not merely present in a rare number of "pathological" counterexamples, but that such difficulties can be expected to arise with some regularity in practice.

As a result, the apportionment method to be used in any given instant is still a matter of debate, because of both practical and theoretical considerations. One is forced to forego one of the properties Q, H, or SP. If house size h or total population P is fixed, then the properties H and perhaps even P may not seem necessary. But for manpower allocations they appear as most essential. In many applications, it seems as though property Q could be allowed to slip, but this could be ruled illegal in some political instances and may violate union rules in some manpower allocations. In short, one must forego some reasonable assumption for the apportionment method he or she employs in this less-than-perfect situation. A serious mathematical investigation seemed essential to reveal this rather "paradoxical" result.

6.2. Applications

The apportionment problem occurs in a great number of applications. These include situations concerned with the sharing or allotting of indivisible goods, tasks, personnel, and costs, as well as in political representation. Applications to distributing personnel to units in the U.S. Navy, as well as to several aspects in a school district, have been investigated. The reader should be able to think of several such possible uses in his own profession or institution.

The apportionment problem is often followed by an attempt to solve the well-known *assignment* or *marriage* problem, which is, e.g., concerned with assigning the best qualified to the different tasks in a most efficient way. This is described in many publications, e.g., see Dantzig [17] or Gale and Shapley [20]. Many other crucial factors may appear in real-world applications that are not resolved by the simple apportionment problem presented here. Different persons may have different skills and thus not be interchangeable. The value of a parcel of land depends upon its quality as well as upon its size. In some cases, a "weighted approach" can make up for such shortcomings. Nevertheless, additional primary or secondary considerations may make the simple apportionment schemes unsuitable for the problem at hand, and completely different models should be employed when such other dominant factors are present. Nevertheless, simple apportionment problems do occur in the early states of many studies concerned with equity and fairness.

References

1. Arrow, K. J. *Social Choice and Individual Values.* Yale University Press, New Haven, 1951; second edition, 1963.
2. Balinski, M. L., and Young, H. P. "A New Method for Congressional Apportionment," *Proceedings of the National Academy of Sciences, U.S.A., 71* (1974), 4602–4606.
3. Balinski, M. L., and Young, H. P. "The Quota Method of Apportionment," *American Mathematical Monthly, 82* (1975), 701–730.
4. Balinski, M. L., and Young, H. P. "The Jefferson Method of Apportionment," *SIAM Review, 20* (1978), 278–284.
5. Balinski, M. L., and Young, H. P. "A Problem of Fair Division: Apportioning the European Paraliament," I.I.A.S.A., Research Memorandum-76-55, 1976.
6. Balinski, M. L., and Young, H. P. "Criteria for Proportional Representation," *Operations Research 27* (1979), 80–95.
7. Balinski, M. L., and Young, H. P. "Apportionment Schemes and the Quota Method," *American Mathematical Monthly, 84* (1977), 450–455.
8. Balinski, M. L., and Young, H. P. "On Huntington's Methods of Apportionment," *SIAM Journal on Applied Mathematics, 33* (1977), 607–618.
9. Balinski, M. L., and Young, H. P. "Quotatone Apportionment Methods," *Mathematics of Operations Research, 4* (1979), 31–38.
10. Balinski, M. L., and Young, H. P. "Stability, Coalitions, and Schisms in Proportional Representation System," *American Political Science Review, 72* (1978), 848–858.
11. Balinski, M. L., and Young, H. P. "The Webster Method of Apportionment," *Proceeding of the National Academy of Sciences, U.S.A.., 77* (1980), 1–4.
12. Balinski, M. L., and Young, H. P. *Fair Representation.* Yale University Press, New Haven, 1982.
13. Bergman, L. M., and Romanovsky, I. V. "Apportionment and Optimization in Allotting Problems," *Operations Research and Statistical Simulation*, Issue 3, pp. 137–162. Edited by I. V. Romanovsky, Leningrad, 1975. (In Russian.)
14. Birkhoff, Garrett. "House Monotone Apportionment Schemes," *Proceedings of the National Academy of Sciences, U.S.A., 73* (1976), 684–686.
15. Chafe, Z. Jr. "Congressional Reapportionment," *Harvard Law Review, 42* (1929), 1015–1047.
16. Chafe, Z. Jr. "Reapportionment of the House of Representatives Under the 1950 Census," *Cornell Law Quarterly, 36* (1951), 643–665.
17. Dantzig, G. B. *Linear Programming and Extensions*, Princeton University Press, Princeton, 1963, 625 pp.
18. Hylland, Aanund. Allotment Methods: Procedures for Proportional Distribution of Indivisible Entities, mimeographed report, December, 1978, 141 pp.
19. d'Hondt, V. *A Practical and Reasonable System for Proportional Representation*, Muquardt, Brussels, 1882. (In French.)
20. Gale, D., and Shapley, L. S. "College Admissions and the Marriage Problem," *American Mathematical Monthly, 69* (1962), 9–15.
21. Huntington, E. V. "The Mathematical Theory of the Apportionment of Representatives," *Proceedings of the National Academy of Science, U.S.A., 7* (1921), 123–127.
22. Huntington, E. V. "A New Method of Apportionment of Representatives," "*Quarterly Publication of the American Statistical Association* (Sept. 1921), 859–870.
23. Huntington, E. V. "The Apportionment of Representatives in Congress," *Transactions of the American Mathematical Society, 30* (1928), 85–110.

24. Lucas, W. F. "Measuring Power in Weighted Voting System," Chapter 9 in this volume.
25. Lucas, W. F., and Housman, D. The Apportionment Problem, Tech. Report No. 501, School of O. R. & I. E., Cornell University, Ithaca, April 1981, 14 pp. Condensed version as: "Apportionment: Reflections on the Politics of Mathematics," *Engineering, Cornell Quarterly*, *16*, No. 1, (Summer, 1981), 16–22.
26. Mayberry, J. P. "Quota Methods of Apportionment are Still Nonunique," *Proceedings of the National Academy of Sciences, U.S.A.*, *75* (1978), 3537–3539.
27. Mayberry, J. P. Allocation for Authorization Management, mimeographed, Feb. 1978, 18 pp.
28. Mayberry, J. P. A Spectrum of Quota Methods of Legislative Apportionment and Manpower Allocation, Brock University, mimeographed, March 1978, 52 pp.
29. Mayberry, J. P. Additional Quota Methods of Apportionment, mimeographed, March 1978.
30. Meder, A. E., Jr. *Legislative Apportionment*. Houghton Mifflin Co., Boston, 1966, 28 pp.
31. Pearcy, G. E. *A Thirty-Eight State U.S.A.*, Plycon Press, 1973.
32. Saari, D. G. "Apportionment Methods and the House of Representatives," *American Mathematical Monthly*, *85* (1978), 792–802.
33. Steinhaus, H. *Mathematical Snapshots*, new edition, Oxford University Press, New York, 1960, 328 pp.
34. Still, J. W. "A Class of New Methods for Congressional Apportionment," *SIAM Journal of Applied Mathematics*, *37* (1979), 401–418.
35. Willcox, W. F. "The Apportionment of Representatives" (American Economic Associations Annual Address of the President), *American Economic Review*, Supplement *6* (1916), 3–16.
36. Willcox, W. F. "Last Words on the Apportionment Problem," in *Legislative Reapportionment*, *17*, No. 2, of *Law and Contemporary Problems* (1952), 290–301.
37. Woods, L. C. "Beware of Axiomatics in Applied Mathematics," *Bulletin of the Institute of Mathematics and its Applications, Oxford* *9* (1973), 40–44.

MIX
Papier aus verantwortungsvollen Quellen
Paper from responsible sources
FSC® C105338
FSC
www.fsc.org

If you have any concerns about our products,
you can contact us on
ProductSafety@springernature.com

In case Publisher is established outside the EU,
the EU authorized representative is:
Springer Nature Customer Service Center GmbH
Europaplatz 3, 69115 Heidelberg, Germany

Printed by Libri Plureos GmbH
in Hamburg, Germany